BLOOMSBURY
GUIDE TO
BETTER ENGLISH

BLOOMSBURY GUIDE TO BETTER ENGLISH

Editor
Martin H. Manser

Consultant Editors
Jonathon Green · Betty Kirkpatrick · John Silverlight

Compilers
Rosalind Fergusson · Jenny Roberts

BLOOMSBURY

First published in 1988 as *Bloomsbury Good Word Guide*. This
edition first published in 1994.

Copyright © 1988, 1990, 1994 by Bloomsbury Publishing Ltd,
2 Soho Square, London W1V 5DE

10 9 8 7 6 5 4 3 2 1

British Library Cataloguing in Publication

A CIP record for this book is available from the British Library.

ISBN 0 7475 1646 4

The moral right of the author has been asserted

Acknowledgments
The editor expresses his thanks to the following: Rosalind
Desmond and Gloria Wren for careful checking, Kathy Rooney
and Tracey Smith, of the publishers, for encouragement at
every stage of the book's production, and on the first edition,
Sarah Peasley for help in compiling the text and Margaret
McPhee for advice on Australian English.

Typeset by Watermark, Cromer, Norfolk
Printed in Britain by Cox & Wyman Ltd, Reading, Berks

INTRODUCTION

These days the term 'communicative skills' has become a vogue expression, being much in evidence in situations vacant columns and playing an important role in educational rethinking. In common with many voguish expressions of the age overuse has left it in danger of not being taken seriously. This is a great pity since the phenomenon which the term describes is of paramount importance in modern life.

Failure to communicate effectively is at the root of many social ills and misfortunes, from war to missed career opportunities, from industrial strife to broken relationships. If only we had been able to persuade the other party of our real intentions, what misunderstandings and conflict might have been averted.

Nowadays there is little excuse for poor communicative skills in those with a basic education, even in those who feel that they missed out at school in this particular area of education. Articulacy is not necessarily inborn; it can be acquired. Never before has there been such a wealth of self-help English language material available to ease the process of this acquiral.

The proliferation of English language reference books is a relatively recent occurrence. Not long ago the average family bookshelves probably stocked, if any reference books, an ancient Bible, a dog-eared, somewhat elderly dictionary, and perhaps a set of out-of-date encyclopedias. In many cases this state of affairs must have changed radically, judging from current sales of English language reference books.

Something of a revolution hit reference book publishing, brought about partly by the arrival of computerization and the new technology and partly by the realization among publishers that reference books, although expensive to produce, represented less of a risk than other branches of publishing. There was probably also an element of response to demand as people came to realize the need for articulacy in the modern world.

For whatever reasons bookshop shelves have become positively crammed with a wide range of attractive, up-to-date English language reference books, most of them extremely reasonably priced. At first most of these were English language dictionaries but soon a wider selection of books joined them. The net result was that the promotional activities involved in bringing these reference wares to the notice of the public made it difficult for people not to be aware of an important fact — that language is subject to change. Newspapers revelled in providing their readers with selected lists of the 'new English', the more bizarre the better.

The speed at which new words are added to the language nowadays is overwhelming, but it is not only the vocabulary that is subject to change. As attitudes and conventions change other areas of language change with them — stylistics, usage, and even, in some cases, pronunciation.

It is all too easy to feel marooned in this sea of change. While the importance of communicative skills cannot be denied, many people find it difficult to set about acquiring them. Getting to grips with something as amorphous as the English language can be a daunting task, particularly for those whose formal education omitted to convey much about the structure or grammar of the language.

Dictionaries obviously provide a great deal of self-help with regard to language but their contribution is frequently restricted to meaning, spelling, or pronunciation. People seeking to extend their competence in the use of English require more varied and in-depth assistance.

Thesauruses are another great boon to those wishing to improve their standard of articulacy but here again they are far from providing all the solutions. Although would-be writers or speakers will undoubtedly find in thesauruses a wide range of inspirational words with which to clothe ideas, they might well feel in need of some guidance as to how exactly these words should be used.

In the present age much more emphasis than hitherto is placed on the importance of being able to produce a high standard of English, whether oral or written. Formerly this aspect tended to be neglected in favour of highly developed reading and interpretative skills but this is now being rectified in these days of mass communication.

Participation in the communication media, for example, is no longer restricted to a few highly educated experts. Audience participation has extended from the realms of the stage to the realms of radio and television. Indeed one wonders what local low-budget radio stations would do without the phone-in contributions of the man/woman in the street, not to mention the chat show featuring the local celebrity who has published a first novel, climbed Everest, or lost more weight than anyone else in the community. All manner of things are of interest to the media.

In order to improve one's oral and written skills it is important to have more than just a dictionary and a thesaurus as self-help material. Of immense help are books that offer guidance in the use of language, particularly those which show language in action by including example sentences or phrases.

Such books provide very valuable ground rules on which to base one's own English usage. Few of us can rely entirely on instinct or even on memory when it comes to the English language for it is full of quirks and inconsistencies. Even the most educated benefit from having a standard authority to fall back on.

Language reference books these days are less didactic than they were. In general we have moved on from the times when they were entirely prescriptive in their comments on language. Now most of them adopt a more descriptive role, restricting themselves to stating what is actually happening in language rather than dictating what ought to be happening.

Inevitably there are people who are unhappy with this change of emphasis. There is a school of thought prevalent mainly among older people which seeks to impose a kind of restriction on language that is no longer imposed on other areas of life. It is as if, in an age of uncertainty and kaleidoscopic change, they look to language to provide a safe, unchanging structure.

This places an impossible burden on language. It does not exist in a vacuum but simply reflects what is happening in society and the world around. If we do not like the words, we probably do not like the events but it is difficult to hold back the tide of change.

At the very least we cannot stem the flow of vocabulary additions which are created in response to new inventions, new discoveries, and new concepts. New labels have to be found and so are born *camcorders*, *E-numbers*, *genetic engineering*, and *teleshopping*, to name but a few of the new words that are invading the language from every area of human activity.

Language change is not confined to new vocabulary additions.

Sometimes the old gets recycled in a new form as words alter their meaning in some way. The classic example is, of course, the word *gay*, which has almost entirely lost its 'merry' associations — except in literature written before the present day — in favour of the modern meaning of 'homosexual'.

There are, however, a growing number of other instances of language change, several based on misconception or error. *Hopefully* was an early example when it came to mean 'it is to be hoped that' as well as 'with hope'. Now *disinterested* is frequently to be found meaning 'not interested' as well as 'unbiased'. There is now a very fine line to be drawn between error and alternative usage — and sometimes the former becomes the latter.

Data, for example, as the plural of *datum* should come accompanied by a plural verb but it is now frequently seen in the presence of a singular verb, particularly in the field of information technology. The same fate has befallen *media*. It is no longer thought of as simply the plural of *medium* but as a word in its own right. As such it is increasingly accompanied by a singular, rather than a plural, verb.

Educational trends frequently have an effect on the state of the language. With the virtual demise of the teaching of classics in schools a knowledge of Latin and Greek in relation to the English language is now quite a rare phenomenon among younger people. So is born the puzzlement over *medium/media* and *datum/data* and the confusion over *stadia/stadiums* and *referendums/referenda*.

The creative writing phase in primary schools was the forerunner of many spelling problems and even more grammatical problems. It is, of course, a good thing to encourage creativity and self-expression, but some knowledge of the structure of the language is necessary if one is to use it with confidence and skill. Attempts are now being made to revive grammar, at least in some form, but what is done cannot be undone and there remain generations to whom it is a closed book.

This has undoubtedly affected modern English as it is used by the man/woman in the street. It may offend purist ears but *less bottles of milk* is challenging *fewer bottles of milk* for supremacy in terms of frequency.

Then there is the nervousness about *me* and *I*. There is a general — and erroneous — feeling that *I* is much more polite and more correct than *me* in all contexts. This accounts for the *between you and I* which so offends those brought up on a diet of parts of speech and parsing.

Prepositions in English are the source of much confusion. Should it be *different from* or *different to*? For that matter should *accompanied* be followed by *with* or *by*? Is either possible and, if so, which is correct in which context?

As formal language training has diminished and public communication has increased, language has become less and less rigid and the distinction between the linguistically correct and the linguistically incorrect has become blurred. But we are not yet at the stage where anything goes; let us hope we never reach it. I think that most of us would prefer a few guidelines to a linguistic free-for-all.

The trouble is that it is difficult to establish such guidelines when the language is in a state of flux. As has already been suggested it is difficult to pigeon-hole language into the correct and the incorrect. The categories are often too black and white; some shades of grey are sometimes necessary.

In any area where extremes are involved it is often advisable to take the middle course. So it is with language, provided the rationale and the terms of reference are clearly explained. By taking such a course and explaining the options you may not please everyone but, on the other hand, you are unlikely to offend everyone.

The *Bloomsbury Guide to Better English*, one of the most wide-ranging English language reference books available, presents the reader with the facts associated with the relevant words and makes recommendations rather than laying down didactic rules. Where a supposed alternative is in fact still generally considered wrong this is clearly stated, but where acceptable alternatives exist these are also stated together with the justifications for these.

Sometimes distinctions have to be made between the habits of the consciously careful users who wish to achieve absolutely correct and elegant English and those of the run-of-the-mill users who simply wish to get their basic message across as speedily and as painlessly as possible. A distressing number of us fall into this latter category although on special occasions, when we are out to impress, we try to mend our ways.

The said special occasions are usually formal occasions when we dress up not only ourselves but our language also. Forms of language associated with particular social situations are called registers. Thus in a formal situation a formal register of language is used.

Many of the entries in the *Bloomsbury Guide to Better English* distinguish between formal and informal registers. The formal/informal distinction is often, although not always, between written and spoken English. We tend to be at our most formal, linguistically speaking, when we are writing letters of a business nature, while informal English is kept for chatty letters to friends and family or everyday conversation. It is important to remember that informal English is neither incorrect nor less correct as long as it is the appropriate register for the context.

The *Bloomsbury Guide to Better English* takes language as it finds it and acts as a navigator through the many potential hazards. All problematic areas are dealt with and explained in a way that is readily understandable by all users. Giving help with language is of very little use if the help itself is more difficult to comprehend than the original linguistic problem.

It tackles two types of **spelling** difficulty — words that for some reason present problems in themselves and words which are problematic because they are likely to be confused with other words that resemble them. Into the first category come such words as *antihistamine, disappoint, innocuous, privilege*, and *wilful*, while the second category covers such duos as *bloc/block, dual/duel, principal/principle*, and *stationary/stationery*. This edition of the *Guide* also includes words and expressions of foreign origin which frequently present spelling and pronunciation problems. Examples include *bête noire* and *tête-à-tête*.

Of course the *Guide* does not confine its help with **pronunciation** to foreign words. The editor has been conscious of the fact that knowing how to pronounce words correctly is essential for confident public speaking, whether in the area of business or leisure. Thus words such as *Celtic, dynasty, flaccid, irrevocable, status*, and many more are listed to save you from red-faced stumbling.

Many people find difficulty with **punctuation** and so hesitate to launch into print. The *Bloomsbury Guide* gives advice on many aspects of this from the basic comma and paragraph to the more esoteric semicolon. Potential authors will find it invaluable.

Grammar is a cause of nervousness in many, mostly because they have never been taught the rudiments of it. One of the great advantages of this book is that the grammatical information is presented in an easily comprehensible, rapid-to-use form as it unfolds the mysteries of the preposition, the conjunction, and the rest.

If your particular linguistic problem centres on **usage** you will find that the *Bloomsbury Guide to Better English* gives sensible answers to a wide range of possible queries, often incorporating examples of the particular words showing the usual context. Should you use *converse* or *inverse*, *impinge* or *infringe*, *soluble* or *solvable*? A quick scan through the alphabetical listing will reveal the answer. Although mindful of the fact that print gives a kind of credence to any statement the editor has sensibly given examples of incorrect usage on occasion to contrast with the correct form.

One of the most innovative features of this book is the concentration on what are known as **buzz words** or vogue words, expressions which, however much we may deprecate them, suddenly leap into fashionable prominence in the general language, often from specialist sources. In many cases objections to buzz words lie not with the words themselves but with their overuse, the user rather than the word being at fault. Too many of us jump on the linguistic bandwagon and reach for the vogue word of the day instead of spending time and effort in finding the more appropriate expression.

What is to be done with buzz words? Should we ignore them and hope they will fade rapidly? Should we embrace them enthusiastically and risk heaping criticism on ourselves? Should we take the middle course and use them sparingly and effectively? The choice is of course yours but this particular volume advocates this last course of action. Appreciate their merits but do not abuse them by overusing them.

If you find yourself tempted by any of them put temptation behind you by consulting the *Guide* for suggested suitable alternatives. Armed with it you will have no excuse for peppering your prose with *the bottom line, catalyst, gravitas, downsizing, leading-edge, parameter, matrix*, and so on unless the context demands it. Many of them are best left to their specialist use. A severe head injury is *traumatic*; missing a bus is just annoying.

In this edition of the *Guide*, two additional tables have been included: *Countries and peoples*, giving guidance on the spelling of words derived from the names of countries – what do you call a person who comes from *the Seychelles*; what is the adjective that derives from *Burkina Faso*? – and *Prepositions*, showing which preposition to use with certain verbs, adjectives, and nouns – do you use *for* or *to* with *liable*; *between* or *with* with *alternate*?

The *Bloomsbury Guide to Better English* is a book for everyone and truly is an invaluable ready reference to English today. Whether you are using it for guidance with spelling, punctuation, pronunciation, or usage — or simply to settle or cause language disputes — you will quickly come to regard it as an old friend. Just remember one thing. Do not blame the book for what is happening to the language.

BETTY KIRKPATRICK
Edinburgh

HOW TO USE THIS BOOK

Entries, listed in a single alphabetical ordering, cover five main areas
of the English language: spelling, pronunciation, grammar and
punctuation, usage, and buzz words. Two tables, of Countries and
Peoples and Prepositions, are also included in the main alphabetical
listing.

Spelling

accommodation The word *accommodation* is often misspelt. Note the
-*cc*- and -*mm*-.

Pronunciation

controversy In the traditional pronunciation of this word, the stress
falls on the first syllable [*kon*trŏversi]. The variant pronunciation, with stress on the second syllable [kŏn*tro*vĕrsi], is widely
heard, but is disliked by many users. See also **STRESS**.

Grammar and punctuation

participles All verbs have *present participles*, which are formed with
-*ing*: □ *seeing* □ *walking*, and *past participles*, formed with -*d* or
-*ed* for regular verbs and in other ways for irregular verbs: □ *loved*
□ *finished* □ *given* □ *gone* □ *thought*.
  ◆ Participles are often used as adjectives: □ *broken promises* □ *a
leaking tap*. They are also used, with an inversion of the usual
sentence construction, to introduce a sentence such as: □ *Sitting in
the corner was an old man.* □ *Attached to his wrist was a luggage
label.* Care should be taken with such introductory participles, as they
are sometimes used to link items that are quite unrelated: see
DANGLING PARTICIPLES.

full stop The principal use of the full stop as a punctuation mark is to
end a sentence that is neither a direct question nor an exclamation.
  ◆ See also **EXCLAMATION MARK; QUESTION MARK; SENTENCES**.
    In creative writing, reference books, etc., the full stop may also mark
the end of a group of words that does not conform to the conventional
description of a sentence: □ *He had drunk six pints of beer and two
whiskies. Two very large whiskies.*
    A full stop is often used in decimal fractions, times, and dates: □ *3.6
metres of silk* □ *at 9.15 tomorrow morning* □ *your letter of 26.6.93.* Full
stops are also used in some **ABBREVIATIONS**.
    A full stop is sometimes called a *stop*, a *point*, or (in American
English) a *period*.
    See also **BRACKETS; QUOTATION MARKS; SEMICOLONS**.

Usage

he or she The use of *he/him/his* as pronouns of common gender, with
reference to a person of unspecified sex, is widely considered to
be misleading and sexist, as is the use of *she/her/hers* for the same
purpose with reference to jobs or activities that are traditionally
associated with women: □ *The candidate must pay his own
travelling expenses.* □ *This book will be of great value to the student nurse preparing for her examinations.* The most acceptable

substitutes for these pronouns are the cumbersome and pedantic expressions *he or she*, *he/she*, *(s)he*, *his or her*, etc.: □ *If a child is slow to learn, he or she will be given extra tuition.* □ *The candidate must pay his or her own travelling expenses.*

In some cases, the problem may be avoided by restructuring the sentence, making the subject plural, or both: □ *Travelling expenses must be paid by the candidate.* □ *Candidates must pay their own travelling expenses.* □ *Children who are slow to learn will be given extra tuition.*

Buzz words—vogue expressions, often originally from specialist subjects

hi-tech The adjective *hi-tech* specifically refers to high technology, or sophisticated electronics; its indiscriminate application to basic electrical appliances or to anything remotely connected with computing is disliked by many careful users: □ *a beautiful hi-tech modern home* □ *high-tech benefits* [a reference to the computerization of the social security benefits system] □ *This transition of the cycle from leisure 'toy' to hi-tech pedal machine* (*Daily Telegraph*).

Most entries are divided into two parts. The first part gives a concise statement of the main points of the word's usage, pronunciation, spelling, etc. The second part, printed on a new line after a ◆, gives additional explanatory information.

fraction Some people dislike the use of *a fraction* to mean 'a small part' or 'a little': □ *We flew there in a fraction of the time it takes to go by sea.* □ *Could you turn the volume down a fraction, please?*

◆ A fraction is not necessarily a small part of the whole: nine-tenths is a fraction.

To avoid possible ambiguity or misunderstanding, a small fraction should be clearly expressed as such: □ *Why dine out when you can eat at home for a small fraction of the cost?* □ *Only a small fraction of the work has been completed.*

Examples of the use of words are preceded by □. Many of the examples are drawn from actual quotations of contemporary usage.

market forces The phrase *market forces* refers to anything that affects or influences the free operation of trade in goods or services, such as competition or demand, as opposed to (artificially imposed) government controls. It is in danger of becoming overused as a vogue term: □ *The printing of this holy work* [the Bible] *should be subjected to market forces* (*The Bookseller*). □ *The Government yesterday unveiled plans to shift the financing of universities and polytechnics away from block grants and towards higher tuition fees in an attempt to expand student numbers through emphasis on market forces* (*The Guardian*). □ *Green market forces are working in the appliance manufacturers' favour* (*Daily Telegraph*).

Indications of incorrect usages are sometimes shown to contrast with the correct forms.

your or **you're**? These two words may be confused. *Your* means 'belonging to you': □ *your house* □ *your rights*. *You're* is a contraction of *you are*: □ *Hurry up, you're going to be late!*

◆ Note also the spelling of *yours*: □ *That's mine not yours*; the spelling with an apostrophe, *your's*, is wrong.

A distinction is made between the use of many words in informal and formal contexts.

affect or **effect**? The noun *effect* means 'result'; the verb *affect* means 'influence' or 'have an effect on', hence its frequent confusion with the verb *effect*, which means 'bring about' or 'accomplish':
□ *The new legislation may have an effect on small businesses.*
□ *The new legislation may affect small businesses.* □ *We have effected a number of improvements. Affect* and *effect* are often misused, one in place of the other: □ *Officials said yesterday the downturn could effect the future of the scheme* (*The Guardian*).
□ *'It will have very little affect,' says ... the chief economist at the merchant bank Morgan Grenfell* (*The Times*).

> ♦ The verb *effect* is largely restricted to formal contexts. The verb *affect* is also used in the sense of 'assume', 'pretend', or 'feign':
> □ *I affected an air of indifference.* □ *She affected to despise them.*
> □ *He affected ignorance.*

incredible or **incredulous**? *Incredible* means 'unbelievable'; *incredulous* means 'disbelieving': □ *He told her an incredible story.*
□ *She looked at him with an incredulous expression.*

> ♦ The use of the adjective *incredible* in the sense of 'wonderful' or 'amazing' should be restricted to informal contexts: □ *We had an incredible holiday.* See also **CREDIBLE, CREDITABLE, OR CREDULOUS**?

Differences between British English and American English spelling, usage, etc., are highlighted.

fulfil Note the spelling of this word: in British English neither *l* is doubled.

> ♦ The spelling of the derived noun in British English is *fulfilment.*
> The spellings *fulfill* and *fulfillment* are almost exclusively restricted to American English. However, the final *l* of the verb is doubled in British English before a suffix beginning with a vowel, as in *fulfilled* and *fulfilling* (see also **SPELLING 1**).

At many entries advice is given to avoid overusing a particular word or expression.

aggravate The use of the verb *aggravate* and its derivatives in the sense of 'annoy', 'irritate', or 'exasperate' dates back to the early 17th century but is still disliked by some people. It is therefore best restricted to informal contexts and the offending word replaced by one of its synonyms: □ *I was aggravated by the noise.*
□ *She has a number of aggravating habits.* □ *His lackadaisical attitude is a constant source of aggravation.*

Cross-references are used to show where an entry may be found or where there is additional information.

uninterested see **DISINTERESTED OR UNINTERESTED**?

government In the sense of 'the group of people who govern a country, state, etc.', *government* may be a singular or a plural noun: □ *The government is blamed for the rise in unemployment.* □ *The government have rejected the proposal.*

> ♦ See also **COLLECTIVE NOUNS; SINGULAR OR PLURAL**?

GUIDE TO PRONUNCIATION

a as in bad

å as in arrest

ah as in father

air as in dare

ar as in carpet

âr as in burglar

aw as in saw

ay as in may

b as in bed

ch as in cheese

d as in dig

dh as in these

e as in get

ê as in open

ee as in see

eer as in here

er as in bird

êr as in butcher

ew as in few

ewr as in pure

f as in fit

g as in go

h as in hat

i as in it

ī as in pencil

ī as in try

j as in jam

k as in keep

kh as in loch

ks as in mix

kw as in quiz

l as in lie

m as in mad

n as in nod

ng as in sing

n(g) as in restaurant

o as in hot

õ as in cannon

ō as in no

oi as in boy

oo as in zoo

oor as in cure

or as in tore

ôr as in doctor

ow as in now

p as in pat

r as in rim

rr as in marry

s as in sat

sh as in ship

t as in take

th as in thin

u as in up

û as in crocus

uu as in push

v as in van

w as in water

y as in yes

yoo as in unite

yoor as in urine

yr as in tire

z as in zoo

zh as in treasure

stressed syllables are shown
in italics: [sistêr].

a or **an**? *A* is the form of the indefinite article used before words or abbreviations that are pronounced with an initial consonant sound, regardless of their spelling; *an* is used before words that begin with a vowel sound: □ *a light* □ *an LP* □ *a unit* □ *an uncle* □ *a horse* □ *an heir* □ *a one-armed bandit* □ *an ostrich* □ *a seat* □ *an SOS* □ *a ewe* □ *an egg* □ *a UFO* □ *an IOU*.

◆ The use of *an* before words that begin with an *h* sound and an unstressed first syllable, such as *hotel, historic, hereditary, habitual,* etc., is optional. Nowadays, the preference is increasingly to use *a* followed by *hotel,* etc., with the *h* sounded, rather than *an* followed by *hotel,* etc., with the *h* not pronounced.

A and *an* are usually unstressed. The pronunciations [ay] and [an] are used only for emphasis: □ *He told you to take* a *biscuit, not the whole plateful!* In this example *a* would be pronounced [ay].

abbreviations Abbreviations are useful space-saving devices. They are used heavily both in informal writing and in technical or specialized writing, but less in formal writing. Some abbreviations stand for more than one thing, and it is better to spell these out unless the context makes the meaning clear. □ *He was a CO in the war* is confusing, as the abbreviation means both 'commanding officer' and 'conscientious objector'.

◆ The main problems with abbreviations concern punctuation. The modern tendency is to omit full stops whenever possible: □ *BBC* □ *AD* □ *D H Lawrence* □ *Prof,* and so on. Full stops are increasingly being omitted from capital abbreviations: □ *USA* □ *EC,* and they are always omitted from acronyms: □ *NATO* □ *UNESCO.* When an abbreviation is a contraction (i.e. the final letter of the abbreviation corresponds with the final letter of the word) there is usually no full stop: □ *Mr* □ *Dr* □ *Rd.* There is more likely to be a full stop when the abbreviation is just the first part of the word: □ *Rev.* □ *Feb.,* although here too the modern trend is to omit it. Abbreviated names can take a full stop or not: □ *C.S. Lewis* □ *A S Byatt.* There should be no full stop if a capital letter does not stand for a whole word: one should not write *T.V.* (television) or *E.S.N.* (educationally subnormal) as *tele-* and *sub-* are not complete words. There are usually no full stops in the abbreviations of weights and measures: □ *km* □ *oz* and never in chemical symbols: □ *Fe* □ *Cu.*

Apostrophes are no longer generally used for shortened forms that are in general use: □ *bus* □ *flu* □ *phone* □ *photo* □ *vet.*

Most abbreviations form their plurals with an *s*: □ *JPs* □ *PhDs.* A few abbreviations form their plurals by doubling: □ *pp* (pages) □ *ll* (lines).

Most abbreviations (except for acronyms) are pronounced by spelling out the letters. When preceded by the indefinite article, those abbreviations that begin with a vowel sound take *an*: □ *an ESN child* □ *an LSE graduate* and those beginning with a consonant sound take *a*: □ *a DBE* □ *a UDR spokesman.*

See also **ACRONYMS.**

aberration This word, meaning 'deviation from the norm': □ *a temporary mental aberration*, is sometimes misspelt. Note the spelling: a single *b* and *-rr-*, as in *error*.

ability see CAPABILITY, CAPACITY, OR ABILITY?

-able or **-ible**? Both forms of this suffix are added to words to form adjectives, *-able* being the suffix that is productive and the more frequently used: □ *washable* □ *comfortable* □ *collapsible*.

◆ The form *-able* is always used for words composed of other English words: □ *drinkable; -ible* being used for some words of Latin origin: □ *credible* □ *defensible*.

On whether to retain the silent final *-e* in words such as *lik(e)able*, see SPELLING 3 and individual entries.

The suffix *-able* may be active or (more frequently) passive in usage. In such words as *washable, eatable, dispensable*, etc. it has the passive meaning of 'able to be washed, eaten, dispensed (with), etc.'. In the adjectives *changeable, perishable*, etc. it has the active meaning of 'able (or likely) to change, perish, etc.'. The suffix is frequently used to produce new words, such as *microwav(e)able*, meaning 'able to be cooked in a microwave oven', and *photocopiable*. Some people dislike the overuse of words coined in this way, preferring *can it be found?* to *is it findable?*, for example.

abled The term *abled* is sometimes used as a synonym for 'able-bodied'; it is also used as an alternative for 'disabled' or 'handicapped': □ *otherly abled* □ *Marshall rejects the term 'disabled' for these children. ... She calls them 'uniquely differently abled'* (*Daily Telegraph*). Users feel that such phrases project a more positive image of people with disabilities, but these alternatives are widely disliked as much by the supposed beneficiaries as by the public at large. See also ABLEISM; CHALLENGED; POLITICAL CORRECTNESS.

ableism The term *ableism* refers to discrimination against people with disabilities, especially in employment and in the provision of facilities in public places. See also POLITICAL CORRECTNESS.

about see AROUND OR ABOUT?

above or **over**? The preposition *above* means 'at a higher level than'; *over* means 'vertically or directly above', 'on top of', or 'across': □ *He raised his hand above his head.* □ *She held the umbrella over her head.* □ *There's a mark on the wall above the radiator.* □ *I've put my towel over the radiator.* □ *The aeroplane flew above the clouds.* □ *The aeroplane flew over Southampton.*

◆ In many contexts the two words are interchangeable: □ *Hang the picture above/over the mantelpiece.* □ *Our bedroom is above/over the kitchen.*

The use of *above* as a noun or adjective, with reference to something previously mentioned, is disliked by some users but acceptable to most: □ *You will need several items in addition to the above.* □ *Please quote the above reference number on all correspondence.*

abridgment or **abridgement**? This word, meaning 'a shortened version of a work such as a book', may be spelt *abridgment* or *abridgement*. Both spellings are fully acceptable.

abscess This word, meaning 'a collection of pus surrounded by inflamed tissue', is often misspelt. Note the *sc* at the beginning of the second syllable.

absence This word is sometimes misspelt, the most frequent error being the substitution of *-sc-* for the *-s-*, as in *abscess*. Note also the *-ence* ending.

absolutely Some users dislike the frequent use of *absolutely* in place of *yes*. Others feel that the adverb is overused as an intensifier, in the sense of 'completely': □ *it's absolutely disgraceful!*

◆ The pronunciation of *absolutely* varies according to its meaning. In normal adverbial use it is stressed on the first syllable [absŏlootli]; in the sense of 'yes' it is stressed on the third syllable [absŏlootli].

absorption Note the spelling of this word. The final *-b* of the verb *absorb* changes to *-p-* in the derived noun.

abstention or **abstinence**? Both these nouns are derived from the verb *abstain*, meaning 'refrain' or 'refrain from voting'. The noun *abstention* is chiefly used in the second of these senses: □ *24 votes for the motion, 16 against, and 5 abstentions*. *Abstinence* refers to the act or practice of abstaining, often from something that is enjoyable but possibly harmful: □ *abstinence from alcohol* □ *total abstinence from sexual intercourse*.

abstractedly or **abstractly**? *Abstractedly* is derived from the adjective *abstracted*, meaning 'lost in thought': □ *He stared abstractedly out of the window*. The adverb *abstractly*, meaning 'in the abstract', is less frequent in usage.

abuse or **misuse**? The noun *abuse* denotes wrong, improper, or bad use or treatment; the noun *misuse*, denoting incorrect or unorthodox use, is more neutral: □ *the abuse of power* □ *child abuse* □ *the misuse of words* □ *misuse of the club's funds*.

◆ The same distinction applies to the verbs *abuse* and *misuse*: □ *to abuse a privilege* □ *to misuse one's time*.

In some contexts the two words are interchangeable: □ *Mr Douglas Hogg, the Home Office minister who chairs the ministerial group on the misuse of drugs ... Miss Mary Tracey, of the Standing Conference on Drug Abuse (Daily Telegraph)*. □ *He predicted that it would not lead to an upsurge in alcohol misuse .... But Action on Alcohol Abuse attacked the move at a time of increased medical concern about excessive drinking (Daily Telegraph)*.

The word *abuse* also refers to insulting language: □ *The president was abused by the crowd.* □ *The pickets shouted abuse at the strikebreakers.*

As in the word *use*, the final [s] sound of the nouns *abuse* [àbews] and *misuse* [misews] changes to [z] in the verbs.

abysmal This word, meaning 'very bad; dreadful': □ *abysmal weather*, is sometimes misspelt. The word comes from *abyss*, hence the *y* in the spelling.

academic The adjective *academic* is widely used in the sense of 'theoretical': □ *an academic question* □ *of academic interest only*, but some people object to its frequent use in place of *irrelevant*: □ *Whether he wins this race or not is academic, because he is already several points ahead of his nearest rival.*

accede or **exceed**? *Accede*, used in formal contexts, means 'agree'; *exceed* means 'go beyond' or 'be greater than': □ *They will accede to our demands.* □ *Do not exceed the speed limit.*

◆ The two verbs are similar in pronunciation but quite different in spelling: *accede* [akseed] ends in *-ede*; *exceed* [ikseed] ends in *-eed*.

The verb *accede* is usually followed by *to*; it can also be used in the expression *to accede to the throne*, meaning 'to become king (or queen)'. Compare *to succeed to the throne*, meaning 'to be the next person to become king or queen, especially as an inheritance'.

accelerate The word *accelerate*, meaning 'speed up', is sometimes misspelt. Note the *-cc-* and single *l*.

accent or **accentuate**? Both verbs can be used in the sense of 'to emphasize'. *Accent* usually refers to the act of stressing a sound in speech or music, whereas *accentuate* is used in a wider range of visual and abstract contexts: □ *He accented the word 'life'.* □ *to accent the first beat in the bar* □ *to accentuate an outline/a problem.*
◆ The word *accent* is stressed on the second syllable [ak*sent*] when it is used as a verb and on the first syllable [*ak*sĕnt] when it is used as a noun.

accents Accents are sometimes used on words that are now accepted into English, though the tendency is increasingly to omit them.
◆ Accents are generally used when they show the pronunciation of the word: the cedilla in *façade* shows that the *c* is soft, the acute accent on *cliché* shows that the word is pronounced [*klee*shay] not [kleesh]. A circumflex accent on the *o* of *role* is unnecessary and is usually omitted.

accentuate see ACCENT OR ACCENTUATE?

accept or **except**? These two verbs should not be confused, being virtually opposite in meaning. *Accept* means 'receive' or 'admit'; *except*, used in formal contexts, means 'exclude' or 'leave out': □ *She was accepted for the job.* □ *He was excepted from the team.* The two words are similar but not identical in pronunciation: *accept* is pronounced [ăk*sept*] and *except* is pronounced [ik*sept*].

access The use of the word *access* as a verb is best restricted to the field of computing, where it means 'gain access to (stored information or a computer memory)': □ *Booksellers can already access teleordering computer to computer or through Prestel viewdata* (*The Bookseller*).
◆ The extended use of the verb in general contexts is disliked by many users: □ *We often receive requests to 'access' our membership lists and these are almost always refused* (*Club Lotus News*).

access or **accession**? The noun *access* refers to the act, right, or means of approaching, reaching, entering, or using: □ *Access to the laboratory is restricted.* The noun *accession* is derived from the verb *accede* (see ACCEDE OR EXCEED?) and is most frequently used in the sense of 'becoming king (or queen)': □ *Elizabeth II's accession (to the throne) in 1952.*

accessory or **accessary**? In British English, the spelling of this word in the sense 'supplementary attachment' is *accessory*: □ *car accessories.*
◆ In the legal sense of 'a person who incites another to commit a crime', the spelling is usually *accessory*, *accessary* being an older variant: □ *an accessory before the fact.*
In American English, *accessory* is the spelling in all senses.

accommodation The word *accommodation* is often misspelt. Note the *-cc-* and *-mm-*.

accompany The passive verb *to be accompanied* may be followed by the preposition *by* or *with*, depending on the sense in which it is used: □ *She was accompanied by her friend.* □ *His words were accompanied with/by a gesture of impatience.* In the first example the verb *accompany* means 'go somewhere with someone as a companion; escort', in the second it means 'supplement'.
◆ *With* is also used with the active verb *accompany*: □ *He accompanied his words with a gesture of impatience.*

accountable The adjective *accountable*, meaning 'answerable', should be applied only to people: □ *Union leaders are accountable to the rank-and-file members.* □ *We were accountable for* *their welfare.*

◆ In other contexts the adjective is often better replaced by its synonym *responsible*: □ *An unexpected fall in demand was responsible* [not *accountable*] *for the company's financial problems.*

The noun *accountability* is best avoided where *responsibility* would be adequate or more appropriate: □ *the individual responsibilities* [not *accountabilities*] *of the directors.*

accumulative or **cumulative**? The adjective *cumulative* refers to something that gradually increases with successive additions: □ *the cumulative total* □ *a cumulative effect.* It should not be confused with *accumulative*, an adjective that is derived from the verb *accumulate* but is rarely used.

acetic see AESTHETIC, ASCETIC, OR ACETIC?

acknowledgment or **acknowledgement**? This word may be spelt with or without the *e* after the *g*; both spellings are fully acceptable.

acoustics The word *acoustics* is often misspelt, the most frequent error being the doubling of the first *c*.

◆ For the use of *acoustics* as a singular or plural noun see -ICS.

acquaint The verb *acquaint* is best avoided where *tell* would be adequate or more appropriate: □ *He acquainted me with his plans*, for example, may be more simply expressed as *he told me his plans.*

◆ The passive form *be acquainted with* can often be replaced by *know*: □ *I am not acquainted with the rules.*

Note the spelling of *acquaint* and its derivatives, particularly the presence and position of the letter *c*.

acquirement or **acquisition**? In the sense of 'something acquired' *acquirement* is largely restricted to abilities or skills and *acquisition*, the more frequent word, to material things or people: □ *Fluency in spoken and written Japanese is one of her many acquirements.* □ *He showed me his latest acquisition.*

◆ Both nouns may be used to denote the act of acquiring: □ *the acquirement/acquisition of knowledge* □ *the acquisition/acquirement of wealth.*

Note the spelling of *acquirement* and *acquisition*, particularly the *-c-* before the *-qu-*.

acronyms An *acronym* is a word formed from the initial letters or syllables of other words: □ *OPEC* (Organization of Petroleum Exporting Countries) □ *radar* (radio detecting and ranging).

◆ The punctuation of acronyms varies. The usual style is capitals without full stops: □ *WHO* □ *NALGO*, although some of the better-known acronyms are sometimes seen with only an initial capital: □ *NATO/Nato* □ *AIDS/Aids*. Acronyms which refer to some piece of technical equipment, rather than an organization: □ *sonar* (sound navigation and ranging) □ *radar* □ *laser* (light amplification by stimulated emission of radiation) □ *scuba* (self-contained underwater breathing apparatus), become so accepted that they are written in lower-case letters like ordinary words and many people do not even realize that they are acronyms. Other acronyms have become so well-known that it is rare to hear their full names: □ *Naafi* □ *Oxfam*.

Recently there has been a tendency to make acronyms correspond with actual English words: □ *SALT* (Strategic Arms Limitation Talks) □ *ASSET* (Association of Supervisory Staff, Executives and Technicians). The more appropriate the word to the organization the better: □ *ASH* (Action on Smoking and Health) □ *PROP* (Preservation of the Rights of Prisoners). It sometimes seems almost as though organizations and systems are made to fit the acronyms, rather than vice versa: □ *In 1984, Holmes, the Home Office Large Major Enquiry System was set up. In spite of its name, Holmes is not an electronic version of the master detective, but a means of investigating crimes through computers* (*The Times*). See also DINKY; NIMBY; YUPPIE.

acrylic This word is sometimes misspelt. Note particularly the *yl*, not *il* in the middle of the word.

act or **action**? Both these nouns mean 'something done', but *action* tends to emphasize the process of doing whereas *act* denotes the deed itself: □ *Terrorist action has increased.* □ *It was an act of terrorism.*

◆ The use of the word *action* as a verb, meaning 'take action on' or 'put into action', is disliked by many people, including Fritz Spiegl (*Daily Telegraph*), who criticized 'the many new verbs spawned by the Caring Industry. They no longer do things. They "action" them.'

active An active verb is one in which the SUBJECT performs the action of the verb (compare PASSIVE). The sentence □ *The mechanic mended my car* contains the active verb *mended*.

◆ Most clauses and sentences containing an active transitive verb can be converted into the passive: □ *My car was mended by the mechanic*, but the result is sometimes clumsy or needlessly complicated.

actualize The verb *actualize*, meaning 'make actual', is disliked by some users as an example of the increasing tendency to coin new verbs by adding the suffix *-ize* to nouns and adjectives: □ *They have actualized their plans.*

◆ See also -IZE OR -ISE?

actually Many people object to the frequent use of the adverb *actually* where it adds nothing to the meaning of the sentence: □ *Actually, I prefer coffee to tea.* □ *We weren't actually very impressed by his performance.* □ *She doesn't live here, actually.*

◆ In some contexts, however, *actually* may serve the useful purpose of contrasting what is actual or real with what is theoretical or apparent: □ *I know how to make a soufflé but I've never actually made one.* □ *It sounds difficult but it's actually quite easy.*
See also IN FACT.

acumen In the traditional pronunciation of this word, which means 'the ability to make good judgments': □ *sound business acumen*, the stress falls on the second syllable [ăkyoomĕn]. The pronunciation with the stress on the first syllable [akyoomĕn] is, however, more frequently heard.

AD and **BC** The abbreviation *AD*, which stands for *Anno Domini*, is traditionally placed before the year number; *BC*, which stands for *before Christ*, always follows the year number: □ *The custom dates back to AD 1462.* □ *The city was destroyed in 48 BC.*

◆ In modern usage *AD* sometimes follows the year number: □ *The battle took place in 1127 AD.*

It is strictly tautological to precede *AD* with *in*, since *Anno Domini* literally means 'in the year of the Lord', but the omission of *in* is generally considered to be unidiomatic: □ *He died in AD 1042.*

BC and *AD* are also applied to centuries, although the use of *AD* for this purpose is disliked by some people and is often unnecessary: □ *since the fourth century BC* □ *until the ninth century AD.*

The abbreviations are always written in capital letters (small capitals are sometimes used in printed texts), with or without full stops (see also ABBREVIATIONS).

address Note the spelling of this word, particularly the *-dd-* and the *-ss* ending.
  ◆ See also **LETTER WRITING 1**.
adherence or **adhesion**? Both these nouns are derived from the verb *adhere*, meaning 'stick'. *Adhesion* is largely confined to the literal sense of the word, whereas *adherence* is used for the figurative senses of 'loyalty' or 'obedience': □ *the adhesion of the tape to the fabric* □ *their adherence to the cause* □ *strict adherence to the rules.*
  ◆ In medical contexts *adhesion* is the abnormal union of usually separated body tissues, for example as a result of inflammation.
ad hoc The Latin phrase *ad hoc* denotes something that is made or done for a particular purpose, rather than as a general rule. It is most frequently used as an adjective: □ *an ad hoc decision* □ *on an ad hoc basis.*
  ◆ The phrase is also used as an adverb: □ *The committee will meet ad hoc, as needs arise.* It is not usually written or printed in italics.
adjectives An *adjective* is a word which provides information about a noun: □ *fat* □ *blue* □ *happy* □ *intelligent* □ *dirty.* The main division of adjectives corresponds to the position that they take. Attributive adjectives come before a noun: □ *a stupid boy.* Predicative adjectives follow a verb: □ *the sky is grey.* Postpositive adjectives follow a noun: □ *the chairman elect.*
  ◆ Of course, some adjectives can be used in all three positions: □ *a long walk* □ *the sides are long* □ *two yards long.* Most can be used attributively and predicatively: □ *sweet tea* □ *The tea is sweet.* Some adjectives can only be attributive: □ *the principal reason*, not *The reason is principal.* Some can only be predicative: □ *The baby is awake*, but not *the awake baby.* Some are used only in the postpositive position: □ *There were drinks galore.*
  Nouns can sometimes be used as attributive adjectives: □ *a glass bowl* □ *a Meissen plate* □ *cotton shirts*, and adjectives can be used as nouns: □ *the poor* □ *the blind* □ *the quick and the dead.* Adjectives are also used in the place of adverbs: □ *They sell their goods dear.* □ *It tastes delicious.* Such words as: □ *fast* □ *late* □ *early* function as both adjectives and adverbs.
  Absolute adjectives are such words as: □ *entire* □ *extreme* □ *total* □ *unique*, which cannot be used in the comparative or superlative, and cannot be modified by words like *very, utterly*, or *totally.* They can, however, be modified by *almost* or *nearly*: □ *an almost total disaster* □ *a nearly perfect round.* Other absolute adjectives cannot be modified in any way: □ *a postgraduate student* □ *a deciduous tree*, but it is occasionally possible to modify an apparently absolute adjective for effect: □ *He looked very dead.*
  The overuse of adjectives should be avoided, particularly when they are tautologous: □ *true facts* (see **TAUTOLOGY**). Care should be taken with choice of adjectives and the less informative ones should be avoided. *He's a nice man* tells one very little about a man; he might be *good-natured, sympathetic, witty, attractive, respectable*, or none of these. Long strings of adjectives should also be avoided in ordinary speech or writing unless they are needed for a precise description: □ *a small brown one-eyed mongrel.* In poetry several adjectives can be used to good effect: □ *A poor, weak, palsy-stricken, churchyard thing* (Keats).
  See also **COMPARATIVE AND SUPERLATIVE**; **NOUNS**.
adjourn This word, which means 'stop for a short time' and 'go', is

sometimes misspelt. Note the *d* in front of the *j*, and the *our*, as in *journey*.

administer or **administrate**? Either verb may be used in the sense of 'manage', 'supervise', 'control', or 'direct', with reference to the work of an administrator: □ *She has administered/administrated the company since the death of her father.*

◆ *Administer* also means 'give', 'apply', or 'dispense': □ *to administer first aid* □ *to administer justice. Administrate* is not used in such contexts.

admission or **admittance**? Both these nouns mean 'permission or right to enter'. *Admission* is the more frequent, *admittance* being largely restricted to formal or official contexts: □ *Admission is by ticket only.* □ *No admittance.* □ *He presents the picture of a boy for whom an early admission could well be advantageous .... Education officials say they blocked his admittance because class sizes at the school were too large (Sunday Times).*

◆ Of the two words only *admission* may be used to denote the price charged or a fee paid for entrance.

The noun *admission* also means 'confession' or 'acknowledgment': □ *an admission of guilt* □ *by her own admission.*

admit In the sense of 'confess' or 'acknowledge' *admit* is generally used as a transitive verb: □ *He admitted his mistake.* □ *I admitted that I had lied.* □ *Do you admit writing this letter?*

◆ The insertion of the preposition *to* in such contexts is disliked by many users: □ *He admitted to his mistake.* □ *Do you admit to writing this letter?*

Admit is followed by *to* in the sense of 'allow to enter' or 'give access': □ *We were not admitted to the club.* □ *This gate admits to the garden.* In the formal sense of 'be open to' or 'leave room for' *admit* is followed by *of*: □ *The phrase does not admit of a different interpretation.*

admittance see ADMISSION OR ADMITTANCE?

adolescence This word is sometimes misspelt. Note particularly the *sc* and the *nc*.

adopted or **adoptive**? The adjective *adopted* is applied to children who have been adopted; *adoptive* relates to adults who adopt another person's child: □ *their adopted daughter* □ *her adoptive parents.*

◆ Careful users maintain the distinction between the two words.

adult The noun *adult* may be stressed on either syllable, but the pronunciation [adŭlt] is heard more frequently than [ădult] in British English.

◆ The adjective *adult*, which principally means 'mature' or 'of or for adults': □ *an adult approach* □ *adult education*, is often used as a euphemism for 'pornographic': □ *adult videos* □ *an adult film.* □ *There is a demand for commercial sex (from prostitution, through massage parlours and blue movies to strip shows and 'adult' magazines) which will not go away ... if repressed (The Guardian).*

advance or **advancement**? The noun *advance* means 'forward motion' or 'progress': □ *the advance of the enemy.* The noun *advancement* is chiefly used in formal contexts to refer to 'promotion' or 'increased status': □ *opportunities for personal advancement.* The two nouns are sometimes confused in the context of progress in development: □ *advances in medical science* □ *the advancement of medical science.* Here, *advancement* refers to the act of assisting progress or development.

advantage or **vantage**? *Advantage* means 'superiority' or 'benefit': □ *to* *have the advantage over one's rivals* □ *the advantages of co-education. Vantage* is chiefly found in the phrase *vantage point*, meaning 'a place that affords a good overall view'.

◆ In tennis, the words *vantage* and *van* are sometimes used as shortened forms of the scoring term *advantage:* □ *(ad)vantage Smith.*

advantageous This word is sometimes misspelt, the most frequent error being the omission of the *-e-*. Note also the pronunciation of this word, stressed on the third syllable [advăn*tay*jŭs].

adverbs Adverbs modify other parts of speech and answer questions such as how? (adverbs of manner): □ *quietly* □ *greedily*, when? (adverbs of time): □ *then* □ *tomorrow*, where? (adverbs of place): □ *there* □ *outside*.

◆ They can modify verbs: □ *She wrote neatly*, adjectives: □ *extremely hot*, other adverbs: □ *fairly well*, whole clauses or sentences: □ *Anyway, it doesn't matter now*, or can be used to link clauses or sentences: □ *I dislike him; nevertheless, I feel responsible for him.* Adverbs are frequently formed by adding *-ly* to an adjective: □ *darkly* □ *wisely*, but this does not apply to all adverbs: □ *to work late* □ *to jump high*.

It is usually acceptable to place an adverb between parts of a verb: □ *I have often spoken about the matter*, but adverbs should not come between a verb and its direct object. Whether the adverb is positioned after the object or before the verb depends on the length of the object clause: □ *They tortured the prisoners cruelly.* □ *They cruelly tortured the political prisoners who had been arrested for demonstrating against the regime.* Careful positioning of the adverb is sometimes necessary in order to avoid ambiguity in a sentence: □ *She disliked intensely sentimental films.* If *intensely* relates to *disliked* it should be placed before the verb.

See also **ADJECTIVES**; **SPLIT INFINITIVE**.

adversary The pronunciation of this word with stress on the second syllable [ăd*ver*sări] is disliked by many users, who prefer the traditional pronunciation with stress on the first syllable [*ad*vĕr-sări]. See also **STRESS**.

adverse or **averse?** *Adverse*, meaning 'unfavourable', 'antagonistic', or 'hostile', usually precedes an abstract noun; *averse*, meaning 'disinclined', 'unwilling', or 'having a strong dislike', usually relates to people and is never placed before the noun it qualifies: □ *adverse criticism* □ *an adverse effect* □ *These working conditions are adverse to efficiency.* □ *The committee was not averse to the proposal.* □ *Her father is not averse to using violence.* □ *They are averse to all publicity.*

◆ The two adjectives are sometimes confused in the sense of 'opposed'.

Averse is often preceded by *not* and may be followed by *to* or *from*, *to* being preferred in modern usage.

Adverse may be stressed on either syllable, but the pronunciation [*ad*vers] is more frequent than [ăd*vers*]. *Averse* is always stressed on the second syllable [ă*vers*].

advertise This word, meaning 'promote or publicize': □ *a brochure advertising holidays*, is sometimes misspelt. This is one of the words ending in *-ise* that cannot be spelt *-ize*; see also **-IZE OR -ISE?**

advise The use of the verb *advise* as a synonym for 'tell', 'inform', 'notify', etc., is widely regarded as **COMMERCIALESE** and is best avoided in general usage: □ *Please advise us of your new address.* □ *I told* [not *advised*] *him that the meeting had been cancelled.*

◆ The *s* of *advise* should not be replaced by *z* in British or American

English. See also COUNSEL OR ADVISE?; -IZE OR -ISE?

adviser or **advisor**? This word, meaning 'person who gives advice',
may be spelt either *adviser* or *advisor*. Both spellings are fully
acceptable.

-ae- and **-oe-** In such words as *archaeology* and *amoeba*, the vowel
combinations *-ae-* and *-oe-* were once represented by the symbols æ and œ. They are now usually written or printed as separate letters and there is an increasing tendency for the *-a-* and
-o- to be omitted.

◆ In American English such words as *haemorrhage, oestrogen,* and
anaesthetic are spelt *hemorrhage, estrogen,* and *anesthetic.* In British
English the *-o-* has already been dropped from *ecumenical* (formerly
oecumenical) and the *-a-* and *-o-* are gradually disappearing from
medi(a)eval, encyclop(a)edia, f(o)etus, etc. This process of
simplification is disliked and resisted by some users.

The *-ae-* ending of such plural nouns as *vertebrae* and *formulae* (see
PLURALS) should not be reduced to *-e*.

See also ARCHAEOLOGY; ENCYCLOPEDIA OR ENCYCLOPAEDIA?;
FOETUS OR FETUS? etc.

aerial This word, meaning 'of the air; from an aircraft' and 'device that
receives or sends out broadcast signals', is sometimes misspelt.
Note particularly the *ae-* at the beginning of this word.

aero or **air**? Both these words may be used adjectivally or as prefixes
in the sense of 'relating to aeroplanes or aircraft': □ *aerobatics*
□ *airliner* □ *aerodrome* □ *airport* □ *an aero engine* □ *the air force*
□ *aerospace* □ *airspace*.

◆ In some American words the prefix *aero-* is replaced by *air-*: the
nouns *aeroplane* and *aerofoil,* for example, are rendered as *airplane*
and *airfoil* in American English.

aeroplane see AERO OR AIR?; PLANE.

aerosol Note the spelling of this word, particularly the *ae-* at the
beginning and the *-ol* at the end. An *aerosol* is a fine spray dispensed from a pressurized container; the noun may refer to the
container or the contents.

aesthetic, ascetic, or **acetic**? These three words should not be confused. The adjective *aesthetic* means 'relating to beauty or good
taste': □ *aesthetic value.* An *ascetic* is a person who practises self-
denial; *acetic acid* is the main component of vinegar.

◆ Note the spelling of *aesthetic,* particularly the *ae-*; the variant
spelling *esthetic* is restricted to American English.

Ascetic and *acetic* are not identical in pronunciation. The middle
syllable of *ascetic* is pronounced with the short [e] sound of *set,*
whereas the middle syllable of *acetic* is usually pronounced like the
word *seat*.

affect or **effect**? The noun *effect* means 'result'; the verb *affect* means
'influence' or 'have an effect on', hence its frequent confusion
with the verb *effect*, which means 'bring about' or 'accomplish':
□ *The new legislation may have an effect on small businesses.*
□ *The new legislation may affect small businesses.* □ *We have
effected a number of improvements. Affect* and *effect* are often
misused, one in place of the other: □ *Officials said yesterday the
downturn could effect the future of the scheme* (*The Guardian*).
□ *'It will have very little affect,' says ... the chief economist at the
merchant bank Morgan Grenfell* (*The Times*).

◆ The verb *effect* is largely restricted to formal contexts. The verb
affect is also used in the sense of 'assume', 'pretend', or 'feign':

□ *I affected an air of indifference.* □ *She affected to despise them.* □ *He affected ignorance.*

affectation or **affection**? *Affectation* is false behaviour that is intended to impress; *affection* means 'fondness' or 'tenderness'. The two nouns are related to different meanings of the verb *affect* and should not be confused.

affinity The use of the preposition *for* with the noun *affinity*, in the sense of 'liking' or 'attraction', is disliked by some users but acceptable to most: □ *He has a natural affinity for young children.*

◆ Those who object to this usage restrict the noun to the meaning 'reciprocal relationship or similarity', in which sense it is followed by *between* or *with*: □ *the affinity between the two friends* □ *her affinity with her brother.*

afflict or **inflict**? To *afflict* is to distress or trouble, to *inflict* is to impose: □ *He afflicted the prisoners with cruel torture.* □ *He inflicted cruel torture on the prisoners.* □ *Egypt was afflicted with a plague of locusts.* □ *A plague of locusts was inflicted on Egypt.*

◆ The direct object of *afflict* is the sufferer; the direct object of *inflict* is the suffering. The two verbs should not be confused.

affront or **effrontery**? *Affront* may be used as a noun or as a verb, meaning 'insult': □ *an affront to his pride* □ *I felt affronted.* The noun *effrontery* means 'impudence': □ *She had the effrontery to suggest we were mistaken.*

afters see DESSERT, SWEET, PUDDING, OR AFTERS?

afterward or **afterwards**? In British English *afterwards* is the usual form of the adverb meaning 'subsequently', the variant *afterward* being more frequently used in American English: □ *I'll do the washing-up afterwards.* □ *His foot was sore for days afterwards.*

◆ See also -WARD OR -WARDS?

again This word may be pronounced either [ăgen] or [ăgayn]. The first of these is probably the more frequently used.

aged This word is pronounced [ayjid] in the sense 'very old': □ *his aged uncle* □ *looking after the aged.* When the word is used with a specific age: □ *She was aged twenty*, it is pronounced [ayjd].

ageing or **aging**? This word, meaning '(the process of) becoming old', may be spelt *ageing* or *aging*.

ageism *Ageism* is discrimination against people on the grounds of age, especially in employment, or the offensive use of stereotypical images of old people. In the first sense the noun is not restricted to old age: any job advertisement that puts an upper (or lower) limit on the age of applicants may be described as *ageist*.

◆ In the second sense, the noun refers to the assumption that all people over retirement age are dependent, unproductive, intolerant, conservative, infirm, senile, unhappy, poor, etc. Such stereotypes are best avoided wherever possible in speech and writing. See also POLITICAL CORRECTNESS.

agenda The word *agenda* is used as a singular noun, with the plural form *agendas*: □ *The agenda for tomorrow's meeting has been changed.* □ *This item has appeared on a number of previous agendas.*

◆ Originally the plural form of the singular noun *agendum*, *agenda* literally means 'things to be done'. The singular form *agendum* remains in occasional very formal use in the sense of 'item on the agenda'.

aggravate The use of the verb *aggravate* and its derivatives in the sense of 'annoy', 'irritate', or 'exasperate' dates back to the early 17th century but is still disliked by some people. It is therefore best restricted to informal contexts and the offending word replaced by one of its synonyms: □ *I was aggravated by the noise.* □ *She has a number of aggravating habits.* □ *His lackadaisical attitude is a constant source of aggravation.*

◆ The principal meaning of *aggravate* is 'make worse': □ *Your resignation will aggravate our problem.* □ *The child's suffering was aggravated by the intense heat.*

Note the spelling of *aggravate*, particularly the *-gg-* and the single *-v-*.

aggressive The use of the adjective *aggressive* in the sense of 'assertive' or 'forceful' is best avoided where there is a risk of confusion with its principal meaning of 'belligerent' or 'hostile': □ *an aggressive salesman* □ *an aggressive approach.*

◆ The derived noun *aggressiveness* may be used for both senses of the adjective but *aggression*, with its connotations of hostility, should be restricted to the principal meaning: □ *the aggressiveness of the salesman's approach* □ *an act of aggression.*

Note the spelling of *aggressive* and *aggression*, particularly the *-gg-* and *-ss-*.

aging see AGEING OR AGING?

ago or **since?** It is wrong to place *ago* and *since* side by side: □ *It was a fortnight ago that* [not *since*] *I posted the letter.* □ *It is a fortnight* [not *a fortnight ago*] *since I posted the letter.*

◆ Note that *ago* is preceded by the past tense and *since* by the present tense in sentences of this type. The first example could be more simply expressed as: □ *I posted the letter a fortnight ago.* The adverbial use of *since* for this purpose: □ *I posted the letter a fortnight since*, is regarded as very old-fashioned.

The word *since* is also used as a preposition: □ *We have lived here since 1984.* If a period of time rather than a specific time is mentioned the preposition *for* should be substituted for *since*: □ *We have lived here for three years.*

agoraphobia This word, describing a fear of open spaces, is sometimes misspelt. Note the *o* after the *ag-*.

◆ The word originates from the Greek word *agora*, 'marketplace'. *Agoraphobia* should not be confused with *acrophobia*, which means 'fear of heights'.

-aholic The suffix *-aholic* (or *-oholic*), derived from the noun *alcoholic*, is being attached to an increasing number of words to denote a person who is obsessed by or addicted to something: □ *golfaholic* □ *shopaholic* □ *spendaholic* □ *chocoholic.*

◆ The noun *workaholic*, coined in the late 1960s, is now firmly established in the English language, but more recent examples are best avoided in formal contexts.

aid The noun *aid* is specifically used to denote a tangible source of help, assistance, or support, such as a device: □ *hearing aid* □ *teaching aids* □ *audiovisual aids* or money, supplies, equipment, etc., given to those in need: □ *overseas aid.*

◆ In the second sense the word has been used in a series of fund-raising campaigns inspired by the rock musicians of *Band Aid* (1984) and the immensely successful rock concert *Live Aid* (1985): □ *Prince Charles has shelved plans to raise millions for Britain's poorest areas .... Inner City Aid, the charity he helped launch last year as 'Band Aid for the inner cities', has stopped campaigning (Sunday*

Times).

The noun *aid* also occurs in certain fixed expressions, such as *legal aid*, *first aid*, and *in aid of*, but its use as a general synonym for 'help', 'assistance', or 'support' is disliked and avoided by many users.

The spelling of *aid* should not be confused with that of *aide*, a noun meaning 'assistant': □ *one of the president's aides*.

ain't As a contraction of *are not, is not, have not*, or *has not, ain't* is wrong. It is however generally widely used in speech and in such jocular expressions as: □ *Things ain't what they used to be.* □ *You ain't heard nothing yet.*

◆ As a contraction of *am not, ain't* is regarded by some users as slightly more acceptable, especially in informal American English in the interrogative form *ain't I*, which is replaced in British English by the grammatically irregular *aren't I* and in formal contexts by the full form *am I not*.

air see **AERO OR AIR?**

air miss or **near miss?** An *air miss* is the near collision of two aircraft in the sky. Such a situation is traditionally called a *near miss*, and both terms are in current use: □ *The Civil Aviation Authority has launched an investigation into a near miss 33,000 feet over Exmoor* (*Daily Telegraph*). □ *The Civil Aviation Authority is investigating an air miss over Sussex this morning* (*BBC South Today*).

◆ The expression *near miss* is also used figuratively to describe something that almost succeeds: □ *It was a near miss failing by just 1%; better luck next time!*

aisle This word is sometimes misspelt, the most frequent mistake being the omission of the silent *s*. Note also the initial *a-*.

alibi The use of the noun *alibi* as a synonym for 'excuse' or 'pretext' is disliked by many people and is best restricted to informal contexts: □ *He used the power cut as an alibi for not finishing his essay.* □ *Her illness provided her with an alibi to leave early.*

◆ The word *alibi*, which literally means 'elsewhere', is principally used in law to denote a defendant's plea (or evidence) that he or she was somewhere other than the scene of a crime: □ *I have an alibi for the afternoon of the robbery – I was at a conference in Birmingham.*

align This word, meaning 'bring or come into line; support', is sometimes misspelt. Note the single *l* and also the silent *g*.

all The use of the preposition *of* between *all* and *the, this, that, these, those*, or a possessive adjective is optional, *all* being preferred in British English and *all of* in American English: □ *All (of) the birds have flown away.* □ *I can't carry all (of) that.* □ *Do all (of) these books belong to you?* □ *All (of) her children are right-handed.* □ *They spent all (of) their leave in France.*

◆ *All* is used alone before nouns that are not preceded by *the, these, my, their*, etc.: □ *All birds have wings.* □ *All leave has been cancelled. All of* is always used before personal pronouns: □ *all of us* □ *all of it.* See also **ALL RIGHT OR ALRIGHT?; ALTOGETHER OR ALL TOGETHER?; NOT.**

allege The verb *allege*, meaning 'state without proof', is sometimes misspelt, the most frequent error being the substitution of *-edge* for the *-ege* ending.

all right or **alright?** The spelling *all right* is correct; the spelling *alright* is wrong.

◆ Some users defend the spelling *alright*, arguing that *altogether* and *already* are analogous spellings. Such users want to distinguish *alright*, 'satisfactory or acceptable': □ *The play was alright for children* from *all right*: □ *The answers were all right*, i.e. all the answers were right.

all together see ALTOGETHER OR ALL TOGETHER?

allude The verb *allude* means 'refer indirectly'; it should not be used in place of the verb *refer* itself: □ *He was alluding to the death of his father when he spoke of the loss of a lifelong friend.* □ *She referred* [not alluded] *to 'the spectre of redundancy' in her speech on unemployment.*

◆ *Allude* should not be confused with *elude* (see AVOID, EVADE, OR ELUDE?). See also ALLUSION, ILLUSION, OR DELUSION?; ALLUSIVE, ELUSIVE, OR ILLUSIVE?

allure or **lure**? Both these words may be used as a noun or as a verb. The verbs *allure* and *lure* are virtually synonymous in the sense of 'entice', 'tempt', or 'attract', but *lure* is by far the more frequent: □ *They tried to lure her away.* The verb *allure* is most frequently found in the form of the present participle, used as an adjective: □ *an alluring proposition.*

◆ The nouns *allure* and *lure* share the meaning 'attraction', but they are used in different contexts. *Lure* refers to the act of attracting, whereas *allure* refers to the attractiveness of the person or thing concerned: □ *the lure of the gambling table* □ *the allure of show business.*

allusion, illusion, or **delusion**? An *allusion* is an indirect reference (see ALLUDE); an *illusion* is a false or misleading impression or perception; a *delusion* is a false or mistaken idea or belief: □ *an allusion to his schooldays at Eton* □ *an optical illusion* □ *to destroy one's illusions* □ *delusions of grandeur* □ *to labour under a delusion.*

◆ The nouns *allusion* and *illusion* are confused because of their similarity in pronunciation, *illusion* and *delusion* because of their similarity in meaning.

Illusion and *delusion* are virtually interchangeable in some contexts but careful users maintain the distinction between them where necessary. An *illusion* is often pleasant and harmless; a *delusion* may be a sign of mental disorder: □ *the illusions of childhood* □ *the delusion that she is Queen Elizabeth I.* An *illusion* temporarily deceives the senses and is sometimes known to be false; a *delusion* is a strongly held opinion that is not easily eradicated.

See also ALLUSIVE, ELUSIVE, OR ILLUSIVE?

allusive, elusive, or **illusive**? The adjectives *allusive* and *illusive* relate to the nouns *allusion* and *illusion* respectively (see ALLUSION, ILLUSION, OR DELUSION?); *elusive* means 'difficult to catch, find, achieve, describe, define, remember, etc.': □ *an allusive style* □ *an illusive hope* □ *an elusive quality.*

◆ *Elusive* and *illusive* are identical in pronunciation [iloosiv]; *allusive* differs only in the pronunciation of the first syllable [ǎloosiv].

Of the three adjectives *elusive* is the most frequent. *Allusive* is rarely used and *illusive* is usually replaced by its synonym *illusory.*

almond This word is sometimes mispronounced. The *-l-* is silent, as in calm; the correct pronunciation is [ahmŏnd].

alone or **lone**? *Alone* and *lone* are both used in the sense of 'solitary' or 'by oneself', but *alone* is always placed after the verb and *lone* before the noun: □ *She was alone.* □ *a lone cyclist* □ *The house stood alone.* □ *a lone tree. Lone* tends to be used more in literary or poetic contexts. There is also some difference in meaning: *alone* is more likely to suggest loneliness or a desire for solitude, whereas *lone* usually describes a person or thing that simply happens to be on his/her/its own.

◆ When *alone* is placed directly after a noun or pronoun it means 'only': □ *He alone can help us.* Care should be taken to avoid ambiguity when *alone* is used in this sense: □ *She drinks whisky alone* probably means that she drinks no other alcoholic liquor, but it could imply that she drinks in solitude.

along with In the phrase *along with,* the word *along* is often superfluous: □ *The package was delivered along with the rest of the mail* could be changed to: □ *The package was delivered with the rest of the mail* without affecting the meaning.

alright see ALL RIGHT OR ALRIGHT?

also The use of the adverb *also* in place of the conjunction *and* is disliked and avoided by many users, especially in formal writing: □ *Please send me a copy of your new catalogue and a list of local stockists* [not ... *a copy of your new catalogue, also a list* ...].

◆ The combination *and also,* however, is generally acceptable: □ *Please send me a copy of your new catalogue and also a list of local stockists.*

In some sentences *also* must be carefully positioned in order to convey the intended meaning: □ *She also* [as well as someone else] *was carrying an umbrella.* □ *She was carrying an umbrella also* [as well as something else]. □ *She was wearing a raincoat and she was also carrying an umbrella.*

See also NOT ONLY ... BUT ALSO.

altar or **alter**? These words are sometimes confused. An *altar* is a place where sacrifices are offered to a god and also the table on which the bread and wine are blessed in Communion services: □ *The priest approached the altar. Alter* with an *e* means 'change': □ *a scheme for radically altering the whole tax system.*

◆ The different words both have the same pronunciation [awltĕr].

alternate or **alternative**? The adjective *alternate* means 'every other' or 'occurring by turns'; the adjective *alternative* means 'offering a choice' or 'being an alternative': □ *on alternate Saturdays* □ *alternate layers* □ *alternative routes* □ *an alternative suggestion.*

◆ The use of *alternate* in place of *alternative* is acknowledged by most dictionaries but disliked by many users. *Alternative* should not be used in place of *alternate.*

Note the difference in pronunciation between the adjective *alternate* [awltĕmăt] and the verb *alternate* [awltĕrnayt].

The adjective *alternative* is used with increasing frequency in the specific sense of 'not conventional' or 'not traditional': □ *alternative medicine* □ *alternative comedy* □ *alternative technology* □ *alternative energy.* This usage is best avoided where there is a risk of ambiguity: □ *I decided to buy an alternative newspaper.*

The noun *alternative* traditionally denotes either of two possibilities, or the opportunity of choosing between them, but is widely used with reference to three or more options or choices: □ *Are the current alternatives to the dole effective?* (*Daily Telegraph*). □ *If Owen had been picked as late as spring this year, so that the Alliance campaign could have presented him as the alternative to Thatcher and Kinnock* (*Daily Mail*). Criticism of this usage on etymological grounds (*alternative* is derived from the Latin word *alter,* meaning 'other (of two)') is dismissed by most authorities as pedantry.

alternative medicine see COMPLEMENTARY MEDICINE OR ALTERNATIVE MEDICINE?

although or **though**? As conjunctions, meaning 'despite the fact that', *although* and *though* are interchangeable in most contexts: □ *We bought the table, although/though it was damaged.*

◆ *Though* is slightly less formal but more versatile than *although*: it may be used in combination with *even* for extra emphasis; in the phrase *as though* (see AS IF OR AS THOUGH?); after an adjective; and as an informal substitute for the adverb *however*: □ *We bought the table, even though it was damaged.* □ *We bought the table, damaged though it was.* □ *Ground coffee tastes better than instant coffee; it's more expensive, though. Although* is not used in any of these contexts.

Though and (less frequently) *although* are also used in the sense of 'but' or 'and yet': □ *They applauded, though not enthusiastically.* □ *It's possible, though unlikely.*

The shortened forms *altho', altho, tho',* and *tho* are best avoided in formal writing.

See also IF.

altogether or **all together**? The adverb *altogether* means 'in all' or 'completely'; *all together* means 'at the same time' or 'in the same place': □ *She has nine pets altogether.* □ *Your system is altogether different from ours.* □ *They disappeared altogether.* □ *They arrived all together.* □ *We keep our reference books all together on a separate shelf.*

a.m. and **p.m.** Full stops are often retained in the abbreviations *a.m.* (for *ante meridiem*, meaning 'before noon') and *p.m.* (for *post meridiem*, meaning 'after noon') to distinguish *a.m.* from the verb *am*.

◆ The use of capital letters is acceptable but rare. See also ABBREVIATIONS.

The abbreviation *a.m.* refers to the hours from midnight to midday; *p.m.* refers to the hours from midday to midnight: □ *12.05 a.m.* is five minutes after midnight; □ *12.05 p.m.* is five minutes after midday. Such phrases as *8.15 a.m. in the morning* and *11.45 p.m. at night* are tautological; either *a.m.* or *in the morning* and either *p.m.* or *at night* should be omitted.

amateur This word, meaning 'person who follows an activity as a pastime rather than as a profession': □ *an amateur golfer*, has several pronunciations, the most frequent being [amătĕ]. The pronunciations [amăchĕ], [amătewr], and [amăter] are also heard.

ambience Some people object to the frequent use of the noun *ambience* as a pretentious synonym for 'atmosphere': □ *the ambience of the restaurant.*

◆ The French spelling *ambiance* and an anglicized form of the French pronunciation are sometimes used in English. The English pronunciation of *ambience* is [ambièns].

ambiguous or **ambivalent**? *Ambiguous* means 'having two or more possible interpretations or meanings' or 'obscure'; *ambivalent* means 'having conflicting emotions or attitudes' or 'indecisive': □ *The phrase 'a French horn player' is ambiguous.* □ *Many people are ambivalent about the issue of disarmament: they recognize the importance of the nuclear deterrent but feel that the money spent on nuclear weapons could be put to better use.*

◆ Careful users maintain the distinction between the two adjectives, avoiding the temptation to use *ambivalent* in place of *ambiguous*. In some contexts, including the above example, *be ambivalent* may be better replaced by *have mixed feelings* or *be in two minds.*

amen The word *amen*, meaning 'so be it', may be pronounced [aymen] or [ahmen]. Both pronunciations are correct.

amend or **emend**? Of these two verbs *amend*, meaning 'correct', 'improve', or 'alter', is the more general, *emend* being restricted to the correction of errors in a printed or written text: □ *The ambiguous wording of the opening paragraph has been amended.* □ *They have amended the rules.* □ *The manuscript was emended by an eminent scholar.*

◆ The pronunciation of *amend* [ămend] is very similar to that of *emend* [imend]. Their derived nouns, however, are quite different: □ *an amendment* □ *an emendation.*

amenity The noun *amenity* is ultimately derived from the Latin word for 'pleasant'. A few users prefer to restrict the term, which is generally used in the plural form *amenities*, to what is conducive to comfort or pleasure, objecting to its extended application to what is merely useful or convenient: □ *The amenities of the hotel include a sauna, swimming pool, licensed restaurant, and 24-hour room service.* □ *The town lacks some of the basic amenities, such as public toilets and a rubbish dump.*

◆ *Amenity* is usually pronounced [ameeniti], with a long *e*, but the pronunciation [ameniti], with a short *e*, is an accepted variant and is usual in American English.

America The word *America* is most frequently used with reference to the United States of America, although it strictly denotes the whole landmass comprising Canada, the USA, Central America, and South America.

◆ *The United States of America* may be shortened to *the United States, the USA, the US,* or (in informal contexts) *the States*: □ *I often go to the States on business. USA* and *US* are sometimes written or printed with full stops (see also **ABBREVIATIONS**).

Like *America*, the adjective *American* is largely restricted in general usage to the meaning 'of the USA'. The abbreviation *US* may be used adjectivally to avoid ambiguity: □ *a US actor.* There is no single noun that specifically denotes a native or citizen of the USA, but *American* is generally used for this purpose: □ *The book was written by an American.*

Americanisms For many years American English has had a significant influence on British English. Although many British purists dislike American English, in some respects its differences arise from greater conservatism than British English. Such words as: □ *gotten* □ *fall* (autumn) as well as many American spellings, were originally the British forms and have changed in Britain but not in the United States. American English is also a fertile ground for new words and idioms and there is no reason why British English should not borrow the more striking ones. Such American words as: □ *truck* □ *commuter* □ *teenager* have become part of British vocabulary.

◆ The most noticeable differences between American and British English are those of vocabulary. Most British people are familiar with the better-known American equivalents: □ *sidewalk* (pavement) □ *elevator* (lift) □ *cookie* (biscuit) □ *vacation* (holiday). It is when the same word or phrase is used with different meanings that confusion arises. If an American says: □ *I put on my vest and pants and washed up,* an English person might think of him washing the dishes in his underwear, while in fact he had put on his waistcoat and trousers and washed his hands.

There are various differences between British and American spellings: □ *tyre – tire* □ *mould – mold.* Many words ending in *-re* in

British English have the ending *-er* in American English: □ *centre –
center* □ *fibre – fiber*; many words ending in *-our* in British English have
the ending *-or* in American English: □ *colour – color* □ *humour –
humor*. British English has in most cases resisted American spellings,
although the American tendency to drop the *o* or *a* in words like *foetus*
or *encyclopaedia* is beginning to be adopted in British spelling. See
also **-AE- AND -OE-**; **SPELLING 1**.

The significant differences in grammar include a few past tenses
like the American *dove* (dived) or *gotten* and the American tendency
to say: □ *Do you have...?* where the British would say: □ *Have you...?*
or: □ *Have you got...?* See also **QUOTATION MARKS; SHALL OR WILL?;
SUBJUNCTIVE; TENSE**.

Much as many British people deplore the adoption of such American
words and phrases as □ *laid-back* □ *no way* □ *hype*, it can be
assumed that such words will continue to cross the Atlantic and that
they will continue to be absorbed into British English.

amiable or **amicable**? *Amiable* means 'friendly', 'pleasant', 'agreeable', or 'congenial'; *amicable* means 'characterized by friendli-
ness or goodwill': □ *an amiable man* □ *an amicable agreement*
□ *She smiled at me in an amiable manner.* □ *The dispute was settled in an amicable manner.*
◆ The two adjectives should not be confused.

amid, amidst, mid, or **midst**? *Amid* and *amidst* are synonymous, and
are used in formal or poetic contexts, but *amidst* is used more
rarely. Both mean 'in the middle of' or 'among': □ *amid the crowd*
□ *amidst the waving reeds*. The word *mid* also means 'in the
middle of'; in modern usage it is chiefly found in combination
with nouns: □ *mid-September* □ *mid-air*. *Midst* is most frequently used as a noun, in the phrases *in the midst of*, meaning
'in the middle of' and *in our/their/etc. midst*, meaning 'among us/
them/etc.': □ *in the midst of the election campaign* □ *There is a
traitor in our midst.*

amok or **amuck**? The work *amok*, pronounced [ămuk] or [ămok] and
used especially in the phrase *run amok*, 'behave in a violent manner; go berserk', has the rarer variant spelling *amuck*, pronounced [ămuk].
◆ The word derives from Malay *amoq* 'frenzied attack'.

among or **amongst**? The words *among* and *amongst* are interchangeable in all contexts, *among* being the more frequent in modern
usage: □ *They hid among/amongst the bushes.*
◆ Some users prefer *among* before a consonant sound and *amongst*
before a vowel sound: □ *among strangers* □ *amongst ourselves*.
See also **BETWEEN OR AMONG?**

amoral or **immoral**? *Amoral* means 'not concerned with morality' or
'having no moral standards'; *immoral* means 'not conforming to
morality' or 'infringing accepted moral standards': □ *an amoral
matter* □ *an amoral politician* □ *immoral behaviour* □ *an immoral
young man* □ *Some people consider vivisection to be immoral,
others have an amoral attitude to the issue.*
◆ Careful users maintain the distinction between the two adjectives,
both of which can be used in a derogatory manner.

The first syllable of *amoral* may be pronounced as a long *a*
[aymorrăl] or a short *a* [amorrăl]; *immoral* is pronounced [imorrăl].
Note the spellings of the two words, particularly the single *m* of *amoral*
and the *-mm-* of *immoral*.

amuck see **AMOK OR AMUCK?**

an see A OR AN?

anaesthetic This word, meaning 'a substance that produces a loss of feeling', is sometimes misspelt. Note the *ae* in the middle of the word.

◆ In the American English spelling, the second *a* is dropped: *anesthetic*. See also -AE- AND OE-.

analogous The adjective *analogous* is best avoided where *similar, equivalent, comparable, corresponding, like*, etc., would be adequate or more appropriate: □ *The new system is analogous to that used in the electronics industry.*

◆ The usual pronunciation of *analogous* is [ănalŏgŭs], with the hard *g* of *goat* and *analogue*, not the soft *g* of *gem* and *analogy*.

analyse The *s* of *analyse* should not be replaced with *z* in British English, *analyze* being the American spelling of the word.

◆ See also -IZE OR -ISE?

Some people object to the use of the verb *analyse* in place of *discuss, examine*, etc.: □ *Your proposal will be analysed at the next committee meeting.* The frequent use of the noun *analysis* in general contexts is also disliked, especially the phrases *in the last analysis, in the final analysis,* and *in the ultimate analysis,* which can usually be replaced by *in the end, at last, finally, ultimately,* etc.

analysis see ANALYSE.

ancillary This word, meaning 'supplementary or subsidiary': □ *ancillary services,* is sometimes misspelt. Note particularly the *c*, the *-ll-*, and the ending *-ary*, not *-iary*.

and The use of *and* at the beginning of a sentence is disliked by some users but acceptable to most. And it can sometimes be an effective way of drawing attention to what follows.

◆ Two or more subjects joined with *and* are used with a plural verb unless they represent a single concept. See also SINGULAR OR PLURAL?

For the use of a comma before *and* in a series of three or more items see COMMA 1. *And* may also be preceded by a comma in other contexts, especially in complex sentences or where there is a risk of ambiguity: □ *Jenny owns the red car, and the black car belongs to her brother.* □ *He unlocked the door with the key that he had found inside the stolen purse, and went in.* □ *She has been to Spain, Portugal, and Italy, and hopes to visit Greece next year.* The omission of the first *and* in the last example and similar sentences is a frequent error.

The use of *and* in place of *to* is best avoided in formal contexts: □ *We'd better try and find it.* □ *I'll come and see you tomorrow.*

See also AND/OR; I OR ME?

and/or The phrase *and/or* should only be used where three possibilities are envisaged: □ *cash and/or postage stamps*, for example, means 'cash, postage stamps, or both'.

◆ The phrase should not be used where *and* or *or* would be adequate: □ *This food is suitable for hamsters and* [not *and/or*] *gerbils.* □ *The bank is not open on Saturdays or* [not *and/or*] *Sundays.*

And/or is best restricted to official, legal, or commercial contexts and replaced elsewhere by a slightly longer phrase: □ *The casserole may be served with potatoes or carrots or both* [not *potatoes and/or carrots*].

angle Some people object to the frequent use of the noun *angle* in place of *point of view, standpoint*, etc.: □ *The report has been written from a unilateralist angle.*

◆ The verb *angle* implies a lack of objectivity: □ *The play was angled* to make the audience sympathize with the criminal.

annex or **annexe**? In British English *annex* is a verb meaning 'add' or 'appropriate'; *annexe* is a noun that denotes a building built or used as an extension: □ *to annex a state* □ *a room in the annexe.*
◆ The variant spelling of the noun without the final *-e* is largely restricted to American English. It is wrong to spell the verb with a final *-e*: □ *He had no ambitions to annexe the Department of Transport* (*The Guardian*).

anonymous This word, meaning 'of unknown origin or identity': □ *an anonymous donor*, is sometimes misspelt, the most frequent error being to replace the *y* with an *i*.

anorexic or **anorectic**? The words *anorexic* and *anorectic* are interchangeable. Either may be used as a noun or as an adjective to describe a person suffering from the disorder anorexia nervosa, although *anorexic* is used more frequently.

-ant or **-ent**? The suffixes *-ant* or *-ent*, identical in pronunciation, cause frequent spelling problems. Either suffix may be used to form nouns and adjectives: □ *the defendant* □ *a superintendent* □ *a defiant child* □ *an irreverent remark.* However, in many cases where both *-ant* and *-ent* forms exist, *-ant* is the usual form for the noun and *-ent* for the adjective (see CONFIDANT OR CONFIDENT?; DEPENDANT OR DEPENDENT?; PENDANT OR PENDENT?).
◆ It may be useful to remember that nouns and adjectives formed from verbs ending in *-ate* take the suffix *-ant* rather than *-ent*: □ *predominant* □ *stimulant* □ *tolerant* □ *mutant.*

ante- or **anti-**? These two prefixes are sometimes confused. *Ante-*, from Latin, means 'before': □ *antenatal* □ *anteroom* □ *antecedent.* *Anti-*, from Greek, means 'against; opposite to': □ *anti-apartheid* □ *anti-aircraft* □ *anti-American* □ *anticlockwise.*
◆ In British English, both prefixes are pronounced [anti]; in American English *anti-* is pronounced [anti] or [anti], *ante-* [anti].
In informal spoken English, *anti* is sometimes used as a preposition, meaning 'opposed to': □ *He's very anti politics* or as an adjective: □ *He's very anti.*

antennae or **antennas**? The noun *antenna* has two plural forms, *antennae* and *antennas.* The plural form *antennae*, pronounced to rhyme with *my* or *tree*, is used to denote an insect's or crustacean's feelers; when *antenna* is used to mean 'aerial' (this sense being of American origin) the plural form *antennas* is preferred.

anti- see ANTE- OR ANTI-?

anticipate The verb *anticipate* is widely used as a synonym for 'expect': □ *We do not anticipate that there will be any problems.* □ *Oil prices showed their expected leap yesterday …. But the rally was not as strong as some traders anticipated* (*Daily Telegraph*). This usage is disliked by many people, who restrict the verb to its accepted more formal senses of 'forestall', 'act in advance of', etc.: □ *Preventative medicine anticipates disease.* □ *They anticipated the attack by boarding up their doors and windows.* □ *You must learn to anticipate his needs.*
◆ The verb is best avoided altogether where there is a risk of ambiguity, as in such sentences as *I anticipated her resignation* and *The driver anticipated the accident.*

antihistamine The word *antihistamine*, which denotes a medicinal substance that is used to treat allergies, is sometimes misspelt. Note the third syllable, *-hist-* (not *-hyst-*), and the *-ine* ending.

antique or **antiquated**? The adjective *antique* is used to describe a piece of furniture or a work of art that is old and valuable: □ *a beautiful antique vase.* The adjective *antiquated,* meaning 'old-fashioned' or 'obsolete', is usually derogatory: □ *an antiquated washing machine* □ *antiquated procedures.*

antisocial, asocial, unsocial, or **unsociable**? These four adjectives are sometimes confused. Both *antisocial* and *unsociable* can mean 'unfriendly', describing somebody who avoids the company of others: □ *Our new neighbours seem rather antisocial/unsociable. Antisocial* is the stronger of the two and may also describe behaviour that causes harm or inconvenience to others: □ *an antisocial act/habit. Asocial,* a much rarer word, implies a deeper hostility to or withdrawal from society; *unsocial* is chiefly used in the phrase *unsocial hours,* referring to the time when most people are not at work: □ *You must be prepared to work unsocial hours.*

◆ See also **SOCIABLE OR SOCIAL?**

any The use of a singular or plural verb with the pronoun *any* depends on the sense and context in which it is used: □ *Is any of the furniture damaged?* □ *Ask him if any of his children watch/ watches the programme.*

◆ In the first example *any,* like *furniture,* must be used with a singular verb. In example of the second type a singular verb is preferred if *any* is used in the sense of 'any one' and a plural verb if *any* imples 'some'. See also **SINGULAR OR PLURAL?**

The use of *any* in place of *at all* is used in American English but should be avoided in British English: □ *Her manners haven't improved any.* See also **ANYBODY OR ANYONE?**

anybody or **anyone**? The pronoun *anybody* and its synonym *anyone* are interchangeable in all contexts.

◆ Both are used with a singular verb but are sometimes followed by a plural personal pronoun or possessive adjective (see **THEY**): □ *Has anybody/anyone finished their work?*

Note the difference between the one-word compound *anyone* and the more specific two-word form *any one,* both of which may be applied to people: □ *Anyone could have started the fire.* □ *Any one of the tenants could have started the fire.* Only the two-word compound is used of things: □ *These tables are not reserved, so you can sit at any one you like.*

apartheid The name of the South African political system *apartheid* may be pronounced in several different ways. Some users prefer the pronunciation [ăpart̄hayt] following the Afrikaans original. Other frequently used pronunciations are [ăpart̄hīt] and pronunciations in which the *h* is not sounded: [ăpart̄īt] and [ăpart̄īd].

apostrophe The apostrophe is used mainly to denote possession and other relationships: □ *Angela's house* □ *the Church of England's doctrines* □ *the rabbits' warren,* and to indicate omitted letters in contractions: □ *can't* □ *you're* □ *there's.*

◆ Difficulties with the possessive use of the apostrophe centre on its presence or absence and its position before or after the *s* (for the basic rules see **'S OR S'**?). Advertisers are particularly guilty of sins of omission: *mens clothes, last years prices, special childrens menu,* and market stalls are particularly prone to forming plurals with apostrophes: *potato's, apricot's.* Other examples mentioned by correspondents to *The Guardian* in March 1989 included: □ *cres's* □ *gateaux's* □ *Beware of the dog's.* Units of measure often have their apostrophes omitted; it should be: □ *50 years' service* □ *a six months' stay in America.* With well-known commercial organizations and products the tendency is now to drop the apostrophe: □ *Barclays Bank* □ *Macmillans* □ *Pears soap*.

Possessive personal pronouns do not take apostrophes: □ *his book* □ *its name* □ *it is ours*, but indefinite pronouns do: □ *anybody's guess* □ *no one's* fault. Purists have maintained that as *else* is not a noun or pronoun it cannot take an apostrophe, and have used the form: □ *someone's else*, but *someone else's* is now generally acceptable.

There are a few exceptions to the rule that apostrophes cannot be used for plurals. They can be used to indicate the plurals of individual letters, words, and numbers in expressions like: □ *It takes two I's in the past tense*. □ *She often begins sentences with and's and but's*. □ *He writes his 7's in the continental way*. The apostrophe is also sometimes used for the plural of some abbreviations: □ *MP's*, but this usage is becoming less frequent.

Apart from the use of the apostrophe to indicate contractions such as *shouldn't, I'm, 'n'* (for *and*: □ *salt 'n' vinegar flavour crisps*), it is used to indicate missing letters in poetic forms such as *e'er, o'er*, in terms such as *o'clock, will-o'-the-wisp*, and in names like *O'Connor*. It might also be used in writing dialogue to indicate Cockney or dialect speech: □ *'E was goin' to 'Ackney*. □ *... 'tis said 'a was a poor parish 'prentice* (Hardy, *The Mayor of Casterbridge*). Apostrophes are also sometimes used to indicate missing numbers: □ *the generation who were young in the '60s*.

Apostrophes are no longer generally used for shortened forms that are in general use: □ *flu* □ *phone* □ *photo* □ *plane*.

See also **CONTRACTIONS; DATES; -ING FORMS; ITS OR IT'S?; POSSESSIVES**.

appal Note the spelling of this verb, especially the *-pp-* and (in British English) the single *l*.

◆ The usual American English spelling of the word is *appall*. In British English the final *-l* is doubled before a suffix beginning with a vowel, as in *appalled* and *appalling* (see also **SPELLING 1**).

apparatus This word is usually pronounced [apăr*ay*tŭs] or [*ap*ăraytus], though the pronunciation [apăr*ahtŭs*] is also sometimes heard.

appendixes or **appendices**? The noun *appendix* has two accepted plural forms, *appendixes* and *appendices*.

◆ The use of the plural form *appendixes* is largely restricted to the anatomical sense of the word: □ *During his early years as a surgeon he removed countless tonsils, adenoids, and appendixes.*

In the sense of 'supplement (to a book, document, etc.)' the plural form *appendices*, pronounced [ăpend*iseez*], is preferred by most users: □ *One of the appendices lists foreign words and phrases in general usage.*

applicable In the more traditional pronunciation of this word, the first syllable is stressed [*ap*likăbl]. The pronunciation with the second syllable stressed [ă*plik*ăbl] is probably more frequently heard, however. See also **STRESS**.

apposition A noun or phrase that is in apposition supplies further information about another noun or phrase. Both nouns or phrases refer to the same person or thing; they are equivalent in meaning. In the sentence □ *Mary Jones, an accountant, was elected*, the phrases *Mary Jones* and *an accountant* are in apposition. In the phrase □ *the accusation that he had stolen the car*, *the accusation* and *that he had stolen the car* are in apposition.

◆ Like relative clauses (see **CLAUSE**), appositive nouns or phrases may be defining or non-defining. The phrase □ *that he had stolen the car* is non-defining in □ *The accusation, that he had stolen the car, was untrue* and defining in □ *The accusation that he had stolen the car was the most upsetting.*

Many names and titles are made up of two nouns in apposition; for example, *Lake* and *Geneva* in □ *Lake Geneva* or *Prince* and *Charles* in □ *Prince Charles*. Longer titles are better placed after the proper noun with which they are in apposition: □ *Mr Green, managing director of the company* (the insertion of *the* before *managing director* is optional).

See also COMMA 3.

appraise, apprise, or **apprize?** To *appraise* is to assess the quality or worth of something; *apprise* means 'inform': □ *She appraised their work.* □ *He apprised me of the details.* *Apprize* is listed in some dictionaries as a less frequent variant spelling of *apprise*; it is also an archaic verb meaning 'appraise'.

◆ The verb *apprise* is largely restricted to formal contexts.

appreciate The frequent use of the verb *appreciate* in place of *realize* or *understand* is disliked by a few users: □ *I appreciate that the child's parents were unaware of the risk.* □ *Do you appreciate our problem?*

◆ The principal senses of *appreciate* are 'be grateful for', 'recognize the worth of', and 'increase in value': □ *He would appreciate some assistance.* □ *She does not appreciate good wine.* □ *Their house has appreciated considerably during the past six months.*

apprehend or **comprehend?** These two verbs are sometimes confused when they have the meaning 'understand'. *Comprehend* implies a complete understanding, sometimes emphasizing the mental activity needed to come to such knowledge: □ *They did not fully comprehend the motives that lay behind her decision.* *Apprehend*, which is used fairly rarely in this sense, implies a perception – not always complete – of the essential quality or significance of something: □ *to apprehend the nature of beauty.*

◆ Both verbs have other meanings. *Apprehend* means 'arrest' and is used in formal contexts: □ *to apprehend a criminal.* In formal contexts *comprehend* means 'include', in which sense it is more frequently found in the form of the adjective *comprehensive* (see COMPREHENS-IBLE OR COMPREHENSIVE?): □ *a comprehensive survey.* The noun *comprehension* means 'understanding'; *apprehension* is rarely used in this sense.

apprise, apprize see APPRAISE, APPRISE, OR APPRIZE?

a priori The Latin phrase *a priori*, which literally means 'from the previous', is applied adjectivally to deductive or presumptive reasoning, arguments, statements, etc.

◆ The phrase is usually pronounced [ay prīorī], the pronunciation [ah preeoree] being an accepted variant.

apropos As a preposition meaning 'with regard to', *apropos* may be followed by *of*: □ *apropos (of) your enquiry* □ *apropos (of) the new development.*

◆ In formal contexts *apropos* is also used as an adjective, meaning 'appropriate', and as an adverb, meaning 'incidentally': □ *Your remark was not quite apropos.* □ *Apropos, have you paid the bill yet?*

Apropos is always written as one word in English, unlike the French phrase *à propos,* from which it is derived. Note that the initial *a* is followed by a single *p*.

The pronunciation of this word is [aprōpō]: the *-s* is not sounded.

apt 24

apt see LIABLE OR LIKELY?

aqueduct The noun *aqueduct*, describing a structure that carries water, is often misspelt. Note that the word begins *aque-*, not *aqua-* (as in *aqualung, aquaplane,* etc.).

Arab, Arabian, or **Arabic**? The adjective *Arab* relates to the people of Arabia and their descendants, *Arabian* to Arabia itself, and *Arabic* to the language of Arabia and other Arab countries: □ *an Arab sheikh* □ *the Arab nations* □ *the Arabian peninsula* □ *the Arabian Sea* □ *an Arabic numeral* □ *Arabic literature.*

◆ All three words are used as nouns, *Arabian* being a rare variant of *Arab*: □ *His sister married an Arab.* □ *Arabic is the official language of Egypt.*

The word *Arab* is also applied to a breed of horse that is used for riding; the *Arabian Nights* is a collection of oriental tales; and *gum arabic* (note the lower-case *a*) is a gum obtained from certain acacia trees.

arbiter or **arbitrator**? An *arbiter* is a person who has the power to judge or who has absolute control; an *arbitrator* is a person who is appointed to settle a dispute: □ *an arbiter of fashion* □ *an arbiter of human destiny* □ *The arbitrator's decision proved acceptable to both parties.*

◆ The general term *arbiter* may be used in place of the more specific *arbitrator*, but the two nouns are not fully interchangeable.

arbitrarily The adverb *arbitrarily* should be stressed on the first syllable [arbitrărĕli].

◆ The pronunciation [arbitrerrĕli], in which the primary stress shifts to the third syllable, is unacceptable to many people.

arbitrator see ARBITER OR ARBITRATOR?

arch- and **archi-** The prefixes *arch-* and *archi-* are both derived from a Greek word meaning 'to rule'. In words beginning with the prefix *arch-* the *-ch-* sound is soft, as in *choose*; in words beginning with the prefix *archi-* the *-ch-* sound is hard, as in *chord*: □ *archbishop* [archbishŏp] □ *architect* [arkitekt].

◆ The word *archangel* [arkaynjĕl] is an exception to this rule. In the suffixes *-arch* and *-archy* the *-ch-* sound is always hard: □ *patriarch* [paytriark] □ *anarchy* [anărki].

archaeology This word, describing the study of the material remains of ancient cultures, is spelt with the vowels *-aeo-* in the middle of the word in British English.

◆ The spelling *archeology* is used in American English. See also -AE- AND -OE-.

archetypal The adjective *archetypal* is best avoided where *typical, characteristic, classic, original,* etc., would be adequate or more appropriate: □ *an archetypal Yorkshire village.*

archi- see ARCH- AND ARCHI-.

Argentine or **Argentinian**? Either word may be used as an adjective, meaning 'of Argentina', or as a noun, denoting a native or inhabitant of Argentina. Though purists prefer *Argentine*, *Argentinian* is more frequent in both senses: □ *the Argentinian/ Argentine flag* □ *an Argentinian/Argentine ship* □ *Her stepfather is an Argentinian/Argentine.*

◆ The word *Argentine* may be pronounced [arjĕntīn] or [arjĕnteen], rhyming with *mine* or *mean.*

The republic of Argentina is sometimes called *the Argentine*: □ *They lived in the Argentine for several years.*

argument Note the spelling of this word. The final *-e* of the verb *argue* is dropped when the suffix -*ment* is added to form the noun.

arise or **rise**? *Arise* means 'come into being', 'originate', or 'result'; *rise* means 'get up', 'move upwards', or 'increase': □ *A problem has arisen.* □ *The quarrel arose from a misunderstanding.* □ *He rose to greet her.* □ *The water level is rising.*

◆ *Arise* may be substituted for *rise* in some senses of the latter, but this usage is largely restricted to formal or poetic contexts and is generally regarded as old-fashioned.

See also **RAISE OR RISE?**

aristocrat In British English this word is usually stressed on the first syllable [áristŏkrat].

◆ Some speakers stress the second syllable [ăristŏkrat], but this is disliked by many people, although standard in American and Scottish English.

around or **about**? In British English *about* is preferred to *around* in the sense of 'approximately': □ *We have about/around 200 employees.* □ *He left at about/around eleven o'clock.*

◆ Many people regard the use of *around* in this sense as an Americanism.

In the sense of 'here and there' *around* and *about* are interchangeable in most contexts: □ *to run around/about* □ *sitting around/about all day* □ *toys scattered around/about the room.* In the sense of 'surrounding' *about* is less frequent than *around* (in American English) and *round* (in British English).

See also **AROUND OR ROUND?**

around or **round**? *Around* and *round* are synonymous in most of their adverbial and prepositional senses, *around* being preferred in American English and *round* in British English: □ *I turned round/around.* □ *The wheels went round/around.* □ *They sat round/around the table.* □ *She wore a gold chain round/around her ankle.*

◆ See also **AROUND OR ABOUT?**

arouse or **rouse**? *Arouse* means 'stimulate' or 'excite'; *rouse* means 'wake' or 'stir': □ *Their curiosity was aroused.* □ *The ban on smoking has aroused widespread opposition.* □ *The noise of the aeroplanes roused the child.* □ *I was roused to anger by his accusations.*

◆ The direct object of *arouse* is usually an abstract noun; the direct object of *rouse* is usually a person or animal. The substitution of *arouse* for *rouse* in the sense of 'wake' is acceptable but rare.

artefact or **artifact**? Both spellings of this noun, referring to an object made by a person, e.g., a tool with special historical interest, are correct. *Artefact* is probably more frequent in British English and *artifact* in American English.

articles see **A OR AN?; THE.**

artifact see **ARTEFACT OR ARTIFACT?**

artist or **artiste**? An *artist* is a person who is skilled in one or more of the fine arts, such as painting or sculpture; an *artiste* is a professional entertainer, such as a singer or dancer: □ *the Dutch artist Vincent Van Gogh* □ *the music-hall artiste Marie Lloyd.*

◆ In its extended sense of 'skilled person' the noun *artist* may be substituted for *artiste*, which is becoming less frequent. Both nouns can be applied to people of either sex.

as The *as ... as* construction may be followed by a subject pronoun or an object pronoun: □ *She loves the child as much as he* [as much as he does]. □ *She loves the child as much as him* [as much as she loves him].

◆ In informal contexts the subject pronoun is sometimes replaced by the object pronoun, especially in simple comparisons: □ *as tall as me* □ *as old as them.* This usage, which is unacceptable to many people, should be avoided in formal contexts.

The *as ... as* construction is sometimes ambiguous: □ *She loves the child as much as her husband,* for example, may mean 'she loves the child as much as her husband does' or 'she loves the child as much as she loves her husband'. In such cases the missing verb may be inserted for clarity.

The substitution of *so ... as* for *as ... as* in negative constructions is optional: □ *He is not so/as clever as his sister.* When the construction is followed by an infinitive with *to*, however, *so ... as* is preferred: □ *I would not be so careless as to leave my car unlocked.*

When the *as ... as* construction is followed by a comparative adjective or adverb, the second *as* is sometimes omitted in informal contexts but is retained by careful users in formal contexts: □ *Her car is as old (as) or older than mine.* □ *He dances as badly (as) or worse than you.*

The use of the *as ... as* construction when *as* alone is required, in the sense of 'though', is widely disliked in British English: □ *Tired as he was* [not *As tired as he was*], *he finished the race.*

The dialectal use of *as* in place of *that* or *who* should be avoided in formal contexts: □ *I don't know that* [not *as*] *I agree.* □ *the man who* [not *as*] *cleans our windows.*

See also AS FAR AS; AS FROM; AS IF OR AS THOUGH?; AS PER; AS TO; AS WELL AS; AS YET; BECAUSE. AS, FOR. OR SINCE?; COMPARATIVE AND SUPERLATIVE; LIKE; SUCH AS OR LIKE?

ascent see ASSENT OR ASCENT?

ascetic see AESTHETIC, ASCETIC, OR ACETIC?

as far as The phrase *as far as ... is concerned* can often be replaced by a simple preposition: □ *The course is a waste of time for the more experienced students* [not *as far as the more experienced students are concerned*].

as for see AS TO.

as from The phrase *as from* is best avoided where *from, on, at,* etc., would be adequate or more appropriate: □ *I shall be available for work from* [not *as from*] *next Monday.* □ *Sunday deliveries will cease on* [not *as from*] *1 November.* □ *The increase will come into effect at* [not *as from*] *midnight.*

◆ *As from* may serve a useful purpose in the context of retrospective payments, agreements, etc.: □ *The reduced interest will be payable as from last July.*

Asian or **Asiatic**? Either word may be used as an adjective, meaning 'of Asia', or as a noun, denoting a native or inhabitant of Asia. *Asian* is preferred in both senses, the use of *Asiatic* with reference to people being considered racially offensive: □ *an Asian/Asiatic country* □ *an Asian* [not *Asiatic*] *doctor* □ *an Asian* [not *Asiatic*] *living in Europe.* See also INDIAN.

◆ The word *Asian* may be pronounced [ayshǎn] or [ayzhǎn].

as if or **as though**? *As if* and *as though* are interchangeable in most contexts: □ *The car looked as if/though it had been resprayed.* □ *She trembled, as if/though aware of our presence.* □ *He opened his mouth as if/though to speak.*

◆ *As if* is preferred in emphatic exclamations: □ *As if it mattered!* □ *As if I needed their advice!* See also SUBJUNCTIVE; WERE OR WAS?

asocial see ANTISOCIAL, ASOCIAL, UNSOCIAL, OR UNSOCIABLE?

as of see AS FROM.

as per The use of the phrase *as per* in place of *according to* is widely
regarded as **COMMERCIALESE**: □ *as per instructions* □ *as per the
specifications.*
     ◆ The use of the jocular expression *as per usual* in place of *as usual*
     is best restricted to informal contexts: □ *The train was ten minutes late,
     as (per) usual.*

asphalt This word, used to describe a material used in road-surfacing,
is often misspelt. Note particularly the *sph.* The preferred pronunciation is [*as*falt], although [*ash*falt] is also heard.

asphyxiate This word, meaning 'suffocate', is sometimes misspelt.
Note particularly the *phy,* as in *physics.*

assassinate This word, meaning 'murder an important person': □ *The
president was assassinated,* is often misspelt. Remember the *-ss-*,
which occurs twice.
     ◆ The nouns *assassin* and *assassination* follow the same spelling
     pattern.

assent or **ascent**? These two words are sometimes confused, being
identical in pronunciation. The noun *assent* means 'agreement'
(see ASSENT OR CONSENT?); the noun *ascent* means 'the act of
ascending', 'a climb', or 'upward slope': □ *She gave her assent.*
□ *the ascent of Everest.*

assent or **consent**? Either word may be used as a verb, meaning
'agree', or as a noun, meaning 'agreement'. The verb *consent*
sometimes implies greater reluctance than *assent:* □ *They readily
assented to our plan.* □ *After hours of persuasion they consented
to end the strike.*
     ◆ The noun *assent* has connotations of acceptance or
     acquiescence, whereas the noun *consent* denotes approval or
     permission: □ *with the assent of my colleagues* □ *without her parents'
     consent.*

assertion or **assertiveness**? An *assertion* is a positive statement or
declaration; *assertiveness* is the state of being dogmatic or
aggressive: □ *to make an assertion* □ *assertiveness training.* Careful users maintain the distinction between the two nouns.
     ◆ The use of *assertion* in place of *assertiveness* is probably due to
     confusion with the noun *self-assertion,* which means 'putting oneself
     forward in a forceful or aggressive manner'.

assignation or **assignment**? Both these nouns may be used to denote
the act of assigning: □ *the assignation/assignment of household
chores.*
     ◆ *Assignation* has the additional meaning of 'secret meeting';
     assignment also means 'task': □ *an assignation with her lover*
     □ *having completed his first assignment.* The two words are not
     interchangeable in either of these senses.

assimilate This word, meaning 'absorb or integrate', is often misspelt.
The only double letters are the *-ss-*.
     ◆ The verb *assimilate* should not be confused with *simulate* (see
     **DISSEMBLE, DISSIMULATE, OR SIMULATE?; SIMULATE OR
     STIMULATE?**).

assume or **presume**? In the sense of 'suppose' or 'take for granted' the
verbs *assume* and *presume* are virtually interchangeable: □ *I
assume/presume you will accept their offer.*
     ◆ In some contexts *assume* may suggest a hypothesis postulated
     without proof and *presume* a conclusion based on evidence: □ *He
     assumed that she was an experienced player and did not offer her any*

advice. □ *From her performance in the opening game he presumed that she was an experienced player.*

Both verbs have a number of additional senses. *Assume* means 'undertake', 'feign', or 'adopt': □ *to assume responsibility* □ *to assume an air of astonishment* □ *to assume a new name. Presume* means 'dare' or 'take advantage of': □ *I did not presume to contradict him.* □ *They presumed on our hospitality.*

assurance or **insurance**? Both *assurance* and *insurance* are used to denote financial protection against a certainty, such as the death of the policyholder: □ *life assurance* □ *life insurance.*

◆ Of the two nouns only *insurance* is used with reference to financial protection against a possibility, such as fire, accidental damage, theft, medical expenses, etc.: □ *motor insurance* □ *household insurance* □ *travel insurance* □ *health insurance.*

The noun *assurance* has a number of other meanings derived from the verb *assure*, such as 'guarantee', 'confidence', etc.: □ *an assurance of help* □ *an air of assurance.*

See also ASSURE, ENSURE, OR INSURE?

assure, ensure, or **insure**? To *assure* is to state with conviction or to convince; to *ensure* is to make certain; to *insure* is to protect financially: □ *He assured me that the carpet would not be damaged.* □ *Please ensure that you do not damage the carpet.* □ *I insured the carpet against accidental damage.*

◆ In American English the word *insure* is sometimes used in place of *ensure.*

See also ASSURANCE OR INSURANCE?

asthma This word, which describes the disorder that makes breathing difficult, is sometimes misspelt, the most frequent error being in the combination of the consonants *sthm.*

◆ It is not easy to pronounce the word in its entirety, and [asmǎ] is probably more frequently heard than the full pronunciation [asthmǎ].

as though see AS IF OR AS THOUGH?

as to Many people object to the unnecessary use of *as to* before *whether, what, why,* etc.: □ *There is some doubt (as to) whether she is suitably qualified.* □ *He offered no explanation (as to) why he was late.*

◆ *As to* is also best avoided where *of, about, on,* etc., would be adequate or more appropriate: □ *Please give me your opinion as to the efficiency of the system.* □ *They received no warning as to the risks involved.*

The phrase *as to* (or *as for*) may serve a useful purpose at the beginning of a sentence, in the sense of 'with regard to' or 'concerning': □ *As to/for the results of the survey, they will be published in next month's magazine.* □ *As for his sister, she survived the accident.*

astrology or **astronomy**? These two nouns are sometimes confused. *Astrology* is the study of the movements of the planets and their effect on human affairs; *astronomy* is the scientific study of the universe.

astronomical The use of the adjective *astronomical* in the sense of 'very large' is best restricted to informal contexts: □ *an astronomical increase in crime* □ *astronomical prices.*

◆ This usage probably originated in the very high figures required to express measurements in astronomy.

astronomy see ASTROLOGY OR ASTRONOMY?

as well as When two or more verbs are linked by the phrase *as well as,* in the sense of 'in addition to', the verb that follows *as well as* is usually an *-ing* form: □ *The burglar broke a valuable ornament, as well as stealing all my jewellery.* □*As well as weeding the borders, the gardener pruned the roses and mowed the lawn.*

◆ For the use of a singular or plural verb after nouns linked by *as well as* see **SINGULAR OR PLURAL?**

As well as is best avoided where there is a risk of confusion with the literal sense of the phrase: □ *Mark plays golf as well as Peter,* for example, may mean 'both Mark and Peter play golf' or 'Mark and Peter are equally good at golf.'

as yet The phrase *as yet*, meaning 'up to now' or 'so far', is best avoided where *yet* would be adequate: □*Have you sold any tickets yet* [not *as yet*]*?* □*I haven't sold any tickets (as) yet.* □*No tickets have been sold (as) yet.* □*Only a few tickets have been sold as yet.*

at or **in**? *At* is traditionally used before the name of a village or small town, *in* before the name of a large town, city, country, etc.: □*He lives at Great Snoring.* □ *They stayed at Keswick.* □ *She works in Southampton.* □ *We have a house in Scotland.*

◆ *At* may be replaced by *in* when the speaker or writer is referring to his or her own place of residence, work, etc.: □ *I live in Southbourne.* In other contexts *at* generally indicates a more exact or specific position than *in*: □ *He lives in North Street.* □ *He lives at 27 North Street.* □ *She works in a bank.* □ *She works at Barclays Bank.*

ate This word, which is the past tense of the verb *eat*, is pronounced [et] or [ayt] in British English.

◆ In American English the usual pronunciation is [ayt], the pronunciation [et] being considered nonstandard.

-ate A number of words ending in *-ate* may be used as adjectives (and/ or nouns) and verbs. In these adjectives and nouns the ending *-ate* is pronounced [-ăt]; in verbs it is pronounced [-ayt]. For example, the adjective *animate* is pronounced [anim*ă*t] whereas the verb is pronounced [*ani*mayt], and the noun *delegate* is pronounced [*deli*gät], whereas the verb is pronounced [*deli*gayt].

attach This word, meaning 'join or fasten', is sometimes misspelt. Note the *-tt-* and the *ch*. There is no *t* before the *ch*.

at the sharp end To be *at the sharp end* of an activity is to be involved in the area in which there is the greatest difficulty or danger: □*football referees at the sharp end of violence on the field and also criticism from the media* □ *'Nurses' ... a repeat of the* [television] *series on life at the sharp end of the National Health Service* (*The Guardian*). Care should be taken to avoid using this expression, which is best restricted to informal contexts.

◆ The expression is a figurative extension of the term *sharp end*, nautical slang for the bows of a ship.

at this moment in time Many people object to the frequent use of the cliché *at this moment in time* in place of *now*: □*I am not in a position to comment on the situation at this moment in time.*

attribute The verb *attribute*, meaning 'ascribe', is generally used with the preposition *to*: □ *They attributed the accident to careless driving.* □ *To what do you attribute your success?* □ *The idea was attributed to his colleague.*

◆ The use of *attribute* with the preposition *with*, in the sense of 'credit', is wrong: □ *His colleague was credited* [not *attributed*] *with the idea.* Note the difference in pronunciation between the verb *attribute* [ă*trib*ewt] and the noun *attribute* [*atrib*ewt]. See also **STRESS.**

attributive see ADJECTIVES.

au fait *Au fait* means 'familiar', 'informed', or 'competent': □ *Are you au fait with the procedure?*

◆ The phrase *au fait* is of French origin and is sometimes written or printed in italics in English texts. It is pronounced [ō *fay*].

aural or **oral**? These two words are sometimes confused, partly because sometimes confused, partly because they both often have the same pronunciation [*awrăl*]. *Aural* means 'of the ear or the sense of hearing', *oral* means 'of the mouth; expressed in speech'. An *aural comprehension* tests a person's ability to understand a spoken language; an *oral examination* is one in which the questions and answers are spoken, not written.

◆ In order to distinguish *aural* and *oral*, the variant pronunciations [*owrăl*] for *aural* and [*oral*] for *oral* are sometimes used.

Australianisms There are fewer differences between Australian and British English than between American and British English, probably because until comparatively recently nearly all settlers in Australia were British or Irish. The words that were adopted by the early settlers from the Aboriginal languages: □ *koala* □ *boomerang*, are now in general use, and most British people are familiar with those Australian words which were coined in the context of the early days of European settlement: □ *outback* □ *bushranger* □ *swagman* □ *digger* □ *walkabout*.

◆ Although the speech of many Australians is not markedly different from British forms, for most British people Australian English is associated with the pronunciation known as *Broad Australian* or *Strine*. In the amusing book *Let Stalk Strine*, published in 1965, examples are given of this characteristic pronunciation: □ *egg nishner* (air conditioner) □ *garbler mince* (couple of minutes) □ *chee semmitch* (cheese sandwich).

Australian English seems particularly adapted to informal use (the very formal British *good day* becomes the informal Australian greeting *g'day*) and it abounds in colourful slang. The word best known in Britain: □ *cobber* is out of date, although □ *dinkum* and □ *pommy* or *pom* (a British person) are still used. The words □ *chunder* (vomit) □ *crook* (ill) □ *rubbish* (as a verb, see NOUNS) are becoming familiar in Britain. Slang words are often formed by adding *-ie* or *-o* to an abbreviated word: □ *arvo* (afternoon) □ *garbo* (refuse collector) □ *sickie* (day taken off work for real or invented illness).

Australian spelling has traditionally been identical to British. In recent years, however, Australian spelling, as well as pronunciation and vocabulary, has been influenced by American English.

author The use of the word *author* as a verb, in place of *write*, is disliked and avoided by careful users in all contexts: □ *She has written* [not *authored*] *a number of books on the subject.*

◆ On the use of *authoress*, see -ESS.

authoritarian or **authoritative**? The adjective *authoritarian* means 'favouring obedience to authority as opposed to individual freedom'; *authoritative* means 'having authority' or 'official': □ *an authoritarian father* □ *an authoritarian regime* □ *an authoritarian policy* □ *an authoritative voice* □ *an authoritative article* □ *an authoritative source.*

◆ The word *authoritarian*, which is also used as a noun, usually has derogatory connotations, whereas *authoritative* is generally used in a complimentary manner.

Authoritative is often misspelt, the most frequent error being the omission of the third or fourth syllable.

avenge see REVENGE OR AVENGE?

averse see ADVERSE OR AVERSE?

avoid, evade, or **elude**? *Avoid* means 'keep away from'; *evade* and *elude* mean 'avoid by cunning or deception': □ *He avoided the police by turning down a side street.* □ *He evaded the police by hiding in the cellar.* □ *He eluded the police by using a series of false names.*

◆ All three verbs have other senses and uses: □ *She managed to avoid managing to avoid damaging the car.* □ *He is trying to evade his responsibilities.* □ *Your name eludes me.*

The difference between the terms tax *avoidance* and tax *evasion*, both of which relate to methods of reducing or minimizing tax liability, is that tax *avoidance* is legal and tax *evasion* is not.

avoidance see AVOID, EVADE, OR ELUDE?

await or **wait**? *Await* is principally used as a transitive verb, meaning 'wait for' or 'be in store for'; *wait* is chiefly used intransitively, often followed by *for*, in the sense of 'remain in readiness or expectation': □ *They awaited the verdict of the jury with trepidation.* □ *I wonder what adventures await you in your new career.* □ *She asked us to wait outside.* □ *He waited for the rain to stop.*

◆ In the sense of 'wait for' *await* is largely restricted to formal contexts, where its direct object is usually an abstract noun. In other contexts *wait for* is preferred: □ *We're waiting for* [not *awaiting*] *a taxi.*

Wait is used as a transitive verb in the phrase *wait one's turn* and similar expressions. The phrasal verb *wait on* means 'serve'; its use in place of *wait for* or *await* is disliked by many people: □ *They're waiting on the results.*

awake, awaken, wake, or **waken**? All these verbs may be used transitively or intransitively in the literal senses of 'rouse or emerge from sleep' and the figurative senses of 'make or become aware': □ *Please waken me at six o'clock.* □ *He wakes earlier in the summer.* □ *Her sister's plight awakened her to the problems faced by single parents.* □ *They awoke to the dangers of drug abuse. Wake* and *waken* are preferred in literal contexts and *awake* and *awaken* in figurative contexts.

◆ The verb *wake*, which is more frequently used than *waken*, is often followed by *up*: □ *Don't wake the baby up.* □ *I woke up in the middle of the night. Woke* and *woken* respectively are the usual forms of the past tense and past participle of *wake*, although *waked* is also used from time to time. *Waken* is a regular verb.

Awaken and (less frequently) *awake* are also used in the sense of 'arouse': □ *His absence from work may awaken/awake her suspicions.* The usual forms of the past tense and past participle of the verb *awake* are *awoke* and *awoken* respectively, *awaked* being an accepted variant. Like *waken, awaken* is a regular verb.

The word *awake* is also used as an adjective, meaning 'not asleep' or 'alert': □ *Did the children manage to stay awake?* □ *The police are awake to the situation.*

award-winning The adjective *award-winning*, which is frequently used in advertising, is meaningless unless the nature of the award is specified: □ *an award-winning design* □ *an award-winning writer.*

◆ It is therefore best avoided or replaced with a more precise synonym, such as *excellent* or *remarkable.*

aware The use of the adjective *aware* before the noun it qualifies, in the sense of 'knowledgeable' or 'alert', is disliked by many users: □ *one of our more aware students* □ *financially aware individuals.*

◆ Aware is usually placed after a noun or pronoun and is often followed by *of*: □ *I am aware of the need for secrecy.*

awesome The adjective *awesome* is used as a slang term of approval, especially by young people: □ *'What was the party like?' 'Awesome!'* In formal contexts it should be restricted to the sense of 'inspiring admiration or dread': □ *an awesome responsibility.*

awful see AWFULLY.

awfully The use of the adverb *awfully* as an intensifier is best restricted to informal contexts: □ *I'm awfully sorry.* □ *It's awfully difficult to decide which to buy.*

◆ The substitution of *awful* for *awfully* in this sense is wrong.

Ultimately derived from the noun *awe*, *awful* and *awfully* are rarely used in their literal senses ('being inspired or filled with awe') today. Their principal meanings in modern usage are 'bad' or 'badly': □ *The weather is awful.* □ *They played awfully in yesterday's match.*

axe In journalese the verb *axe* is frequently used in the sense of 'dismiss', 'terminate', 'remove', etc.: □ *Britain's biggest teaching union, the National Union of Teachers, is to axe a third of its head office staff* (Sunday Times). □ *Coloroll, the wallpaper and furnishing company, is to axe 120 jobs* (Daily Telegraph). □ *Saturday Review, the BBC's current arts magazine programme ... will be axed after a final series starting in October* (Sunday Times).

◆ This usage is best avoided in general contexts.

axes *Axes* is the plural of *axe* or *axis*: □ *axes for chopping wood* □ *the horizontal and vertical axes.* The plural of *axe* is pronounced [aksiz] and the plural of *axis* is pronounced [akseez].

-babble Many people dislike the increasing use of the suffix *-babble* to coin new words for particularly incomprehensible types of jargon: □ *technobabble* □ *psychobabble* □ *Eurobabble* □ *ecobabble*. See also **-SPEAK**.

bachelor This word, meaning 'unmarried man': □ *a confirmed bachelor*, is sometimes misspelt. The most frequent error is to insert a *t* before the *ch*.

back burner The phrase *on the back burner* is often used, especially in informal contexts, in the figurative sense of 'deferred' or 'postponed': □ *'People are examining things on a long-term basis, not on an expedient basis,' a London Underground spokeswoman said. 'Priorities will be made, and some things will be put on a back burner.' (The Guardian).* Care should be taken not to overuse this phrase.

back formation Back formation is a way of creating new words, usually verbs, by removing an affix from an existing word: □ *donate* (from *donation*) □ *extradite* (from *extradition*). Many such words have been used for so long that they are no longer recognized as back formations: □ *edit* (from *editor*) □ *laze* (from *lazy*) □ *burgle* (from *burglar*) □ *enthuse* (from *enthusiasm*).

◆ Back formations often arise as a result of false assumptions about the composition of a word. People hearing the word *scavenger* might assume incorrectly that the noun comes from a verb *scavenge* and so come to use this verb. Often, however, the removed affix is not a genuine affix at all. The 19th-century writer on obesity and slimming, William Banting, invented a system of diet which became known as *the banting system*, which in turn gave rise to the verb *to bant*.

New verbs are regularly being formed in this way: □ *televise* □ *automate* □ *explete* □ *euthanase*. Many, like *liaise* (from *liaison*), are disliked when newly coined, but when such verbs are created from a genuine need for them in the language, they tend to be retained.

background Some people object to the use of the word *background* to mean 'the circumstances that relate to, lead up to, or explain an event or experience', preferring to use such words as *circumstances, conditions, context,* or *setting* instead.

◆ Recently *background* has also been used for a person's work or professional experience and training: □ *The successful applicant will probably have a building background (Executive Post).*

backlash *Backlash* is used metaphorically to describe a strong adverse reaction to a recent event or political/social development or tendency: □ *the backlash against the Government's radical new changes in education policy.*

◆ The metaphor suggests a sudden reaction, but in fact the word is often used in describing a gradual reaction, perhaps over years: □ *The philosophy of the New Right can be seen as a backlash against the pacifism and permissiveness of the 1960s.*

backward or **backwards**? In British English *backward* is principally used as an adjective, *backwards* being the usual form of the adverb meaning 'towards the back' or 'in reverse': □ *a backward step* □ *a backward child* □ *walking backwards* □ *written backwards*.

◆ The adverb *backward* is more frequently used in American English. See also **-WARD** OR **-WARDS**?

bacteria The term *bacteria* refers to all microorganisms exhibiting certain characteristics. They are thought of as disease-bearing, but in fact many are harmless and some essential to human life, although others do cause disease.

◆ *Bacteria* is a plural noun so expressions like: □ *I think it's caused by a bacteria* are incorrect; the singular term is *bacterium*.

bad The adjective *bad* is used as a slang term of approval, especially by young people. The potential ambiguity of this usage is obvious. See also **WICKED**.

◆ This sense derives originally from American black English.

bade *Bade* is a form of the past tense of the verb *bid*: □ *He bade them farewell*. Its traditional pronunciation is [bad], but [bayd] is also acceptable.

bail or **bale**? The spellings of these words are often confused. The primary senses of these words are as follows. *Bail* is the security deposited as a guarantee of the appearance of an arrested person; a *bale* is a large quantity of hay, old newspapers, etc. The associated verbs also follow these spellings: □ *Davies was released on £10,000 bail.* □ *His friends bailed him out for £10,000.* □ *bales of old papers* □ *to bale hay*.

◆ In the senses of scooping water out of a boat, helping someone out of a difficult situation, and escaping from an aircraft in an emergency by using a parachute, either *bail out* or *bale out* can be used.

The *bails* are the two crosspieces over the stumps in cricket.

baited or **bated**? These two words are occasionally confused. *Baited* means 'provoked or teased' or 'hooked or trapped with food to attract a fish or animal'. *Bated* is used only in the expression *with bated breath*, meaning 'tense with anxiety or excitement': □ *They waited for news of the missing child with bated breath*.

balance Some people dislike the frequent use of the noun *balance* in the sense of 'remainder', especially in nonfinancial contexts: □ *The balance of the work will be completed by the end of the month*.

bale see **BAIL** OR **BALE**?

baleful or **baneful**? The adjective *baleful* means 'harmful' or 'menacing': □ *a baleful stare*. It should not be confused with the adjective *baneful*, meaning 'destructive' or 'fatal', which is very rare in modern usage.

balk or **baulk**? Either spelling may be used for this word: □ *He balked* [or *baulked*] *at paying such a high price.* □ *The horse balked* [or *baulked*] *at the fence.* □ *As usual she was balked* [or *baulked*] *in her ambitions by a man*.

ball game or **ballpark**? Both these terms have informal idiomatic uses, of American origin. In the phrase *a whole new ball game, ball game* means 'state of affairs'; in the phrases *in the right ballpark* and *not in the same ballpark, ballpark* means 'range' or 'area': □ *a ballpark figure* is an estimate or approximate figure. The two terms are sometimes confused, producing such expressions as: □ *It was a completely new ballpark*.

balmy or **barmy**? These words are sometimes confused. *Balmy* means 'mild and pleasant': □ *a balmy evening*. *Barmy*, an informal word in British English, means 'foolish': □ *I've never heard of such a barmy idea!*

◆ *Balmy* derives from *balm*, a plant with fragrant leaves that is used for flavouring foods and for scenting perfumes. The word derives from the Latin *balsamum* 'balsam'. *Barmy* comes from the Old English *beorma* 'the yeasty froth of fermenting beer'.

In American English and sometimes in British English, *balmy* is the main spelling for both senses.

baneful see BALEFUL OR BANEFUL?

banister A *banister*, a handrail supported by posts fixed alongside a staircase, has the less common variant spelling *bannister*.

baptismal name see FIRST NAME, CHRISTIAN NAME, FORENAME, GIVEN NAME, OR BAPTISMAL NAME?

barbarian, barbaric, or **barbarous**? *Barbaric* means 'crude, primitive, uncivilized': □ *They discovered a barbaric tribe living in the bush*; or sometimes merely 'uncultured, unsophisticated': □ *Most teenagers have barbaric tastes in music*. *Barbarian* as a noun means 'someone living barbarically' and as an adjective is synonymous with *barbaric*. *Barbarous* means 'cruel, harsh, or inhuman': □ *Torture is condemned as a barbarous practice*.

◆ *Barbaric* is often used with the same condemnatory meaning as *barbarous*, although it can be used approvingly: □ *The dance had a barbaric vitality*.

barbecue The word *barbecue* is often misspelt. The most frequent error is the substitution of *-que* for the *-cue* ending, perhaps influenced by advertisements that use the nonstandard phonetic spelling *bar-b-q*.

barely see HARDLY.

barmy see BALMY OR BARMY?

base or **basis**? Both *base* and *basis* mean 'a foundation, substructure, or support'. *Base* is usually used to refer to the bottom support of a tangible object: □ *the base of a pillar*, while *basis* is used for abstract or theoretical foundations: □ *on the basis of all the evidence received* □ *The new pay scale provides a sound basis for the new contract*.

◆ *Base* is also used to mean 'a principal ingredient': □ *The cocktail has a whisky base*, and 'a centre', as in: □ *We used the flat as our London base*. *Base* can be used as a verb: □ *The company is based in Sheffield*, and an adjective: □ *base unit*.

The plural of both *base* and *basis* is *bases* but the plural of *base* is pronounced [baysiz] and the plural of *basis* [bayseez].

basically The literal sense of *basically* is 'concerning a base or basis, fundamentally': □ *His argument has a superficial persuasiveness but it is basically flawed.* □ *I believe she is basically a good person.*

◆ It is often used to mean no more than 'importantly': □ *It is basically the case that fats can cause heart disease*; and it has recently become fashionable to put it at the beginning of a sentence, where its presence is often wholly superfluous. This usage is disliked by some: □ *Basically, I don't think he should have been offered the job.*

basis see BASE OR BASIS?

bated see BAITED OR BATED?

bath or **bathe**? In British English the verb *bath* means 'have a bath (in a bathroom)', or 'wash someone else in a bath': □ *bath the baby*, while the noun means 'the vessel in which one baths, or the act of washing in a bath'. *Bathe* means 'immerse in liquid, apply water or soothing liquid to (a wound)', or 'swim, usually in the sea, for pleasure': □ *Who's coming for a bathe?* In American English *bathe* is used to mean 'to have a bath' and does not have the transitive use of *bath*.

◆ *Bath* is pronounced [bahth] and *bathe* [baydh]. The past tense of both verbs is *bathed* and the present participle *bathing*, but the pronunciation differs: *bath*: [bahtht], [*bah*thing]; *bathe*: [baydhd], [*bay*dhing].

bathroom see TOILET, LAVATORY, LOO, OR BATHROOM?

battalion The word *battalion*, denoting a military unit, is sometimes misspelt. Note the consonants *-tt-* and *-l-*, which are the same as those in the word *battle*.

baulk see BALK OR BAULK?

BC see AD AND BC.

be The infinitive *be* is used in some British dialects in place of other parts of the verb: □ *It be a fine day*. In standard speech it is used mainly in imperatives: □ *Be quiet!*, after *to*: □ *You ought to be careful*, and after an auxiliary verb: □ *He should be home soon.*

◆ Two common uses after an auxiliary verb concern age and money: □ *She'll be 40 tomorrow.* □ *That'll be £10 exactly. Be* is often used to mean 'become': □ *What do you want to be when you grow up?*

beat or **beaten**? *Beat* is the past tense and *beaten* the past participle of the verb *beat*: □ *He beat the eggs.* □ *She has beaten the champion.*

◆ The use of *beat* as a variant form of the past participle is largely restricted to the informal phrase □ *dead beat*, meaning 'exhausted'.

beautiful This word, meaning 'delightful to the senses': □ *a beautiful woman* □ *a beautiful sunset*, is sometimes misspelt. Note particularly the first letters *beau-*.

◆ The word derives from the Old French word *biau* and comes ultimately from the Latin *bellus*, meaning 'pretty'.

because The conjunction *because* means 'for the reason that': □ *You're cold because you need warmer clothes.*

◆ It is often used incorrectly in such constructions as: □ *The reason her accent is so good is because her mother is French*, which should be: *Her accent is so good because her mother is French*, or: *The reason for her accent being so good is that her mother is French*. Another mistaken use of *because* is to mean 'the fact that': □ *Because he's deaf doesn't mean he's daft*. See also NOT; REASON.

because, as, for, or **since**? All these words are used to introduce clauses which give the reason for whatever has been said in the main clause.

◆ *As* and *since* are similar in use, although *since* is rather more formal. They are used more often at the beginning of a sentence than *because*, and tend to be used when the reason is already well known or when the reason is considered not as important as the main statement: □ *As you're only staying a little while, we'd better have tea now.* □ *He refrained from smoking between courses, since he knew that was generally thought to be impolite.* □ *As/Since we went there in the summer, the weather was gloriously hot. Because* tends to put the emphasis on the cause: □ *He married her because she was rich. Because* is also sometimes used to introduce a reason for stating a fact: □ *You must have forgotten to invite him, because he didn't turn up. For* would be better here although it would have a more formal sound. *For* always comes between the elements it joins and places equal emphasis on the main statement and the reason: □ *She never saw him again, for he returned to Greece soon afterwards.*

Ambiguity in the use of *as* should be avoided, since it can mean both 'while' and 'because': □ *As Hugh went out to do the shopping, Sandra looked after the baby.*

because of see DUE TO, OWING TO, OR BECAUSE OF?

befriend Some people dislike the increasing use of the verb *befriend* in the sense of 'make friends with': □ *She soon befriended her new neighbours.* The traditional meaning of the verb is 'act as a friend to (by giving assistance or showing kindness)': □ *They befriended me when I first came to work at the hospital.*

beggar This word, describing a person who begs, is sometimes misspelt. Note the ending *-ar*, not *-er*.

◆ This spelling is different from other 'doer' words such as *hunter*, *miner*, and *writer*.

beg the question To *beg the question* is sometimes used as if it meant 'evade the question skilfully' or even 'raise the question'. In fact it means 'base an argument on an assumption whose truth is the very thing that is being disputed'.

◆ For example, to argue that God must exist because one can see evidence of his creation in the natural beauties that surround us is *begging the question*, for the premise that these natural beauties are evidence of God's creation is unproved, and dependent on the truth of God's existence, which is supposed to be the conclusion of the argument.

behalf To speak or act *on behalf of* someone else is to act as the representative of that person or those people: □ *I am speaking on behalf of my union.*

◆ In American English *in behalf of* is also used and a distinction is sometimes drawn between *on behalf* (acting for) and *in behalf* (in the interest of). A frequent mistake is to use *on behalf* instead of *on the part*: □ *That was a serious error on behalf of the Government.*

beige This word, describing a very pale brown colour, is sometimes misspelt. Note the *ei* and the soft *g*. See also SPELLING 5.

bells and whistles The phrase *bells and whistles* is used in informal English to refer to the nonessential facilities and special features that are used to promote sales of a particular computer, software package, or similar product: □ *This system's got fewer bells and whistles, but it's half the price.* The phrase should not be overused.

beloved This word, meaning 'dearly loved', may be pronounced [bi*luv*id] or [bi*luvd*]. Either is acceptable.

below, beneath, under, or **underneath**? These words all mean 'lower than', and the distinctions between them are subtle.

◆ *Below* and *under* are often synonymous; *below* is contrasted with *above*, and *under* with *over*. *Below* alone is used to refer to written material following: □ *See chapter 5 below*, and is more often used in comparison of levels: □ *She lives in the flat below.* □ *He was below me in rank. Under* is used in reference to being subject to authority: □ *He served under Montgomery. Underneath* is used mainly for physical situations, and often suggests proximity: □ *She kept her savings underneath her mattress. Beneath* can be synonymous with *underneath* but sounds either old-fashioned or poetic; it is now used mainly to mean 'unworthy of': □ *beneath contempt.*

beneficent, beneficial see BENEVOLENT, BENIGN, BENEFICENT, OR BENEFICIAL?

benefit Note the single -*t*- in the spelling of the past tense: □ *benefited* and the present participle: □ *benefiting*.
   ◆ The *t* is not doubled, because the syllable containing this consonant is not stressed. See also **SPELLING 1**.

benevolent, benign, beneficent, or **beneficial**? These are all adjectives suggestive of doing or intending good. *Benevolent* means 'disposed to do good; charitable': □ *a donation from a benevolent well-wisher*. *Benign* means 'kind, mild, and well-disposed' and can be used of things as well as people: □ *a benign climate*; it is also used as a medical term meaning 'non-cancerous': □ *a benign tumour*. *Beneficent* means 'doing good; promoting good' and is used of people, while *beneficial* means 'promoting good or well-being' and is often used of things: □ *The waters are said to be beneficial to one's health*.

bereft *Bereft* was formerly synonymous with *bereaved* but is now used mainly to suggest loss or deprivation of any nonmaterial thing: □ *He was now bereft of all hope*.
   ◆ When used of death, *bereft* suggests the desolation of loss more forcefully than does *bereaved*: □ *A year after his death she still wandered through the silent house, bereft*. It should not be used merely as a synonym for 'without', with no sense of loss, as in: □ *I was unable to help, being bereft of any mechanical skill*.

beside or **besides**? *Beside* means literally 'by the side of': □ *Come and sit beside me*, and is also used in the expression *beside oneself*, meaning 'extremely agitated': □ *He was beside himself with grief*. *Besides* can mean 'moreover': □ *I won't be able to go; besides, I don't want to*, 'as well as': □ *Besides the usual curries, the restaurant offers some unusual tandoori specialities*, and 'except for; other than': □ *He's interested in nothing besides cricket*.
   ◆ This last use is always inclusive, not exclusive as with *except*: □ *Besides Ben, my colleagues are all Jewish* implies that Ben is Jewish; while *Except for Ben* ... implies that he is not.

best-before date see **SELL-BY DATE**.

best-selling *Best-selling* is the adjective derived from *best-seller*, which is applied to anything which has sold very well, but particularly a book which has sold a great number of copies: □ Sue Townsend, author of the best-selling *Adrian Mole* books.
   ◆ The term *best-selling* is applied to the author as well as the books: □ *best-selling novelist, Frederick Forsyth*.

bet or **betted**? *Bet* is the usual form of the past tense and past participle: □ *They bet me £10 I wouldn't do it*.
   ◆ *Betted* is a much rarer word, preferred in more general intransitive contexts: □ *He has never betted in his life*, but even here a phrase such as *place a bet* is more common: □ *He has never placed a bet in his life*.

bête noire A *bête noire* is something that a person fears or hates: □ *Rock music is her bête noire*. The phrase is of French origin and is sometimes written or printed in italics in English texts.
   ◆ Note the spelling of the phrase, particularly the accent on the first -*e*- and the -*e* ending of *noire*. The plural is formed by adding *s* to both words: □ *What are your bêtes noires?*

betted see **BET OR BETTED**?

better The phrase *had better* means 'ought to' or 'should': □ *You had better close the window*. □ *She'd better stay here*. Careful users do not drop the word *had* (or its contraction '*d*), even in informal contexts: □ *I'd better apologize*, not *I better apologize*. This last form, without *had* or '*d*, is common in informal speech, but it should be avoided when writing.

◆ The negative form of the phrase is *had better not*: □ *He had/He'd better not be late,* but *better hadn't* is also heard in informal speech: □ *He better hadn't be late.*

between The preposition *between* is used either before a plural noun: □ *the interval between the acts* or in conjunction with *and*; it should not be used with *or*: □ *You must choose between your family life and* [not *or*] *your work.*

◆ *Between* should not be used with *each* or *every* followed by a singular noun: □ *There is a gap of one foot between the skittles* [not *between each skittle*].

See also I OR ME?

between or **among**? *Between* is traditionally used when speaking of the relationship of two things, and *among* of three or more: □ *There was a clear hostility between George and Henry.* □ *There was dissent among the committee members.*

◆ However, in current usage *between* is acceptable as a substitute for *among*: □ *agreement between the NATO countries,* although *among* is still only used for several elements. *Between* is also used when discussing the joint activities of a group: □ *The carol-singers collected £50 between them,* and in the expression *between ourselves,* meaning 'in confidence': □ *Between ourselves, I think he's heading for a nervous breakdown.*

See also AMONG OR AMONGST?

bi- The prefix *bi-* always means 'two' but sometimes in the sense of doubling: □ *bicycle* □ *bifocal,* and sometimes halving: □ *bisection.* This is particularly confusing with words like *biweekly,* which sometimes means 'every two weeks' and sometimes 'twice a week'. It is probably best to avoid *biweekly* and *bimonthly* and express in a fuller form what is intended.

◆ *Biannual* means 'twice a year', while *biennial* means 'every two years'.

A *bicentenary* (or *bicentennial*) is a 200th anniversary. *Bicentennial* is used more frequently in American English and can also be used as an adjective: □ *bicentennial celebrations.*

bias The doubling of the final *s* of the word *bias* before a suffix beginning with a vowel is optional. Most dictionaries give *biased,* with *biassed* as an acceptable alternative.

◆ See also SPELLING 1.

Bible or **bible**? The noun *Bible* is spelt with a capital *B* when it refers to the sacred writings of the Christian religion: □ *the first book of the Bible* □ *a Bible reading.* When the noun refers to a copy of the book containing these writings, it may be spelt with a lower-case *b-*: □ *I bought her a bible for Christmas.* The noun is also spelt with a lower-case *b-* when it refers to an authoritative book on a particular subject: □ *the gardener's bible.*

◆ The adjective *biblical* is usually spelt with a lower-case *b-*: □ *in biblical times.*

bid The noun *bid,* normally meaning 'an offer', takes on a new meaning in popular journalism, where it is used, particularly in headlines, to mean 'an attempt or effort': □ *Athlete's bid for title* □ *Rescue bid fails* □ *Vicar's bid to cut family breakdowns.*

big bang The *big-bang theory* is a cosmological theory that suggests that the universe originated in an explosion of a mass of material.

◆ The *Big Bang* is also a vogue expression to describe the radical reorganization of the London Stock Exchange which took place in

1986: □ *British Rail is to set up a new region for East Anglia, the first since nationalisation in 1948, to cope with growth in the area caused largely by the effects of the Big Bang in the City of London* (*The Guardian*).

The term is increasingly used in general contexts to denote any sudden radical change or reform: □ *the big-bang approach to solving the problems of the National Health Service.*

billion *Billion* has traditionally meant 'one million million' in Britain. However, in the United States it means 'one thousand million' and this usage has been increasingly adopted in Britain and internationally.

◆ When used with specific figures the word *of* is not used: □ *Five billion dollars*, not *five billion of dollars*. When used informally to mean 'a great number', *billions of* is sometimes used: □ *Billions of people are living in poverty.*

bimbo *Bimbo* is a slang term used in a derogatory manner, especially by the media. It is applied to an attractive but unintelligent young woman, especially one who has a much-publicized affair with somebody who is in the public eye: □ *She was portrayed by the tabloid press as a money-grabbing bimbo.*

bio- The prefix *bio-* comes from the Greek word *bios*, meaning 'life', and words beginning with it have a connection with life or living organisms: □ *biology* □ *biography* □ *biopsy.*

◆ There are several recently coined words having the *bio-* prefix: □ *bionic* 'the application of knowledge about living systems to the development of artificial systems' □ *biodegradable* 'able to decompose organically without harming the environment' □ *biorhythms* 'supposed regular cycles in human physiological processes that affect emotions and behaviour' □ *bioethics* 'study of moral problems connected with issues like euthanasia, surrogate motherhood, genetic engineering, etc.'.

bivouac The verb *bivouac* adds a *-k-* before the suffixes *-ed* and *-ing*: □ *We bivouacked halfway up the mountain.* See also SPELLING 1.

bizarre Note the spelling of this word, meaning 'eccentric or odd', particularly the single *-z-* and the *-rr-*.

◆ Do not confuse *bizarre* with *bazaar*, 'a type of market'.

black *Black* is the word now usually applied to dark-skinned people of Afro-Caribbean origins and is the term most black people themselves prefer: □ *black power* □ *black consciousness*. In Britain it is sometimes extended to include other nonwhite races. *Coloured* is considered offensive as it groups all non-Caucasians. In South Africa it is a technical term used to refer to South Africans of mixed descent. The terms *Negro* and *Negress* are also considered offensive.

◆ *Black* is used in many words and phrases, usually having negative connotations: □ *black magic* □ *blackleg* □ *black market*. Some black people resent the association of the colour black with evil and unpleasantness and, while it is difficult to find synonyms for established words like *blackmail*, it is desirable to avoid such possibly offensive terms as: □ *a black look* □ *an accident black spot* □ *blacken someone's name.*

black hole The term *black hole*, originally used in astronomy, is increasingly found in figurative contexts, where it is used with a variety of meanings: □ *If a region of the UK gets into trouble through high wages, underinvestment or because it is regarded by business as an economic black hole, Whitehall can bail it out* *with grants* (*The Guardian*). □ *It is likely that many of the 'black holes' in BCCI's accounts ... can be put down to transactions connected with the nuclear bomb project* (*The Guardian*).

◆ In astronomy, a *black hole* is a hypothetical region of space with such a high gravitational field that nothing can escape from it.

blame *Blame*, as a verb, means 'hold responsible; place responsibility on': □ *He was blamed for the accident.* The expression *blame (it) on:* □ *They all blame it on me* is disliked by some careful users, who would substitute: □ *They blame me for it* or: *They put the blame on me.* However, the usage is well-established and is acceptable in all but very formal contexts.

blanch or **blench**? Both these verbs mean 'make or become white' or 'make or become pale'. *Blanch* may be applied to people or things and is more frequently used as a transitive verb: □ *The sun had blanched the rug.* □ *Her face was blanched with fear.* *Blench* is chiefly applied to people and is more frequently used as an intransitive verb: □ *He blenched with shock.*

◆ In this sense the verb *blench* is a variant of *blanch*, which is derived from the Old French *blanc* 'white'. There is an unrelated verb *blench*, meaning 'recoil (in fear)', which is derived from the Old English *blencan* 'to deceive'.

In cookery, the verb *blanch* refers to the process of immersing vegetables, nuts, etc., in boiling water: □ *blanched almonds.*

blatant or **flagrant**? *Blatant* and *flagrant* are both concerned with overtly offensive behaviour but their usage is not identical. *Blatant* means 'crassly and conspicuously obvious': □ *The article was blatant propaganda.* *Flagrant* means 'conspicuously shocking or outrageous': □ *The European parliament sees the tougher measures as a 'flagrant violation of human rights and justice'* (*Sunday Times*).

◆ *Blatant* can be used of a person: □ *a blatant liar*, but *flagrant* is used only of abstract things and carries a stronger suggestion of moral disapproval.

blench see BLANCH OR BLENCH?

blends A *blend*, also known as a *portmanteau word*, is a new word that is formed by joining parts of two other words, usually the beginning of one and the end of the other, such as: □ *brunch* (*br*eakfast + l*unch*) □ *motel* (*mo*tor + ho*tel*). Many of these words fill a genuine gap in the English language; others are best restricted to informal contexts.

◆ Some people dislike the increasing number of neologisms coined in this way: □ *camcorder* ([video] *cam*era + re*corder*) □ *dramadoc* (*drama* + *doc*umentary) □ *magalog* (*maga*zine + cata*log*ue) □ *infotainment* (*info*rmation + enter*tainment*) □ *gazundering* (*gazum*ping + *under*) □ *Chunnel* (*Ch*annel + t*unnel*) □ *Japlish* (*Jap*anese + Eng*lish*).

blessed This word sometimes causes problems with pronunciation. The word *blessed*, the past tense of the verb *bless*: □ *He blessed the child*, is pronounced [blest]. The noun or adjective *blessed*: □ *the Blessed Sacrament*, is usually pronounced [blesid] but is occasionally pronounced [blest].

blip *Blip*, a term used in radar, has developed the figurative sense of 'sudden change or interruption; temporary minor problem'. It became a vogue word in the late 1980s when the Chancellor of the Exchequer, Nigel Lawson, dismissed a sudden rise in the Retail Price Index as a 'temporary blip'. The word should not be overused in this figurative sense.

◆ A *blip* on a radar screen is the sharp peak or flash of light that indicates the position of something.

bloc or **block**? The noun *bloc* denotes a group of people or nations that have political aims or interests in common: □ *the Communist bloc*. It should not be confused with *block*, which has a wide range of meanings and uses: □ *a block of wood* □ *a mental block* □ *a block of flats.*

blond or **blonde**? These two spellings of the word meaning 'light in colour' are sometimes confused. *Blond* is used when the subject is masculine: □ *He has blond hair; blonde* is used when the subject is feminine: □ *She is a blonde.*

blue The verb *blue* has the slang sense 'squander': □ *He blued the prize money on drink*. It is synonymous with the verb *blow*, used in the slang sense 'spend freely or recklessly': □ *She blew her inheritance*. The two verbs are virtually interchangeable; neither should be used in formal contexts. Ambiguity or confusion may arise from the fact that *blue* (present tense of *blue*) and *blew* (past tense of *blow*) are identical in pronunciation.

blue-chip *Blue-chip* is originally a Stock Market term referring to a share issue which is considered to be both reliable and profitable: □ *a blue-chip investment.*

◆ It is extended to companies and any extremely worthwhile asset or property: □ *one of the world's most successful manufacturers ... with a blue-chip reputation* (*Sunday Times*). The meaning has now become further extended, to 'fashionable and exclusive' or 'of the highest standard': □ *polo, the blue-chip sport* (*Daily Telegraph*) □ *Parents in Britain believe they are entitled to blue-chip facilities when they go out and about with their children* (*Daily Telegraph*). Many people dislike the use of the word in this way.

blueprint A *blueprint* is literally a print used for mechanical drawing, engineering, and architectural designs. The word is used metaphorically to mean any plan, scheme, or prototype: □ *a blueprint for a successful life* □ *the London launch of a policy document, 'A Blueprint for Urban Areas'* (*The Times*). Although a literal blueprint is a finished plan, the metaphorical use, very popular as a jargon and journalistic term, is just as often applied to preliminary schemes. Care should be taken, however, not to overuse this word.

blush or **flush**? Both these verbs mean 'go red in the face'. To *blush* may be a sign of modesty, embarrassment, shame, or guilt; to *flush* may indicate any of these emotions as well as stronger feelings, such as anger, or the effects of alcohol or physical causes.

◆ The verb *flush* is also used transitively, often in the passive or in the form of the past participial adjective: □ *He was flushed with rage*. To be *flushed* may also indicate excitement or be the result of exertion or illness: □ *You look flushed – have you got a temperature? Blush* cannot be used in this way.

boat or **ship**? The use of *boat* or *ship* is mainly a matter of size. *Boat* is usually applied to smaller vessels, especially those that stay in shallow or sheltered waters: □ *a rowing boat* and: □ *lifeboat*, and *ship* to larger vessels that travel the open seas: □ *steamship* □ *warship.*

◆ The rule is by no means invariable: cross-Channel ferries are informally described as *boats*. Most sailing expressions refer to ships even when applied to boats: □ *amidships* □ *aboard ship* □ *The fishing boat was shipwrecked.*

bona fide *Bona fide* is an adjective meaning 'of good faith; genuine or sincere': □ *I will accept any bona fide offer. Bona fides* is a singular noun, meaning 'good faith, sincerity, honest intention': □ *He had no documentary proof but we did not doubt his bona fides.*

◆ *Bona fide* is also sometimes used to mean 'authentic' as in: □ *It's not a reproduction; it's a bona fide Matisse.*

Bona fide is pronounced [bōnă fīdi] in British English, but sometimes [bōnă fīd] in American English. *Bona fides* is pronounced [bōnă fīdeez].

born or **borne**? These two spellings are sometimes confused. *Borne* is the past participle of the verb *bear*: □ *They had borne enough pain.* □ *The following points should be borne in mind.* □ *His account is simply not borne out by the facts.* □ *It was borne upon him that the decision was irrevocable.* □ *airborne supplies.* In the sense of 'giving birth', *borne* is used in phrases where the mother is the subject: □ *She has borne six children*, and also in the passive with *by*: □ *borne by her. Born* is used for all other passive constructions without *by*: □ *He was born in Italy.* □ *Twins were born to her.* □ *a born leader* □ *his Burmese-born wife.*

born again The term *born again* was originally confined to the context of evangelical Christianity, to mean 'converted': □ *a born-again believer.*

◆ The term is now often used generally to refer to a conversion to any cause or belief, particularly when accompanied by extreme enthusiasm or fervour: □ *a born-again conservationist* □ *In their 'born again' zeal, some former opponents of the EEC may develop dangerous illusions on the possibilities of ... reform of EEC institutions* (*The Guardian*). Occasionally, *born-again* is also used to mean 'renewed; fresh, new, or resurgent': □ *a born-again car* □ *born-again post offices with refurbished premises* □ *Starring Neil Kinnock as the evangelical leader of born-again Labour, it is, of course a party political broadcast* (*The Guardian*).

The origin of the term *born again* is John 3:3 in the Bible.

borne see BORN OR BORNE?

borrow Besides its literal meaning of 'take something for a limited period with the intention of returning it': □ *I borrowed this book from the library, borrow* can also be used metaphorically to refer to words, ideas, etc., taken from other sources: □ *Wagner borrowed this theme from Norse mythology.* □ *Some American slang is borrowed from Yiddish.*

◆ One borrows *from*, not *off* someone: □ *I borrowed it off my friend* is generally considered wrong. See also LEND OR LOAN?

both *Both* is used as a determiner, a pronoun, and a conjunction: □ *Both legs were amputated.* □ *I like both.* □ *He is both an artist and a writer.* It should not be used where more than two elements are involved, as in: □ *She's both selfish, mean, and malicious.*

◆ The constructions □ *Both his parents are teachers* and □ *Both of his parents are teachers* are equally acceptable. However, in possessive constructions it is usually necessary to use *of*: □ *the opinion of both of them*, not *both of their opinion.*

When two things are being considered separately, it is often better to use *each* to avoid ambiguity. □ *We were both given a box of chocolates* might involve two boxes or one shared box. In general one should be careful about placing the word *both* in order to avoid ambiguity: □ *He has insulted both his aunts and his grandmother* might suggest *his two aunts*.

Both as a conjunction goes with *and*, and as with all such pairs of conjunctions must link grammatically similar things. So one can say: □ *She is both charming and intelligent* but not *She is both charming and an intellectual*.

Both is often used redundantly, when some other phrase in the sentence conveys the same sense: □ *They are both identical.* □ *Both of them are equally to blame.*

bottleneck *A bottleneck* is a term originally applied only to narrow stretches of road which cause traffic hold-ups. It is now extended to anything that holds up free movement or progress: □ *A bottleneck at the Traffic Area Office is resulting in long waits for driving tests.*

◆ As a vogue word it is sometimes overworked and its literal meaning forgotten. The original metaphor refers to the narrowness of the neck of a bottle, which makes such phrases as: □ *an enormous bottleneck* □ *an increasing bottleneck* □ *reducing the bottleneck* absurd.

bottom line *Bottom line* is a vogue expression, taken from financial reports where the final line registers the net profit or loss. It can mean 'the most important or primary point or consideration': □ *The bottom line is that we have no more resources for the project*; or 'the final result': □ *The bottom line was their divorce.* Care should be taken not to overuse this phrase.

◆ It is also sometimes used as an adjective to mean 'having a pragmatic concern for cost and profit': □ *He has a bottom-line approach to running the company.*

bottom out To *bottom out* was formerly used to describe a levelling out of something that has reached its lowest point: □ *Industrial output is now bottoming out.* It is more recently being used to suggest that the low point is prior to an upsurge: □ *The market has now bottomed out and is expected to improve by the spring.*

bouquet Some users prefer to pronounce the first syllable of this word [boo-] rather than [bō-], and to stress the second syllable [boo*kay*].

bourgeois This word, meaning 'middle class': □ *a bourgeois mentality*, is sometimes misspelt. Note the first syllable *bour* and the *e* which softens the *g* in the second syllable.

◆ The word comes from the Old French word *borjois*, meaning 'burgher or merchant'.

bow The word *bow* has two pronunciations. The noun and verb *bow*, referring to the bending of (part of) the body as a sign of respect, etc., are pronounced to rhyme with *how*. The same pronunciation is used for the noun meaning 'front of a boat or ship'. The noun *bow*, meaning 'looped knot', the *bow* that is used as a weapon, the *bow* that is used to play a violin, etc., and the verb *bow*, meaning 'curve', are pronounced to rhyme with *toe*.

◆ In the adjective *bow-legged* and the noun *bow window*, the word *bow* is pronounced to rhyme with *toe*.

boy A *boy* is a male child or adolescent. The use of the noun as a synonym for 'man' is largely restricted to informal contexts: □ *one of the boys* □ *a local boy* □ *the new boy* □ *a night out with the boys.*

boycott This word, meaning 'refuse to deal with': □ *boycott the Olympic games*, is sometimes misspelt. Note the -*tt* at the end of the word.

◆ The term originates from the name of Charles Cunningham *Boycott*

(1832–97), an Irish land agent who was ostracized for refusing to grant reductions in rent.

bracket Some people object to the frequent use of the noun *bracket* in place of *group, level, range,* etc.: □ *the 25–35 age bracket* □ *a lower income bracket.*

brackets The most frequently used kind of brackets are round brackets, also known as parentheses. They are used to enclose supplementary or explanatory material that interrupts a complete sentence: □ *William James (1842–1910) was the brother of the novelist Henry James.* □ *He asked his scout (as college servants are called in Oxford) to wake him at nine.* The material in parentheses could be removed without changing the meaning or grammatical completeness of the sentence. Round brackets are used, in preference to commas or dashes, when the interruption to the sentence is quite a marked one.

◆ Punctuation within brackets is that appropriate to the parenthetic material, but even if it is a complete sentence, capital letters and full stops are usually not used. Punctuation of the sentence containing the brackets is unaffected, except that any punctuation which would have followed the word before the first bracket is placed after the second bracket: □ *Worst of all, their confidence is undermined by a lurking fear of the meaninglessness of those basic questions in themselves (is this good? is this right?), which yet they find themselves unable to cease from asking* (Richard Hoggart, *The Uses of Literacy*). If the parenthetic material comes at the end of a sentence the full stop falls outside the second bracket. The only time when a full stop appears inside brackets is when the parenthetic material in brackets comes between two sentences, rather than within a sentence: □ *He came from a humble background. (His mother was a charwoman.) Yet he mixed with people of all classes.*

Round brackets are also used for letters or numbers in a series: □ *The Chartists demanded (1) annual elections, (2) universal manhood suffrage, (3) equal electoral districts ....* They are also used to indicate alternatives or brief explanations: □ *boy(s)* (meaning 'boy' or 'boys') □ *it cost 10 francs (roughly £1)* □ *the payment of VAT (value added tax).*

Square brackets are used for brackets within brackets: □ *Browning's wife (the poet Elizabeth Barrett Browning [1806–61]) was an invalid.* They are also used to indicate editorial comment or explanation in quoted matter: □ *The Young Visiters [sic]* □ *'who would fardels [burdens] bear'.* To use ordinary round brackets implies that the words inside them are part of the original quotation.

brake or **break**? These words are sometimes confused. A *brake* is a device to slow something down: □ *the handbrake on a car. Break* has many meanings including '(cause to) fall into pieces', 'stop', and 'transgress': □ *break a vase* □ *break for lunch* □ *break the law.*

bratpack The noun *bratpack*, often spelt *brat pack*, is a slang term applied (especially by the media) to any group of young people, usually precociously rich and famous, noted for their rowdy or ill-mannered behaviour.

◆ The term, originally applied to a group of up-and-coming American film stars in the mid-1980s, should not be overused.

bravado, bravery, or **bravura**? These three nouns are sometimes confused. *Bravery* means 'courage'; *bravado* is a false or outward display of courage or daring; *bravura* is an ostentatious or brilliant display of daring, skill, etc.

breach or **breech**? The word *breach* means 'the breaking or violating of a rule or arrangement': □ *a breach of the peace. Breach* should not be confused with *breech*, 'the rear part of the body' and 'the part of a gun behind the barrel': □ *a breech birth.*

◆ The nouns *breach* and *breech* are pronounced [breech], but the plural noun *breeches*, meaning 'knee-length trousers', may be pronounced [*breech*iz] or [*brich*iz].

break see BRAKE OR BREAK?

breakthrough *Breakthrough* as a metaphor meaning 'a sudden advance in (particularly scientific or technological) knowledge' has become something of a journalistic cliché. One reads, for example, of: □ *a major breakthrough in cancer research* so frequently that it has lost all impact.

◆ *Breakthrough* is also sometimes used to mean 'success': □ *Olympic breakthrough for British athletes* or 'new idea': □ *The Great Borrowing Breakthrough* (advertisement for a loan company).

breech, breeches see BREACH OR BREECH?

Brit The noun *Brit*, meaning 'British person', is often used derogatorily. It should be restricted to informal contexts. A British person may be called a *Briton*, but this term is most frequently found in newspaper reports about the British abroad: □ *A coach carrying 58 Britons ... was preparing last night to spend a third night trapped in a motorway service area south of Paris (Daily Telegraph).* The informal term *Britisher* is chiefly used by people of other English-speaking nations, not by the British themselves.

Britain The expression *Britain* is often used vaguely, sometimes as a substitute for *Great Britain*, sometimes for the *United Kingdom* or the *British Isles*. As an abbreviation of *Great Britain* it means England, Scotland, and Wales.

◆ The *United Kingdom* includes Northern Ireland as well as England, Scotland, and Wales. The *British Isles* includes all the United Kingdom, together with the Republic of Ireland, the Isle of Man, and the Channel Islands.

Briticisms British English is the basis on which the English of America, Australia, New Zealand, South Africa, the West Indies, and the rest of the English-speaking world is built. To greater or lesser degrees the English of these countries has gone its own way, producing distinct varieties of English, while the English spoken in Britain has its own characteristics, known as Briticisms.

◆ Specifically British, usually in contrast to American, usage of grammar, spelling, and so forth, is discussed under various headings in this book. It is vocabulary and idiom that mark the speaker or writer of British English. A sentence like: □ *I rang you from a call box but the line was engaged* marks the speaker as British; in other English-speaking countries it would have been: *I called you from a phone booth but the line was busy.* Such familiar words or phrases as: □ *bank holiday* □ *fortnight* □ *white coffee* □ *spring onion* □ *Father Christmas* □ *roundabout* (in the senses of both merry-go-round and traffic junction) are peculiarly British uses.

Of course there is no one standard form of English spoken throughout Britain; marked differences in pronunciation, vocabulary, grammar, and usage are found in the different countries and regions of Britain. See also DIALECT.

Britisher, Briton see BRIT.

Brittany *Brittany*, the English name of a region of northwest France, is often misspelt. Note the *-tt-* and single *-n-*, unlike *Britannia*.

broach or **brooch?** A *brooch* is a piece of jewellery that is pinned to a garment: □ *a diamond brooch*. *Broach*, a rare variant spelling of this noun, is most frequently used as a verb, meaning 'introduce' or 'mention': □ *to broach a subject*. Both words are pronounced [brōch].

◆ To *broach* a barrel or a bottle is to open it in order to use the contents: □ *We broached a second bottle of champagne*.

In nautical contexts, *broach* means 'to swerve dangerously in a following sea, so as to lie broadside to the waves'.

brochure This word is usually pronounced [brōshĕr], although the French-sounding [brōshoor] is also possible.

◆ Note also the *ch*, not *sh* in the spelling.

brooch see BROACH OR BROOCH?

brownie points *Brownie points* are notional marks of approval for an action or achievement, especially something that is deliberately or ostentatiously done to win favour: □ *You should get some brownie points for that*. □ *There are political brownie points in opening hospitals* (*The Guardian*).

◆ The phrase may be spelt with a capital *B-* or with a lowercase *b-*. It is best restricted to informal contexts. The expression derives from the erroneous belief that Brownie Guides receive points for doing something good.

buffet In the senses 'a counter where food is served' and 'food set out on tables': □ *a buffet car* □ *a buffet lunch*, *buffet* is pronounced [buufay]. In the sense 'strike sharply': □ *buffeted by the wind*, the pronunciation is [bufit].

bulk *Bulk* means 'thickness, volume, or size; a heavy mass': □ *the vast bulk of the castle walls*. It is also used in the expression *in bulk* to mean 'in large quantities': □ *We buy rice in bulk*.

◆ *Bulk* is frequently used to mean 'the greater part of, the majority': □ *The bulk of the population support the new legislation*. Some people object to the application of *bulk* to anything other than mass or volume, but this usage is well-established and generally acceptable.

bulletin This word, meaning 'statement of news': □ *No further bulletin will be issued this evening*, is sometimes misspelt. Note the *-ll-* and single *t*, as in *bullet*.

bulwark This noun, meaning 'fortification', is sometimes mispronounced. The second syllable is unstressed; the *-ark* ending has the same pronunciation as the *-ock* ending of *hillock*.

buoy The noun and verb *buoy*, meaning 'type of float' or 'keep afloat', and the derived adjective *buoyant*, are sometimes misspelt. The most frequent mistake is to place the *-u-* and the *-o-* in the wrong order.

◆ *Buoy* should not be confused with the noun BOY, which is identical in pronunciation in British English. In American English *buoy* is pronounced [booi].

bureaucracy Note the spelling of this word: the first *u*, the vowels *eau*, and the suffix *-cracy* (not *-crasy*).

burgle, rob, or **steal?** To *steal* is to take other people's possessions without permission: □ *He stole her jewellery*. *Burgle* is a back-formation from *burglar* and means 'break into a building in order to steal': □ *Their house was burgled when they were on holiday*. *Burglary* always involves unlawful entry. To *rob* is to steal money or property from a person or place, often with violence: □ *rob a bank* □ *rob an old lady*. *Rob* is sometimes incorrectly used in place of *steal*: □ *to rob a car* is to take things from a car, not to take the car itself.

◆ The verb *burglarize* is chiefly confined to American English.

burned or **burnt**? Either word may be used as the past tense and past participle of the verb *burn*. In transitive contexts *burned* is preferred in American English and *burnt* in British English; in intransitive contexts *burned* is the preferred form in both: □ *We burnt/burned the letters.* □ *He has burnt/burned his hand.* □ *She burned with anger.* □ *The fire had burned all night.*

◆ See also **-ED OR -T**?

Burnt is also used as an adjective in British and American English: □ *burnt toast* □ *a burnt offering.*

Burned may be pronounced [bernd] or [bernt]; *burnt* is always pronounced [bernt].

bus Although the noun *bus* was originally short for *omnibus* it is now never spelt with an apostrophe.

◆ The word was rarely used as a verb until the 1960s, when the controversy in the United States over the practice of sending schoolchildren by bus to different districts in order to achieve a racial balance in the schools gave rise to the need for such a verb. The problem of how to spell the various forms of the verb has not been wholly resolved. Traditional British spelling rules dictate *bussed* and *bussing*, but the American preference was for *bused* and *busing* and these spellings have now been widely accepted in Britain.

business This noun, meaning 'occupation', 'commercial activity', or 'matter', is sometimes misspelt. The most frequent mistake is the omission of the letter *-i-*, which is silent in speech.

◆ *Business* is a two-syllable word, pronounced [*biz*nis]. It should not be confused with the noun *busyness*, meaning 'the state of being busy', which has three syllables and is pronounced [*biz*inis].

but There are various problems with the usage of the word *but*. As a conjunction it is used to link two opposing ideas: □ *He lives in Surrey but works in London.* It should not be used to link two harmonious ideas: □ *She is not British-born, but originates from Kenya*, and should not be used in a sentence with *however*, which conveys the same meaning: □ *But their suggestions for improvement, however, were ill-received.*

◆ The problem with *but* used to mean 'except' is whether it should be followed by an object or subject pronoun; is it *all but he* or *all but him*? There is no absolute rule here but a rough guide to natural usage is to use the object when it falls at the end of a clause and the subject when it comes in the middle: □ *They had all escaped but her.* □ *All but she had escaped.*

The use of *but* at the beginning of a sentence is disliked by some users. But it is acceptable to most and can be used to good effect.

The expressions *can but* and *cannot but* are slightly formal and old-fashioned but still used: □ *setting a standard others can but hope to follow* (advertisement, *Sunday Times*). The oddity is that the expressions mean much the same thing, for the *not* of *cannot* combines with the *but* to form a double negative. When used with *help* in *can't help but* a triple negative is formed, but in fact the expression is used positively: □ *I can't help but regard your attitude as hostile.* The phrase is clumsy and should be avoided. The combination *cannot help but* is awkward and should be avoided; the expressions *can but* and *cannot but* can also be rephrased: □ *I can only regard your attitude as hostile.* □ *I can't help regarding your attitude as hostile.* See also CONJUNCTIONS; HELP; NOTHING BUT; NOT ONLY ... BUT ALSO.

buyout A *buyout* is the purchase of a company, often by a group of managers: □ *MFI Furniture, the independent company resulting from the management buy-out from Asda-MFI* (*The Guardian*). □ *And ... certainly in the UK ... management buyouts are currently a very popular flavour* (*The Bookseller*).

◆ The word *buyout* is most commonly printed or written without a hyphen.

buzz word A *buzz word* is a vogue word or expression, especially one that is first used in technical jargon and subsequently enters everyday language, usually in a figurative sense. Examples of buzz words that are dealt with in this dictionary are: *bottom line, gravitas, matrix, traumatic.*

by or **bye?** These spellings are sometimes confused. Note the spelling of the following compounds and expressions: □ *by-election* (occasionally, *bye-election*) □ *by-law* (sometimes, *bye-law*) □ *by-pass* □ *by-product* □ *by and by* ('later') □ *by and large* ('generally') □ *by the bye* (occasionally, *by the by*, 'incidentally') □ a *bye* in sports, and □ *bye-bye* (informal for *goodbye*).

by the same token *By the same token* is a fashionable expression meaning 'for the same reason; in a similar way': □ *Middle-aged men should avoid overworking because of the effects of stress on the heart; and by the same token they should avoid fatty foods.* Care should be taken to avoid overusing this phrase.

cadre Note the pronunciation of this noun, which means 'unit or nucleus of personnel'. Of French origin, *cadre* is usually pronounced [*kah*dĕ], rhyming with *larder*, in British English. The variant pronunciation [*kah*drĕ], which is closer to the French original, is less frequent but not incorrect.

Caesarean This word, meaning 'of or relating to any of the Caesars', is used particularly in the expression *Caesarean section*, 'the surgical operation for the delivery of a baby by cutting through the wall of the mother's abdomen and into the womb'. The variant spellings *Caesarian*, and, in American English, *Cesarean* or *Cesarian*, are also used. Note, too, that any of these spellings may be written with a lower-case *c*: □ *She had a caesarean*.
   ◆ The word derives from Julius *Caesar*, who, it is traditionally thought, was born by this method.

café or **cafeteria**? The noun *café* refers to any small restaurant or coffee-bar serving nonalcoholic drinks, snacks, light meals, etc.: □ *a seaside café*. The noun *cafeteria* is more specific, meaning 'self-service restaurant': □ *There is a cafeteria on the third floor*.
   ◆ Note the spelling of *café*, particularly the acute accent, which should never be omitted. The noun may be pronounced [*ka*fay] or [*ka*fi].
   Cafeteria should not be confused with the noun *cafetière*, denoting a type of coffee-pot with a plunger, in which coffee can be brewed and served. The grave accent on the second *-e-* of *cafetière* is optional in English.

caffeine *Caffeine*, pronounced [*ka*feen], is a stimulant substance found in tea and coffee. Note the spelling of the word, especially the *-ff-* and the vowel sequence *-ei-*. It is an exception to the '*i* before *e*' rule (see SPELLING 5).
   ◆ *Caffein* is a rare variant spelling of the word.

calendar, calender, or **colander**? These words are often confused. A *calendar* tells the date, a *calender* is a machine used to smooth paper or cloth, and a *colander* is a perforated bowl used for draining food.
   ◆ The first two words are pronounced in the same way [*ka*lindĕ]. *Colander* is pronounced [*ko*lăndĕ] or [*ku*lĕndĕ]. This second pronunciation of *colander* is reflected in the variant spelling *cullender*.

callous or **callus**? *Callus* is a noun, denoting a hardened or thickened area of skin, especially on the hand or foot. The adjective *callous* is related to this noun, but is most frequently used in the figurative sense of 'unfeeling' or 'insensitive': □ *a callous attitude to the poor*.

calorie Note the spelling of this word, which is a unit for measuring the energy value of food and also a measurement of heat.

calvary see CAVALRY OR CALVARY?

camouflage This word, meaning 'disguise': □ *The trees provided*

50

excellent camouflage, is sometimes misspelt. Note the *ou* and the soft *g*.

can or **may**? The verb *can* means 'be permitted' or 'be able'; the verb *may* means 'be permitted' or 'be likely'. In the sense of 'be permitted', *may* is preferred in formal contexts and *can* is best restricted to informal contexts: □ *Can I come to your party?* □ *May I borrow your pen, please?*

◆ The negative contraction *mayn't* is disliked by many people and is usually replaced with *can't*: □ *Can't* [not *Mayn't*] *she stay?*

Both verbs can be ambiguous: □ *He can go* may mean 'he is permitted to go' or 'he is able to go'; □ *He may go* may mean 'he is permitted to go' or 'he is likely to go'. *Could* and *might*, the past tenses of *can* and *may* respectively, are equally ambiguous: □ *She said he could go.* □ *She said he might go.*

Could and *might* are also used in polite requests: □ *Could/Might I have another cup of tea, please?*

See also **BUT**; **CANNOT AND CAN'T**; **HELP**; **MAY OR MIGHT**?

candelabra The word *candelabra*, meaning 'a branched candlestick or lamp', was originally a plural noun, from the singular *candelabrum*. Purists therefore consider it incorrect to speak of: □ *a valuable candelabra* or to say: □ *There were candelabras in every room*, although such usage is widespread.

◆ *Candelabra* are often confused with *chandeliers*, which hang from the ceiling, while *candelabra* stand on surfaces.

cannon or **canon**? These two words are sometimes confused. A *cannon* is a large gun and a shot in billiards, a *canon*, with a single *n*, is a ruling laid down by the church, or a title given to a clergyman.

cannot and **can't** In American English *can not* is sometimes written as two words but in British English *cannot* is standard. It may be necessary to write *can not* when the *not* is stressed: □ No, I can *not* lend you any more money, or in sentences like: □ *It can not only blend vegetables but also grind coffee beans*, where the *not* goes with *only*, rather than *can*.

◆ Care should be taken when using *cannot* in constructions like: □ *Her work cannot be too highly praised.* □ *You cannot put too much pepper in*, where ambiguity can arise. Was her work excellent or poor? Should a large or small amount of pepper be put in?

The contraction *can't* is normally used in speech and often in writing. The standard British English pronunciation is [kahnt].

See also **BUT**; **CAN OR MAY**?; **HELP**.

canon see **CANNON OR CANON**?

can't see **CANNOT AND CAN'T**.

canvas or **canvass**? *Canvas* is a certain type of woven cloth: □ *a canvas bag* □ *a painting on canvas*. *Canvass*, with *-ss* at the end, means 'solicit votes': □ *He canvassed for the Labour Party*.

-cap The suffix *-cap* relates to restrictions imposed by central government on local council spending and taxation. Under the system of domestic rates, councils could be *rate capped*; the introduction of the community charge (or poll tax) led to such terms as *charge-capping*. The verb is sometimes used independently: □ *The government threatened to cap a number of councils*.

capability, capacity, or **ability**? These words all refer to the power to do something. *Capability* suggests having the qualities needed to do something: □ *She has the capability to handle the work*. *Capacity* suggests being able to absorb or receive: □ *Children are born with* *the capacity to acquire language. Ability* can sometimes suggest above-average skills: □ *He has considerable mathematical ability.*

◆ *Capacity* has several other meanings: 'volume': □ *The pot has a capacity of two litres,* '(maximum) output': □ *The factory is working at (full) capacity,* 'a particular role': □ *I am speaking in my capacity as treasurer.* It is also used as an adjective in the journalistic phrase: □ *a capacity crowd at the ground.*

capital letters Capital letters are used to draw attention to a particular word. There are some generally accepted rules for their use, but some areas where it is a matter of choice.

◆ Capitals are used to mark the first word of a sentence, a direct quotation, or a direct question within a sentence (see also **QUESTION MARK; QUOTATION MARKS; SENTENCES**). They are sometimes used after a colon (see **COLON**). They are used for the first word of each line of poetry: □ *Forewarned of madness/In three days time at dusk/The fit masters him* (Robert Graves), and for the major words of titles of literary, musical, or artistic works: □ *The Mill on the Floss* □ *Peter and the Wolf.*

Capitals are used for proper nouns and most adjectives derived from them: □ *John Brown* □ *New York* □ *Sainsbury's* □ *Oxford Street* □ *French* □ *Jewish* □ *Freudian.* If an adjective is not closely connected with its original proper noun it does not usually take a capital: □ *brussels sprouts* □ *french windows,* and capitals are not used for verbs derived from proper nouns: □ *anglicize* □ *boycott* (see also **EPONYMS; TRADE NAMES**). Titles of people or places are capitalized when part of a proper name but not when used alone: □ *my aunt* □ *Aunt Jane* □ *redbrick universities* □ *Cambridge University* □ *a professor of history* □ *Professor Thomson.* For institutions the rule is that capitals are used in specific references but not in general ones: □ *many world governments* □ *the Government has agreed* □ *he goes to a Baptist church* □ *St Mark's Church* □ *the Church of England.* The pronoun *I* always takes a capital, but no other pronouns apart from those referring to God, where some people choose to capitalize *He, Him, His.*

Capitals are used for days of the week, months, holidays, and religious holidays: □ *Monday* □ *February* □ *Easter* □ *Yom Kippur,* but not for seasons. They are used for historical, cultural, and geological periods: □ *the Restoration* □ *the Enlightenment* □ *the Spanish Civil War* □ *the Stone Age.*

Capitals should never be used for emphasis; italics should be used for this purpose: □ *an enormous* [not ENORMOUS] bear!

See also **ABBREVIATIONS; HYPHEN; COLON; EAST, EAST, OR EASTERN?; NORTH, NORTH, OR NORTHERN?; SOUTH, SOUTH, OR SOUTHERN?;WEST, WEST, OR WESTERN?**

carat or **caret**? These words are sometimes confused. A *carat* is a unit for measuring the weight of precious stones and a unit for measuring the purity of gold; in this second sense, the spelling *karat* is usually used in American English. A *caret,* spelt with an *e,* is a character used in written or printed matter to indicate that an insertion should be made.

carburettor Note the spelling of this word, particularly the *-u-,* the *-tt-,* and the *-or* ending.

◆ The spelling in American English is *carburetor.*

carcass This word, which describes the body of a dead animal: □ *a chicken carcass,* may be spelt *carcass* or *carcase* in British English.

◆ In American English only *carcass* is used.

caret see **CARAT OR CARET?**

caring *Caring* has been used in recent years in such phrases as: □ *the caring professions* □ *the caring services*, to describe people professionally involved in various kinds of social work, sometimes also including health care and education.

◆ It combines the idea of 'taking care of' and the idea of 'concerned': □ *The welfare state itself, and all the caring professions, seemed to be plunging into ... uncertainty, self-questioning, economic crisis* (Margaret Drabble, *The Middle Ground*).

The noun *carer* is increasingly used to denote a person who looks after a sick or old relative: □ *The new benefit is payable to carers and their dependants.*

case *Case* is very often loosely used to mean 'state of affairs, the truth' in sentences where it is either redundant or could be replaced by simpler or more specific wording: □ *Is it the case that you are his aunt?* could be changed to: *Are you his aunt?* □ *Teenage pregnancies are now less common than was the case ten years ago* could be changed to: *... than they were ten years ago.* The expression is acceptable in sentences like: □ *This rule applies in your case.*

◆ *In case* is used as a conjunction: □ *in case it rains.* The use of *just in case*, with no clause: □ *Take your mac, just in case* is acceptable only in informal contexts.

caster or **castor**? For the senses 'a swivelling wheel on furniture' and 'a container from which sugar may be shaken', the spelling may be either *castor* or *caster*. Finely granulated white sugar is usually *caster sugar*, although the spelling *castor sugar* is also found. The medicinal or lubricating oil, *castor oil*, is, however, always spelt with an *o*.

catalyst A *catalyst* is a scientific term that applies to a substance which speeds up a chemical reaction though itself remaining chemically unchanged. It is also used as a metaphor to apply to a person or event that, by its action, provokes significant change: □ *The shooting of Archduke Ferdinand acted as the catalyst for the outbreak of World War I.* Overuse of the word *catalyst* is disliked by some.

catarrh This word, which describes an inflammation of the throat and nasal passages, is sometimes misspelt. Note particularly the single *t* and the *rrh*.

catastrophic The adjective *catastrophic* comes from *catastrophe* which was originally used in Greek drama to describe the denouement of a tragedy. The word should be applied to extremely severe disasters and tragic events: □ *the catastrophic earthquake in Mexico City.*

◆ It is often used informally for quite minor disasters: □ *Do you remember that catastrophic dinner party when I burnt the casserole?*

catch-22 In Joseph Heller's novel *Catch 22*, published in 1961, the catch in question was that airmen could be excused from flying missions only if they were of unsound mind, but a request to be excused from flying missions was a sign of a concern for personal safety in the face of danger and therefore evidence of a rational mind, so it was impossible to escape flying missions. *A catch-22 situation* is any such circular dilemma or predicament from which there is no escape, and is often extended to any situation or problem where the victim feels that it is impossible to gain a personal benefit or make the right decision.

Catholic or **catholic**? The word *catholic*, with a lower-case *c-*, is an adjective meaning 'general, wide-ranging, or comprehensive': □ *It is a catholic anthology which includes poems by Shelley, Auden, and Allen Ginsberg. Catholic*, with a capital, as a noun or adjective, usually refers to the Roman Catholic Church: □ *He's a good Catholic.* □ *They go to a Catholic school.*

◆ As some 'high' Anglicans prefer to refer to themselves as *Catholics*, it is advisable to use the term *Roman Catholic* when speaking in a specifically theological context.

cavalry or **calvary**? These words are sometimes confused. *Cavalry* is used to refer to soldiers trained to fight on horseback and the branch of the army that uses armoured vehicles. *Calvary* is the hill near Jerusalem where Christ was crucified.

caviar or **caviare**? Both of these spellings are acceptable for the word which describes the salted roe of the sturgeon.

ceiling *Ceiling* is frequently used, particularly in economic jargon, to mean 'an upper limit': □ *The organization is urging the Government to put a ceiling on rent rises.* As the word *ceiling*, in its literal meaning, is in constant use, it can sound odd to speak of *increasing* or *reducing a ceiling*, an *unworkable ceiling*, and so on: □ *Sir Gordon Borrie ... said, 'If money and manpower ceilings were to become too tight in relation to the demands put upon my office, then the taxpayer ... would be likely to pay the price in other ways'* (*The Guardian*).

celibate *Celibacy* means 'the state of being unmarried, often because of a religious vow'. *Celibate* is used as a noun to describe a person living in a state of celibacy and, by implication, chastity: □ *As celibates, priests find it difficult to give advice on marital problems*, and as an adjective: □ *She never married but chose a celibate life.*

◆ The word is sometimes used to mean 'abstaining from sexual intercourse': □ *After twenty years of marriage, they decided to live a celibate life together*. Careful users consider this usage to be incorrect.

Celsius, centigrade, or **Fahrenheit**? All these terms denote scales of temperature. The Celsius and centigrade scales are the same; the degree Celsius is now the principal unit of temperature in both scientific and nonscientific contexts.

◆ The Fahrenheit scale, on which water freezes at 32° and boils at 212°, remains in informal use, particularly with reference to the weather: □ *The temperature reached the eighties today.* The centigrade scale, on which water freezes at 0° and boils at 100°, is now known as the Celsius scale, to avoid confusion with other units of measurement.

Celsius and *Fahrenheit* should always begin with a capital letter, being the surnames of the scientists who devised the scales.

Celtic The word *Celtic*, referring to a language or people of Scotland, Wales, Ireland, or Brittany, is usually pronounced [*k*eltik], with a hard initial *C-*.

◆ The variant pronunciation [*se*ltik], with a soft initial *C-*, is most frequently associated with the Scottish football team of that name.

censure, censor, or **censer**? The verbs *censure* and *censor* are often confused. *Censure* means 'to blame, criticize strongly, or condemn': □ *The judge censured them for the brutality of the attack.* *Censor* means 'examine letters, publications, films, etc., and remove any material which is considered obscene, libellous, or contrary to government or official policy': □ *All prisoners' mail is censored.* The person who examines letters, etc., in this way is also known as a *censor.*

◆ The adjective from *censor* is *censorial* and from *censure*, *censorious*.

Censor should not be confused with the noun *censer*, meaning 'a vessel used for burning incense'.

centenary or **centennial**? Both *centenary* and *centennial* are used to mean a hundred-year anniversary: □ *1982 was the centenary of Joyce's birth. Centennial* is used more frequently in American English and can also be used as an adjective: □ *a centennial celebration.*

◆ The recommended pronunciation of *centenary* is [senteenări], although some people pronounce it [sentenări]. *Centennial* is pronounced [senteniăl].

centigrade see CELSIUS, CENTIGRADE, OR FAHRENHEIT?

centre or **middle**? *Centre* and *middle* are sometimes used virtually synonymously: □ *Put it in the centre/middle of the table. Centre* is used as a precise geometrical term: □ *the centre of the circle,* whereas *middle* is more often used generally in situations where the geometric centre is not obvious or measurable: □ *the middle of the sea.*

◆ *Centre* is also used to mean a place where activity is concentrated: □ *shopping centre. Middle* is used to mean the point equally distant from extremes, either literally: □ *middle name*, or figuratively: □ *middle-of-the-road politics.*

centre on or **centre around**? The verb *centre* can be used with *on* or *upon* or (of a place) *at:* □ *His argument centres on Marxist theory.* □ *The European Parliament is centred at Brussels.*

◆ The expressions *centre round* and *centre around:* □ *The film centres around the Vietnam War.* □ *Her hobbies centred around the arts* are frequently used, although they are disliked by many careful users as being illogical, as, it is argued, a centre cannot be *around* anything.

Since this usage is so widely objected to, it is best avoided.

centrifugal There are two pronunciations for this word. The traditional pronunciation stresses the second syllable [sen*tri*fyoogăl], but the alternative pronunciation [sentri*fyoog*ăl] is widely used in contemporary English.

centuries People often become confused about when centuries start and end and how one should refer to them. As there was no year 0 AD, we calculate in hundred years from the year 1 AD. This means that the twentieth century began on 1 January 1901 (not 1900) and will end on 31 December 2000.

◆ So although the expressions *the 1800s* and *the nineteenth century* are almost synonymous, in fact the 1800s means 1800–1899 inclusive and the nineteenth century 1801–1900 inclusive.

cereal or **serial**? These two words are sometimes confused. A *cereal* is a plant that produces grain for food: □ *breakfast cereals.* A *serial* is a novel or play produced in several parts and at regular intervals: □ *a television serial.*

ceremonial or **ceremonious**? The adjectives *ceremonial* and *ceremonious* are sometimes confused. *Ceremonial* means 'marked by ceremony or ritual': □ *The Queen wears her crown only on ceremonial occasions like the opening of Parliament. Ceremonious* means 'devoted to formality and ceremony' and usually carries a slightly pejorative suggestion of overpunctiliousness or pomposity: □*She presided over the dinner table with a ceremonious air.*

certainty or **certitude**? Both these nouns mean 'the state of being certain'. *Certainty* is by far the more frequent, and is used in a wider range of contexts: □*a feeling of certainty* □*the certainty of death.* *Certitude* is a formal or literary word, largely restricted to the state of mind of somebody who is certain: □*Nothing could disturb his certitude.*

◆ *Certainty* may also be used as a countable noun: □*She may win, but it's not a certainty. Certitude* is not used in this sense.

cervical There are two pronunciations for this word, both of which are perfectly acceptable: [*servi*kăl] and [sĕr*vī*kăl].

cession or **cessation**? These two nouns should not be confused. *Cession* is derived from the verb *cede*, meaning 'yield'; *cessation* is derived from the verb *cease*, meaning 'stop': □*the cession of territory* □*the cessation of warfare.*

◆ Both words are largely restricted to formal contexts. See also **CESSION OR SESSION?**

cession or **session**? *Cession* is the act of yielding (see **CESSION OR CESSATION?**); a *session* is a meeting or a period of time devoted to a specific activity: □*the cession of rights/property* □*a parliamentary session* □*a recording session* □*The court is in session.*

◆ The two nouns are identical in pronunciation; *session* is the more frequent in usage and should not be misspelt.

chafe or **chaff**? The verb *chafe* means 'rub'; the old-fashioned verb *chaff* means 'tease': □*These boots chafe my ankles.* □*She was chaffed by her colleagues.* The two verbs should not be confused.

◆ *Chaff* is also a noun, meaning 'husks (of wheat, etc.)', and is used figuratively in the phrase *to separate the wheat from the chaff*, meaning 'separate the good from the bad'.

chain reaction *Chain reaction* is an expression from scientific terminology that refers to a chemical or nuclear reaction which creates energy or products that cause further reaction. It is now more often used to mean any series of events where each one sets off the next one, though this usage is disliked by some: □*The shooting started a chain reaction which culminated in the street riots.*

chair The noun *chair* is sometimes used to denote a person presiding over a meeting, committee, etc., to avoid the potentially sexist terms *chairman* and *chairwoman* and the controversial neologism *chairperson*: □*The new chair will be elected next week.*

◆ This usage is disliked by many. See also **PERSON**.
The verb *chair*, meaning 'preside over', is acceptable to most users: □*The leader of the Union chaired the conference.*

challenge Some people object to the frequent use of the word *challenge* in the sense of 'stimulate' or, as a noun, 'something that is stimulating or demanding': □*Gifted children need challenging work.* □*The job presents a challenge.*

◆ The verb *challenge* sometimes means little more than 'interest; excite': □*The film challenged us visually and musically.*

challenged *Challenged* is a vogue word used to form euphemisms for disability or disadvantage: □*physically challenged.* See also **ABLED; POLITICAL CORRECTNESS.**

◆ The use of this term is widely satirized by opponents of political

correctness, who have coined such phrases as *follicularly
challenged*, 'balding'. It is often used facetiously or ironically: □ *Robert
Lindsay ... is about to play the nasally challenged Cyrano de Bergerac
in the West End* (*Daily Telegraph*). □ *The Borrowers are a vertically
challenged family – 6in tall, to be exact* (*Sunday Times*). □ *Financially
challenged souls cannot afford to cast aside the clothes that have
been key fashion investments over the past three years* (*Daily
Telegraph*). □ *The usual assumption made about those still watching
the TV of their youth – that they're sad, socially challenged creatures*
(*Sunday Times*).

chamois This word may cause problems with pronunciation and
spelling. The antelope *chamois* is pronounced [*sham*wah]. The
leather *chamois* made from the skin of this animal or a sheep is
usually pronounced [*sham*i].

changeable This word, meaning 'liable to change': □ *changeable
weather*, is sometimes misspelt. Note the *e* of *change* which is
retained before the suffix *-able*.
  ◆ See also SPELLING 3.

chaperon or **chaperone**? An older woman who accompanies a young
unmarried woman on social occasions is known as a *chaperon* or
a *chaperone*. The noun, and its derived verb, may be spelt with
or without the final *e*.
  ◆ The usual pronunciation for both spellings is [*shapērōn*].

character The word *character* can be used of the distinguishing qualities that make up individual people or things, of people with
unusual traits, of people portrayed in works of fiction, and of
moral firmness and integrity: □ *Such behaviour did not seem
consistent with what I knew of her character.* □ *It is a lively town
with a great deal of character.* □ *Everyone knows him – he's a real
character.* □ *Mrs Gamp is a minor character in Martin
Chuzzlewit.* □ *Anyone who takes this job on will need character
and determination.*
  ◆ *Character* is often used vaguely in such phrases as: □ *the strange
  character of this declaration* □ *programmes of an intellectual
  character* □ *the intimate character of our conversation*. Where it is
  used to mean no more than 'type' or 'quality', *character* would be
  better replaced or omitted.

charisma The word *charisma* was originally used only in theological
contexts to refer to supernatural spiritual gifts of healing, speaking in tongues, etc. A *charismatic church* is one where emphasis
is placed on the exercise of these gifts. *Charisma* and *charismatic*
are now often used to describe a person with unusual qualities
of leadership, personal appeal, and magnetism, though care
should be taken to avoid overusing these words: □ *Lange is planning to run a presidential-style election campaign, based on his
own charisma* (*Sunday Times*).
  ◆ The word *charismatic* is sometimes used more loosely to mean
  'charming or showing a confident efficiency': □ *Our client ... is looking
  for two charismatic sales managers* (advertisement, *Daily Telegraph*).

charted or **chartered**? A *chartered accountant/surveyor/engineer/*etc.
is a person who has the required professional qualifications and
experience. A *chartered yacht* is a hired yacht. *Chartered* should
not be confused with *charted* (derived from the word *chart*):
□ *charted territory.*
  ◆ Similarly, the adjective *uncharted*, describing something that has
  not been mapped or surveyed: □ *uncharted waters*, should not be

misspelt as *unchartered*.

chattering classes The *chattering classes* are educated middle- and upper-class liberals who frequently air their opinions in the media: □ [Rupert] *Murdoch is contemptuous of the views of those to whom he and ... Andrew Neil obsessively refer as the 'chattering classes'* (*The Bookseller*). This vogue term is generally used in a derogatory manner.

chauvinism The word *chauvinism* means 'excessive or fanatical patriotism' and comes from Nicolas *Chauvin*, a soldier of Napoleon's army who was noted for his overzealous patriotism. It is used more loosely to describe any prejudiced belief in the superiority of a group or cause, particularly in the term *male chauvinism* which is often applied by feminists to male supremacists: □ *'The media ... fanned the flames of male chauvinism, stereotyping all women who took a serious interest in the issues as bra-burners'* (Elaine Storkey, *What's Right with Feminism*).

◆ Some people, encountering the word for the first time in the context of male chauvinism, wrongly assume *chauvinist* to be synonymous with *sexist*: □ *Her husband's an awful chauvinist*. The word should not be used in this sense unless preceded by *male*.

chequered Note the spelling of this adjective, meaning 'varied; marked by many changes in fortune', most frequently used in such phrases as a *chequered career* and *chequered past*. In British English the adjective is spelt *chequered*; *checkered* is the American English spelling.

chick or **chicken**? A *chick* is a young bird: □ *The chicks have hatched.* □ *eagle chicks.* A *chicken* is a type of domestic fowl and *chicken* is the meat of this fowl: □ *He keeps geese and chickens.* □ *roast chicken.* Either noun may be applied to the young of a domestic fowl: □ *a hen and her chicks* [or *chickens*].

◆ *Chick* is also used offensively as a slang term for a young woman.

chihuahua Note the unusual spelling of this word, which denotes a breed of tiny dog. These dogs are named after the state of *Chihuahua* in Mexico; the noun is sometimes written with a capital *C-*.

◆ *Chihuahua* is usually pronounced [chiwahwah] or [chiwahwä].

chilblain A sore that is caused by exposure to the cold is known as a *chilblain*. The word is sometimes misspelt, the most common error being to retain the second *l* of *chill* which has been lost in the formation of this compound noun.

childish or **childlike**? *Childish* is almost always used in a pejorative sense to indicate immaturity and the less endearing characteristics of childhood: □ *She refused to tolerate his selfish behaviour and childish outbreaks of temper.* □ *The drawings looked like childish scribbles.* *Childlike* is usually applied to the attractive qualities of childhood, such as enthusiasm and innocence: □ *At 85, she retains a childlike curiosity about her environment.*

Chinese *Chinese* as an adjective means 'of or from China': □ *Chinese writing*; it is also used as a singular or plural noun for a person or people of Chinese nationality: □ *I took a party of Chinese around London.* □ *There is a Chinese studying at my college.*

◆ The singular expression *a Chinese* sounds odd to some people, who prefer to say *a Chinese man/woman*. The term *Chinaman* is out-of-date, derogatory, and offensive.

chiropodist This word, describing a person who treats and looks after people's feet, may be pronounced [kiropödist] or [shiropödist], although the first of these is preferred by many users.

cholesterol This word is sometimes misspelt. The most frequent error is the omission of the second *e*, often silent in speech.

◆ Remember also that the first syllable is *chol-* and not *chlo-* as in *chlorine*.

chord or **cord**? These spellings are sometimes confused. In the musical or mathematical senses the spelling is *chord*. *Chord* is also used when describing an emotional reaction: □ *He struck the right chord.* In the anatomical sense: □ *umbilical cord* □ *spinal cord*, either spelling is acceptable, although in *vocal cords* the word is nearly always spelt without the *h*. The word which describes any type of string is spelt *cord*: □ *nylon cord.*

Christian name see FIRST NAME, CHRISTIAN NAME, FORENAME, GIVEN NAME, OR BAPTISMAL NAME?

chronic *Chronic* means 'long-standing; permanently present': □ *She has suffered from chronic asthma all her life.* □ *Malnutrition is a chronic problem in the Third World.*

◆ It is often confused, in its medical context, with *acute*, which means 'intense and of sudden onset': □ *I suddenly got an acute* [not *chronic*] *pain in my shoulder*. Because *chronic* is so often used of pains and illnesses that are very bad it is also sometimes used in informal British English to mean 'bad' or 'dreadful': □ *Drink! my word! Something chronic'* (Shaw, *Pygmalion*).

chutzpah *Chutzpah* or *chutzpa* is a Yiddish expression now in general use which, in one word, conveys 'cheek, gall, effrontery, audacity, cool nerve, brazen self-confidence, arrogance'.

◆ In *The Joys of Yiddish*, Leo Rosten writes 'Chutzpa is that quality enshrined in a man who, having killed his mother and father, throws himself on the mercy of the court because he is an orphan.'
It is pronounced [*khuuts*på].

circumstances *In the circumstances* and *under the circumstances* are used in slightly different ways. *In the circumstances* is more general, and merely acknowledges the existence of a situation: □ *In the circumstances you had better do nothing.* *Under the circumstances* suggests more of a connection between the circumstances and the action: □ *He was starving and under the circumstances cannot be blamed for stealing food.*

◆ *Under* is more often used than *in* in a negative context: □ *Under no circumstances will I allow it.*

cirrhosis This word, denoting a disease of the liver, is sometimes misspelt. Note particularly the -*rrh*- combination.

city or **town**? In general a *city* is a place that is larger and more important than a *town*: □ *She had only lived in small towns before and was apprehensive about moving to the city.*

◆ The British 'rule' that the possession of a cathedral confers city status on a town is misleading. It is the monarch who grants a town the right to call itself a city, and though cities very often do have cathedrals this is not always the case. Cambridge, for example, was granted city status and has no cathedral.

civic, civil, or **civilian**? These words all refer to citizenship but have different meanings. *Civic* means 'of a city': □ *civic centre*, or is used of the attitudes of citizens to their city: □ *a sense of civic pride. Civil* relates to citizens of a state, rather than a city: □ *civil rights*, or is used as distinct from criminal, religious, or military: □ *civil law* □ *civil marriage* □ *civil defence. Civilian* refers to a person who is not a member of the armed forces, police, or other official uniformed state organization: □ *The major had been a bank manager in civilian life.*

◆ *Civil* is also used to mean 'polite or courteous': □ *The proprietor was very civil to us.*

clad or **clothed**? *Clad* means the same as *clothed* but, except in expressions like *thinly clad* or *ill-clad*, is considered archaic or poetic. It can be used of things other than clothes: □ *rose-clad trellises*, or of clothes where the note of archaism is appropriate: □ *clad in armour*, but for ordinary dress, *clothed* is used: □ *She was clothed completely in black.*

◆ *Clothed,* not *clad,* may be used as the opposite of *naked:* □ *With that paunch, he looks sexier clothed these days.*

claim The verb *claim* means 'demand something as a right': □ *The dismissed workers are claiming redundancy pay*; 'take something one rightfully owns or that is one's due': □ *He claimed his father's estate.* □ *She claimed the prize*, and 'assert forcefully, especially when faced with possible contradiction': □ *He claims that there have been no composers of genius since Beethoven.*

◆ This last use was at one time disliked, having no connection with the recognition of rights, but it is now widely used and accepted. It should, however, be avoided when the assertion is not particularly forceful or controversial, when *maintain, allege, contend,* or sometimes just *say,* is often better.

clandestine This word, meaning 'secret', is generally stressed on the second syllable [klan*des*tin], although it is acceptable to stress the word on the first syllable [*klan*dèstin].

classic or **classical**? There is some overlap in the meanings of *classic* and *classical*, but they have distinct separate meanings. *Classic* means 'typical of or unusually fine in its class': □ *classic symptoms of diabetes* □ *a classic example of 1960s pop art. Classical* essentially means 'of the classics, i.e. the literature, history, and philosophy of ancient Greece and Rome': □ *a classical education.*

◆ *Classic* is also used to mean 'elegant and unlikely to date': □ *a classic dress* □ *a classic design*, and 'definitive, absolute': □ *Your behaviour was a dirty trick of classic dimensions ... (The Guardian).* While *the classics* are the works of ancient Greece and Rome, *a classic* is any work of high standard and enduring quality, whatever its date: □ *the jazz classic 'St Louis Blues'.*

Classical, too, can suggest elegance, but there is a definite link with the standards and forms of ancient Greece and Rome. *Classical music,* in its narrowest sense, is the music of about 1750–1830, which is characterized by its formal beauty. The term is, however, widely applied to all serious music, as distinct from jazz, folk, and popular music.

clause A *clause* is a group of words, including a finite verb, within a compound or complex sentence. A *main clause* can stand alone as a sentence in its own right; it is expanded by a *subordinate clause.* A *relative clause* modifies the subject or object of a sentence.

◆ In the sentence □ *She stayed at home because it was raining, She stayed at home* is the main clause and *because it was raining* is the subordinate clause. The sentence □ *She stayed at home but her sister went out* contains two main clauses.

Relative clauses may be defining (identifying) or non-defining (non-identifying). They are usually introduced by *that, which, who,* etc. A defining clause provides essential information; a non-defining clause provides parenthetical information. The clause *who lives in India* is non-defining in the sentence □ *My sister, who lives in India, is coming home for Christmas* and defining in □ *My sister who lives in India is coming home for Christmas*. The first sentence implies that she is the only sister the speaker has; the second sentence implies that the speaker's other sisters are not coming home for Christmas. See also COMMA 3; THAT OR WHICH?

claustrophobia The fear of being in confined spaces is known as *claustrophobia*. Note the *claustro-* in the spelling.

clean or **cleanse**? While *clean* functions as adjective, noun, adverb, and verb, *cleanse* is used only as a verb. The two words are almost synonymous but *cleanse* has more of a suggestion of very thorough cleaning which also purifies: □ *I'll just clean the flat quickly.* □ *The wound must be cleansed before a dressing is applied.*

◆ *Cleanse* has a more formal sound than *clean* and is sometimes used figuratively to mean 'purify', as it is in the older translations of the Bible: □ *Wash me throughly from mine iniquity, and cleanse me from my sin* (Psalm 51:2).

clench or **clinch**? These two words are sometimes confused. The verb *clench* means 'close tightly' or 'grasp firmly': □ *to clench one's teeth* □ *She clenched the key in her hand*. The verb *clinch* is most frequently used in the figurative sense of 'settle definitely': □ *to clinch a deal*.

◆ The literal meaning of the verb *clinch* is 'secure by bending over the protruding point of a driven nail'. *Clinch* is also used as a noun and verb to refer to two people holding each other tightly with the arms in boxing or wrestling or in an amorous embrace.

clichés The word *cliché*, referring to a phrase or idiom that has become stale through overuse, is almost always used pejoratively. Examples of clichés are: □ *from time immemorial* □ *as old as the hills* □ *last but not least*.

◆ Not all fixed phrases are necessarily bad. Some clichés were quite apt when first used but have become hackneyed over the years. One can hardly avoid using the occasional cliché, but clichés that are inefficient in conveying their meaning or are inappropriate to the occasion should be avoided.

There are various categories of cliché. There are overworked metaphors and similes: □ *leave no stone unturned* □ *as good as gold*, overused idioms: □ *to add insult to injury* □ *a blessing in disguise*, the clichés of public speakers: □ *someone who needs no introduction* □ *in no uncertain terms* □ *without fear or favour*, and the quotation (or usually misquotation) from the Bible or Shakespeare: □ *pride goes before a fall* □ *a poor thing, but mine own*. Journalists are perhaps the worst offenders. To them all countries at war are *strife-torn*, all battles are *pitched*, and all denials *categorical*.

Many clichés have become such through many years of use. But it can take a very short time for a newly-coined phrase to become a cliché. Some modern examples are: □ *at the end of the day* □ *at this moment in time* □ *keep a low profile*.

client or **customer**? A *client* is someone who receives the services of a professional person or organization, while a *customer* is someone who buys goods from a shop or other trading organization: □ *The solicitor had several Asian clients.* □ *She was a regular customer at the fish market.*

◆ A collective noun for regular clients is *clientele*, and this word is also sometimes used for customers, particularly if there is a suggestion of superiority in the shop or its customers: □ *The customers at the Co-op have less exacting tastes than the clientele of Harrods.* The rather formal word *patron* is also sometimes used in place of *customer*, when there is a sense of them bestowing the favour of their custom on an establishment.

clientele The preferred pronunciation of this word, which means 'clients' (see CLIENT OR CUSTOMER?): □*an exclusive clientele*, is [kleeon*tel*]. Note also the spelling, particularly the *-ele* (not *-elle*) ending.

climactic or **climatic**? These two words have completely different meanings. *Climactic* is the adjective from *climax*: □ *This aria marks the climactic point of the opera. Climatic* is the adjective from *climate*: □ *The climatic conditions are unsuitable for outdoor activities.*

◆ Both words should be distinguished from the noun *climacteric*, which means 'a crucial stage in life; the menopause or corresponding male equivalent'.

climate The word *climate* has been extended in meaning to embrace not just the atmosphere as regards the weather, but atmosphere in general: □*a climate of hope.* It is used rather more specifically of the prevailing state of affairs or the attitudes and opinions of people at a particular time: □ *the economic climate* □ *the change in the moral climate of America* (Franklin D. Roosevelt).

climatic see CLIMACTIC OR CLIMATIC?

clinch see CLENCH OR CLINCH?

clique The noun *clique*, often used pejoratively to denote a small exclusive group of people, may be pronounced to rhyme with *teak* or *tick.*

◆ The first of these pronunciations, [kleek], is closer to the French original and is preferred by many users.

clone *Clone* is a word taken from genetic science, where it means 'the asexually, and often artificially, produced offspring of a parent, which are genetically identical to the parent and to each other'. Despite the dislike of some people, the word is now used popularly to suggest anything very similar to something else: □*Marketing the Arts* is a new magazine, tabloid size, a clone of *Campaign* (*Daily Telegraph*). It is also used synonymously with *lookalike*: □*a dozen Elvis Presley clones.*

close or **closed**? Confusion between these two words sometimes arises when they are used in compounds, especially *close/closed season* (the period of time when the killing of certain animals, birds, or fish is forbidden). In British English *close season* is preferred; in American English, *closed season.*

◆ In most other compounds *close* and *closed* are not interchangeable: □*a close shave* □*a closed-shop agreement* □*at close quarters* □*closed-circuit television.*

In all these compounds *close* is pronounced [klōs] and *closed* is pronounced [klōzd].

close proximity *Proximity* means 'being close or near in space or time': □*Its proximity to the station made the house particularly convenient.* As 'close' is part of the meaning of the word, it is never necessary to add *close* before *proximity*: □*His close proximity made me feel uneasy.*

◆ See also TAUTOLOGY.

clothed see CLAD OR CLOTHED?

clout Some people object to the overuse of the noun *clout* to mean 'influence; political power': □ *financial clout* □ *The union doesn't carry much clout with the government.* This usage is best restricted to informal contexts.

co- The prefix *co-* is increasingly attached without a hyphen in modern usage. Some users prefer to retain the hyphen when the prefix is attached to a word beginning with *o-*: □ *co-ordinate* □ *co-operate* (see also **HYPHEN 1**). Some dictionaries retain the hyphen in words referring to a person who does something jointly with another: □ *co-author* □ *co-star*, but the spellings *coauthor, costar*, etc., are acceptable.

coarse or **course**? These words are sometimes confused. *Coarse* means 'rough or crude': □ *coarse behaviour* □ *coarse cloth.* The noun *course* means 'progression of events': □ *in the course of time*, or 'route': □ *The ship steered a difficult course.* The verb *course* means 'hunt or pursue'; *coursing* is the sport in which hares are hunted with dogs.
    ◆ *Coarse* [not *course*] *fishing* is the activity of catching freshwater fish other than salmon or trout.

cocoon This word, which means 'protective covering': □ *The butterfly emerged from its cocoon*, is sometimes misspelt. Note the second *c* and the *-oo-*.

coherent or **cohesive**? *Coherent* and *cohesive* have the same roots in the verb *to cohere*, but they are used differently. *Coherent* means 'logically consistent; comprehensible': □ *a coherent argument* □ *coherent speech. Cohesive* means 'clinging or sticking together': □ *the cohesive properties of the mortar*, but is more frequently used figuratively of anything that holds together or has unity: □ *Union members should think of themselves as a cohesive group.*

coiffure This word, meaning 'hairstyle', is usually pronounced [kwah*fewr*]. This should be clearly distinguished from the pronunciation of *coiffeur* meaning 'hairstylist' [kwah*fer*].
    ◆ Note the different endings of these nouns and also the *-ff-* in the spelling.

colander see **CALENDAR, CALENDER, OR COLANDER**?

collaborate or **cooperate**? Both *collaborate* and *cooperate* mean 'work together for a common purpose': □ *The two scientists have collaborated/cooperated for years on various projects. Collaborate* has the extra sense of working with or assisting an enemy, particularly an enemy occupier of one's country: □ *The French politicians who had collaborated with the Nazis were discredited after the war.*
    ◆ *Collaborate* is more likely to be used of a cooperative enterprise of an intellectual or artistic nature; people might *collaborate* in writing a book but *cooperate* in organizing a party.

collective nouns The term *collective noun* applies to such nouns as: □ *flock* □ *gang* □ *troop*, which are usually followed by *of* and another noun: □ *a flock of sheep*, to other nouns which apply to groups, such as: □ *audience* □ *orchestra* □ *crowd*, and to 'class' collectives, which include various things of a certain kind: □ *furniture* □ *underwear* □ *greengrocery* □ *cutlery.*
    ◆ Some collective nouns have very restricted uses. A *pride* can only be of lions; a *school* only of fish and other aquatic animals. Others, such as *herd* or *heap*, have a more general use.
    The main problem with collective nouns is whether to treat them as

singular or plural. With some nouns there is no choice. Class collectives always take a singular verb: □ *My luggage is missing.* Words for people in general or a particular class of person: □ *folk* □ *the police,* take a plural verb: □ *The clergy are up in arms about it.* It is with group nouns such as: □ *audience* □ *jury* □ *committee* that problems arise. British English tends to treat such words as plural: □ *The Government are undecided,* while American English treats them as singular: □ *The Government is undecided.* For the use of singular and plural verbs see individual entries at SINGULAR OR PLURAL?

colon A *colon* introduces a clause or word which amplifies, interprets, explains, or reveals what has gone before it: □*He was beginning to be anxious: they had been gone for five hours.* □ *Only one party cares: Labour.* Its other main uses are to introduce lists: □ *The Thames Valley Police Authority covers three counties: Berkshire, Buckinghamshire, and Oxfordshire,* and to introduce lengthier quotations, often when quotation marks are not used and the quoted material is indented.

◆ The clause preceding a colon should usually be able to stand on its own grammatically.

Capitals should be used after colons only if the word following is a proper noun; if the first word of a quotation is capitalized; if the colon follows a formal salutation or brief instruction: □ *To whom it may concern:* □ *Note:* □ *Warning:* or sometimes if the material following the colon is a whole sentence or sentences expressing a complete thought.

Colons are also used to introduce speech in plays: □ *Cecily: Are you called Algernon? Algernon: I cannot deny it.* They are used between titles and subtitles: □ *Men Who Play God: The Story of the Hydrogen Bomb*; in biblical references between chapter and verse: □ *James 2:14–17*; in business correspondence: □ *To:* □ *Reference:* and to show the relationship of one number to another: □ *The ratio was 2:1.* Colons are also used in books such as this to introduce examples.

The use of the dash following a colon is restricted to lists, usually where each item starts on a new line and is indented. Even then the practice is old-fashioned and not recommended. See also DASH.

colonnade Note the spelling of this noun, meaning 'row of columns', particularly the *-l-* (as in *column*) and the *-nn-*.

coloration Note that the *u* of *colour* is omitted in this derived form of the word, which refers to a pattern or arrangement of colours: □ *the distinctive coloration of the feathers.*

◆ The same principle applies to the noun *discoloration,* derived from the verb *discolour.*

coloured see BLACK.

colourize The verb *colourize* refers to the process of adding colour to black-and-white films: □ *the controversial practice of colourizing classic films.* Note that the verb is spelt *-our-* in British English (the American spelling is *colorize*), unlike the verb *decolorize,* meaning 'remove the colour from', which is spelt *-or-* in British and American English.

columnist The *n* of this word is sometimes not sounded in speech. The pronunciation [kŏlŭmnist] is strictly correct, but [kŏlŭmist] is becoming increasingly common; [kŏlŭmist] reflects the pronunciation of *column,* with its silent *n.*

comic or **comical**? *Comic* and *comical* are not quite synonyms. *Comic* means 'of comedy, intended to cause laughter or amusement': □ *a comic actor* □ *a comic poem. Comical* means 'having the effect of causing laughter or amusement': □ *a comical sight*.

◆ Something can be *comic*, in that it is intended to be funny, even if it fails actually to arouse mirth: □ *His comic songs did not raise a smile*. *Comical* is often used in cases where the humour is unintentional: □ *It was comical to see their attempts to appear sophisticated*.

comma Of all the punctuation marks, the comma is the most likely to cause confusion or ambiguity through its misuse, overuse, or omission. Some of the conventions that formerly governed its use are now regarded as optional; it is important, however, to be consistent within a single piece of writing. Excessively long sentences containing many clauses separated by commas are best divided into shorter units; short sentences that require many commas for clarity should be reworded if possible. The principal uses of the comma are listed below.

◆ **1** The individual items of a series of three or more are separated by commas; the final comma preceding *and* or *or* is optional: □ *We have invited Paul, Michael, Peter, and Mark*. □ *She plays tennis, hockey and netball*. □ *He doesn't like cabbage, carrots, or beans*.

The same conventions apply to series of longer units: □ *I closed the window, drew the curtains, and went to bed*. Omission of the final comma may cause confusion if the last or penultimate item contains *and*: □ *They only serve pies, fish and chips, and beefburgers*.

2 The use of a comma between adjectives that precede the noun they qualify is optional in most cases: □ *a large, red, juicy tomato* □ *a small round black button*.

When the final adjective has a closer relationship with the noun, it should not be preceded by a comma: □ *a picturesque French village* □ *an impertinent little boy* □ *an eccentric old woman*.

In the following examples, omission of the comma could cause ambiguity or confusion: □ *bright, blue curtains* □ *a freshly ironed, neatly folded shirt*.

3 Commas separate non-defining or parenthetical clauses and phrases from the rest of the sentence: □ *The mayor, who is very fond of gardening, presented the prizes at the flower show*. □ *My diamond necklace, a valuable family heirloom, has been stolen*.

It is important to ensure that both commas are present (unless the clause or phrase falls at the end of the sentence) and that they enclose the appropriate information: it should be possible to remove the words between the commas without affecting the basic message of the sentence. As a general rule, the subject of a sentence should not be separated from its verb by a single comma. Commas are not used around defining or essential clauses or phrases: □ *The classical guitarist Andrés Segovia has died*. □ *The skirt that I bought last week has a broken zip*.

In some cases, the removal or insertion of parenthetical commas can alter the meaning of a sentence: □ *My daughter Elizabeth is a doctor* implies that the speaker has two or more daughters, one of whom is called Elizabeth; □ *My daughter, Elizabeth, is a doctor* implies that the speaker has only one daughter.

See also **APPOSITION; BRACKETS; CLAUSE; DASH; THAT OR WHICH?**

4 The use of the comma or commas to separate such words and phrases as *however, therefore, nevertheless, of course, for example*, and *on the other hand* from the rest of the sentence is optional: □ *I wondered, however, whether he was right*. □ *The holiday will include visits to some of the local attractions, for example the caves and the pottery*. □ *We could go by train or of course we could use the car*.

5 Commas are always used to separate terms of address, interjections, and closing quotation tags from the rest of the sentence: □ *I'm sorry to have troubled you, madam.* □ *Please sit down, Mr Smith, and tell me what happened.* □ *Oh, what a beautiful garden!* □ *It's cold today, isn't it?*

6 The main clause of the sentence may be separated from a preceding subordinate clause or participial phrase by a comma. The comma is often omitted after a short clause or phrase: □ *After loading all their luggage into the car and locking up the house and garage, they set off on their holidays.* □ *When it stops raining we will go out.* See also **DANGLING PARTICIPLES**.

7 Two or more main clauses linked by a coordinating conjunction (*and, or, but,* etc.) may be separated with a comma if necessary. The comma is usually omitted if the clauses have the same subject or object: □ *Tom washed the dishes and Sarah dried them.* □ *He shut the door but forgot to turn out the light.* If the clauses are fairly short the comma is optional: □ *The lorry overturned but the driver was uninjured.* □ *The hotel is very comfortable, and the food is excellent.*

Between longer or more complex main clauses, a comma is often necessary to avoid ambiguity or confusion. (Where such clauses are not linked by a coordinating conjunction, they should be separated by a **SEMICOLON** rather than a comma.)

8 A comma may be used in place of a repeated verb in the second of two related clauses: □ *She speaks French and German; her husband, Spanish and Italian.* See also **DATES; LETTER WRITING; NUMBERS; QUOTATION MARKS**.

commandant, commander, or **commandeer?** *Commandant* and *commander* are nouns; *commandeer* is a verb. The noun *commandant* refers to an officer in command of a particular group or establishment, such as a military academy or prisoner-of-war camp; the noun *commander* refers to an officer in command of a military operation, ship, etc. *Commander* is also the name of a rank in the Navy and is used in nonmilitary contexts to denote anybody who is in command: □ *the commander of the expedition.* The verb *commandeer* means 'seize, especially for military or public use': □ *They commandeered our car.*

commemorate This word, meaning 'remember with a ceremony': □ *They commemorated the 50th anniversary of the revolution,* is sometimes misspelt. Note particularly the *-mm-* followed by a single *m*.

commence *Commence* means the same as *begin* or *start* but should be used only in formal contexts, where its opposite is *conclude,* rather than *end*: □ *The meeting will commence at 9.30 a.m. and conclude at noon.*

◆ It sounds affected or pompous if one uses *commence* in contexts where *begin* or *start* is appropriate: □ *I shall commence my new job tomorrow.* □ *The car commenced making a rattling noise.*

Commencement is the noun from *commence* and should be used in similar contexts: □ *the commencement of the financial year.* It has a special meaning in the United States, where *Commencement* is the ceremony at which students receive degrees.

commensurate *Commensurate* means 'equal in measure or extent; proportionate': □ *The rent charged is commensurate with the flat's current value.* The word is frequently used in connection with job salaries: □ *Remuneration will be commensurate with the importance of this key role* (*Executive Post*).

commercialese *Commercialese* is a usually pejorative term applied to the jargon used in the business and commercial world.
  ◆ Typically such jargon is found in business letters and includes such abbreviations as: □ *inst.* (this month) □ *ult.* (last month) □ *prox.* (next month), as well as such phrases as: □ *Please find enclosed* □ *Further to your letter* □ *I beg to remain* □ *your esteemed favour* □ *your communication to hand.* Unlike other forms of jargon, commercialese is becoming distinctly old-fashioned and most modern companies prefer to conduct their correspondence in plain English.

commissionaire This word, meaning 'attendant in uniform': □ *the commissionaire at the theatre*, is sometimes misspelt. Note the *-mm-*, *-ss-*, single *-n-*, and the *-aire* ending.
  ◆ Do not confuse this word with *commissioner*, meaning 'an important official of a government, etc.': □ *a high commissioner* □ *the police commissioner.*

commitment The sense of *commitment* which means 'loyalty to a cause or ideology' is an increasingly popular one: □ *a genuine Christian commitment* □ *his commitment to the animal rights movement* □ *As my commitment to the struggle for racial justice intensified, I wanted to go further in my relationship with the black community* (Jim Wallis, *The New Radical*). Many users dislike this word's overuse.
  ◆ Note the *-mm-* and single *t* of *commit.* The *-t* is not doubled in *commitment*, unlike *committed, committing*, etc.

committee The noun *committee* may be singular or plural: □ *The committee meets on Thursdays.* □ *The committee were unable to reach a unanimous decision.*
  ◆ See also COLLECTIVE NOUNS; SINGULAR OR PLURAL?
  Note the spelling of *committee*, particularly the *-mm-*, *-tt-*, and *-ee*.

common see MUTUAL, COMMON, OR RECIPROCAL?

communal This word, meaning 'of a community': □ *communal living*, has two different pronunciations. Both [*kom*yuunăl] and [kŏ*mew*năl] are widely used. Careful speakers, however, prefer the first of these pronunciations.

community *Community* has become a vogue word in two different ways. The application of the word to a recognizable group within a larger society: □ *the Jewish community* □ *the black community*, has given the word an association with minority racial groups, and now a *Council for Community Relations*, a *community relations officer*, and so on, are those that deal with the problems of black and Asian minorities in Britain.
  ◆ *The community* is also used in a much vaguer sense to mean 'society in general'. When psychiatric patients are discharged from hospital and are recommended to be *cared for in the community* it usually means no more than that they are to live in society.

comparable The traditional pronunciation of this word is [*kom*-părăbl]. The variant [kŏm*parr*ăbl] is avoided by careful speakers. See also STRESS.

comparative and **superlative** The *comparative* form of an adjective or adverb is used when two things or people are compared: □ *Anne is smaller than her sister*, while the *superlative* is used as the highest degree of comparison between three or more things: □ *Anne is the smallest girl in her class.*
  ◆ The two main ways of forming comparatives and superlatives are by adding the suffixes *-er* and *-est*, or preceding the word with *more* or *most*: □ *sad–sadder–saddest* □ *eager–more eager–most eager.*

One-syllable words always take -er and -est, as do two-syllable words ending in -y: □ *big–bigger* □ *pretty–prettiest*. Two-syllable words ending in -le, -ow, -er sometimes also take -er and -est: □ *little–littlest* □ *shallow–shallower* □ *clever–cleverer*. Other two-syllable words and all words of three or more syllables take *more* and *most:* □ *more abject* □ *most horrific* □ *most interesting*. Most compound adjectives can use either form: □ *fairer minded* □ *more fair-minded*. There are two well-known words with irregularly formed comparatives and superlatives: □ *good/well–better–best* □ *bad/badly–worse–worst*.

More is used instead of -er, even with one-syllable words, in certain contexts: when two adjectives are being compared with each other: □ *He's really more shy than aloof*; and when the aptness of an adjective is being challenged: □ *She's no more fat than a stick insect!*

Absolute adjectives (see **ADJECTIVES**) cannot be used in comparative or superlative forms. One cannot say *more total* or *emptier*. It is, however, possible to use comparative forms when suggesting a closer approximation to perfection: □ *A fuller description will be given tomorrow*.

Mistakes concerning comparatives and superlatives include the use of the comparative in phrases like: *three times wider, ten times more expensive,* instead of: □ *three times as wide* □ *ten times as expensive*, although when an actual measure is specified it is appropriate to say: □ *three feet wider* □ *ten pounds more expensive*. Another mistake is the use of *more* or -er in phrases like: □ *one of the more promising of the new novelists*, when it is clear that more than two things or people are being compared, and the use of *most* or -est when only two things or people are being compared: *We have two sons; Tom is the youngest*. A (possibly deliberate) mistake much used by advertisers is the use of the comparative when it is unclear what is being compared: □ *X washes whiter and cleaner!* □ *Y gives you a better, closer shave!*, and the unbridled use of superlatives: □ *The most luxurious holiday ever!*

Finally, a frequent mistake is the misspelling of *comparative* as *comparitive*, probably based on *comparison*.

comparatively *Comparatively* means 'relatively, as compared with a standard': □ *It was comparatively inexpensive for vintage champagne*.
◆ It is often used as a synonym for 'rather, fairly, or somewhat', with no question of comparison: □ *It is a comparatively small resort*, but many people dislike this usage.

compare to or **compare with**? *Compare to* and *compare with* are not interchangeable. *Compare to* is used when things are being likened to each other: □ *He compared her skin to ivory*. *Compare with* is used when things are being considered from the point of view of both similarities and differences: □ *Tourists find London hotels expensive compared with those of other European capitals*. When *compare* is used intransitively, *with* should always be used: □ *His direction compares with early Hitchcock*.
◆ In American English *compared to* and *comparable to* are frequently used where *with* is appropriate: □ *Compared to my brother, I'm poor*. □ *It's not comparable to the home-made version*, and these uses are coming into British English.

compel or **impel**? Both these verbs mean 'force', but they differ in usage. *Compel* is used with human and non-human subjects and implies strong obligation: □ *They compelled us to take part*. □ *Financial necessity compelled him to accept the job. Impel* is chiefly used with non-human subjects and implies an urge rather than an obligation: □ *She felt impelled to protest.* □ *Fear impelled him to turn back.*

competition or **contest**? *Competition* and *contest* both involve rivalry with an opponent or opponents and can be synonymous: □ *At 18 she won a contest/competition for young musicians.* However, *contest* is restricted to the sense of organized competitive events or exertions to achieve victory over opponents: □ *the contest for nomination as candidate. Competition* is used more generally of rivalry: □ *There will be keen competition for tickets*, and is also used of the people or organization against which one is competing: □ *We must assess the strengths and weaknesses of the competition.*

complacent or **complaisant**? A *complacent* person is smug or self-satisfied; a *complaisant* person is obliging or willing to comply. Both adjectives may be applied to the same noun: □ *'We can't lose,' she said with a complacent smile.* □ *He opened the door with a complaisant smile.*

◆ The two words should not be confused. They are similar in pronunciation but quite different in spelling: *complacent* [kŏm*plays*ĕnt] ends in -*cent*; *complaisant* [kŏm*playz*ănt] ends in -*sant*.

Complacent is the more frequent word, *complaisant* being rather old-fashioned.

complement The *complement* of a clause or sentence provides essential additional information about the SUBJECT or OBJECT. A complement may be a noun, adjective, pronoun, or phrase.

◆ A subject complement usually follows such verbs as *be, become, turn, look, appear, seem, feel,* and *sound.* In the sentence □ *He became a teacher, a teacher* is the complement. In □ *They felt disappointed, disappointed* is the complement. The clause □ *where we live* is the complement of the sentence *This is where we live.*

An object complement usually follows the direct object of such verbs as *make, find, declare, elect,* and *call.* In the sentence □ *You made me very proud, very proud* is the complement. In □ *The judges declared him the winner, the winner* is the complement.

See also COMPLEMENT OR COMPLIMENT?; COMPLEMENT OR SUPPLEMENT?

complement or **compliment**? These two words are often confused. Both as a noun and a verb, *complement* suggests the addition of something necessary to make something whole or complete: □ *a ship's complement* □ *The flowers complemented the room's decor perfectly. Compliment* is used as a noun and verb to refer to an expression of praise, respect, or admiration: □ *She complimented her host on the excellent meal.* □ *with the compliments of the management.* To avoid mistakes remember the *e* of *complement* is also in *complete.*

◆ The derived adjectives *complementary* and *complimentary* are also confused, particularly when *complimentary* is used in the sense of 'given free': □ *a complimentary* [not *complementary*] *copy of his latest book* □ *two complimentary* [not *complementary*] *tickets to the exhibition.*

complement or **supplement**? *Complement* and *supplement* have a distinct difference in meaning. Both as noun and verb, *complement* suggests the addition of something necessary to make something whole or complete: □ *The closures were forced by the hospital's* *inability to recruit 92 nurses out of its full complement of nearly 800* (*Daily Telegraph*). □ *The music complemented the mime aptly. Supplement* suggests an addition to something that is already complete: □ *Her fees for private tuition supplemented her teacher's salary.* □ *Most Sunday newspapers publish a colour supplement.*

complementary medicine or **alternative medicine**? *Complementary medicine* is the treatment of illnesses by such techniques and systems as osteopathy, acupuncture, and homoeopathy. The term *complementary medicine* suggests that the treatments and therapies complement – fit in with and work alongside – orthodox medicine; the term *alternative medicine* emphasizes that such treatments, etc., are completely different from those of 'conventional' medicine.

complete When used to mean 'total' *complete* is an absolute adjective (see **ADJECTIVES**) and many people dislike any modification of it: □ *We were in almost complete darkness.* However, *complete* also has the meaning of 'thorough': □ *a complete overhaul*, and in that sense can be modified with *more* or *most*: □ *This is the most complete study of the period yet published.*

complex The noun *complex* is taken from psychoanalysis, where it means 'a set of subconscious repressed ideas and emotions which can cause an abnormal mental condition': □ *an Oedipus complex* □ *an inferiority complex.* The term has been taken up and used popularly to mean any behavioural problem or obsession, even if it is completely conscious. This usage is disliked by some. □ *She's got a complex about spiders.* □ *'You're crazy,' Clevinger shouted … 'You've got a Jehovah complex'* (Joseph Heller, *Catch 22*).

◆ *Complex* is also used to mean 'something made up of interrelated parts' and this is now often applied to a group of buildings as in: □ *shopping complex* □ *housing complex.*

complex or **complicated**? *Complex* and *complicated* are very similar in meaning and the differences in usage are subtle ones. Both mean 'consisting of many parts which are intimately combined': □ *This is a complex/complicated problem.*

◆ *Complicated* emphasizes the fact that the multifaceted nature of a thing makes it difficult to solve or understand, and there is sometimes a negative connotation to it – a suggestion that it could possibly be simpler: □ *Compared with Scottish procedure, housebuying in England is unnecessarily complicated. Complex* is more neutral and emphasizes the intricacy of the combination of parts rather than the resulting difficulties: □ *The blood-clotting system is a complex mechanism.*

compliment, complimentary see **COMPLEMENT OR COMPLIMENT**?

compose, comprise, or **constitute**? All these verbs are concerned with parts making up a whole. *Compose* and *constitute* are both used to mean 'come together to make (a whole)' but *compose* is usually used in the passive and *constitute* in the active: □ *The team is composed of several experts.* □ *the commodities that constitute the average household diet. Comprise* can only be used to mean 'consist of': □ *The house comprises three bedrooms, a living room, kitchen, and bathroom.* Its use in place of *constitute*: □ *Eleven players comprise a team* is not generally considered acceptable; its use in place of *compose*: □ *The team is comprised of eleven players* is wrong.

◆ See also CONSIST OF OR CONSIST IN?

compound A *compound* is a word that consists of two or more other words joined together, with or without a space or hyphen: □ *breakdown* □ *forget-me-not* □ *dining room*.

◆ There are no absolute rules governing the use of spaces and hyphens in many compounds (see HYPHEN 2).

The plural of a compound noun is usually formed by making the noun element plural: □ *passers-by* □ *sons-in-law*. See also PLURALS.

The coining of new compound verbs, such as *to drug-test*, is disliked by some people: □ *Students starting degree courses in 1990 will be among the first to job-hunt in the single European market* (*The Guardian*). See also VERBS.

As a noun or adjective, the word *compound* is stressed on the first syllable [*kom*pownd]; as a verb it is stressed on the second syllable [köm*pownd*].

comprehend see APPREHEND OR COMPREHEND?

comprehensible or **comprehensive**? These two adjectives are derived from different senses of the verb *comprehend* (see APPREHEND OR COMPREHEND?). *Comprehensible* means 'understandable'; *comprehensive* means 'including all or most things': □ *The explanation must be comprehensible to the average reader.* □ *fully comprehensive car insurance.*

compulsive or **compulsory**? Both these adjectives are derived from the verb *compel*, meaning 'force'. *Compulsive* refers to something that one is forced to do by an internal or psychological urge; *compulsory* refers to something that one is forced to do by an external rule or law: □ *a compulsive gambler* □ *a compulsory payment.*

computerate The word *computerate* means 'able to operate a computer; experienced in computing'. It is a blend of the synonymous phrase *computer literate* (see LITERAL, LITERARY OR LITERATE?) and is often used in job advertisements: □ *Applicants must be computerate and able to work under pressure.*

concede This verb, meaning 'admit' or 'yield', is sometimes misspelt. Note the *-cede* ending, as in the verb *cede*, which is similar in meaning.

concept The precise meaning of *concept* is 'an idea of a category or thing which is formed by generalization from particular instances'. The meaning has widened to embrace ideas in general, and is often now used to mean 'an accepted idea of a particular thing': □ *the concept of alternative medicine*. It is frequently used very loosely to mean little more than 'an idea or notion', particularly in advertising. Many people dislike this usage: □ *a new concept in slimming*.

◆ *Conceptualize* means 'form a concept' or 'interpret conceptually': □ *The Greeks conceptualized all their experiences in terms of the gods*. It should not be used to mean 'think', 'imagine', or 'visualize'.

concerned The adjective *concerned* may be followed by *about* or *for* when it means 'anxious' and by *with* when it means 'on the subject of': □ *We are very concerned about pollution.* □ *The article is concerned with pollution.* □ *They are concerned for his health.* □ *The organization is concerned with public health.*

◆ For discussion of the phrase *as far as ... is concerned*, see AS FAR AS.

concerning *Concerning* means 'relating to, on the subject of, or about': □ *The head teacher is available to talk to people concerning their* *career choices.*

◆ It is normally used between two clauses rather than at the beginning of a sentence and is rather more formal than *about.*

condition or **precondition**? A *condition* is a requirement or stipulation on which an agreement or contract depends: □ *I will let you go on condition that you are back before midnight.* While a condition can be fulfilled either before or after the agreement is made, a *precondition* is a requirement that must be satisfied in advance of an agreement being made: □ *Assent to the manifesto was a precondition of membership.*

◆ *Condition* can be used, not just of agreements, but also of situations and states of being: □ *the condition of the world* □ *in good/poor condition.* The words *condition* and *precondition* are used synonymously to mean anything which has to be true or occur before something else can happen: □ *The establishment of a just society is an essential condition/precondition for peace.*

conduit This word, which describes a pipe or channel conveying liquid, has various pronunciations. The most widely used is [*kon*dit], but [*kun*dit], [*kon*dyuuit], and [*kon*dwit] are also heard.

confidant or **confident**? A *confidant*, feminine *confidante*, is someone in whom one can confide. Both words are pronounced either [*kon*fidant] or [konfi*dant*]. These nouns should not be confused with the adjective *confident* which means 'assured or certain': □ *a confident young man.*

confrontation A *confrontation* is a face-to-face meeting, especially in the context of opposition, challenge, or defiance: □ *St George's confrontation with the dragon.* Popular journalism has now weakened the meaning so that any disagreement or conflict of ideas is now inevitably referred to as *a confrontation.*

◆ Similarly, anyone with a tendency to argumentativeness is described as *confrontational:* □ *Mr Underhill said Mr Senchak's style 'was that of the old-fashioned confrontational "us and them" union official'* (*The Times*).

congenial, genial, congenital, or **genetic**? Both *congenial* and *genial* mean 'pleasant'; *congenial* is usually applied to abstract nouns and *genial* to people: □ *a congenial atmosphere* □ *He finds the work congenial.* □ *a genial host. Congenial company* refers to people who share one's interests or attitudes; *genial company* refers to people who are friendly and cheerful.

Congenital means 'existing from birth'; *genetic* means 'relating to genes': □ *congenital brain damage* □ *genetic engineering.* A *congenital defect* is not hereditary or inherited; a *genetic defect* is hereditary or inherited.

◆ The adjectives *congenital* and *congenial* are sometimes confused, being similar in spelling. Note that the *e* of *congenital* is short, as in *men,* whereas the *e* of *congenial* is long, as in *mean.*

conjunctions *Conjunctions* are words which link two or more words, clauses, or sentences: □ *and* □ *but* □ *or* □ *because* □ *when.*

◆ *And, but, yet,* and *or* are known as coordinating conjunctions. They connect words and clauses of the same grammatical type: □ *Martha and Mary* □ *I love Mozart but I detest Mahler.* They often connect clauses which share a common verb and this does not need to be repeated: □ *She is young yet surprisingly wise. But* and *yet* can be used only to link two sentence elements, but *and* and *or* can link more than two: □ *I'm tired and cold and hungry and miserable.*

Conjunctions such as *because, when, if, though, unless* are known as subordinating conjunctions, as they connect a subordinate clause to its main clause: □ *He's fat because he eats too much.* □ *It won't work unless everyone cooperates.*

Correlative conjunctions are the pairs *either ... or* and *neither ... nor* which are always used together: □ *Neither Williams nor Jenkins is now an MP.* □ *He's either wicked or mad.*

Few people still have objections to sentences starting with the conjunctions *and, but,* and *or*, which can be effective if used sparingly.

See also individual entries for conjunctions and **SINGULAR OR PLURAL?**

conjurer or **conjuror**? Either spelling is perfectly acceptable.

connection or **connexion**? This word, meaning 'a relationship between two things; joint': □ *His death must have had some connection with the stormy weather.* □ *faulty electrical connections,* is usually spelt *connection. Connexion* is a rarer variant spelling, especially in British English.

connoisseur A person who is an expert within a certain field is called a *connoisseur.* Note the *-nn-, -oi-,* and *-ss-.*

connote or **denote**? These two verbs are sometimes confused. *Denote,* the more frequent of the two, refers to the literal or primary meaning of something: □ *The word 'bachelor' denotes an unmarried man.* □ *Tears do not always denote sadness. Connote,* a more formal word, means 'imply' or 'suggest', referring to secondary meaning or association: □ *For some people, the word 'bachelor' connotes freedom.*

conscience Note the spelling of this word, particularly the *-sci-* in the middle and the *-ce* ending. The second syllable is identical in spelling (but not in pronunciation) with the noun *science.*

conscientious This word, meaning 'diligent and careful': □ *She was a conscientious worker,* is sometimes misspelt. Note in particular the *t.*

consensus *Consensus* means 'opinion shared unanimously, a view generally held or accepted': □ *He had broken the pro-nuclear consensus shared by all postwar leaders (Sunday Times).*

◆ As the meaning contains the idea of a generally held opinion, the frequently used expressions *general consensus* and *consensus of opinion* are tautologies, and are avoided by careful users.

Consensus is frequently misspelt as *concensus,* perhaps from a mistaken belief that it is connected with the word *census.* In fact it derives from the same root as *consent.*

consent see **ASSENT OR CONSENT?**

consequent or **consequential**? *Consequent* means 'following as a direct result': □ *She was knocked down by a lorry and her consequent injuries left her a permanent invalid. Consequential,* a rarer word than *consequent,* is also used to mean 'following as a direct result': □ *the improvement in the local economy and the consequential loss of the area's special status. Consequential* also means 'important': □ *Their decisions were becoming increasingly consequential in determining the direction of the company.* It is also used in legal expressions such as *consequential loss* to mean 'an indirect result' and has the additional meaning of 'self-important; pompous': □ *His manner was pretentious and consequential.*

consequent or **subsequent**? *Consequent* and *subsequent* are sometimes confused. While *consequent* means 'following as a direct result', *subsequent* simply means 'occurring after': □ *her*

bereavement and consequent grief □ her bereavement and subsequent remarriage. Consequent takes the preposition on, while
subsequent takes to: □ increase in salaries consequent on the pay
review □ his behaviour subsequent to his arrival.

consequential see CONSEQUENT OR CONSEQUENTIAL?

conservative or **Conservative**? The word conservative with a lower-
case c- means 'tending to support tradition and established
institutions, opposed to change, moderate, cautious, conventional': □ The college has a reputation for being conservative and
still refuses to admit women students. □ He has conservative
tastes and dresses in sombre colours. □ A Conservative is someone who supports or is a member of the Conservative Party in
Britain or elsewhere; it is also used as an adjective: □ a Conservative MP.
   ◆ A conservative estimate is one that is cautious and moderate, but
   the term is often used to mean 'a low estimate': □ It's worth a million
   pounds at the most conservative estimate.

consider Consider means 'regard as being': □ I consider him a non-
entity, 'think about carefully': □ I have considered all aspects of
the problem, and 'regard sympathetically': □ We will not fail to
consider your feelings on the matter.
   ◆ In the first sense given above, consider is more or less synonymous
   with regard as, and this leads some people to add as to consider: □ He
   considered their work as vitally important. This construction is wrong.
   There is, however, nothing wrong with using as when consider is used
   in the sense of 'think about, give consideration to': □ The songs are
   tuneful but considered as an opera, the work lacks solidity.

considerable Considerable means 'worth consideration; significant':
□ She has made a considerable contribution to biochemical
research. It has been extended to mean 'large in amount': □ They
have saved a considerable amount of money, although some
people dislike the imprecise nature of this use.
   ◆ Considerable is usually attached to abstract nouns: □ a
   considerable quantity □ considerable numbers of, but in American
   English it can be used with concrete nouns: □ They have mined
   considerable gold. This use is not yet acceptable in British English
   although when the meaning is 'significant' one can attach
   considerable to a concrete noun: □ a considerable pianist.

consist of or **consist in**? Consist of means 'comprise, be made up of':
□ Breakfast consists of bread, croissants, jam, and coffee. Consist
in means 'have its essence in': □ The appeal of the writing consists in its use of language rather than its content.
   ◆ Consist of usually precedes a list of concrete nouns, while consist
   in is usually applied to abstract nouns.

consonant A consonant is the sound represented by any of the letters
b, c, d, f, g, h, j, k, l, m, n, p, q, r, s, t, v, w, x, y, and z in the English
language. Compare VOWEL.
   ◆ The presence of a consonant at the beginning of a word may affect
   the form or pronunciation of the preceding word (see A OR AN?; THE).
   Note that in such words as party and rhyme, the letter -y- functions
   as a vowel.

consortium or **consortia**? Consortia is a plural form of the noun consortium, which means 'association of companies': □ a consortium of insurance brokers. The plural form -ia is sometimes
wrongly used in place of the singular noun: □ Now only
Phonepoint, a consortia led by British Telecom, and Byps,

owned by Hutchison Telecom UK, are keen to offer the mobile phone service (*The Guardian*).

◆ The plural form *consortiums* is also acceptable.

constable A police officer of the lowest rank is known as a *constable*. The word has two pronunciations: [*kun*stăbl] or [*kon*stăbl], both of which are acceptable.

constitute see COMPOSE, COMPRISE, OR CONSTITUTE?

constrain or **restrain**? Both these verbs mean 'hold back' or 'limit', but there are differences of usage and application between them. *Constrain* is more formal and implies an abstract or undesirable restriction; to *restrain* may involve physical force: □ *Such strict guidelines constrain creativity.* □ *He struggled to restrain the dog.*

◆ *Constrain* has the additional and more frequent meaning of 'compel': □ *I felt constrained to resign.*

contact The meanings of *contact* as a noun include 'the state of touching': □ *He avoided all physical contact with dogs,* 'link or relationship': □ *The two towns have commercial contacts,* and 'communication': □ *I am in regular contact with her.* A modern use is 'a person one knows who may be useful to one': □ *I have a good contact at the Home Office.*

◆ The use of the verb *contact* to mean 'communicate with': □ *I will contact you next week* is still disliked as an Americanism by some people. It is, however, particularly useful in cases where one wishes to avoid specifying whether communication will be made by letter, telephone, message, or personal visit.

contagious or **infectious**? *Contagious* and *infectious* are both used of diseases that can be passed on to others. *Contagious* diseases are those that are passed on by physical contact, like venereal diseases or impetigo; *infectious* diseases are those passed on by airborne or waterborne microorganisms, like measles or influenza.

◆ In figurative use the words are synonymous: □ *His optimistic mood was infectious/contagious.*

containerize *Containerize* is a verb formed from the noun *container* in its sense of a large packing case in which goods are transported by road and sea, being handled mechanically throughout. To *containerize* means both 'pack into containers for transport and transport in this method': □ *The beans must be containerized before the end of the week;* and 'change over to the use of containers': □ *We are containerizing our shipping procedures.*

contemporary The primary meaning of *contemporary* is 'happening or living at the same time as': □ *Joyce was contemporary with the Bloomsbury group, though not a member of it.* It has more recently been used to mean 'happening at the present time; current': □ *Contemporary values are materialistic and selfish.*

◆ A development of this meaning has been the use of *contemporary* to mean 'modern, up-to-date', sometimes qualified with *very, extremely,* etc.: □ *They sell the most contemporary fashions in town.* This use is disliked by many people and is best avoided. One should beware of ambiguities between the first and second meanings of *contemporary:* □ *a contemporary biography of Shelley* may mean one written when Shelley was alive, or one written recently.

contemptible or **contemptuous**? Both *contemptible* and *contemptuous* are concerned with *contempt,* but they have distinctly different meanings. *Contemptible* means 'despicable; deserving scorn or contempt': □ *His meanness was contemptible. Contemptuous* means 'scornful, feeling or showing contempt': □ *She observed his feeble efforts with a contemptuous smile.*

contest see COMPETITION OR CONTEST?

contingency A *contingency* is 'something that happens by chance; something unforeseen that might possibly occur in the future': □ *We must prepare ourselves for every contingency.*

◆ In modern use the word almost always appears in the phrase *contingency plans* and is usually applied, not to unforeseen future events, but to those that are predictable, although not inevitable: □ *The council have made contingency plans in case of a severe winter.*

continual or **continuous**? *Continual* means 'frequently repeated'; *continuous* means 'without break or interruption': □ *Our neighbour's continual complaints forced us to move house.* □ *The continuous noise from the generator kept him awake all night.*

◆ The fundamental difference in sense, which also applies to the adverbs *continually* and *continuously*, is that something *continual* stops from time to time, whereas something *continuous* does not stop until it reaches its natural end. It is acceptable in certain contexts to interchange the two words, but this may lead to ambiguity and is therefore best avoided if possible. *Continual* is not used of physical objects, such as *a continuous roll of paper*, nor may *continuous* be substituted for *continual* in such phrases as: □ *continual interruptions*.

continuance, continuation, or **continuity**? All three nouns are derived from the verb *continue*. *Continuance* is the act of continuing, usually without a break, whereas *continuation* may be the act of continuing after a break: □ *the continuance of the strike* □ *a continuation of yesterday's discussion.* In some contexts, such as the first example above, *continuance* and *continuation* are interchangeable. *Continuity* is the state of being continuous (see CONTINUAL OR CONTINUOUS?): □ *the continuity of the action.*

continuous see CONTINUAL OR CONTINUOUS?

contractions The most common contractions in English are those of the verbs *am, are, is, have, has, had, will, shall, would,* and the word *not* combined with an auxiliary verb: □ *I'm* □ *you're* □ *she's* □ *we've* □ *he'll* □ *they'd* □ *can't* □ *shouldn't.*

◆ An apostrophe indicates the missing letter(s), although in the contraction *shan't*, where there are actually two sets of missing letters, only the missing *o* is indicated. The contracted form *'d* can stand for either *had* or *would*, and *'s* can be either *is* or *has* – or *us* when used in the word *let's*; it should always be clear from the context which word is intended. Two irregular contractions are *won't* (will not) and *aren't* (are not), which can also mean *am not*, as in: □ *Aren't I right?* □ *Aren't I clever!*

Contractions are almost always used in speech. They should always be used in written passages of dialogue, and they are generally acceptable in all but the most formal writing. Some contractions are more likely to be written than others. □ *He's late* and: □ *Jill's late* are more acceptable in writing than: □ *Dinner's late* □ *The train's late,* and the *'ll* contraction (except when used with personal pronouns: □ *I'll*): □ *Tim'll be there.* □ *The bus'll be on time* is not usually used in writing.

Care should be taken with the placing of the apostrophe. A frequent mistake is placing it where the syllables break, rather than where the letter is missing: □ *wouldn't* [not *would'nt*].

See also AIN'T; 'S OR S'?

contrary This word, meaning 'opposed in position': □ *On the contrary,*

I would like to go for a walk, is stressed on the first syllable [kon-trări]. Only in the sense 'perverse or stubborn': □ *such a contrary girl*, is it stressed on the second syllable [kŏntrairi].

contribute In the traditional pronunciation of this word, the stress is on the second syllable [kŏn*trib*yoot]; some users dislike the pronunciation with the word stressed on the first syllable [*kon*tribyoot].

controversy In the traditional pronunciation of this word, the stress falls on the first syllable [*kon*trŏversi]. The variant pronunciation, with stress on the second syllable [kŏn*trov*ĕrsi], is widely heard, but is disliked by many users. See also **STRESS**.

convalescence This word, meaning 'recovery after an illness', is sometimes misspelt. Note the combinations *sc* and *nc*.

converse, inverse, obverse, or **reverse**? These four words share the sense of 'opposite'; in some contexts they are interchangeable. The noun *converse* specifically denotes something that is opposite in meaning: □ *the converse of this statement. Inverse* is more frequently used as an adjective in such phrases as □ *in inverse proportion*; *obverse*, a formal word and the least common of the four, refers to a counterpart: □ *The obverse of the company's success is the failure of its rivals. Reverse*, the most frequent and general of the four words, may be used as a verb, noun, or adjective: □ *to reverse a decision* □ *to do the reverse* □ *in reverse order.*

◆ *Obverse* and *reverse* may also refer to the two sides of a coin, *obverse* being 'heads' and *reverse* 'tails'.

The *converse* of a statement or proposition is one that reverses the elements of the proposition: □ *You say that your mother dislikes you but in fact the converse is true – you dislike your mother.* The word is now usually used much more loosely to mean 'opposite': □ *The previous speaker claimed that nuclear weapons help to preserve peace, but I maintain the converse.* The adverb *conversely*, similarly, is now used to mean just 'on the other hand': □ *In such an emergency one can stop the car or, conversely, one can accelerate out of danger.*

The noun or adjective *converse* is stressed on the first syllable [*kon*vers]. The verb *converse*, meaning 'have a conversation', is stressed on the second syllable [kŏn*vers*].

convertible This word, meaning 'capable of being changed': □ *convertible car*, is sometimes misspelt. The ending is *-ible*, not *-able*.

cooperate see **COLLABORATE OR COOPERATE**?

cord see **CHORD OR CORD**?

co-respondent see **CORRESPONDENT OR CO-RESPONDENT**?

corps or **corpse**? The noun *corps*, meaning 'body of people', should not be confused with the noun *corpse*, meaning 'dead body': □ *the diplomatic corps* □ *The corpse lay undiscovered for several weeks.*

◆ Both are ultimately derived from the Latin *corpus* 'body', via the French noun *corps*. The English word *corps* retains the French pronunciation [kor], whereas *corpse*, which entered English from Old French some 400 years earlier, is pronounced [korps].

correspond There are two main meanings of *correspond*. One is 'communicate with someone by exchange of letters': □ *He met his Italian penfriend after they had corresponded for years.* The other meaning is 'match or be equivalent or comparable in some respect': □ *Your account corresponds exactly with the description of the other witnesses.* □ *The French lycée roughly corresponds to the British grammar school.*

◆ In this second meaning *correspond to* is considered correct by many careful users, although *correspond with* is often used.

correspondent or **co-respondent**? A *correspondent* is someone who communicates by letter: □ *She has correspondents in three continents*, or someone who contributes news reports to a newspaper or to radio or television programmes: □ *And now a report from our Middle East correspondent*. A *co-respondent* is the person cited in divorce proceedings as the lover of the husband or wife who has been accused of adultery: □ *Divorced couples hobnobbed with each other and with each other's co-respondents* (Noel Coward, *Present Indicative*).

cosmetic Some people dislike the use of *cosmetic* as an adjective to apply to anything that improves the outward appearance of something: □ *One supplier of decaffeinated coffee ... plans to switch from the chemical process ... although a spokesman insisted this was necessary for 'cosmetic' reasons only* (*Sunday Times*).

◆ It is extended further to anything which makes a superficial improvement but does not make any fundamental change:
□ *Opposition claims that the Government's inner-city plans would have only a cosmetic effect were hotly denied by the Department of the Environment.*

cost or **price**? *Cost* and *price* are often used synonymously as nouns to mean 'the amount paid or charged for something': □ *We were afraid the cost/price would be more than we could afford. Cost* is more likely to refer to an amount paid and *price* to an amount charged: □ *An increase in manufacturing costs will result in higher prices.*

◆ *Price* is more often used when preceded by an adjective: □ *an exorbitant price* □ *bargain prices*, and when speaking of the amount needed in order to bribe someone: □ *'All those men have their price'* (Sir Robert Walpole). *Cost* is used in the plural for the expenses of a lawsuit: □ *The court awarded him costs*, and either *cost* or *price* is used to describe the expenditure in terms of effort and sacrifice made in order to achieve an end: □ *'To give and not to count the cost'* (St Ignatius Loyola). □ *This was indeed a high price to pay for success.*

couch potato The slang term *couch potato* originated in American English in the mid-1970s and entered British English in the later 1980s. It is applied to people who spend most of their leisure time watching television: □ *We are inexorably mutating into a coast-to-coast allotment of couch potatoes* (*The Guardian*). The term is best avoided in formal contexts.

could see CAN OR MAY?

council or **counsel**? The noun *council* means 'a body of people meeting for discussion and consultation': □ *the county council.* The noun *counsel* means 'advice': □ *She always gave wise counsel*, and has the corresponding verb *to counsel* meaning 'give advice to someone': □ *She was counselled about her future career.* □ *He was counselled against acting rashly.* □ *psychiatric counselling.*

◆ A *councillor* (in American English, sometimes *councilor*) is a person who belongs to a *council*, just as a *counsellor* (in American English, sometimes *counselor*) is a person who *counsels*: □ *marriage-guidance counsellors.*

A *counsel* is a lawyer or group of lawyers: □ *Queen's Counsel* □ *the counsel for the defence.*

counsel or **advise**? In many instances *counsel* and *advise* are synonymous, although *counsel* is rather more formal: □*I would advise/counsel you not to drink any more if you're driving home. Advise* is more likely to be used in informal contexts and when the advice is not of great importance: □*He advised me to go on the ring road. Counsel* is more appropriate when the advice is serious and when it is given by trained or professional counsellors: □*He has been counselled by social workers, doctors, and clergy but he still can't sort out his problems.*

COUNTRIES AND PEOPLES

The right-hand column lists the words used as adjectives and nouns referring to the countries in the left-hand column and their people. A single item in the right-hand column, such as 'Albanian', indicates that the same word is used as adjective and noun. 'Argentinian *or* Argentine' indicates that either of these words may be used as an adjective or a noun.

Where the adjective and noun are not identical, they are separated by a semicolon, with the adjective first: 'Danish; a Dane' indicates that *Danish* is the adjective and *Dane* the noun.

Most of the nouns can be converted to plural or collective form by adding -*s*: □*the Albanians* □*a party of Danes.* However, the plural and collective form of nouns ending in -*ese* and -*ois* is identical to the singular form: □*the Chinese* □*the Seychellois.* Other irregular plurals and collective forms are separated from the singular noun by a second semicolon, as at 'Lesothan; a Mosotho ...; the Basotho ...' and 'Irish; an Irishman (*or* -woman); the Irish'.

Cross-references, e.g. see CHINESE, are also included to main entries in the *Guide to Better English.*

Afghanistan	Afghan
Albania	Albanian
Algeria	Algerian
Andorra	Andorran
Angola	Angolan
Antigua and Barbuda	Antiguan
Argentina	Argentinian *or* Argentine
(see ARGENTINE OR ARGENTINIAN?)	
Armenia	Armenian
Austria	Austrian
Azerbaijan	Azeri *or* Azerbaijani
Bahamas, the	Bahamian
Bahrain	Bahraini
Bangladesh	Bangladeshi
Barbados	Barbadian
Belarus	*see* Byelorussia
Belgium	Belgian
Belize	Belizean
Benin	Beninese *or* Beninois
Bermuda	Bermudan *or* Bermudian
Bhutan	Bhutanese
Bolivia	Bolivian
Bosnia-Herzogovina	Bosnian
Botswana	Botswanan
Brazil	Brazilian
Brunei	Bruneian

Bulgaria	Bulgarian
Burkina Faso	Burkinabé
Burma	*see* Myanmar
Burundi	Burundian
Byelorussia	Byelorussian
Cambodia	Cambodian
Cameroon	Cameroonian
Canada	Canadian
Cape Verde	Cape Verdian *or* Cape Verdean
Cayman Islands, the	Caymanian; a Cayman Islander
Central African Republic, the	Central African
Chad	Chadian
Chile	Chilean
China	Chinese
(see **CHINESE**)	
Colombia	Colombian
Commonwealth of Independent States, the *or* the CIS	
Comoros, the	Comoran
Congo	Congolese
Costa Rica	Costa Rican
Côte d'Ivoire	Ivorian
Croatia	Croatian; a Croat *or* a Croatian
Cuba	Cuban
Cyprus	Cypriot
Czechoslovakia	Czech *or* Czechoslovak *or* Czechoslovakian
Denmark	Danish; a Dane
Djibouti	Djibouti
Dominica	Dominican
Dominican Republic, the	Dominican
Ecuador	Ecuadorean *or* Ecuadorian *or* Ecuadoran
Egypt	Egyptian
El Salvador	Salvadorean *or* Salvadorian *or* Salvadoran
England	English; an Englishman (*or* -woman); the English
Equatorial Guinea	Equatorial Guinean
Estonia	Estonian
Ethiopia	Ethiopian
Falkland Islands, the	Falklands; a Falkland Islander
Fiji	Fijian
Finland	Finnish; a Finn
France	French; a Frenchman (*or* -woman); the French
Gabon	Gabonese
Gambia *or* the Gambia	Gambian
Georgia	Georgian
Germany	German
Ghana	Ghanaian
Gibraltar	Gibraltarian
Great Britain	British; a Briton; the British
(see **BRITAIN: BRIT**)	
Greece	Greek
(see **GREEK OR GRECIAN?**)	

Grenada	Grenadian
Guatemala	Guatemalan
Guinea	Guinean
Guinea-Bissau	Guinea-Bissauan
Guyana	Guyanese *or* Guyanan
Haiti	Haitian
Holland	*see* Netherlands, the
Honduras	Honduran
Hong Kong	Hong Kong; a Hong Konger
Hungary	Hungarian
Iceland	Icelandic; an Icelander
India	Indian
Indonesia	Indonesian
Iran	Iranian
Iraq	Iraqi
Ireland, Republic of (Eire)	Irish; an Irishman (*or* -woman); the Irish

(*see also* Northern Ireland *in table*)

Israel	Israeli
Italy	Italian
Ivory Coast	*see* Côte d'Ivoire
Jamaica	Jamaican
Japan	Japanese
Jordan	Jordanian
Kazakhstan	Kazakh
Kenya	Kenyan
Kiribati	Kiribati
Korea	Korean

(*see also* North Korea, South Korea *in table*)

Kuwait	Kuwaiti
Kyrgyzstan	Kyrgyz; a Kyrgyzstani
Laos	Laotian *or* Lao
Latvia	Latvian *or* Lettish; a Latvian *or* a Lett
Lebanon	Lebanese
Lesotho	Lesothan; a Mosotho *or* a Lesothan; the Basotho *or* the Lesothans
Liberia	Liberian
Libya	Libyan
Liechtenstein	Liechtenstein; a Liechtensteiner
Lithuania	Lithuanian
Luxembourg	Luxembourg *or* Luxembourgian *or* Luxembourger; a Luxembourger
Macao	Macao; a Macanese
Macedonia	Macedonian
Madagascar	Madagascan *or* Malagasy; a Madagascan *or* a Malagasy
Malawi	Malawian
Malaysia	Malaysian
Maldives, the	Maldivian
Mali	Malian
Malta	Maltese
Mauritania	Mauritanian
Mauritius	Mauritian

Mexico	Mexican
Moldavia *or* Moldova	Moldavian
Monaco	Monacan *or* Monegasque
Mongolia	Mongolian *or* Mongol
Montenegro	Montenegrin
Montserrat	Montserratian
Morocco	Moroccan
Mozambique	Mozambican
Myanmar (Burma)	Myanmar *or* Burmese
Namibia	Namibian
Nauru	Nauruan
Nepal	Nepalese
Netherlands, the	Dutch; a Netherlander *or* a Dutchman (*or* -woman) *or* a Hollander; the Dutch
New Zealand	New Zealand; a New Zealander
Nicaragua	Nicaraguan
Niger	Nigerien
Nigeria	Nigerian
Northern Ireland	Northern Irish; a Northern Irishman (*or* -woman); the Northern Irish
North Korea	North Korean
Norway	Norwegian
Oman	Omani
Pakistan	Pakistani
Panama	Panamanian
Papua New Guinea	Papua New Guinean
Paraguay	Paraguayan
Peru	Peruvian
Philippines, the	Philippine; a Filipino
Poland	Polish; a Pole
Portugal	Portuguese
Puerto Rico	Puerto Rican
Qatar	Qatari
Romania	Romanian
Russia	Russian
Rwanda	Rwandan
St Lucia	St Lucian
St Vincent and the Grenadines	St Vincentian
San Marino	San Marinese *or* Sanmarinese
São Tomé and Príncipe	São Toméan
Saudi Arabia	Saudi Arabian *or* Saudi
Scotland	Scottish; a Scot *or* a Scotsman (*or* -woman); the Scots *or* the Scottish

(see **SCOTCH. SCOTS. OR SCOTTISH?**)

Senegal	Senegalese
Serbia	Serbian *or* Serb
Seychelles, the	Seychellois
Sierra Leone	Sierra Leonean
Singapore	Singaporean
Slovenia	Slovenian
Solomon Islands, the	Solomon Islands; a Solomon Islander

Somalia	Somalian *or* Somali; a Somalian *or* a Somali
South Africa	South African
South Korea	South Korean
Spain	Spanish; a Spaniard; the Spanish
Sri Lanka	Sri Lankan
Sudan	Sudanese
Suriname	Surinamese
Swaziland	Swazi
Sweden	Swedish; a Swede
Switzerland	Swiss; a Swiss; the Swiss
Syria	Syrian
Tadjikistan	Tadjik
Taiwan	Taiwanese
Tanzania	Tanzanian
Thailand	Thai
Togo	Togolese
Tonga	Tongan
Trinidad and Tobago	Trinidadian *or* Tobagoan
Tunisia	Tunisian
Turkey	Turkish; a Turk
Turkmenistan	Turkmen
Tuvalu	Tuvaluan
Uganda	Ugandan
Ukraine	Ukrainian
United Arab Emirates, the	Emirian
United Kingdom, the *or* the UK (*see also* Great Britain, Northern Ireland *in table*)	British; a Briton; the British
United States of America, the *or* the USA *or* the US	American
Uruguay	Uruguayan
Uzbekistan	Uzbek
Vanuatu	Vanuatuan
Venezuela	Venezuelan
Vietnam	Vietnamese
Wales	Welsh; a Welshman (*or* -woman); the Welsh
Western Samoa	Western Samoan
Yemen	Yemeni
Yugoslavia	Yugoslavian *or* Yugoslav
Zaïre	Zaïrean *or* Zaïrian *or* Zaïrese
Zambia	Zambian
Zimbabwe	Zimbabwean

country or **countryside**? Both these words may be used to denote a rural area: □ *We went for a walk in the country/countryside.* *Countryside* is commonly preceded by *the* and usually only *country* occurs before a noun: □ *the English countryside* □ *a country cottage/lane.*

◆ In the sense of 'nation' or 'state', the noun *country* cannot be replaced by *countryside*: □ *A flu epidemic is sweeping the country* [not *countryside*].

country or **nation**? These words are often used interchangeably: □ *the poorer countries/nations of the world.* Strictly speaking *country* should be used when the context is one of geographical characteristics: □ *Wales is a mountainous country*, and *nation* when speaking of the people or of social and political characteristics: □ *Wales is a nation of musicians and orators.*

◆ *Nation* carries a suggestion of a people with a common culture, language, and traditions, and is often better replaced with the more general *people* when describing a multicultural society like modern Britain.

countryside see COUNTRY OR COUNTRYSIDE?

course see COARSE OR COURSE?; OF COURSE.

crafted This word, meaning 'skilfully made', is sometimes used simply as a synonym for 'made' or 'produced' in exaggerated sales descriptions: □ *fitted cupboards crafted from the finest wood.* Many people dislike this usage.

crash The adjectival use of *crash* in the sense of 'intensive' is best restricted to the few phrases in which it is most familiar: □ *a crash diet* □ *a crash course.*

◆ The word should not be used in contexts that may be associated with its sense of 'collision': □ *an intensive* [not *crash*] *course in air-traffic control.*

creative The adjective *creative* traditionally refers to originality and imagination used for artistic purposes: □ *a creative mind* □ *She is very creative.* It is increasingly used in a less favourable sense, describing something that stretches the limits of convention, legality, or truth: □ *creative accounting/bookkeeping.*

-cred The slang term *-cred*, short for *credibility*, is derived from *street-cred* (or *street credibility*), meaning 'acceptance by young people or people who are familiar with the latest trends, fashions, topical issues, etc.' (see STREET-). It is occasionally attached to other nouns to denote acceptance by a specific group of people: □ *The new chief inspector has force-cred.* □ *Wearing last winter's looks ..., with precisely the same accessories, will do little for up-to-date morale and nothing for one's style-cred* (*Daily Telegraph*).

◆ See also CREDENCE OR CREDIBILITY?

credence or **credibility**? *Credence* is the state of believing something; *credibility* is the state of being believable: □ *He gave credence to her explanation.* □ *Her explanation lacked credibility.* The two nouns should not be confused.

◆ *Credence*, a formal word, is also used in the phrase *letters of credence*, meaning 'credentials'.

Credibility is increasingly used as a vogue word meaning 'power to convince or impress': □ *Labour ... has broken through the important credibility barrier by demonstrating that it can win elections again* (*Daily Telegraph*).

Credence and *credibility* should not be confused with *creed*, 'a set of beliefs'.

See also -CRED; CREDIBLE, CREDITABLE, OR CREDULOUS?; STREET-.

credibility gap *Credibility gap* is a fashionable expression used to describe the lack of trust created by a discrepancy between what is said officially and what is actually seen to happen: □ *The public cynically accepts the credibility gap between election promises and the Government's subsequent policies.*

credible, creditable, or **credulous**? The three adjectives *credible, creditable*, and *credulous*, and their corresponding nouns *credibility, credit*, and *credulity* are sometimes confused. *Credible* means 'believable': □ *My story may sound barely credible but I assure you it's true.* *Creditable* means 'deserving praise': □ *Her* *readiness to forgive her attacker is creditable. Credulous* means 'gullible; too ready to believe': □ *Only the most credulous person could believe such nonsense.*

◆ There is a further, fashionable use of *credible* to mean 'authentic; convincing': □ *They serve a credible paella.* See also **CREDENCE OR CREDIBILITY?**

creed see **CREDENCE OR CREDIBILITY?**

crescendo *Crescendo* is a musical term that is frequently misused in both its technical and figurative senses. In music it describes a gradual increase in volume: □ *The brass sections take up the theme as the crescendo builds up.* It can be used of other sounds or to describe any build-up of intensity: □ *The baby's whimpering increased in a crescendo to a howl.* □ *Public interest in the matter has risen in a crescendo.*

◆ Because people sometimes mistakenly refer to *building up/rising to a crescendo*, the word is often interpreted to mean the loud climax which is actually the culmination of a crescendo, and it is used to mean both 'a loud noise' and, in figurative contexts, 'peak, climax, or milestone': □ *The drum solo ended in a deafening crescendo.* □ *She reached the crescendo of her career before she was 30.*

crisis *Crisis* literally means 'turning point' and it should be used for situations that have reached a turning point for better or worse, for decisive moments in dramas, for crucial states of affairs where significant changes are likely: □ *The illness had passed its crisis and it was clear that she would live.* □ *the worsening economic crisis* □ *It is feared that the crisis which resulted in the military coup may lead to civil war.*

◆ To the dislike of some people, *crisis* is now often applied to situations which are worrying or serious but without any definite implication of imminent change: □ *Independent television is facing a crisis through declining audiences* (*Daily Telegraph*), or for quite trivial problems: □ *I've got a crisis here – my zip's broken.*

Note the spelling of the plural of *crisis*, which is *crises*, pronounced [*krīseez*].

criterion or **criteria?** The word *criterion*, meaning 'a standard by which to judge or evaluate something', is a singular noun: □ *Exam results were the only criterion for deciding whether candidates should be interviewed.* The plural of *criterion* is *criteria*: □ *on the condition that the basic criteria of the code are accepted and met* (*The Bookseller*).

◆ Many people take *criteria* to be a singular noun with the plural *criterias*. This is wrong.

critic or **critique?** A *critic* is someone who criticizes. The word is sometimes used in the sense of someone who finds fault or expresses disapproval: □ *Acupuncture has many critics in the medical profession.* It is also used of someone who is employed to evaluate works of art, music, or literature: □ *The public loved the play but the critics did not have a good word to say for it.* A *critique* is a work of criticism, usually applied to an academic work which analyses and discusses ideas in depth: □ *This is a thoughtful critique of logical positivism.*

critical *Critical* means 'inclined to judge severely': □ *My mother is so critical of the way I bring up the children*; 'involving careful or scholarly evaluation': □ *a critical account of Jung's work*; 'involving a turning point; crucial': □ *We are at a critical point in our negotiations.*

◆ This last use is often applied to serious or dangerous illnesses or injuries: □ *in a critical condition* and has in its turn led to such uses as: □ *A woman was later described as 'critical' in hospital, with one wrist almost severed* (*Daily Telegraph*).

critique see CRITIC OR CRITIQUE?

crochet or **crotchet**? The noun *crochet* refers to a type of needlework; the noun *crotchet* is the name of a note in music.

◆ *Crochet* is a word of French origin that retains the French pronunciation [krōshay] in English. The past tense of the verb *crochet* is *crocheted*, spelt with a single -*t*- and pronounced [krōshayd].

The noun *crotchet*, pronounced [krochit], has the derived adjective *crotchety*, which means 'irritable' in informal English.

cross-section A *cross-section* is a piece of something which has been cut off at right angles or a drawing of the dimensions revealed by such a cutting: □ *The diagram shows an artery in cross-section.* The expression is more often used popularly to mean 'a typical or representative sample': □ *Over five thousand people were interviewed as a cross-section of the general public.*

crotch or **crutch**? Either noun may be used to denote the angle between a person's legs (hence, the genital area) or the corresponding part of a garment (such as a pair of trousers). The term *crotch* is more frequently used in these senses, but *crutch* is not incorrect.

◆ The principal meaning of the noun *crutch* is 'support used by people with injured legs or feet': □ *She was on crutches for three months after the accident.*

crotchet see CROCHET OR CROTCHET?

crucial The use of *crucial* as a synonym for *important* is best avoided in formal speech and writing, where it should be restricted to the sense of 'decisive' or 'critical': □ *constituencies where the self-employed vote could be crucial to the outcome of the election* (*Daily Telegraph*).

◆ *Crucial* is widely used in informal contexts, and increasingly by journalists, broadcasters, advertisers, and others, to emphasize the importance of events or issues that are by no means decisive or critical. The word has the same derivation as *crux*, meaning 'a decisive point', which is most frequently encountered in the expression *the crux of the matter*.

crutch see CROTCH OR CRUTCH?

cuisine The word *cuisine* is used to describe a style of cooking food, particularly one which is typical of a particular country or region: □ *Peppers and tomatoes are characteristic of Basque cuisine*; for the food itself: □ *Their cuisine is excellent*; and in various phrases which convey a particular style of cooking: □ *nouvelle cuisine* □ *cuisine minceur*.

◆ *Cuisine* carries a suggestion of good food skilfully cooked so its use in such a sentence as: □ *It was typical service-station cuisine – chips with everything* is either inappropriate or jocular.

cullender see CALENDAR, CALENDER, OR COLANDER?

culminate *Culminate* means 'form a summit; reach the highest or most crucial point': □ *The church culminates in a steeple.* □ *Her rise in society culminated in her marriage to an earl.*

◆ The word is very often used as though it were merely a synonym for *result* or *conclude*: □ *The growing unrest culminated in industrial action.* This use is so widespread as to be generally accepted, although some careful users object to it.

cult Some people dislike the adjectival use of the word *cult* to refer to a particular person, idea, activity, etc., that arouses great popular interest, especially for a short period of time: □ *a cult movie* □ *a cult book* □ *a cult figure*. Care should be taken to avoid overusing the word in this way.

cultured or **cultivated**? *Cultured* and *cultivated* are almost synonymous in that they are both used to mean 'educated, refined'. *Cultured* is particularly applied to education in terms of an understanding and appreciation of the arts: □ *They were cultured people who attended concerts and art galleries*, while *cultivated* is applied to behaviour and speech: □ *He gradually dropped his Cockney twang and spoke in a soft, cultivated accent.*

◆ Both *cultured* and *cultivated* also have connections with things that are produced artificially: □ *cultured pearls* □ *cultivated plants*.

cumulative see ACCUMULATIVE OR CUMULATIVE?

curb or **kerb**? These two spellings may sometimes be confused. *Curb* means 'check or control': □ *He curbed his anger*. A *kerb* is the edge of a pavement; in American English this word is spelt *curb*.

currant or **current**? A *currant* is a small seedless dried grape used in cookery: □ *She always put lots of currants in her cakes*, or any of several different soft fruits: □ *redcurrant jam* □ *blackcurrant juice*. A *current* is a steady flow: □ *They did not swim because the current was very strong.* □ *250 volts, alternating current.*

current The adjective *current* means 'occurring in or belonging to the present time; presently existing or in progress': □ *Current techniques for treating the disease are acknowledged to be inadequate*; and 'accepted or prevalent at this time': □ *The current opinions of American Catholics are in conflict with the Vatican.*

◆ *Current* and *currently* are often used superfluously where there is no need to emphasize that one is talking about the present as contrasted with the past or future: □ *The company currently employs over a thousand people*.

curriculum This word, meaning 'programme of available courses in a school or college': □ *a wide-ranging sixth-form curriculum*, is sometimes misspelt. Note that the only double letters are -rr-, as in *current*.

◆ A *curriculum vitae*, often abbreviated to *CV*, is a summary of a person's career and qualifications that is often required when applying for a job. *Vitae* may be pronounced [*veetī*] or [*vītee*].

curtsy or **curtsey**? The noun and verb *curtsy* refer to a formal greeting made by a girl or woman in which the head and shoulders are lowered, the knees are bent and the skirt is held outwards with both hands: □ *She curtsied to the Queen*. The alternative spelling *curtsey* is also acceptable.

customer see CLIENT OR CUSTOMER?

cutting edge Some people dislike the frequent use of the phrase *cutting edge* in the figurative sense of 'forefront': □ *at the cutting edge of information technology*. See also LEADING-EDGE.

cymbal or **symbol**? Note the spelling of these words, which have the same pronunciation [*simbăl*]. A *cymbal* is a circular brass percussion instrument; a *symbol* is a sign or design that represents something else: □ *the clash of cymbals* □ *The dove is a symbol of peace.*

cynical or **sceptical**? A *cynical* person is one who has a distrust of human nature and sincerity, believing others to be motivated by self-interest: □ *He had a cynical belief that nobody took up law or medicine for any reason but the money.* Sceptical (American English, *skeptical*) means 'doubtful, unwilling to believe without rational proof': □ *While accepting Jesus' moral teachings she remained sceptical about the miracles and the resurrection.*

czar see TSAR OR CZAR?

dais This word, meaning 'a raised platform', is usually pronounced [*day*is]. It was formerly pronounced as only one syllable [days], but this is now rarely heard.

dangling participles Participles are often used to introduce a phrase which is attached to a later-mentioned subject: □ *Startled by the noise she dropped her book.* □ *Being by now very tired, we stopped at a pub.* There is a tendency, though, for such introductory participles to become apparently attached to the wrong noun: □ *Startled by the noise, her book fell to the floor.* □ *Being by now very tired, a pub was a welcome sight.* It was not the book that was startled or the pub that was tired. Then there is the sentence where the participle appears to have no subject at all, which is the thought behind the term *dangling participle* (also known as *unattached,* or *unrelated participle*): □ *Lying in the sun, it felt as though it had always been summer.* Who, or what, was lying in the sun?

♦ Some participles are habitually used in a manner where they might be thought to dangle, but such use is usually being used as prepositions or conjunctions, and such use is acceptable: □ *Speaking of fruit, does anyone want an apple?* □ *Considering the odds against them, they did well.* □ *Regarding your enquiry, I have pleasure in enclosing our catalogue.* On the borderline is the increasingly popular use of *having said that:* □ *Having said that, the West Indies still look certain to win,* which is considered unacceptable by many people.

dare The verb *dare* can be used in two different ways. It can be used as a full verb, followed by an infinitive with *to:* □ *I dare you to jump.* □ *We'll see if she dares to contradict him;* or it can be an auxiliary or modal verb, followed by an infinitive without *to:* □ *He dared not go there at night.* □ *How dare you say that?*

♦ As an auxiliary the verb is only used in the forms *dare* and *dared,* and only in negative and interrogative constructions.

The expression *dare say* means 'suppose, expect, or think likely': □ *I dare say we'll go to Bognor again.* It is only used in the present tense and in the first person, and is sometimes written as one word: □ *I daresay.*

dash Dashes can be used both singly and in pairs. Though the dash is useful, most of its functions can be performed by other punctuation marks, and excessive use of the dash is sometimes considered to be a mark of a careless writer. A sentence should never contain more than one dash or pair of dashes.

♦ The double dash is used to mark a break in a sentence, very much in the same way as round brackets: □ *My mother – a Yorkshire-woman by birth – had little time for Londoners.* As with parentheses, the material enclosed by dashes should be able to be removed leaving the sentence grammatically complete. Commas should not be used with double dashes.

A single dash is used to introduce a statement summarizing what has gone before: □ *Beer, chips, and cigarettes – these are the main threats to the nation's health.* It is also used to introduce an afterthought or a sharp change in subject or continuity: □ *I'm surprised to see Nigel here – he's usually late.* □ *You take two eggs – but perhaps you don't even like omelettes?* □ *I don't believe it – caviare!*

Dashes are used to indicate an unfinished sentence or hesitant speech: □ *I think he's – □ I – um – er – I don't er – know.* They are often used to precede the attribution of a quotation: □ *'No man is an island' – Donne.* They are, occasionally, used to indicate an omission of part of a name, and to replace all or part of an obscenity: □ *I travelled to the small mountain town of L——.* □ *It's none of your ——ing business.* They are also used between points in space or time, where they are equivalent to *to*: □ *London–Paris* □ *1914–18.*

A dash may be thought of as a less formal punctuation mark than a colon, indicating an afterthought: □ *This word means 'like a goat' – Lloyd George was known as 'the Goat'.* For dashes with colons see **COLON.**

data *Data* means 'facts, information that can be used as a basis for analysis, etc.': □ *We have data on road accidents for the past thirty years.*

◆ *Data* is actually a plural, with the singular *datum*, but this singular is rarely used and *data* has come to be regarded as a collective noun, which is appropriate to its use for a body or aggregate of information. There is still considerable controversy as to whether it should take a singular or plural verb. In American English the singular verb is now usual: □ *This is essential data*, and this use is becoming increasingly frequent in British English. However, some careful users still insist on using the noun as a plural: □ *These are essential data.*

The pronunciation [*daytă*] is preferred, although [*dahtă*] is sometimes used and is usual in American English.

dates It is usual to write dates in figures, rather than words, except in some very formal contexts, such as legal documents. There are various ways of expressing dates: □ *5 October 1994* is becoming the standard form in Britain in preference to *5th October, 1994* and *October 5th, 1994*. The standard form in the United States is *October 5 1994*.

◆ The abbreviated form *5.10.94* or *5/10/94* is acceptable in informal use but it should be used with caution as this abbreviation would mean the tenth of May in the United States, where the fifth of October would be abbreviated to *10.5.94*.

Centuries may be written as numbers or written out in full: □ *the 19th century* or □ *the nineteenth century*, and the abbreviation AD usually precedes the date, while BC follows it: □ *AD 527* □ *1000 BC*. See also **AD AND BC.**

The apostrophe in a series of years is nowadays generally omitted: □ *in the 1990s* □ *the 1800s*.

de- The prefix *de-* is used to signify 'the opposite or reverse': □ *de-classify*, 'removal': □ *descale*, or 'reduction': □ *degrade*.

◆ As a productive prefix, *de-* is constantly being used to create new words: □ *desegregate* (to reverse a practice or law involving racial segregation), □ *de-escalate* (to decrease in scope or extent), □ *deinstitutionalize* (to release patients from an institution), □ *delist* (to remove from a list of approved items), □ *demerger* (the separation of previously merged companies). Some users object to the coining of such forms.

deadly or **deathly**? *Deadly* means 'likely to cause death'; *deathly* refers to a characteristic of death: □ *a deadly weapon* □ *a deathly silence. Deadly* is sometimes used in place of *deathly* in figurative contexts: □ *'Goodbye,' she said, with a deadly finality.*

◆ Both words may be used adverbially: □ *deadly quiet* □ *deathly pale.* In informal contexts the adjective *deadly* can also mean 'extremely boring': □ *The party was deadly.*

debris This word, meaning 'rubble or remains': □ *They removed the debris from the building site*, is stressed on the first syllable [*debr*i]. The variant pronunciation [*day*bri] is widely used, and this pronunciation should be used when the word is written with an acute accent: □ *débris.*

debut *Debut*, meaning 'first appearance': □ *He made his debut in a James Bond film*, may be pronounced [*day*bew] or [*deb*ew]. If the word is spelt with an acute accent: □ *début*, the first pronunciation should be used.

◆ The use of *debut* as a verb: □ *She debuted last month*, is disliked by many users.

deca- or **deci-**? The prefix *deca-* means 'ten times'; the prefix *deci-* means 'one tenth': □ *decagon* □ *decibel.* A *decametre* is ten metres; a *decimetre* is one tenth of a metre.

◆ Note the difference in pronunciation, particularly the hard *-c-* [k] of *deca-* and the soft *-c-* [s] of *deci-.*

deceitful or **deceptive**? Both *deceitful* and *deceptive* imply misleading appearances or cheating. However, *deceitful* suggests an intention to deceive or mislead, even if not successful, and therefore carries negative moral overtones: □ *It was deceitful of you to pretend to be an orphan. Deceptive* applies to a misleading effect or result rather than dishonest motivation, and something might be unintentionally deceptive: □ *The ring's dull appearance was deceptive, for on closer inspection it turned out to be gold.*

decent or **decorous**? Both these adjectives can mean 'socially acceptable': □ *decent/decorous behaviour. Decorous*, a formal word, is largely restricted to this sense, whereas *decent* has the additional meanings of 'not obscene', 'adequate', 'morally correct', 'obliging; pleasant', etc.: □ *decent language* □ *a decent meal* □ *to do the decent thing* □ *He's a decent enough fellow.*

◆ In the sense of 'not obscene', *decent* is not as common as its opposite *indecent* ('obscene').

deceptive see DECEITFUL OR DECEPTIVE?

deceptively The adverb *deceptively* suggests misleading appearances and is used to indicate that something is not as it seems. *A deceptively healthy man* is actually a sick man; *a deceptively slimming meal* is, in fact, fattening.

◆ The word is frequently misused to mean 'surprisingly' or 'contrary to appearances': □ *a semi-detached house offering deceptively spacious accommodation* (advertisement, *Chichester Observer*).

deci- see DECA- OR DECI-?

decidedly or **decisively**? *Decidedly* usually means 'definitely; unquestionably': □ *It was a decidedly welcome suggestion.* It is also sometimes used to mean 'firmly; resolutely', and *decisively* is used in the same way: □ *'I'm going ahead with it,' she said decidedly/decisively. Decisively* is also used to imply decision-making which is marked by firmness, confidence, and lack of wavering: □ *He studied the options briefly before decisively choosing the second one.*

◆ *Decisive* can be applied to anything which makes a particular outcome inevitable: □ *a decisive goal* is the one that decides the result of the match; and *decisively* is also used in this sense: □ *Her conduct at the interview influenced the board decisively.*

decimate *Decimate* literally means 'destroy one in ten', from the Roman practice of killing every tenth soldier as a punishment for mutiny. The word is now used popularly to mean 'inflict considerable damage; destroy a large part of': □ *The weather decimated today's sports programme* (BBC TV). This use probably arises from the mistaken belief that the word means 'to destroy all but a tenth' and, although the usage is very widespread, many careful users still dislike it. *Decimate* should not be used to mean 'annihilate totally', or in such constructions as: □ *badly decimated* □ *utterly decimated* □ *Some 75 per cent of the cattle were decimated by the disease.*

decisively see DECIDEDLY OR DECISIVELY?

decolorize see COLOURIZE.

décor The noun *décor*, meaning 'interior decoration' or 'stage decoration', may be spelt with or without the acute accent in English. The pronunciation is [*day*kor] or [*de*kor].

◆ The spelling *décor* and the pronunciation [*day*kor], being closer to the original French, are preferred by some users.

decorous see DECENT OR DECOROUS?

decriminalize or **legalize**? These two verbs are virtually interchangeable in the sense of 'make no longer illegal': □ *to legalize* [or *decriminalize*] *the smoking of cannabis. Legalize* is the more frequent, and is used in a wider range of contexts in the sense of 'make legal': □ *to legalize independent radio stations.*

◆ The verb *decriminalize* emphasizes the (former) criminality of the practice to which it refers, and it may be more emotive than *legalize*: □ *He was an ardent supporter of the campaign to decriminalize homosexuality.*

dedicated In technology, the word *dedicated* is applied to machines, parts, accessories, computer programs, etc., that are designed to fulfil a single specific function: □ *a dedicated word-processing package.* The term is increasingly used in more general contexts: □ *Three companies gave their proposals to the Commons select committee on broadcasting for a new 'dedicated' parliamentary channel* (The Guardian).

deduce or **deduct**? To *deduce* is to come to a logical conclusion; to *deduct* is to subtract: □ *I deduced that she was lying.* □ *He deducted £10 from the bill.* The two verbs have the derived noun *deduction* in common: □ *the deduction that she was lying* □ *a deduction of £10.*

defective or **deficient**? *Defective* means 'having a fault; not working properly': □ *The washing machine I bought yesterday turned out to be defective. Deficient* means 'having a lack': □ *She sings well but her voice is deficient in power.*

◆ While *deficient* can be applied to concrete as well as abstract nouns: □ *Your diet is deficient in calcium,* it is not usually applied to manufactured objects. *Defective* is usually applied to concrete nouns, including manufactured objects, but can be applied to some abstract nouns, particularly those denoting some physical quality: □ *His colour vision is defective.*

defence The noun *defence:* □ *the importance of the country's defence,* is spelt with a *c* in British English, while the adjective *defensive*

is spelt with an *s*: □ *The players adopted a defensive strategy.*
◆ In American English the noun is spelt with an *s*.

deficient see DEFECTIVE OR DEFICIENT?

definite or **definitive**? These two words are sometimes confused, although their meanings are different. *Definite* means 'precise, exact, or unambiguous': □ *The rules draw a definite distinction between professionals and amateurs.* *Definitive* means 'final; conclusive': □ *This is the definitive game in the tournament,* and is frequently used in criticism in the sense of 'authoritative' to describe a work or performance that is unlikely to be improved on: □ *Painter has written the definitive biography of Proust.*
◆ Careful users avoid the vague use of *definite* for emphasis: □*He has a definite resemblance to Winston Churchill.*

definite article see THE.

definitely This word, meaning 'certainly': □ *He was definitely going to win,* is sometimes misspelt, the most frequent error being the replacement of the second *i* with an *a*.

definitive see DEFINITE OR DEFINITIVE?

defuse or **diffuse**? To *defuse* is to remove the device that causes a bomb to explode; to *diffuse* is to spread: □ *The bomb was defused.* □ *The light was diffused.*
◆ The two verbs are sometimes confused, being similar in pronunciation: *defuse* is pronounced [dee*fewz*] and *diffuse* is pronounced [di*fewz*]. The adjective *diffuse*, meaning 'widely spread', has a final *s* sound [di*fews*].
The verb *defuse* is also used in figurative contexts, meaning 'make less tense': □ *Mrs Thatcher sought to defuse the growing Tory revolt over the poll tax last night* (*Daily Telegraph*).

degree The phrase *to a degree* has two meanings, 'somewhat' and 'extremely': □ *The match was exciting to a degree.* This may give rise to ambiguity, as in the above example: how exciting was the match?
◆ The use of the phrase in the sense of 'extremely' should be restricted to informal contexts.
The phrases *to a surprising/considerable/lesser/etc., degree* are often better replaced by a simple adverb, such as *surprisingly/considerably/less/etc.* *To what degree ... ?* may be replaced by *How much ... ?* or *To what extent ... ?*

deity The pronunciation of *deity* is either [*day*iti] or [*dee*iti]. Although the former is widely used, the latter is the more traditional pronunciation.

delirious Note the spelling of this adjective, particularly the first two vowels *-e-* and *-i-*. The correct pronunciation is [di*lirri*ŭs], with the short [i] of *squirrel*, not [di*leeri*ŭs].
◆ *Delirious* is the adjective that derives from *delirium*, 'a confused mental state because one is suffering from a feverish illness' or 'a state of great excitement or happiness'.

deliver Some people dislike the intransitive use of the verb *deliver* in the sense of 'fulfil a promise or commitment': □ *The government has failed to deliver on tax cuts.* □ *We don't just want people with good ideas; we want people who will deliver.*
◆ This usage is derived from the very informal expression *deliver the goods,* which originated in American slang about 1850 and has the same meaning.

deliverance or **delivery**? Both these nouns are derived from the verb *deliver. Deliverance* specifically refers to the act of delivering from danger, captivity, evil, etc., and is used in formal or literary contexts; *delivery* is used in the many other senses of the verb: □ *to pray for deliverance* □ *the delivery of a baby* □ *postal deliveries* □ *the delivery of a speech.*

delusion see ALLUSION, ILLUSION, OR DELUSION?

demi-, hemi-, or **semi-?** All three prefixes mean 'half': □ *demigod* □ *hemisphere* □ *semicircle.* Semi- is the most frequent, and may be used to form new words: □ *semiprofessional* □ *semi-independent.* Hemi- is found in a number of scientific terms: □ *hemihydrate* (a term used in chemistry) □ *hemiplegia* (paralysis of one side of the body). Demi- is chiefly found in words of French origin: □ *demitasse* (a small cup) □ *demilune* (a crescent-shaped formation).

◆ The noun *hemidemisemiquaver*, the name of a note in music that is one eighth of the length of a quaver, is the only word in English that makes use of all three prefixes.

demise The original meaning of *demise* was 'the transfer of an estate or of sovereignty', and because such a transfer was frequently the result of death, the word came to mean 'death': □ *We were sad to hear of the demise of your husband.* This usage is formal and somewhat outdated.

◆ *Demise* can be used figuratively to mean 'the ending of existence or activity': □ *The demise of the steel industry in Consett caused massive unemployment in the area.* Its use to mean merely 'failure' or 'decline': □ *the demise of the cinema* should be avoided.

demonstrable This word may cause problems with pronunciation. The most widely used pronunciation is [dimŏnstrăbl] which is stressed on the second syllable. Some careful speakers prefer the traditional [demŏnstrăbl] which is stressed on the first syllable.

denationalization see PRIVATIZATION OR DENATIONALIZATION?

denote see CONNOTE OR DENOTE?

denouement This word, meaning 'final outcome': □ *the stunning denouement of the novel,* may be spelt *denouement* or *dénouement.* Note the *oue* vowels in the middle of the word.

◆ The usual pronunciation is [daynoomon(g)] although in American English the word may be stressed on the first or third syllables.

deny see REFUTE OR DENY?

depend *Depend* means 'be contingent': □ *It depends on the weather,* or 'be reliant on': □ *They depend on Social Security.* It is normally used with *on* or *upon,* except in certain constructions where *it* is the subject: □ *It depends whether I'm well enough.* □ *It depends what you mean by socialism.*

◆ This usage is widespread but disliked by some careful users who insist on the word *on* or *upon* following *depend* in all cases. The expression: □ *It all depends,* as a complete utterance, is acceptable only in informal speech.

dependant or **dependent?** The adjective, meaning 'reliant', is spelt *dependent*: □ *industries that are dependent on North Sea gas* □ *He is completely dependent on other people's help.* The noun, meaning 'someone who relies on another person for financial support', is spelt *dependant*: □ *Apart from your children, do you have any dependants?* The two are often confused, as in a leaflet for *Exmoor Area Tourist Attractions*: □ *But this freedom will remain largely dependant upon visitors respecting the life of the countryside.*

◆ Note that in American English the noun *dependant* is often spelt *dependent.*

dependence or **dependency?** Either noun may be used to mean 'the state of being dependent', but *dependence* is the more frequent in this sense: □ *his dependence/dependency on his parents* □ *her dependence/dependency on alcohol.* See also **DEPENDANT OR DEPENDENT?**

◆ *Dependency* can also mean 'territory that is controlled by another nation': □ *one of Britain's dependencies.* It cannot be replaced by *dependence* in this sense.

Note the spellings of the two words. The endings *-ance* and *-ancy* are American variants.

dependent see **DEPENDANT OR DEPENDENT?**

deploy *Deploy* is a military term meaning 'organize troops or equipment so that they are in the most effective position': □ *the decision to deploy Cruise missiles at Greenham Common.* Careful users object to the frequent use of the word with reference to any utilization or organization of resources: □ *It will be up to you to set ambitious revenue targets and then train, develop, and deploy your team-members to ensure that those targets are met and surpassed* (*Daily Telegraph*).

deprecate or **depreciate?** *Deprecate* means 'express disapproval': □ *She deprecated the Government's record on equal opportunities. Depreciate* means 'reduce in value', where it is usually used intransitively: □ *It depreciates by about £100 every year,* and 'belittle or disparage': □ *He depreciated their attempts to talk English.*

◆ *Deprecate* is often used instead of *depreciate* in the sense of 'disparage' and is also extended to mean 'play down; show modesty'. This usage of *deprecate* is disliked by some people, although it is acceptable in the well-established use of *self-deprecating*: □ *Jewish humour tends to be ironical and self-deprecating.*

deprived *Deprived* means 'having something taken away or withheld': □ *Brain damage can occur if a baby is deprived of oxygen during labour.* It should properly be applied to things which were once possessed or would be possessed in normal circumstances, but the modern tendency is to connect it with basic necessities and rights. As an adjective it has become a vogue word often meaning little more than 'poor': □ *It is always the most deprived women, usually with housing problems or of low intelligence, who are involved* (*The Times*).

derail Some people dislike the increasing use of the verb *derail* in a figurative sense: □ *The British Government ... would not be allowed to use its presidency of the European Community to derail progress to greater political union or a 'social Europe'* (*The Guardian*). This usage is best restricted to informal contexts.

derisive or **derisory?** *Derisive* means 'expressing derision; mocking or scornful': □ *His speech was received with derisive mirth. Derisory* means 'deserving derision': □ *It was a derisory performance.*

◆ *Derisory* is used particularly in the sense of 'ridiculously inadequate; contemptibly small': □ *He was retired with a derisory pension* (BBC Radio).

derived words Derived words are formed by adding fixed groups of letters at the beginning or end of another word. The noun □ *sadness* is derived from the adjective *sad*; the adjective □ *readable* is derived from the verb *read*; the adverb □ *boldly* is derived from the adjective *bold*; the noun □ *membership* is derived from the noun *member*.

◆ Sometimes the base form of the word changes in the derived form:

the *-y* of *happy*, for example, changes to *-i-* in the derived forms *happily* and *happiness*.

New words are also formed by adding prefixes (see **PREFIXES AND SUFFIXES**) or inflectional endings, such as *-s, -ed, -ing, -er,* and *-est*: □ *unhappy* □ *members* □ *reading* □ *bolder*. Some derived words are more complex: □ *unknowingly*, for example, consists of the base form *know* plus *un-, -ing,* and *-ly*.

deselect The verb *deselect*, referring to an MP who is not selected for re-election, is one of a number of new words formed with the prefix **DE-**: □ *a number of Labour MPs have been deselected by their local constituency parties.*

desert or **dessert**? These words are sometimes confused. *Dessert* is the last course of a meal (see **DESSERT, SWEET, PUDDING, OR AFTERS?**): □ *a deliciously sweet dessert* □ *a dessert spoon. Desert* is used in all other contexts: □ *the Sahara desert* □ *She got her just deserts.* □ *a deserted city.*

desiccated This word, meaning 'dried': □ *desiccated coconut*, is sometimes misspelt. Note the single *s* and *-cc-*.

◆ It is worth remembering the Latin words *de* and *siccare*, meaning 'to dry', from which the word originates.

design see **INVENT, DESIGN, OR DISCOVER?**

designer *Designer* has become a vogue adjective which is applied to clothes and other manufactured goods which are produced by a well-known company with a reputation for fashionable design: □ *designer jeans* □ *designer watches* □ *He won't wear anything without a designer label.*

◆ The use has been extended to mean 'chic; trendy' and is applied, sometimes jocularly, to anything that is in fashion: □ *designer stubble* (a fashionably unshaven appearance) □ *designer water* (mineral water) □ *The arrival of the designer salad has increased our enthusiasm for French dressing (Sunday Times).* □ *... as the world gets the first glimpse of the light, roomy designer terminal* [at Gatwick airport] *(The Guardian)* □ *Designer Nazis rise on the tide of German fear* (headline, *Sunday Times*).

desirable or **desirous**? *Desirable* means 'worth desiring or having': □ *a desirable residence* □ *Confrontation with the union is not desirable at this stage. Desirous*, which means 'desiring; wanting', is a more formal adjective, usually placed after the verb and followed by *of*: □ *to be desirous of peace* □ *The president is desirous of your opinion.* The two adjectives should not be confused.

despair or **desperation**? The noun *despair* means 'loss of hope': □ *a feeling of utter despair* □ *She gave up in despair.* The noun *desperation* is often applied to a reckless act that results from despair: □ *In desperation he jumped out of the window.*

◆ Note the spelling of *desperation*, particularly the second *-e-*, which is sometimes wrongly replaced with the *-a-* of *despair*.

despatch or **dispatch**? Both of these spellings are acceptable for the verb meaning 'send quickly' or the noun meaning 'message or report': □ *The letter was immediately despatched/dispatched.* □ *The despatch/dispatch arrived that afternoon.*

desperate This word, meaning 'having no hope': □ *a desperate man* □ *a desperate situation*, is sometimes misspelt. The middle part of the word is spelt *per*, not *par* as in *separate*.

desperation see **DESPAIR OR DESPERATION?**

despicable *Despicable*, meaning 'contemptible': □ *It was a despicable act*, is usually stressed on the second syllable [di*spik*ăbl]. Careful users, however, prefer the traditional pronunciation with the stress on the first syllable [*despi*kăbl].

despite or **in spite of**? *Despite* and *in spite of* are completely interchangeable: □ *Despite/In spite of his injury, his playing was superb. In spite of* is used rather more frequently, although *despite* has the advantage of brevity.

♦ *Despite* needs no preposition; *despite of* is incorrect, and it is never necessary to precede either *despite* or *in spite of* with *but*.

dessert, sweet, pudding, or **afters**? The question of how the sweet (usually) last course of a meal is referred to in Britain is not fixed. Usage not only varies slightly from one individual, family, etc., to another, but also is probably currently changing. Generally, *dessert* is found in both spoken and written contexts: □ *For dessert we were offered ice cream and fruit. Sweet* is more informal, is found in spoken English, and is considered by some middle- and upper-class people to be unacceptable. Such users prefer the word *pudding*, but this may be becoming slightly old-fashioned to refer generally to the last course of a meal. *Afters* is used in very informal spoken English: □ *What's for afters, Mum?*

♦ *Pudding* has a number of other culinary senses. It may refer to a cooked sweet or savoury dish containing flour, eggs, etc.: □ *treacle pudding* □ *Yorkshire pudding*, or to a sausage-like savoury preparation □ *black pudding*. These connotations may make it seem an inappropriate term for a light dessert, such as ice cream or fruit.

Dessert, especially formerly, is the course of fruit, dates, nuts, etc., served at the end of a meal.

See also **DESERT** OR **DESSERT**?

destined *Destined* means 'being determined or intended in advance; directed towards, or having a particular purpose or end': □ *She believed her son was destined to be the messiah.* □ *The convict ship was destined for Australia.*

♦ Some people object to the use of *destined* as a synonym for *intended*, with no suggestion of *destiny*. The use of *was destined to be* to mean 'later became': □ *He was destined to be prime minister* is also disliked. However, these uses are well-established and generally acceptable.

desultory This word, meaning 'unmethodical', should be stressed on the first syllable [*des*ŭltri].

detach The verb *detach*, meaning 'separate', is often misspelt, the most frequent error being the substitution of *-tch* for the *-ch* ending.

detract or **distract**? *Detract* means 'to take away from; diminish' and is usually used figuratively to describe the diminishing of some desirable quality: □ *The new hotels can only detract from the resort's charm. Distract* means 'take one's mind off something; divert attention elsewhere': □ *I tried to concentrate but I was distracted by the noise outside.*

development Since Third World countries have been referred to as *underdeveloped countries*, and then *developing countries*, the word *development* has come to have a specialized meaning in terms of the economic growth and improvements in living conditions of these countries: □ *the World Development Movement* □ *The rich world need provide only $5 billion a year in development assistance* (Ronald Sider, *Rich Christians in an Age of Hunger*).

◆ Note the spelling: there is no *e* after the *p*.

device or **devise**? These words are sometimes confused. *Device* is a noun meaning 'contrivance or gadget': □ *a device for opening bottles*, or 'scheme or ploy': □ *It was a cunning device to get his own way*. *Devise* is a verb meaning 'plan': □ *They devised a new method of classifying the books*.

◆ Note that *devise* is one of the few verbs that cannot be spelt *-ize*: see also **-IZE OR -ISE**?

devotee The noun *devotee*, meaning 'enthusiast', 'supporter', or 'follower', is sometimes mispronounced. The correct pronunciation is [devŏ*tee*], with the stress on the last syllable. The first two syllables rhyme with *clever*: they do not have the same vowel sounds as the verb *devote*.

dexterous or **dextrous**? This word, meaning 'skilful or nimble': □ *a dexterous artisan*, may be spelt *dexterous* or *dextrous* although the former is the more frequently used spelling.

◆ Note that *ambidextrous* is always spelt without the extra *e*.

diagnosis or **prognosis**? Both *diagnosis* and *prognosis* are most often used in medical contexts. A *diagnosis* is the identification of a disease, from studying the symptoms: □ *The doctor's diagnosis, based on her spots, was chicken-pox*. A *prognosis* is a forecast of the likely course of an illness and the prospect of recovery: □ *The doctor's prognosis is that he will never fully regain his eyesight*.

◆ Both *diagnosis* and *prognosis* can be used of problems in general, with the meanings, respectively, of 'an analysis of the cause of the problem' and 'a forecast of the course and outcome of a problem': □ *They diagnosed a major fault in the wiring.* □ *His prognosis indicated that the company was heading for bankruptcy.*

The plural of both nouns is formed by changing the *-sis* ending to *-ses*: □ *diagnoses* □ *prognoses*.

dialect *Dialect* usually refers to an established variety of a language, confined either to a region or to a social group or class.

◆ The dialect used by educated middle- or upper-class people is often regarded as the standard form of a language and other dialects as nonstandard (see **PRONUNCIATION**). At one time nonstandard regional dialects were a handicap to acceptance in 'civilized' English society; now even some BBC announcers have regional accents, although nonstandard grammar or vocabulary is still considered unacceptable.

Dialect is seen not only in pronunciation: vocabulary, grammar, and sentence construction vary too. Compare the Northern English: □ *He'll not be coming* with the Southern: □ *He won't be coming*, or the North-East English: □ *You suit that dress* with the standard: □ *That dress suits you*. An example from William Trevor shows the Irish use of *the* for *a*: □ *'Well, Bridie, isn't that the grand outfit you have on'* (*The Ballroom of Romance*). Social dialects are often associated with the working-class dropping of *h*'s, use of double negatives, and so on, but upper-class cultures have their own dialect forms too.

There is a wealth of dialect words. Often the same word has different meanings in different regions. *Canny* means 'thrifty or shrewd' in Scotland, but 'pleasant or agreeable' in North-East England.

dialectal or **dialectic**? *Dialectal* is an adjective, meaning 'relating to dialect': □ *a dialectal term*. *Dialectic* is a noun, meaning 'disputation'; it has a number of specialized uses in logic and philosophy.

◆ *Dialectic* is also a variant of the adjective *dialectical*, meaning 'relating to dialectic'.

dialogue *Dialogue* is now rarely used for an ordinary conversation between two or more people, but is increasingly applied to exchanges of opinion and high-level negotiation between organizations and individuals who are usually ideologically opposed or have a conflict of interest: □ *We must bring about meaningful dialogue between management and unions.* □ *Mr Gorbachev said, 'The meeting ... might start a peaceful chain-reaction in the sphere of strategic offensive arms ... and many other items on a possible agenda of international dialogue'* (*The Times*).

◆ *Dialogue* is used as a verb in American English: □ *We must dialogue with each other*, but this use is not generally acceptable in British English.

diaphragm A *diaphragm* is a separating membrane and especially refers to the partition that separates the chest from the abdomen. The word also refers to a contraceptive device. In spelling, note the *ph* and the silent *g*.

diarize Some people dislike the verb *diarize*, meaning 'write in one's diary', as an example of the increasing tendency to coin new verbs by adding the suffix *-ize* to nouns and adjectives: □ *to diarize one's appointments.* See also **-IZE** OR **-ISE**?

diarrhoea This word is often misspelt. Note particularly the *rrh* and also the *-oea* ending.

◆ In American English the *o* is usually omitted. See also **-AE-** AND **-OE-**.

dice *Dice* was originally the plural form of a singular noun *die*, but this singular form is now almost never used except in the expression: □ *The die is cast. Dice* is used now both as a singular and as a plural: □ *He made a dice out of a sugar cube.* □ *You need two dice for that game.*

◆ The word is also used for a gambling game played with dice: □ *'I cannot believe that God plays dice with the cosmos'* (Albert Einstein).

dichotomy A *dichotomy* is a division of two things which are sharply contrasted, especially if they are mutually exclusive, contradictory, or irreconcilably different: □ *the dichotomy between Christianity and atheism.* It has become a vogue word used generally to mean 'conflict, split, schism, or difference': □ *A new dichotomy is developing in the Church of England.* This usage is disliked by some people, both for its lack of precision and for its pretentiousness.

◆ The usual pronunciation of *dichotomy* is [dīkotŏmi], with the long *-i-* of *die*.

dietician or **dietitian**? A person who studies the principles of nutrition is known as a *dietician* or *dietitian*. Both spellings of the word are perfectly acceptable.

◆ Note that the science itself is called *dietetics*.

different from, different to, or **different than**? It is possible to follow *different* with *from, to,* or *than. Different from* is the most frequently used form and the most acceptable: □ *Your life is different from mine. Different to* is often used in informal British English: □ *The happy situation he finds himself in is very different to the experiences of graduates in the early 1980s* (*Sunday Times*). It is, however, disliked by some people and not used in American English. *Different than* is in frequent use in American English but is disliked by many users of British English and generally should be avoided.

◆ *Different than* is considered most acceptable when followed by a clause: □ *My values now are different than they were when I was a teenager,* as it removes the need for clumsy phrases such as: □ *from those that I had.*

differential *Differential,* as adjective and noun, is a term in mathematics and has the nontechnical meanings of 'based on a difference; a difference between comparable things'. It is now most frequently used in reference to differences in pay rates for various jobs in the same industry, based on differences in skills, work conditions, etc.: □*Pay differentials between nursing and administrative staff have widened.*

◆ The use of *differential* in place of *difference*: □ *a differential of £20 a week* is inappropriate, as a *differential* is a discrepancy based on related differences, not the difference itself.

different than, different to see DIFFERENT FROM, DIFFERENT TO, OR DIFFERENT THAN?

diffuse see DEFUSE OR DIFFUSE?

digital The adjective *digital* has specific technical uses in computing and sound recording: □ *a digital computer* □ *a digital recording. Digital* also refers to the presentation of information in the form of digits rather than pointers on a dial or scale: □ *digital watch* □ *digital display* □ *digital thermometer.*

◆ The use of *digital* with reference to high technology in general is disliked and avoided by careful users: □ *the digital revolution.*

dilapidated This word, meaning 'falling into ruin': □ *a dilapidated cottage,* is sometimes misspelt, the most frequent mistake being to begin the word with *de-,* rather than the correct *di-.*

dilemma A *dilemma* is a situation where one is faced with two equally unsatisfactory alternatives: □*It was a hopeless dilemma – she could stay with her husband and be miserable, or she could leave him and lose the children.*

◆ It is usually considered acceptable to use *dilemma* when more than two choices are involved, provided they are equally unattractive, but one should not use *dilemma* for desirable things: □ *His mouth watered as he pondered the dilemma of whether to choose the chocolate soufflé or the pistachio icecream. Dilemma* is often used to mean just 'a problem', where there is open choice or no element of choice at all: □ *the dilemma of what to wear* □ *the dilemma of how to attract new members.* Careful users dislike this imprecise use of the word.

The *-i-* of *dilemma* may be short [di*lem*ă] or long [dī*lem*ă]. The first of these pronunciations is preferred by some users.

dimension The literal uses of *dimension* are concerned with measurement, *dimensions* being also used figuratively to mean 'scope or extent': □ *They were now in a position to assess the dimensions of the tragedy.* The word is also fashionably used as a synonym for *aspect* or *factor*: □ *The fact that one of the applicants was black and one a woman added a new dimension to their decision.*

◆ Some people dislike the overuse of the nonliteral senses of this word.

diminution This word means 'decrease in size, intensity, etc.': □*the possible diminution in readers.* Note the spelling and the pronunciation [dimi*new*shŏn].

dinghy or **dingy**? These words are sometimes confused. A *dinghy* is a small boat; *dingy* is an adjective meaning 'gloomy or shabby': □*a dingy basement flat.*

◆ *Dinghy* is pronounced with a hard *g* [*ding*gi] or [*ding*i]. The pronunciation of *dingy* is [*din*ji].

dining room see LOUNGE.

dinky *Dinky*, an acronym of 'dual (or 'double') income, no kids', is used with reference to a childless couple earning above-average salaries. The final *-y* is sometimes interpreted as 'yet'.

◆ Of American origin, the acronym is one of many contrived to identify perceived categories of society (see also NIMBY, YUPPIE). Others include *lombard* (lots of money but a right dickhead), *sinbad* (single income, no boyfriend, absolutely desperate), *woopie* (well-off older person), and *pippie* (person inheriting parents' property). Few of these will outlive the vogue for coining such terms, and most, except for established formations, e.g. *nimby* and *yuppie*, are best confined to informal contexts.

There is also the British adjective *dinky*, 'pretty; neat'.

dinner, lunch, tea, or **supper**? The question of how meals and meal-times are referred to in Britain is fraught with class and regional considerations. In general, middle- and upper-class people have their main meal in the evening and call it *dinner* or *supper*; *lunch* is taken around midday and is usually a light meal or snack, although Sunday lunch may be the main meal of the day. *Tea* (or *afternoon tea*), if it is taken, is eaten late in the afternoon and consists of small sandwiches and cakes. *High tea* is a meal eaten in the late afternoon rather than *dinner* or *supper* later in the evening. Some people, especially those living in Northern England and Scotland have *dinner* at midday, while *tea* is a substantial meal eaten at about six o'clock. *Supper* is always the last meal of the day and is sometimes a light bedtime snack for those who have had a large tea, or it can be the main evening meal for those who choose not to call the main evening meal *dinner* or *tea*.

◆ See also LUNCH OR LUNCHEON?

diphtheria This word causes problems with spelling and pronunciation. Note the *phth* in the spelling. The *ph* sound is pronounced f by careful users [dif*theer*iă] or p [dip*theer*iă].

diphthong Note the *phth* in the spelling. The *ph* sound is pronounced f by careful users [*dif*thong] or p [*dip*thong].

direct speech *Direct speech* is a record of the actual words used by a speaker. These words are usually enclosed in QUOTATION MARKS and followed or preceded by a verb such as *said, whispered, shouted*, etc.: □ *'Get out!' he cried.* □ *She replied, 'I don't know.'* See also REPORTED SPEECH.

◆ In passages of conversation, the words of different speakers are often placed in separate paragraphs. The verbs that follow or precede the direct speech are sometimes omitted once the identity of the speakers has been made clear.

dis- or **dys-**? Confusion between these two prefixes can cause spelling mistakes. *Dis-* is the more frequent, indicating lack, reversal, negation, removal, etc.: □ *disagreement* □ *discontinue* □ *dissimilar*. *Dys-* means 'abnormal', 'faulty', 'difficult', or 'bad' and is chiefly found in technical words relating to physical or mental problems: □ *dyspepsia* □ *dyslexia* □ *dysfunction*.

disadvantaged Like UNDERPRIVILEGED and DEPRIVED, *disadvantaged* has become a fashionable euphemism for 'poor', with particular emphasis on the lack of a reasonable standard of housing, living conditions, and opportunities for gaining basic rights: □ *Up to 100 teachers from each country are to spend one or two months studying such matters as how to motivate disadvantaged children* (The Times).

disappear Note the spelling of this word, particularly the single -*s*- and the -*pp*-.

disappoint The verb *disappoint* and its derivatives are often misspelt, the most frequent error being the doubling of the -*s*-. Note also the -*pp*-.

disassemble see DISSEMBLE OR DISASSEMBLE?

disassociate see DISSOCIATE OR DISASSOCIATE?

disastrous This word is sometimes misspelt. Note that the *e* of *disaster* is dropped before the suffix -*ous* is added.

◆ In pronunciation careful users avoid sounding the *e* of *disaster*: [dizahstrĕs] rather than [dizahstĕrĕs].

The overuse of this word, to describe something very bad in its performance or results, is disliked by many.

disc or **disk**? These spellings are sometimes confused. A *disc* is a flat round or circular shape: □ *a slipped disc* □ *compact disc*. In American English this word is usually spelt *disk*. In British English *disk* is reserved for use in computer science, to describe a thin plate on which data is stored: □ *a floppy disk*. This is occasionally spelt *disc*.

discipline Note the *c* following the *s* in the spelling of this word.

discoloration see COLORATION.

discomfit or **discomfort**? There is some overlap between these words and often confusion as to the distinction between them. *Discomfit* means 'defeat or thwart': □ *He discomfited his opponent*, and 'disconcert, confuse, or embarrass': □ *They were discomfited by his strange manner*. *Discomfort* means 'make uncomfortable or uneasy'. This might be physical distress: □ *The hard seats discomforted her*, or mental uneasiness, in which case the distinction between *discomfort* and *discomfit* often becomes blurred: □ *His ominous tone discomforted them*.

◆ *Discomfort* is both a verb and a noun, but the noun from *discomfit* is *discomfiture*.

discover see INVENT, DESIGN, OR DISCOVER?

discreet or **discrete**? These two words are sometimes confused. *Discreet* means 'judicious or prudent': □ *You can confide in him; he is very discreet*; *discrete* means 'separate or distinct': □ *discrete elements in the composition*.

discrepancy or **disparity**? Both these nouns mean 'difference'. A *discrepancy* is a difference between things that should be the same; a *disparity* is a greater difference that suggests imbalance or inequality: □ *a discrepancy between the accounts of the two witnesses* □ *a disparity between the wages of factory and office workers*.

discriminating or **discriminatory**? Both these adjectives are derived from *discrimination* and are connected with 'distinguishing, making distinctions' but they are used in very different ways. *Discriminating* is applied to someone who is discerning in matters of taste and able to tell the difference between good and poor quality: □ *We'd better serve the Bordeaux because Paul is discriminating when it comes to wine*. *Discriminatory* is now almost always applied to discrimination that is unjust and based on prejudice: □ *Feminists are organizing a boycott of the bank because of its discriminatory practices*.

disinterested or **uninterested**? *Disinterested* means 'impartial; having no self-interest': □ *As a disinterested party he felt free to intervene in the dispute*. *Uninterested* means 'having no interest;

indifferent; bored': □*I was quite uninterested in their holiday photos.*

◆ Perhaps because *uninterested* is not in frequent use, *disinterested* is now often used in its place to mean 'lacking interest', which was, in fact, the original meaning of *disinterested*: □ *Charles, in turn, appeared cold and disinterested in his wife* (Sunday Times). However, its use in this sense is objected to by many people: □ *'It was nothing but copying documents and tedious things like that, canceled checks and invoices, little chits of things. I've never been so disinterested.' Macon stirred and said, 'Don't you mean uninterested?'* (Anne Tyler, *The Accidental Tourist*).

disk see DISC OR DISK?

disorganized or **unorganized**? Either adjective may be used in the sense of 'not organized'. As the past participle of the verb *disorganize, disorganized* specifically refers to something organized that has been thrown into confusion, but it is also used in a general informal sense: □ *I'm a bit disorganized this morning. Unorganized* is more neutral and less frequent: □ *an unorganized method of working.*

disorient or **disorientate**? *Disorient* and *disorientate* are interchangeable and mean 'cause to lose bearings or sense of identity; confuse': □ *They had organized a one-way traffic system since his last visit and he was completely disoriented/disorientated.* □ *After years of being institutionalized she was disoriented/disorientated after her discharge. Disorient* is preferred by some users as the shorter and simpler alternative; it is also the standard form in American English, while *disorientate* is more frequently used in British English.

◆ See also ORIENT OR ORIENTATE?

disparity see DISCREPANCY OR DISPARITY?

dispassionate, impassioned, or **impassive**? The adjectives *dispassionate* and *impassive* are sometimes confused because of their similarity in meaning; *impassioned* and *impassive* because of their similarity in form. *Dispassionate* means 'not influenced by emotion; objective', whereas *impassive* means 'showing no emotion': □ *a dispassionate assessment of the problem* □ *She remained impassive, ignoring his cries. Impassioned* means 'full of passion': □ *an impassioned attack on the government.*

dispatch see DESPATCH OR DISPATCH?

dispel or **disperse**? *Dispel* means 'scatter; drive away' and is often used for abstract things: □ *He allowed them to see the original document so as to dispel their doubts about its authenticity. Disperse* means 'break up': □ *The family were dispersed over Europe,* 'spread over a wide area': □ *The gas dispersed over half the town,* and 'dissipate, evaporate, or vanish': □ *The mist had now dispersed and visibility was normal.*

dispute The noun *dispute* may be pronounced with the stress on the first syllable [*dis*pewt] or the second [dis*pewt*]. The first of these pronunciations is becoming increasingly frequently heard, although it is disliked by many users.

◆ The verb *dispute* is always stressed on the second syllable.

dissect This word, meaning 'separate or cut up for analysis', is spelt with -*ss*-, unlike *bisect*.

◆ Although *dissect* is often pronounced to rhyme with *bisect* [dīsekt], careful users prefer [disekt].

dissemble or **disassemble**? *Dissemble*, a literary word, means 'pretend' or 'conceal'; *disassemble* means 'take apart': □ *He dissembled his excitement.* □ *She disassembled the machine.* The two verbs should not be confused.

◆ Note the spellings of the words, particularly the -*s*- and -*ss*-.

dissemble, dissimulate, or **simulate?** The verbs *dissemble* and *dissimulate,* both of which are formal, mean 'pretend not to have; conceal'; *simulate* means 'pretend to have; feign': □ *to dissemble* [or *dissimulate*] *one's anger* □ *to simulate enthusiasm.* See also SIMULATE OR STIMULATE?

dissension or **dissent?** The noun *dissension* refers to a state of disagreement, discord, or conflict: □ *The proposal caused much dissension.* The noun *dissent,* the opposite of *assent,* means 'difference of opinion'; it refers to the act of disagreeing or an expression of disagreement: □ *a voice of dissent.*

◆ Confusion between the two nouns may lead to the misspelling of *dissension,* with -*t*- in place of the third -*s*-.

dissimulate see DISSEMBLE, DISSIMULATE, OR SIMULATE?

dissociate or **disassociate?** *Dissociate* and *disassociate* are interchangeable opposites of *associate:* □ *One of the committee members told me after the meeting that she wished to dissociate/disassociate herself from what the chair had said.*

◆ Most careful users prefer the form *dissociate.*

distil In British English the verb *distil* ends in a single *l,* which is doubled before a suffix beginning with a vowel: □ *distilled* □ *distillery.*

◆ The American English spelling of the verb is *distill.*
See also SPELLING 1.

distinct or **distinctive?** These two adjectives are frequently confused although they are not interchangeable. *Distinct* means 'definite; clearly perceivable or distinguishable': □ *There's a distinct taste of garlic in this stew. Distinctive* means 'characteristic, peculiar to, distinguishing': □ *He had the distinctive rolling gait of a sailor.*

distract see DETRACT OR DISTRACT?

distrust or **mistrust?** *Distrust* and *mistrust* are often used interchangeably: □ *Somehow I distrust/mistrust the whole business. Distrust* is more frequently used and has a far more emphatic suggestion of suspicion and lack of trust: □ *I have known him to be deceitful in the past and I have come to distrust everything he says. Mistrust* is rather more tentative and is used for a less positive lack of trust or when the doubt is directed against oneself: □ *There was something about her manner that made me uneasy and I found myself beginning to mistrust her.* □ *I mistrust my critical judgment when it comes to my own writing.*

disturb or **perturb?** *Disturb* can mean 'interrupt; inconvenience': □ *His reverie was disturbed by a ring at the doorbell.* □ *I hope I'm not disturbing you by phoning so late,* 'throw into disorder': □ *The cleaner had disturbed all her papers,* and 'upset; destroy the mental composure of': □ *I was deeply disturbed by this revelation.* In this last use, *disturb* is virtually synonymous with the less frequently used word *perturb,* which means 'cause disquiet to; cause mental disturbance': □ *His violent language and abrupt departure had perturbed her.*

dived or **dove?** In British English the past tense of *dive* is almost always *dived:* □ *They all dived for cover.* However, the past tense *dove* exists in some British dialects and is the standard form in

several regions of the United States and Canada: □*She dove
beautifully, and a moment later she was swimming back to the
side of the pool* (Philip Roth, *Goodbye Columbus*).

◆ The use of *dove* (pronounced [dōv]) is now generally considered
acceptable in all but the most formal writing in American English. It is
still considered nonstandard in British English.

divorcee A divorced person is known as a *divorcee* [divaw*see*]. A
divorced man is called a *divorcé* [divaw*say*] or [divaw*see*], and
a divorced woman is called a *divorcée* [divaw*see*].

do *Do* is used as an informal replacement for various different verbs,
for example 'prepare': □*Shall I do you a sandwich?*, 'clean': □*I'm
just going to do my teeth*, 'visit': □*We're doing the British
Museum tomorrow*, 'perform': □The local rep are doing *The
Cherry Orchard*, 'study': □*She's doing maths at Cambridge*, 'provide': □*Do they do breakfasts?*

◆ There are also the slang meanings of 'cheat': □ *You've been done!*,
'arrest': □ *He was done for burglary*, 'rob': □ *They did the bank last
night*, 'attack': □ *I'll do you*, 'have sexual intercourse with': □*Glober did
me on the table* (Anthony Powell, *Temporary Kings*). *Do* is also used
informally as a noun to mean 'a party or social event': □ *I'm going to
the firm's Christmas do*.

The addition of *do* in constructions when a previously mentioned
verb is omitted: □ *They behaved just as I wanted them to do* is best
reserved for informal use.

Do is also used as an auxiliary verb in questions: □ *Do you like it?*, in
negative sentences: □ *They don't want to go*, and for emphasis: □ *I do
wish he'd phone!*

document *Document* is used as a verb to mean 'provide documentary
evidence or information to act as factual support': □*His essay
was well documented with authoritative references*. It is also
used in reference to the production of a written, filmed, or broadcast work that has plentiful detailed factual information: □ *The
programme documents life in a women's prison*.

Domesday or **doomsday**? The *Domesday Book* is the survey of England carried out during the reign of William I. The noun *doomsday*, sometimes spelt with a capital *D*-, means 'Judgment Day;
Last Judgment' in the Christian religion, and 'day of reckoning'
or 'end of the world' in general usage. The phrase *till doomsday*
means 'for ever': □ *You can wait till doomsday, but I won't
change my mind*.

◆ Both words are pronounced [*doomz*day].

dominate or **domineer**? To *dominate* means 'rule, exert power or
control over': □*Her charm and energy were such that she came
to dominate the whole company*. It can also mean 'occupy a
preeminent position': □*Our products dominate the pet-food
market*, and 'overlook from a superior height': □ *The church is
built on a hill and dominates the town*. *Dominate* is often used
in a negative way that would be better reserved for *domineer*
which means 'tyrannize, exert power in an arbitrary or overbearing manner'. It is most frequently used as a present participle that functions as an adjective: □*his cruel domineering
manner*.

doomsday see DOMESDAY OR DOOMSDAY?

doorstep The verb *doorstep* is disliked by some people as an example
of the increasing tendency to use nouns as verbs. It originally
referred to the practice of selling door-to-door, then to the

practice of canvassing door-to-door, and later to the practice (favoured by investigative journalists, press photographers, etc.) of waiting outside the house or office of somebody in the public eye and accosting that person when he or she appears.

do's and don'ts In the phrase *do's and don'ts*, note that the apostrophe in *don'ts* comes after the *n* and not after the *t*. The apostrophe in *do's* is sometimes omitted.

double negative The double negative, as in: □ *I didn't do nothing.* □ *He hasn't had no tea*, is always avoided by careful users. The objection to such constructions is that the negatives cancel each other out and reverse the meaning of the sentence.

◆ When two negatives are intended to cancel each other: □ *She is not without talent.* □ *It is not impossible*, they are, however, acceptable. Another generally acceptable, if colloquial, use is in such sentences as: □ *I shouldn't be surprised if it doesn't snow.*

The cruder double negative is not difficult to avoid. It is more likely to occur with the semi-negative adverbs *hardly, scarcely, barely*: □ *They were left for hours without hardly any food*, or in complex sentences where the various negative words and phrases might get muddled: □ *Despite his injury, he denied that it was unlikely that he would not play again this season.*

The word *neither* should not be used in sentences that are already negative: □ *I'm not hungry and I'm not thirsty neither.* □ *I didn't neither.*

double whammy A *double whammy* is a double blow, or any problem or difficulty that has a two-pronged effect: □ *We have been hit by a double whammy: a cut of £30 million below meagre expectations ... and major cost increases for equipment and international subscriptions following the devaluation of sterling* (*Daily Telegraph*).

◆ The phrase *double whammy* gained a certain vogue in Britain during the general election of 1992, when it was used by the Conservatives with reference to Labour's twin economic threats: raised taxes and the abolition of the ceiling for National Insurance contributions.

The term *whammy*, meaning 'devastating blow', has been used in American English since the 1940s, where it originally (in the Li'l Abner cartoon strip) referred to the evil eye: the use of one eye is a whammy; the use of both, only in an emergency, is a *double whammy*.

doubling of consonants On the general rule of doubling consonants in such words as: □ *drop – dropped* □ *refer – referred*, see individual entries and **SPELLING 1**.

doubt The main problem with *doubt* is what preposition or conjunction to use with it. When *doubt* is used as a noun it is most often followed by *about*: □ *I have my doubts about it*, but it can be followed by *that* in a negative construction: □ *There is no doubt in my mind that he is telling the truth.* When *doubt* is used as a verb it can only be followed by *that* in negative constructions: □ *I don't doubt that you are right*, and in most other constructions it is followed by *whether*: □ *They doubted whether she would be welcome.*

◆ *If* is a possible alternative to *whether* but it is suitable for more informal use: □ *I doubt if I can make it.*

doubtful or **dubious**? Both *doubtful* and *dubious* mean 'giving rise to doubt, uncertain, questionable' and they are often more or less interchangeable: □ *They were doubtful/dubious whether the car* *was safe. Doubtful* is more neutral and is more likely to be used when expressing uncertainty: □ *The eventual result remains doubtful. Dubious* carries more negative overtones and is often used to suggest a suspicion that a person or practice is underhand or dishonest in some way: □ *He was involved with some dubious export company.*

◆ *Doubtful* is always preferable in constructions starting *it is*: □ *It is doubtful whether he has ever actually visited Germany.*

doubtless see UNDOUBTEDLY.

douse or **dowse**? Either spelling of this verb may be used in the sense of 'soak' or 'extinguish', pronounced [dows]. *Douse* is the more frequent: □ *doused with petrol* □ *to douse a candle.* The verb *dowse*, in the additional meaning 'search for water using a divining rod' and pronounced [dowz], should never be spelt *douse.*

dove see DIVED OR DOVE?

downside The vogue word *downside* means 'unfavourable aspect'; it is best avoided where *disadvantage* would be more appropriate: □ *the downside of the new system* □ *Every scientific breakthrough has its downside.*

downsizing *Downsizing* is the act of reducing in size. In America in the late 1970s it referred to the production of smaller cars: □ *With the whole industry downsizing, big-car addicts will find fewer alternatives* (*Time*). In Britain in the late 1980s it referred to redundancy: □ *downsizing the workforce* □ *In the case of the latest cuts – 55 jobs to go at US investment bank L.F. Rothschild – downsizing is something of an understatement* (*The Guardian*).

◆ The term is also used in computing: □ *'Downsizing' simply means that firms are tending to buy smaller computers to do jobs which used to require big ones* (*The Guardian*).

downward or **downwards**? In British English *downward* is principally used as an adjective, *downwards* being the usual form of the adverb meaning 'to a lower level': □ *a downward slope* □ *to look downwards.*

◆ The adverb *downward* is more frequently used in American English. See also -WARD OR -WARDS?

dowse see DOUSE OR DOWSE?

draft see DRAUGHT OR DRAFT?

dramatist or **playwright**? *Dramatist* and *playwright* are synonymous words, both dating from the late seventeenth century and meaning 'a person who writes plays': □ *He is a poet as well as a dramatist/playwright.*

◆ There may be a slight tendency to apply *dramatist* to those who write more serious plays or plays which conform to the traditional categories of drama: □ *Racine was a dramatist writing in the classical tradition,* and *playwright* to modern writers and those whose work is less serious: □ *playwrights like Neil Simon who are popular on both sides of the Atlantic.*

Note the spelling of the final syllable of *playwright: -wright*, not *-write.*

draught or **draft**? These words are sometimes confused. A *draft* is a preliminary outline: □ *a rough draft of the essay.* A *draft* is also a money order and a group of soldiers. *Draught* is the spelling for: □ *draught beer* □ *draught animals* □ *a draught from an open door.* The American English spelling of *draught* is *draft.*

◆ A person who draws up a rough version of a document is a *draftsman;* an artist or someone who prepares detailed drawings of buildings, machinery, etc., is a *draughtsman* (feminine, *draughtswoman*; American English *draftsman*).

The board game called *draughts* in British English is known as *checkers* in American English.

drawing room see **LOUNGE**.

dreamed or **dreamt**? Either word may be used as the past tense and past participle of the verb *dream*: □*I dreamed/dreamt I was in Australia.*

◆ See also **-ED OR -T**?

Dreamed may be pronounced [dreemd] or [dremt]; *dreamt* is always pronounced [dremt].

drier or **dryer**? *Drier* is the usual spelling of the comparative form of the adjective *dry*; both are equally common for the noun derived from the verb *dry*: □*These socks are drier/dryer than those.* □*a hair-dryer/drier* □*a spin-dryer/drier.*

drunk or **drunken**? Both *drunk* and *drunken* are adjectives applied to alcoholic intoxication, but *drunk* is normally used after a verb: □*She got drunk on cheap white wine,* while *drunken* is normally used before a noun: □*We were just sipping sherry – it was hardly a drunken orgy.* □*the campaign against drunken driving.*

◆ However, *drunk* implies temporary intoxication, while *drunken* suggests a habitual state of being drunk. When this distinction is being emphasized it is possible to reverse the usual rule and use *drunk* before a noun: □*drunk driving* and, though less frequently, *drunken* after a verb: □*He was drunken, foul-mouthed, and inconsiderate.*

dryer see **DRIER OR DRYER**?

dual or **duel**? These two words are sometimes confused, being identical in pronunciation. *Dual* is an adjective, meaning 'double'; *duel* is a noun or verb referring to a rather formal fight between two people: □*dual-purpose* □*a dual carriageway* □*the duel of the champions* □*to settle a quarrel by duelling.*

◆ Note that in British English the final *l* of *duel* is doubled before *-ed, -ing, -er,* etc.

dubious see **DOUBTFUL OR DUBIOUS**?

duel see **DUAL OR DUEL**?

due to, owing to, or **because of**? Although these phrases have roughly the same meanings they are not used in the same way. *Due to* should be used only adjectivally: □*His shakiness is due to Parkinson's disease;* whereas *owing to* and *because of* can be used either adjectivally or as prepositions: □*The delay was owing to an electrical fault on the line.* □*Because of poor health he took early retirement.* □*She was now rich, owing to her successful venture.*

◆ Although the use of *due to* as a preposition is objected to by careful users, this usage is becoming increasingly widespread: □*Due to the sheer size of the operation, we now need additional people to join our ... Membership Recruitment and Corporate Marketing Departments* (*Sunday Times*).

duplication or **duplicity**? The noun *duplication* is derived from the verb *duplicate*, meaning 'copy' or 'repeat'; the more formal noun *duplicity* means 'deception' or 'double-dealing': □*There may be some duplication in the text.* □*They were unaware of his duplicity.* The two nouns should not be confused.

dwarfs or **dwarves**? Either spelling is acceptable as the plural of the noun *dwarf, dwarfs* being the more frequent.

dwelled or **dwelt**? Either word may be used as the past tense and past participle of the verb *dwell*. *Dwelled* is more frequent in American English than in British English, but *dwelt* is the preferred form in both: □ *He dwelt on her infidelity.*

◆ See also **-ED** OR **-T**?

dying or **dyeing**? These spellings are sometimes confused. *Dying* is the present participle of the verb *die*, meaning 'cease to live': □ *Her son is dying.* □ *his dying words. Dyeing* is the present participle of the verb *dye*, meaning 'change the colour of': □ *She was dyeing her hair blonde.*

dynamic *Dynamic* is an overworked vogue word meaning 'lively, forceful, or energetic': □ *The Party needs young, dynamic leadership.*

◆ Its frequent use, particularly in job advertisements, has considerably weakened its impact: □ *If you are aged 28+, a dynamic team leader and an imaginative business organiser (Daily Telegraph).* □ *Self-motivated, dynamic person required (The Times).*

dynasty The preferred British English pronunciation of *dynasty*, which means 'series of hereditary rulers', is [dĭnăsti]. The American English pronunciation [dīnăsti] is sometimes also used in British English.

dys- see **DIS-** OR **DYS-**?

dyslexic or **dyslectic**? The words *dyslexic* and *dyslectic* are interchangeable; either may be used as a noun or adjective to describe a person suffering from dyslexia, though *dyslexic* is used much more frequently.

each When *each* is used as a determiner or as a pronoun which is the subject of a sentence, the rule is that subsequent verbs and pronouns should be singular: □ *Each man has his price.* □ *Each of the operas was sung in English.*
◆ The rule is frequently broken, partly because those who are sensitive to sexism in language prefer: □ *Each student had a paper handed to them* [rather than *to him*]. Of course, one can avoid both sexism and grammatical error by rephrasing such sentences: □ *All the students had a paper handed to them.* When *each* follows a plural noun or pronoun which is the subject of the sentence, the verb following is plural: □ *The cakes each have cherries on top.*

each or **both**? see BOTH.

each and every *Each and every* is used for emphasis in such phrases as: □ *Each and every person has a vital part to play.* □ *I am deeply grateful to each and every one of you.* It is disliked by most careful users as a cliché and as an unnecessarily wordy construction for which *each, everyone,* or *all* can often be substituted.

each other or **one another**? The traditional rule is that *each other* is used when two elements are involved and *one another* when more than two are involved: □ *Helen and Charles love each other deeply.* □ *All the people at the party already knew one another.* However, there is no particular reason for this rule and most people feel free to ignore it.
◆ There is a slight difference between the two phrases in that *each other* tends to emphasize each individual element whereas *one another* sounds more general. So it would be preferable to say: □ *They were throwing one another into the swimming pool* rather than *throwing each other*; the former gives a general impression of horseplay and allows for the odd person who was neither thrown nor throwing, while the latter suggests something much more systematic.

earthly or **earthy**? *Earthly* relates to the earth as opposed to heaven; *earthy* refers to earth in the sense of 'soil': □ *our earthly life* □ *an earthly paradise* □ *an earthy taste/texture.* The two adjectives are not interchangeable.
◆ Both words have other meanings. *Earthly* is used informally in the sense of 'possible', usually in negative contexts or in questions: □ *What earthly reason could she have for saying that?* □ *They haven't an earthly chance of success.* Earthy means 'coarse' or 'crude': □ *an earthy remark.*

east, East, or **eastern**? As an adjective, *east* is always written with a capital *E* when it forms part of a place-name: □ *East Anglia* □ *the East End.* The noun *east* is usually written with a capital *E* when it denotes a specific region, such as the countries of Asia: □ *She has travelled extensively in the East.* □ *East-West relations.*
◆ In other contexts, and as an adverb, *east* is usually written with a lower-case *e*: □ *They sailed east in search of land.* □ *The east wind*

chilled him to the marrow. □ *The sun rises in the east.*

The adjective *eastern* is more frequent and usually less specific than the adjective *east*: □ *the eastern shore* □ *in eastern Australia.*

Like *east*, *eastern* is written with a capital *E* when it forms part of a proper name, such as: □ *the Eastern Orthodox Church.* With or without a capital *E*, it also means 'of the East': □ *eastern/Eastern philosophy.*

eatable or **edible**? *Eatable* means 'palatable', but with the suggestion of 'not actually tasting unpleasant' rather than 'delicious': □ *He had managed to get together a reasonably eatable meal. Edible means 'suitable for eating as food':* □ *Common sorrel is edible but wood sorrel is poisonous.*

◆ If something is not *edible* it would be either impossible or dangerous to eat it, but a substance can be *edible* without being *eatable*, for example, raw potatoes. Despite these differences the two words are often used interchangeably in informal contexts: □ *The cabbage was overcooked but just about eatable/edible.*

The distinction between *eatable* and *edible* is also applicable to their antonyms, *uneatable* and *inedible*: □ *The meal was uneatable.* □ *Toadstools are inedible.*

EC or **EEC**? The abbreviation *EC* and its full form *European Community* have now replaced the abbreviation *EEC* and *European Economic Community.*

echelon *Echelon* is a military expression applying to the formation of units or to a division of a supply organization. It is now often used as a fashionable synonym for *grade, rank, level of power,* or to describe the people at that level: □ *the management echelon* □ *the higher echelons of the civil service.*

◆ Note the spelling: *ch* not *sh*, and although the word comes from the French *échelon* there is no acute accent on the English word.

The usual pronunciation is [esh*ă*lon], although [aysh*ă*lon] is sometimes heard.

eco- The growing popularity of the science of *ecology*, the study of living things in their relation to the environment, has given rise to several words with the prefix *eco-*, some legitimate terms in ecology: □ *ecospecies* □ *ecotype* □ *ecosystem,* and some more modern coinages: □ *ecocatastrophe* □ *eco-freak* □ *ecotourism* □ *ecotoxicology.*

◆ New *eco-* words are being spawned all the time: □ *a new magazine ... described as the journal of eco-politics* (The Guardian) □ *the eco-warriors of Greenpeace* (Sunday Times) □ *WWF has continued to express keen interest in the issue of eco-labelling* (WWF Review).

economic or **economical**? *Economic* is the adjective from *economics* or *the economy* and is concerned with the production, distribution, and structure of wealth: □ *Friedman's economic theories* □ *the Government's economic policies. Economical* is the adjective from *economy* and is concerned with thrift and the avoidance of waste: □ *an economical car* □ *a large economical pack.* An *economic price* is one that benefits the seller, but an *economical price* benefits the buyer.

◆ Although careful users keep the distinction between the two words, each is frequently used with the meaning belonging to the other: □ *Labour gave fewer details of their economical brief* (BBC Radio). □ *Buying a whole chicken makes economic sense* (advertisement, *Bejam* magazine).

The initial *e-* of both words may be short [ek*ŏ*nomik(l)] or long [eek*ŏ*nomik(l)].

economics see -ICS.

ecstasy This word, meaning 'intense emotion', especially of happiness, is sometimes misspelt. Note particularly the *cs* and the *-asy* ending, as in *fantasy*.

ecu The noun *ecu* is an acronym of *European Currency Unit*, the currency unit of the European Community. It is sometimes written *ECU*.

◆ *Ecu* is usually pronounced [*ay*kew]. This pronunciation is influenced by *écu*, the name of a former French coin, but in the sense of 'European Currency Unit' the noun should not be spelt with an acute accent on the *e*-.

-ed or **-t**? The past tense and past participle of the verbs *burn*, *dream*, *dwell*, *kneel*, *lean*, *leap*, *learn*, *smell*, *spell*, *spill*, and *spoil* may end in *-ed* or *-t*.

◆ In most cases the *-ed* form is preferred in American English and the *-t* form is slightly more frequent in British English. For further discussion and specific information on pronunciation and adjectival use see the entries at the individual words.

edible see EATABLE OR EDIBLE?

-ee or **-er**? In general, the suffix *-ee* can be applied to the recipient of an action denoted by the verb to which the suffix is attached, and the suffix *-er* is applied to the thing or person who performs the action: □ *employer–employee* □ *trainer–trainee*. However, this rule does not apply in all cases. The suffix *-ee* can sometimes indicate someone who behaves in a particular way: □ *absentee* □ *arrestee* □ *escapee*, and the suffix *-er* can be applied to something that is a suitable object for an action: □ *prisoner* □ *cooker* (type of apple).

◆ The suffix *-ee* is also found as a substitute for *ie* or *y*, suggesting smallness, in the word *bootee*, and is sometimes applied to people or things associated with a particular noun: □ *townee* □ *goatee*, although *-er* is more often used in this way: □ *docker* □ *villager*.

EEC see EC or EEC?

effect see AFFECT OR EFFECT?

effective, effectual, efficacious, or **efficient**? The distinction between these words is subtle. *Effective* means 'having or producing the desired effect': □ *The talks were effective in settling the dispute.* *Effectual*, a formal word, means 'capable of achieving the desired effect': □ *All plans to reduce the trade deficit have not so far proved effectual*, and in religious contexts: □ *effectual prayer* □ *God's effectual calling of his people*. *Efficacious*, also a formal word, means 'having the power to achieve the desired effect' and is usually applied to medical treatment: □ *an efficacious remedy*. *Efficient* is applied to people or things producing results through a good and economical use of resources: □ *an efficient machine* □ *an efficient secretary*.

◆ Similar distinctions apply to *ineffective*, *ineffectual*, and *inefficient*: □ *an ineffective remedy* □ *an ineffectual policy/leader* □ *an inefficient system/clerk*.

Effective is used in various other ways. It can mean 'impressive': □ *an effective performance*, 'operative; in force': □ *The law is effective as from today*, and 'actual; in practice if not theory': □ *He had become the effective leader*.

effrontery see AFFRONT OR EFFRONTERY?

e.g. and **i.e.** The abbreviation *e.g.* stands for *exempli gratia* and means 'for example'. It is used before examples of what has previously been mentioned: □ *We could show you some of the sights, e.g. Buckingham Palace and the Tower of London.* The abbreviation *i.e.*, often used in error for *e.g.*, stands for *id est* and means 'that is'. It is used before amplifications or explanations of what has previously been mentioned: □ *They were vegans, i.e. vegetarians who also avoid eggs and dairy products.*

◆ The abbreviations *e.g.* and *i.e.* are best confined to official writing or very informal writing; in other contexts and in speech *for example* and *that is* should be used.

egoism or **egotism?** The words *egoism* and *egotism* are frequently used interchangeably but there are differences between them. *Egoism* is applied to the ethical theory that all actions and motivation are based on self-interest. An *egoist* is a believer in this theory or, much more often, a person who is selfish and self-seeking: □ *His conduct was characterized by ruthless egoism.* *Egotism* means 'being self-obsessed; self-centred'. The typical *egotist* is vain, boastful, and uses the word *I* constantly: □ *Her egotism makes her oblivious to other people's concerns.*

◆ The conspicuous self-obsession of *egotists* often makes them absurd pathetic figures, whereas *egoists* may pursue their own interests in a covert, though calculating, manner.

egregious The adjective *egregious*, used in formal contexts and meaning 'very bad', is sometimes misspelt and/or mispronounced. Note the *-egi-* in the middle of the word. The correct pronunciation is [i*greej*ŭs].

eighth Note that in the spelling of this word the letter *h* occurs twice: *eight* plus *h*.

either As an adjective or pronoun *either* is used with a singular verb: □ *Is either child left-handed?* □ *Is either of your children left-handed?*

◆ In the *either ... or* construction, a singular verb is used if both subjects are singular and a plural verb is used if both subjects are plural: □ *Either David or Peter is responsible.* □ *Either their parents or their teachers are responsible.* The use of a plural verb with the pronoun *either* or with singular subjects in an *either ... or* construction is avoided by careful users, especially in formal contexts.

When a combination of singular and plural subjects occurs in an *either ... or* construction, the verb traditionally agrees with the subject that is nearest to it: □ *Either David or his parents are responsible.* □ *Either his friends or his brother is responsible.* The same principle is applied to singular subjects that are used with different forms of the verb: □ *Either you or I am* [not *are*] *responsible.* If the resulting sentence sounds awkward or unidiomatic it may be reordered or rephrased.

The alternatives presented in an *either ... or* construction should be grammatically balanced: □ *Dilute the soup either with milk or water* may be changed to: *Dilute the soup either with milk or with water* or: *Dilute the soup with either milk or water.*

As a pronoun *either* should be used only of two alternatives: □ *I haven't seen either of my parents since June.* □ *Any* [not *Either*] *of the four knives may be used to cut vegetables.* However, the use of the *either ... or* construction with three or more subjects is acceptable to some: □ *Either Sarah, Jane, or Pauline will be there.*

The first syllable of *either* may be pronounced to rhyme with *try* or *tree.* The pronunciation [*ī*dhĕr] is more frequent in British English.

See also **NEITHER; OR.**

eke out The original meaning of *eke out* is 'make something more adequate by adding to it': □ *She eked out the meal with extra rice.* It is frequently used in two other senses: 'make something last longer by using it economically': □ *They eked out the supplies over two weeks*, and 'make (a living) with laborious effort': □ *The children eked out a living by selling wild flowers to tourists.*

◆ Both these uses, particularly the latter, are disliked by some careful users, but they are well-established and generally acceptable.

elder, eldest, older, or oldest? *Elder* and *eldest* are applied only to people, and usually within the context of family relationships: □ *my eldest brother* □ *She is the elder of my two daughters.* One cannot say: *Rachel is elder than Sarah* or: *He is elder/eldest* without adding *the*. *Older* and *oldest* can be used of things as well as people and in a far wider range of constructions: □ *I am older than David.* □ *He is older.* □ *It is the oldest church in Yorkshire.*

◆ *Elder* is also used in such expressions as: □ *I am his elder by eighteen months*, although: □ *I am older than him by eighteen months* sounds less formal. It is also used for people noted for age and experience: □ *an elder statesman* □ *village elders* □ *one's elders and betters*; and for an officer in various nonconformist churches.

See also **COMPARATIVE AND SUPERLATIVE**.

electric or electrical? *Electric* and *electrical* can both mean 'worked by electricity' although *electric* tends to be applied more to specific, and *electrical* to general things: □ *electric lighting* □ *an electric motor* □ *electrical appliances* □ *electrical equipment*.

◆ *Electric* is also applied to things that produce or carry electricity: □ *an electric socket* □ *electric current* □ *an electric shock*, and is used figuratively to describe something stimulating or thrilling: □ *The atmosphere was electric*. *Electrical* is also used to mean 'concerned with electricity': □ *electrical engineering*.

elemental or elementary? *Elemental* means 'of or like the elements or forces of nature': □ *This evoked a flood of elemental passion*. It is also sometimes used to mean 'fundamental or essential': □ *an elemental truth of Christianity*. It should not be confused with *elementary* which means 'very simple; introductory': □ *I know nothing about computers so I need an elementary manual.*

◆ A further possible mistake is the confusion of *elementary* with *alimentary* which means 'to do with the provision of nourishment': □ *the alimentary canal.*

elicit see **ILLICIT OR ELICIT?**

eligible see **ILLEGIBLE OR ELIGIBLE?**

ellipse or ellipsis? An *ellipse* is an oval; *ellipsis* is a term used in grammar and linguistics (see **ELLIPSIS**). The two nouns share the derived adjective *elliptical*: □ *an elliptical shape* □ *an elliptical phrase*. *Elliptical* also means 'ambiguous' or 'obscure' in formal contexts: □ *an elliptical reference.*

ellipsis There are two meanings of the term *ellipsis* in grammar: one is for the punctuation marks ..., usually indicating omission; the other is for the omission of words in a sentence, as an abbreviation or in order to avoid repetition: □ *See you Friday.* □ *I ought to write some letters and make some phone calls.*

◆ The ellipsis ... is used mainly to indicate an omission from a quoted passage: □ *'There's rosemary, that's for remembrance ... and there is pansies, that's for thoughts.'* If the quotation does not start at the beginning of a sentence the ellipsis precedes it: □ *'... a good fellow of infinite jest'*, and when the end of a sentence is omitted the three dots

of the ellipsis are sometimes followed by a fourth, to indicate a full
stop: □ *'Cudgel thy brains no more ....'*; if a whole sentence is left out
the sentence before the omitted one has a full stop and the ellipsis
follows. An ellipsis is always three dots, or four if a full stop is included,
except when a whole line of poetry is omitted, when a row of dots can
be used to fill the length of the line.

The ellipsis is also used in the same manner as the dash, to indicate
halting speech, an unfinished sentence, or an omitted obscenity (see
DASH). When used for an unfinished sentence, a dash suggests a
more abrupt break, while an ellipsis gives an impression of speech
tailing off: □ *'I suppose I had hoped that you might ...'*. An ellipsis
should not be used at the end of a passage to suggest that the rest of
an episode can be left to the reader's imagination.

When using ellipsis in sentences to avoid repetition, the danger is
that the omitted word(s) might not correspond with the word(s)
repeated, as in the following two examples. In: □ *I know him as well or
even better than you do*, a second *as*, after *as well*, is omitted, but this
is not repeated. In: □ *No one has ever or will ever solve the mystery*,
the omitted word is *solved*, not *solve*. The only case in which such a
false ellipsis is acceptable is when the omitted word is part of the verb
to be: □ *I'm going to London and Sarah to Edinburgh*.

elliptical see **ELLIPSE OR ELLIPSIS**?

else *Else* is often followed by either *than* or *but*: □ *Nothing else than
revolution is possible*. □ *Anybody else but him would be preferable*. Some careful users object to following *else* with *but* and
difficulties can be avoided by substituting such phrases as *nothing but* or *anyone other than*.

◆ The use of *else* as a conjunction: □ *Stop, else you'll have an
accident* is also disliked by many people. Unless it is used in very
informal speech *or else* should be substituted.

For possessive forms see **APOSTROPHE**.

elude see **AVOID, EVADE, OR ELUDE**?

elusive see **ALLUSIVE, ELUSIVE, OR ILLUSIVE**?

embarrass This word, meaning 'cause to feel shy, ashamed, or self-
conscious': □ *She was embarrassed by her brother's behaviour*, is
often misspelt. Note the *-rr-*, the *-ss-*, and the last vowel, which
is an *a*, not an *e*.

emend see **AMEND OR EMEND**?

emigrant or **immigrant**? An *emigrant* is someone who is migrating
from his or her country: □ *Thousands of emigrants left Britain for
Australia under the assisted passage scheme*. An *immigrant* is
someone who is migrating into another country: □ *Some of the
immigrants had only been in the country for a week*.

◆ The word *immigrant* should not be applied to nonwhite British
residents unless one is sure that they were actually born abroad.

The word *émigré* is applied to someone who has been forced to
leave a country, usually because of a repressive political regime or
intellectual atmosphere. The reasons for leaving are generally less
pressing than for those described as *refugees*, and *émigré* carries a
suggestion of refined class and intellect that *refugee* lacks:
□ *Nabokov is the most famous of Russian émigré writers*.

eminent, imminent, or **immanent**? *Eminent* means 'outstanding, notable, or distinguished' and is particularly applied to people who
have achieved some distinction or fame in their profession, or in
the arts or sciences: □ *an eminent barrister* □ *an eminent poet*.
Imminent means 'impending; about to happen; threatening': □ *It*

now seemed that war was imminent.

◆ *Imminent* should not be confused with the far less frequently used word *immanent*, which means 'inherent, indwelling', and has the respective philosophical and theological meanings of 'inherent' and 'pervading all things throughout the universe'.

emotive or **emotional**? *Emotive* means 'causing or arousing emotion, especially as opposed to reason': □ *Taxation is always an emotive subject* (*Mind Your Own Business*). *Emotional* means 'expressing emotion, showing excessive emotion': □ *an emotional woman* □ *an emotional meeting.*

◆ *Emotive* is often used when *emotional* is intended, especially since the word has become more fashionable: □ *She is very emotive and gets emotionally involved herself* (*The Times*). *Emotional* is also sometimes used when *emotive* would be better, although it is acceptable to use *emotional* in this sense: □ *It features television spots of almost wrenching pathos, and is being supported by equally emotional posters* (*Sunday Times*).

empathy *Empathy* means 'an imaginative identification with another's feelings or ideas': □ *He read all he could about the king, and meditated on his character, so by the time he came to play the part he felt a real empathy with Henry.* It has recently become a fashionable word and its frequent use as a mere synonym for *sympathy* is disliked by some: □ *Essential attributes are ... an empathy for the ideals within a voluntary organisation* (*Daily Telegraph*).

emulate *Emulate* means 'attempt to equal or do better than, especially by close imitation': □ *Since the company's success all our competitors are trying to emulate our products.*

◆ The word is often used in the sense of 'imitate closely' without the idea of rivalry: □ *As a teenager he had admired John Lennon devotedly and had tried to emulate him in his dress and speech.* This usage is disliked by some.

encyclopedia or **encyclopaedia**? Both spellings of this word are acceptable, *encyclopaedia* being the more traditional in British English. In American English *encyclopedia* is the more frequent spelling and this spelling is becoming adopted in British English. See also -AE- AND -OE-.

endemic or **epidemic**? *Endemic*, a formal word, is most frequently used as an adjective, meaning 'occurring in a particular area': □ *an endemic disease* □ *The plant is endemic in* [or *to*] *Africa.* An *epidemic* is the widespread occurrence or rapid spread of a disease: □ *a flu epidemic* □ *an epidemic of measles.*

◆ *Endemic* may also be used as a noun and *epidemic* as an adjective. Both words have figurative uses: □ *Vandalism is endemic in the inner cities.* □ *There was an epidemic of resignations after the takeover.*

end product and **end result** *End product* usually means 'the final product of a process, or series of processes': □ *We use the best materials so that the end product is a quality item.* □ *These young men are the end products of expensive public schools and the most exclusive colleges.*

◆ Both phrases may simply mean 'the eventual outcome', as is the phrase *end result*: □ *The agreement is the end product/end result of many years of negotiation.* Many careful users dislike both these phrases as the *end* is clearly redundant.

enervate *Enervate* means 'weaken, to lessen vitality or strength': □ *It*

was an enervating climate and they felt listless most of the time.
◆ It is sometimes used as though it meant quite the opposite, as a
synonym for *invigorate* or *energize*, and is also sometimes used as
though it meant 'irritate' or 'get on someone's nerves'. *Enervate* is most
often used in the forms *enervated* or *enervating*.

England see BRITAIN.

enhance *Enhance* means 'improve, increase the value or attractiveness of': □ *The new windows have enhanced the value of the
house.* □ *This week's running debacle over Labour's defence
policies has hardly enhanced Mr Kinnock's appeal to any Tories
who might be wavering (Sunday Times).*
◆ It has become a fashionable word, particularly used by employers
in connection with extra benefits offered to employees: □ *Excellent
salaries are enhanced by a wide range of benefits including
relocation assistance (Daily Telegraph).*

enormity or **enormousness**? *Enormity* means 'the quality of being outrageous or wicked, a very wicked act': □ *Those experiences
alerted him to the enormity of what was being done to the Jews
(The Guardian). Enormousness* means 'the quality of being
extremely large': □ *They were daunted by the enormousness of
the task.*
◆ *Enormity* is frequently used as though it meant *enormousness* but,
although this usage is now acceptable in American English, most
careful users of British English still dislike it.

enquiry or **inquiry**? For many users of British English the spellings of
the nouns *enquiry* and *inquiry* (and of the verbs *enquire* and
inquire) are completely interchangeable. Some users, however,
maintain that *enquire* and *enquiry* are used for simple requests
for information: □ *He enquired after her health.* □ *an enquiry
office* □ *directory enquiries*, and *inquire* and *inquiry* are used for
investigations, especially official ones: □ *The police are now
inquiring into the events that led up to his disappearance.* □ *MPs
are calling for a public inquiry into the causes of the disaster.*
◆ In American English, the general preference is to use *inquiry*.

enrol In British English the verb *enrol* ends in a single *l*, unlike the
word *roll*. The *l* is doubled before suffixes beginning with a
vowel: □ *enrolled* □ *enrolling*.
◆ Note that the derived noun *enrolment* has only one *l* in British
English. The American spellings are *enroll* and *enrollment*.

ensure see ASSURE, ENSURE, OR INSURE?

-ent see -ANT OR -ENT?

enterprise Some people dislike the overuse of the noun *enterprise* in
the context of self-employment and the setting up of new small
businesses: □ *the enterprise culture* □ *the government's Enterprise Allowance Scheme* □ *a network of Local Enterprise Agen-
cies* □ *Britain's enterprise economy* □ *the enterprise initiative.*
◆ An *enterprise* is also simply a business or company: □ *several large
industrial enterprises. Private-enterprise* is industry and business
owned by independent individuals or groups, i.e. not receiving
financial help from the government.
   The indiscriminate application of the word *enterprise*, which is
traditionally reserved for ventures that are particularly risky, bold, or
innovative, was encouraged by the Conservative government of the
late 1980s: □ *It was confirmation that Docklands had become the
showpiece of Thatcherism's enterprise culture (The Guardian).* See
also ENTREPRENEUR.

Note the spelling of *enterprise*, which always ends in *-ise*, unlike the word *prize*.

enthral In British English the verb *enthral* ends in a single *l*, which is doubled before suffixes beginning with a vowel: □ *enthralled* □ *enthralling*.

◆ Note that the derived noun *enthralment* has only one *l* in British English. The American spellings are *enthrall* and *enthrallment*.

enthuse The verb *enthuse* is a back formation from *enthusiasm* and means 'show enthusiasm': □ *The critics enthused over her new play*, or 'make enthusiastic': □ *Mr Neil Kinnock's achievement has been to mobilise and enthuse the traditional Labour vote (Sunday Times)*.

◆ Although it has been in use, especially in American English, for over a century, it is still disliked by many people and is perhaps best avoided in formal use.

entomology or **etymology**? *Entomology* is the study of insects; *etymology* is the study of the origin and development of words. The two nouns should not be confused.

◆ An *etymologist* may think that all centipedes have a hundred legs, as the word is derived from Latin *centum* 'hundred' and *pes* 'foot', but an *entomologist* knows that they do not.

entourage Of French origin, the noun *entourage*, meaning 'attendants; retinue', is pronounced [ontuu*rahzh*] in English.

entrepreneur Like ENTERPRISE, the noun *entrepreneur* is losing its traditional connotations of risk and initiative and is indiscriminately applied to any person who becomes self-employed or sets up a new small business: □ *Skills appear to be the main requirement for successful entrepreneurship ... in contrast with the simple traditional view of the entrepreneur as someone who is risk loving (The Guardian)*. □ *She regularly scoured the Businesses for Sale columns of the papers for the inspiration that would turn her into an entrepreneur (Daily Telegraph)*.

◆ Of French origin, the noun *entrepreneur* is frequently misspelt. Note that it begins with *entre-*, not *enter-*, and ends in *-eur*, not *-er*.

E-numbers *E-numbers*, which appear on food labels as E401, E218, etc., denote additives that have been approved for use throughout the European Economic Community. The belief that E-numbers denote harmful artificial substances is a popular misconception: E440(a), for example, is pectin, which occurs naturally in ripe fruit and vegetables; E270 is lactic acid, which is found in dairy products; and E150 is caramel. The term was popularized by Maurice Hanson in *E for Additives* (1984).

envelop or **envelope**? The verb *envelop* means 'enclose, surround, or enfold' and is used both literally and figuratively: □ *He was enveloped in a blanket and barely visible*. □ *She spent a happy childhood, enveloped in love and security*. The noun *envelope* means 'something that envelops, a wrapper (particularly for a letter)': □ *It arrived in a plain brown envelope*.

◆ *Envelop* is pronounced [inve*lŏp*]. The preferred pronunciation of *envelope* is [*env*ălōp], although [*onv*ălōp] is also heard.

enviable or **envious**? Both these adjectives are derived from the word *envy* (see ENVY OR JEALOUSY?). *Enviable* means 'causing envy'; *envious* means 'feeling envy': □ *the enviable task of showing the film star around the building* □ *He was envious of his sister's success*. The two words are not interchangeable.

environment *Environment* can be applied to the surrounding conditions of people and other organisms and can include physical and social influences, though many people are careful not to overuse this word.

◆ *Environment* and its derived noun *environmentalism* have become fashionable words in the context of ecology and the protection of the world's physical environment from pollution: □ *The CBI is now viewing the present wave of environmentalism not as a passing fad but as a long term influence on the market* (*Daily Telegraph*). See also **-FRIENDLY; GREEN.**

envisage or **envision**? Both *envisage* and *envision* mean 'have a mental image of, especially of something hoped for in the future': □ *They envisaged/envisioned a world where war and poverty no longer existed. Envisage* is more often used in British English and *envision* in American English.

◆ The words should not be used as mere synonyms for 'expect': □ *A further downward trend in share prices is envisaged.* Careful users avoid using these words with *that*: □ *We envisage* [not *envisage that*] *the situation will improve.*

envy or **jealousy**? *Envy* involves the awareness of an advantage possessed by someone else, together with a desire to have that advantage oneself: □ *She gazed at his car with envy.* □ *I envy your ability to relax. Jealousy* involves a concern to avoid the loss of something that one regards as one's own, and includes the tendency to be suspicious of rivalry and infidelity in relation to a person one is close to: □ *Her husband's jealousy forced her to conceal even the most innocent encounters with other men,* as well as vigilance in preserving a possession: □ *They guarded their professional reputation jealously.*

ephemeral This word, meaning 'lasting only a short time': □ *the ephemeral pleasures of life,* is sometimes misspelt. Note particularly the *ph*, pronounced [f], and the sequence of vowels.

epic *Epic* originally applied to long narrative poems on a grand, heroic scale, like Homer's *Iliad* and *Odyssey* or the Finnish *Kalevala.* It was extended to other works with some of these qualities or to series of events or episodes which might be fit subjects for an epic: □ *a marvellous epic novel* (*Newsweek,* review of Salman Rushdie's *Midnight's Children*) □ *the epic battle between Greenpeace and the whaling ships.*

◆ It is also sometimes used of anything more than usually large and impressive: □ *an epic gathering,* but it is preferable not to use the word so that it entirely loses its connection with its heroic origins.

epidemic see **ENDEMIC OR EPIDEMIC?**

epigram, epigraph, epitaph, or **epithet**? These four nouns should not be confused. An *epigram* is a short witty saying; an *epigraph,* the least common of the four words, is a quotation or motto printed at the beginning of a book or engraved on a monument. An *epitaph* is a commemorative statement about a dead person, often inscribed on a gravestone; an *epithet* is a short descriptive word or phrase applied to a person, such as *Lionheart* in *Richard the Lionheart.*

◆ Some people dislike the extended euphemistic use of the word *epithet* in the sense of 'term of abuse': □ *shouting epithets at each other.*

epitome This word, meaning 'typical example': □ *He is the very epitome of the absent-minded professor,* is sometimes mispronounced. Note that there are four syllables [ip*i*tōmi].

eponyms An *eponym* is a person from whose name a word is derived: □ *sandwich* □ *quisling* □ *cardigan* □ *ampere*. There are eponymous nouns: □ *martinet* □ *salmonella* □ *listeria* □ *watt*, adjectives: □ *quixotic* □ *herculean*, and verbs: □ *bowdlerize* □ *guillotine*.

◆ The only problem with the use of eponymous words is whether or not they are written with a capital letter. The rough rule is that the closer the connection between the word and the name, the more likely it is that a capital should be used. When one calls a young man given to amorous adventures a *Romeo*, one is making a definite allusion to the Shakespearean character and would use a capital. One would use a capital when referring to *Platonic forms* but not when referring to *platonic love*, a concept further removed from Plato. There are no firm rules with things named after the person who invented or popularized them. Generally such words are more likely to be capitalized when used adjectivally than when used as nouns: □ *Wellington boots* □ *wellingtons*, but this is very much a matter of custom. *Pullman cars* and *Bunsen burners* are nearly always capitalized, while *diesel engine* hardly ever is. Eponymous verbs such as: □ *boycott* □ *pasteurize* never have capital letters.

equable or **equitable**? *Equable* means 'regular, moderate, not given to extremes' and is frequently applied both to climates which are consistently mild and not subject to sudden changes, and to people who are placid and even-tempered. *Equitable* means 'fair, reasonable, impartial': □ *It was an equitable agreement which both parties found satisfactory*.

equally The word *equally* should not be followed by *as* in such sentences as: □ *She is a brilliant pianist, and her brother is equally talented* [not *equally as talented*].

◆ The word *equally* may, however, be replaced by *as* in the above example, in which case it is stressed.

In the sentence: □ *This dress is as expensive as that one*, the first *as* should not be preceded or replaced by *equally*. The sentence can, however, be rephrased as: □ *The two dresses are equally expensive*.

equal to or **equal with**? When briefly indicating identity, equivalence, or similarity *equal* is used as a verb with no preposition: □ *x equals 5* or as an adjective followed by *to*: □ *x is equal to 5*. In longer constructions, using *equal* as an adjective, it is preferable to use *equal with*, rather than *equal to*: □ *The Bradford team have gained five points and are now equal with the team from Liverpool*. *Equal to* has the specific meaning of 'capable of meeting the requirements of': □ *He seemed too young and inexperienced to be equal to the task*.

equitable see EQUABLE OR EQUITABLE?

-er see -EE OR -ER?

-er or **-or**? The suffix *-er* is used to form nouns to indicate an occupation: □ *lawyer* □ *bricklayer*, or an action performed by a person: □ *steeple-chaser* □ *messenger* □ *enquirer*. The suffix *-or* is used in the same way with other words, normally those formed from Latin roots. Often these are words where there is no English verb base: □ *sponsor* □ *doctor* □ *author* □ *mentor*, but this is not always the case: □ *actor* □ *investigator* □ *sailor*.

◆ It is not always possible to guess which ending should be used and sometimes both are acceptable: □ *adviser/advisor* □ *vendor/vender*. The *-er* ending is more frequent and more likely with recently coined nouns and those that do not have Latin roots.

See also **-EE OR -ER?**

erogenous *Erogenous* zones are the parts of the body that are sensitive to sexual stimulation. Note the spelling of the word *erogenous*: a single *r* and *-gen-*, not *-gyn-* as in *misogynist*.

erupt or **irrupt**? These two verbs (and their derived nouns *eruption* and *irruption*) are identical in pronunciation but different in meaning. *Erupt* means 'burst out; come or go out with force', whereas *irrupt*, a more formal word, means 'burst in; enter with force': □ *The crowd erupted onto the street.* □ *The police irrupted into the building.*

◆ The verb *erupt* is also used with reference to volcanoes, with reference to the sudden appearance of a rash on the skin, and in the figurative sense of 'begin suddenly and violently': □ *Fighting erupted along the border.* The verb *irrupt* should not be used in this sense. Note the single *-r-* of *erupt* and the *-rr-* of *irrupt*.

escalate *Escalate* is a back formation from *escalator*, and as a vogue word meaning 'expand, rise, intensify' tends to be overused. It is best confined to the description of an upward movement that increases step by step: □ *Rents have escalated over the last five years.* □ *Officials killed by mine as Tamil attacks escalate* (*The Times*).

especially or **specially**? These adverbs are often used interchangeably, but there is a difference in their meanings. *Especially* means 'more than usual, in particular, above all': □ *He was especially hungry.* □ *I hate dogs, especially big ones.* *Specially* means 'specifically, purposely, in this particular way': □ *The car is specially designed for handicapped people.* □ *I made it specially for you.*

◆ *Specially* is often used where *especially* is intended, and sometimes, as in the last example, this might lead to confusion as *specially for you* might mean 'for you above all' or 'specifically for you'.

-ess The use of the feminine suffix *-ess* is sometimes regarded as patronizing or sexist and is often unnecessary.

◆ Such nouns as *author, poet, sculptor, editor, manager,* etc., can be applied to people of either sex, making *authoress, poetess, sculptress, editress,* and *manageress* redundant. *Actress* and *hostess* are retained in some contexts, although *actor* and *host* are generally considered to be of neutral gender. Certain occupational titles, such as *waiter* and *steward,* tend to be used as masculine nouns, *waitress* and *stewardess* being their feminine equivalents. The suffix *-ess* is obligatory in such words as *princess, duchess, countess,* and *marchioness.*

See also SEXISM.

essentially *Essentially* should be used primarily to mean 'basically, inherently, or most importantly': □ *The play is essentially a tragedy although there is some comic relief.*

◆ It tends sometimes also to be used with a weaker meaning of 'in general terms': □ *It was essentially a good match,* or 'importantly': □ *Your view isn't essentially different from mine.* This usage is disliked by some.

establishment *The Establishment* refers to the powerful figures in government (especially the civil service), the legal system, the established church, the armed forces, and the City of London, who are thought to control the country: □ *The Prime Minister, the Archbishop of Canterbury, and the Lord Chief Justice were among the Establishment figures present. The Establishment* (sometimes with a lower-case *e*) is thought to have a conservative outlook, generally opposing changes to the existing order, and as such is often used as a derogatory term.

◆ A further meaning of *establishment* is 'a controlling or influential group': □ *the pedigree dog establishment.*

esthetic see AESTHETIC, ASCETIC, OR ACETIC?

estimation, estimate, or **esteem**? *Estimation* is the act of estimating; an *estimate* is a figure, idea, etc., arrived at by the process of estimation: □ *an estimate of the time it will take. Esteem,* a more formal word, means 'great respect': □ *He held her in high esteem.*

◆ The noun *estimation* also means 'opinion' or 'regard': □ *What, in your estimation, is the cause of the problem?* □ *She went down in their estimation when the truth came out.*

et al. *Et al.* is an abbreviation of *et alii* and means 'and other people'. It is used particularly in writings of a formal technical nature to indicate the omission of other names: □ *Similar findings have been recorded by Jones, Bernstein, et al.*

◆ It should not be used in ordinary writing or in speech, and should be used only when a list is specific and does not start with *for example* or *such as.*

etc. The abbreviation *etc.* stands for *et cetera*, which means 'and other things, and so forth': □ *The college offers several non-academic subjects – home economics, physical education, craft and design, etc.*

◆ It is used in technical or informal writing, but in formal writing *and so on* or *and so forth* are preferred. One should not write *and etc.* or use it in a list preceded by *for example* or *such as*. There is never any point in writing *etc. etc.*, although it is sometimes used in informal speech.

The correct pronunciation of *etc.* is [etsetèrà] or [etsetrà], not [ekset(ê)rà].

ethics see -ICS.

ethnic The original meaning of *ethnic* is 'to do with groups of people classed by common race, traits, or customs': □ *There are many different ethnic groups in the USA.* As a vogue word *ethnic* is now used to mean 'to do with race': □ *Shooting continued last night in Sukhumi, ... more than 24 hours after the start of ethnic clashes in which 11 people have been killed (Daily Telegraph),* 'foreign': □ *But a great deal of ethnic food is not hot, but spiced, with pronounced flavours (Sunday Times),* and 'nonwhite': □ *Labour now has three other ethnic MPs (Sunday Times).*

ethnic cleansing The phrase *ethnic cleansing* is a euphemism applied to the deportation and murder of thousands of Muslims and Croats living in Bosnia.

◆ The term is gaining wider recognition, and is sometimes used as a synonym for the extermination of Jews, the 'cleansing' to create Jew-free areas, by the Nazis in the 1930s.

Stephen Burgen (*The Guardian*) warns against the adoption of euphemisms coined by the perpetrators of atrocities: 'Already some newspapers have started taking ethnic cleansing out of quotation marks, thus moving the phrase one more step along the road to respectability.'

etymology see ENTOMOLOGY OR ETYMOLOGY?

euphemisms A *euphemism* is an inoffensive term that is used as a substitute for one that might give offence. Euphemisms tend to be used particularly when referring to sexual and bodily functions: □ *private parts* (genitals) □ *smallest room* (toilet) □ *pass* *water* (urinate), and to death: □ *She passed away.* □ *I lost my wife two years ago.*

◆ Some euphemisms have arisen out of genuine feelings of sensitivity, but many are an attempt to cover up something reprehensible: □ *the Nazi final solution* (mass extermination of the Jews) □ *being economical with the truth* (lying).

The invention of new euphemisms in the business and professional worlds is becoming almost an art form: □ *At one international computer company the accepted wording for falling behind is 'achieving schedule overrun' (Sunday Times).* □ *[An American] hospital recently announced the relapse of an important patient by saying he 'did not fully achieve his wellness potential.' He later experienced a 'terminal episode' ... previously known as death (The Times).*

Euro- Although the United Kingdom is part of Europe, British people have traditionally spoken of *Europe* to mean all the continent apart from the United Kingdom. When United Kingdom membership of the European Community was mooted, it was often referred to as *going into Europe*, and *Europe* is now quite often used as a synonym for the EC.

◆ The prefix *Euro-* is sometimes used in words which are connected with Europe in general: □ *Eurocommunism* □ *Eurobond* □ *Eurovision* □ *Eurobank* but more often with those having connections with the EC: □ *Euro-sceptic* □ *Europhile* □ *Eurocurrency* □ *Eurocrat* □ *Demand for the 'rare breed' of Euro-manager will far outstrip the supply in the single market (Daily Telegraph).*

evade, evasion see AVOID, EVADE, OR ELUDE?

even The position of the word *even* in a sentence can influence its meaning. Compare the following sentences and their implications: □ *Even I like opera on television* (so other people would like it still more). □ *I like even opera on television* (presumably I would prefer things other than opera). □ *I like opera even on television* (though it is inferior on television). In formal writing it is best to put *even* before the word it modifies, in order to make the meaning unambiguous, although in speech it is often more natural to put *even* before the verb: □ *He doesn't even stop working on holiday.*

eventuate *Eventuate* is used, usually in formal contexts, to mean 'result': □ *If the proposed merger takes place, this might eventuate in the new company having a monopoly of the market.* It is disliked by many people as pompous and affected, and conveying nothing that is not conveyed by simpler and more usual words.

ever The use of *ever* with superlatives in such constructions as: □ *the largest pie ever* □ *his fastest speed ever,* is disliked by some people as they feel that *ever* includes the future, as well as the past. The usage is well-established, but the criticism can be met by changing the constructions slightly: □ *the largest pie ever baked* □ *his fastest speed to date/the fastest he has ever run.*

◆ The expressions *ever so* and *ever such* as intensives: □ *He's ever so clever.* □ *It's ever such a nice house* should be confined to informal contexts, and *ever so* without an adjective or adverb following: □ *Thanks ever so* is better avoided.

On whether to write *whatever* or *what ever*, *wherever* or *where ever*, etc., in such sentences as: □ *What ever did he say next?* □ *Wherever you travel you'll find businesses that accept our credit card,* see **WHATEVER OR WHAT EVER?**

every *Every* is used with singular nouns and all related words should be in the singular form: □*Every machine is equipped with a safety device.* The temptation to use plurals arises when one wishes to avoid such gender-specific constructions as: □*I hope every committee member has remembered to bring his agenda.* Rather than use the ungrammatical *their agendas* or the rather clumsy *his or her agenda* it is better to rephrase the sentence: □*I hope all committee members have remembered to bring their agendas.*

everybody or **everyone**? The pronoun *everybody* and its synonym *everyone* are interchangeable in all contexts.

◆ Both are used with a singular verb but are sometimes followed by a plural personal pronoun or possessive adjective (see **THEY**): □*Everybody/Everyone has paid their fare.*

Note the difference between the one-word compound *everyone* and the more specific two-word form *every one*, both of which may be applied to people: □*Everyone knew the answer.* □*Every one of the contestants knew the answer.* Only the two-word compound is used of things: □*I bought six glasses and every one was cracked.*

evince *Evince* is a formal verb meaning 'show clearly; make apparent': □*Her writing evinces keen perception and skills of observation.* Some careful users believe it should be applied only to qualities, not to attitudes or emotions, although it is generally acceptable in such applications.

ex As a prefix, *ex-* means 'former' or 'outside': □*the ex chairman* □*an ex-directory telephone number.* It is usually attached with a hyphen. The noun *ex*, meaning 'former wife' or 'former husband', should be restricted to informal contexts: □*She had a letter from her ex this morning.*

◆ The preposition *ex* is used in financial contexts in the sense of 'without' or 'excluding': □*ex interest* □*£150 ex VAT.* In commercial contexts it means 'from': □*ex stock* □*ex warehouse* □*ex works.* The phrase *ex stock* is sometimes misinterpreted as 'no longer in stock', through confusion with the prefix *ex-* in the sense of 'former'.

exaggerate This word, meaning 'represent as greater than is true', is sometimes misspelt. Note the *-gg-* and single *-r-*, as in *stagger*.

exalt or **exult**? *Exalt* means 'elevate' or 'praise'; *exult* means 'rejoice' or 'triumph': □*She was exalted to the position of sales director.* □*to exalt a hero* □*He exulted at his success.* □*to exult in victory.*

◆ Both words are formal and more frequently found in their derived forms, such as the adjectives *exalted* and *exultant* and the nouns *exaltation* and *exultation.*

exceed see **ACCEDE OR EXCEED?**

except It is usually better to use *except* rather than *except for*: □*We all went for a walk except Flora.* The exceptions are at the beginning of a sentence: □*Except for Stuart, we are all under 40,* and when a whole statement is being qualified and *except for* means 'if it were not for': □*The room was silent except for the occasional squeak of a pen.*

◆ *Except for* is also used with the meaning 'without; but for': □*I wouldn't have got this far except for your support,* but this is an informal use and some careful users dislike it.

Except as a preposition should be followed by the object form: □*except me* [not *I*] □*except him* [not *he*].

See also **ACCEPT OR EXCEPT?**

exceptional or **exceptionable**? *Exceptional* means 'out of the ordinary;

uncommon': □ *Apart from the exceptional quiet day, we've been kept busy all month*, and 'unusually good': □ *This is an exceptional wine.* In British English *exceptional* is often used of people to mean 'above average; superior; gifted': □ *an exceptional student* □ *an exceptional musician.* In American English, however, *exceptional* is applied to children of both below and above average ability, and is now applied particularly to physically or educationally handicapped children. *Exceptional* should not be confused with *exceptionable*, which means 'objectionable; something to which exception might be taken': □ *His words were not offensive in themselves but there was something in his manner that we found exceptionable.*

exclamation mark Exclamation marks are used to indicate strong feeling or urgency: □ *Hurray!* □ *Go away!* □ *Help!* Exclamation marks may come at the end of a sentence, as a substitute for a full stop, or at the end of a quotation, within quotation marks: □ *'Ouch!' he cried.* Occasionally, they may occur in the middle of a sentence.

◆ Exclamation marks are used after interjections, oaths, and words representing loud noises: □ *Oh!* □ *Ow!* □ *Crash!* □ *Damn!* □ *Gracious!*, after alarms and commands: □ *Look out!* □ *Quiet!* □ *Fire!*, and after insults and curses: □ *You bastard!* □ *Rot in hell!* They are used after various exclamations expressing surprise, indignation, pleasure, or displeasure, often starting with *how* or *what*, and some which have the form of questions: □ *How beautiful!* □ *What fun!* □ *What a mess!* □ *How we laughed!* □ *Aren't you silly!* They are also used after longer sentences when strong emotion is being expressed: □ *I'm absolutely sick to death of the lot of you!*

There are no words or utterances that always need an exclamation mark. The presence or absence of one indicates the intonation required when reading a word or sentence. □ *You can't be serious!* would be read with a different intonation from: *You can't be serious?* or: *You can't be serious.*

Exclamation marks should be used sparingly, and never doubled or trebled. The excessive use of exclamation marks in writing, particularly when used in an attempt to create an atmosphere of excitement, fun, or humour, generally has a negative effect on the reader.

exclamations Exclamations are words, phrases, or sentences that express a strong feeling, such as surprise, anger, shock, excitement, etc.: □ *Gosh!* □ *Get out!* □ *Oh dear!* They are always followed by an EXCLAMATION MARK.

◆ In writing, exclamations are best restricted to direct speech. They may also be used in informal letters, but they become less effective if overused.

exclude or **preclude**? *Exclude* means 'leave out' or 'prevent from entering'; *preclude* is used in formal contexts and means 'make impossible' or 'prevent from happening': □ *A number of items were excluded from the list.* □ *Lack of resources precluded further research.* The two verbs should not be confused.

executive An *executive* is a senior businessman or businesswoman. Many people object to the increasing use of the word in the sense of 'fashionable', 'luxurious', or 'expensive', describing items that are designed to appeal to those who aspire to the social level of an executive or the (supposed) high income of an executive: □ *an exclusive development of executive homes* □ *an executive* *bathroom.*

◆ The adjectival use of the noun to describe items that are intended for or used by the executives of a company is more acceptable: □ *the executive restaurant* □ *an executive jet.*

exercise or **exorcise**? These two words should not be confused. *Exercise* is a noun and verb with various meanings, including 'a set of energetic movements', 'a short piece of school work', and, in formal contexts, 'make use of': □ *You should take more exercise.* □*He exercised his right to remain silent.* The verb *exorcise* means 'expel evil spirits from': □ *The house had been exorcised.*

◆ Both words are sometimes misspelt with *-xc-* in place of the *-x-*. Note also the *-ise* endings: *exercise* is one of the few words in which *-ise* cannot be replaced by *-ize* (see **-IZE OR -ISE?**). *Exorcise* has the variant spelling *exorcize*, but the *-ise* ending is sometimes preferred by those who use the *-ize* form for other verbs.

    The two words are not identical in pronunciation. The unstressed *-or-* in the middle of *exorcise* is pronounced [-or-], whereas the unstressed *-er-* in the middle of *exercise* has the weak sound of the final - *er* of *baker, tumbler,* etc.

exhausting or **exhaustive**? *Exhausting* means 'extremely tiring': □*I find Christmas shopping very exhausting.* It should not be confused with *exhaustive*, which means 'thorough; comprehensive; considering all possibilities': □ *They made exhaustive enquiries but to no avail.* □ *This is an exhaustive study, covering every aspect of the subject.*

exhilarate This word, meaning 'thrill or excite': □*an exhilarating experience*, is sometimes misspelt. Frequent errors include the omission of the *-h-* and the substitution of *-ler-* for *-lar-*.

existential *Existential* usually means 'relating to existence, particularly human existence': □*an existential statement*, or 'grounded in human existence; empirical': □*an existential argument for the existence of God.* It is also sometimes used to mean 'existentialist, based on existentialist philosophy': □*existential angst* □*Sartre's existential theories.*

◆ It is also sometimes used as a vogue word to mean 'referring to a subjective intellectual viewpoint', but such use is generally considered pretentious.

exorbitant This word, meaning 'excessive': □*an exorbitant price to pay*, is sometimes misspelt. There is no *h* in the spelling, unlike *exhilarate.*

exorcise see **EXERCISE OR EXORCISE?**

exotic The original meaning of *exotic* is 'from another country, not native to the place it is found': □ *exotic flowers.* By this definition the potato would be an exotic vegetable in Britain but it is never spoken of as such, because *exotic* is now almost always used with the meaning of 'unusual, excitingly different, interestingly foreign': □*exotic food* □*exotic dances* □*travel to distant exotic lands.*

expatriate The word *expatriate*, meaning 'a person who is living in a country that is not his or her native country', is sometimes misspelt. Note the spelling of the ending of this word: *-iate*, not *-iot* as in *patriot.*

expeditious or **expedient**? *Expeditious* and *expedient* come from the same root, but have quite different meanings. *Expeditious* means 'speedy; efficient': □ *Our courier service is the most expeditious method of sending parcels. Expedient* means 'convenient for a particular situation or aim': □*It would not be expedient to change the law at the present time.*

◆ *Expedient* is associated with practical action and often also a concern for self-interest rather than moral considerations: □ *You can't learn too soon that the most useful thing about a principle is that it can always be sacrificed to expediency* (W. Somerset Maugham, *The Circle*).

explicable In the traditional pronunciation of this word, which means 'able to be explained': □*no explicable reason for their behaviour*, the stress was on the first syllable [*eks*plikǎbl]. It is now more usual and perfectly acceptable to stress the second syllable [ik*splik*ǎbl]. See also STRESS.

explicate *Explicate* means 'explain in detail; analyse and explore the implications of': □ *This series of lectures aims to explicate Kant's critical philosophy and explore its influence on German idealism.* It is a formal word, usually confined to intellectual contexts, and it is pretentious to use it merely as a synonym for *explain.*

explicit or **implicit**? *Explicit* means 'clear; unambiguous, stated or shown in a direct manner': □ *He gave them explicit instructions so there was no question of their making a mistake. Implicit* means 'implied; understood although not directly expressed': □*He detected an implicit criticism in her words,* and 'without reservation; unquestioning': □*I have implicit faith in your organizational abilities.*

◆ Because *explicit* is often used in phrases like: □*explicit scenes of sex and violence*, some people now use the word to mean 'frankly portraying (usually) sexual material': □*It is very explicit and is not suitable for family viewing.* It would be preferable to say *explicitly sexual* or *sexually explicit*, if that is what is meant.

exquisite *Exquisite*, meaning 'very delicate and beautiful': □*exquisite carvings,* may be pronounced in two ways. Some users prefer the stress to fall on the first syllable [*eks*kwizit]. Other users find this pronunciation slightly affected and prefer to stress the second syllable [ik*skwi*zit].

◆ Overuse of this word is disliked by many users.

extant or **extinct**? *Extant*, a formal word, means 'surviving' or 'still in existence': □*Seven of Sophocles' plays are extant.* □*an extant law. Extinct* is usually applied to a species of animal or plant that has died out or to a volcano that is no longer active: □ *The African elephant is in danger of becoming extinct.* The two adjectives are virtually opposite in meaning.

extempore or **impromptu**? These two words have similar meanings but are not quite interchangeable. Both are applied to speeches and performances which are not rehearsed in advance. However, *extempore* suggests that nothing has been memorized or written down beforehand, although the speaker or performer may have thought about the content in advance: □*He never wrote his sermons down but preached extempore. Impromptu* suggests something improvised on the spur of the moment, with no prior notice: □ *She was surprised to be asked to address them but managed a splendid impromptu speech.*

extemporize or **temporize**? To *extemporize* is to act, make a speech, play music, etc., without preparation; to *temporize* (a rarer word) is to gain time by delaying, stalling, or being evasive: □*He extemporized an accompaniment on the piano.* □*She temporized, being unable to think of a reasonable excuse.* The two verbs should not be confused.

◆ Note the spellings, especially the *-or-* in the middle, unlike the *-er* ending of *temper*.

extensive or **extended**? *Extensive* means 'large' or 'widespread'; *extended* means 'lengthened in time or space': □ *an extensive search* □ *an extended contract.* Both adjectives may be applied to the same noun: □ *an extensive discussion* covers a wide range of subjects; □ *an extended discussion* goes on for longer than usual or longer than planned.

exterior, external, or **extraneous**? *Exterior* means 'on the outside; relating to the outside': □ *The house needs some minor exterior repairs.* □ *Beneath his charming exterior he has a cold and selfish nature. External* means 'outwardly visible; suitable for the outside; coming from the outside; not essential': □ *He has a few external injuries.* □ *This ointment is for external use only.* □ *The paper will be marked by the external examiners.* □ *Do not be misled by these external details. Extraneous* means 'from the outside; not essential or relevant to the issue': □ *We try to impart our values to our children but they are influenced by extraneous pressures.* □ *Let's concentrate on the main issue and ignore those extraneous points.*

extinct see EXTANT OR EXTINCT?

extract or **extricate**? Both these verbs have the sense of 'remove' or 'withdraw', but *extricate* is more formal and specifically refers to disentanglement or setting free from a difficult situation: □ *to extract a tooth* □ *to extract information* □ *to extricate oneself from a complex relationship* □ *to extricate a ball from a thorn bush.*

extraordinary This word, meaning 'unusual or exceptional': □ *an extraordinary memory for details*, is sometimes misspelt, the most frequent mistake being the omission of the first *a*. Remember the two elements of the word: *extra* plus *ordinary*.

extrapolate Apart from specialized mathematical uses, *extrapolate* is usually applied to the estimation or prediction of unknown factors by the examination, analysis, and extension of known data and past experience: □ *We can extrapolate from the existing figures and our knowledge of the previous trends in mobility and birth control to produce an estimate of the populations of major cities in twenty years' time.* Careful users, however, are aware that this word is in danger of overuse.

extricate see EXTRACT OR EXTRICATE?

extrinsic see INTRINSIC OR EXTRINSIC?

extrovert or **introvert**? *Extrovert* and *introvert* are terms coined by the psychologist Jung that are now in general use. *Extroverts* are people who are more concerned with their environment than with their own inner selves; they are generally sociable, outgoing, and confident: □ *He is an extrovert and enjoys nothing better than a noisy, crowded party. Introverts* are primarily concerned with their own mental and emotional lives. They are withdrawn and quiet, and prefer reflection to activity: □ *She tends to be an introvert and is happiest in her own company.*

◆ The original spelling was *extravert*, and this is still more frequently used than *extrovert* in American English. The spelling *extrovert* was formed by analogy with *introvert* and is now standard in British English.

exuberant This adjective is sometimes misspelt, a common error being the insertion of *-h-* after the *-x-*. Note also the *-ant* ending.

exult see EXALT OR EXULT?

façade This word, which means 'front', as in: □ *the palace's ornate façade*, is usually spelt with a cedilla under the *c* in British English.

◆ The spelling is sometimes anglicized by dropping the cedilla, but the French pronunciation [fås*ahd*] is retained.

face or **face up to**? Some users object to *face up to* as an unnecessary extension of the verb *face*, meaning 'confront' or 'accept', but there is a slight difference in sense and usage between the two: *to face up to one's punishment* suggests a greater degree of effort and courage than *to face one's punishment*.

◆ The verb *face* often requires qualification: □ *He faced death with equanimity.* □ *They face the future with hope/fear. Face up to*, on the other hand, conveys the subject's feelings of resignation, determination, etc., by implication: □ *I will just have to face up to the prospect of redundancy*.

facetious This word, which means 'jocular' or 'flippant', as in: □ *a facetious remark*, is sometimes misspelt.

◆ It is worth remembering that *facetious* is one of the few words in the English language in which each vowel appears just once and in alphabetical order.

facia see FASCIA.

facile In the sense of 'easily achieved' or 'superficial', the adjective *facile* is often used in a derogatory manner: *facile prose* is produced with little effort and lacks substance; a *facile argument* is glib and lacks sound reasoning.

◆ The usual pronunciation of *facile* is [fasīl], rhyming with *mile*; the alternative pronunciation [fasil], rhyming with *mill*, is an accepted but rarer variant.

facilitate The verb *facilitate* means 'make easier'; it should not be used as a synonym for 'help' or 'assist': □ *His cooperation facilitated our task.* □ *We were helped* [not *facilitated*] *in our task by the information he gave us.*

◆ *Facilitate* is largely restricted to formal contexts.

facility or **faculty**? These two words are sometimes confused in the sense of 'ability'. *Facility* is ease or skill that is often gained from familiarity; *faculty* is more likely to denote a natural power or aptitude: □ *a facility for public speaking* □ *a faculty for understanding complex scientific concepts.*

◆ Both words have additional meanings. A *faculty* is a division of a college or university: □ *the faculty of arts.*

A *facility* provides the means for doing something; with this sense, referring to buildings or equipment, the word is usually found in the plural: □ *conference facilities* □ *sports facilities* □ *facilities for the blind.*

The extended use of *facility* or *facilities* as synonyms for 'premises', 'factory', or 'shop' (or, euphemistically, for 'toilet' – as in: □ *'May I use your facilities?'* – or 'hospital') is avoided by careful users.

faction This word, a blend of *fact* and *fiction*, was coined in the mid-1960s and is used especially by critics to denote a book, play, film, etc., that describes historically true events, using the techniques of fiction.

◆ John Silverlight (*Words*) notes that the term tends to have 'a dismissive quality'. The word is best avoided where there is a risk of confusion with the more generally known sense of *faction*, denoting a minority group within a larger party: □ *the anti-merger faction within the party.*

factitious or **fictitious**? Both these adjectives mean 'not genuine', but they differ in usage and application and should not be confused. *Factitious*, which is largely confined to formal contexts, means 'artificially created' or 'unnatural': □ *factitious enthusiasm. Fictitious* means 'false' or 'invented': □ *a fictitious address.* See also FICTIONAL OR FICTITIOUS?

factor A *factor* is a contributory element, condition, or cause; many people object to its frequent use as a synonym for 'point', 'thing', 'fact', 'event', 'constituent', etc.: □ *A rise in the cost of raw materials and a fall in demand were important factors in the company's collapse.* □ *We must discuss all the relevant points* [not *factors*].

faculty see FACILITY OR FACULTY?

Fahrenheit Note the spelling of this word, which should always begin with a capital letter.

◆ See also CELSIUS, CENTIGRADE, OR FAHRENHEIT?

fail Some people dislike the frequent use of the verb *fail* as a simple negative: □ *Those who fail to pay the tax will be imprisoned.* The principal meaning of *fail* is 'try unsuccessfully (to do something)'; the verb should not be used with reference to something that is deliberately not done.

◆ This misuse of *fail* can lead to ambiguity: □ *The driver of the car failed to stop* may mean that the driver applied the brakes ineffectively, or that he or she made no attempt to stop.

faint or **feint**? *Faint* means 'not clear' or 'not strong'; it is also a noun or verb referring to a brief loss of consciousness. *Feint*, derived from the verb *feign*, refers to an action or movement intended to distract or mislead: □ *On hearing the news she fell to the floor in a faint.* □ *The boxer made a feint with his left fist then struck with his right.*

◆ The confusion between these two words may be due to the use of *feint* by printers and stationers to denote the fine lines on ruled paper. In this sense either spelling is acceptable, *feint* being by far the more frequent.

fait accompli A *fait accompli* is something that has already been done and that therefore cannot be changed: □ *She was afraid he might not agree to her selling the car, so she decided to present him with a fait accompli* [i.e. She did not tell him until she had sold the car].

◆ Of French origin, the phrase is sometimes written or printed in italics in English texts. The plural is formed by adding s to both words: □ *faits accomplis.* The anglicized pronunciation is [fayt ăkomplee].

fallible or **fallacious**? These two adjectives, both of which are formal, are sometimes confused. *Fallible* means 'capable of making an error' or 'imperfect'; *fallacious* means 'containing an error' or 'illogical': □ *All human beings are fallible.* □ *fallacious reasoning.* The adjective *fallible* may be applied to people; *fallacious* is applied only to abstract nouns.

◆ Both adjectives are derived from the Latin verb *fallere* 'to deceive'. Note the spelling of *fallible* and its opposite *infallible*, particularly the *-ible* ending. The first syllable is pronounced [fal-], to rhyme with *pal*, not [fawl-], as in *fall*.

falsehood, falseness, or **falsity**? All three nouns are formal and are derived from the adjective *false*, meaning 'untrue', 'not genuine', or 'disloyal'. *Falsehood* and *falsity* are largely restricted to the first sense: □ *the difference between truth and falsehood/falsity*. A *falsehood* is a lie; a *falsity* is an act of deception. *Falseness* may be used in all three senses, occurring most frequently in the sense of 'disloyalty': □ *the falseness of his statement/name/behaviour*.

fantastic The use of *fantastic* as a synonym for 'excellent' or 'very great' is best restricted to informal contexts: □ *a fantastic holiday* □ *fantastic wealth*.

◆ *Fantastic*, related to the noun *fantasy*, originally meant 'fanciful' or 'unreal': □ *a fantastic tale*. The word should be used with care, however, even in these senses, to avoid misinterpretation through association with its informal usage.

farther, farthest, further, or **furthest**? In the sense of 'more (or most) distant or advanced', as the COMPARATIVE and SUPERLATIVE of *far*, *farther* is interchangeable with *further* and *farthest* with *furthest*: □ *London is farther/further from Manchester than it is from Bristol*. □ *Which of the three can run the farthest/furthest?*

◆ Some users restrict *farther* and *farthest* to physical distance, using *further* and *furthest* for more figurative senses: □ *the farthest country* □ *further from the truth*.

In the sense of 'additional', *further* is more acceptable than *farther*: □ *further supplies* □ *further questions*. *Further* is also preferred in certain set phrases, such as: □ *further education* □ *until further notice* □ *Further to your letter of ....*

Farther is not interchangeable with *further* when the latter is a verb, meaning 'advance' or 'promote': □ *to further one's career*.

fascia The noun *fascia* may be spelt *facia*, without the *-s-*, but many careful users prefer *fascia*, the spelling of the Latin noun from which the word is derived. The word is pronounced [fayshĕr].

fascinate This word, meaning 'attract and capture the interest of', as in *fascinating tales about her experiences in China*, is sometimes misspelt. The most frequent error is the confusion of the *-sc-*.

◆ The term originates from the Latin *fascinare* 'to bewitch'.

fast-forward Some people dislike the use of the word *fast-forward*, normally applied to video recorders, cassette players, etc., as a verb and adjective in figurative contexts: □ *Fast-forwarding through the years* (*Sunday Times*) □ *Fast-forward reviewers dependent on the index* (*The Guardian*).

fast lane The *fast lane* (or *fast track*) is the quickest and most competitive way to success. People who are *in the fast lane* or *in the fast track* or who are described as *fast-lane* or *fast-track* have great ambitions, are involved in a lot of intense hectic activity, and are promoted rapidly: □ *He tells Carol Price how he copes with the critics, the fame, the fortune and a career in the fast lane* (*TV Times*). □ *fast-track executives*. These fashionable modern expressions should not be overused and are best restricted to informal contexts.

◆ The expressions derive from literal senses: the *fast lane* of a motorway is for drivers who want to overtake slower cars and a *fast* horse-racing *track* is one on which the horses race at high speeds.

fast-moving This expression is often used in commerce and advertising to describe products that sell quickly: □ *one of the world's most successful manufacturers and marketers of fast-moving consumer goods* (*Sunday Times*).

◆ *Fast-moving* is also used in similar contexts to create the impression of an enterprising up-to-date company: □ *one of Britain's most innovative and fast-moving building societies*. Although these usages are widely accepted in the business world, they may not be understood by lay people and are best avoided in more general contexts.

fast track see FAST LANE.

fatal or **fateful**? *Fatal* means 'causing death or ruin'; *fateful* means 'decisively important': □ *a fatal illness* □ *a fatal mistake* □ *their fateful meeting* □ *that fateful night.*

◆ Both words are related to *fate*: *fatal* originally meant 'decreed by fate'; *fateful* means 'controlled by fate'.

In its extended sense of 'having momentous and disastrous effects', *fatal* is sometimes interchangeable with *fateful*: □ *a fatal/fateful decision*. *Fatal* should not be used in this sense if there is a possibility of misinterpretation: □ *a fateful journey* may change one's life; *a fatal journey* may end in death.

It is also worth remembering that the consequences of something *fateful* can be good, although the word is very rarely used in this sense.

Fateful may not be substituted for *fatal* in such phrases as: □ *fatal wounds.*

faux pas A *faux pas* is a social blunder: □ *Inviting her ex-husband to the party was a faux pas.*

◆ Of French origin, the phrase literally means 'false step'. It is occasionally written or printed in italics in English texts. The plural form is the same as the singular: □ *faux pas*. The anglicized pronunciation is [fô *pah*].

fax The word *fax*, short for *facsimile* (a system for transmitting documents telegraphically), has established itself in the English language as a noun (referring to the system of transmission, the machine used for transmission, or the document transmitted) and as a verb: □ *by fax* □ *a combined fax, photocopier, and answering machine* □ *fax number* □ *a fax from head office* □ *I faxed the details to the agency.* This abbreviation is acceptable in most contexts.

◆ *Fax* is also used as a respelling of the plural noun *facts*, as in the trade names *Ceefax* and *Filofax*. This usage is less acceptable and may be confused with the sense of 'facsimile'; it is best restricted to informal contexts.

faze or **phase**? *Faze* is a verb, meaning 'worry' or 'daunt': □ *She was not fazed by the accusation. Phase* is a noun, meaning 'stage': □ *the next phase of the development* □ *He went through a rebellious phase in his early teens*, or a verb, often found in the phrasal forms *phase in/out*, meaning 'introduce/withdraw gradually': □ *The benefit will be phased out over a period of five years.*

◆ *Faze* is regarded by some people as an Americanism and is best restricted to informal contexts.

Compare the spelling of *phase*, particularly the *ph* and *s*, with that of *faze*, which is spelt exactly as it sounds.

fearful or **fearsome**? Both adjectives can mean 'frightened' or 'frightening', but *fearful* is the more frequent and principally used in the sense of 'frightened': □ *fearful of what might happen* □ *a fearsome sight.*

◆ Either adjective may also be used in informal contexts as an intensifier, meaning 'extremely bad': □ *I had a fearful cold.* □ *fearsome weather.*

feasible The use of *feasible* to mean 'probable', 'likely', or 'plausible' is avoided by many careful users, especially in formal contexts, where the word is restricted to its original sense of 'practicable' or 'capable of being done': □ *The committee decided that the project was feasible.*

◆ In informal usage, *feasible* now shares the double meaning of *possible*, describing something that can be done or something that might happen, and is therefore equally ambiguous: □ *Raising prices is a feasible solution to the problem.*

Note the spelling of the word: *feasible* ends in *-ible*, not *-able*.

feature The verb *feature* is best avoided where *have, include, display, appear*, etc., may be more appropriate; to *feature* is principally used in the entertainment world: □ *The concert features such stars as George Harrison and Eric Clapton.* □ *a new leisure centre, featuring squash and badminton courts and an indoor swimming pool with flumes.*

◆ Both as a noun and as a verb, *feature* should be reserved for what is prominent, distinctive, characteristic, or important: □ *The spiral staircase is a feature of the house, which also has* [not *features*] *central heating, double glazing, and fitted carpets.*

February This month name causes problems of spelling and pronunciation, the most frequent being the omission of the first *r*.

◆ The full pronunciation of the word is [febrooåri]. In informal speech, however, the simplified pronunciation [febråri] and [febewri] are often heard. The first of these is more acceptable than the second.

feedback The use of *feedback* as a synonym for 'response' or 'reaction' is disliked by some people, who prefer to restrict the term to its scientific or technical usage.

◆ In science and technology, *feedback* is the return of part of the output of a system, device, or process to its input, the most familiar example being the high-pitched whistle heard when the output from a loudspeaker returns to the microphone.

Both in scientific contexts and in general usage, *feedback* often leads to modification: □ *We must try to get as much feedback as possible from the public to see if our ideas are being successfully put over.* □ *Feedback from customers helped us choose the most practical design.*

feel Some people dislike the use of the noun *feel* in the sense of 'impression' or 'quality', as in the phrases *a nice feel about it, a different feel about it*, etc.: □ *The car has a strange feel about it.*

◆ Such expressions may be more succinctly worded by using the verb *feel*: □ *The car feels strange.*

feel-good factor The phrase *feel-good factor* refers to a feeling of optimism amongst the general public about the state of the nation, for example the economic situation: □ *The 'feel-good factor' – as it has come to be known – has plummeted since the time of the General Election in April (Daily Telegraph)*. The phrase is disliked by some people and should not be overused.

feet see FOOT OR FEET?

feint see FAINT OR FEINT?

fellow- The word *fellow* may be combined with other nouns to denote female   134

a person in the same category: *fellow passengers* are the people
with whom one is travelling; *fellow workers* are people who
work in the same place. The two words are sometimes hyphenated in British English: □*fellow-students* □*fellow-sufferers.*
See also HYPHEN 2.
   ◆ A *fellow-traveller* is someone who sympathizes with the aims of a
   political party (especially the Communist Party), but is not actually a
   member of it.
female or **feminine**? The adjective *female* refers to the sex of a person,
animal, or plant; it is the opposite of MALE: □*a female giraffe*
□*female reproductive cells. Feminine* is applied only to people
(or their attributes) or to words (see GENDER); it is the opposite of
MASCULINE: □*feminine charms.*
   ◆ With reference to people, *female* is used only of the childbearing
   sex; it is used to distinguish women or girls from men or boys but has
   no further connotations: □ *There are more female students than male
   students at the college.* See also WOMAN.
   Feminine, on the other hand, may be used of both sexes; it refers to
   characteristics, qualities, etc., that are considered typical of women
   or are traditionally associated with women: □*a feminine hairstyle* □*a
   feminine voice.*
   Feminine is occasionally confused with *feminist,* which refers to the
   movement or belief (*feminism*) that women should have the same
   rights, opportunities, etc., as men, particularly in economic, political,
   and social fields. A *feminist* is a person who supports feminism,
   especially someone who is actively trying to bring about change:
   □*She regards herself as a staunch feminist.*
ferment or **foment**? These two verbs are virtually interchangeable in
the sense of 'to stir up': □*to foment/ferment trouble.*
   ◆ This figurative sense is now the most frequent use of *foment*; in
   medical contexts it retains its original meaning of 'to bathe or apply
   warmth to'.
   The principal meaning of *ferment,* however, is 'to undergo
   fermentation', referring to the chemical reaction involved in the
   formation of alcohol. Its figurative usage is an extension of this sense.
   Confusion may be caused by the identical pronunciation of the two
   words [fĕ*ment*]; they may be more clearly distinguished, if necessary,
   by using the variant pronunciation of *foment* [fŏ*ment*].
fête This word, used as a noun or verb, is usually spelt with a circumflex accent over the first *e* in British English.
   ◆ The word may be pronounced to rhyme with *gate* or *get,* the first of
   these being the more frequent.
fetid or **foetid**? Both spellings of this adjective, which describes something that has a very unpleasant smell, are acceptable. The
spelling *fetid* is preferred in British English and is standard in
American English. See also -AE- AND -OE-.
   ◆ The first syllable of *fetid* may be pronounced with a short *e* [*fet*id] or
   with a long *e* [*fee*tid]; *foetid* is usually pronounced [*fee*tid].
fetus see FOETUS OR FETUS?
few The difference between *few* and *a few* is one of expectation or
attitude rather than number; both expressions mean 'some, but
not many': □*They brought few books.* □*They brought a few
books.*
   ◆ The first of these sentences suggests that more books were
   expected; the second, that no books were expected. The actual
   number of books may be the same in both cases.

Few has negative force, contrasting with *many*; *a few* has positive force, contrasting with *none*: □ *I have many acquaintances but few friends.* □ *There are no pears left, but there are a few apples.*

The same principles may be applied to *little* and *a little*: □ *I added little salt to the soup.* □ *I added a little salt to the soup.*

For the distinction between *(a) few* and *(a) little* see FEWER OR LESS?

fewer or **less**? *Fewer*, the comparative of *few*, means 'a smaller number of'; *less*, the comparative of *little*, means 'a smaller amount or quantity of': □ *fewer cars* □ *less unemployment.* The general rule is that *fewer* (or *few*) is used with plural nouns and *less* (or *little*) with singular nouns, whether the nouns are concrete or abstract: □ *fewer pleasures* □ *few chairs* □ *less wood* □ *little hope* □ *fewer noises* □ *less noise.*

◆ The use of *less* in place of *fewer* occurs widely in informal speech and also, occasionally, in more formal contexts: □ *Please remember, on Tuesdays and Thursdays there are less queues in the afternoon* (Post Office advertisement, *The Guardian*). Many people find this usage ungrammatical and therefore unacceptable in formal speech and writing.

The same principles apply to the phrases *fewer than* and *less than*: □ *fewer than four people* □ *less than a pint of milk.* However, plural units of measurement, time, money, etc., are regarded as singular in such cases: □ *It took less than ten seconds.* □ *He earned less than £50 last week.*

fiancé or **fiancée**? An engaged woman's future husband is her *fiancé*; an engaged man's future wife is his *fiancée*.

◆ The feminine form is sometimes misspelt, the second *e* being dropped in error.

Unlike some other words of French origin, *fiancé* and *fiancée* are always written with an acute accent over the (first) *e*.

The pronunciation of both words is identical [fionsay].

fictional or **fictitious**? *Fictional* means 'of fiction' or 'not factual'; *fictitious* means 'false' or 'not genuine': □ *a fictional detective* □ *his fictional works* □ *a fictitious address* □ *her fictitious companion.*

◆ The two words are largely interchangeable in the sense of 'imaginary', 'invented', or 'not real': □ [of Tom Sharpe's *Porterhouse Blue*] *he reassured dons that the college was fictitious and that no individual tutors had been singled out* (*Sunday Times*).

However, *fictional* is more frequently used with direct reference to stories, novels, plays, etc.; *fictitious* is preferred for deliberate justification that is intended to deceive: □ *Fagin, Scrooge, and other fictional characters* □ *this fictitious character you claim to have met in the park.*

See also FACTITIOUS OR FICTITIOUS?

fifth The second *f* in this word is sometimes not sounded in speech.

◆ The pronunciations [fifth] and [fith] are both acceptable, but some people object to the omission of the second *f*.

fill in or **fill out**? In British English, application forms and other official documents are usually *filled in* rather than *filled out*: □ *Fill in this form and give it to the receptionist.*

◆ *Fill out* is the more frequent verb in American English and is disliked by some British users for this reason alone. It is also considered less appropriate – the blank spaces are to be *filled in*, like holes, to make the form complete. *Fill out* suggests enlargement or extension.

The verb *fill up* is also occasionally used for this purpose.

finalize The verb *finalize* is best avoided where *complete*, *finish*, *conclude*, *settle*, etc., would be adequate or more appropriate: □ *The preparatory work must be finished* [not *finalized*] *as soon as possible.*

◆ The word does, however, serve a useful purpose in some official contexts, combining the senses of 'to reach agreement on' and 'to put into final form': □ *The committee met to finalize arrangements for the prime minister's visit.*

finite verb A *finite verb* is a verb in any of the forms that change according to the person or number of the subject or according to the tense in which the verb is used. □ She *helps.* □ The train *stopped.* □ I *am* cold. □ They *were* leaving. □ He *has* lost his key. The following verbs are not finite: □ *going* to school □ *covered* with dew □ I want to *leave.*

fiord or **fjord**? Both spellings of this word are acceptable.

◆ Derived from the Old Norse *fjörthr*, the word is usually applied to the narrow inlets of the sea along the Scandinavian coastline. *Fjord*, the Norwegian spelling of the word, is preferred by some users.

first or **firstly**? *Firstly* may be used in place of the adverb *first* when enumerating a list: □ *There are three good reasons for not buying the house: firstly, it is outside our price range; secondly, it is too close to the railway; thirdly, the garden is too small.*

◆ The use of *first ... secondly ... thirdly*, in accordance with a former convention that rejected the word *firstly*, remains acceptable and is still favoured by some users. Others, however, find this usage inconsistent, preferring *first ... second ... third* or *firstly ... secondly ... thirdly*, according to the context.

Firstly should not be substituted for *first* in any of its other adverbial uses: □ *When he first* [not *firstly*] *came to this country, he could hardly speak any English.* □ *Janet came in first* [not *firstly*], *followed by the others.*

first name, Christian name, forename, given name, or **baptismal name**? All these expressions are used to denote the name or names borne in addition to one's surname; in British English *first name* is replacing *Christian name* as the most frequent choice: □ *a dictionary of first names.*

◆ The principal objection to *Christian name* is that it is inapplicable, and possibly offensive, to non-Christians. For this reason the expression is generally avoided on official forms. It remains in regular use, however, in informal contexts: □ *We never address our teachers by their Christian names.*

The term *first name* may lead to confusion among people who bear more than one such name: □ *My first name is Leonard but I prefer to be called by my middle name, Mark.*

Forename is widely used on official forms but is rarely heard in informal speech. It is not, however, the ideal solution, being inappropriate for people whose surname precedes their other names (Hungarians or the Chinese, for example). The same problem may occur with the use of *first name.*

Given name is the preferred expression in American English.

The term *baptismal name* is occasionally used in British English; like *Christian name*, it is inapplicable to non-Christians.

fish or **fishes**? The plural of *fish* is *fish* or *fishes*; *fish* is used in a wider range of contexts than the alternative form: □ *Fish live in water and breathe through their gills.* □ *There are five fish in the pond.* □ *Dace, bream, roach, and burbot are all freshwater fishes/fish.*

◆ Considered as a food item, *fish* usually remains in the singular: □*Fish is more expensive than some cuts of meat.*

The plural form *fishes* is most frequently found in technical contexts, often with reference to individual groups or species: □ *The major division in this group is between jawless and jawed fishes* (*Longman Illustrated Animal Encyclopedia*).

fix or repair? Both these verbs are used in the sense of 'mend', *repair* being more formal than *fix*: □*Have you fixed the radio yet?* □*He was ordered to repair the damaged boat.*

◆ The verb *fix* has a number of other meanings, principally 'make firm' or 'fasten'.

fjord see FIORD OR FJORD?

flaccid The formal adjective *flaccid*, meaning soft and limp, may be pronounced [*flak*sid] or [*flas*id]. The first pronunciation is more widely accepted than the second.

flagrant see BLATANT OR FLAGRANT?

flagship The noun *flagship*, which denotes the ship that carries the commander of a fleet, is increasingly used in figurative contexts with reference to the most important of a group of products, projects, services, etc.: □ *The Labour leader, Mr Neil Kinnock, amid uproar, said the Government's flagship* [the community charge] *had been 'badly holed' and was 'sinking fast'* (*The Guardian*). □ *The* [Laura Ashley] *company has recently opened a furnishing flagship store in Madison Avenue, New York* (*The Bookseller*).

flair or flare? The noun *flair* means 'a natural aptitude or instinct'; *flare* is a noun or verb referring to a sudden burst of flame: □*a flair for cookery* □*the flare of the torch.*

◆ The two words are sometimes confused, though not always with the humorous effect of an advertisement from the *Gloucestershire Echo* quoted by 'Peterborough' in the *Daily Telegraph*: □ *Chef/Cook. Really talented person with flare required at Burlington Court Hotel, experience essential.*

Both words have additional senses: *flair* is an informal synonym for 'stylishness'; a *flare* is a light signal used especially at sea. To *flare* may also mean 'to become wider': □*a flared skirt.*

flak The use of *flak* in the sense of 'heavy adverse criticism or opposition' is best restricted to informal contexts: □*Civil-service bureaucrats come in for a lot of flak from the general public.*

◆ The principal meaning of *flak* is 'antiaircraft fire'; of German origin, the word is an acronym of *Flieger* (flyer) *Abwehr* (defence) *Kanonen* (guns).

The spelling *flack*, an anglicized variant, is also occasionally used.

flammable see INFLAMMABLE.

flare see FLAIR OR FLARE?

flaunt or flout? *Flaunt* means 'show off' or 'display ostentatiously'; *flout* means 'treat with contempt' or 'disregard': □*to flaunt one's wealth* □*to flout the rules.*

◆ The use of *flaunt* in place of *flout* is avoided by careful users in all contexts, but the confusion occurs with some frequency: □*If Christians are to campaign against total deregulation* [of the laws on Sunday trading] ... *they must be seen to obey, and not flaunt, the present law* (Jubilee Centre leaflet). This confusion may be due to the sense of openness that is conveyed by both verbs: the open disregard shown by one who *flouts* a law may be seen as an open display, or *flaunting*, of contempt.

flavour of the month The phrase *flavour of the month* is applied to something that is popular or fashionable for a short time: □ *Political correctness is flavour of the month at colleges and universities across the country.* The phrase is often used in a derogatory manner. Its overuse should be avoided.

flee or **fly**? The rather literary verb *flee* means 'run away (from)': □ *You must flee the town.* □ *They have fled.* □ *I fled from the danger.* The verb *fly* is also occasionally used in this sense in literary contexts: □ *You must fly the town,* but is more frequently found in its principal sense of '(cause to) move through the air': □ *Most birds can fly.* □ *The children were flying a kite.* □ *We flew to Paris.*

◆ Note the potential ambiguity of the last example, which can mean 'We travelled to Paris by air' or 'We ran away to Paris', although the second meaning is far less likely.

Both verbs are irregular: *fled* is the past tense and past participle of *flee*; *flew* and *flown* are the past tense and past participle, respectively, of *fly*.

A *fly* is also an insect, but the name of the insect that sounds like *flee* is spelt *flea*, with a final *-a*.

fleshly or **fleshy**? *Fleshly* refers to the body as opposed to the spirit; *fleshy* refers to the flesh of a person, animal, fruit, or plant: □ *fleshly desires* □ *fleshly delights* □ *fleshy thighs. Fleshly* is occasionally used in place of *fleshy*, but some users prefer to maintain the distinction between the two adjectives.

flier or **flyer**? The spellings *flier* and *flyer* are interchangeable in the sense of 'person or thing that flies' and in such compounds as □ *high-flier/high-flyer.*

floor or **storey**? Both these nouns are used to denote a particular level of a building or the rooms on this level. The word *floor* is more frequently used with reference to the interior of the building, *storey* with reference to the exterior or structure. □ *He lives on the fourth floor.* □ *The new office block will be ten storeys high.*

◆ In American English the *first floor* of a building is at ground level. In British English this is known as the *ground floor*, the *first floor* being the floor above (called the *second floor* in American English). This difference in usage does not apply to the word *storey*.

See also STOREY OR STORY?

flounder or **founder**? To *flounder* is to struggle, move with difficulty, or act clumsily; to *founder* is to fail, break down, collapse, or sink. Both verbs can be used literally or figuratively: □ *They floundered in the mud.* □ *She floundered on to the end of the speech.* □ *The project foundered through lack of support.* □ *The ship foundered at the harbour entrance.*

◆ The two verbs are often confused, especially in figurative contexts, *flounder* being used in place of *founder*: □ [of the Stoke Mandeville Wheelchair Games] *future Games could flounder unless £2.5 million is raised* (*Bucks Advertiser*).

The two words are not unrelated: *flounder* is probably a blend of *founder* and *blunder. Founder* itself is ultimately derived from the Latin *fundus* 'bottom'.

flout see FLAUNT OR FLOUT?

flu The word *flu* – the shortened form of *influenza* – is more frequent in general and some technical contexts than *influenza*: □ *She's off work with (the) flu.*

◆ *Influenza* tends to be restricted to very formal contexts. See also ABBREVIATIONS; APOSTROPHE.

Flu should not be confused with the noun *flue*, which denotes a shaft or pipe in a chimney or organ. (*Flue* was once a variant spelling of *flu*, but is no longer used for this purpose.)

fluorescent This word, which is usually applied to light fittings, colours, paint, etc., may cause spelling problems.

◆ Note the order of the vowels in the first syllable (as in *fluoride*), the -*sc*- combination, and the -*ent* ending.

flush see BLUSH OR FLUSH?

fly see FLEE OR FLY?

flyer see FLIER OR FLYER?

fob or **foist**? Both these verbs may refer to the disposal of something unwanted or worthless: □*He fobbed the damaged toys off on Christmas shoppers.* □*She always foists the boring jobs on her assistant.*

◆ The insertion of *off* after *foist*: □ *She always foists the boring jobs off on her assistant*, on the model of *fob off on*, is disliked and avoided by many careful users.

The verb *fob off* may also be used in the sense of 'appease' or 'put off': □ *They fobbed us off with the usual excuses. Foist* may not be substituted for *fob* in this sense.

focus The doubling of the final *s* of the verb *focus* before a suffix beginning with a vowel is optional. Most dictionaries give *focused, focuses, focusing*, etc., as the preferred spellings, with *focussed, focusses, focussing*, etc., as acceptable variants.

◆ The noun *focus* has two plural forms, *focuses* and *foci* [fōsī], the latter being largely restricted to technical contexts. The final *s* of the noun *focus* is never doubled before the plural ending. See also SPELLING 1.

The noun *focus* is often used in the figurative sense of 'centre of attention or activity': □ *The proposed route for the new bypass is the focus of today's meeting.* It is better avoided, however, where *emphasis, object, point*, etc., would be more appropriate: □ *the emphasis* [not *focus*] *on unemployment in the Labour Party's manifesto.*

foetid see FETID OR FOETID?

foetus or **fetus**? There are two possible spellings for this word. The first is more frequent in British English, and the second in American English. See also -AE- AND -OE-.

foist see FOB OR FOIST?

folk The use of the noun *folk* as a synonym for 'people' is generally considered to have slightly old-fashioned and sentimental associations: □*country folk* □*old folk* □*a name that will be familiar to many folk.*

◆ The word is chiefly used adjectivally, in the sense of 'traditional': □ *folk music* □ *folk dance* □ *folklore*.

Like *people*, the noun *folk* is used with a plural verb: □ *Poor folk often dream of a life of luxury. Folks*, the plural form of the word, is largely restricted to informal contexts, in the sense of 'relatives': □ *My folks are coming here tomorrow* or 'people in general': □ *That's all, folks!*

following The preposition *following* may be confused with the present participle; it is best avoided where *after* or *because of* would be adequate or less ambiguous: □ *They went home after* [not *following*] *the party.*

◆ *Following* may serve a useful prepositional purpose in the dual sense of 'after and as a result of': □ *Following the burglary we fitted additional locks to the doors and windows.*

Following is also used as an adjective meaning 'next' or 'about to be mentioned': □ *I left the following morning*. □ *The following tools will be required* ....

foment see FERMENT OR FOMENT?

foot or **feet**? The plural of *foot*, as a unit of measurement, may be *foot* or *feet*: □ *a six-foot fence* □ *five feet tall* □ *nine feet eight inches long* □ *a pane of glass measuring two foot six by four foot three*.

◆ In compound adjectives that precede the noun, the singular form *foot* is always used: □ *a three-foot rod*. The same convention applies not only to other units of measurement but also to such expressions as *a two-car family, four-star petrol, a five-year-old child*, etc., and to compound nouns such as *trouser leg, toothbrush*, etc.

For measurements in feet and inches, *feet* is preferred in more formal and precise contexts: □ *seven feet four inches*. In informal usage the word *inches* is omitted and the plural form *foot* is more frequent: □ *seven foot four*.

In such expressions as *three feet high* or *ten foot wide*, the same distinctions of formality and precision may be applied: □ *The wall must be exactly three feet high.* □ *The room is about ten foot wide.* For larger measurements, such as the height of a mountain, *feet* is preferred in all contexts.

for see BECAUSE, AS, FOR, OR SINCE?

for- or **fore-**? The prefix *for-* usually indicates prohibition (*forbid*), abstention (*forbear*), or neglect (*forsake*). The prefix *fore-* means 'before': □ *foreboding* □ *forecast* □ *forefather*.

◆ Confusion of these two prefixes may lead to spelling mistakes. See also FORBEAR OR FOREBEAR?; FORGO OR FOREGO?

forbade *Forbade*, the past tense of the verb *forbid*, may be pronounced [fŏrbad] or [fŏrbayd].

◆ The first of these pronunciations, rhyming with *mad* rather than with *made*, is the more frequent.

Forbad, an alternative spelling of *forbade*, is always pronounced [fŏrbad].

forbear or **forebear**? *Forbear* is the only accepted spelling of the verb, which means 'to refrain': □ *I shall forbear from criticizing her appearance*. The noun, meaning 'ancestor', may be written *forebear* or *forbear*, the spelling *forebear* being the more frequent: □ *His forebears were wealthy landowners*.

◆ See also FOR- OR FORE-?

The two words are not identical in pronunciation: the verb is stressed on the second syllable [for*bair*]; the noun, whichever spelling is used, is stressed on the first syllable [*for*bair].

forbid or **prohibit**? Both these verbs are used in the sense of 'refuse to allow', *prohibit* being more authoritative than *forbid*: □ *I forbid you to visit her.* □ *The rules prohibit us from visiting her*.

◆ Note the difference in construction: *forbid* is followed by an infinitive with *to*; *prohibit* is followed by an *-ing* form with *from*.

See also FORBADE.

forceful or **forcible**? *Forceful* means 'having great force'; *forcible* means 'using force': □ *a forceful personality* □ *forcible expulsion*.

◆ Something that is *forceful* may be contrasted with something that has little force; something that is *forcible* may be contrasted with something that uses no force.

In many contexts, in the sense of 'powerful' or 'effective', the two words are virtually interchangeable: □ *a forceful/forcible reminder*. (Some people may interpret a *forceful* reminder as one that is powerfully presented, a *forcible* reminder as one that has a powerful effect.)

Forcible should not be replaced by *forceful* where physical force or violence is involved or implied: □ *forcible entry*.

fore- see FOR- OR FORE-?

forebear see FORBEAR OR FOREBEAR?

forego see FORGO OR FOREGO?

forehead This word is usually pronounced [*for*rid], rhyming with *horrid*.
♦ The variant pronunciations [*for*hed] and [*for*red] are widely used and accepted.

forename see FIRST NAME, CHRISTIAN NAME, FORENAME, GIVEN NAME, OR BAPTISMAL NAME?

forever or **for ever**? The adverb *forever* may be written as a single word in all contexts, but some people prefer to use the two-word form *for ever* for the principal sense of 'eternally': □ *We shall remember her for ever.* □ *It will stay there for ever.* □ *Liverpool for ever!*
♦ In the sense of 'continually' or 'incessantly', *forever* is preferred to *for ever*: □ *He is forever changing his mind.*
The use of *forever* to mean 'a very long time' is best restricted to informal contexts: □ *It will take forever to get this carpet clean.*

foreword or **preface**? Both these nouns are used to denote the statement or remarks that often precede or replace the introduction to a book.
♦ *Preface* is the older of the two words and the more frequent; some authorities suggest that a *foreword* is usually written by a person other than the author of the book: □ *The foreword will be written by a distinguished historian.* □ *Have you read the author's preface?*
See also FORWARD OR FORWARDS?; PREFIX OR PREFACE?

forgo or **forego**? *Forgo* is the usual spelling of the verb that means 'do without' or 'give up', *forego* being an accepted variant spelling of this verb: □ *The union will not forgo the right to strike.*
♦ The verb *forego*, meaning 'go before' or 'precede', is most frequently found in the adjectival forms *foregoing* or *foregone*, which have no alternative spellings: □ *the foregoing instructions* □ *a foregone conclusion*. See also FOR- OR FORE-?

formally or **formerly**? These two adverbs are sometimes confused, being identical in pronunciation. *Formally* means 'in a formal manner'; *formerly* means 'in the past': □ *formally dressed* □ *Sri Lanka, formerly called Ceylon.*

former and **latter** Of two previously mentioned items or people, *the former* denotes the first and *the latter* the second: □ *On Monday evening there will be a lecture on local history and a meeting of the chess club: the former will be held in the main hall, the latter in the lounge.*
♦ *The former* or *the latter* should not be used to refer to a single previously mentioned item; the item may be repeated or a simple pronoun, such as *it* or *this*, may be used: □ *The killer left the scene of the crime in a stolen car; the car/this* [not *the latter*] *was later found abandoned in a lay-by.*
Of three or more items or people, the first-mentioned should be referred to as *the first*, *the first-named*, or *the first-mentioned* (not *the former*) and the last-mentioned should be referred to as *the last*, *the last-named*, etc. (not *the latter*): □ *The secretary, the treasurer, and the chairman had a meeting at the house of the first-named* [not *the former*] *yesterday evening.*
For the sake of simplicity or clarity, *the former, the latter, the*

first-named, the last-mentioned, etc., should be avoided if possible by restructuring the sentence or by repeating the names of the items or people concerned.

formerly see FORMALLY OR FORMERLY?

formidable This word may be stressed on the first syllable [*form*idăbl] or the second syllable [förm*id*ăbl].

◆ The first of these pronunciations is the more widely accepted in British English. See also STRESS.

formulae or **formulas**? The noun *formula* has two accepted plural forms, *formulae* and *formulas*.

◆ *Formulae*, pronounced to rhyme with *tree*, is largely restricted to scientific contexts: □ *chemical formulae*.

For other senses of *formula*, the plural form *formulas* is preferred by most users: □ *no easy peace formulas that will resolve the dispute* □ *There are many different formulas for success.*

forte The noun *forte*, denoting a person's strong point, may be pronounced as two syllables [*for*tay] or as a single syllable [fort].

◆ The first of these pronunciations is the more frequent of the two, although the second is closer to the French original (*forte* is an English feminine rendering of French *fort*, meaning 'strong; strength').

The two-syllable pronunciation may possibly have been influenced by the musical term *forte*, meaning 'loud' or 'loudly'. Pronounced [*for*ti] or [*for*tay], this word is of Italian origin.

fortuitous or **fortunate**? *Fortuitous* means 'happening by chance' or 'accidental'; *fortunate* means 'having or happening by good fortune' or 'lucky': □ *a fortuitous meeting* □ *a fortunate child.*

◆ A *fortuitous* occurrence is not necessarily good, but the similarity between the two words, and their frequent confusion, has led to the increasing acceptance of 'fortunate' as a secondary meaning of *fortuitous*. Many people object to this usage, which can result in ambiguity: □ *a fortuitous discovery* may be accidental, or lucky, or both.

Unlike *fortunate*, the adjective *fortuitous* is not applied to people: □ *You were fortunate to find another job so quickly.*

forward or **forwards**? As an adjective, *forward* is never written with a final *s*: □ *forward motion* □ *a forward remark* □ *forward planning.* In some of its adverbial senses, the word may be written *forward* or *forwards*: □ *He ran forward/forwards to greet his father.*

◆ Some users restrict the adverb *forwards* to physical movement in the opposite direction to *backwards*; some use *forwards* in the wider adverbial sense of 'ahead in space or time'; others use *forward* for all adverbial senses of the word.

In idiomatic phrasal verbs, such as *come forward*, *put forward*, *look forward to*, etc., and in the sense of 'into a prominent position', the adverb *forward* is never written with a final *s*: □ *She came forward as a witness.* □ *I put forward the proposals at the meeting.*

The word *forward* is also used as a noun (denoting a player or position in various sports) and as a verb: *to forward a letter.* See also -WARD OR -WARDS?

Forward, pronounced [*for*wărd], should not be confused with *foreword*, pronounced [*for*werd], the introduction to a book. See also FOREWORD OR PREFACE?

founder see FLOUNDER OR FOUNDER?

foyer In British English this word, meaning 'an entrance hall or lobby in a theatre, hotel, etc.', is usually pronounced [*foi*ay].

◆ The pronunciations [*foi*èr] and [*fwah*yay] are also acceptable, the last of these being an approximation of the French original.

fraction Some people dislike the use of *a fraction* to mean 'a small part' or 'a little': □ *We flew there in a fraction of the time it takes to go by sea.* □ *Could you turn the volume down a fraction, please?*

◆ A fraction is not necessarily a small part of the whole: nine-tenths is a fraction.

To avoid possible ambiguity or misunderstanding, a small fraction should be clearly expressed as such: □ *Why dine out when you can eat at home for a small fraction of the cost?* □ *Only a small fraction of the work has been completed.*

See also HYPHEN 6.

fraught *Fraught with* means 'filled with' or 'charged with': □ *fraught with problems* □ *The expedition was fraught with danger.* The use of the adjective *fraught* alone, in the sense of 'tense' or 'anxious', is disliked by some people and is best restricted to informal usage: □ *a fraught evening* □ *He looked fraught.*

-free The adjective *free* is frequently used in combination to indicate the absence of something undesirable or unpleasant: □ *lead-free petrol* □ *rent-free accommodation* □ *additive-free food* □ *pollution-free water* □ *duty-free spirits* □ *a trouble-free life.*

◆ Some careful users object to this usage, preferring to replace some compounds by a paraphrase: □ *accommodation, for which no rent is paid* □ *water that has not been polluted.*

freeze or **frieze**? The verb *freeze* means 'change from liquid into solid form': □ *Water freezes at 0°C.* The noun *frieze* denotes a decorative or ornamental band or strip on a wall: □ *a frieze depicting the history of the town.* The two spellings should not be confused.

◆ *Freeze* is also used figuratively: □ *to freeze prices* □ *a pay freeze.*

friable The adjective *friable*, a technical term, means 'crumbly' or 'easily broken up': □ *friable soil.* It has no etymological connection with the verb *fry.*

-friendly Some people object to the vogue for attaching the adjective *friendly* to an increasing number of nouns, on the model of USER-FRIENDLY: □ *customer-friendly* □ *Readers ... voted M & S Britain's least parent-friendly high street store* (*Daily Telegraph*) □ *ozone-friendly* □ *environment-friendly* □ *dolphin-friendly.*

◆ In the last three examples, *-friendly* has developed the extended sense of 'not harmful': □ *Supermarkets ... realised that green products, from ozone-friendly aerosols to bleach-free nappies, can give a marketing edge* (*Daily Telegraph*).

Environment-friendly has further evolved into the phrase *environmentally friendly*, sometimes hyphenated: □ *The technical problems and costs of the environmentally-friendly route chosen for Chunnel services* (*The Guardian*).

The opposite of *-friendly* is *-hostile* or *-unfriendly*: □ *user-hostile* □ *ozone-unfriendly.*

See also ENVIRONMENT; GREEN.

frieze see FREEZE OR FRIEZE?

frolic The verb *frolic* adds a *k* before suffixes beginning with a vowel: □ *frolicked* □ *frolicking* □ *frolicky.* There is no *k* in the derived adjective *frolicsome.* See also SPELLING 1.

front-line In military contexts, the *front line* is the most advanced or exposed position in a battle. Some people dislike the use of the phrase in figurative or nonmilitary contexts: □ *a front-line* *defender of government policy* □ *front-line inner city areas.*

fuchsia Note the spelling of this plant name, particularly the silent *ch*. It is pronounced [*fewshă*].

◆ The plant name honours the German botanist Leonhard *Fuchs* (1501–66).

-ful For nouns ending in *-ful*, such as *cupful, spoonful, sackful, handful, mouthful,* etc., most users prefer the plural form *-fuls*: □ *two cupfuls* □ *three spoonfuls.*

◆ The plural form *-sful*, as in: □ *three cupsful* □ *two spoonsful*, is regarded by some authorities as rare or old-fashioned and by others as incorrect; it is best avoided.

It is important to recognize the difference between *-ful* and *full*: □ *a bucketful of water* denotes the quantity of water held by a bucket, but not the bucket itself; *a bucket full of water* denotes both the bucket and the water it contains.

The tendency to confuse *-ful* with *full* sometimes leads to the misspelling of both nouns and adjectives, such as *spoonful, doubtful*, etc., with the ending *-ll* (see also **FULLNESS OR FULNESS?**).

fulfil Note the spelling of this word: in British English neither *l* is doubled.

◆ The spelling of the derived noun in British English is *fulfilment*. The spellings *fulfill* and *fulfillment* are almost exclusively restricted to American English. However, the final *l* of the verb is doubled in British English before a suffix beginning with a vowel, as in *fulfilled* and *fulfilling* (see also **SPELLING 1**).

full see **-FUL**.

fullness or **fulness**? Both spellings are acceptable, *fullness* being the more frequent in British English.

◆ In the nouns derived from adjectives ending in *-ful*, the *l* is never doubled: □ *faithfulness* □ *hopefulness.*

full stop The principal use of the full stop as a punctuation mark is to end a sentence that is neither a direct question nor an exclamation.

◆ See also **EXCLAMATION MARK; QUESTION MARK; SENTENCES.**

In creative writing, reference books, etc., the full stop may also mark the end of a group of words that does not conform to the conventional description of a sentence: □ *He had drunk six pints of beer and two whiskies. Two very large whiskies.*

A full stop is often used in decimal fractions, times, and dates: □ *3.6 metres of silk* □ *at 9.15 tomorrow morning* □ *your letter of 26.6.93.* Full stops are also used in some **ABBREVIATIONS.**

A full stop is sometimes called a *stop*, a *point*, or (in American English) a *period*.

See also **BRACKETS; QUOTATION MARKS; SEMICOLONS.**

fulsome *Fulsome praise, fulsome compliments*, etc., are offensively excessive, exaggerated, or insincere.

◆ Derived from *full* and the suffix *-some*, the word originally meant 'abundant'; its derogatory connotations may have developed from a mistaken etymology that associated *fulsome* with *foul*.

fun The use of the word *fun* as an adjective, meaning 'enjoyable' or 'amusing', is disliked by some users and is best restricted to informal contexts: □ *a fun game* □ *a fun person* □ *a fun-size packet of sweets.*

function The verb *function* is best avoided where *work, perform, operate, serve, act*, etc., would be adequate or more appropriate, particularly in general, nontechnical contexts: □ *The machine* *never works* [not *functions*] *properly in very hot weather.* □ *The automatic lock serves* [not *functions*] *as a safety device.*

◆ Some people also object to the excessive use of the noun *function* as a synonym for 'duty', 'role', 'party', etc.: □ *What are the precise functions of bishops and priests in the modern world?*

fundamental The adjective *fundamental* means 'basic', 'essential', 'primary', or 'principal'; it is best avoided where *important, major, great*, etc., would be more appropriate: □ *the fundamental difference between the two systems* □ *a major* [not *fundamental*] *improvement in East-West relations.*

◆ The noun *fundamental*, which is more frequently used in the plural form, denotes a basic principle, constituent, etc.: □ *the fundamentals of the issue.*

funeral or **funereal**? The adjective *funereal* means 'like a funeral; suggestive of death; mournful; gloomy': □ *funereal music* □ *The atmosphere was funereal.* It should not be confused with the noun *funeral* used adjectivally: □ *a funeral service* □ *a funeral cortege.*

fungi *Fungi*, one of the plural forms of *fungus*, may be pronounced to rhyme with *try* or *tree*; the *g* may be hard, as in *gum*, or soft, as in *germ*.

◆ The pronunciations [*fung*gī] and [*fun*jī], rhyming with *try*, are the most frequent. The first of these is closer to the singular form, which has a hard *g* sound. See also SPELLING.

Funguses is an alternative plural of *fungus*.

furore The final *e* of the noun *furore*, meaning 'uproar' or 'craze', can cause problems of spelling and pronunciation.

◆ In British English the *e* is never omitted in spelling; *furor* is the usual American spelling of the word.

Furore is usually pronounced as a three-syllable word stressed on the second syllable [few*ror*i]. It is occasionally pronounced as a two-syllable word stressed on the first syllable [*few*ror]; this is also the pronunciation of the American spelling.

further, furthest see FARTHER, FARTHEST, FURTHER, OR FURTHEST?

Gaelic or **Gallic**? *Gaelic* is a noun or adjective that refers to the Celtic languages of Scotland and Ireland: □ *to speak Gaelic* □ *a Gaelic word*. *Gallic* is an adjective, meaning 'of France or the French': □ *a Gallic custom*.

The pronunciation of *Gaelic* is [*gay*lik], with the alternative pronunciation [*ga*lik] used especially in regions where the language is spoken. This second pronunciation is identical to that of *Gallic*, and so may cause confusion or ambiguity in some contexts.

gaiety *Gaiety*, meaning 'a cheerful and carefree manner' or 'festivity', is sometimes misspelt.

◆ Note the middle vowels *-aie-*.
See also **GAY**.

gallant The adjective *gallant*, 'brave and courageous', as in: □ *put up a gallant fight*, is stressed on the first syllable [*gal*ănt].

◆ The sense 'courteous to women' may have the same pronunciation or may, in rather old-fashioned English, be stressed on the second syllable [gă*lant*].

Gallic see **GAELIC** OR **GALLIC**?

gallop Note the spelling of this verb, particularly the *-ll-* and the final *p*, which is not doubled before *-ed*, *-ing*, etc.: □ *The horse galloped across the field.* □ *galloping inflation.*

gamble or **gambol**? The verb *gamble* means 'take a risk on a game of chance'; *gambol* means 'skip and jump playfully'.

◆ The spelling of these words is sometimes confused although their meanings are very different: □ *He went to the casino to gamble.* □ *lambs gambolling in the fields.*

gaol see **JAIL** OR **GAOL**?

garage This word may be pronounced [*ga*rahzh] or [*ga*rij]. Many users prefer the former pronunciation.

◆ The stress falls on the first syllable in British English, although in American English [ga*rahzh*], the second syllable is stressed.

gases or **gasses**? The plural of the noun *gas* is *gases* or, less commonly, *gasses*.

◆ *Gasses* is also a form of the verb *gas*, meaning 'affect with a gas' or 'talk idly'. See also **SPELLING 1**.

-gate The suffix *-gate*, derived from the *Watergate* affair (a scandal involving Richard Nixon, then President of the USA, in 1972), is sometimes attached to other words to denote a political scandal: □ *Irangate/Contragate* (an American scandal in 1987 involving the sale of arms to Iran and use of the profits to supply arms to the anti-Communist Contras in Nicaragua) □ *Yuppiegate* (a scandal involving five young Wall Street employees in 1986) □ *The 'Dianagate' scandal, the disclosure of intimate tapes of conversations believed to be between the princess and James Gilbey, her close friend* (*Sunday Times*).

◆ Many of these coinages are inevitably ephemeral in usage and are best avoided in formal contexts.

gauge This word, which means 'measure or standard', is frequently misspelt. The *u* comes after the *a* and not before it.

◆ The correct pronunciation is [gayj]. A mispronunciation [gawj] may arise from the unusual spelling.

gay The adjective *gay* is so widely used as a synonym for 'homosexual' that its use in the original sense of 'cheerful', 'merry', or 'bright' may be open to misinterpretation in some contexts: □ *a gay bachelor* □ *a gay party.*

◆ The noun *gay* is principally applied to homosexual men, *lesbian* being the preferred term for homosexual women: □ *a community centre for gays and lesbians.* The noun derived from *gay* in the sense 'homosexual' is *gayness*; in other senses it is *gaiety*.

In the sense of 'homosexual', *gay* is becoming increasingly acceptable in formal contexts.

gender The word *gender* refers to the grammatical classification of nouns as masculine, feminine, or neuter. The use of *gender* as a synonym for 'sex' is avoided by many users in formal contexts: □ *Applications are invited from suitably qualified candidates of either sex* [not *gender*].

◆ The frequency of this usage is attributable both to the use of the word *sex* as a synonym for 'sexual intercourse' and to the association in English grammar between gender and sex.

In many languages all nouns are of masculine or feminine gender: the French word for *flower* is feminine; the Italian word for *carpet* is masculine. In English, however, masculine nouns refer to male people, animals, etc., and feminine nouns to female people, animals, etc.: *king*, *brother*, *drake*, and *bull* are masculine nouns; *heroine*, *queen*, *mother*, *vixen*, and *cow* are feminine nouns.

In some compounds in informal use, *gender* is used instead of *sex*, e.g. *gender-bending*, 'the blurring of the difference between the sexes, for example by transvestism'.

See also SEXISM.

general or **generic**? The adjective *general* has a wide range of meanings, including 'widespread', 'overall', and 'not specialized or specific': □ *general opinion* □ *general knowledge*. *Generic* means 'referring to a whole class or group': □ *a generic term for products that do not damage the environment.*

◆ *Generic* is also used in the sense 'cheaper, because it does not have a trade name': □ *a generic drug.*

genetic, genial see CONGENIAL, GENIAL, CONGENITAL, OR GENETIC?

gentleman *Gentleman* is used as a synonym for 'man' in some formal or official contexts and as a term of politeness: □ *Show the gentleman to his room.* □ *Ladies and gentlemen, may I introduce tonight's guest speaker?*

◆ The noun *gentleman* has connotations of nobility, chivalry, and good manners: □ *a country gentleman* □ *If you were a gentleman you'd stand up and give me your seat.*

See also MAN; WOMAN.

geriatric Many people object to the increasing use of the noun and adjective *geriatric* as derogatory synonyms for 'old person' or 'elderly': □ *These geriatric drivers should be banned from the roads.* □ *The country is governed by a bunch of geriatrics.*

◆ *Geriatrics* is the branch of medical science concerned with the diseases of old age and the care of old people; the use of *geriatric* in such contexts as *the geriatric ward of the hospital* is acceptable to all users.

gerunds see INFINITIVE; -ING FORMS.

get In formal contexts *get* can often be replaced with an appropriate synonym, such as *become, buy, obtain, receive,* etc.: □*It is becoming* [not *getting*] *increasingly difficult to obtain* [not *get*] *impartial advice on financial matters.* However, if the synonym sounds clumsy or unnatural in context, or causes ambiguity, *get* should be retained or the sentence restructured.

◆ The same principles apply to phrasal verbs, idioms, and other expressions containing *get*, such as *get out* (escape), *get by* (survive), *get dressed* (dress), *get well* (recover): □ *I often get up/rise at six.* □ *They will get married/marry in the spring.* See also GOT.

geyser The noun *geyser,* meaning 'hot spring' or 'water heater', is usually pronounced [geezĕr] in British English and [gīzĕr] in American English.

gibe, jibe, or **gybe**? The word *gibe,* or variant spelling *jibe,* means 'jeer or taunt': □*gibes/jibes and insults.*

◆ *Gybe,* sometimes spelt *gibe* or *jibe,* is a nautical term referring to the movement of a ship's sail.

gild or **guild**? *Gild* is a verb, meaning 'cover with gold' (see also GILT OR GUILT?) or 'make golden in colour': □*gilded picture frames* □ *The setting sun gilded the leaves.* *Guild* is a noun, denoting an organization of craftsmen, tradespeople, or other people with similar or related interests: □ *a guild of wine merchants* □*She belongs to the Townswomen's Guild.*

◆ *Gild* is also a rare variant spelling of the noun *guild.*

gilt or **guilt**? *Gilt* is a variant form of the past participle of the verb *gild* (see GILD OR GUILD?) used as an attributive adjective in the sense of 'covered with gold': □*a gilt candlestick.* As a noun, *gilt* denotes the gold or other substance used for this covering: □*Some of the gilt had worn away.* It should not be confused with the noun *guilt,* meaning 'responsibility for wrongdoing': □*a feeling of guilt* □*He admitted his guilt.*

gipsy or **gypsy**? This word, meaning 'wanderer', has two spellings: *gipsy* and *gypsy.*

◆ Some users prefer the *i* spelling, but the *y* spelling indicates the derivation from *Egyptian.* At one time this migrant people was thought to have originated from Egypt.

girl see WOMAN.

given name see FIRST NAME, CHRISTIAN NAME, FORENAME, GIVEN NAME, OR BAPTISMAL NAME?

glacier The first syllable of this word, which means 'a vast area of ice', may be pronounced to rhyme with *mass* [glaseer] or with *clay* [glayseer].

◆ Both pronunciations are acceptable in British English, while [glayshĕr] is the usual American English pronunciation.

glamorous Some people object to the frequent use of the adjective *glamorous* as a synonym for 'beautiful', 'romantic', 'exciting', 'interesting', etc.: □*a glamorous setting* □*a glamorous career.*

◆ The adjective is best restricted to the combination of showy attractiveness, fashion, romance, excitement, charm, and fascination that is known as *glamour*: □*a glamorous film star* □*a glamorous lifestyle.*

The *u* of *glamour* is usually omitted in the adjective *glamorous,* although some dictionaries acknowledge the rare variant spelling *glamourous.*

glasnost *Glasnost*, a Russian word, is used to denote the increased
openness, both in East-West relations and in internal policies
and reforms, that became a characteristic of the Soviet statesman
Mikhail Gorbachev's regime in the mid-1980s: □ *We need to
maintain the atmosphere of openness in our society through
glasnost, democratisation and criticism* (Mr Gorbachev, *The
Guardian*). See also **PERESTROIKA**.
     ◆ The increasing use of the term in the Western world is disliked by
     some people: □ In a rare example of Foreign Office *glasnost*, he was
     invited to spend a week with the British ambassador (*Daily
     Telegraph*). □ *In the spirit of the 'period of glasnost at BT' recently
     announced by its new chairman* (*The Guardian*).

global The adjective *global* is increasingly used with specific reference to ecological or environmental issues that affect the whole
world: □ *global consciousness* □ *global politics* □ *The Clinton
team is likely to be far more European-minded on global issues
such as energy consumption* (*Daily Telegraph*). This usage is
probably influenced by the phrase *global warming* (see
GREENHOUSE EFFECT).
     ◆ The use of *global* in such contexts may cause confusion with the
     more general sense of 'worldwide'.

gobbledygook The noun *gobbledygook* is used in informal contexts to
denote the pretentious or incomprehensible **JARGON** of bureaucrats, especially the circumlocutory language of official documents, reports, etc.
     ◆ The alternative spelling *gobbledegook* is in regular use. See also
     OFFICIALESE.

gobsmacked The adjective *gobsmacked*, meaning 'astounded; flab-
bergasted; speechless with amazement', is a slang term that
should not be used in formal contexts: □ *I was gobsmacked when
I found out how much it would cost.* □ *There was a long pause
(maybe he was gobsmacked at the prospect of me staying at home
for another year), then an unconvincing 'Never mind'* (*The
Guardian*).

god or **God**? A *god* is any of a number of beings worshipped for their
supernatural powers. *God*, written with a capital *G*, is the sup-
reme being worshipped in many religions as the creator and
ruler of all: □ *the god of war* □ *the Greek gods* □ *to believe in God*
□ *for God's sake.*
     ◆ Compounds and derivatives of the noun, whether they refer to
     a *god* or to *God*, are usually written with a lower-case *g*: □ *godly*
     □ *godless* □ *godchild* □ *godsend*. The adjectives *god-fearing* and
     god-forsaken, however, may be written with a capital or lower-case *g*;
     God-forsaken is usually hyphenated.

gold or **golden**? The word *gold* is used adjectivally to describe things
that are made of gold or contain gold: □ *a gold medal* □ *a gold
mine*. The adjective *golden* usually refers to the colour of gold:
□ *golden hair* □ *golden syrup*.
     ◆ In the four examples above *gold* and *golden* are not
     interchangeable; however, *gold* is sometimes used in the sense of
     'gold-coloured' and *golden* in the sense of 'made of gold': □ *fabric with
     blue and gold stripes* □ *a golden necklace.*
     Golden has a number of other meanings, such as 'prosperous':
     □ *golden age*, 'important': □ *golden rule*, and 'fiftieth': □ *golden
     anniversary*. The phrase *golden handshake*, denoting a large sum of

money paid to a retiring employee, has given rise to *golden hello* (a similar sum paid to a new employee), *golden handcuffs* (a payment made to discourage an employee from leaving), and *golden parachute* (a guarantee of compensation if the employee is dismissed or demoted following a takeover). A *golden share* is the control held by a national government in a privatized company in order to prevent the company from being taken over by foreign business interests.

goodwill or **good will**? The term meaning 'a feeling of kindness and concern', as in: □ *a gesture of good will*, can be written either as one word or as two.

◆ Some users prefer the latter, unless the term is being used in the commercial sense when it is written *goodwill*. □ *They paid £12,000 for the goodwill of the shop and £6000 for the stock.*

gorilla see GUERILLA, GUERRILLA, OR GORILLA?

got *Got*, the past participle of *get*, is often superfluous in the expressions *have got* (meaning 'possess') and *have got to* (meaning 'must'): □ *He has (got) grey hair and a small moustache.* □ *They have (got) to win this match to avoid relegation.*

◆ In informal contexts, especially in negative sentences, questions, and CONTRACTIONS, *got* is often retained: □ *We haven't got any milk.* □ *Have you got enough money?* □ *I've got to write to my brother.*

In some contractions, the occasional omission of *got* may cause confusion: □ *She's a cat* may mean 'she is a cat' or 'she has a cat'; *She's got a cat* is unambiguous.

Used alone, *got* is the past tense of *get*; it should not be used in place of *have* or *have got*: □ *They have/have got* [not *They got*] *three children.* □ *I got a new car last week.*

Gotten is an American variant of the past participle *got*; in British English its use is restricted to such expressions as *ill-gotten gains*.

gourmand or **gourmet**? A *gourmand* enjoys the pleasurable indulgence of eating, with or without regard to the quality of the food. *Gourmet*, the more common and also more complimentary of the two terms, refers only to a connoisseur of fine food or drink: □ *The size of the meals will satisfy the gourmand; their quality should please the most discriminating gourmet.* To avoid ambiguity, *gourmand* may be replaced by *glutton* in the sense of 'one who eats greedily or to excess'.

◆ Many people object to the increasing use of *gourmet* to describe restaurants, meals, etc., in which the food is elaborate and expensive but not necessarily of high quality.

Gourmand is usually pronounced [*goor*mănd] or [*goor*mon(g)]; *gourmet* is pronounced [*goor*may]. Both words are occasionally stressed on the second syllable.

government In the sense of 'the group of people who govern a country, state, etc.', *government* may be a singular or a plural noun: □ *The government is blamed for the rise in unemployment.* □ *The government have rejected the proposal.*

◆ See also COLLECTIVE NOUNS; SINGULAR OR PLURAL?

graceful or **gracious**? *Graceful* refers to movement, actions, forms, shapes, etc., that have *grace*, in the sense of beauty, charm, or elegance: □ *a graceful dance*. *Gracious* means 'kind', 'courteous', 'benevolent', or 'compassionate': □ *a gracious gift*.

◆ The two words are not interchangeable, although they may occasionally qualify the same noun: □ *a graceful gesture* is a beautiful or elegant movement; □ *a gracious gesture* is an act of kindness or courtesy.

The adjective *gracious* may also occasionally imply condescension: □*She thanked the waiter with a gracious smile.* In such expressions as *gracious living*, the word conveys an impression of luxury, comfort, elegance, and indulgence.

graffiti Nowadays very few people still object to the widespread use of *graffiti* as a singular noun: □*Graffiti covers the walls of the community centre.* □*Some of this graffiti is quite obscene.*

◆ *Graffito*, the singular of this Italian borrowing, meaning 'a little scratch', is used only very occasionally to refer to a single inscription or drawing: □ *The first graffito appeared the day after the room was repainted.*

Note the spelling of the word, particularly the *-ff-* and single *-t-*.

grammar The word *grammar*, which denotes the rules of a language or a type of school: □*Latin grammar* □*a grammar school*, is often misspelt. The most frequent error is the substitution of *-er* for the *-ar* ending. Note also the *-mm-*.

grand- or **great-**? Both these prefixes are used to denote family relationships that are two or more generations apart. Either prefix may be used for the aunts and uncles of one's parents and the children of one's nephews and nieces, *great-* being more frequent than *grand-*: □*great-niece* □*grandnephew* □*great-uncle* □*grandaunt*.

◆ The prefix *grand-* is always used for the parents of one's parents and the children of one's children: □ *granddaughter* □ *grandfather* □ *grandchild* □ *grandma*.

The prefix *great-* is also used for the parents of one's grandparents and the children of one's grandchildren: □ *great-grandmother* □ *great-grandson* □ *great-grandparent*. (The father of one's *great-grandfather* is one's *great-great-grandfather*, and so on.)

grass roots Some people object to the widespread use of this term both in political or industrial contexts and as a noun meaning 'the fundamental level' or as an adjective 'fundamental' or 'basic': □*the grass roots of the problem* □*at the grass-roots level* □*support for the party at the grass roots* □*grass-roots opinion.*

◆ The noun *grass roots* came originally from mining in the USA, referring to the soil immediately below the surface. It was subsequently applied to the ordinary people as opposed to the political leaders of society. The *grass roots* of a trade union or other organization are its rank-and-file members.

gratuitous The adjective *gratuitous* is most frequently used in the sense of 'unwarranted' or 'uncalled-for': □*gratuitous violence* □*gratuitous criticism.*

◆ The original meaning of the word is 'free' or 'given without payment'.

gravitas The noun *gravitas*, meaning 'serious or solemn nature or manner; weight, substance, or importance', is a vogue word that is increasing in frequency: □ *The most mentioned attribute which best equips him* [Peter Sissons] *for sustained political encounters is the gravitas he clearly was born with* (*The Guardian*). □ [Jonathan] *Dimbleby is felt to be a safe pair of hands, with sufficient stature to give the book gravitas* (*Daily Telegraph*). Some users consider the word to be a pretentious and unnecessary synonym for 'seriousness'.

◆ The implication, since this is a Latin word, is the high solemnity of the mythical ancient Roman official.

gray see GREY OR GRAY?

graze The verb *graze*, traditionally applied to animals in the sense of 'eat', is increasingly used in human contexts with three specific meanings: 'eat small amounts of food throughout the day', 'eat food from supermarket shelves while shopping', and 'eat standing up'. The first sense is the most frequent in British English: □ *doing away with family meals and replacing them, as the report suggests, with 'grazing ... eating'* (*Daily Telegraph*).

◆ The second and third senses are largely restricted to American English but are becoming increasingly common in British English.

great- see GRAND- OR GREAT-?

Great Britain see BRITAIN.

Greek or **Grecian**? The adjective *Greek* means 'of Greece, its people, or its language'; *Grecian* means 'in the simple but elegant style of classical Greece': □ *Greek history* □ *a Grecian vase.*

◆ The adjective *Grecian* was formerly applied to the art, architecture, literature, culture, etc., of ancient Greece; in these senses it has been largely superseded by *Greek*.

The noun *Greek* denotes a native or inhabitant of Greece; a *Grecian* is a scholar of classical Greek language or literature.

green The adjective *green* is becoming overused in its application to any product, policy, or ideology that is connected with the protection of the environment: □ *green consumerism* □ *green issues* □ *to buy green* □ *to go green* □ *Ministers moved ... to restore the Government's 'green' credentials by introducing a range of environmental safeguards into plans to sell the electricity and water industries* (*Daily Telegraph*). □ *The Whole Thing is a mail order company dedicated to providing a wide range of over 150 of the greenest products available* (advertisement, *The Guardian*).

◆ Usage is currently in flux regarding whether the word when used as a noun is spelt with a capital or lower-case initial letter. Spelt with a lower-case or capital initial letter, the noun denotes a person who supports the protection of the environment. Spelt with a capital *G-*, the word specifically denotes a political party that is chiefly concerned with the protection of the environment: □ *to vote Green* □ *The Greens have shaken Britain's three big parties by winning 2.25m votes and 15% of the poll in the European elections* (*Sunday Times*).

A *green field site* is a rural undeveloped site, often near a town or city, that has not been designated as part of a green belt and so is available for development, e.g. for technical parks or starter homes.

The verbal noun *greening* has been coined to denote the process of removing environmentally harmful substances: □ *the greening of the city streets* □ *the greening of the washing machine* (a reference to 'environment-friendly' detergents).

See also ENVIRONMENT; -FRIENDLY.

greenhouse effect The *greenhouse effect* is the warming of the earth's atmosphere (*global warming*) caused by an accumulation of gases that trap the radiated heat from the sun: □ *Flood defences along Britain's coasts will fail to prevent large tracts of farmland from being flooded when sea levels rise because of the greenhouse effect* (*Daily Telegraph*). The gases thus function like the glass in a greenhouse, hence the name. Sometimes called *greenhouse gases*, they include carbon dioxide produced by the burning of coal, oil, stubble, and the tropical rainforests that would normally absorb carbon dioxide from the air.

grey or **gray**? This word can be spelt with an *e* or an *a*, although the former is far more frequent in British English.

◆ *Gray* is standard in American English.

grievous The correct pronunciation of this word, most frequently encountered in the phrase *grievous bodily harm*, is [greevŭs], not [greeviŭs]. Note the spelling of the word, particularly the order and position of the vowels.

grill or **grille**? A *grill* is 'a framework of bars used for cooking food'. A *grille* is a grating over a window or door.

◆ These words are occasionally confused, especially as *grille* can also sometimes be spelt *grill*.

grisly or **grizzly**? The spellings of these words may sometimes be confused. *Grisly* means 'gruesome'; *grizzly* means 'partly grey': □ *a grizzly bear*, or 'whining fretfully': □ *a grizzly toddler*.

growth The word *growth* is used adjectivally, in the sense of 'rapidly developing or increasing', in economic and commercial spheres: □ *a growth industry* □ *a growth economy*.

◆ In other contexts it is often better replaced by a paraphrase: □ *Canoeing is a growth sport* could well be changed to: *The sport of canoeing is increasing in popularity.*

guarantee This word, which is often misspelt, means 'an assurance that a certain agreement will be kept': □ *The washing-machine was still under guarantee.*

◆ It is worth remembering that the vowels of the first syllable are like those in *guard*: □ *A guarantee guards the rights of the consumer.*

guerilla, guerrilla, or **gorilla**? *Guerilla/guerrilla* means 'fighter within an independent army': □ *a guerrilla war*; a *gorilla* is a large ape. The spellings *guerilla* and *guerrilla* are both acceptable, although the latter is preferred by some users since it derives from the Spanish *guerra* 'a war', with *-rr-*.

◆ The usual pronunciation of both words is [gĕrilē]. However, *guerilla/guerrilla* may be pronounced [gerilē] to make it distinct from *gorilla* [gĕrilē].

guest The use of the word *guest* as a verb, in the sense of 'be a guest (on a television or radio show)', is disliked by some users and is best restricted to informal contexts: □ *She guested on his chat show last month.*

◆ Unlike *host*, the verb *guest* is not used outside the entertainment industry: □ *He was a guest at our wedding* [not *He guested at ...*].

GUI The acronym *GUI*, used in computing, is short for *graphical user interface*, an on-screen interface using visual icons: □ *The increasing success of the so-called 'graphical user interfaces' or GUIs, which are supposed to be making using PCs easy and 'intuitive'* (*Daily Telegraph*).

◆ *GUI* is usually pronounced [gooi].

guidelines Some people object to the increasing use of the plural noun *guidelines* in place of *advice, policy, instructions, rules*, etc.: □ *New guidelines to establish minimum sentences in rape cases* (*The Guardian*). □ *The series is within the BBC's guidelines on violence* (*Daily Telegraph*).

◆ The noun *guidelines*, which is rarely used in the singular, is now usually written as one word; the hyphenated form *guide-lines* is an accepted but less frequent variant.

guild see GILD OR GUILD?

guilt see GILT OR GUILT?

gut The use of the word *gut* as an adjective, meaning 'instinctive', 'strong', 'basic', or 'essential', is best restricted to informal contexts: □ *a gut reaction* □ *a gut feeling* □ *gut issues*.

gybe see GIBE, JIBE, OR GYBE?

gymkhana This word, meaning 'competition for horses and their riders', is sometimes misspelt.

◆ It is worth remembering that *gym* is spelt as in *gymnastics*, and *khana* as in *khaki*.

gynaecology This word, meaning 'the branch of medicine concerned with women's diseases', is frequently misspelt. Note the *y* and, in British English *ae*, or American English *e*. See also -AE- AND -OE-.

◆ This word is pronounced [gīnīkolōji].

gypsy see GIPSY OR GYPSY?

haemorrhage This noun, meaning 'immense loss of blood', is often misspelt. Note the *-rrh-* and the British English *-ae-*, which is reduced to *-e-* in American English (see *-AE-* AND *-OE-*).

hail or **hale**? The noun *hail* means 'frozen rain'; the verb *hail* means 'call' or 'be a native of': □ *hail a taxi* □ *She hails from Scotland.* *Hail* should not be confused with *hale*, meaning 'vigorous and healthy': □ *hale and hearty.*

half Although *half* is a singular noun, it is followed by a plural verb when it denotes a number rather than an amount: □ *Half of the books are missing.* □ *Half of the water has evaporated.* In most cases the word *of* is optional: □ *Give him half (of) the money.*

◆ Such expressions as *a half-hour* and *half an hour, a half-dozen* and *half a dozen, a mile and a half* and *one and a half miles,* etc., are equally acceptable in most contexts. However, the insertion of an extra indefinite article before *half an hour, half a dozen,* etc., is avoided by careful users. See also **HYPHEN 4.**

half- or **step-**? One's *step-parent* (*stepmother* or *stepfather*) is the new spouse of a divorced or widowed parent. Any children of this step-parent by previous partners become one's *stepbrothers* or *stepsisters.* Any children of one's father or mother by this step-parent (or any other partner) are one's *half-brothers* or *half-sisters.*

◆ Confusion arises because half-brothers and half-sisters are usually the offspring of one's stepmother or stepfather. A person may have both half-brothers (or half-sisters) and stepbrothers (or stepsisters).

Note that *half-* is always attached with a hyphen in this sense, whereas *step-* is attached without a hyphen (except in the case of *step-parent*).

hallo see **HELLO, HALLO, OR HULLO?**

handful Most users prefer to form the plural *-fuls*: □ *handfuls.*

◆ See *-FUL.*

handicap The final *p* of the word *handicap* is doubled before a suffix beginning with a vowel: □ *handicapped* □ *handicapping.* See also **SPELLING 1.**

hands-on This expression refers to practical or personal involvement in a task: □ *This is not a desk job. It is a 'hands-on' sales role* (*Daily Telegraph*). □ *The Prime Minister returned to London last night to resume hands-on control of the Gulf crisis* (*The Guardian*).

◆ The term *hands-on* is often used in the expression *hands-on experience,* practical experience 'in ... learning – where students can obtain real experience of possible future jobs – or in business, where there is a similar implication of rolling up one's sleeves and getting involved, rather than simply reading or talking, or in a variety of situations where the practical is seen as improving on the merely theoretical' (Jonathon Green, *Dictionary of Jargon*).

hangar or **hanger**? These words are often misspelt. A *hangar* is a building for storing aircraft; a *hanger* is an apparatus on which articles can be hung: □ *coat hanger*.
◆ To avoid mistakes, remember the *a* in *aircraft* and in *hangar*.

hanged or **hung**? *Hung* is the past tense and past participle for most senses of the verb *hang*; *hanged* is restricted to the meaning 'suspended by the neck until dead', in the context of capital punishment or suicide: □ *He hung his coat on the peg*. □ *The picture was hung up in the hall*. □ *The conspirators were hanged for treason.* □ *Her father hanged himself.*

hanger see HANGAR OR HANGER?

hang-up The noun *hang-up* is an informal name for a mental or emotional problem or inhibition: □ *She's got a hang-up about answering the phone*. The word should not be used in formal contexts.
◆ *Hang-up* is usually hyphenated in British English but may be written as one unhyphenated word in American English. The plural of *hang-up* is *hang-ups*.

hara-kiri *Hara-kiri* is the traditional spelling of this Japanese term, which refers to a ritual act of suicide by cutting open the abdomen: □ *to commit hara-kiri*. It is pronounced [harrǎ kirri].
◆ The variant spelling *hari-kari*, pronounced [harri karri] or [hari kari], is best avoided.

harangue This word, which means ' a vehement and lengthy speech', as in: □ *a long harangue about the state of the economy*, is sometimes misspelt.
◆ The *-gue* ending is the same as in *meringue*.

harass This word, meaning 'trouble persistently', is spelt with a single *-r-* and ends in *-ss*. It is pronounced [harǎs]. The American pronunciation [hǎras] has recently come into British English but is disliked by some people.
◆ Note that the same spelling rules apply for *harassment*.

hardly In the sense of 'only just' or 'almost not' the adverb *hardly*, like its synonyms *scarcely* and *barely*, is used with negative force; it is unnecessary to add another negative to the clause or sentence: □ *I can* [not *can't*] *hardly see you*. See also DOUBLE NEGATIVE.
◆ Careful users avoid using *than* in place of *when* in the constructions *hardly ... when*, *scarcely ... when*, or *barely ... when*: □ *She had hardly begun to speak when* [not *than*] *he interrupted her*. □ *Scarcely had they reached the end of the road when* [not *than*] *the rain began*. This confusion may be due to the use of *than* in the construction *no sooner ... than*: □ *No sooner had I stepped into the bath than* [not *when*] *the doorbell rang*.
Hardly is rarely used as the adverbial form of the word *hard*, which functions both as an adjective and as an adverb: □ *a hard surface* □ *to work hard* □ *hard-earned money*.

have got (to) see GOT.

he see HE OR SHE.

headed for or **heading for**? The phrase *be headed for* is sometimes wrongly used in place of *be heading for*. When the verb *head* is used intransitively, the correct phrase is *be heading for*: □ *We were heading* [not *headed*] *for Southampton*. □ *The government is heading* [not *headed*] *for defeat.*

head up Many people dislike the use of this phrasal verb in place of the simpler *head*, meaning 'lead' or 'be in charge': □ *to head up a team of workers*.

healthful or **healthy**? *Healthy* can mean 'having good health' or

'promoting good health': □*a healthy child* □*a healthy diet.*
Healthful is a less frequent synonym of *healthy* in both these
senses, but in modern usage it is largely restricted to the sense of
'promoting good health': □*foods that are both healthful and rela-*
tively inexpensive.

heaved or **hove**? *Heaved* is the usual form of the past tense or past participle of the verb *heave*: □*He heaved the crate up the steps.*
□*She heaved a sigh of relief. Hove* is an archaic variant of *heaved*
that is used facetiously or in nautical contexts, in the past tense
or past participle of *heave to*, meaning 'stop', and *heave into*
sight (or *view*), meaning 'appear': □*We hove to for lunch.* □*A*
ship hove into sight.

◆ The phrase *heave into sight* (or *view*) is also used in non-nautical
(but fairly literary) contexts, usually in the past tense: □*As they*
rounded the corner the house hove into view.

heavy-duty The term *heavy-duty* should be restricted to articles,
materials, etc., that are designed to withstand hard wear or frequent use: □*heavy-duty overalls* □*heavy-duty plastic sheeting.*

◆ In other contexts the adjectives *tough* or *strong* may be adequate
or more appropriate.

height This word refers to the distance from the base to the top of an
object or person: □*the height of the mountain.* It also means
'most intense point': □*at the height of summer. Height* is sometimes misspelt with the ending *-th*, on the model of *length,*
width, etc.

heinous This word, meaning 'extremely evil': □*a heinous crime*, is
often misspelt and mispronounced. Note the *ei* spelling and the
stress on the first syllable [*hay*nĕs].

◆ The pronunciation [*heen*ĕs] is also acceptable but [*hī*nĕs] is best
avoided.

hello, hallo, or **hullo**? This word of greeting has various spellings
which are all acceptable. The first spelling is probably the most
frequent in contemporary usage.

help Many people object to the phrases *cannot/can't/could not/*
couldn't help but, as in: □*I couldn't help but laugh*, preferring
either *I couldn't help laughing* or, less frequently, *I couldn't but*
laugh.

◆ The idiomatic *cannot/can't/could not/couldn't help* construction,
where *help* means 'refrain from', is followed by a present participle.
See also **BUT**.

In the sense of 'assist' or 'contribute' *help* is usually followed by a
direct object and/or an infinitive, with or without *to*: □ *These pills will*
help you (to) sleep. □ *They all helped (to) tidy the house.* Some users
prefer to retain *to* in the absence of a direct object: □ *This money will*
help to pay for the new car. □ *This money will help us pay for the new*
car.

hemi- see **DEMI-, HEMI-,** OR **SEMI-**?

hence *Hence* means 'from this time' or, more rarely, 'from this place';
it is therefore unnecessary to precede the adverb with *from*:
□ *The concert will begin three hours hence.*

◆ The use of *hence* in the sense of 'from this place' is largely restricted
to very formal or archaic contexts. See also **THENCE**.

Hence is also used to mean 'for this reason' or 'therefore': □ *My route*
is more direct, and hence faster, than yours. □ *Her father drowned at*
sea, hence her reluctance to go sailing. In the second of these
examples, note that *hence* is often followed by a noun rather than a

verb; to replace *hence* with *therefore* would involve rewording the clause: □ *... therefore she is reluctant to go sailing.*

he or she The use of *he/him/his* as pronouns of common gender, with reference to a person of unspecified sex, is widely considered to be misleading and sexist, as is the use of *she/her/hers* for the same purpose with reference to jobs or activities that are traditionally associated with women: □ *The candidate must pay his own travelling expenses.* □ *This book will be of great value to the student nurse preparing for her examinations.* The most acceptable substitutes for these pronouns are the cumbersome and pedantic expressions *he or she, he/she, (s)he, his or her,* etc.: □ *If a child is slow to learn, he or she will be given extra tuition.* □ *The candidate must pay his or her own travelling expenses.*

In some cases, the problem may be avoided by restructuring the sentence, making the subject plural, or both: □ *Travelling expenses must be paid by the candidate.* □ *Candidates must pay their own travelling expenses.* □ *Children who are slow to learn will be given extra tuition.*

◆ Various attempts to coin new pronouns, such as *s/he, tey, hesh,* etc., have met with little success; it has also been suggested that the pronoun *it,* already used of babies, should be extended to human beings of all ages. Some consider that the solution is already in the making, with the increasing use of *they, them, their,* and *theirs* as singular pronouns (see **THEY**).

hereditary or **heredity**? *Hereditary* is an adjective, meaning 'genetically transmitted' or 'inherited'; *heredity* is the noun from which it is derived: □ *The disease is not hereditary.* □ *Is intelligence determined by heredity or environment?*

◆ The two words are sometimes confused, being similar in pronunciation (the *a* of *hereditary* is often elided in speech).

heritage or **inheritance**? The noun *heritage* most frequently refers to cultural items, natural features, or traditions of the past that are handed down from generation to generation and are considered to be of importance to modern society: □ *The pyramids are part of Egypt's heritage.* An *inheritance* is money or property that an heir receives from an ancestor who has died: □ *He squandered his inheritance.*

◆ *Inheritance* may also refer to the inheriting of physical or mental characteristics from one's parents. In its broader sense, *heritage* denotes anything that one inherits at birth; it is thus interchangeable to some degree with *inheritance*: □ *the family's rich intellectual heritage/inheritance.*

Some people dislike the indiscriminate application of the word *heritage* to any historical event, building, custom, etc., especially as a means of exploiting its commercial potential in the tourism industry: □ *heritage tours of the docklands.* □ *Tourism and the heritage industry inevitably distort the past by making imitations of historic buildings or changing their use* (*The Guardian*).

hesitance, hesitancy, or **hesitation**? The nouns *hesitance* and *hesitancy* refer to the state of being hesitant (i.e. wavering, irresolute, indecisive, reluctant, etc.). *Hesitancy* is the more frequent of these synonyms: □ *There was a note of hesitancy in her voice.* The noun *hesitation* refers to the act or an instance of hesitating: □ *after a slight hesitation* □ *He accepted the offer without hesitation.*

hiatus The noun *hiatus* is best avoided where *gap, break,* or *pause* would be adequate or more appropriate: □ *a hiatus in our discussions.*

hiccup or **hiccough**? Both spellings of this word are acceptable but *hiccup* is the more frequent.

◆ The word refers to a sudden intake of breath resulting in a characteristic sound. It has the additional informal sense of 'small problem': □ *The project is going well apart from a few minor hiccups.*

hidden agenda The phrase *hidden agenda* is generally used in a derogatory manner, referring to a secret intention or ulterior motive concealed behind a public statement, political policy, etc.: □ *Ministers have assured their critics that there is no hidden agenda.* The phrase is regarded by some people as a vogue cliché and should not be overused.

high or **tall**? Both these adjectives mean 'of greater than average size, measured vertically', but there are differences of sense, usage, and application between them: □ *a high mountain* □ *a tall woman.*

◆ The adjective *tall* is largely restricted to people, animals, and plants and to things that are narrow in proportion to their height; it is the opposite of *short*: □ *a tall tree* □ *a tall chimney. High* has the additional meaning of 'situated at a great distance above the base'; it is the opposite of *low*: □ *a high branch* □ *a high shelf.*

The two adjectives may be applied to the same noun in different senses: *a high window* is a long way from the floor; *a tall window* is relatively large from top to bottom. The size of the *high* window and the position of the *tall* window are unspecified.

Like other adjectives of magnitude (*long, deep, wide,* etc.), *high* and *tall* are used in combination with specific measurements regardless of size: □ *He is only five feet tall.* □ *The wall is less than one metre high.*

high-profile see PROFILE.

hijack The verb *hijack*, meaning 'seize control of (a vehicle in transit)', is increasingly used in figurative contexts: □ *The plane has been hijacked by terrorists.* □ *One of their most successful authors has been hijacked by a rival company.*

◆ *Highjack* is a rare variant spelling of the verb.

him or **his**? see -ING FORMS.

Hindi or **Hindu**? *Hindi* is a language of India; *Hindu* is a noun or adjective relating to the Indian religion of Hinduism: □ *She speaks Hindi.* □ *He is (a) Hindu.* The two words should not be confused.

hire or **rent**? Both verbs mean 'have or give temporary use of something in return for payment': □ *He hired a suit for the wedding.* □ *We rented a flat in the town centre.* □ *They hire/rent (out) cars at competitive rates.*

◆ The basic difference in sense between the two verbs concerns the length of the period of temporary use and, to some extent, the nature of the item in question: a room or building may be *hired* for a party or conference or *rented* for a longer period of time. Clothes are *hired* (usually for a single occasion), not *rented*; television sets are *rented* (sometimes for a number of years), not *hired*. Cars may be *hired* or *rented*.

The verbs *let* and *lease* are also used in this context, usually with reference to buildings or land: □ *She lets the cottage to tourists.* □ *Room to let.* □ *They leased the land from the council.* □ *The council leased them the land.* □ *All the company cars are leased.* The subject of *let* is usually the owner of the property rather than the person who pays for temporary use.

his or her see HE OR SHE.

historic or **historical**? The adjective *historic* relates to events, decisions, etc., that are memorable or important enough to earn a place in recorded history; *historical* relates to the study of history and to the past in general: □ *a historic election* □ *historical records* □ *The king's visit to the town was not a historic occasion, it is of historical interest only.* The adjective *historical* is also applied to people, events, etc., that existed or happened in fact, as opposed to fiction or legend: □ *a historical character.*
◆ The two adjectives are not fully interchangeable, although both may be applied to the same noun. *A historic voyage*, for example, is contrasted with one that is of no lasting significance, whereas *a historical voyage* is contrasted with one that never took place: the voyage of Christopher Columbus to the New World was both *historic* and *historical*. See also A OR AN?
Some people dislike the overuse of *historic* with reference to events that are of ephemeral significance: □ *Western Samoa produced the first major upset of the World Cup with a historic victory over Wales ... yesterday (The Guardian).*

histrionic or **hysterical**? The adjectives *histrionic* and *hysterical* are both used of emotional outbursts but should not be confused: *histrionic* behaviour is a display of insincerity, being deliberately exaggerated for melodramatic effect; *hysterical* behaviour is the result of an involuntary loss of control.
◆ The same distinction may be applied to the nouns *histrionics* and *hysterics*, both of which are used with plural verbs, adjectives, etc., in this context (see -ICS).
Histrionics and *histrionic* originally referred to actors and the theatre; *hysterics* and *hysterical* also relate to the mental disorder of hysteria.

hi-tech The adjective *hi-tech* specifically refers to high technology, or sophisticated electronics; its indiscriminate application to basic electrical appliances or to anything remotely connected with computing is disliked by many careful users: □ *a beautiful hi-tech modern home* □ *high-tech benefits* [a reference to the computerization of the social security benefits system] □ *This transition of the cycle from leisure 'toy' to hi-tech pedal machine (Daily Telegraph).*
The word *hi-tech* has a number of variant spellings: *high-tech, high tech, hi-tec, high-tec*, etc. It is also used as a noun: □ *Reflecting the world of high tech* [spelt *hi-tech* in the headline], *the first museum devoted to the chemical industry opens today (The Guardian).*

hoard or **horde**? A *hoard* is 'a store reserved for future use'; a *horde* is 'a large crowd': □ *hordes of tourists.*
◆ These words are often confused, as they have the same pronunciation.

holey see HOLY, HOLEY, OR WHOLLY?

holistic The adjective *holistic* is used of any system, method, theory, etc., that deals with the whole rather than with individual parts or members: □ *holistic medicine* □ *a holistic approach to life.*
◆ The term relates to the concept of wholes that are greater than the sum of their parts, of the natural tendency to form such wholes, and of a universe that is composed of such wholes. Many people take care not to overuse or misuse this word.

holocaust The use of the noun *holocaust* to denote any major disaster, especially one that involves great loss of life, is disliked by some users, who prefer to restrict the word to its original meaning of 'total destruction by fire': □ *the nuclear holocaust.*

◆ The *Holocaust*, usually written with a capital *H*, refers to the massacre of the Jews by the Nazis during World War II.

holy, holey, or **wholly**? These three spellings should not be confused. The adjective *holy* means 'sacred'; the adjective *holey*, only used facetiously or informally, means 'having holes'; the adverb *wholly* means 'completely': □ *holy relics* □ *holey socks* □ *wholly convinced.*

◆ *Holy* and *holey* are pronounced [*hō*li]; the pronunciation of *wholly* [*hō*li] reflects the *-ll-* spelling.

homely In British English the adjective *homely* is complimentary, meaning 'like home', 'unpretentious', or 'sympathetic'; in American English it has the derogatory sense of 'ugly' or 'unattractive': □ *a homely room* □ *a homely child.*

◆ Misunderstanding is most likely to occur when the adjective is applied to a person, in which case it may be replaced by an appropriate synonym.

homogeneity The traditional pronunciation of this word, derived from *homogeneous* (see **HOMOGENEOUS OR HOMOGENOUS**?) is [homōjĕn*ee*iti], although [homōjĕn*ay*iti] is sometimes heard.

homogeneous or **homogenous**? These two adjectives are virtually interchangeable in the sense of 'similar, identical, or uniform in nature, structure, or composition', *homogeneous* being the more frequent: □ *a homogeneous mixture.*

◆ In biology, the adjective *homogenous* specifically refers to correspondence or similarity due to common descent.

The two words are closer in spelling and meaning than in pronunciation: *homogeneous* is usually pronounced [homō*jee*niŭs] and *homogenous* [hōmō*ji*nŭs].

homophobia The noun *homophobia,* meaning 'fear or dislike of homosexuals', and the derived noun *homophobe* and adjective *homophobic* are used with increasing frequency: □ *The Church has been accused of homophobia.* □ *a homophobic police officer.* Some people object to these coinages, on the basis that the *homo-* element can only mean 'same' (as in the word *homosexual* itself) or 'man'.

homosexual This word may be pronounced in several ways, two of the most frequent being [homō*seks*yool] and [hōmō*seks*yool].

◆ Some people prefer [hom-] to [hōm-] because, in this case, *homo* is from the Greek *homos* 'same' and not the Latin *homo* 'man'.
See also **GAY.**

honorary or **honourable**? *Honorary* means 'given as an honour, without the usual requirements or obligations' or 'unpaid': □ *an honorary degree* □ *an honorary member of the society* □ *the honorary secretary. Honourable* means 'worthy of honour' or 'showing honour' and is also used as a title of respect: □ *an honourable man* □ *an honourable deed* □ *the Right Honourable Margaret Thatcher.*

◆ The two adjectives are not interchangeable in any of their senses, but both may be abbreviated to *Hon.* in titles: □ *the Hon. Sec.* □ *the Rt Hon. Margaret Thatcher.*

Note the spellings of the two words: the *u* of *honour* is always absent from *honorary*; it is present in the British spelling of *honourable* but absent from the American spelling of this word.

hoofs or **hooves**? Either *hoofs* or *hooves* is acceptable as the plural of *hoof*, 'the hard bony part of the foot of a horse, cow, etc.'.

hopefully The use of *hopefully* to mean 'it is (to be) hoped (that)' or 'I/ we hope (that)' is disliked by some users and is best restricted to informal contexts: □ *Hopefully the rain will stop before we leave.*

◆ The resistance to this usage is based on a number of arguments, of which the most valid is the possible confusion with the traditional adverbial sense of *hopefully* – 'with hope' or 'in a hopeful manner'. Ambiguity is most likely to occur when the adverb is placed directly before the verb: □ *They will hopefully wait for us* may mean 'I hope they will wait for us' or 'they will wait for us with hope'; *Hopefully they will wait for us* and *They will wait for us hopefully* are less ambiguous renderings of the two senses. See also **ADVERBS**.

Hopefully is favoured by some users as a less cumbersome alternative to 'it is (to be) hoped (that)' and a more impersonal alternative to 'I/we hope (that)'.

horde see **HOARD OR HORDE?**

horrible, horrid, horrific, or **horrendous**? *Horrible* and *horrid* are virtually interchangeable in the sense of 'very unpleasant'; *horrific* and *horrendous* convey a stronger sense of horror: □ *a horrid sight* □ *a horrible dream* □ *a horrific attack* □ *the horrendous prospect of nuclear war.*

◆ All four adjectives are ultimately derived from the Latin verb *horrēre*, meaning 'to tremble or bristle (with fear)'; in formal contexts they are principally used in the sense of 'causing fear or dread'.

The use of *horrible* and *horrid* to mean 'disagreeable' or 'unkind': □ *a horrid man* □ *a horrible meal*, is best restricted to informal contexts, as is the use of *horrendous* to describe exorbitant prices, very bad weather, etc.

hors d'oeuvre An *hors d'oeuvre* is an item of food served before or as the first course of a meal. Of French origin, the phrase is sometimes misspelt: note particularly the vowel sequence *-oeu-*. The two words are sometimes hyphenated: □ *hors-d'oeuvre.*

◆ The plural is usually *hors d'oeuvres*, but *hors d'oeuvre*, without the final *-s*, is also acceptable.

The anglicized pronunciation of *hors d'oeuvre* is [or *der*vr] or [or *der*v]: the *h-* and *-s* are silent. If the final *-s* of the plural form *hors d'oeuvres* is sounded, the pronunciation is [or *der*vz]: it can be difficult to say [or *der*vrz].

hospitable This word may be stressed on the first syllable [*hos*pitäbl] or the second syllable [ho*spit*äbl]. Some users prefer the former, more traditional pronunciation.

hospitalize The verb *hospitalize*, meaning 'send or admit to hospital', is disliked by some users as an example of the increasing tendency to coin new verbs by adding the suffix *-ize* to nouns and adjectives: □ *She was hospitalized in the eighth month of her pregnancy.*

host The verb *host*, meaning 'act as host at' or 'be the host of', is disliked by some users: □ *He hosted the firm's Christmas party.* □ *She is to host the BBC's new quiz show.*

◆ See also **GUEST**.

-hostile see **FRIENDLY**.

hove see **HEAVED OR HOVE?**

however The principal adverbial senses of *however* are 'nevertheless', 'in whatever way', and 'no matter how': □ *The car doesn't have a large boot; it does, however, have plenty of room inside.* □ *However I wash my hair, and however carefully I dry it, it* *always looks untidy.* For the distinction between *however* and *how ever* see WHATEVER OR WHAT EVER?

◆ In the sense of 'nevertheless', *however* often serves the same purpose as *but*; careful users avoid using both words in the same sentence or clause unless *however* is being used in one of its other senses: □ *The girl screamed; she did not, however, try to escape.* □ *The girl screamed, but she did not try to escape.* □ *The girl struggled, but however hard she tried, she could not escape.*

Some users always separate *however* (in the sense of 'nevertheless') from the rest of the sentence with commas or other punctuation marks; others use punctuation marks only where there is a possibility of ambiguity or confusion. See also COMMA 4.

In the sense of 'nevertheless', *however* is usually placed immediately after the word or phrase that it serves to contrast or emphasize: □ *my friend, however, does not like the colour* suggests that I like the colour but my friend does not; *my friend does not, however, like the colour* suggests that my friend likes some other feature of the object in question but does not like the colour.

Some users object to the positioning of *however* (in the sense of 'nevertheless') at the beginning or end of a sentence or clause; however, this is generally acceptable in most contexts.

hullo see HELLO, HALLO, OR HULLO?

human Some people dislike the use of *human* as a noun, preferring *human being* (or *man, woman, child, person,* etc.): □ *This job can be done more efficiently by a robot than by a human (being).*

◆ Most dictionaries acknowledge the noun *human* as a synonym for *human being*. See also INHUMAN OR INHUMANE?

humanism or **humanity**? *Humanism* is a philosophy that values human beings and rejects the need for religion. The noun *humanity* refers to human beings collectively; it also means 'kindness': □ *for the sake of humanity.* The two nouns should not be confused.

◆ *Humanism* also refers to a cultural movement of the Renaissance. *The humanities* are academic subjects such as history, art, literature, language, and philosophy, as distinct from science.

humanist or **humanitarian**? A *humanist* is a person who supports the philosophy of humanism (see HUMANISM OR HUMANITY?); a *humanitarian* is a philanthropist, a person who works for the welfare of human beings.

◆ The word *humanitarian* is also used as an adjective: □ *a humanitarian organization.*

humanity see HUMANISM OR HUMANITY?

humiliation or **humility**? *Humiliation* is a feeling of shame, embarrassment, or loss of pride sometimes caused deliberately by other people; *humility* is the quality of being humble or modest: □ *the humiliation of failure* □ *the nun's humility.*

humorist The noun *humorist,* meaning 'humorous writer, speaker, etc.' is often misspelt. As in the adjective HUMOROUS, the *-mour* ending of *humour* is changed to *-mor* before the suffix *-ist.*

humorous This word, meaning 'amusing or funny', is often misspelt. The second *u* of *humour* is dropped before the suffix *-ous.*

◆ *Humorous* must not be confused with *humerus,* the long bone in the upper arm.

hung see HANGED OR HUNG?

hygiene This word, meaning 'science of ensuring good health', is often misspelt. Note *hy-* and not *hi-* at the beginning of the word, and the *-ie-* in the middle.

hype The word *hype*, used as a noun or verb with reference to extravagant and often deceptive publicity of books, films, etc., is generally regarded as a slang term: □ *The launch owed more to hype than to literary merit* (*Sunday Times*). □ *the biggest money-making hype in sports history* (*Publishers Weekly*) □*Hyping books is big business* (*The Bookseller*).

◆ The word is of uncertain origin: many authorities associate it with the slang use of *hype* as an abbreviation for *hypodermic*; others have suggested a connection with the prefix *hyper-*, meaning 'excessive', as in *hyperbole*.

hyper- or **hypo-**? These two prefixes are often confused. This may result in misunderstanding when each is joined to its relevant suffix. *Hyper-* means 'above or excessively': □ *a hyperactive child*; *hypo-* means 'beneath or under': □ *a hypodermic syringe*.

◆ The prefix *hyper-* is increasingly used as an adjective in its own right, in the sense of 'hyperactive': □ *Her son is rather hyper*.

hyperbola or **hyperbole**? These two nouns should not be confused. *Hyperbola* is a technical term used in mathematics to describe a type of symmetrical curve; *hyperbole* means 'exaggeration used for effect in speech or writing': □ *I've warned him a million times* is an example of *hyperbole*. Both nouns originate from the same Greek word and they share the derived adjective *hyperbolic(al)*.

◆ Note that the final *-e* of *hyperbole* is pronounced, producing the four-syllable word [hīperbŏli]. *Hyperbola* is pronounced [hīperbŏlār].

hypercritical see HYPOCRITICAL OR HYPERCRITICAL?

hyphen The principal uses of the hyphen in English are to join two or more words together, either as a fixed compound or to avoid ambiguity, and to indicate that a word has been broken at the end of a line through lack of space.

◆ There are a number of other situations in which the use of the hyphen is optional.

1 Most standard prefixes are attached without a hyphen: □ *unimportant* □ *multicoloured* □ *prefabricated*.

Some users prefer to hyphenate words prefixed with *non-* and words in which the absence of the hyphen would result in a doubled vowel: □ *non-flammable* □ *pre-eminent* □ *co-ordinate*. Such words are widely and increasingly accepted in the single-word forms: □ *nonflammable* □ *preeminent* □ *coordinate*, etc. However, the double *i* of words prefixed by *anti-*, *semi-*, etc., is usually split by a hyphen: □ *anti-inflationary* □ *semi-independent*.

Words prefixed with *ex-* (in the sense of 'former') and *self-* are usually hyphenated: □ *ex-wife* □ *self-sufficient*.

A hyphen is sometimes inserted after the prefix to avoid ambiguity or confusion; for example, to distinguish between the nouns *co-op* (a cooperative) and *coop* (an enclosure), or between the verbs *re-cover* and *recover* (see also RE-), and to clarify the pronunciation and meaning of such words as *de-ice*. See also CO-.

A hyphen is always used to join a prefix to a word beginning with a capital letter: □ *anti-British* □ *un-Christian*.

See also -LIKE.

2 Many compounds can be written with or without a hyphen, depending on convention, frequency of usage, the writer's personal preference, or the publisher's house style: □ *dining room* or *dining-room* □ *hard-hearted* or *hardhearted* □ *boy-friend* or *boyfriend*. There is a growing tendency towards minimal hyphenation, with the substitution of two words or one word as appropriate.

Some fixed compounds of three or more words, such as *son-in-law*, *happy-go-lucky*, etc., are always hyphenated; two-word compound adjectives in which the second element ends in *-ed*, such as *light-hearted*, *blue-eyed*, *short-sighted*, etc., are usually hyphenated (see also **4** below).

Some compounds derived from phrasal verbs are always hyphenated: □ *broken-down*; some are always solid: □ *breakthrough*; others may be hyphenated or solid: □ *takeover* or *take-over* □ *run-down* or *rundown*.

3 Compounds of two or more words used adjectivally before the noun they qualify are usually hyphenated: □ *a used-car dealer* sells used cars; □ *a plain-chocolate biscuit* is coated with plain chocolate; □ *a three-month-old baby* is three months old; □ *a once-in-a-lifetime opportunity* occurs only once in a lifetime. These hyphens are often essential to avoid ambiguity: □ *a red-wine bottle* is a bottle for red wine; □ *a red wine bottle* may be a wine bottle that is red.

4 Adjectives or participles preceded by an adverb are not hyphenated if the adverb ends in *-ly*: □ *a neatly written letter* □ *a letter that is neatly written*. Compounds containing other adverbs, especially those that may be mistaken for adjectives (*well*, *ill*, *best*, *little*, *half*, etc.) are usually hyphenated when they are used adjectivally before a noun, to avoid ambiguity: □ *a half-cooked loaf* □ *his best-known novel*. When such compounds occur after the noun, the hyphen is sometimes optional.

5 A common element need not be repeated in groups of two or more hyphenated compounds but the hyphen must not be omitted; the same convention applies to solid compounds, in which the common element may be replaced by a hyphen: □ *long- or short-haired dogs* □ *salesmen and -women*. Some users dislike this convention, preferring to retain the full compound in all cases.

6 A hyphen is inserted when numbers between 21 and 99 are written out in full: □ *twenty-one* □ *thirty-seven* □ *eighty-six* □ *four hundred and fifty-three*.

A hyphen is used when fractions are written out, to separate the numerator and denominator: □ *three-tenths* □ *thirteen-sixteenths* □ *two-thirds*.

7 The other major use of the hyphen is at the end of a line, splitting a word that is to be continued at the beginning of the next line.

There are a number of conventions relating to the points at which a word may be divided; these recommended breaks are marked in some dictionaries. There is an increasing tendency for word division to be influenced by phonetic rather than etymological principles; for example, *photog-rapher* [fōtogrǎfêr], not *photo-grapher*.

A word should always be split between syllables, ideally at a natural break: after an existing hyphen; between the elements of a one-word compound; after a prefix, such as *semi-*, *inter-*, etc.; or before a suffix, such as *-ness*, *-ment*, etc. Words of one syllable should not be broken. Words should not be broken immediately after the first letter or immediately before the last.

It is also important to ensure that the letters on either side of the break will not mislead the reader, especially if they form a word in their own right: □ *mace-rate* □ *the-rapist* □ *mans-laughter* □ *not-able* □ *rear-range* □ *leg-end*, and that the hyphen will not be mistaken for a fixed hyphen: □ *re-creation* □ *un-ionized* □ *de-crease* □ *ex-tractor*.

8 In handwritten and typewritten texts a hyphen is often used in place of a **DASH**.

hypo- see **HYPER- OR HYPO-**?

hypocrisy The noun *hypocrisy* is sometimes misspelt, a common error being the substitution of *-cracy* (as in *democracy*) for the *-crisy* ending. Note also the prefix *hypo-*, not *hyper-*.

hypocritical or **hypercritical**? These two words are often confused. *Hypocritical* means 'insincere' or 'two-faced'; *hypercritical* means 'excessively critical': □*It would be hypocritical of me to say I enjoyed the concert, when really I thought it was awful.* □*He's so hypercritical about the way his wife lays the table.*

◆ As well as being misspelt, these words are sometimes mispronounced. *Hypocritical* is pronounced [hipĕkritĭkl], *hypercritical* is pronounced [hīpĕkritĭkl].

hysterical, hysterics see **HISTRIONIC OR HYSTERICAL?**

I or **me?** The subject pronoun *I* and the object pronoun *me* are sometimes confused in informal speech, especially in the phrases *It's me* and *Between you and I*.

◆ After verbs and prepositions, the object pronoun *me* should be used; before verbs, the subject pronoun *I* should be used: □ *They have invited my mother, my father, and me* [not *I*] *to the wedding.* □ *He works with Mary and me* [not *I*]. □ *My friend and I* [not *me*] *will help.* Confusion and errors occur in the highest places: □ *She* [Margaret Thatcher] *could give a better answer than that to I and to my honourable friends* (said by Neil Kinnock during Prime Minister's Question Time).

These problems rarely arise when the pronoun stands alone; any confusion may therefore be resolved by mentally removing the other item(s) and assessing the result: □ *They have invited me to the wedding.* □ *He works with me.* □ *I will help.*

The verb *to be*, according to grammatical convention, is an exception: in formal contexts *It is me* is unacceptable to a few careful users, who prefer *It is I*. However, in informal contexts the idiomatic *It's me* is generally considered to be more natural than the pedantic *It's I* and is acceptable to most users. See also **IT**.

The phrase *between you and I* is avoided by many users in all contexts, although it is often heard in informal speech. *Between you and me*, which conforms to grammatical convention, is the preferred usage.

See also **AS**; **LET**; **MYSELF**; **PRONOUNS**; **THAN**.

-ible see **-ABLE** OR **-IBLE?**

-ic or **-ical?** Many adjectives are formed by the addition of the suffixes *-ic* or *-ical*: □ *cubic* □ *symmetrical* □ *phonetic* □ *geographical*.

◆ Sometimes either suffix may be added to the same root. The pairs of words thus created may be virtually interchangeable, such as: □ *metric–metrical* □ *philosophic–philosophical*, although one is usually more frequent or more specialized than the other. In other pairs the two words may differ in meaning or usage: see **CLASSIC** OR **CLASSICAL?**; **COMIC** OR **COMICAL?**; **ECONOMIC** OR **ECONOMICAL?**; **ELECTRIC** OR **ELECTRICAL?**; **HISTORIC** OR **HISTORICAL?**; **MAGIC** OR **MAGICAL?**; **POLITIC** OR **POLITICAL?**

Some adjectives, especially those related to nouns ending in *-ic*, are found only in the *-ical* form: a *critic* may be *critical*; a *sceptic* is *sceptical*. Others, such as *static* or *tragic*, are very rarely, if ever, found in the *-ical* form.

With the exception of *politic* and *public*, all adverbs derived from adjectives ending in *-ic* or *-ical* have the suffix *-ically*: □ *tragically* □ *critically*.

-ics A number of words ending in *-ics* may be singular or plural nouns, depending on the sense in which they are used: □ *Acoustics is the study of sound.* □ *The acoustics of the room have been* *improved and are now excellent.*

◆ Such nouns are usually singular when they denote a science or some other area of study or activity: □ *Mathematics was not my favourite subject at school.* □ *Gymnastics is just one of her many hobbies.* □ *Economics is taught in the sixth form, but politics is not on the curriculum.*

In other contexts, the same nouns may become plural, when they refer to a system, set of principles, group of activities, etc. □ *His politics are very left-wing.* □ *What are the economics of the coal industry?*

Some nouns, such as *tactics*, *statistics*, and *ethics*, may be singular or plural as described above but also exist in a singular -*ic* form: □ *military tactics* □ *vital statistics* □ *professional ethics* □ *her latest tactic* □ *an alarming statistic* □ *the work ethic.*

Nouns relating to behaviour, such as *heroics* and *hysterics*, are usually plural.

See also **SINGULAR OR PLURAL?**

identical with or **identical to**? The adjective *identical* may be followed by *with* or *to*: □ *This picture is identical with/to the one we saw in the shop.*

◆ Some users dislike the phrase *identical to*, considering *with* to be the more acceptable preposition in this context.

identify Some people dislike the frequent use of *identify* as a synonym for 'associate', 'link', or 'connect': □ *They have been identified with a number of extreme right-wing organizations.*

◆ In the sense of 'share the ideas or feelings of', *identify with* is sometimes used reflexively: □ *I cannot identify (myself) with the heroine.*

In commercial and bureaucratic contexts, *identify* is increasingly used as a synonym for 'find', 'discover', or 'recognize': □ *to identify a gap in the market.*

idioms An *idiom* is a more or less fixed expression, such as *out of hand*, *in spite of*, *to come into one's own*, or *a storm in a teacup*, the meaning of which is distinct from the individual senses of the words it contains. See also **METAPHORS; SIMILES.**

◆ Many idioms, such as □ *have egg on one's face* 'be shown to be foolish' and □ *be dog tired* 'to be very tired after exertion' are best restricted to informal contexts; others, such as □ *the salt of the earth*, 'people regarded as having praiseworthy qualities' are acceptable at all levels.

idiosyncrasy This word is often misspelt, the most frequent error occurring when the ending -*asy* is replaced by -*acy*. The correct ending is like *fantasy* and not like *privacy*.

◆ Note also that *i* and *y* each occurs twice.

idle, idol, or **idyll**? The adjective *idle* means 'not active; lazy': □ *an idle machine* □ *an idle fellow* □ *He is never idle.* An *idol* is an object of worship or admiration: □ *a pop idol* □ *They bowed before the idol.* An *idyll* is (a piece of writing that depicts) a pleasant or idealized scene or situation: □ *an idyll of life on the Pacific island.*

◆ *Idle* and *idol* are sometimes confused, being identical in pronunciation: [īdl]. *Idyll* is pronounced with a short initial *i*: [*id*il]. *Idyll* is more usually found in the derived adjectival word *idyllic*.

idyllic The first *i* of *idyllic* is usually pronounced as in *ill*, although it may be pronounced as in *item*.

◆ The stress occurs on the second syllable in both cases; [*idil*ik] or [*īdil*ik].

i.e. see **E.G.** AND **I.E.**

if The use of *if* in place of *though* often causes ambiguity: □ *The work, if difficult, is rewarding.* □ *The service was good, if not excellent.*
 ◆ The first of these examples may mean 'the work is difficult but rewarding' or 'difficult work is rewarding'. It is impossible to ascertain from the second example whether the service was excellent or not.
  The use of *if* in place of *whether* may also be confusing in certain contexts: □ *Ask him if it is raining* probably means 'ask him whether it is raining (or not)', but it may also mean 'if it is raining, ask him (for a lift, to close the window, etc.)'. See also **SUBJUNCTIVE; WERE OR WAS?; WHETHER.**

if and when Many people object to the frequent use of the phrase *if and when*, which can usually be replaced by *if* or *when* alone: □ *We'll move to a larger house if and when we start a family.*
 ◆ The phrase sometimes serves a useful purpose, however. In the example above the users may not wish to commit themselves on the subject of parenthood: *if* would imply doubt; *when* would imply certainty.

ignoramus The only plural form of the noun *ignoramus*, which means 'ignorant person', is *ignoramuses*. Although the word is of Latin origin, implying a possible *i* ending in the plural (see **PLURALS**), it is not a noun in Latin but a verb, meaning 'we do not know'.

ilk The use of *ilk* as a synonym for 'type' or 'sort', in the phrase *of that ilk*, is widely accepted in many contexts but is disliked by some users: □ *Barbara Cartland and other writers of that ilk.* The word *that* is sometimes replaced by *your, their, his, her*, etc.: □ *Barbara Cartland and other writers of her ilk.*
 ◆ The phrase *of that ilk* is traditionally used to denote the landed gentry of Scotland, meaning 'of that estate': □ *Glengarry of that ilk is Glengarry, laird of Glengarry.* In such contexts the phrase is often misinterpreted as 'of that family'.

ill see **SICK** OR **ILL**?

illegal see **ILLICIT, ILLEGAL, OR ILLEGITIMATE?**

illegible or **eligible**? The adjective *eligible*, meaning 'qualified; suitable; worthy': □ *to be eligible for a competition* □ *an eligible bachelor*, should not be confused with *illegible* (see **ILLEGIBLE** OR **UNREADABLE?**).
 ◆ Note the differences in spelling between the two words, particularly the *-ll-* and *i-e-* vowel sequence of *illegible* and the *-l-* and *e-i-* vowel sequence of *eligible*.
  Illegible is stressed on the second syllable, [i*le*jĭbl]; *eligible* on the first, [*el*ijĭbl].

illegible or **unreadable**? The adjective *illegible* describes something that cannot be deciphered and is therefore impossible to read; *unreadable* means 'uninteresting' or 'badly worded', describing something that cannot be read with enjoyment, ease, or understanding: □ *Her handwriting is illegible.* □ *He has produced another unreadable novel.* □ *The document is unreadable; it must be reworded.*
 ◆ *Unreadable* may be used as a synonym for 'illegible' in certain contexts, but it can cause ambiguity: □ *This paragraph is totally unreadable* may be a criticism either of the handwriting (or printing quality) or of the content or wording.

illegitimate see **ILLICIT, ILLEGAL, OR ILLEGITIMATE?**

illicit or **elicit**? The adjective *illicit* (see **ILLICIT, ILLEGAL, OR ILLEGITIMATE?**) should not be confused with the verb *elicit*, meaning 'draw out' or 'evoke': □ *illicit dealings* □ *to elicit the truth.*

◆ The two words have the same pronunciation [i*lisit*].

illicit, illegal, or **illegitimate?** All these adjectives mean 'unlawful', but there are differences of sense, usage, and application between them: □ *illicit trade* □ *illegal parking* □ *an illegitimate attack.*

◆ *Illicit* means 'not permitted or approved by law': □ *The Government should seek the co-operation of the unions, business and revenue authorities to eradicate illicit and irregular earnings (Daily Telegraph).* The word is also used to describe something that is contrary to social custom: □ *an illicit relationship.* See also **ILLICIT OR ELICIT?**

Illegal means 'forbidden by law': □ *The hippies defied the council's notice to leave common land where they had set up an illegal camp.* The word is also used to describe something that contravenes the regulations of a sport, etc.: □ *an illegal tackle.*

The adjective *illegitimate* is principally applied to children born of unmarried parents: □ *the president's illegitimate daughter.* It also describes something that defies reason or logic: □ *an illegitimate explanation.*

illusion see ALLUSION, ILLUSION, OR DELUSION?

illusive, illusory see ALLUSIVE, ELUSIVE, OR ILLUSIVE?

illustrative In British English the adjective *illustrative*, as in: □ *illustrative examples*, is stressed on the first syllable, [*i*lŭstrătiv]. In American English the second syllable is stressed, [i*lu*strătiv].

image The frequent use of *image* as a synonym for 'reputation' is disliked by some users: □ *This scandal will not be good for the president's image.*

◆ In many contexts, however, *image* has a wider range of meaning than *reputation*: an advertising campaign can improve the *image*, but not necessarily the *reputation*, of a political party, for example. The *reputation* of a person, product, organization, etc., is based largely on past performance; the word *image* denotes a more general impression, which may also be influenced by presentation, appearance, association, etc.

imaginary or **imaginative?** *Imaginary* means 'unreal' or 'existing only in the imagination'; *imaginative* means 'having or showing a vivid or creative imagination': □ *an imaginary house* □ *an imaginative designer* □ *an imaginative story.*

◆ The two adjectives are not interchangeable, although both may occasionally be applied to the same noun: □ *an imaginary friend* does not exist; *an imaginative friend* has a lively imagination.

Note the spelling of *imaginary*, particularly the -*ary* (not -*ery*) ending.

imbroglio An *imbroglio* is a confused situation: □ *a political imbroglio.* Note the spelling of this word, particularly the silent *g*. It is used in formal contexts and is of Italian origin; the anglicized pronunciation is [im*brō*liō].

◆ The plural is formed by adding -*s*, not -*es*: *imbroglios.*

I mean The phrase *I mean* may be used in informal speech to clarify, expand, or correct a previous statement, question, etc.: □ *Is your foot very painful, I mean too painful to walk on?* □ *She lives in Plymouth, I mean Portsmouth.*

◆ In some contexts the phrase serves no useful purpose and may be omitted: □ *You could have bought a new umbrella, (I mean) they're not very expensive.*

immanent see EMINENT, IMMINENT, OR IMMANENT?

immigrant see EMIGRANT OR IMMIGRANT?

171   **impersonate**

imminent see EMINENT, IMMINENT, OR IMMANENT?
immoral see AMORAL OR IMMORAL?
immune from or **immune to**? The adjective *immune* is followed by *to*
in the literal sense of 'protected against or resistant to disease'
and figurative extensions of this sense: □ *The plant is immune to
fungal disease.* □ *She is immune to criticism.* In the figurative
sense of 'exempt', *immune* is followed by *from*: □ *Nobody is
immune from punishment.*
immunity or **impunity**? *Immunity* is exemption or freedom from obligation or duty; *impunity* is exemption or freedom from punishment or harm: □ *Diplomatic immunity provides foreign
ambassadors with immunity from taxation and enables them to
infringe the law with impunity.*
◆ *Impunity* is a restricted form of *immunity*; the word occurs most
frequently in the phrase *with impunity*.
Immunity also means 'resistance to disease': □ *This vaccination
may not confer total immunity.*
impact The use of *impact* as a synonym for 'effect', 'impression', or
'influence' is best restricted to contexts in which the effect,
impression, etc., is particularly powerful: □ *the impact of the
government's resignation on the stock market* □ *The new packaging has had little effect* [not *impact*] *on sales.*
◆ Some people object to all figurative uses of the noun, reserving it
for physical collisions and their effects: □ *the impact of the bullet on
the car door.*
The use of *impact* as a verb meaning 'affect' is best avoided: □ *The
cutbacks impacted secondary education negatively* could be
reworded as: *The cutbacks had a bad effect on secondary education.*
impasse The formal word *impasse*, meaning 'deadlock; stalemate':
□ *to reach an impasse,* is of French origin and has a number of
anglicized pronunciations. The first syllable may be pronounced
[am-], [im-], or [om-]; the second syllable [-pahs] or [-pas]; and
the stress may be on either syllable. The pronunciation [am*pahs*]
is closest to the French.
impassioned, impassive see DISPASSIONATE, IMPASSIONED, OR IMPASSIVE?
impeccable This word, meaning 'faultless': □ *She spoke impeccable
Italian,* is often misspelt. Note particularly the *-able* ending as in
acceptable, and not *-ible* as in *sensible.*
impel see COMPEL OR IMPEL?
imperial or **imperious**? The adjective *imperial* means 'of an emperor,
empress, or empire'; *imperious* means 'overbearing' or 'arrogant': □ *the imperial palace* □ *an imperious gesture.*
◆ The two words are sometimes confused in the extended sense of
imperial – 'majestic', 'regal', or 'commanding': *imperial powers* are
those that are as majestic as an emperor's, not those that are
domineering and arrogant. Both are derived from the Latin noun
imperium, meaning 'command'.
The adjective *imperial* also refers to the British system of weights
and measures (pounds and ounces, feet and inches, gallons and
pints, etc.), which is gradually being replaced by the metric system.
impersonate, personate, or **personify**? To *impersonate* is to imitate or
pretend to be somebody else: □ *The comedian impersonated
Humphrey Bogart.* □ *It is a crime to impersonate a police officer.*
To *personify* is to represent or embody something abstract or
inanimate as a human being: □ *He personifies the greed of modern society.* The rare verb *personate* is sometimes used in place

of *impersonate* or *personify*.

impinge or **infringe**? Either verb may be used in the sense of 'encroach': □ *They are impinging/infringing on our rights.* Note that both verbs are followed by *on* (or *upon*) in this sense. *Impinge* is used with more abstract nouns: □ *everything that impinges on our consciousness.*

◆ To *impinge on*, in formal contexts, also means to strike: □ *The bullet impinged on the side of the vehicle. Infringe*, used transitively without *on*, means 'break' or 'violate': □ *to infringe the rules.*

impious This word should be stressed on the first syllable [*im*piŭs].

◆ This contrasts with *impiety*, which is stressed on the second syllable [imp*i*iti].

implement The verb *implement* is best avoided where *carry out, fulfil, accomplish*, or *put into action* would be adequate or more appropriate: □ *His absence will enable us to carry out* [not *implement*] *our plan.*

◆ Originally a legal term, the verb *implement* is widely used in official contexts: □ *Townsend Thoresen ... could pull out of an operating deal with a Belgian ferry company if it did not implement safety measures introduced in the wake of the Zeebrugge disaster* (Daily Telegraph).

As a noun, *implement* denotes a tool or instrument: □ *agricultural implements.* There is a slight difference in pronunciation between the verb and the noun: the final syllable of the verb is sounded [-ment], rhyming with *tent*; the final syllable of the noun is unstressed [-mĕnt], as in *garment.*

implicit see **EXPLICIT OR IMPLICIT?**

imply or **infer**? The verb *imply* means 'suggest' or 'hint at'; *infer* means 'deduce' or 'conclude': □ *She implied that there would be some redundancies in the factory.* □ *I inferred from what she said that there would be some redundancies in the factory.* To *imply* involves speech, writing, or action; to *infer* involves listening, reading, or observation.

◆ The two verbs are frequently confused, *infer* being used in place of *imply*, to the extent that some dictionaries now list 'imply' as an additional sense of *infer*. Many people object to this usage, however; it is therefore advisable to maintain the distinction between the two words. Similarly, the noun *inference* is sometimes used instead of *implication*, but it is preferable to maintain the distinction between these two words: □ *the implications* [not *the inferences*] *of the report.*

Infer is stressed on the second syllable; the final *r* is doubled before *-ed, -ing*, and *-er*. The noun *inference*, in which the stress shifts to the first syllable, has a single *r*. See also **SPELLING 1.**

important or **importantly**? *More important* (short for *what is more important*) is sometimes regarded as an adverbial phrase, the adjective *important* being changed to *importantly*: □ *His assistants are very conscientious and, more important(ly), they are utterly trustworthy.*

◆ The phrase *more important* is preferred by many users in formal contexts, although *more importantly* is becoming increasingly acceptable.

impostor or **imposter**? This word, meaning 'person who fraudulently pretends to be another person', has two spellings, though the spelling *impostor* is more frequently used than *imposter.*

impractical or **impracticable**? see **PRACTICAL OR PRACTICABLE?**

impresario An *impresario* is a theatrical producer or sponsor. Note the spelling of the word, particularly the single *s*, unlike *impress.*

The usual pronunciation is [imprĕsariō]; the variant [imprĕsairiō] is disliked by some people.

◆ The plural is formed by adding -s, not -es: *impresarios*.

impromptu see EXTEMPORE OR IMPROMPTU?

impunity see IMMUNITY OR IMPUNITY?

in see AT OR IN?; INTO OR IN TO?

inaccessible Note the spelling of this adjective, particularly the single -n-, the -cc- and -ss-, and the -ible ending.

inapt or **inept**? The adjective *inapt* means 'inappropriate' or 'unsuitable'; its synonym *inept* is more frequently used in the sense of 'incompetent' or 'clumsy': □ *an inapt comparison* □ *an inept mechanic.*

◆ Both adjectives are ultimately derived from the Latin word *aptus*, meaning 'fit', and the negative prefix *in-*; *inept* entered the English language via the Latin adjective *ineptus*.

inasmuch as This phrase may also be written *in as much as*, although *inasmuch as* is far more frequent: □ *The result was significant inasmuch as it demonstrated the power of the individual.* See also IN SO FAR AS.

incident The noun *incident* is frequently used in the mass media to denote an action or occurrence that has or is likely to have serious, violent, or political consequences: □ *The latest wave of terrorist attacks was sparked off by an incident in Londonderry.*

◆ In other contexts the noun *incident* is principally used with reference to events of minor importance: □ *The unfortunate incident was soon forgotten.*

incomparable This word, meaning 'without comparison', is often mispronounced. The stress falls on the second syllable and not the third. The correct pronunciation is [inkompĕrĕbl].

incontrovertible The adjective *incontrovertible*, meaning 'undeniable; indisputable', and the derived adverb *incontrovertibly*, are sometimes misspelt. Note the -ible (not -able) ending. Another frequent error is the substitution of -a- for the second -o-.

incredible or **incredulous**? *Incredible* means 'unbelievable'; *incredulous* means 'disbelieving': □ *He told her an incredible story.* □ *She looked at him with an incredulous expression.*

◆ The use of the adjective *incredible* in the sense of 'wonderful' or 'amazing' should be restricted to informal contexts: □ *We had an incredible holiday.* See also CREDIBLE, CREDITABLE, OR CREDULOUS?

indecent see DECENT OR DECOROUS?

indefinite article see A OR AN?

indefinitely This word is often misspelt, the most common error being the substitution of an *a* for the final *i*.

◆ It is worth remembering that the word *finite* has the same sequence of vowels.

independence and **independent** These words are sometimes misspelt, the most frequent error being the substitution of an *a* for the final *e*.

◆ Note, however, that the noun *dependant*, 'person who relies on another for financial support', is spelt with a final *a*.

in-depth The adjective *in-depth* is disliked by many users; it can usually be replaced by *thorough* or *detailed*, for which it is an unnecessary synonym: □ *an in-depth knowledge of the latest electronic equipment* □ *an in-depth study of child abuse.*

indexes or **indices**? The noun *index* has two accepted plural forms, *indexes* and *indices*. The use of the plural form *indices*, pronounced [*indiseez*], is largely restricted to mathematics, economics, and technical contexts.

◆ For other senses of *index*, especially that of 'alphabetical list', the plural form *indexes* is preferred by most users: □ *This cookery book has two indexes: one lists recipes by name; the other lists principal ingredients.* □ *Book titles and authors' names are entered in separate indexes.*

Indian The adjective and noun *Indian* may refer to India and its inhabitants or to the indigenous peoples of America: □ *the Indian Empire* □ *an Indian reservation.*

◆ This common confusion can be blamed on the explorer Christopher Columbus, who mistook the New World for India.

The term *American Indian* is used to distinguish these peoples from the Indians of Asia; it is preferred to the older British term *Red Indian*, which refers to the Indians of North America, and is now generally considered offensive.

An inhabitant of Pakistan, part of the Indian subcontinent, is a *Pakistani*. Asian Indians and Pakistanis living in Britain are usually referred to as *Asians*. See also ASIAN OR ASIATIC?

Further confusion may be caused by the term *West Indian*, which refers to inhabitants of the West Indies and their descendants.

indicate In the field of medicine the verb *indicate* can mean 'require; show the need for or advisability of', usually in the passive: □ *A course of antibiotics was indicated.* Some people object to the use of *indicated* in this sense in nonmedical contexts, in place of *shown to be necessary, advisable,* etc.: □ *Redundancies were indicated.* □ *Upgrading of the computer system is indicated.*

indices see INDEXES OR INDICES?

indict or **indite**? The words *indict* and *indite* are both pronounced [*indīt*], but they have different meanings. *Indict* – note the *c* that is not pronounced – means 'accuse; formally charge'; *indite* is an older word that means 'write down'.

◆ The derived nouns are spelt *indictment* and *inditement*.

indifferent The adjective *indifferent* should be followed by *to* or *as to*, not *for* or *about*: □ *He is indifferent to your criticism.* □ *I am indifferent as to the outcome of the trial.*

◆ The two principal senses of *indifferent* have undergone a gradual change, from 'impartial' to 'unconcerned' or 'uninterested' and from 'neither good nor bad' to 'below average' or 'poor'. Used in either of its original senses, or even in one of its modern senses, the word is sometimes open to misinterpretation or confusion: □ *an indifferent referee* may be uninterested, neither good nor bad, or poor.

indigenous see NATIVE.

indirect speech see REPORTED SPEECH.

indiscriminate or **undiscriminating**? Both adjectives refer to a lack of discrimination (in the sense of 'discernment' rather than 'prejudice'); *indiscriminate* has the extended meaning of 'random' or 'unselective': □ *indiscriminate killings* □ *an undiscriminating palate.*

◆ There is a tendency for *undiscriminating* to be preferred to *indiscriminate* with direct reference to people: □ *undiscriminating viewers* □ *indiscriminate viewing.* See also DISCRIMINATING OR DISCRIMINATORY?

indispensable This word, meaning 'absolutely essential': □ *In this job, a car and a telephone are indispensable assets*, is sometimes misspelt.

◆ The ending is *-able*, and not *-ible* as in *indestructible*.

indite see INDICT OR INDITE?

individual The use of the noun *individual* in place of *person* is disliked by some users, who reserve *individual* for contexts in
which a single person is contrasted with a group: □ *the rights
of the individual* □ *the person* [not *individual*] *who wrote this
article*.

◆ The noun *individual* is also used, with a derogatory, contemptuous,
or humorous effect, to denote a particular kind of person: □ *an
unpleasant individual* □ *an eccentric individual*. This usage is best
restricted to informal contexts.

indoor or **indoors**? *Indoor* is an adjective; *indoors* is an adverb: □ *an
indoor aerial* □ *to go indoors* □ *Indoor games are played indoors*.

industrial or **industrious**? These two adjectives should not be confused. *Industrial* is derived from the noun *industry* in the sense
of 'manufacturing or commercial enterprises'; *industrious*
means 'hard-working' (from *industry* in the sense of 'diligence;
assiduity'): □ *an industrial town* □ *an industrious student*.

industrial action The term *industrial action* may denote any of a
number of measures (such as a strike, sit-in, go-slow, work-to-
rule, or overtime ban) used by protesting or dissatisfied
employees to put pressure on their employers: □ *Industrial
action by electricity workers may result in power cuts*. The term
is, however, misleading and contradictory, as a strike is characterized by a *lack* of action, rather than action.

◆ The expression *industrial action*, which originated in the early
1970s, is not confined to industry (in the sense of 'manufacturing or
commercial enterprises'): civil servants, teachers, hospital staff, etc.,
may take industrial action.

industrious see INDUSTRIAL OR INDUSTRIOUS?

inedible see EATABLE OR EDIBLE?

ineffective, ineffectual, inefficient see EFFECTIVE, EFFECTUAL, EFFICA-
CIOUS, OR EFFICIENT?

inept see INAPT OR INEPT?

inequality, inequity, or **iniquity**? *Inequality* is the state of being unequal
or different; *inequity* means 'unfairness'; *iniquity* is wickedness:
□ *the inequality of their ages* □ *the inequity of the law* □ *a den of
iniquity*. *Inequity* and *iniquity* are much more formal words than
inequality.

◆ All three nouns may be used in the sense of 'injustice', with different
connotations: □ *The inequality of the tax system* means that some
people pay more tax than others; □ *The inequity of the tax system*
implies that the system is unfair; □ *The iniquity of the tax system*
suggests that the system is morally wrong.

in fact The phrase *in fact* is largely used for emphasis or to expand on
a previous statement: □ *This legislation will not in fact improve
housing conditions in inner-city areas*. □ *I'm not familiar with
the machine, in fact I've only used it once*.

◆ Since *in fact* means 'actually' or 'in reality', the addition of *actual* is
considered by many users to be superfluous: □ *He often spends his
holidays in France, but in (actual) fact he hates the French*.

infamous or **notorious**? Both adjectives mean 'well-known for something bad': *notorious* emphasizes the well-known aspect; *infamous* emphasizes the bad aspect: □ *the execution of this infamous/
notorious criminal* □ *his notorious lack of punctuality* □ *That
junction is notorious for accidents*. □ *one of Richard III's most*

infamous deeds.

◆ Note the pronunciation and stress pattern of *infamous* [ínfâmŭs], which is quite different from that of *famous* [fáymŭs].

infectious see CONTAGIOUS OR INFECTIOUS?

infer, inference see IMPLY OR INFER?

infinite or **infinitesimal**? *Infinite* means 'having no limits' or 'extremely great'; *infinitesimal* means 'negligible' or 'extremely small': □ *She has infinite patience.* □ *The difference is infinitesimal.* An *infinite* amount is so great that it cannot be measured; an *infinitesimal* amount is so small that it cannot be measured.

infinitive The *infinitive* of a verb, often preceded by *to*, is its basic form, without any of the changes or additions that relate to tense, person, number, etc.: *(to) go* is the infinitive of the verb from which the past participle *gone* is derived.

◆ The infinitive is used without *to* after a number of auxiliary verbs: □ *you can leave* □ *they must wait* □ *he may object* □ *we should succeed*, etc.

After a number of other verbs, the infinitive is used with *to*: □ *I hope to see it.* □ *She refused to come.* □ *It never fails to amuse him.* □ *Do you wish to go home?* The infinitive (with *to*) is also used after adjectives and nouns: □ *easy to mend* □ *a book to read.*

In some constructions the infinitive functions as a verbal noun and may be interchangeable with its gerund (see -ING FORMS): □ *We love walking/to walk.* □ *He began writing/to write.* □ *To teach/Teaching young children requires great patience.* □ *To find/Finding another job is not always easy.*

In other constructions the infinitive and gerund are not interchangeable: □ *able to win–capable of winning* □ *a tendency to cheat–a habit of cheating* □ *He volunteered to help–he considered helping.*

Replacing an infinitive with a gerund sometimes changes the meaning of a sentence: □ *He stopped* [i.e. paused] *to read the notice.* □ *He stopped reading the notice* [i.e. He finished reading it]. □ *I remembered to lock the door* [i.e. I didn't forget to do it]. □ *I remembered locking the door* [i.e. I recalled having locked it]. See also SPLIT INFINITIVE.

inflammable The adjective *inflammable* describes something that will catch fire and burn easily: □ *This liquid is highly inflammable.* *Inflammable* may be wrongly interpreted as the opposite of its synonym *flammable* (by analogy with *sensitive–insensitive*; *visible–invisible*; *edible–inedible*; *capable–incapable*; etc.). The potential danger of such confusion has led to a preference, especially on warning signs and labels, for the less ambiguous terms *flammable* (denoting an inflammable substance) and *non-flammable* (denoting a substance that is not (in)flammable).

◆ *Inflammable* also means 'easily angered or excited': □ *an inflammable situation.* In this figurative sense it cannot be replaced by *flammable.*

The adjectives *inflammable* and *inflammatory* should not be confused; something *inflammatory* tends to arouse strong or violent feelings: □ *an inflammatory speech.*

inflation Inflation is a general increase in the level of prices: □ *The rate of inflation has risen to 16%.* The word is widely used, especially in informal contexts, to denote the rate of inflation: □ *Inflation has risen to 16%.*

◆ *Inflation* is sometimes misinterpreted as being synonymous with the level of prices: □ *They say inflation's going down, but my housekeeping money isn't going any further than it did.* A fall in (the rate of) inflation does not mean a fall in prices; it simply denotes a slower increase.

inflection *Inflection* is the term used for the change in form that words undergo in order to denote distinctions of number, tense, gender, case, etc. It is also used to describe the grammatical relation of a word to its root by inflection. See **DERIVED WORDS**.

◆ So one can say that the word *tables* is formed by inflection from *table*; *walked* is formed by inflection from *walk*; *heroine* is formed by inflection from *hero*; *them* is formed by inflection from *they*.

The spelling *inflexion* is occasionally seen in British English. This is not incorrect but it is now considered virtually obsolete and *inflection* is the preferred spelling.

inflict see **AFFLICT OR INFLICT?**

influenza see **FLU**.

info- Some people dislike the increasing use of *info-*, short for *information*, to form new blends and compounds, especially in informal contexts. □ *infotainment* (informative entertainment) □ *infomania* (preoccupation with information for its own sake) □ *infotech* (information technology).

◆ The noun *info* 'information' should be used only in informal contexts.

inform The verb *inform* is best avoided where *tell* would be adequate or more appropriate: □ *Please tell* [not *inform*] *your husband that his car is ready for collection.*

◆ Unlike *tell*, *inform* should not be followed by an infinitive: □ *They told* [not *informed*] *him to leave.* □ *They informed me of his departure.*

Inform is also used in the sense of 'inspire', which is closer to the meaning of the Latin verb *informare* 'give shape to', from which it is derived: □ *His learning informs his whole discourse.*

informant or **informer**? An *informant* is a person who gives information; an *informer* is a person who gives the police information about criminals and their activities: □ *The professor was one of the author's most useful informants.* □ *The police were tipped off about the robbery by an informer.*

◆ The noun *informer* may also be used in the neutral sense of *informant*, but to avoid misunderstanding it is best restricted to its more specific meaning.

infringe see **IMPINGE OR INFRINGE?**

ingenious or **ingenuous**? *Ingenious* means 'clever' or 'inventive'; *ingenuous* means 'innocent', 'naive', or 'frank': □ *an ingenious idea* □ *an ingenuous smile*. The two adjectives are not interchangeable, but are sometimes confused.

◆ The noun form *ingenuity*, originally derived from *ingenuous* and formerly used for both adjectives, is now restricted to the sense of 'cleverness' or 'inventiveness'; *ingenuousness* is the noun form of *ingenuous*.

Note the pronunciations of the two adjectives: the *e* of *ingenious* is long, as in *mean*; the *e* of *ingenuous* is short, as in *men*.

-ing forms The *-ing* form of a verb may be a present participle or a gerund (verbal noun): □ *I am learning Japanese* [present participle]. □ *Learning Japanese is not easy* [gerund]. It is sometimes difficult, and often unnecessary, to distinguish between a gerund and a present participle.

◆ Problems of usage arise when the gerund has its own subject: □ *She disapproves of your using the car.* □ *She disapproves of the house where she spent her childhood being demolished.* According to grammatical convention, the possessive form should always be used in such cases. The substitution of *you* for *your* in the first example (or of *me/him/us/them* for *my/his/our/their* in similar cases) would be unacceptable to many users, even in informal contexts. However, the substitution of *childhood's* for *childhood* in the second example would be clumsy, unidiomatic, and also unacceptable to many users.

Between these two extremes – the simple personal pronoun and the complex noun phrase – the possessive form is used with varying degrees of acceptability.

For personal names and nouns relating to people, animals, etc., the possessive form is usually preferred in formal contexts but is sometimes rejected in informal contexts: □ *She disapproves of Peter's using the car.* □ *She disapproves of the gardener's using the car.* If more than one name or noun is involved, the possessive form is usually rejected in all contexts: □ *She disapproves of Michael and Peter using the car.* □ *She disapproves of the cook and the gardener using the car.*

For abstract nouns and nouns relating to inanimate objects, which are rarely used with the possessive ending -'s, the possessive form is usually rejected: □ *She disapproves of the house being demolished.* □ *She disapproves of religion being taught in schools.*

In the four preceding examples, the absence of the possessive ending may cause confusion: the reader or listener is momentarily led to believe that *she disapproves of Michael/the cook/the house/religion.* Such confusion can often be avoided by restructuring the sentence or by replacing the gerund with a noun: □ *She disapproves of the demolition of the house.*

The use of the possessive form with such words as *painting, writing, meeting, cooking,* etc., which may denote either an action or its result, can be ambiguous in some contexts: □ *We were not informed of their meeting* [that they intended to hold a meeting]. □ *We were not informed of their meeting* [that they had met].

In other contexts, the use of the possessive form may alter the meaning of a sentence: □ *They watched the girl dancing* places the emphasis on the girl; □ *They watched the girl's dancing* places the emphasis on the dancing.

See also **APOSTROPHE; DANGLING PARTICIPLES; INFINITIVE; PARTICIPLES; 'S OR S'?; WANT.**

inherent This word, meaning 'essential or intrinsic', has two possible pronunciations: [in*heer*ĕnt] or [in*herr*ĕnt]. The first of these is the more traditional and is preferred by many users.

inheritance see **HERITAGE OR INHERITANCE?**

inhuman or **inhumane?** Careful users maintain the distinction between *inhuman* and *inhumane. Inhumane,* the opposite of *humane,* means 'lacking in compassion and kindness; cruel; not merciful': □ *inhumane treatment. Inhuman,* the opposite of *human,* is stronger and has a wider scope than *inhumane.* To be *inhuman* means to lack all human qualities, not only compassion and kindness: □ *inhuman violence* □ *inhuman living conditions.*

◆ *Inhuman* has the additional meaning of 'not having human form': □ *An inhuman shape appeared at the window.*

iniquity see **INEQUALITY, INEQUITY, OR INIQUITY?**

in-law The use of the plural noun *in-laws,* denoting a person's relatives by marriage, is best restricted to informal contexts: □ *My*

in-laws are coming for dinner on Saturday.
♦ The plural of *mother-in-law, father-in-law, son-in-law, daughter-in-law,* etc., is formed by adding s to the first element of the compound: *mothers-in-law, fathers-in-law,* etc.

in lieu The phrase *in lieu (of)* is best avoided where *instead (of)* would be adequate or more appropriate: □*She drove to the airport instead* [not *in lieu*] *of taking the train.*
♦ *In lieu (of)* is chiefly used in formal contexts with reference to the replacement of one thing with another or others of equivalent value or importance: □ *If they have to work on Christmas Day they should be given time off in lieu.* □ *We are sending two bottles of dessert wine in lieu of the champagne you ordered.*
The word *lieu* may be pronounced [lew] or [loo].

innocuous The adjective *innocuous,* meaning 'harmless': □*a few innocuous remarks,* is sometimes misspelt. Note the -*nn*-, the single *c*, and the vowel sequence -*uou*-.

innovative Many people dislike the frequent use of *innovative* in place of *new, creative, imaginative, progressive,* etc.: □*an innovative method of contraception* □*an innovative sales manager* □*an innovative company.*

inoculate or **vaccinate**? The verbs *inoculate* and *vaccinate* are virtually synonymous in the sense of 'introduce a vaccine into the body of a person or animal to provide immunity': □ *She has been inoculated* [or *vaccinated*] *against whooping cough. Inoculate* has a wider range of usage: it may refer to the introduction of a substance other than a vaccine and is also used in figurative contexts in the sense of 'instil': □*He inoculated his students with egalitarian ideals.*
♦ Note the spelling of *vaccinate,* particularly the -*cc*- and the single -*n*-.

inoculation This word is often misspelt, the most frequent error being the addition of an extra *n* as in *innocent*. Note the single *c* and the single *l*.

in order that and **in order to** The phrase *in order that* is followed by *may, might, shall,* or *should* rather than *can, could, will,* or *would*: □*He moved his suitcase in order that we might* [not *could*] *open the door.* □ *She drove him to the station in order that he should* [not *would*] *not miss his train.*
♦ These restrictions do not apply to the simpler expression *so that* (see **so**), which is often preferable to *in order that* in such contexts.
If the subordinate clause has the same subject as the main clause, *in order that* may be replaced by *in order to* followed by an infinitive: □ *He moved his suitcase in order to open the door.*
The phrase *in order to* is best avoided where *to* would be adequate: □ *He turned the key to* [not *in order to*] *open the door.*

input Many people object to the use of the noun *input* as a synonym for 'contribution': □ *We hope to have some input from the teaching staff at tomorrow's meeting.* □*positive input* 'approval or encouragement' □*negative input* 'criticism'.
♦ As a noun, *input* may be used to denote the power, energy, data, etc., put into a system or machine, or the resources, labour, raw materials, etc., required for production.
The verb *input* refers to the process of entering data into a computer: □ *Travel agents will be able to input data direct to a central computer.* In other contexts, use of the verb *input* is generally deprecated, other verbs being preferred: □ *contribute* [not *input*] *ideas to a meeting*

□ *provide with* [not *input*] *equipment.*

inquiry see ENQUIRY OR INQUIRY?

inside of Many people dislike the prepositional phrase *inside of*, meaning 'within' or 'in less than', in which the word *of* is incorrect. The phrase should not be used in formal contexts: □ *There was a cheque inside* [not *inside of*] *the envelope.* □ *The job was completed inside* [not *inside of*] *two weeks.*

◆ The addition of this superfluous *of* to the preposition *inside* may be influenced by the phrase *on the inside*, which is followed by *of* when it is used prepositionally: □ *a coupon on the inside of the wrapper.*

in so far as This expression may be written *in so far as* or *insofar as*, the latter being more frequent in American English: □ *I'll help you in so far as it is appropriate.*

◆ See also INASMUCH AS.

in spite of see DESPITE OR IN SPITE OF?

install or **instal**? Both spellings of this word are correct, although the first is more frequently used: □ *install a central-heating system.*

◆ If the spelling *instal* with a single *l* is followed, then this doubles before the suffixes beginning with a vowel: *installing, installed, installer, installation.*

In British English, *instalment* has a single *l*, in American English it usually has a double *l*.

instantly or **instantaneously**? The adverbs *instantly* and *instantaneously* are virtually interchangeable in the sense of 'immediately' or 'without delay': □ *He replied instantly/instantaneously.*

◆ *Instantaneously* has the additional meaning of 'very quickly' or 'almost simultaneously': □ *She was hit by the car and died instantaneously.*

instil This word, meaning 'introduce gradually', is often misspelt. It ends in a single *l* in British English.

◆ It is worth remembering that the *l* must be doubled before a suffix is added: *instilled.* See also SPELLING 1.

In American English the spelling is usually *instill*.

institute or **institution**? Both nouns are used to denote certain professional bodies and established organizations founded for research, study, charitable work, the promotion of a cause, etc.: □ *the Institute of Metals* □ *the British Standards Institution* □ *the Royal National Institute for the Blind* □ *the Royal National Lifeboat Institution.* The nouns also denote the buildings or premises used by these organizations.

◆ *Institution* has a range of additional meanings: 'the act of instituting': □ *the institution of a new electoral system*; 'an established social custom or practice': □ *the institution of marriage*; 'a school or hospital': □ *an educational institution* □ *He spent years in a mental institution.*

The verb *institute* means 'establish', 'initiate', or 'install'.

instructional or **instructive**? *Instructional* is the rarer word and means 'providing instruction(s)'; *instructive* is used in the wider sense of 'informative; enlightening': □ *an instructional leaflet* □ *an instructive experience.*

◆ Both adjectives may sometimes be applied to the same noun: □ *an instructional course* in intended to instruct and may succeed or fail in this objective; □ *an instructive course* succeeds in instructing, whether or not this was the intention.

insurance see ASSURANCE OR INSURANCE?

insure see ASSURE, ENSURE, OR INSURE?

integral Some people object to the frequent use of the phrase *integral part*, in which the adjective *integral* is often superfluous: □ *The study of local history is an integral part of the syllabus.* Most parts are *integral*, i.e. 'essential to the completeness of the whole', by definition.

◆ In many contexts the word *integral* would be better replaced by *essential, important*, etc.: □ *Cash registers have become an integral part of even the most backward industries in these competitive days.*

The usual pronunciation of *integral* is [íntigrăl], stressed on the first syllable; the variant pronunciation [intégrăl], stressed on the second syllable, is disliked by many users.

integrate The verb *integrate* is widely used in the sense of 'make or become part of a social group': □ *One of the aims of our organization is to integrate ethnic minorities into the community.* □ *Newcomers to the village often find it difficult to integrate.*

◆ In other contexts *integrate* is often better replaced by *mix, amalgamate, join, combine*, etc.: □ *a new television programme that combines* [not *integrates*] *learning with entertainment.*

Note the spelling of *integrate*, which does not begin with the prefix *inter-*.

intense or **intensive**? *Intense* means 'extreme' or 'very strong'; *intensive* means 'concentrated' or 'thorough': □ *intense pain* □ *intense heat* □ *intensive training* □ *an intensive search.* The two adjectives are not interchangeable, although both may be applied to the same noun: *intense/intensive study*.

◆ Both adjectives have additional senses: *intense* describes a person who has very strong and deep feelings; *intensive* has specialized meanings in grammar and agriculture and is used in such compounds as *intensive care* and *labour-intensive*.

inter see INTERMENT OR INTERNMENT?

inter- or **intra-**? The prefix *inter-* means 'between' or 'reciprocally'; *intra-* means 'within': □ *intercontinental* □ *interdependent* □ *intravenous* □ *intramural*.

◆ The two prefixes should not be confused: *international* means 'of two or more nations'; *intranational* means 'within one nation'.

The prefix *intra-* is most frequently found in medical contexts: □ *intracranial* □ *intramuscular* □ *intrauterine*.

interactive In computing, the adjective *interactive* refers to direct communication between the user and the computer: □ *The disks are interactive, which means that they pose questions on the screen, and you only get further information by answering* (*Daily Telegraph*). The term is also applied to television programmes, video games, etc., in which the viewer or player is physically involved in the progress or completion of the programme, game, etc.

intercede This verb, meaning 'mediate', is sometimes misspelt. Note the *-cede* ending, as in *concede, precede*, etc. (unlike *proceed, succeed*, etc.).

interface In science, computing, etc., the noun *interface* denotes a surface forming a common boundary or a point of communication. Its extended use as a synonym for 'interaction', 'liaison', 'link', '(point of) contact', etc., is disliked by many people: □ *the interface between professionals and lay people in the caring professions* □ *the interface of history and literature* □ *at the interface between design and technology*.

◆ The verb *interface* is also best restricted to technical contexts:

□ *The office microcomputers will interface with the main computer.*

interjections see EXCLAMATIONS.

interment or **internment**? *Interment* means 'burial'; *internment* means 'imprisonment': □ *the interment of the corpse* □ *the internment of the terrorists.*

◆ The two words should not be confused.

The noun *interment* and the verb *inter* (from which it is derived) are formal words that refer to the depositing of a dead body in the earth or in a tomb.

The noun *internment* is derived from the verb *intern*, which refers to the confinement of enemy aliens, prisoners of war, etc.

In both nouns and both verbs the stress falls on the second syllable.

The noun *intern*, stressed on the first syllable, is an American name for someone in the final stages of professional training, especially in medicine.

internecine The adjective *internecine* may refer to slaughter or carnage, mutual destruction, or conflict within a group: □ *an internecine battle* □ *internecine warfare* □ *an internecine dispute.*

◆ The first of these, the original meaning of the word, is the least frequent of the three; it is no longer listed in some dictionaries.

In British English the word is pronounced [intĕrneesīn]; the variant pronunciation [intĕrnesīn] is regarded by some as an Americanism.

internment see INTERMENT OR INTERNMENT?

interpersonal The adjective *interpersonal*, meaning 'between people', is disliked by some people as a vogue term and can often be replaced by a synonym, such as *social*, or by a simple paraphrase: □ *interpersonal skills* are social skills; □ *in an interpersonal situation* means 'with people'.

interpretive or **interpretative**? Either adjective may be used, but *interpretative* is the more frequent: □ *The appendix contains interpretative/interpretive notes on the text.*

intestinal The adjective *intestinal* is usually stressed on the third syllable, [intestīnl]. The variant pronunciation [intestinl], with the stress on the second syllable, is also heard.

in that The phrase *in that* means 'because' or 'to the extent that': □ *He is unsuitable for the job in that he has no relevant experience.* □ *The two machines are different in that one is fully automatic and the other is manually controlled.*

◆ In some contexts, however, *in that* may be better replaced by *because* or one of its synonyms: □ *We are in financial difficulties because* [not *in that*] *my wife has unfortunately recently been made redundant.*

in the fast lane, in the fast track see FAST LANE.

in the near future The phrase *in the near future* is disliked by some users as an unnecessarily wordy substitute for *soon*: □ *The electronics company is considering relocating to Swindon in the near future.*

in this day and age The cliché *in this day and age* is best avoided where *nowadays, today, now*, etc., would be adequate or more appropriate: □ *In this day and age a good education is not a passport to a successful career.*

into or **in to**? *Into* is a preposition with a variety of meanings; *in to* is a combination of the adverb *in* and the preposition or infinitive marker *to*: □ *I went into the house.* □ *I went in to fetch a book.* □ *I went in to tea.*

◆ It is important to recognize and maintain the distinction between these uses.

As prepositions, *into* and *in* are occasionally interchangeable: □ *He put the letter into/in his pocket. Into* usually suggests movement from the outside to the inside, whereas *in* suggests being or remaining inside. In many contexts the two prepositions are not interchangeable: □ *They sailed into the harbour at four o'clock.* □ *They sailed in the harbour all afternoon.*

intonation *Intonation* is a change in pitch that adds to the meaning of a spoken word, phrase, or sentence. It should not be confused with STRESS, which relates to loudness or emphasis, although the two are often used in combination.

◆ In English intonation is most noticeable in **QUESTIONS**, where the pitch of the voice tends to rise towards the end: □ *When did she arrive?* □ *Saturday?* The sentence □ *Jane doesn't want a cat,* spoken with rising intonation, means 'Does Jane want a cat?' or 'Is it true that Jane wants a cat?'; with falling intonation it is a neutral statement of fact. Other variations in the intonation of the sentence and the stress on individual words may produce a number of alternative interpretations, such as 'I don't believe that Jane wants a cat', 'Jane would like a pet of some sort, but not a cat', and 'Other people want a cat, but not Jane'.

Rising intonation is also heard in lists; falling intonation indicates the end of the list: □ *You can have carrots, peas, cabbage, or cauliflower.*

in toto The Latin phrase *in toto* means 'entirely' or 'completely': □ *He did not disagree in toto.*

◆ It is acceptable, but not necessary, to use italics when writing or printing this expression.

intra- see INTER- OR INTRA-?

intransitive see VERBS.

intrinsic or **extrinsic**? The adjective *intrinsic* means 'inherent', 'essential', or 'originating from within': □ *The discovery is of great intrinsic interest. Extrinsic,* the opposite of *intrinsic,* is less frequent in general usage: □ *The document is of extrinsic interest only.*

◆ The *intrinsic* value of a pound coin, for example, is the value of the metal from which it is made; its *extrinsic* value is one pound.

introvert see EXTROVERT OR INTROVERT?

Inuit The term *Inuit* refers to the people of North America and Greenland traditionally known as Eskimos. The term *Inuit* (meaning 'people') is preferred to *Eskimo* (meaning 'eater of raw flesh'), by the Inuit themselves. It may also be used to distinguish this people from the Eskimos of the Aleutian Islands and Siberia.

◆ *Inuit,* sometimes spelt *Innuit,* is pronounced [*in*yooit]. The plural is *In(n)uit* or *In(n)uits.*

invalid The adjective sense of 'not valid' is pronounced with the stress on the second syllable [in*val*id]. The noun sense of 'someone who is ill' is pronounced with the stress on the first syllable, either as [*in*vălid] or [*in*văleed].

◆ The verb sense, 'disable' or (usually followed by *out*), 'remove from active service because of illness or injury', may be pronounced [*in*vălid], [*in*văleed], or [invă*leed*].

inveigh or **inveigle**? To *inveigh* is to protest strongly; to *inveigle* is to persuade cleverly: □ *She inveighed against the inequity of the law.* □ *He inveigled us into signing the form. Inveigh,* an intransitive verb, is followed by *against,* whereas *inveigle* is transitive and often used with *into.*

◆ The two verbs are both formal and are sometimes confused. Note the *ei* spelling of both.

Inveigh is always pronounced [invay]; *inveigle* may be pronounced [invaygl] or [inveegl].

invent, design, or **discover**? *Invent* and *design* refer to the creation of something new; *discover* refers to the finding of something that is already in existence: □ *to invent a machine* □ *to design a new computer* □ *to discover a cure for cancer.*

◆ The three words sometimes overlap in usage. A scientific *discovery* may lead to an *invention,* and inventions have to be *designed.* Some people dislike the use of *invent* in place of *design:* a new type of car, for example, that is modelled on existing styles and uses a traditional method of propulsion, is *designed,* not *invented.*

inventory The noun *inventory,* unlike *invent* and *invention,* is stressed on the first syllable. The usual British pronunciation is [inventri]; in American English the -o- may be sounded: [inventori].

inverse see CONVERSE, INVERSE, OBVERSE, OR REVERSE?

inversion *Inversion* is a reversal of the normal order of the elements of a sentence or clause so that the subject follows the verb: □ *There goes the bus.* □ *In came Michael.* □ *At the bottom of the heap was the missing book.*

◆ Inversion is most frequently used in QUESTIONS: □ *Am I late?* It is also used after *so, neither,* and *nor:* □ *So are they.* □ *Neither do we,* and after some negative words and phrases: □ *Never have I heard such nonsense!* □ *On no account should he go.* The use of inversion in conditional clauses: □ *Had she known about his past, she would not have married him.* □ *There's a fire extinguisher here, should you need it,* is rather more formal than the use of an *if* clause: □ *If she had known ...* □ *... if you should need it.*

Inversion is optional after direct speech, but is best avoided if the subject is a pronoun: □ *'Go away!' cried the boy.* □ *'Go away!' he cried.* In poems and stories inversion is sometimes used for effect or variety: □ *In a hole in the tree lived a wise old owl.* □ *Stands the Church clock at ten to three?* (Rupert Brooke).

inverted commas see QUOTATION MARKS.

invite The use of the word *invite* as a noun, in place of *invitation,* is disliked and avoided by many users, even in informal contexts: □ *Have you had an invite to their party?* □ *Thank you for your invitation, which I am very pleased to accept.*

◆ Note that the stress pattern of the noun *invite* is different from that of the verb: the noun is stressed on the first syllable; the verb is stressed on the second syllable. See also STRESS.

involve Some people object to the frequent use of the verb *involve* and its derivatives in place of more specific or more appropriate synonyms: □ *This proposal will entail* [not *involve*] *further cuts in expenditure.* □ *Some changes may be necessary* [not *involved*]. □ *I have a number of questions concerning* [not *involving*] *teaching methods and discipline.* □ *These fingerprints are evidence of his participation* [not *involvement*] *in the robbery.*

◆ Many authorities recommend that *involve* and its derivatives be restricted to the sense of entanglement and complication: □ *the chairman's involvement in the scandal* □ *a long-winded and involved account of the incident.*

inward or **inwards**? In British English *inward* is principally used as an adjective, *inwards* being the usual form of the adverb meaning 'towards the inside': □ *inward feelings* □ *to push inwards.*

◆ The adverb *inward* is more frequently used in American English. See also **-WARD** OR **-WARDS**?

IQ This abbreviation for 'intelligence quotient': □ *The average IQ is one hundred*, must always be written with capital letters. The abbreviation may be written with full stops, *I.Q.*, but this form is becoming less frequent in modern usage (see **ABBREVIATIONS**).

◆ The abbreviation with lower-case letters, *i.q.*, stands for *idem quod*, a Latin phrase meaning 'the same as'.

irascible The formal word *irascible*, meaning 'easily angered', is sometimes misspelt. *Irascible* has a single *r* and ends in *-ible*, unlike its synonym *irritable*. Note also the *sc*.

ironic, ironical, ironically see IRONY.

iron out The phrasal verb *iron out* is widely used in the metaphorical sense of 'settle', 'resolve', 'solve', or 'remove': □ *We have a few more problems to iron out before work can begin.*

◆ It is best avoided, however, in contexts that may be associated with its literal meaning of 'smooth with an iron': □ *The laundry workers have ironed out their difficulties.* □ *The last stumbling block was ironed out at yesterday's meeting.*

irony *Irony* is the use of words to express the opposite of their accepted meaning, often for satirical or humorous effect.

◆ Some people object to the frequent use of the noun *irony* and its derivatives with reference to something paradoxical, incongruous, or odd: □ *She resigned when they rejected her proposals; the irony of the situation is that they have now adopted the system she proposed.* □ *It's ironic that he should win a skiing holiday just after breaking his leg.* □ *Ironically, it was the police inspector's car that was stolen.*

The adjectives *ironic* and *ironical* are both in use, *ironic* being the more frequent.

Irony may be used as a form of *sarcasm*, but the two words should not be confused: an *ironic* remark is more witty and less cruel than a *sarcastic* remark.

irrefutable This word, meaning 'impossible to be disproved': □ *irrefutable evidence*, may be stressed on the second or on the third syllable: [iref*yoot*ăbl] or [irif*yoot*ăbl]. The second pronunciation is becoming more common.

irregardless The word *irregardless* is a nonstandard blend of *irrespective* and *regardless*. Most dictionaries do not acknowledge its existence, but it is frequently heard in colloquial usage: □ *'Irregardless of what we say about Robbo, he done a good job,' was a near-miss by Elton Welsby for ITV in Bologna (The Guardian).* The word should be avoided in all contexts; either *irrespective* or *regardless* may be used in its place (see IRRESPECTIVE).

irrelevant This word is frequently misspelt. Note the *-rr-* and the vowels *i-e-e-a*.

irreparable This word, meaning 'unable to be repaired', is often mispronounced. The stress should fall on the second syllable and not the third [irep*ă*răbl].

◆ See also REPAIRABLE OR REPARABLE?

irresistible Note the spelling of this adjective, particularly the *-rr-* and the *-ible* (not *-able*) ending.

irrespective The word *irrespective* is most frequently used in the prepositional phrase *irrespective of*, meaning 'regardless of': □ *Applications are invited from all suitably qualified candidates, irrespective of age, sexual orientation, nationality, disability or religion.*

◆ The expression *irrespectively of* is generally considered to be unidiomatic.

Unlike *regardless*, *irrespective* should not be used adverbially in other contexts: □ *It soon began to rain but they carried on with their game regardless* [not *irrespective*].

See also **IRREGARDLESS**.

irrevocable In its general sense of 'not able to be changed': □ *an irrevocable decision*, the word *irrevocable* is stressed on the second syllable, [irevŏkǎbl]. The pronunciation [irivŏkǎbl], stressed on the third syllable, is restricted to a few legal or financial contexts, where the sense is literally 'not able to be revoked': □ *irrevocable letters of credit*.

irrupt see **ERUPT OR IRRUPT**?

-ise see **-IZE OR -ISE**?

-ism Some people object to the increasing use of the suffix *-ism*, in the sense of 'discrimination', to coin new words modelled on the nouns *racism* and *sexism*: □ *legislation against ageism* □ *the controversial issue of heterosexism* □ *ableism* □ *heightism*.

◆ The use of the suffix to form new nouns in the conventional sense of 'doctrine' or 'system' is acceptable in moderation: □ *the prospect of another five years of Thatcherism.*

-ist or **-ite**? Both these suffixes may be used to denote an adherent, follower, advocate, or supporter of a particular doctrine: □ *Stalinist* □ *Luddite* □ *communist* □ *Labourite*. The suffix *-ite* is sometimes used in a derogatory manner: people who call themselves *Trotskyists*, for example, may be described by opponents of Trotskyism as *Trotskyites*.

◆ The suffix *-ist*, which is also used to form adjectives, may face the same objection as **-ISM**: □ *ageist principles* □ *heterosexist attitudes* □ *classist* □ *genderist.*

isthmus The noun *isthmus*, meaning 'narrow strip of land', causes problems of spelling and pronunciation. Note the four adjacent consonants *-sthm-*. The [th] sound is not heard in the usual pronunciation [ismǔs]; the full pronunciation [isthmǔs] is no more or less correct.

it The pronoun *it* has a wide range of uses: to replace an abstract noun or the name of an inanimate object, as the subject of an impersonal verb, etc.: □ *He washed the towel and hung it out to dry.* □ *It hasn't rained for a week.* □ *I find it difficult to make new friends.* □ *It's obvious that she doesn't like him.* For this reason, the use of *it* may sometimes cause ambiguity or confusion: □ *She took her purse out of her handbag and put it on the table* [the purse or the handbag?]. □ *You can open the window if it gets too hot* [the window or the weather?].

◆ The constructions *it is/was … who* and *it is/was … that* should be used only for emphasis: □ *It was she who broke the window, so I don't see why you should pay for the repair.* □ *It's the weather that's making me feel tired – I'm not ill.*

In such constructions the verb agrees with the pronoun or noun that follows *is* or *was*, not with the word *it*: □ *It's I who wish* [not *wishes*] *to complain.* □ *It was they who were* [not *was*] *at fault.* □ *It is the books that make* [not *makes*] *the trunk so heavy.* (Note the use of *I* and *they*, rather than *me* and *them*; see also **I OR ME?; PRONOUNS**.)

The construction is not used with *where* or *when*: □ *It is in France that the best cheeses are to be found* [not *It is France where …*]. □ *It was in 1986 that he won the championship* [not *It was 1986 when ..*].

However, the construction should not be confused with such
statements as *It was dark when we arrived* and *It's snowing where my
parents live* or such expressions as *it is believed that ...* and *it is
possible that ....*

See also ITS OR IT'S?; THAT OR WHICH?

italics The word *italic* denotes a sloping typeface that is used for a
variety of purposes in English. In handwritten or typewritten
texts, underlining is generally used to indicate italics.

◆ The principal uses of italics are:

1 For the titles of books, newspapers, magazines, plays, films, works
of art, musical works, etc.: □ *The Economist* □ *An Ideal Husband*, by
Oscar Wilde □ Elgar's *Enigma Variations.*

2 For the names of ships, boats, trains, aircraft, etc.: □ Sir Francis
Chichester sailed round the world in *Gipsy Moth IV.*

3 For the Latin names of plants, animals, etc.: □ The tiger, *Panthera
tigris*, is found in Asia.

4 For foreign words and phrases that are not fully integrated into the
English language: □ This was his *pièce de résistance*. □ The teacher
is *in loco parentis*. It is sometimes difficult to judge whether a foreign
word or phrase should be italicized or not. Some dictionaries offer
guidance on this matter.

5 To indicate stress or emphasis: □ Is it *still* raining? □ I don't *like*
spiders, but I'm not afraid of them. Excessive italicization for the
purpose of stress or emphasis is avoided by careful users.

6 To draw attention to a particular word, phrase, or letter: □ How do
you pronounce *controversy*? □ Her surname is spelt with a double *s.*

-ite see -IST OR -ITE?

itinerary This word, meaning 'planned route of a journey', is sometimes misspelt. The careful pronunciation [ītiněrări] should
ensure its correct spelling.

its or **it's**? *It's*, a contraction of *it is* or *it has*, should not be confused
with *its*, the possessive form of *it*: □ *It's easy to tell the difference.*
□ *It's been raining for several hours.* □ *The lion has escaped from
its cage.* See also APOSTROPHE; CONTRACTIONS; 'S OR S'?

◆ The insertion of an apostrophe in the possessive form *its* is wrong
in all contexts, although it occasionally finds its way into print: □ *It's aim
is to encourage new ideas and developments in the field of learning
and teaching English* (advertisement for The English-Speaking
Union, *The Guardian*).

The omission of the apostrophe in the contraction *it's* is less
frequent, but equally unacceptable.

-ize or **-ise**? In British English, the sound [-īz] at the end of many
verbs may be spelt *-ize* or *-ise*: □ *baptize/baptise* □ *realize/realise*
□ *recognize/recognise* □ *organize/organise*; etc. Most modern
dictionaries, partly because of the American international influence, list *-ize* as the preferred spelling, giving *-ise* as an accepted
variant. Otherwise, *-ise* is generally as common as *-ize* in British
English.

◆ There is etymological justification for both spellings, the suffix being
derived via French *-iser* from Latin *-izare* and Greek *-izein.*

Whichever spelling is preferred, it is important to be consistent
within a single piece of writing, both in the choice of other *-ize/-ise*
words and in the spelling of any derivatives ending in *-ization/
-isation, -izer/-iser, -izable/-isable*, etc.

Capsize is the only *-ize* verb of more than one syllable that is never
spelt *-ise.*

However, there are a number of *-ise* verbs that cannot be spelt *-ize*; the most common of these are *advertise, advise, chastise, circumcise, comprise, compromise, despise, devise, enfranchise, excise, exercise, improvise, revise, supervise, surmise, surprise,* and *televise*. See also $\overline{\text{EXERCISE}}$ OR **EXORCISE**?

Verbs ending in *-yse*, such as *analyse* and *paralyse*, are never spelt *-yze* in British English.

In American English, *-ize* is always used for verbs that can have either ending in British English, but *-ise* is usually retained for verbs of the *advertise ... televise* group. *Analyse, paralyse,* etc., are spelt with z in American English.

Some people object to the modern tendency to create new verbs by the addition of *-ize/-ise* to a noun or adjective: □ *pedestrianize* □ *hospitalize* □ *prioritize* □ *finalize*. Such verbs are best avoided where a simpler form or synonym exists: *to martyrize* may be replaced with *to martyr, to finalize* can often be replaced with *to finish*. However, *-ize/-ise* verbs (and their derivatives) that have neither a one-word equivalent nor a simple paraphrase often serve a useful purpose: □ *to computerize the stock-control system* □ *the decimalization of British currency*.

jail or **gaol**? In British English these two spellings are both acceptable, although *jail* is preferred by many people. In American English *jail* is the only accepted spelling.

jargon *Jargon* is the technical language used within a particular subject or profession, such as science, computing, medicine, law, accountancy, etc.: □ *CVA or cerebral vascular accident is medical jargon for a stroke.*

◆ The term is also used to denote the complex, obscure, pretentious, or euphemistic language used by estate agents, journalists, sociologists, advertisers, bureaucrats, politicians, etc.: □ *In sociological jargon the class system has been replaced with a series of socioeconomic groups.*

Jargon of both types is acceptable, and often indispensable, in professional journals and in written or spoken communications between members of the same group. It should be avoided, however, in articles, brochures, insurance policies, etc., that are to be read and understood by lay people and in conversations with members of the general public. Jargon should not be used to impress, intimidate, confuse, or mislead the outsider. See also **COMMERCIALESE**; **JOURNALESE; OFFICIALESE.**

Jargon sometimes finds its way into everyday language in the form of **CLICHÉS** or vogue words, e.g. *interface, traumatic, user-friendly.* Such words and expressions are disliked and avoided by many users. Jargon should not be confused with **DIALECT** or **SLANG.**

jealousy see **ENVY** OR **JEALOUSY?**

jeopardize This word, meaning 'expose to danger', is often misspelt, the most frequent error being the omission of the letter *o*.

◆ Note that the vowel pattern is the same as in *leopard*.

jewellery or **jewelry**? This word has two spellings in British English. Both are acceptable although *jewelry*, standard in American English, is less frequent in British English.

◆ The preferred pronunciation is [*joo*ėlri] rather than the dialectal or nonstandard [*joo*lĕri].

jibe see **GIBE, JIBE,** OR **GYBE?**

jodhpurs This word, meaning 'riding trousers', is often misspelt, the *h* being either incorrectly placed or omitted completely.

◆ The word originates from *Jodhpur*, a city in India, hence the unusual spelling.

join or **joint**? The nouns *join* and *joint* are synonymous (but not interchangeable) in the sense of 'place where two parts are joined'. *Join* most frequently refers to the visual effect of the act of joining, the line or seam between two flat or flexible parts (such as paper, fabric, carpet, string, etc.): □ *You can hardly see the join.* A *joint* is more practical or functional, joining two rigid three-dimensional parts: □ *The pipe was leaking at one of the joints.* □ *the joint between the shaft and the head.*

journalese

journalese *Journalese* is a derogatory name for the style of writing or language that is considered to be typical of newspapers.

◆ It is characterized by the use of CLICHÉS and short sensational synonyms, e.g. *axe*, *bid*, *probe*, which occur especially in headlines. The telegraphic style of newspaper headlines sometimes gives rise to ambiguity or confusion: □ *Merseyside pioneers abuse teaching pack for schools* (*The Guardian*). This headline was intended to mean 'A teaching pack about child abuse has been launched on Merseyside', but it could be interpreted as 'Pioneers on Merseyside are misusing a teaching pack'.

Careful users avoid such techniques and devices in formal writing. See also JARGON.

judgment or **judgement**? Either spelling of this word is acceptable, although *judgement* is probably more common in British English and *judgment* in American English.

◆ Some authorities that follow the British spelling *judgement* in general contexts prefer the spelling *judgment* in legal works.

Whichever spelling of *judg(e)ment* is adopted, it is advisable to be consistent in the spelling of this word and words such as *abridg(e)ment* and *acknowledg(e)ment*.

judicial or **judicious**? *Judicial* means 'of judgment in a court of law' or 'of the administration of justice'; *judicious* means 'having or showing good judgment' or 'prudent': □ *judicial proceedings* □ *a judicious choice*.

◆ The two adjectives are not interchangeable, although both may be applied to the same noun: □ *a judicial decision* is the decision of a court of law; □ *a judicious decision* is a wise decision.

Judicial may also mean 'of a judge; impartial; fair'; it is in this sense that it is most likely to be confused with *judicious*.

juncture The phrase *at this juncture* refers to a critical point in time; many people object to its frequent use in place of *now*: □ *The leader's resignation at this juncture would have a disastrous effect on the members' morale.* □ *I suggest that we take a short break for refreshments now* [not *at this juncture*].

◆ This use of *juncture* has developed from its meaning of 'concurrence or conjunction of events or circumstances'. The noun is rarely used in its original sense, as a synonym of 'junction' or 'joint'.

junta This word refers to a controlling political council and has various pronunciations. The preferred pronunciation is [*juntă*].

◆ Other alternatives such as [*huuntă*] and [*juuntă*] have arisen in imitation of the Spanish pronunciation.

just *Just* has a variety of adverbial senses: 'at this moment', 'exactly', 'only', etc. For this reason it must be carefully positioned in a sentence in order to convey the intended meaning: □ *Your son has just eaten two cakes* [i.e. a short time ago]. □ *Your son has eaten just two cakes* [i.e. not one or three, etc.]. □ *Just your son has eaten two cakes* [i.e. only your son; no one else]. Transposing *just* and *not* may also change the meaning of a sentence: □ *I'm just not tired.* □ *I'm not just tired; I'm hungry too.*

◆ In the sense of 'in the very recent past', *just* should be used with the perfect tense in formal contexts: □ *They have just arrived at the station.* Its use with the past tense in this sense (*They just arrived* ...) is regarded as an Americanism and is avoided by many careful users, even in informal contexts.

Just may be used in place of, but not in addition to, *exactly*: □ *That's just* [not *just exactly*] *what I need.*

K The letter *K*, short for *kilo-*, is increasingly used to represent 1000, especially in sums of money: □ *a salary of £50K plus company car* □ *houses priced from £250K upwards.* The abbreviation is also used in spoken language: □ *She was earning a hundred K in the City.*

◆ This usage was adopted from the jargon of computing, where *K* may represent 1000 or 1024.

kaleidoscope This word is sometimes misspelt. Note particularly the *-ei-* and the first *o* from the Greek *eidos*, meaning 'form'.

◆ The correct pronunciation is [kălīdóskŏp].

karaoke The noun *karaoke*, denoting a form of entertainment in which people sing along with a pre-recorded tape, causes problems of spelling and pronunciation. Of Japanese origin, the word may be pronounced [karrăōki] or [karriōki] in English.

kerb see CURB OR KERB?

key Some people object to the increasingly frequent use of the word *key* as an adjective, in the sense of 'fundamental', 'essential', 'crucial', 'most important', 'indispensable', etc.: □ *a number of key individuals to manage their top UK stores* □ *setting up a policy committee that will take key decisions* (*Sunday Times*).

◆ In many contexts it is better replaced by one of its synonyms.

kibbutzim *Kibbutzim* is the plural form of the noun *kibbutz*, denoting a collective community in Israel. *Kibbutz* is pronounced [kibuuts], rhyming with *puts*; *kibbutzim* is stressed on the final syllable [kibuutseem].

kick-start The figurative use of the verb *kick-start* in the sense of 'take action to set in motion (again)' is becoming rather hackneyed, especially in the phrase *kick-start the economy*: □ *Plans to balance income tax cuts with measures to boost business and kickstart the economy will form a key element in the chancellor's strategy* (*Sunday Times*). □ *to kick-start the housing market.*

◆ The metaphor is derived from the world of motorcycling, where the verb refers to the act of starting an engine by kicking or pressing a pedal.

kid The use of the noun *kid* as a synonym for 'child' or 'young person' is best restricted to informal contexts: □ *Things were very different when I was a kid.* □ *One of the local kids broke the window.* □ *Have you got any kids?*

kidnap The final *p* of the word *kidnap* is doubled before a suffix beginning with a vowel: □ *kidnapped* □ *kidnapper.* See also SPELLING 1.

kilo The word *kilo*, pronounced [keelō], is most frequently used as an abbreviation for *kilogram*: □ *a kilo of sugar* □ *50 kilos of coal.*

◆ Some dictionaries also list *kilo* as an abbreviation for *kilometre*, but this usage is very rare.

Note that the first syllable of the prefix *kilo-*, in such words as *kilometre*, *kilogram*, etc., is pronounced like the word *kill*, not *keel*.

kilometre This word may be stressed on the first syllable [kilŏmeetĕ] or on the second syllable [kilomitĕ].

◆ The first of these pronunciations is the more widely accepted in British English. The second, regarded by some as an Americanism, is probably becoming more current in British English. See also **METER OR METRE?**; **STRESS**.

kindly The word *kindly* may be used as an adjective, meaning 'kind' or 'sympathetic', or as an adverb, meaning 'in a kind way': □ *a kindly policeman* □ *a kindly smile* □ *They treated us kindly.*

◆ The adjective *kindly* has no one-word adverbial form: □ *He smiled in a kindly manner.*

The adverb *kindly* is also used in polite or angry requests or commands: □ *Patrons are kindly requested to refrain from smoking.* □ *Kindly allow me to tell you what happened.* □ *Would you kindly take your hand off my knee!* In such contexts it is often better replaced by *please*.

kind of In formal contexts the phrases *kind of, sort of,* and *type of,* in which *kind, sort,* and *type* are in the singular, should be preceded by *this* or *that* (rather than *these* or *those*) and followed by a singular noun: □ *this kind of story* □ *that sort of biscuit.*

◆ Such expressions as *these kind of stories, those sort of biscuits,* etc., are sometimes heard in informal contexts but are disliked and avoided by careful users.

A plural noun may be used if the expression is rephrased: □ *Stories of this kind are very popular.* Note that the verb agrees with *stories,* not *kind.*

Where more than one kind, sort, or type is concerned, the whole expression may be put into the plural: □ *She specializes in detective stories and horror stories: these kinds of stories are very popular.* In such cases, the noun that follows *kinds/sorts/types of* may remain in the singular: ... *these kinds of story are very popular.* (Note that the verb here agrees with *kinds,* not *story.*)

The same principles apply to *kind of, sort of,* and *type of* in other contexts: □ *a different type of vegetable* □ *many different types of vegetable/vegetables.* See also **SINGULAR OR PLURAL?**

The use of *kind of* or *sort of* in place of *rather* or *somewhat* is best restricted to informal contexts: □ *I sort of like him.* □ *It's kind of warm in here.* The spelling *kinda* is sometimes used in writing to denote 'kind of' in casual speech.

knee-jerk In figurative contexts, the term *knee-jerk* is applied to an automatic, predictable, and/or unthinking reaction, as opposed to a more considered response: □ *A knee-jerk reaction to the problem could make matters worse.* □ *Industrial action is the knee-jerk response of many union leaders.* The term should be confined to informal usage and not be overused.

◆ A knee-jerk reaction or response is the metaphorical equivalent of the physical reflex action that results from a light blow just below the kneecap.

kneeled or **knelt**? Either word may be used as the past tense and past participle of the verb *kneel. Knelt* is more frequent in British English: □ *He knelt on the grass*; *kneeled* in American English.

◆ See also **-ED OR -T?**

knit or **knitted**? *Knitted* is the more frequent form of the past tense and past participle of the verb *knit,* especially in the literal sense: □ *I (have) knitted a cardigan for the baby.* □ *She was wearing a knitted jacket.*

◆ *Knit*, an alternative form of the past tense and past participle, is largely restricted to figurative contexts, especially in combination with an adverb before a noun: □ *a closely knit family* □ *a well-knit athlete*.

knock-on effect The phrase *knock-on effect* refers to a series of related causes and effects: □ *The reduction in taxes will have a knock-on effect throughout the economy.*

◆ It should not be used when the word *effect* would be adequate: □ *the effects* [not *knock-on effects*] *of the new safety regulations.*

know see YOU KNOW.

knowledgeable This word, meaning 'having clear knowledge or understanding', is sometimes misspelt. Note that the final *-e* of *knowledge* is retained before the suffix *-able*.

laboratory The usual pronunciation of this word in British English is [lăborrătŏri], with the stress on the second syllable; the second *o* is sometimes not sounded. In American English the stress falls on the first and fourth syllables, [labŏrători]; the first *o* is sometimes not sounded.

laborious The word *laborious* is sometimes misspelt, the most frequent error being the insertion of a *u* after the first *o*, as in *labour*.

lack When using the verb *lack*, *lack for* in place of *lack* is unacceptable to many people, and the superfluous *for* is best omitted: □ *She did not lack* [not *lack for*] *friends.*

◆ The use of *lack for* may be influenced by the synonymous phrase *want for*, in which the optional preposition *for* serves the useful purpose of avoiding ambiguity or confusion with *want* in the sense of 'desire': □ *She did not want for friends.*

lacquer This word is sometimes misspelt. Note that it has only one *-u-*: the word ends in *-er*, and not *-eur* as in *liqueur*.

laden or **loaded**? *Laden*, a past participle of the verb *lade*, is principally used as an adjective, meaning 'weighed down' or 'burdened'; *loaded* is the past tense and past participle of the verb *load*: □ *The tree was laden with apples.* □ *We overtook a heavily laden lorry.* □ *He (has) loaded the car.* The verb *lade*, meaning 'load with cargo', is rarely used in modern times in any other form, except in the term *bill of lading.*

◆ *Loaded* is also used as an adjective in literal and figurative senses: □ *a loaded gun* □ *a loaded question,* 'one that contains hidden implications or is misleading'.

The two adjectives should not be confused: □ *The van is laden with furniture* implies that the van is weighed down or full to overflowing with furniture; □ *The van is loaded with furniture* simply means that the van contains furniture.

lady see WOMAN.

laid, lain see LAY OR LIE?

lama or **llama**? The spelling of these words is sometimes confused. A *lama* is a Lamaist monk, the order of Lamaism being a form of Buddhism of Tibet and Mongolia. A *llama* is a South American mammal related to the camel. Note the *ll-* at the beginning of this word.

lamentable This word has two pronunciations. The traditional British English pronunciation is [lamĕntăbl].

◆ The stress may also fall on the second syllable [lămentăbl], although this is disliked and avoided by some users.

languor Note the spelling of this word, particularly the unusual *-uor* ending. *Languor* is a formal word that means 'laziness; weariness'; the derived adjective is spelt *languorous*.

lasso A *lasso* is a rope with a noose, used for catching horses or cattle. There are two acceptable pronunciations although [lasoo] is the

194

more frequent in contemporary British usage.

◆ The second pronunciation [*lasō*] was once standard but is now less frequent.

last To avoid ambiguity, the adjective *last* should be replaced, where necessary, with an appropriate synonym, such as *latest*, *final*, or *preceding*: □ *His latest* [not *last*] *novel was published in June.* □ *His final* [not *last*] *novel was published in June.* □ *The final* [not *last*] *chapter contains a list of useful addresses.* □ *The preceding* [not *last*] *chapter contains a list of useful addresses.*

◆ The use of *last* may also cause confusion in such phrases as *last Wednesday*, used on a Friday, which may mean 'two days ago' or 'nine days ago'. If the context is clearly in the past, *last* may be replaced by *on* before days of the current week: □ *I posted it on* [not *last*] *Wednesday*. See also NEXT OR THIS?

Last may be retained where the context makes its meaning clear: □ *His last novel was published posthumously.* □ *The identity of the narrator is not revealed until the last chapter.*

late Used directly before a noun denoting a person, the adjective *late* may mean 'dead' or 'former': □ *The widow gave her late husband's clothes to charity.* □ *The late president has written his memoirs.* To avoid confusion, *late* (in the sense of 'former') is often better replaced by *ex-* or *former*: □ *the ex-chairman* □ *my former flatmate.*

lath or **lathe**? These two nouns should not be confused. A *lath* is a thin strip of wood; a *lathe* is a machine for shaping wood, metal, etc. Note that it is the noun *lath*, not *lathe*, that is used in the simile *as thin as a lath.*

◆ *Lath* is pronounced [lahth]; *lathe* is pronounced [laydh].

lather This word has various pronunciations. The traditional pronunciation rhymes with *gather*, but the pronunciation rhyming with *father* is becoming more frequent in contemporary usage.

◆ The pronunciation [*laythèr*] is incorrect.

latter see FORMER AND LATTER.

launch The verb *launch* is widely used in the figurative sense of 'set in motion', 'start', or 'introduce': □ *The campaign will be launched next month.* □ *They have just launched their new perfume.*

◆ *Launch* is also used figuratively as a noun: □ *He gave a party to celebrate the launch of his latest novel.*

Some people object to the frequency of this usage, replacing *launch* with an appropriate synonym wherever possible.

lavatory see TOILET, LAVATORY, LOO, OR BATHROOM?

law and order Careful speakers pronounce this phrase without an intrusive [r] sound between the words *law* and *and*. Similar care should be taken with the pronunciation of other words and phrases containing the sound [aw] followed by a vowel, such as *drawing, awe-inspiring, I saw it.*

lawful, legal, or **legitimate**? All these adjectives mean 'authorized by law', but there are differences of sense, usage, and application between them: □ *the lawful owner* □ *a legal contract* □ *a legitimate organization.*

◆ *Lawful* means 'allowed by law' or 'rightful'; it is largely restricted to formal contexts or set phrases, such as *one's lawful business.*

Legal is more widely used, having the additional meaning of 'relating to law': □ *the legal profession* □ *legal advice* □ *the legal system* □ *legal action.*

The adjective *legitimate* is principally applied to children born in wedlock: □ *the king's legitimate son.* It also means 'reasonable', 'logical', 'genuine', or 'valid': □ *a legitimate excuse* □ *a legitimate reason.*

lay or lie? The verb *lay*, which is usually transitive – i.e. has an object – is often confused with *lie*, which is intransitive, i.e. does not have an object: □ *I'll lay the towel on the sand to dry.* □ *She's going to lie down for a while.*

◆ Careful users maintain the distinction between the two verbs in all contexts.

This confusion is probably due to the fact that the word *lay* also serves as the past tense of *lie*: □ *The baby lay in his cot and screamed.* □ *You'd better lay the baby in his cot.*

The past participle of *lie* is *lain*; the word *laid* (note the spelling) is the past tense and past participle of *lay*: □ *They have lain in the sun for too long.* □ *We (have) laid our coats on the bed.*

This verb *lie*, meaning 'rest in a horizontal position', should not be confused with the unrelated verb *lie*, meaning 'be untruthful'. The past tense and past participle of the latter are regular: □ *He (has) lied about his age.* The present participle of both these verbs is *lying*; the present participle of the verb *lay* is *laying.*

The verb *lay* has a number of specific uses: □ *to lay eggs* □ *to lay the table* □ *to lay a ghost*; etc. The expression *to lay low*, meaning 'to bring down', should not be confused with *to lie low*, meaning 'to stay in hiding'.

The verb *lay* is rarely used without a direct object, a notable exception being the sense of 'produce eggs': □ *If the hens don't lay there will be no eggs for breakfast.* The verb *lie* never has a direct object.

lead or led? These two words are often confused. *Lead* means 'guide by going in front': □ *He was leading the walking party*, and is pronounced [leed]. The past tense of this verb is *led*. This is sometimes wrongly spelt as *lead* because the pronunciation is the same as that of the metal: □ *as heavy as lead*, pronounced [led].

leadership *Leadership* is the state or rank of a leader; it also denotes qualities associated with a good leader: □ *elected to the leadership* □ *to lack leadership potential.* The use of the noun in place of *leaders* is disliked by some people: □ *China's leadership appeared to be stepping up efforts to promote its version of recent history* (*Daily Telegraph*).

leading-edge The adjectival use of *leading-edge* is best avoided where *advanced* or *up-to-date* would be adequate or more appropriate: □ *leading-edge technology* □ *a leading-edge project.*

◆ The noun *leading edge* denotes the forward edge of an aerofoil, wing, etc. The noun is also used figuratively, in the vogue expression *at the leading edge*: □ *This impressive product is at the leading edge of both lexicographical and computer technology* (Harrap catalogue). See also CUTTING EDGE.

leading question A *leading question* suggests or prompts the expected or desired answer, such as: □ *Did you see the defendant stab his wife with a kitchen knife?* □ *Do you approve of the wholesale slaughter of innocent animals for their fur?*

◆ Many people object to the frequent use of the term with reference to questions that are challenging, unfair, embarrassing, etc.: □ *'Are there going to be any redundancies at the factory?' 'That's a leading question.'*

leak The use of the verb and noun *leak* with reference to the unofficial, surreptitious, or improper disclosure of secret information is acceptable in most contexts: □*Details of the report were leaked to the press.* □*The managing director's secretary denied all responsibility for the leak.*

◆ The verb *leak* is used both transitively and intransitively in this sense: □*He leaked the story.* □*The story leaked out.*

leaned or **leant**? Either word may be used as the past tense and past participle of the verb *lean*: □*She leaned/leant forwards to open the window.*

◆ *Leaned* may be pronounced [leend] or [lent]; *leant* is always pronounced [lent]. See also **-ED OR -T?**

leaped or **leapt**? Either word may be used as the past tense and past participle of the verb *leap*: □*They leaped/leapt across the very wide ditch.*

◆ *Leaped* may be pronounced [leept] or [lept]; *leapt* is always pronounced [lept]. See also **-ED OR -T?**

learn or **teach**? The use of the verb *learn* in place of *teach* is wrong: □*He's teaching* [not *learning*] *me to swim.*

◆ To *learn* is to gain knowledge; to *teach* is to impart knowledge. See also **LEARNED OR LEARNT?**

learned or **learnt**? Either word may be used as the past tense and past participle of the verb *learn*: □*Have you learned/learnt the words of the song?*

◆ The past tense and past participle *learned* may be pronounced [lernd] or [lernt]; it should not be confused with the two-syllable adjective *learned* [*le*rnid], meaning 'erudite': □*a very learned professor.*

See also **-ED OR -T?**; **LEARN OR TEACH?**

learning curve The phrase *learning curve* refers to the process of acquiring new knowledge or experience as if represented by a graph. (The rate of learning is usually not uniform: the curve may rise steeply at the beginning, when a large amount of knowledge is acquired in a relatively short time.) It is a vogue term, often found in business contexts, and should not be overused: □*to help new employees up the learning curve* □*Most schools have only just started their second year of LMS and head teachers admit to being on a steep learning curve* (*The Bookseller*).

learnt see **LEARNED OR LEARNT?**

lease see **HIRE OR RENT?**

leave or **let**? The use of the verb *leave* in place of *let*, especially in the expressions *let go* and *let be*, is regarded as incorrect and avoided by many users: □*You mustn't let* [not *leave*] *go of the rope.* □*I told the children to let* [not *leave*] *him be.* The expressions *leave alone* and *let alone*, however, are virtually interchangeable in the sense of 'refrain from disturbing, bothering, interfering with, etc.': □*Leave/Let the dog alone.*

◆ *Leave alone* also means 'allow or cause to be alone', in which sense it cannot be replaced by *let alone*: □*Please don't leave me alone – I'm afraid of the dark.*

Let alone is also used as a set phrase meaning 'not to mention' or 'still less': □*They can't afford minced beef, let alone fillet steak.* See also **LET**.

led see **LEAD OR LED?**

leeward This word has two possible pronunciations. The generally accepted pronunciation is [*lee*wărd] but [looărd] is used in nautical contexts.

legal see LAWFUL, LEGAL, OR LEGITIMATE?

legalize see DECRIMINALIZE OR LEGALIZE?

legendary The use of the adjective *legendary* in the sense of 'very famous or notorious' may be misleading or confusing: □ *The legendary Dick Turpin rode a horse called Black Bess.* □ Listening to recordings of the legendary Andrés Segovia during the 1930s ... (*Reader's Digest*).

◆ The context of the second example makes it clear that Andrés Segovia existed in fact, not legend, but the first example is ambiguous.

legible or **readable**? The adjective *legible* describes something that can be deciphered and read; *readable* describes something that may be read with interest, enjoyment, or ease: □ *legible handwriting* □ *a very readable novel.*

◆ *Readable* is also used as a synonym for 'legible': □ *The text is barely readable without a magnifying glass.*

See also ILLEGIBLE OR UNREADABLE?

legionary see LEGIONNAIRE.

legionnaire Note the spelling of this word, particularly the *-nn-*. A *legionnaire* is a (former) member of a military legion, such as the French Foreign Legion, the British Legion, or the American Legion; the noun also occurs in the name of a serious disease, *legionnaires' disease.*

◆ *Legionnaire* should not be confused with the noun *legionary*, which has a single *n* and specifically refers to a member of an ancient Roman legion.

legitimate see LAWFUL, LEGAL, OR LEGITIMATE?

leisure This word, meaning 'time spent free from work', is sometimes misspelt. Note the *-ei-* spelling.

◆ *Leisure* is commonly pronounced [*lezhĕ*] in British English and [*leezhăr*] in American English.

leisurely The word *leisurely* may be used as an adjective or, more rarely, as an adverb, meaning 'without haste': □ *stroll at a leisurely pace* □ *She walked leisurely up the garden.*

lend or **loan**? The word *lend* is used only as a verb; in British English *loan* is used principally as a noun: □ *He lent me his pen.* □ *Thank you for the loan of your lawn mower.* The use of *loan* as a verb is widely regarded as an Americanism. It is becoming increasingly acceptable, however, with reference to the lending of large sums of money, valuable works of art, etc.: □ *The bank will loan us the money we need to finance the setting up of the new venture.* □ *This picture has been loaned to the gallery by the Duke and Duchess of Kent.*

◆ The use of the verb *lend* in place of *borrow* is wrong: □ *Can I borrow* [not *lend*] *your umbrella, please?* To *lend* is to give for temporary use; to *borrow* is to take for temporary use.

lengthways or **lengthwise**? Either word may be used as an adverb in British English: □ *Fold the sheet lengthways/lengthwise before ironing it.*

◆ As an adjective, and as an adverb in American English, *lengthwise* is preferred to *lengthways*. See also -WISE OR -WAYS?

lengthy The adjective *lengthy* means 'tediously, excessively, or unusually long'; it should not be used in place of *long* as a neutral antonym of *short*: □ *The children became very restless during the headmaster's lengthy speech.* □ *She has long* [not *lengthy*] *dark hair and brown eyes.*

◆ *Lengthy* may be pronounced [*leng*thi] or [*lenk*thi]. Note the consonant sequence *-ngth-* in the spelling.

leopard This word is sometimes misspelt. The most frequent error is the omission of the *o* which is not pronounced.

less see FEWER OR LESS?

let Used in the imperative, *let* should be followed by an object pronoun rather than a subject pronoun: □ *Let them try.* □ *Let him finish his meal first.* □ *Let Paul and me* [not *I*] see the letter.

◆ *Let's*, an informal contraction of *let us*, is used to introduce a suggestion or proposal made to the other member(s) of one's group: □ *Let's stay here.*

The preferred negative form of *let's* is *let's not*, although *don't let's* is also used in British English: □ *Let's not go to the party.* See also **HIRE OR RENT?; LEAVE OR LET?**

letter writing There are a number of conventions relating to the style and layout of a formal or semiformal letter.

◆ **1** The sender's address, followed by the date, should appear at the top of the letter, usually in the right-hand corner. The recipient's name and address appear below this, on the left-hand side of the page. Punctuation of the address – a comma at the end of each line (except the final line, which has a full stop) and sometimes after the house number – is optional.

2 The salutation (*Dear Sir, Dear Madam, Dear Miss Jones, Dear Mr Brown*, or, increasingly, under American influence, *Dear James Chapman*, etc., where the writer wants to avoid the formality of *Dear Mr Chapman* and the informality of *Dear James*) is set on a separate line, beginning with a capital letter and ending with a comma in British English, a colon in American English. See also **ABBREVIATIONS; MS, MRS, OR MISS?**

3 The letter itself should be divided into paragraphs, with or without indentation. The style and content of the letter depend on the level of formality (see also **COMMERCIALESE**).

4 The letter is closed with any of a number of fixed phrases, the most frequent being *Yours sincerely* (if the recipient's name is used in the salutation) or *Yours faithfully* (if an impersonal salutation, such as *Dear Sir* or *Dear Madam*, is used). Like the salutation, this phrase is set on a separate line, beginning with a capital letter and ending with a comma.

5 The signature is usually followed by the sender's name, title, and office (if appropriate).

6 Some of these conventions also apply to informal letters: the position of the sender's address, the punctuation and layout of the salutation and closing phrase, etc. An informal letter may begin with the recipient's first name and end with any of a number of expressions, such as *Best wishes, Yours, Love*, etc. The recipient's name and address are usually omitted and it is rarely necessary to add the sender's name after the signature.

leukaemia This word is sometimes misspelt. Note the three sets of vowels: *eu*, *ae*, and *ia* in British English. The American English spelling is *leukemia*.

level The noun *level* serves a useful purpose in a variety of literal and figurative senses but is sometimes superfluous or unnecessarily vague: □ *a high level of unemployment* (high unemployment) □ *an increase in the noise level* (more noise) □ *decisions made at management level* (decisions made by the management).

level playing field The phrase *level playing field* is increasingly used in figurative contexts, denoting a situation where all can compete on equal terms: □ *These* [the single European market rules] *are meant to establish a level playing field for competition between community countries in the single market* (*The Guardian*). □*I don't mind trying to compete on a level playing field with the rest of the book trade, but ...* (*The Bookseller*).

liable or **likely**? Both adjectives are used to express probability, followed by an infinitive with *to*. *Liable* refers to habitual probability, often based on past experience; *likely* refers to a specific probability that may be without precedent: □ *The dog is liable to bite strangers.* □ *The dog is likely to bite you if you pull his tail.* □ *The shelf is liable to collapse when it is filled with books.* □ *The shelf is likely to collapse if it is filled with books.* Careful users maintain the distinction between the two words.

◆ The adjectives *apt* and *prone*, which are similar in sense and usage to *liable*, principally refer to disposition, inclination, or tendency: □ *He is apt/prone to lose his temper.*

Liable also means 'responsible (for)' or 'subject (to)': □ *She is liable for their debts.* □ *He is liable to epileptic attacks. Prone* is interchangeable with *liable* in the second of these senses: □ *She is prone to indigestion.* See also LIKELY.

liaison The noun *liaison* and its derived verb *liaise* are often misspelt, the most frequent error being the omission of the second *i*.

◆ Some people object to the widespread use of *liaison* and *liaise* as synonyms for 'communication', 'communicate', or '(maintain) contact', and the use of *liaison* to refer to an illicit sexual relationship: □ *Closer liaison between teachers and social workers might have prevented this tragedy.* □ *Overseas travel will be necessary to liaise with subsidiaries and distributors in Europe, North America, and the Far East.* □ *His wife found out about his liaison with his secretary.*

libel or **slander**? Both words refer to defamatory statements: *libel* is written, drawn, printed, or otherwise recorded in permanent form; *slander* is spoken or conveyed by gesture.

◆ In informal contexts the word *libel* is often used in place of *slander*. Both words may be used as nouns or as verbs. The final *l* of *libel* is doubled before a suffix beginning with a vowel in British English; the final *r* of *slander* is never doubled. See also SPELLING 1.

library The pronunciation of this word is [*lī*brări]. Careful users avoid dropping the second syllable [*lī*bri], but this pronunciation is frequently heard.

licence or **license**? In British English, the noun is spelt *licence*, the verb *license*: □ *a television licence* □*an off-licence* □*poetic licence* □ *to license one's car* □ *(un)licensed premises* □ *licensing hours.* In American English, both the noun and verb are spelt *license.*

lichen This word has two pronunciations [*lī*kĕn] or [*litch*ĕn]. Some people prefer the first of these, which is the same pronunciation as *liken.*

licorice see LIQUORICE.

lie see LAY OR LIE?

lieu see IN LIEU.

lieutenant This word is often misspelt, the most frequent errors occurring in the first syllable: *lieu-*. The pronunciation of this syllable varies. The most frequent pronunciation in British English is as in *left*, in nautical contexts the pronunciation is as in *let*, and in American English, the pronunciation is as in *loot.*

lifelong or **livelong**? The adjective *lifelong* means 'lasting or continuing for a lifetime': □ *my lifelong friend* □ *his lifelong admiration for her work*. The adjective *livelong*, meaning 'very long' or 'whole', is chiefly used in the old-fashioned poetic expression *all the livelong day*.

◆ *Lifelong* is usually written as a solid compound, the hyphenated form *life-long* being an accepted but rare variant.

Livelong, which is etymologically unrelated to the word *live*, is pronounced [*liv*long].

lifestyle Some people object to the frequent use of the term *lifestyle*, a synonym for 'way of life', by advertisers, journalists, etc.: □ *urban lifestyle* □ *consumer lifestyle values* □ *lifestyle packaging* □ *The spread of Aids is likely to have tremendous effects on the personal lifestyles of many people*.

◆ Kenneth Hudson (*The Dictionary of Even More Diseased English*) notes a connection between lifestyle and possessions: 'Cars, houses, holidays, clothes and furniture have a great deal to do with "lifestyle". A naked savage living in a reed hut ... would be allowed "a way of life", but not a "lifestyle".'

There is an increasing tendency for *lifestyle* to be written as a one-word compound. It is sometimes hyphenated (*life-style*) but not usually written as two separate words.

lighted or **lit**? Either word may be used as the past tense and past participle of the verb *light*. *Lit* is the more frequent in British English: □ *Have you lit the fire?* □ *He lit his pipe.* □ *The hall was lit by candles*.

◆ Used adjectivally before a noun, *lighted* is the preferred form: □ *a lighted torch* □ *a lighted match* □ *a lighted cigarette*. If the adjective is modified by an adverb, however, *lighted* may be replaced by *lit*: □ *a well-lit room* □ *a badly lit stage*.

lightning or **lightening**? These two words are often confused. *Lightning* is a flash of light produced by atmospheric electricity: □ *thunder and lightning*. *Lightning* is also used as an adjective to describe things that happen very quickly: □ *the lightning strike by postal workers*. *Lightening* is the present participle/gerund of the verb *lighten*: □ *lightening someone's load*.

light-year A *light-year* is a unit of distance, not time; careful users avoid such expressions as: □ *It happened light-years ago.* □ *The wedding seemed light-years away*.

◆ A *light-year* is the distance travelled by light in one year (approximately six million million miles); the term is used in astronomy.

likable see LIKEABLE OR LIKABLE?

like The use of *like* as a conjunction, introducing a clause that contains a verb, is disliked by many users and is best avoided in formal contexts, where *as*, *as if*, or *as though* should be used instead: □ *The garden looks as if* [not *like*] *it has been neglected for many years*. □ *As* [not *like*] *the headmaster said, corporal punishment is not used in this school*.

◆ The use of *like* as a preposition, introducing a noun, pronoun, or noun phrase, is acceptable in all contexts: □ *The garden looks like a jungle*. □ *Like the headmaster, she disapproves of corporal punishment*. □ *His sister writes like him*. □ *Like you and me, they are keen amateur photographers*. (Note that the preposition *like* is followed by the object pronouns *him*, *me*, etc., not the subject pronouns *he*, *I*, etc.)

The use of *as* in place of the preposition *like* may change the meaning of the sentence: □ *As your father, I have a right to know.* □ *Like your father, I have a right to know.* □ *She plays like a professional.* □ *She plays as a professional.* In other contexts, the two prepositions may be virtually interchangeable: □ *He was dressed as/like a policeman.* □ *They treat me like/as an idiot.*

See also **AS; SUCH AS OR LIKE?**

-like The suffix *-like* may be attached with or without a hyphen in British English: □ *spadelike* or *spade-like* □ *autumnlike* or *autumn-like.*

◆ When *-like* is added to one- or two-syllable words that do not end in *-l,* the hyphen is often omitted: □ *dreamlike* □ *birdlike* □ *paperlike,* particularly in words that are well-established in the English language, such as *lifelike* and *ladylike.* Words that end in *-l,* especially those that end in *-ll,* and words of three or more syllables, usually retain the hyphen when adding *-like:* □ *coal-like* □ *model-like* □ *doll-like* □ *potato-like.*

likeable or **likable**? Both spellings of this word are acceptable. See **SPELLING 3.**

likely In British English the adverb *likely,* meaning 'probably', is not used on its own in formal contexts; it is usually preceded by *very, quite, more,* or *most:* □ *They will very likely arrive tomorrow morning.* □ *I'll most likely see you at the party.*

◆ Some people avoid the problem by using *probably* or by rephrasing the sentence to make *likely* an adjective: □ *They will probably arrive tomorrow morning.* □ *They are likely to arrive tomorrow morning.*

As an adjective, *likely* may stand alone or be modified by an adverb: □ *a likely effect* □ *a more likely explanation.* See also **LIABLE OR LIKELY?**

limited Some people object to the use of the adjective *limited* as a synonym for 'small', 'little', 'few', etc.: □ *a limited income* □ *with limited assistance* □ *of limited education.*

◆ *Limited* is best reserved for its original meaning of 'restricted': □ *Their powers are limited.* □ *We have a limited choice.* □ *He finds it difficult to work in a limited space.*

lineage or **linage**? The noun *lineage,* pronounced [*lin*iij], means 'line of descent' or 'ancestry'; the noun *linage,* pronounced [*līn*ij], means 'number of printed or written lines': □ *the emperor's lineage* □ *payment based on linage.*

◆ Neither word is in frequent use: *lineage* is largely restricted to formal contexts, *linage* to the world of printing and publishing.

Lineage is also used as a variant spelling of *linage,* in which case it is pronounced [*līn*ij].

lineament or **liniment**? The noun *lineament,* meaning 'feature', is largely restricted to formal or literary contexts: □ *the noble lineaments of his face.* It should not be confused with the noun *liniment,* denoting a liquid rubbed into the skin to relieve pain or stiffness: □ *a bottle of liniment.*

linguist The noun *linguist* may denote a person who knows a number of foreign languages or a specialist in linguistics, the study of language. □ *Mr Evans, an accomplished linguist, was a great help to us on our European tour.* □ *At yesterday's lecture the linguist Noam Chomsky expounded his theory of language structure.*

◆ A *modern linguist* is someone who can speak or is studying modern European languages such as French, German, and Spanish. Although the noun *linguist* is rarely ambiguous in context, it may be replaced, if necessary, by the synonym *polyglot* (for the first sense) or *linguistician* (for the second sense).

liniment see LINEAMENT OR LINIMENT?

liquefy or **liquify**? Both spellings of this word are acceptable, although the first is generally preferred.

liqueur or **liquor**? The spellings of these words are sometimes confused. A *liqueur* [li*kyoor*] or, less commonly, [li*ker*] is a sweet alcoholic drink taken after a meal. *Liquor* [*li*kĕ] is any alcoholic beverage.

liquidate or **liquidize**? The verb *liquidate* is used in finance: □ *to liquidate a company* □ *to liquidate one's assets,* and as an informal euphemism for 'kill': □ *He liquidated his rivals.* To *liquidize* is to make something liquid, usually in a blender or liquidizer: □ *Liquidize the fruit and add it to the whipped cream.*

liquify see LIQUEFY OR LIQUIFY?

liquor see LIQUEUR OR LIQUOR?

liquorice There are two possible pronunciations of this word. The traditional pronunciation [*li*kŏris] is preferred by many, but [*li*kŏrish] is also acceptable and widely used.

◆ In American English the noun is spelt *licorice.*

lit see LIGHTED OR LIT?

literal, literary, or **literate**? *Literal* means 'word for word; exact'; *literary* means 'relating to literature'; *literate* means 'able to read and write; (well-)educated': □ *a literal translation* □ *the literal meaning of the word* □ *literary works* □ *a literary critic* □ *They are barely literate.* □ *a highly literate candidate.*

◆ All three adjectives are ultimately derived from Latin *littera* 'letter', but they are not interchangeable in any of their senses.

Some people avoid using *literate* to mean 'well-educated' where there is a risk of ambiguity. In a job advertisement, for example, *literate* may refer to anything from a basic ability to read and write to degree-level qualifications.

In such combinations as □ *computer literate,* the word *literate* is reduced to the sense of 'competent; able; experienced'.

literally The use of the adverb *literally* as an intensifier, especially in figurative contexts, is disliked by many users: □ *It literally rained all night.* □ *I was literally tearing my hair out by the time they arrived.*

◆ The effect of this usage may be misleading or ambiguous: □ *We were literally starving,* or quite absurd: □ *She literally laughed her head off.*

As the opposite of *figuratively, literally* may be used to indicate that a metaphorical expression is to be interpreted at its face value: □ *The dog had literally bitten off more than it could chew.*

literary, literate see LITERAL, LITERARY, OR LITERATE?

literature Some people object to the use of the noun *literature,* with its connotations of greatness, to denote brochures, leaflets, and other written or printed matter: □ *They're sending us some literature about holidays in the Far East.*

◆ The principal objection is not that *literature* is an unnecessary synonym for some other noun – it has no one-word equivalent in general use for this sense – but 'that so reputable a word should be put to so menial a duty' (H.W. Fowler, *A Dictionary of Modern English Usage*).

little see FEW; FEWER OR LESS?

live The adjective *live,* meaning 'not prerecorded': □ *a live broadcast* □ *live music,* is increasingly used in the extended sense of 'actually present': □ *They have never performed in front of a live audience.*

◆ This usage inevitably leads to humorous associations with the principal meaning of *live*, i.e. 'living' or 'alive', in contrast to 'dead'. See also **AID**.

livelong see LIFELONG OR LIVELONG?

livid The adjective *livid* may be used to describe a range of colours, from the dark purple colour of a bruise, through the greyish-blue colour of a *livid* sky, to the pale complexion of somebody who is *livid* with fear.

◆ *Livid* is perhaps most frequently used in the sense of 'very angry': □*His mother will be livid when she finds out.* This usage is best restricted to informal contexts.

living room see LOUNGE.

llama see LAMA OR LLAMA?

loaded see LADEN OR LOADED?

loadsamoney The word *loadsamoney*, from the name of a character created by the alternative comedian Harry Enfield, is used as a noun or adjectivally with reference to excessive or ostentatious wealth: □ *the loadsamoney economy* □ *making loadsamoney in the City.*

◆ The prefix *loadsa-*, derived from *loadsamoney*, is sometimes attached to other nouns in the sense of 'a lot of': □*Labour has loadsapolicies to push, but no cash for a campaign* (*The Guardian*). All these terms are best restricted to informal contexts.

loan see LEND OR LOAN?

loath, loth, or **loathe**? *Loath* and *loth* are adjectives, meaning 'unwilling' or 'reluctant'; *loathe* is a verb, meaning 'detest': □*He was loath/loth to move to London.* □*He loathes working in London. Loath* and *loathe* are frequently confused: □ *The Independent ... would be loathe to see Mr Kinnock turn the clock back* (*Sunday Times*). For this reason some users prefer *loth*, the more distinctive variant spelling of the adjective.

◆ The adjectives *loath* and *loth* are pronounced [lōth], with the final *th* sound of *bath*; the verb *loathe* is pronounced [lōdh], with the final *th* sound of *bathe*.

Note the spelling of the adjective *loathsome*, which may be pronounced [*lōdh*sõm] or [*lōth*sõm].

locale, locality, or **location**? All three nouns mean 'place', but they are not altogether synonymous. *Locale*, the most formal of the three, refers to a place that is connected with a particular event or series of events: □*an unlikely locale for a human rights convention* (example adapted from COBUILD corpus). *Locality* often refers to a neighbourhood or geographical area: □ *There are a number of bookshops in the locality. Location* means 'site' or 'situation' and is often used as a formal or pretentious substitute for the nouns *place, position,* etc. (see also **LOCATE**): □*to move to a different location* □*the location of the town hall.*

locate The verb *locate* and its derived noun *location* are best avoided where *find, situate, place, position,* etc., would be adequate or more appropriate: □*I can't find* [not *locate*] *my front-door key.* □ *The shrub should be planted in a sheltered position* [not *location*]. □*Offices in a prestigious part of the City* [not *a prestigious City location*].

location see LOCALE, LOCALITY, OR LOCATION?

lone see ALONE OR LONE?

longevity This word, meaning 'long length of life', is usually pronounced [lon*jev*īti] although [long*jev*īti] is also frequently used.
◆ The pronunciation [long*gev*īti] is nonstandard.

longitude This word, referring to the distance west or east of the Greenwich meridian, may be pronounced with a *j*-sound [*lon*jityood] or a *g*-sound [*long*gityood].

loo see TOILET, LAVATORY, LOO, OR BATHROOM?

lookalike The noun *lookalike* denotes someone who closely resembles another person, usually a famous person: □ *a Prince Charles lookalike* □ *the Marilyn Monroe lookalike competition.*
◆ Some users consider *lookalike* to be an unnecessary synonym, of American origin, for the noun *double*.
Lookalike is sometimes written as a hyphenated compound, *look-alike*.

loose or **loosen**? The verb *loose* means 'release', 'set free', or 'undo'; the verb *loosen* means 'make or become less tight': □ *She loosed the lion from its cage.* □ *He loosened his belt.* The two verbs are not interchangeable.
◆ The adjective *loose*, which means 'free' or 'not tight', may be applied to something that has been *loosened*: □ *The lion was loose.* □ *His belt was loose.*
The verb *loose* is rarely used in modern times. It is occasionally confused with the verb *lose*, which is similar in spelling and pronunciation (*loose* is pronounced [loos]; *lose* is pronounced [looz]).

lose see LOOSE OR LOOSEN?

lot The expressions *a lot (of)* and *lots (of)* are best avoided in formal contexts, where they may be replaced by *many, much, a great deal (of), a good deal (of),* etc.: □ *We have many* [not *lots of*] *books.* □ *They received a great deal of* [not *a lot of*] *help.*
◆ See also MANY; MUCH; SINGULAR OR PLURAL?

loth see LOATH, LOTH, OR LOATHE?

lots see LOT.

loud or **loudly**? *Loud* may be used as an adjective or adverb: □ *a loud noise* □ *He shouted as loud as he could.* The adverb *loudly* may be substituted for *loud* in all its adverbial uses except the phrase *out loud*, meaning 'audibly': □ *She read the poem out loud* (not *out loudly*). It is not always acceptable, however, to use the adverb *loud* in place of *loudly*: □ *They protested loudly* [not *loud*] *and angrily.* □ *loudly* [not *loud*] *dressed in a blue-and-yellow striped jacket.*

lounge The *lounge* of a private house or flat is the room used for relaxation, recreation, and the reception of guests, as opposed to the *dining room*: □ *She showed the vicar into the lounge.* Some people consider the synonyms *sitting room* and *living room* to be less pretentious than *lounge*.
◆ The word *lounge* also denotes a room in a hotel, pub, club, or airport: □ *Coffee will be served in the lounge.* □ *The passengers waited in the departure lounge.*
The noun *parlour*, an old-fashioned synonym for *lounge*, is derived from the French verb *parler*, meaning 'to speak': □ *The maid has tidied the parlour.* The word *parlour* also has a number of specific uses: □ *beauty parlour* □ *ice-cream parlour.*
The term *drawing room* (short for *withdrawing room*), another synonym, has connotations of grandeur and formality: □ *The ladies retired to the drawing room.*
Sitting room, living room, drawing room, and dining room are

sometimes hyphenated in British English.

low or **lowly**? The adjective *low*, the opposite of *high*, has a number of senses: □ *a low wall* □ *a low temperature* □ *a low voice* □ *low morale* □ *to feel low*. The adjective *lowly*, meaning 'humble' or 'inferior', is much more restricted in usage and is formal: □ *their lowly abode* □ *a lowly job*.

◆ Both adjectives may be applied to the same noun with different connotations: □ *the low status of women in 18th-century society* □ *the lowly status of the gardener*.

As an adverb, *lowly* can mean 'in a low manner' or 'in a lowly manner', but it is very rarely used in either sense. The word *low* may be used adverbially: □ *to lie low* □ *to bow low* □ *low-heeled shoes* □ *a low-cut neckline*.

low-key Some people object to the frequent use of the adjective *low-key*, meaning 'of low intensity', in place of *modest, restrained, subdued, unassertive*, etc.: □ *The reception was a very low-key affair*.

◆ The variant *low-keyed* is also used from time to time.

lowly see LOW OR LOWLY?

low-profile see PROFILE.

Ltd see PLC.

lumbar or **lumber**? These two words are identical in pronunciation and are sometimes confused. *Lumbar* is an adjective used in medical contexts, referring to the lower part of the back and sides: □ *a lumbar puncture* □ *the lumbar vertebrae*. *Lumber* is used as a noun or verb. In the sense of 'unwanted articles', the noun *lumber* is chiefly found in British English: □ *the lumber room*; in the sense of 'timber' it is chiefly found in American English: □ *heaps of lumber*. The verb *lumber* means 'move heavily, awkwardly, etc.': □ *An elephant lumbered past*; in the sense of 'burden' it should be restricted to informal contexts: □ *I got lumbered with the job of delivering the leaflets*.

lunch or **luncheon**? Both nouns denote a midday meal: a *luncheon* is usually a formal social occasion; *lunch* is often a light informal meal or a fuller meal at which business is conducted: □ *The Princess of Wales was the guest of honour at the luncheon*. □ *We stopped at a pub for lunch*. □ *They discussed the terms of the contract at their business lunch*.

◆ The use of *luncheon* as a synonym for 'lunch' is generally considered to be old-fashioned, surviving only in such terms as *luncheon meat* and *luncheon voucher*.

See also DINNER, LUNCH, TEA, OR SUPPER?

lure see ALLURE OR LURE?

luxuriant or **luxurious**? *Luxuriant* means 'profuse', 'lush', or 'fertile'; *luxurious* means 'sumptuous' or 'characterized by luxury': □ *luxuriant vegetation* □ *a luxurious hotel*. The two adjectives are not interchangeable: *luxuriant* is principally applied to things that produce abundantly; *luxurious* to things that are very comfortable, expensive, opulent, self-indulgent, etc.

◆ The noun *luxury* is also used as an adjective, meaning 'desirable but not essential': □ *luxury goods*. Its use as a synonym for 'luxurious', especially in advertisements: □ *a luxury car* □ *a luxury hotel* □ *luxury flats*, etc., is disliked by some.

lying see LAY OR LIE?

mac see MACINTOSH OR MACKINTOSH?

macabre Note the spelling of this word, which ends in *-re* in both British and American English. It means 'relating to death; gruesome': □ *a macabre tale.* The *r* is not always sounded in speech, the pronunciations [mǎ*kahb*ĕ] and [mǎ*kahb*rĕ] being equally acceptable to most people.

machinations This word, meaning 'devious plots or conspiracies', is traditionally pronounced [mak*inaysh*ŏnz], although the alternative pronunciation [mash*inaysh*ŏnz] is becoming increasingly common.

machismo The noun *machismo,* denoting aggressive masculinity: □ *the machismo of the leader,* may be pronounced [ma*kiz*mō] or [ma*chiz*mō]. Note that the *ch* does not have the *sh* sound of *machine.*

◆ Derived from a Spanish word meaning 'male' (see MACHO), it is a derogatory word that is disliked by some users of British English and is best restricted to informal contexts.

macho The adjective *macho,* the Spanish word for 'male', has derogatory connotations in English, describing a man who displays his masculinity in an aggressive or ostentatious way: □ *a macho image* □ *the macho hero.* Like MACHISMO, *macho* should not be used in formal contexts or overused in informal contexts: it is sometimes better replaced by *masculine, virile, male,* etc.

◆ The *ch* in *macho,* unlike *machismo,* is always pronounced [ch], not [k]: [*macho*].

macintosh or **mackintosh**? The noun *mac(k)intosh,* meaning 'raincoat', may be spelt with or without the *-k-.* Similarly, the informal abbreviation of the noun may be spelt *mac* or *mack.*

◆ The spelling *mackintosh* is more frequent than *macintosh,* whereas *mac* is more frequent than *mack.*

The word derives from the name of the Scottish chemist Charles *Macintosh* (1760–1843), who patented a waterproof fabric made of rubberized cloth in 1823.

mack, mackintosh see MACINTOSH OR MACKINTOSH?

macro- and **micro-** *Macro-* means 'large'; *micro-* means 'small'. Both prefixes are used in scientific and technical terms, such as: □ *macroeconomics* □ *microorganism* □ *macrobiotic* □ *microwave* □ *macrocosm* □ *microcosm* □ *macroscopic* □ *microscopic* □ *microprocessor* □ *microchip.* The use of *macro-* and *micro-* in other contexts, e.g. □ *macrocontract* □ *microskirt,* in place of the adjectives *large, great, small, tiny,* etc., is best avoided.

◆ The insertion of a hyphen between the prefix *macro-* or *micro-* and a word beginning with a vowel is optional: *macroeconomics* and *microorganism,* for example, may be replaced with *macro-economics* and *micro-organism.* See also HYPHEN 1.

Madam or **Madame**? *Madam* is a polite term of address for a woman;

the word may be written with a capital or lower-case *m*: □ *Would madam like a cup of coffee?* □ *Can I help you, Madam? Madame,* written with a capital *M*, is the French equivalent of *Mrs*: □ *Wax models of famous people are displayed at Madame Tussaud's.*

◆ The usual English pronunciation of both words is [*mad*ăm]; *Madame* is pronounced [mădam] or [mădahm], anglicized forms of the French pronunciation.

Madam is also used as an impersonal salutation in **LETTER WRITING** and as a formal title of respect: □ *Dear Madam* □ *Madam President*. In both these uses the word is always written with a capital *M*.

Mesdames, the plural of the French word *Madame*, also serves as the plural form of *Madam*. It is usually pronounced [*may*dam] in English.

The noun *madam* denotes a woman who runs a brothel or a girl who is impudent, conceited, precocious, badly behaved, etc.

magic or **magical**? The adjective *magic* is more closely related to the art or practice of magic than *magical*, which is used in the wider sense of 'enchanting': □ *a magic wand* □ *a magic potion* □ *a magic spell* □ *a magical experience* □ *the magical world of make-believe*.

◆ The two adjectives are virtually interchangeable in many contexts, although *magic* is retained in certain fixed expressions, such as: □ *magic carpet* □ *magic lantern*, etc., and *magical* is sometimes preferred for things that happen as if by magic: □ *a magical transformation*. *Magic*, but not *magical*, is also used in informal contexts to mean 'wonderful': □ *The holiday was magic!*

magnitude The noun *magnitude* is best avoided where *size, extent, importance, greatness*, etc., would be adequate or more appropriate: □ *the magnitude of the problem*.

◆ The expression *of the first magnitude* is used in astronomy to describe the brightness of a star; its figurative use, in the sense of 'greatest' or 'most important', is disliked by some people: □ *a disaster of the first magnitude*.

Mahomet see **MUSLIM OR MOSLEM?**

maintenance The noun *maintenance*, which is related to the verb *maintain*, is often misspelt, a common error being the substitution of *-tain-* for *-ten-* in the middle of the word. Note also the *-ance* ending.

major Some people dislike the frequent use of the adjective *major* in place of *great, important, chief, principal, serious*, etc.: □ *There was certainly major news interest in the details of the background of a man convicted of murdering five members of his family* (*Daily Mail*).

◆ Although *major* is an accepted synonym of these words, it should not be used to excess.

majority and **minority** *Majority* means 'more than half of the total number'; *minority* means 'less than half of the total number': □ *the majority of the books* □ *a minority of his friends*.

◆ *Majority* and *minority* should not be used to denote the greater or lesser part of a single item: □ *the greater part* [not *the majority*] *of the house* □ *less than half* [not *the minority*] *of the meal*.

A *majority* may be as small as 51%; a *minority* may be as large as 49%. For this reason, *majority* and *minority* are best avoided where *most, a few*, etc., would be more appropriate.

Majority and *minority* may be singular or plural nouns. If the people or items in question are considered as a group, a singular verb is used; if they are considered as individuals, a plural verb is used: □ *Only a minority was in favour of the proposal.* □ *The majority have refused to pay.* See also **COLLECTIVE NOUNS; SINGULAR OR PLURAL?**

The two nouns also denote the difference between the greater and lesser numbers; in this sense they are always singular: □ *The Labour candidate's majority has increased.*

male or **masculine**? The adjective *male* refers to the sex of a person, animal, or plant; it is the opposite of **FEMALE**: □ *a male kangaroo* □ *male genital organs. Masculine* is applied only to people (or their attributes) or to words (see **GENDER**); it is the opposite of **FEMININE**: □ *masculine strength.*

◆ With reference to people, *male* is used only of the sex that does not bear children; it is used to distinguish men or boys from women or girls but has no further connotations: □ *We have a male French teacher and a female German teacher.*

Masculine, on the other hand, may be used of both sexes; it refers to characteristics, qualities, etc., that are considered typical of men or are traditionally associated with men: □ *a masculine walk* □ *masculine clothes.*

The noun *male* is best reserved for animals and plants, *man* and *boy* being the preferred terms for male human beings, unless the question of age makes these nouns inappropriate: □ *Haemophilia is almost exclusively restricted to males.*

See also **BOY; CHAUVINISM; MAN.**

malevolent, malicious, or **malignant**? All these adjectives mean 'wishing harm to others', but there are differences of sense, usage, and application between them: □ *a malevolent look* □ *malicious gossip* □ *cruel, malignant intentions.*

◆ *Malignant* is the strongest of the three, describing an intense desire for evil. It is common in medical contexts, in the sense of 'cancerous', 'resistant to treatment', or 'uncontrollable': □ *a malignant tumour.*

The adjectives *malevolent* and *malicious* are interchangeable in many contexts. *Malicious*, the more frequent, is also used in law with reference to premeditated crime: □ *malicious intent.*

man Many people consider the use of the noun *man* as a synonym for 'person' to be ambiguous and/or sexist: □ *the best man for the job* □ *All men are equal.* With reference to individual human beings of unspecified sex, it is usually possible to use *person, people, human being, individual, everyone, worker(s), citizen(s),* etc., in place of *man* or *men*: □ *the best person for the job* □ *All people are equal.*

◆ Idiomatic expressions, such as *the man in the street, to a man, as one man,* or *be one's own man,* and compounds, such as *manhole, manpower, man-made,* or *man-hour,* should not be changed but may be replaced with a synonym or paraphrase if necessary: □ *without exception* (for *to a man*) □ *be independent* (for *be one's own man*) □ *workforce* (for *manpower*) □ *synthetic* (for *man-made*).

Some users also object to the verb *man*, preferring *operate, staff, work, run,* etc.

The use of *man* in the sense of 'male adult' dates from around the 11th century. Before this time, in Old English, the noun *man* denoted a human being of either sex and the nouns *wer* and *wīf* were used to distinguish between male and female (respectively). *Wīf* was subsequently combined with *man* to form *wīfman*, from which the noun *woman* is derived. The word *wīf* also survives in the noun *wife* and in compounds such as *fishwife* and *midwife*, where the *-wife* element simply means 'woman' and does not necessarily refer to a married woman.

See also **BOY; CHAIR; GENTLEMAN; MALE OR MASCULINE?; MANKIND; SEXISM; WOMAN.**

manageable This word, meaning 'able to be controlled': □ *manageable in small numbers*, retains the -*e*- to indicate the softness of the *g*.

mandatory The adjective *mandatory* is usually pronounced [mandătŏri].

◆ The alternative pronunciation [mandaytŏri] is disliked by many users and is best avoided.

Some people object to the frequent use of *mandatory* as a synonym for 'compulsory', 'obligatory', or 'essential': □ *A degree in archaeology is desirable, but not mandatory, for this post.*

mankind The use of the noun *mankind* to denote human beings collectively may be confused with its second sense of 'men in general' (as opposed to *womankind*, meaning 'women in general'): □ *the future of mankind.*

◆ The word *humankind*, coined as a replacement for the first sense of *mankind*, is disliked by many users. *Humanity* may be ambiguous, having the additional meaning of 'kindness', but *the human race* is acceptable to most: □ *the future of the human race.* See also **MAN.**

man-management The term *man-management* denotes the management of people rather than processes, usually in an industrial environment: □ *An honours graduate is required, with 3 years man-management experience.*

◆ Like other *man*- compounds, the term is disliked and avoided by some users: □ *You will need to have skills in people management* (*Daily Telegraph*). See also **MAN.**

manoeuvre This word is sometimes misspelt. Note the vowel sequence -*oeu*- and the -*re* ending in British English. The American spelling is *maneuver*. See also -AE- AND -OE-.

◆ The derived adjective is *manoeuvrable* in British English, *maneuverable* in American English.

mantel or **mantle**? A *mantel*, or more commonly a *mantelpiece*, is a shelf forming part of an ornamental structure round a fireplace. A *mantle* is a cloak or something that covers: □ *shrouded in a mantle of secrecy.*

◆ The spelling *mantle* is also possible for the fireplace shelf, but is much rarer. The spelling *mantlepiece* is not acknowledged by many dictionaries and is best avoided.

many In formal contexts the adjective *many* may be used in place of the informal expressions *a lot (of)* and *lots (of)* (see **LOT**). *Many* is also used in informal contexts, especially in negative and interrogative sentences: □ *She doesn't buy many clothes.* □ *Have you got many pets?* In some positive sentences, however, *a lot of* and *lots of* are more idiomatic than *many* in informal contexts: □ *We have a lot of* [not *many*] *books.*

◆ *Many* denotes a large number (as opposed to *much*, which denotes a large amount); it is therefore used with a plural verb: □ *Many have disappeared.* □ *Many houses were destroyed.* However, in the idiomatic expressions *many a ...* and *many's the ...* a singular verb is used: □ *Many a child has dreamt of becoming a film star.* □ *Many's the time I've walked down this road.*

margarine The usual pronunciation of this word has a soft *g* [marjăreen].

◆ The original pronunciation, with a hard *g*, as in *Margaret*, is now rarely used, even though it is more in keeping with the spelling and the etymology of the word.

marginal Some people object to the use of the adjective *marginal* as a synonym for 'small' or 'slight': □ *marginal changes* □ *a marginal improvement* □ *a marginal effect* □ *a student of marginal ability.*

◆ *Marginal* means 'close to a margin or limit', sometimes with reference to a lower limit: □ *marginal profits* □ *a ceremony of marginal, not primary importance.*

The adjective also has a number of specific uses, notably in politics: □ *a marginal seat* (or *constituency*) is one in which the Member of Parliament has only a small majority. *Marginal* is also used to describe land on the edge of cultivated areas that is too poor to produce many crops.

marginalize The verb *marginalize* means 'treat as unimportant' or 're-legate to the fringes (of society, an organization, etc.)'. Some-times spelt *marginalise* (see -IZE OR -ISE?), it is chiefly used in the passive: □ *Britain risks being marginalized in the EC.* □ *Peter Shore ... has paid the price for his consistent opposition to party orthodoxy by being marginalised on the back benches and har-ried by his constituency party* (*The Guardian*). □ *The arts are no longer marginalised* (*The Guardian*). A vogue term, *marginalize* is disliked by some people as an example of the increasing tend-ency to coin new verbs by adding the suffix *-ize* to nouns and adjectives. It is best restricted to informal contexts.

marital see MARTIAL OR MARITAL?

market forces The phrase *market forces* refers to anything that affects or influences the free operation of trade in goods or services, such as competition or demand, as opposed to (artificially imposed) government controls. It is in danger of becoming overused as a vogue term: □ *The printing of this holy work* [the Bible] *should be subjected to market forces* (*The Bookseller*). □ *The Govern-ment yesterday unveiled plans to shift the financing of univer-sities and polytechnics away from block grants and towards higher tuition fees in an attempt to expand student numbers through emphasis on market forces* (*The Guardian*). □ *Green market forces are working in the appliance manufacturers' favour* (*Daily Telegraph*).

marquess or **marquis**? A *marquess* is a British nobleman who ranks below a duke and above an earl; a *marquis* is a nobleman of cor-responding rank in other countries. The word *marquis* is some-times used in place of *marquess.*

◆ Note that *marquess* is a masculine title, despite the apparently feminine ending *-ess*. The female counterpart of a marquess or marquis is called a *marchioness,* although the term *marquise* is sometimes used for the non-British feminine title.

Marquess and *marquis* have the same pronunciation, [*mark*wis], in British English, but the non-British title is sometimes pronounced [*mark*ee].

marshal see MARTIAL OR MARSHAL?

martial or **marital**? These two adjectives are sometimes confused, being similar in spelling. *Martial* means 'of or relating to war or military matters': □ *martial music* □ *martial arts* □ *martial law.* *Marital* means 'of or relating to marriage': □ *marital problems* □ *marital status* □ *marital vows.* The word *marital* is also found in the adjectives *extramarital, premarital,* etc., and *martial* in the compound noun and verb *court-martial.*

martial or **marshal**? The pronunciation of these two words is identical and they are sometimes confused. The adjective *martial* means 'of or relating to war or military matters' (see **MARTIAL OR MARITAL?**). *Marshal* may be used as a noun, meaning 'officer' or 'official', or as a verb, meaning 'arrange', 'assemble', or 'guide': □ *Field Marshal Montgomery* □ *One of the marshals pushed the damaged car off the racetrack.* □ *to marshal the facts* □ *We were marshalled into the courtroom.*

◆ Note that the second element of the compound noun and verb *court-martial* is *-martial* not *-marshal*.

The word *marshal* is sometimes misspelt with *-ll* at the end. The *-l* should be doubled only before *-ed*, *-ing*, and *-er* (in British English), and in the surname *Marshall*.

masculine see **MALE OR MASCULINE?**

massage The verb *massage* is increasingly used in the figurative sense of 'manipulate (figures, data, etc.) to make them more acceptable': □ *to massage the accounts* □ *to massage the results of the survey.* This usage is best restricted to informal contexts.

masterful or **masterly**? *Masterful* means 'domineering'; *masterly* means 'very skilful': □ *His masterful approach made him unpopular with the staff.* □ *West Germany reached their fifth World Cup final with a display of masterly efficiency* (*The Guardian*).

◆ The two adjectives relate to different senses of the noun *master*, from which they are both derived: 'person in authority' (*masterful*) and 'expert' (*masterly*).

Masterful is sometimes used in place of *masterly*: □ *a masterful performance by the soloist*, but many users prefer to maintain the distinction between the two words.

mat, matt, or **matte**? The adjective *matt*, meaning 'not shiny', has the variant spellings *mat* and *matte*. *Matt* is the most frequent spelling in British English: □ *a matt finish* □ *matt black paint.* The spelling *mat* is preferred in American English.

materialize The use of the verb *materialize* in place of *happen* or *turn up* is disliked by some users: □ *The threatened strike is unlikely to materialize.* □ *Her friends didn't materialize so we left without them.*

◆ In formal contexts the word is best restricted to its original meaning of 'make or become real': □ *They watched in horror as the spirit materialized before their very eyes.*

mathematics see **-ICS**.

matrimony This word, describing the state of marriage, is sometimes mispronounced.

◆ The correct pronunciation is [matrimōni] with the stress on the first syllable.

matrix The noun *matrix* denotes the substance or environment within which something originates, develops, or is contained. It is also a technical term in fields such as mathematics, computing, printing, anatomy, and linguistics. In general contexts *matrix* is disliked by many as a vogue word and often better replaced by *setting, background, framework, environment*, etc.: □ *the matrix in which primitive societies evolved.*

◆ *Matrix* has two plural forms, *matrices* or *matrixes*, either of which is acceptable to most users.

matt, matte see **MAT, MATT, OR MATTE?**

mattress Note the *-tt-* and the *-ss* in this word, which is often misspelt.

maximal, maximize see **MAXIMUM**.

maximum The noun and adjective *maximum* refer to the greatest possible quantity, amount, degree, etc.: □ *a maximum of twenty* guests □ *the maximum dose.*

◆ The noun *maximum* has two plural forms, usually in technical contexts, *maximums* and *maxima.*

The adjective *maximum* is more frequent than its synonym *maximal.*

The verb *maximize* means 'increase to a maximum'; it is best avoided where *increase* would be adequate or more appropriate: □ *The initial brief is to maximize sales of existing products.* Some people also dislike the use of *maximize* to mean 'make maximum use of': □ *to maximize resources.*

may or **might**? *Might* is the past tense of *may* (see CAN OR MAY?): □ *She may win.* □ *May we sit down?* □ *I thought she might win.* □ *He said we might sit down.* In the last two examples, *might* cannot be replaced with *may.* In the first two examples, however, *might* can be substituted for *may* with a slight change of meaning: □ *She might win* expresses a greater degree of doubt or uncertainty than *She may win.* □ *Might we sit down?* is a more tentative request than *May we sit down?*

◆ *May* and *might* are both used in the perfect tense. *May have* expresses a possibility that still exists; *might have* expresses a possibility that no longer exists: □ *She may have won: I didn't hear the result.* □ *She might have won if she hadn't fallen on the last lap.*

maybe or **may be**? *Maybe*, meaning 'perhaps': □ *Maybe the letter will come tomorrow*, is often confused with the phrase *may be*, the verb *may* and the verb *be*: □ *It may be that she has missed the train.*

mayoress A *mayoress* is the wife of a male mayor or a woman who assists or partners a mayor of either sex at social functions and on ceremonial occasions. The use of the term *mayoress* to denote or address a female mayor is incorrect.

me see I OR ME?

me or **my**? see -ING FORMS.

mean see I MEAN.

meaningful The adjective *meaningful* should be avoided where *important, significant, serious, worthwhile*, etc., would be adequate or more appropriate: □ *a caring, loving, and meaningful relationship* □ *a meaningful experience.*

◆ *Meaningful* is best reserved for its literal sense of 'having meaning': □ *meaningful utterances* □ *a meaningful smile* □ *a highly meaningful pause.*

means In the sense of 'method', *means* may be a singular or plural noun; in the sense of 'resources' or 'wealth' it is always plural: □ *A means of reducing engine noise was developed.* □ *Several different means of transport were used.* □ *His means are insufficient to support a large family.* See also SINGULAR OR PLURAL?

meantime or **meanwhile**? *Meantime* is chiefly used as a noun, in the phrases *in the meantime* and *for the meantime*; *meanwhile* is chiefly used as an adverb: □ *He wrote a letter in the meantime.* □ *We have enough for the meantime.* □ *Meanwhile, I had phoned the police.*

◆ *Meantime* may also be used as an adverb, in place of *meanwhile*, and *meanwhile* as a noun, in place of *meantime*, but these uses are less frequent.

medal or **meddle**? These two words should not be confused. *Medal* is a noun, denoting a metal disc, cross, etc., given as an award; *meddle* is a verb, meaning 'interfere': □ *a gold/silver/bronze medal* □ *Don't meddle in other people's affairs.*

media The word *media*, frequently used to refer to television, radio, newspapers, etc., as means of mass communication, is one of the plural forms of the noun *medium*: □ *The media act as publicity agents for writers.* □ *Television is an influential medium.*

◆ The plural of *medium* in the sense of 'spiritual intermediary' is *mediums*. Either plural form may be used for other senses of the noun: 'agency through which something is transmitted': □ *the mediums* [or *media*] *of air and water for transmitting sound,* 'means of communication': □ *English and French are the media* [or *mediums*] *of instruction.*

The increasing use of *media* as a singular collective noun is unacceptable to many people and is best avoided: □ *There has been a failure to educate the young to the benefits of trade unions, leaving the field open for a hostile media* (*The Guardian*). *Media* is also used adjectivally in front of other nouns: □ *a media event* is an event that is deliberately created for extensive coverage by the mass media.

mediaeval see MEDIEVAL OR MEDIAEVAL?

medicine The word *medicine* is sometimes misspelt, the most frequent error being the substitution of *e* for the first *i*. This letter is sometimes not sounded in speech, resulting in the two-syllable pronunciation [*meds*in]. Some users prefer the full pronunciation [*medi*sin].

medieval or **mediaeval**? The two spellings of this word are both acceptable. The spelling *medieval* is far more frequent in British English and is standard in American English. See also -AE- AND -OE-.

mediocre This word, meaning 'of indifferent quality', is sometimes misspelt. Note the ending -*cre*.

◆ Some users object to such expressions as *quite mediocre* and *very mediocre*, considering that something either is or is not mediocre.

Mediterranean Note the spelling of this word, particularly the single *t*, the -*rr*-, and the -*ean* ending. It may help to associate the central syllables with the Latin word *terra*, meaning 'earth; land', from which they are derived.

medium, mediums see MEDIA.

meet with In British English the phrasal verb *meet with* should be restricted to the sense of 'experience' or 'receive': □ *I hope he hasn't met with an accident.* □ *Does it meet with your approval?*

◆ The American use of *meet with* in the sense of 'have a meeting with' is disliked by many British users: □ *We met with the managing director this morning.*

The phrasal verbs *meet up with* and *meet up* are widely regarded as unnecessary synonyms for 'meet' and are best avoided, especially in formal contexts: □ *I met (up with) her at the theatre.* □ *They met (up) in the park.*

mega- Some people object to the increasing use of the prefix *mega-*, meaning 'great' or 'large', in nontechnical contexts, as in : □ *mega-motorway* □ *mega-trend* □ *mega-merger* □ *mega-bid* □ *megabucks* □ *megathon*.

◆ The prefix is increasingly used as an adjective in its own right, meaning 'very large and impressive': □ *The new leisure complex is really mega*. This usage is best restricted to informal contexts.

In science, the prefix *mega-* means 'one million': a *megaton* is one million tons. In computing, the prefix *mega-* means 2^{20}: a *megabyte* is 1,048,576 bytes.

meltdown In nuclear physics, the noun *meltdown* refers to the melting of the core of a nuclear reactor, caused by a defect in the cooling system. It is also used figuratively with reference to any disastrous event, especially a stock-market crash: □*Meltdown Monday.*

◆ Given the very serious nature of a meltdown (in the literal sense of the word), some people object to the figurative application of the term to comparatively trivial issues, such as a fall in company profits.

melted or **molten**? *Melted* is the past tense and past participle of the verb *melt*; it is also used as an adjective: □ *The chocolate (has) melted.* □ *Serve the asparagus with melted butter. Molten* is used only as an adjective, meaning 'melted' or 'liquefied': □*molten iron* □*molten rock.*

◆ The use of the adjective *molten* is restricted to substances that become liquid at very high temperatures.

membership *Membership* is the state of being a member: □ *to apply for membership.* The noun is also used to denote the number of members of an organization: □*Membership has increased this year.* Its frequent use in place of *members,* however, is disliked by some people: □ *We must consult the membership.*

memento The word *memento* is sometimes misspelt, the most frequent error being the substitution of *o* for the first *e*, through confusion with such words as *moment* and *momentum.* It may help to associate the *mem-* with *memory* and *remember.*

◆ *Memento* has two acceptable plural forms, *mementos* and *mementoes.*

mental The use of the adjective *mental* as a synonym for 'stupid', 'foolish', 'mentally ill', 'mentally deficient', etc., should be restricted to very informal contexts: □ *They must be mental to set off in such terrible weather.* □*Her youngest son's a bit mental, and the other children tease him.*

◆ The principal meaning of *mental* is 'of or involving the mind': □*mental illness* □*mental arithmetic.* The adjective is also used in the sense of 'relating to disorders of the mind': □*a mental hospital* □*a mental patient.*

mentholated or **methylated**? These two words should not be confused. *Mentholated* refers to the addition of *menthol,* a medicinal substance found in peppermint oil; *methylated* refers to the addition of the poisonous substance *methanol:* □*a mentholated lozenge* □*methylated spirits.*

meretricious or **meritorious**? *Meretricious* means 'superficially attractive' or 'insincere'; *meritorious* means 'having merit' or 'praiseworthy': □*meretricious glamour* □*a meritorious deed.* Both adjectives are fairly formal in usage.

◆ The adjective *meretricious* originally meant 'of a prostitute'; like *meritorious*, it is ultimately derived from the Latin verb *merēre*, meaning 'to earn' or 'to deserve'.

Note the spellings of the two words, particularly the second vowel: *meretricious* has the *e* of its Latin root; *meritorious* has the *i* of *merit*.

meta- Some people object to the increasing use of the prefix *meta-* in the sense of 'transcending' or 'of a higher order': □*A suggestion of metafiction, of uncertainties found to be themselves fictionally productive* (*London Review of Books*).

◆ The prefix has a number of other accepted meanings: 'change': □*metamorphosis*; 'after', 'behind', or 'beyond': □*metatarsus.*

metal or **mettle**? These two words, which have the same pronunciation, are sometimes confused. A *metal* is one of a group of mineral substances that are good conductors of heat and electricity. *Mettle* means 'strength of character': □*He was given no chance to prove his mettle.*

◆ The confusion may arise from the fact that *mettle* was originally derived from *metal*.

metallurgy This word, meaning 'the science of metals', is usually pronounced [met*a*lĕrji], although it can be stressed on the first and third syllables [met*ă*lerji].

◆ The second pronunciation is rarer in British English but standard in American English.

metamorphosis The usual pronunciation of this word is [met*ă*maw-fŏsis] with the stress on the third syllable.

◆ The alternative pronunciation [met*ă*maw*fŏ*sis] is possible but disliked by many people.

metaphors A *metaphor* is a figure of speech in which a word or phrase is used, not with its literal meaning, but to suggest an analogy with something else. The comparison is implicit, not introduced by *like* or *as*: □ *the winds of change* □ *an icy voice* □ *stone deaf*.

◆ Many expressions used in everyday speech are metaphorical but they are so frequently used that they are hardly thought of as metaphors: □ *the arm of a chair* □ *a branch of a bank*, and many occur in well-known idioms: □ *not up my street* □ *feel under the weather* □ *if you play your cards right*.

Metaphors have been used very successfully with striking effect in literature. There are biblical examples: □ *Thy word is a lamp unto my feet* (Psalm 119:105) and countless poetic ones: □ *I see a lily on thy brow ... and on thy cheek a fading rose* (Keats, *La Belle Dame Sans Merci*). However, as used by modern politicians and journalists, metaphors can often be tired and overworked: □ *the cure for unemployment* □ *fighting against inflation* □ *light at the end of the tunnel*.

Mixed metaphors, where two or more different metaphors are used in one sentence, should be avoided: □ *In resurrecting these allegations they are just fuelling the flames of racism.* □ *The committee's task was to iron out all the bottlenecks in the system.*

meter or **metre**? The spelling of these words is often confused, probably partly because the American spelling of the measurement *metre* is *meter*. In British English, a *meter* is a measuring instrument: □ *gas meter* □ *speedometer*. A *metre* is the basic metric measurement of length and is used in derived measurements: □ *kilometre* □ *millimetre*.

◆ *Metre* is also the technical term for the regular rhythmic arrangement of syllables in poetry. Note however that in compounds describing such measures, the spelling *-meter* is followed: □ *pentameter*, 'a line having five stresses'.

methodology The noun *methodology* denotes a body or system of methods, rules, principles, etc., used in a particular area of activity: □ *the methodology of teaching*.

◆ The use of the noun in other contexts, especially as a synonym for 'method': □ *experimental design methodology* □ *unstructured pragmatic methodologies*, is disliked by many people and is best avoided.

methylated see MENTHOLATED OR METHYLATED?

meticulous The adjective *meticulous* is widely used and accepted as a synonym for 'painstaking' or 'scrupulous': □ *meticulous attention to detail* □ *a meticulous secretary*.

◆ Some people, however, object to the use of the adjective in a complimentary manner, restricting it to the pejorative sense of 'fussy' or 'excessively careful': □ *If you weren't so meticulous you'd have finished the cleaning hours ago.*

Meticulous originally meant 'timid', being ultimately derived from *metus*, the Latin word for 'fear'.

metre see METER OR METRE?

mettle see METAL OR METTLE?

mezzanine This word, meaning 'intermediate storey between two floors', is usually pronounced [*mez*äneen]. The alternative [*mets*äneen] is sometimes used and is closer to the original Italian.
  ◆ The last syllable in both pronunciations should rhyme with *keen* and not with *line*.

micro- see MACRO- AND MICRO-.

mid see AMID, AMIDST, MID, OR MIDST?

middle see CENTRE OR MIDDLE?

midst see AMID, AMIDST, MID, OR MIDST?

midwifery This word is sometimes mispronounced. In British English the correct pronunciation is [*mid*wifĕri].
  ◆ In American English *wif* may be pronounced like *wife*.

might see CAN OR MAY?; MAY OR MIGHT?

migraine The usual pronunciation of this word, meaning 'a severe and recurrent headache', is [*mee*grayn].
  ◆ The alternative pronunciation [*mī*grayn] is also acceptable and is standard in American English.

mileage or **milage**? *Mileage* is the more frequent spelling of this word, *milage* being an accepted but rare variant: □ *The exceptionally low mileage makes this car a good buy.* See also SPELLING 3.
  ◆ In its figurative sense of 'benefit' or 'usefulness', the noun is avoided by some users in formal contexts: □ *It was an interesting subject, though, and the chairman ... got the maximum intellectual mileage out of it* (*The Guardian*).

militate or **mitigate**? The verb *militate*, which is usually followed by the preposition *against*, means 'have a powerful influence or effect': □ *His left-wing opinions militated against his appointment as headmaster.* The verb *mitigate* means 'moderate' or 'make less severe': □ *The judge's decision did little to mitigate the suffering of the bereaved parents.* □ *mitigating circumstances.*
  ◆ The two verbs are occasionally confused, *mitigate* being wrongly used in place of *militate*.

millennium This word is often misspelt, the most frequent error being the omission of the second *n*: □ *Over the millenia, as earth movements cause new formations* (Reader's Digest advertisement for *Marvels and Mysteries of the World around Us*).
  ◆ Spelling mistakes may be avoided by associating the word, which means 'a thousand years', with the *-ll-* of *millipede* and *millimetre* (from Latin *mille* 'thousand') and the *-nn-* of *annual* and *perennial* (from Latin *annus* 'year').

millionaire The word *millionaire* is sometimes misspelt. Note the *-ll-*, but only one *n*.

mimic This word, meaning 'imitate': □ *He likes mimicking the teachers*, is sometimes misspelt. Note that a *k* is added before the suffixes *-ed*, *-ing*, and *-er*. *Mimicry* does not, however, have a *k*. See also SPELLING 1.

mincemeat The noun *mincemeat* principally denotes the sweet mixture of dried fruit, suet, sugar, and spices that is used to fill mince pies, traditionally baked and eaten at Christmas. To avoid confusion, meat that has been minced (*minced meat*) is usually called *mince* in British English and *ground meat* in American English.

miniature *Miniature*, meaning 'small in size', is sometimes misspelt. Note the spelling *-iat-*.

minimal, minimize see MINIMUM.

minimum The noun and adjective *minimum* refer to the smallest possible quantity, amount, degree, etc.: □ *a minimum of four employees* □ *the minimum requirements.*

◆ The noun *minimum* has two plural forms, usually in technical contexts, *minimums* or *minima.*

The frequent use of *minimal* in the sense of 'very small' is disliked by some users: □ *The response to our advertisement was minimal – we received only two applications.* □ *minimal effort* □ *minimal risk.*

The verb *minimize* means 'reduce to a minimum'; it is best avoided where *reduce* would be adequate or more appropriate: □ *The new safety regulations should minimize the danger.* Some people also object to the widely accepted use of *minimize* to mean 'play down' or 'belittle': □ *to minimize one's achievements.*

minority see MAJORITY AND MINORITY.

minus The use of the preposition *minus* in the sense of 'without' or 'lacking' is best restricted to informal contexts: □ *She came home minus her umbrella.*

◆ Some people also avoid using the noun *minus* as a synonym for 'disadvantage' in formal contexts: □ *Having to move to the South is one of the minuses of my new job: we'll never be able to afford to buy a house there.* See also PLUS.

minuscule This word is often misspelt, the most frequent error being the substitution of an *i* for the first *u*. The word is pronounced [mi*nŭs*kyool].

minutiae The plural noun *minutiae*, meaning 'small, minor, or trivial details,' may be pronounced [mi*new*shiee] or [mī*new*shiee]: □ *The minutiae of the problem are of no interest to me.*

◆ *Minutia,* the singular form of the noun, is rarely used.

The noun *minutiae* is best avoided where *details* would be more appropriate: □ *discuss the details* [not *minutiae*] *of a contract.*

Note the spelling of *minutiae,* particularly the three final vowels *-iae.*

miscellaneous This word, meaning 'of a variety of items', is sometimes misspelt. Note particularly the *-sc-*, the *-a-*, and the *-eous* ending.

mischievous The correct pronunciation of this word is [*mis*chivŭs].

◆ The mispronunciations [mis*chee*vŭs] and [mis*chee*viŭs] are heard from time to time but are avoided by careful speakers. The word is often misspelt: particular attention should be paid to the order and position of the vowels.

misogynist Note the spelling of *misogynist,* which refers to a person who hates women. The word derives from Greek *misos* 'hatred' and *gynē* 'woman' as in *gynaecology,* the branch of medicine concerned with women's diseases.

◆ *Misogynist* is usually pronounced [mi*soj*inist], although the first syllable is very occasionally pronounced with a long *i,* as in *my.*

Miss see MS, MRS, OR MISS?

miss The verb *miss,* meaning 'regret the loss or lack of', is sometimes wrongly used with *not*: □ *I miss not having a car* means 'I was happier before I had a car', not 'I wish I had a car'.

◆ This error is not confined to informal spoken contexts: □ *Passengers ... ask me* [a ship's doctor] *if I miss not being a 'proper' doctor* (*Reader's Digest*).

See also AIR MISS OR NEAR MISS?

misspelled or **misspelt**? Either word may be used as the past tense and past participle of the verb *misspell*: □ *You have misspelt/*

misspelled my name.
- ◆ See also -ED OR -T?
  Misspelled may be pronounced [mis*spelt*] or [mis*speld*]; *misspelt* is always pronounced [mis*spelt*].
  Note the spellings of the two words, particularly the single *l* of *misspelt* and the -*ss*- of both words.

mistrust see DISTRUST OR MISTRUST?

misuse see ABUSE OR MISUSE?

mitigate see MILITATE OR MITIGATE?

mix Some people object to the increasing use of the noun *mix* in place of *range*: □ *A wide mix of subjects will be taught at the college.*
- ◆ In the sense of 'combination' or 'mixture', *mix* is found in compounds such as *marketing mix*, 'the various elements that need to be coordinated in a marketing plan'. Some users, however, object to its use in formal contexts.

mnemonic The word *mnemonic*, referring to something that aids the memory (e.g. the spelling rule '*i* before *e* except after *c*'), causes spelling and pronunciation problems. The initial *m* is silent; the word is pronounced [ni*mon*ik].

moccasin This word, used to describe a soft leather shoe without a heel, is sometimes misspelt. Note the -*cc*- but single *s*.

modal see VERBS.

modern or **modernistic**? The adjective *modern* means 'of the present time' or 'contemporary'; *modernistic* means 'characteristic of modern trends, ideas, etc.' and is sometimes used in a derogatory way: □ *modern society* □ *modernistic architecture.*
- ◆ *Modern* has a wider range of sense and usage than *modernistic*, which is largely restricted to objects, designs, thoughts, etc., that are conspicuously modern or unconventional.

modus vivendi The Latin phrase *modus vivendi* is principally used in formal English to denote an arrangement or compromise between conflicting parties: □ *This modus vivendi enabled them to complete the job without further disruption.*
- ◆ The literal meaning of the phrase *modus vivendi* is 'way of living', but some people object to its use in place of the English expression *way of life*.
  The word *modus* may be pronounced [*mō*dŭs] or [*mod*ŭs]; *vivendi* may be pronounced [vi*ven*dee] or [vi*ven*dī].

Mohammed see MUSLIM OR MOSLEM?

molten see MELTED OR MOLTEN?

momentary or **momentous**? *Momentary* means 'lasting for a very short time'; *momentous* means 'of great significance': □ *a momentary lapse* □ *The Commons last night took the momentous step of opening its doors to the television cameras for the first time* (*The Guardian*).
- ◆ The two adjectives relate to different senses of the noun *moment*, from which they are both derived: 'a very short time' (*momentary*) and 'significance' (*momentous*).
  Note the difference in stress between the two adjectives: *momentary* is stressed on the first syllable, *momentous* on the second. The adverb *momentarily* should also be stressed on the first syllable [*mō*mĕntărĭli]; the pronunciation [mōmĕn*ter*rĭli] is unacceptable to many people.

mongoose The plural of the noun *mongoose* is *mongooses*; the word should not be treated as a compound of the noun *goose* (the plural of which is *geese*).

◆ *Mongoose* is derived from the word *mangūs*, of Indian origin, and is etymologically unrelated to *goose*.

monogram or **monograph?** A *monogram* is a design made up of a person's initials: □ *There was a monogram on the corner of the handkerchief.* A *monograph* is a learned book, treatise, etc., about a single subject: □ *He wrote a monograph on Oliver Cromwell.* The two nouns should not be confused.

moot The adjective *moot*, meaning 'debatable' or 'open to question', rarely occurs outside the fixed phrase *a moot point*: □ *Whether she will accept this offer is a moot point.*

◆ The verb *moot*, meaning 'put forward for debate', is most frequently used in the passive in formal contexts: □ *The subject was mooted at our last meeting.*

moral or **morale?** These two spellings are sometimes confused. *Moral* means 'concerned with the principles of right and wrong': □ *the gradual erosion of moral standards.* *Morale* is the extent of confidence and optimism in a person or group: □ *After the election defeat, the party's morale sank to an all-time low.*

◆ *Moral* is stressed on the first syllable [morrăl]. *Morale* is stressed on the second syllable [morahl].

more The adverb *more* is used to form the comparative of a number of adjectives and adverbs: □ *She is more intelligent than her sister.* □ *The trains run more frequently in the summer months.* *More* should not be used with adjectives that already have the comparative ending *-er*, such as *happier*, *older*, etc.

◆ Other uses of the word *more* – as the comparative of *much* or *many*, or in the sense of 'further' or 'additional' – may lead to confusion: □ *She has more beautiful dresses* may mean 'her dresses are more beautiful (than mine/yours/etc.)', 'she has other dresses that are more beautiful (than this one)', 'she has a greater number of beautiful dresses (than you/me/etc.)', or 'she has other beautiful dresses (in addition to this one)'.

The phrase *more than one*, although it implies a plural subject, is used with a singular verb: □ *More than one accident has happened at this junction.* If the sentence is reworded, however, a plural verb is used: □ *More accidents than one have happened at this junction.* See also **COMPARATIVE AND SUPERLATIVE; SINGULAR OR PLURAL?**

mortgage This word is sometimes misspelt, the most frequent error being the omission of the silent *t*.

mortgagee or **mortgagor?** A *mortgagor* is a person who borrows money by means of a mortgage; a *mortgagee* is the person or organization, e.g. a building society or bank, that lends the money. The two nouns should not be confused: the *mortgagors* are the people who are mortgaging their property, i.e. using it as security for a loan; the *mortgagees* are those who receive this security, not the recipients of the loan itself.

Moslem see **MUSLIM OR MOSLEM?**

most The adverb *most* is used to form the superlative of a number of adjectives and adverbs: □ *This is the most expensive picture in the shop.* □ *The prize will be awarded to the child who writes the most neatly.* *Most* should not be used with adjectives that already have the superlative ending *-est*, such as *saddest*, *youngest*, etc.

◆ Other uses of the word *most* – as the superlative of *much* or *many*, or in the sense of 'very' – may cause ambiguity: □ *This teacher has the most intelligent pupils* may mean 'this teacher has the greatest number of intelligent pupils' or 'this teacher's pupils are the most intelligent in the school'; □ *She danced most gracefully* may mean 'she danced very gracefully' or 'she danced more gracefully than the other dancers'. See also COMPARATIVE AND SUPERLATIVE.

The use of *most* in place of *very* is generally best avoided, although it is acceptable in certain contexts: □ *I am most grateful for your assistance.* □ *He spoke most rudely of his former employers.*

The adverb *mostly*, meaning 'mainly' or 'usually', should not be confused with *most*: □ *He writes mostly* [not *most*] *for children.* □ *Old people are most* [not *mostly*] *at risk.* In some contexts the substitution of *most* for *mostly*, or vice versa, changes the meaning of the sentence: □ *Our friends are mostly helpful. – Our friends are most helpful.* □ *The shop sells most books. – The shop sells mostly books.*

motif or **motive**? These words are sometimes confused. A *motif* is a recurrent feature which establishes a pattern throughout a work of art, etc.: □ *a design with a feather motif.* A *motive* is a reason for a course of action: □ *no apparent motive for the crime.*

motivation The use of the noun *motivation*, which means 'incentive' or 'drive', in place of *reason* or *motive* is disliked and avoided by many users: □ *his reason* [not *motivation*] *for deserting his wife and family*.

◆ Some people also object to the frequent use of the noun in its accepted sense of 'providing with an incentive' in the context of industrial psychology: □ *the motivation of the workforce.* As Roland Gribben remarked in the *Daily Telegraph*: 'Motivation is a grossly overworked and abused term for getting the best or more out of people.'

Similar objections may be applied to the use of the verb *motivate* in place of *cause* and of *motivated* as a synonym for 'keen': □ *an action that may cause* [not *motivate*] *her to change her mind* □ *a highly motivated sales manager* □ *a self-motivating entrepreneur.*

motive see MOTIF OR MOTIVE?

mouse The plural of the noun *mouse,* in the sense of 'small animal', is *mice.* In computing contexts, where a *mouse* is an electronic device used to move the cursor on the screen, the preferred plural form is *mice,* though the plural form *mouses* is used by some computer scientists.

mousse The noun *mousse* denotes a creamy or foamy preparation. Some types of mousse are for eating: □ *chocolate mousse* □ *salmon mousse*; some are for cosmetic purposes: □ *styling mousse* □ *body mousse.* Note the spelling of this word, which should not be confused with the animals *moose* and *mouse.*

◆ The pronunciation of this word is [moos].

moustache This word is sometimes misspelt. The most frequent error is the substitution of *u* for *ou* in British English. The British English spelling is *moustache*; the American English spelling *mustache.* Note also the *-che* ending.

movable or **moveable**? This word has two different spellings. Both are acceptable although the first spelling *movable,* which omits the *e* before the suffix *-able,* seems to be more frequent in contemporary usage.

◆ See also SPELLING 3.

movers and shakers *Movers and shakers* is an expression used informally to refer to people who get things done, either through their own power and influence or by urging or encouraging others to take action: □ *the movers and shakers of the film industry.* The phrase should not be overused.

move the goalposts To *move the goalposts* is to change the rules, requirements, etc., usually to the advantage of the person or organization that sets and changes the rules: □ *The Government is moving the goalposts again from April 6, with the cut-off point* [for eligibility for income support] *reduced to 16 hours a week* (*The Guardian*).

◆ The verb *move* is sometimes replaced by *shift* or *change*. The expression is best restricted to informal contexts.

mowed or **mown**? Either word may be used as the past participle of the verb *mow*: □ *Have you mowed/mown the grass yet?*

◆ When the participle is used as an adjective, *mown* is preferred to *mowed*: □ *a neatly mown lawn* □ *new-mown hay*.

The past tense of the verb *mow* is always *mowed*: □ *I mowed the grass yesterday*.

Mr see MS, MRS, OR MISS?

Ms, Mrs, or **Miss**? *Ms, Mrs*, and *Miss*, shortened forms of the archaic title *Mistress*, are used before the names of girls and women, according to age and marital status, in letter writing and as polite terms of address.

◆ *Miss* is traditionally used for girls, unmarried women, and married women who have retained their maiden name: □ *Miss Mary Baker* □ *Miss Davies* □ *Miss Elizabeth Taylor*. In formal contexts, two or more girls or unmarried women with the same surname should be referred to as *the Misses Brown/Smith*/etc. rather than *the Miss Browns/Smiths*/etc.

Mrs, pronounced [misiz], is used before a woman's married name: □ *Mrs Anne Johnson* □ *Mrs Peter Johnson* □ *Mrs Johnson*.

Ms, pronounced [miz] or [mīz], is used before the name of a woman of unknown or unspecified marital status. It was introduced as a feminine equivalent of the masculine title *Mr*, which makes no distinction between married and unmarried men. Because of its feminist associations, however, the title *Ms* is disliked by some people. *Ms* is most frequently used in place of *Miss*, but is best avoided when referring to elderly unmarried women or young girls. See also SEXISM.

The titles *Ms*, *Mrs*, and *Mr* are usually written without a full stop. See also ABBREVIATIONS.

much The use of the adjective *much* in positive sentences is best restricted to formal contexts: □ *They own much land.* □ *There is much work to be done.*

◆ Even in formal contexts, some users prefer to replace *much* with *a large amount of, a great deal of*, etc.: □ *They own a large amount of land.* □ *There is a great deal of work to be done.*

In informal contexts, *much* may be replaced with *a lot of* or *lots of*: □ *There is a lot of work to be done.* See also LOT.

In negative and interrogative sentences, *much* is acceptable in all contexts: □ *They don't own much land.* □ *Is there much work to do?* See also MANY; VERY.

mucous or **mucus**? These two words are sometimes confused. *Mucous* is the adjective from the noun *mucus*; *mucus* is the secretion produced by *mucous membranes*.

muesli The noun *muesli*, denoting a type of breakfast food, causes problems of spelling and pronunciation. Note the *-ue-* in the first syllable, and the *-li* ending. The usual pronunciation is [mewzli], with the first syllable pronounced as in *music*, but the pronunciation [moozli] is also acceptable.

Muhammad see MUSLIM OR MOSLEM?

multi- Some people object to the increasing use of the prefix *multi-*, meaning 'many', to coin new words that are often better expressed by a paraphrase: □*a multirole device* □*a multistage process* □*her outstanding multi-tasking abilities* ('her abilities to perform many tasks at the same time'). □*Specialist skills are now ignored or swamped in the drive for multi-skilling* (*The Guardian*).

◆ In neologisms of this kind a hyphen is sometimes inserted between the prefix and the word to which it is attached.

municipal The adjective *municipal* should be stressed on the second syllable [mewn*i*sipăl], not the first or the third.

Muslim or **Moslem**? Nowadays the preferred spelling for a follower of the Islamic faith is *Muslim*, rather than the older spelling *Moslem*.

◆ *Muslim* is pronounced with the vowel sound as in *put* [*muuz*lim], or as in *cup* [*muz*lim].

The most accepted spelling of the name of the prophet of Islam is *Muhammad*, rather than *Mohammed* or *Mahomet*.

must The auxiliary verb *must* expresses obligation, compulsion, necessity, resolution, certainty, etc.: □ *We must obey the rules.* □ *They must go.* □ *I must finish writing this letter.* □ *You must be very thirsty.* In other tenses, and in the negative, *must* is usually replaced by *have to*: □ *We had to obey the rules.* □ *They don't have to go.*

◆ The negative form *must not* (or *mustn't*) expresses prohibition: □ *They must not go.*

The past tense *must have* is used only to express certainty: □ *You must have been very thirsty.*

The use of *must* as a noun, meaning 'something necessary or essential', is best restricted to informal contexts: □ *Waterproof clothing is an absolute must for a sailing holiday.*

mutual, common, or **reciprocal**? A *mutual* action or emotion is done or felt by each of two or more people to or for the other(s): □*mutual help/destruction/admiration/hatred/*etc. □ *The feeling is mutual.*

◆ The adjective *mutual* is superfluous in such phrases as: □*a mutual agreement* □*a mutual exchange* □*their mutual love for each other*.

The frequent use of *mutual* in place of *common*, meaning 'shared' or 'joint', is disliked by many users: □*a mutual friend* □*mutual interests* □*a mutual problem*. However, the other senses of *common* can cause ambiguity: □*a common friend* may mean 'an unsophisticated, rude friend' as well as 'a friend shared by two people'. Thus expressions such as □*our joint friend* □*the friend we have in common* □*the friend we share* could be used instead.

Reciprocal and *mutual* are synonymous in the principal sense of the latter: □*reciprocal help* □*reciprocal hatred. Reciprocal* can also be used to describe an action or emotion that is done or felt in return: □*He praised her new novel, and she expressed reciprocal admiration for his latest film.*

my or **me**? see -ING FORMS.

myself The use of the pronoun *myself* for emphasis is acceptable to most users but disliked by some: □*I disapprove of such behaviour myself.* □*I myself have never met her.*

◆ *Myself* should not be used in place of *I* or *me* in the following sentences and similar constructions: □*My sister and I* [not *myself*] *will do the gardening.* □ *The bill was paid by Richard and me* [not *myself*].

See also **I OR ME?**; **SELF**.

mythical or **mythological**? *Mythical* means 'imaginary'; *mythological* means 'of mythology': □ *a mythical danger* □ *a mythological kingdom*.

◆ Both adjectives also mean 'of a myth or myths', in which sense they are virtually interchangeable: □ *a mythical/mythological character*.

naff The adjective *naff* is a derogatory slang term meaning 'inferior or worthless; vulgar or tasteless; not stylish': □ *a naff film* □ *That tie is really naff.* The adjective should be restricted to informal contexts.

naive, naïve, or **naïf?** This word, meaning 'innocent' or 'credulous', is most commonly spelt *naive* or *naïve*.

◆ *Naïf*, the French masculine adjective, is no longer used, *naive* (or *naïve*) being used to describe people of both sexes.

The derived noun is most commonly spelt *naivety* or *naïvety*, although the variants *naiveté* and *naïveté* are also found.

Naive is pronounced [nīeev] or [naheev]. *Naivety* is pronounced [nīeevěti] or [naheevěti].

naked or **nude?** A person wearing no clothes at all may be described as *naked* or *nude*: □ *pictures of naked/nude men.*

◆ The adjective *naked*, however, has a wider range of usage and application than *nude*, which is largely restricted to artistic or pornographic human nakedness or to nudism: □ *nude photography* □ *nude bathing* □ *a naked* [not *nude*] *body buried in a shallow grave* □ *naked* [not *nude*] *children playing in the sand.*

Naked is also used as a synonym for 'bare' or 'uncovered' in other contexts: □ *a naked room* □ *a naked flame.*

naphtha This word, meaning 'petroleum', is sometimes misspelt. Note the consonant sequence *-phth-*.

◆ Note also the spellings of the compounds *naphthalene* and *naphthene*.

nation see COUNTRY OR NATION?

native The word *native*, used in the sense of 'non-white person' (originally applied to the indigenous inhabitants of lands colonized by the West), is derogatory and offensive: □ *The settlers intermarried with the natives.*

◆ The noun and adjective *native* may be applied to a person or people born in a specified place: □ *a native of Sweden* □ *native Spaniards.* This usage is generally acceptable, but some people prefer to avoid the word *native* where there is a danger of confusion with the derogatory sense: □ *the indigenous inhabitants* [not *natives*] *of Tasmania.*

naturalist or **naturist?** A *naturalist* is a person who studies animals and plants or an advocate of naturalism (in art, literature, philosophy, etc.); a *naturist* is a nudist: □ *Naturalists will appreciate the flora and fauna of the island; naturists can take advantage of its secluded beaches.*

nature Such phrases as *of this/that nature* and *in the nature of* are often better replaced by more concise or less vague expressions: □ *Crimes like that* [for *of that nature*] *should be severely punished.* □ *This new method of assessment is like* [for *in the nature of*] *an examination.*

◆ The word *nature* is used in other unnecessary circumlocutions: □ *a problem of a difficult nature* is *a difficult problem* □ *a remark of a flippant nature* is *a flippant remark*; etc.

naturist see NATURALIST OR NATURIST?

naught or **nought**? These two words are sometimes confused. *Naught* means 'nothing' and is used in idiomatic expressions such as *set at naught* 'consider unimportant' and *come to naught* 'produce no successful results': □ *All our plans came to naught.* In British English *nought* is used to represent the figure *0* (see also ZERO): □ *The number 100 has two noughts.* □ *play the game of noughts and crosses.*

◆ In American English, however, *naught* is used for the mathematical sense.

nauseous The use of the adjective *nauseous* in the sense of 'nauseated' or 'suffering from nausea' is acceptable in American English but is best avoided in British English: □ *I feel sick* [not *nauseous*].

◆ The principal meaning of *nauseous* in British English is 'nauseating' or 'causing nausea': □ *a nauseous smell.*

naval or **navel**? These two words are sometimes confused. *Naval* is used to describe something connected with the navy: □ *a naval officer* □ *naval warfare.* The *navel* is the small depression in the middle of the abdomen where the umbilical cord was formerly attached, and the word is also used in the phrase *navel orange.*

near or **nearly**? In the sense of 'almost', the adverb *near* is sometimes interchangeable with *nearly*: □ *I nearly* [or *near*] *forgot.* □ *It's near* [or *nearly*] *impossible.* This use of *near* may be considered informal or archaic, and *nearly* is a safer choice in most contexts.

◆ Used in combination with an adjective, especially one that is placed before the noun, *near* may be preferred to *nearly* and is usually attached with a hyphen: □ *a near-perfect copy* □ *a near-successful attempt.*

nearby or **near by**? There is often confusion as to whether this term should be one word or two. *Nearby* is the preferred form for both adjectival and adverbial senses: □ *Wolverhampton, Dudley, and other nearby towns.*

◆ *Near by* may still be used in the adverbial sense: □ *a town near by.* □ *He lives near by.*

nearly see NEAR OR NEARLY?

near miss see AIR MISS OR NEAR MISS?

necessarily There are two possible pronunciations for this word. In the traditional pronunciation, the first syllable is stressed [*nĕsĕsĕrĭli*], but this is very difficult to say unless one is speaking slowly and carefully. Many users dislike the alternative pronunciation, which has the main stress on the third syllable [*nĕsĕserrĭli*].

necessary This word, meaning 'essential', is often misspelt. Note the single *c* and the *-ss-*.

née *Née*, the feminine form of the French word for 'born', is used to indicate the maiden name of a married woman: □ *Mrs Susan Davies, née Eliot.*

◆ The pronunciation of *née*, which is sometimes written without an accent, is [nay].

Née should not be used to indicate a man's original name or pseudonym or a remarried woman's previous married name: □ *Ringo Starr, norn* [not *née*] *Richard Starkey* □ *Jacqueline Onassis, formerly* [not *née*] *Jacqueline Kennedy.*

need *Need* may be used as a full verb, in the sense of 'require' or 'be obliged', or as an auxiliary or modal verb, indicating necessity or obligation: □ *We need help.* □ *Your daughter needs to wear glasses.* □*He need not leave.* □*Need she reply?*

◆ The use of *need* as an auxiliary verb is indicated by the absence of *-s* in the third person singular and the omission of *to* in the following infinitive.

The auxiliary verb *need* is used only in questions and negative sentences (see the last two examples above) and in certain constructions that have negative force, such as: □*All she need buy is food.* □ *He need do no more than wait.* □ *You need only ask.* □ *Nobody need suffer.*

The full verb *need* may also be used in questions and negative sentences: □*He doesn't need to leave.* □*Does she need to reply?*

In the sense of 'require', *need* is followed by the *-ing* form of the verb or by a past participle preceded by *to be*, not by the past participle alone: □ *This shirt needs washing* [not *washed*]. □ *This shirt needs to be washed.*

needless to say The idiomatic expression *needless to say* is frequently used for emphasis, especially in informal contexts: □*Needless to say, the unions intend to campaign against the proposed legislation.*

◆ The expression is disliked by those who choose to interpret it literally, but is acceptable to most people.

negative A negative word is one that is used to deny or contradict something. Words such as *no, not, nobody, never,* and *nothing* make the clause in which they appear a negative one. Care must be taken as to where a negative word is placed in a sentence. □*She didn't explain definitely* does not have the same meaning as: □*She definitely didn't explain.* Usually the negative word is placed with the clause whose truth is being denied: □*He said he had never been there.* □*He never said he had been there.*

◆ The exception is with verbs such as *believe, think, expect, imagine,* etc., where the negative word is generally placed before the verb: □ *I don't think you know who you're talking about.* □ *She didn't expect them before dark.*

The adjective *negative* is now often used in a very general way to mean not only 'lacking in positive features', but also 'pessimistic; unenthusiastic': □ *You're taking a rather negative view.* □ *I felt very negative about all his suggestions.*

See also **DOUBLE NEGATIVE.**

neglectful, negligent, or **negligible?** Both *neglectful* and *negligent* mean 'careless' or 'heedless'; *negligible* means 'very small', 'trivial', or 'insignificant': □ *a neglectful mother* □ *a negligent driver* □ *a negligible effect.*

◆ The adjectives *neglectful* and *negligent* are not completely synonymous: *negligent* often implies habitual or more serious neglect or negligence, which may be punishable by law.

Note the spelling of *negligible*, especially the two *i*'s.

negotiate The usual pronunciation of this verb is [nigōshiayt]. The variant pronunciation [nigōsiayt], in which the *sh* sound is replaced by *s*, is disliked by some people.

Negress, Negro see **BLACK.**

neither As an adjective or pronoun *neither* is used with a singular verb: □ *Neither towel is clean.* □ *Neither of the towels is* [not *are*] *clean.*

◆ In the *neither ... nor* construction, a singular verb is used if both subjects are singular and a plural verb is used if both subjects are plural: □ *Neither his brother nor his sister has* [not *have*] *been invited.* □ *Neither his parents nor his friends have been invited.*

The use of a plural verb with the pronoun *neither* or with singular subjects in a *neither ... nor* construction is avoided by careful users, especially in formal contexts, but nevertheless occurs with some frequency: □ *Neither the coal industry nor British Rail are likely to be privatised in the short term* (*Daily Telegraph*).

When a combination of singular and plural subjects occurs in a *neither ... nor* construction, the verb traditionally agrees with the subject that is nearest to it: □ *Neither his brother nor his parents have been invited.* □ *Neither his friends nor his sister has been invited.* The same principle is applied to singular subjects that are used with different forms of the verb: □ *Neither you nor he has* [not *have*] *been invited.* □ *Neither my husband nor I have* [not *has*] *been invited.* If the resulting sentence sounds awkward or unidiomatic it may be reordered or rephrased.

The alternatives presented in a *neither ... nor* construction should be grammatically balanced: □ *She travelled neither by boat nor train* may be changed to: □ *She travelled neither by boat nor by train* or: □ *She travelled by neither boat nor train.*

As a pronoun *neither* should be used only of two alternatives: □ *There are two cars outside, but neither is mine.* □ *None* [not *Neither*] *of the three candidates arrived on time.* However, the use of the *neither ... nor* construction with three or more subjects is acceptable to some people: □ *They eat neither meat nor fish nor eggs.*

The first syllable of *neither* may be pronounced to rhyme with *try* or *tree.* The pronunciation [nīdhĕr] is more frequent in British English.

See also **DOUBLE NEGATIVE; EITHER; NOR.**

nephew There are two different pronunciations for this word. Both [nevew] and [nefew] are acceptable, although some people prefer the first pronunciation.

◆ In American English [nefew] is standard.

nerve-racking see **RACK OR WRACK?**

net or **nett?** The word *net,* referring to what remains after the deduction of tax, expenses, loss, packaging, etc., is sometimes spelt *nett:* □ *net* [or *nett*] *income* □ *net* [or *nett*] *profit* □ *net* [or *nett*] *weight* □ *500 kg net* [or *nett*] □ *to net* [or *nett*] *£2000 a month.* Both spellings are acceptable in British English, but *net* is the more frequent.

network The word *network* is used as a verb in telecommunications, computing, and the media; it is also increasingly used in general contexts to mean 'communicate or make contact with other people in a similar situation': □ *to network with clients* □ *Women also often mentioned the help, advice and support they had received from networking with other women* (*The Bookseller*). □ *Those four people ... network extensively and draw on specialist help as appropriate* (*Alpha*). □ *Networking ... is one of the current buzz-words of the enterprise industry* (*The Guardian*).

◆ In computing, *networking* is the connecting of computers in different places to one another as a means of transferring and sharing information.

never The use of *never saw/took/went/*etc. in place of *did not see/take/go/*etc., usually for emphasis, is avoided by careful users in all but a few informal spoken contexts: □ *I never said a word! Never* means 'at no time' and should not be used when referring to a single occasion: □ *I never met his wife.* □ *I did not meet his wife in town yesterday.*

◆ *Never* is sometimes used informally as a substitute for a simple negative when expressing surprise: □ *He never expected that to happen.* □ *We never thought it would work.* □ *I never knew you could play the guitar.*

nevertheless see NONE THE LESS OR NEVERTHELESS?

New Age The *New Age* movement, of American origin, is defined in the *Oxford Dictionary of New Words* as 'a cultural movement ... characterized by rejection of (modern) Western-style values and culture and the promotion of a more integrated or 'holistic' approach in areas such as religion, medicine, philosophy, astrology, and the environment': □ *New Age philosophy* □ *New Age music* □ *New Age publishing* □ *the widespread distrust of New Age travellers.*

next or this? The adjective *this* is often used in place of *next* with reference to days of the current week, months of the current year, etc.: □ *I'm not going to the club this Friday.* □ *She's getting married this September.*

◆ As a result, the use of *next* in similar contexts may lead to ambiguity or confusion: the phrase *next Friday*, used on a Tuesday, for example, may mean 'three days hence' or 'ten days hence'. See also LAST.

nice The adjective *nice*, in the sense of 'pleasant', 'agreeable', 'kind', 'attractive', etc., is often better replaced by an appropriate synonym, especially in formal contexts: □ *an attractive* [not *nice*] *garden* □ *a pleasant* [not *nice*] *afternoon.*

◆ In the sense of 'subtle' or 'precise', *nice* is acceptable in all contexts: □ *a nice distinction.*

Nice is ultimately derived from the Latin adjective *nescius*, meaning 'ignorant'; it was originally used in the now obsolete sense of 'foolish'.

niceness or nicety? Both these nouns are derived from NICE. *Niceness* is used in the general senses of 'pleasantness', 'kindness', etc.; *nicety* is restricted to the sense of 'subtlety; precision' and specifically refers to refined details: □ *the niceness of the weather/his sister* □ *a nicety of grammar* □ *the niceties of etiquette.*

niche This word may be pronounced to rhyme with *pitch* or *leash*. The second of these pronunciations is closer to the French origin, but the anglicized [nich] is the more frequent.

◆ The word *niche* is increasingly used with reference to a gap in the market, especially a gap that can be profitably filled: □ *niche marketing* □ *Niche retailers like Sock Shop, Tie Rack and Knobs & Knockers have shown that they struggle when times get hard* (*The Guardian*).

-nik The suffix *-nik*, of Russian or Yiddish origin, is used to denote somebody who is connected with or does the word that precedes it: □ *beatnik* □ *peacenik* □ *refusenik*. It should not be indiscriminately attached to other nouns and verbs.

◆ A *refusenik* was originally a Jew who had been refused permission to leave the Soviet Union. However, the word is increasingly used in more general contexts to denote somebody who refuses to do something: □ *a proposal that should satisfy the remaining refuseniks.*

nil see ZERO.

nimby *Nimby*, an acronym of 'not in my back yard', is used with reference to a person or people who object to proposed new developments, such as roads or power stations, in the vicinity of their houses: □*the Nimby syndrome* □*If he has changed his mind, and is now a true non-Nimby, he should withdraw his objection to having homes at the bottom of his garden* (*The Guardian*).

◆ The noun *nimbyism* has been coined to denote this selfish opposition (the protesters usually have no objection to the development being sited elsewhere): □ *Their deep dislike of the kind of gung-ho development and growth-at-all-costs going on in their communities ... is not crude Nimbyism, as Nicholas Ridley would have us believe* (*Daily Telegraph*).

no see NO ONE OR NO-ONE?; YES AND NO.

nobody see NO ONE OR NO-ONE?

noisome The adjective *noisome* means 'offensive' or 'noxious'; it has no connection, etymological or otherwise, with the noun *noise*: □*a noisome smell*.

◆ *Noisome* is derived from the verb *annoy*. It is largely restricted to formal contexts.

non- The prefix *non-* is used to form a simple or neutral antonym of the word to which it is attached: □*a nonprofessional golfer* □*non-Christian religions*.

◆ The prefix *un-*, attached to the same words, may have stronger negative force: an *unprofessional* or *un-Christian* act, for example, violates professional ethics or Christian principles.

Many people object to the frequent use of the prefix *non-* to coin unnecessary antonyms: □ *nonpresence* (for *absence*) □ *nonpermanent* (for *temporary*) □ *nonsuccess* (for *failure*) □ *nonobligatory* (for *optional*).

See also HYPHEN 1; INFLAMMABLE.

none The use of a singular or plural verb with the pronoun *none* depends on the sense and context in which it is used: □*None of the milk was spilt.* □*None of my friends has/have seen the film.* In the first of these examples *none*, like *milk*, must be used with a singular verb. In examples of the second type some people prefer a singular verb in formal contexts, especially if *none* is used in the sense of 'not one'. In informal contexts, or in the sense of 'not any', a plural verb is more frequent.

See also SINGULAR OR PLURAL?

none the less or **nevertheless**? These two synonyms are sometimes confused. Traditionally *none the less* has been written as three separate words, although *nonetheless* is gradually being accepted. *Nevertheless* is always written as one word.

◆ In American English both words are written as single words.

nonflammable see INFLAMMABLE.

no one or **no-one**? Many users prefer the two-word compound *no one* to the hyphenated form *no-one*. Unlike *anyone, everyone,* and *someone, no one* should not be written as a one-word compound.

◆ The pronoun *no one* and its synonym *nobody* are interchangeable in all contexts. Both are used with a singular verb but are sometimes followed by a plural personal pronoun or possessive adjective (see THEY): □ *No one/Nobody likes to see their children suffer.*

nor *Nor* is used in place of *or* in the *neither ... nor* construction (see NEITHER) and to introduce a negative alternative that stands as a separate clause: □*I speak neither German nor Spanish.* □*She* *hasn't been to America, nor has her sister.* □ *He never watches television, nor does he listen to the radio.*

◆ In many other contexts *nor* and *or* are interchangeable: □ *The library is not open on Thursday mornings, nor/or at the weekend.* □ *We have no food to eat nor/or clothes to wear.*

Many users prefer *or* to *nor* where the negative force of an auxiliary verb covers both alternatives: □ *They cannot sing or dance.* □ *She has not eaten her biscuits or drunk her tea.*

The use of *nor* at the beginning of a sentence is generally acceptable: □ *Nature is slow to compensate for deforestation. Nor has man been able to make good the damage* (*Daily Telegraph*).

normalcy or **normality**? These two nouns are synonymous derivatives of the adjective *normal*. *Normality* is the preferred form in British English; *normalcy* is chiefly used in American English.

north, North, or **northern**? As an adjective, *north* is always written with a capital *N* when it forms part of a proper name: □ *North America* □ *the North Sea*. The noun *north* is usually written with a capital *N* when it denotes a specific region, such as the northern part of England: □ *House prices are lower in the North*. In other contexts, and as an adverb, *north* is usually written with a lower-case *n*: □ *We travelled north for ten days.* □ *They live in north London.* □ *The wind is blowing from the north.*

◆ The adjective *northern* is more frequent and usually less specific than the adjective *north*: □ *the northern part of the country* □ *in northern France.*

Like *north*, *northern* is written with a capital *N* when it forms part of a proper name, such as *Northern Ireland*. With or without a capital *N*, it also means 'of the North': □ *a northern/Northern accent.*

no sooner see HARDLY.

nostalgia The noun *nostalgia* and its derivatives are most frequently used with reference to a wistful or sentimental yearning for the past: □ *She remembered the seaside holidays of her childhood with a deep nostalgia.* □ *Listening to old records always makes me nostalgic.* Some people object to this usage, restricting the term to its original meaning of 'homesickness'.

◆ The use of the adjective *nostalgic* in the sense of 'causing nostalgia', rather than 'feeling nostalgia', is also disliked and avoided by some users: □ *the nostalgic sound of the church bells.*

not The position of the word *not* in a negative sentence may affect its meaning and can sometimes lead to ambiguity: □ *All children are not afraid of the dark.* □ *We did not go because it was raining.* □ *He is not trying to win.* □ *He is trying not to win.* The first of these examples, which literally means 'No children are afraid of the dark', is easily reworded: □ *Not all children are afraid of the dark*. The second example may be reordered or expanded for clarity: □ *Because it was raining we did not go.* □ *We did not go because it was raining, we went because we were bored.*

◆ See also NOT ONLY ... BUT ALSO.

notable, noted, or **noteworthy**? *Noted* means 'famous': □ *a noted scientist* □ *The area is noted for its spectacular scenery*. *Notable* and *noteworthy* both mean 'worthy of notice or of being noted': □ *a notable* [or *noteworthy*] *achievement*, but *noteworthy* is usually used to describe facts or events rather than people: □ *It was noteworthy that the average price remained the same despite the effects of inflation.*

◆ A person or thing that is *notable* or *noteworthy* deserves notice, admiration or renown; a person or thing that is *noted* has already received notice, admiration, or renown.

notable or **noticeable**? The adjective *notable* means 'remarkable' or 'worthy of note'; *noticeable* means 'perceptible' or 'obvious': □ *a notable achievement* □ *a noticeable change in temperature.* The two words should not be confused.

◆ The final *-e* of the verb *notice* is retained in *noticeable,* whereas the final *-e* of *note* is omitted in *notable.*

noted, noteworthy see NOTABLE, NOTED, OR NOTEWORTHY?

nothing but The phrase *nothing but ...* is used with a singular verb, even if the noun that follows *but* is plural: □ *Nothing but crumbs was* [not *were*] *left on the plate.*

◆ When *nothing but* is followed by an infinitive, the word *to* is omitted: □ *They have done nothing but cry since you left.*

noticeable see NOTABLE OR NOTICEABLE?

not only ... but also The words or clauses that follow *not only* and *but also* must be grammatically balanced: □ *I have lost not only my purse but also my car keys* [not *I have not only lost ...*]. □ *They not only broke the world record for long-distance swimming but also raised several thousand pounds for charity* [not *They broke not only ...*].

◆ In many contexts the word *also* can be omitted: □ *He not only wrote to the headmaster but (also) consulted his solicitor.*

notorious see INFAMOUS OR NOTORIOUS?

nougat The standard pronunciation of this word is [*noo*gah], after the French. The alternative pronunciation [*nu*găt] is widely used.

nought see NAUGHT OR NOUGHT?

nouns Nouns are the names of things, places, or people. The main division of nouns is into countable and uncountable nouns. Countable nouns are those which can be preceded by *a* or *the* or a number or word denoting number: □ *a goat* □ *three lemons* □ *the priest* □ *several books.* Uncountable nouns are not able to be counted because they are nouns of mass: □ *flour* □ *water.* Some words can be countable or uncountable, according to how they are used: □ *Have a beer.* □ *Beer is fattening.*

◆ Proper nouns refer to a single particular person or thing and begin with a capital letter: □ *Trevor Jones.* Exceptionally, proper nouns can be made plural: □ *the Americas* □ *There are two Susans on the staff.*

Nouns can often be used as adjectives, when they sometimes form one word with another noun, or are hyphenated, or remain as two words: □ *postbox* □ *tea-tray* □ *birthday present.* They are more likely to be hyphenated when the two nouns are used together adjectivally: □ *Christmas-cake decorations* □ *a bathroom-fittings shop.* See also **HYPHEN 3.**

The use of nouns as verbs has a long history. We use the verb *to question* without thinking that it was originally a noun. Such phrases as: □ *to paper a room* □ *to tin fruit* □ *to pencil it in* are also so frequently used as to be wholly acceptable. However, more modern innovations, such as: □ *Let me example that for you.* □ *They host dinner parties every month.* □ *He rubbished their policies.* □ *to modern*, are disliked by many people. See also **VERBS.**

noxious or **obnoxious**? Both these adjectives can mean 'extremely unpleasant', but *obnoxious* usually refers to a person and *noxious* to something that is physically or morally harmful: □ *their obnoxious children* □ *noxious fumes.*

◆ Both words are ultimately derived from the Latin *noxa* 'injury'.

nubile The adjective *nubile*, derived from the Latin word for 'marriageable', is frequently applied to any sexually attractive young woman, especially in jocular or informal contexts: □ *His friend's nubile sister was sunbathing in the garden.* Some people object to this usage, restricting the term to its original meaning.

◆ The use of the adjective *nubile* to describe attractive married women or unattractive unmarried women is therefore best avoided.

nuclear The occasional use of *nuclear* as a noun, meaning 'nuclear power': □ *a national debate about nuclear,* is disliked and avoided by most people.

◆ This usage is potentially confusing, as the word *nuclear* may also refer to nuclear warfare, nuclear missiles, nuclear fission, nuclear energy, etc. The term *nuclear winter* refers to a period with very little light, heat, or growth that would follow a nuclear war.

In the phrase *nuclear family* the adjective *nuclear* simply means 'forming a nucleus'.

nude see NAKED OR NUDE?

number The phrase *a number of* ... is used with a plural verb; the phrase *the number of* ... is used with a singular verb: □ *A number of pupils were late.* □ *The number of pupils has increased.*

◆ See also SINGULAR OR PLURAL?

numbers Numbers that occur in printed or written texts may be expressed in figures or written out in full, according to the nature of the work, the context, the writer's personal preference, or the publisher's house style.

◆ In mathematical, scientific, technical, commercial, or statistical texts numbers are usually expressed in figures throughout.

In other works specific measurements or sums of money, page numbers, dates, and numbers higher than one hundred (except two hundred, three hundred, four thousand, five million, etc.) are usually expressed in figures.

Some writers and publishers spell out numbers from one to ten only; some spell out numbers from one to twenty; others spell out all numbers up to one hundred. It is important to be reasonably consistent within a single piece of writing, but some users prefer not to mix figures and words in the same sentence: □ *There are nine boys and fifteen* [not *15*] *girls in his class.* □ *We invited 130 guests but only 80* [not *eighty*] *turned up.*

The time may be expressed in words or figures: □ *twenty past three* □ *3.20* □ *eight o'clock* □ *8 o'clock.*

Times using the 24-hour clock are written as figures: □ *16.25* □ *0700 hours.* See also A.M. AND P.M.; DATES.

Numbers of five or more digits are separated by commas or spaces into groups of three: □ *45,069/45 069* □ *3,728,960/3 728 960.*

Four-digit numbers are usually printed or written without commas or spaces: □ *5069* □ *8960.*

See also HYPHEN 6.

nutritional or **nutritious**? *Nutritional* means 'relating to nutrition (the process of taking food into the body and absorbing it)'; *nutritious* means 'nourishing': □ *the nutritional requirements of a baby* □ *a very nutritious meal.*

◆ The adjective *nutritional* is increasingly used with reference to the content of processed and other foods: □ *Nutritional labelling must be made compulsory* (*Sunday Times*). □ *People should have enough nutritional information to make dietary changes* (*Daily Telegraph*).

The more formal adjective *nutritive* may be used in place of

nutritional or *nutritious*, but it more frequently replaces the former:
□ *New recommendations have been made by the Ministry of Agriculture, Fisheries and Food for the way in which nutritive values are displayed* (Kellogg's Rice Krispies packet).

nutritive see NUTRITIONAL OR NUTRITIOUS?

O or oh? *O*, always written with a capital, is a rarer, more poetic variant of the exclamation *oh*: □ *O come all ye faithful.* □ *O* [or *Oh*] *for the school holidays!* □ *'I can't come and see you later, I'm afraid.' 'Oh well, never mind.'* □ *She burst into tears, crying, 'Oh dear! Oh dear! Oh dear!'* □ *I just thought ... oh, never mind.*

obeisance *Obeisance* is a very formal word that means an attitude or gesture of deference or respect: □ *to pay obeisance* □ *to make an obeisance.* It is not synonymous with *obedience*, although both nouns are derived from Old French *obeir*, 'to obey'.

◆ Note the spelling of *obeisance*, particularly the *ei* and the *-ance* ending.

object The *object* of a clause or sentence is the noun, pronoun, or phrase that is affected by the verb. The object usually follows the verb.

◆ An object may be *direct* or *indirect*. In the sentence: □ *The dog buried the bone, the bone* is the direct object and there is no indirect object. In the sentences: □ *I gave the child a book* and □ *She bought the child a book, a book* is the direct object and *the child* is the indirect object. Many sentences that contain both a direct and an indirect object can be rephrased using the prepositions *to* or *for*: □ *I gave a book to the child.* □ *She bought a book for the child.*
Compare SUBJECT.

objective or subjective? The adjective *objective* means 'not influenced by personal feelings, beliefs, or prejudices'; its antonym *subjective* means 'influenced by personal feelings, etc.': □ *This is a subjective opinion: I find it hard to be objective when we're discussing my own daughter's career.*

◆ Some users consider the adjectives to be unnecessary synonyms for *fair, impartial, personal, biased*, etc.
The noun *objective* is best avoided where *goal, aim, purpose, object*, etc., would be adequate or more appropriate: □ *the purpose* [not *objective*] *of this meeting.* □ *Our aim* [not *objective*] *is to provide equal opportunities for all.*

objet d'art The plural of the phrase *objet d'art*, meaning 'small object of artistic worth', is formed by adding *-s* to the first word, *objets d'art.*

◆ Of French origin, the phrase is sometimes written or printed in italics in English texts. Note the spelling of *objet*, which lacks the *c* of the English word *object*.

obliged or obligated? Both these adjectives may be used in the sense of 'morally or legally bound': □ *He felt obliged/obligated to report the accident.*

◆ The use of *obligated* is largely restricted to formal contexts.
Obliged has the additional meaning of 'physically constrained' or 'compelled': □ *They were obliged to remain in their seats.*

oblivious The adjective *oblivious* is often used in the sense of

235

'unaware' or 'heedless': □ *He remained in the shelter of the tree, oblivious of the fact that the rain had stopped.*

◆ Some people object to this usage, restricting the adjective to its original sense of 'no longer aware' or 'forgetful': □ *Oblivious of the need for caution, she stepped out of the car to photograph the lions.*

The frequent use of the phrase *oblivious to*, rather than *oblivious of*, is unacceptable to some users and is best avoided in formal contexts: □ *oblivious of* [not *to*] *the dangers* □ *oblivious of* [not *to*] *my presence.*

obnoxious see NOXIOUS OR OBNOXIOUS?

obscene Some people object to the increasing use of *obscene* as a general term of strong disapproval: □ *Recent large pay awards to some company directors are obscene, the Bishop of Manchester ... has told the General Synod in York* (*Daily Telegraph*).

◆ The primary meaning of *obscene* is 'offensive to accepted standards of decency': □ *obscene language* □ *an obscene picture.*

The word *obscene* is sometimes misspelt: note that the second syllable is identical with the word *scene.*

observance or **observation**? The noun *observance* denotes either the act of complying or a ritual custom or practice; *observation* denotes either the act of watching or noticing or a remark or comment: □ *observance of the rules* □ *religious observances* □ *their observation of human behaviour* □ *an observation made by his client.*

obverse see CONVERSE, INVERSE, OBVERSE, OR REVERSE?

obviate To *obviate* something is to make it unnecessary or to dispose of it: □ *A reduction in inflation would obviate the need for higher pay rises.* □ *The management's new proposals obviated our complaints.* It is largely restricted to formal contexts and should not be used as a pretentious synonym for 'remove' or 'get rid of'.

◆ The verb *obviate* is unconnected in meaning to the adjective *obvious*, although the two words are etymologically related.

occasion The verb *occasion* is best avoided where *cause, bring about,* etc., would be adequate: □ *The accident was caused* [not *occasioned*] *by a fault in the braking system.*

◆ Note the spelling of the word *occasion*, particularly the -*cc*- and single *s*.

occupied or **preoccupied**? Applied to a person, *occupied* means 'busy'; *preoccupied* means 'absorbed in a particular train of thought (often to the exclusion of all else)': □ *I was occupied with the preparations for the carnival.* □ *Try to keep everybody occupied.* □ *He was preoccupied with his marital problems.* □ *She seemed preoccupied.*

◆ Being *occupied* may involve the mind and/or the body, whereas being *preoccupied* usually involves the mind alone.

occurrence This word is often misspelt. A frequent error is the substitution of -*ance* for the -*ence* ending. Note also the -*cc*- and -*rr*-, as also in *occurred* and *occurring*.

octopus The plural of the noun *octopus*, denoting a sea animal with eight tentacles, is *octopuses*. As the word is ultimately of Greek origin, the plural form *octopi* is incorrect; *octopodes* is permissible but pedantic.

oculist see OPTICIAN, OPHTHALMOLOGIST, OPTOMETRIST, OR OCULIST?

odious or **odorous**? *Odious* means 'extremely unpleasant'; *odorous*, a very formal word, means 'having a particular smell': □ *an odious man* □ *an odorous room.* The two adjectives should not be confused.

◆ Like the noun *odour, odorous* may refer to a pleasant or an unpleasant smell. Note that the *u* of *odour* is dropped before the *-ous* ending of *odorous*.

The word *odious*, not *odorous*, is used in the saying 'Comparisons are odious'.

-oe- see **-AE- AND -OE-.**

of The preposition *of* is sometimes wrongly substituted for the verb *have* or, more frequently, its contraction *'ve*: □ *They should have* [not *of*] *refused*. □ *She must've* [not *must of*] *forgotten*. This substitution, caused by the similarity in pronunciation between the two words when unstressed, is wrong.

◆ The use of such phrases as *of a Friday, of an evening*, etc., in place of *on Fridays, in the evening*, etc., should be restricted to informal contexts: □ *I go shopping of a Tuesday afternoon.*

See also **OFF**; **'S OR S'?**; **SINGULAR OR PLURAL?**

of course The phrase *of course* serves a number of useful purposes, but should not be used to excess.

◆ It has a variety of connotations, some of which may cause offence. Used for emphasis, either alone or to introduce a reply, the phrase may convey impatience or politeness: □ *'Did you remember to post my letter?' 'Of course (I did).'* □ *'May I use your telephone?' 'Of course (you may).'*

Used in the sense of 'naturally' or 'admittedly', it may be patronizing, superior, sympathetic, or apologetic: □ *It is of course impossible to communicate with the dead.* □ *I knew his uncle, of course. I don't believe you ever met him, did you?* □ *Of course you're tired, you've had a long journey.* □ *I may be wrong, of course.*

off The use of the preposition *off* in place of *from*, to indicate the source of an acquisition, is considered wrong by many people, even in informal contexts: □ *I bought if from* [not *off*] *my sister.*

◆ The phrase *off of* is also wrong and should be avoided in all contexts: □ *He jumped off* [not *off of*] *the wall.* □ *Take your feet off* [not *off of*] *the table.*

The word *off* is usually pronounced to rhyme with *scoff*; the variant pronunciation [awf] is generally considered to be old-fashioned or affected.

See also **OFF-LIMITS.**

offence This word, meaning 'action causing displeasure; illegal act', is sometimes misspelt. Note the *-c-* not *-s-* in British English (American English, *offense*).

◆ The derived adjective is spelt *offensive* in both British and American English.

offer or **proffer**? Both verbs mean 'present for acceptance': □ *He proffered* [or *offered*] *his passport.* □ *She offered* [or *proffered*] *her sympathy. Offer* has a much wider range of usage; *proffer* is largely restricted to formal contexts, and should not be used as a pretentious substitute for *offer*.

◆ *Proffer* cannot be used in place of *offer* in more complex constructions: □ *He offered* [not *proffered*] *her a glass of champagne.* □ *They offered* [not *proffered*] *us £2000 for the car.*

official or **officious**? The adjective *official* means 'authorized', 'formal', or 'of an office'; *officious*, which is generally used in a derogatory manner, means 'interfering', 'bossy', 'self-important', or 'offering unwanted advice or assistance': □ *an official strike* □ *an official visit* □ *an officious clerk.* The two words should not be confused.

◆ In the field of diplomacy the adjective *officious* means 'informal' or 'unofficial': □ *an officious agreement*. This sense is not in general usage.

officialese *Officialese* is a derogatory name for the style of writing or language that is considered to be typical of official forms, reports, memoranda, letters, leaflets, and other bureaucratic documents.

◆ Known informally as *gobbledygook*, officialese is characterized by the use of pompous and wordy language, obscure jargon, and long unintelligible sentences. An example quoted by Tom Vernon in *Gobbledegook* is from a Department of Employment form: □ *In certain circumstances that condition may be modified to enable those persons who claim benefit early in their insurance life to treat as paid in one tax year all class 1 (standard rate) contributions paid in the period starting with the year in which they first became liable for such contributions, and ending with the day from which benefit is claimed.*

Widely satirized in the media, government departments have tried in recent years, with some success, to eliminate officialese by simplifying vocabulary and circumlocutory phrases, shortening sentences, and personalizing instructions. See also JARGON.

officious see OFFICIAL OR OFFICIOUS?

off-limits The term *off-limits,* meaning 'out of bounds' or 'forbidden', originated in American military contexts and is now entering general British usage: □ *This part of the factory is off-limits to visitors.* Many users prefer to retain the more traditional synonyms.

off-the-wall The adjective *off-the-wall* is used in informal contexts, especially in American English, to mean 'amusingly unusual; eccentric or unexpected; zany': □ *off-the-wall humour.* Care should be taken to avoid overusing this expression.

often The words *oftener* and *oftenest* are accepted comparative and superlative forms of the adverb *often*, but many users prefer *more often* and *most often*, especially in formal contexts: □ *It rains most often in the autumn.* □ *Which car do you use oftener?*

◆ The *t* of *often* is rarely sounded, the most frequent pronunciation of the word being [ofèn]. The pronunciation [oftèn] is heard from time to time, but the variant [awfèn], which sounds like *orphan*, is generally considered to be old-fashioned or affected.

oh see O OR OH?

OK or **okay**? The term *OK* or *okay*, denoting agreement or approval, may be used as an adjective, adverb, noun, or verb: □ *That's OK.* □ *The meeting went OK.* □ *Has she given us the OK/okay?* □ *They are unlikely to okay/OK the suggestion.*

◆ As the term is most frequently used in informal speech, the variations in its written form are not of great importance.

In informal writing, the extended form *okay* is generally preferred for the verb, especially if inflectional endings are to be added: □ *The project has been okayed by the committee.*

The two-letter form *OK* is sometimes written with full stops: □ *It looks O.K. to me.*

old age pensioner see SENIOR CITIZEN OR OLD AGE PENSIONER?

older, oldest see ELDER, ELDEST, OLDER, OR OLDEST?

omelette This word is sometimes misspelt. In British English the spelling is *omelette*, in American English *omelet*. Note the first *e*.

◆ The word is pronounced [omlit].

omission This noun, meaning 'the act of omitting' or 'something omitted', is often misspelt. The most frequent error is the substitution of *-mm-* for the single *-m-*. Note also the *-ission* ending

239

239

(not *-ision* or *-ition*).

on see ONTO OR ON TO?; UPON OR ON?

one The pronoun *one*, representing an indefinite person, is usually followed in British English by *one's, oneself,* etc., rather than by *his, himself,* etc.: □ *One should be kind to one's friends.*

◆ If the resulting sentence sounds clumsy or unidiomatic, it may be paraphrased: □ *When one lives on one's own one often talks to oneself,* for example, may be changed to: *People who live on their own often talk to themselves.*

In American English, however, *one* is usually followed in such contexts by *his, himself,* etc.: □ *One often talks to himself.* □ *One should be kind to his friends.* This can lead to ambiguity: in the last example *his friends* may refer to the friends of some other person.

When the pronoun *one* represents a specific person it is always followed by *his, her,* etc.: □ *The twins' tastes are not identical: one drinks her* [not *one's*] *coffee black, the other drinks it white.*

In formal contexts the impersonal pronoun *one* is generally preferred to *you.* The use of *one* in place of *I* or *we,* however, is widely considered to be affected and is best avoided, especially in informal contexts: □ *I have* [not *One has*] *never been very good at sport.* □ *We hope* [not *One hopes*] *that the situation will improve.* See also YOU.

The constructions *one in three/five/ten/*etc. and *one of the ...,* followed by a plural noun, should be used with a singular verb: □ *One in four teachers is in favour of corporal punishment.* □ *One of the eggs is broken.* However, a plural verb is often seen or heard after the construction *one in ...:* □ *One in ten men are thought to have a drink problem* (BBC radio news). The constructions *one of those ... who* and *one of the ... that* are followed by a plural verb: □ *He is one of those people who are never satisfied.* □ *It is one of the shortest books that have ever been published.* See also SINGULAR OR PLURAL?

In some contexts the word *one* is superfluous: □ *His smile was not a friendly one,* for example, may be more concisely expressed as: *His smile was not friendly.*

See also EACH OTHER OR ONE ANOTHER?

onerous This word, meaning 'demanding or troublesome': □ *onerous tasks,* has two acceptable pronunciations, [onĕrŏs] and [ōnĕrŏs].

one-stop The term *one-stop* refers to the modern trend towards combining various related facilities or services in one place or package: □ *a one-stop system* □ *The report ... suggests local authorities can offer 'one-stop shops' where employers can find child-care, training and other contacts under one roof* (*Daily Telegraph*). It is a vogue word disliked by some people.

◆ *One-stop shopping* originally referred to shops that sell a wide range of essential items – food, newspapers, books, toys, clothes, gardening and household goods, etc.

ongoing Many people object to the use of the adjective *ongoing* in place of *continuing, developing, in progress,* etc.: □ *ongoing research* □ *an ongoing investment programme in manufacturing technology.* The cliché *ongoing situation* is also widely disliked.

◆ The word *ongoing* sometimes appears in hyphenated form: □ *We put you through the world's most advanced management training courses, followed by on-going personal development* (*Executive Post*).

on-line The term *on-line,* which relates to equipment that is directly connected to and/or controlled by a central computer, is sometimes used in the extended sense of 'in direct communication'

with': □ *on-line to the president.* It should not be confused with
ON-STREAM: □ *Rent A Film ... will be getting in the party spirit
to celebrate a very special service which has just come on line
at their plush, newly-refurbished premises* (*Littlehampton
Guardian*).

only In some written sentences the adverb *only* must be carefully
positioned, as near as possible to the word it refers to, in order to
convey the intended meaning: □ *She eats fish only on Fridays*
[i.e. not on other days]. □ *She eats only fish* [i.e. nothing else] *on
Fridays.* □ *Only she* [i.e. She is the only one who] *eats fish on Fridays.*

◆ In speech, where the stress and intonation of the sentence should
eliminate any ambiguity, and in written sentences that are not open to
misinterpretation, *only* may be placed in its most idiomatic position,
i.e. between the subject and the verb: □ *They have only sold three
books.*

The use of *only* as a conjunction, in place of *but* or *however*, is best
restricted to informal contexts: □ *I'd like to go to Canada, only I can't
afford the air fare.*

Some people object to the use of the phrase *only too* as an
intensifier, reserving it for the sense of 'regrettably': □ *I am very* [not
only too] *pleased to help.* □ *The new container, which is supposed to
be childproof, is only too easy to open.*

See also **NOT ONLY ... BUT ALSO.**

onomatopoeia *Onomatopoeia* is the formation of words that imitate
the sound associated with an object or action: □ *cuckoo* □ *moo*
□ *clang* □ *croak* □ *hiss* □ *twitter.*

◆ It also refers to the use of words, usually in poetry, in such a way as
to suggest the sound described. An example is:

Keeping time, time, time,
    In a sort of Runic rhyme,
To the tintinnabulation that so musically wells
    From the bells, bells, bells, bells.
    (Edgar Allan Poe, *The Bells*)

on-stream The term *on-stream* relates to an industrial process or plant
that is in production or about to go into production or operation
or to the launching of a new advertising campaign, etc.: □ *Collec-
tions* [of mail on Sundays] *will start in five districts in October,
.... A further five districts will be added next January with the rest
of the country coming on stream by the end of 1990* (*The Guardian*).

◆ It is sometimes possible to replace the phrase *come on-stream* with
open, begin, etc.

onto or **on to**? The preposition *onto* may be written as one or two
words: □ *She drove onto/on to the pavement.* On to may also be
a combination of the adverb *on* and the preposition or infinitive
marker *to*, in which case it should not be written as one word:
□ *She drove on to London.* □ *She drove on to find a hotel.*

onward or **onwards**? In British English *onward* is principally used as
an adjective, *onwards* being the usual form of the adverb meaning 'ahead': □ *onward motion* □ *to march onwards.*

◆ The adverb *onward* is more frequently used in American English.
See also **-WARD** OR **-WARDS**?

operative The frequent use of the noun *operative* in place of *worker*,
especially in nonindustrial contexts, is disliked by many users:
□ *a strike by cleaning operatives at the hospital.*

ophthalmologist see OPTICIAN. OPHTHALMOLOGIST. OPTOMETRIST. OR OCULIST?

opposite The noun *opposite* is followed by *of*, not *to*: □ *Hot is the opposite of* [not *to*] *cold.* As a preposition, *opposite* may be followed by *to* (not *of*) but usually stands alone: □ *the car park opposite (to) the station.*

◆ The adjective *opposite* may be used with *to* or *from*: □ *He sat on the opposite side to/from her.*

oppress, repress, or **suppress**? These verbs are similar in meaning: all three refer to subjugation or restraint. *Oppress* means 'subjugate by force, cruel treatment, etc.'; the direct object of the verb is usually a group of people: □ *a regime that oppresses women* □ *the oppressed workers.* The verb *repress* is also used in this sense, but more frequently refers to the act of concealing or controlling one's feelings: □ *I repressed the urge to hit him.* □ *a repressed desire.* In psychology, *repress* means 'banish or exclude (thoughts, feelings, etc.) from one's conscious mind or awareness', an act that may lead to psychological problems: □ *repressed sexuality.* The verb *suppress* has the more general meaning of 'restrain' or 'control': □ *She couldn't suppress her laughter. Suppress* also means 'withhold' or 'crush': □ *to suppress information* □ *to suppress a rebellion.*

◆ Note the differences in spelling, particularly the *-pp-* of *oppress* and *suppress* and the single *-p-* of *repress*.

optician, ophthalmologist, optometrist, or **oculist**? All four nouns denote people who are concerned with defects or diseases of the eye.

◆ The word *optician*, which is probably the most familiar, may denote an *ophthalmic optician* or a *dispensing optician*.

An *ophthalmic optician* is qualified to test eyesight and prescribe corrective lenses. A *dispensing optician* makes and sells glasses (and other optical equipment).

An *ophthalmologist* is a doctor who specializes in eye diseases. *Optometrist* is a less frequent name for an *ophthalmic optician; oculist* is synonymous with *ophthalmologist.*

The word *ophthalmologist* is sometimes misspelt, the most frequent error being the omission of the first *h*. It is usually pronounced [ofthalmolŏjist]; the pronunciation of the first syllable to rhyme with *hop*, rather than *scoff*, is disliked by many users.

optimal see OPTIMUM.

optimistic Many people object to the frequent use of the adjective *optimistic* as a synonym for 'hopeful', 'confident', 'cheerful', 'favourable', 'encouraging', etc.: □ *She is optimistic that the car will be found.* □ *They have produced an optimistic report on the company's prospects.*

◆ In general usage *optimistic* principally relates to a tendency to see or expect the best or to take a favourable view of things: □ *Throughout his illness he remained optimistic.*

optimize see OPTIMUM.

optimum The adjective and noun *optimum* refer to the most favourable or advantageous condition, amount, degree, etc.: □ *the optimum speed* □ *A temperature of 15°C is the optimum.*

◆ The noun *optimum* has two plural forms, usually in technical contexts, *optimums* and *optima.*

The frequent use of the adjective *optimum* and its synonym *optimal* in the sense of 'best' is disliked by many users: □ *a manufacturing programme designed to make optimum use of all available resources (Executive Post).* □ *A combination of olive oil and butter will produce the optimal result.*

The verb *optimize* means 'make the most of' or 'make as efficient as possible': □ *to optimize the potential of the business* □ *to optimize the production process.*

opt in see OPT OUT.

optometrist see OPTICIAN, OPHTHALMOLOGIST, OPTOMETRIST, OR OCULIST?

opt out *Opt out* means 'choose not to participate or be involved', with the implication that a person or organization that does not opt out is automatically included: □ *to opt out of society* □ *schools that have opted out (of local government control).* In the opposite situation, where people or organizations are automatically excluded unless they choose to participate, the verb *opt in* may be used: □ *A survey into public attitudes to kidney donation found that most people are willing to donate their kidneys but they are against a scheme to 'opt out' of donorship rather than the present scheme of 'opting in'* (*New Scientist*).

opus The formal noun *opus,* denoting a musical work or other artistic composition, may be pronounced [ōpŭs], with the long *o* of *open,* or [opŭs], with the short *o* of *operate.* Both pronunciations are acceptable, but the first is more frequent.

◆ *Opus* also has two plural forms, *opuses* and *opera.* As the word *opera* exists as a singular noun in its own right, some users prefer *opuses*: the phrase *Mozart's opera,* for example, may refer to a single operatic composition or to all Mozart's musical works.

or When *or* connects two or more singular subjects a singular verb is used: □ *Perhaps Peter or Jane knows* [not *know*] *the answer.* A plural verb is used if both subjects are plural: □ *Carrots or parsnips are served with this dish.*

◆ In a combination of singular and plural alternatives the verb traditionally agrees with the subject that is nearest to it: □ *One large pot or two small ones are needed.* □ *Two small pots or one large one is needed.* The same principle is applied to singular subjects that are used with different forms of the verb: □ *Are you or your wife going to the concert?* If the resulting sentence sounds inelegant or unidiomatic, a second verb may be added: □ *Am I the winner or is he?*

The use of *or* at the beginning of a sentence is generally acceptable: □ *We may go to London tomorrow. Or we may stay at home.*

For the use of a comma before *or* in a series of three or more items see COMMA 1. *Or* may also be preceded by a comma in other contexts, especially if it introduces a synonym rather than an alternative: □ *the policy of glasnost, or openness.*

See also AND/OR; EITHER; NOR.

oral see AURAL OR ORAL?; VERBAL OR ORAL?

ordinance or **ordnance**? An *ordinance* is a decree or regulation; the noun *ordnance* denotes military supplies or artillery.

◆ Neither word is in frequent use: *ordinance* is largely restricted to local government contexts; *ordnance* is chiefly associated with Ordnance Survey maps.

The similarity in spelling often leads to confusion between the two words.

organic The adjective *organic* is applied to methods of food production that do not make use of chemical fertilizers, pesticides, etc.: □ *organic farming* □ *organically produced fruit.* Some people dislike the increasing tendency to apply the adjective directly to the produce itself: □ *organic food* □ *organic vegetables.*

◆ This objection is based on the fact that all meat, fruit, and vegetables may be described as *organic* in the principal sense of 'relating to or derived from living plants or animals'.

orient or **orientate**? Both forms of the verb are acceptable: *orient*, the standard form in American English, is preferred by some users as the shorter and simpler alternative, but *orientate* is the more frequent in British English.

◆ To *orient* originally meant 'to face east'; the variant *orientate* was probably a **BACK FORMATION** from the noun *orientation*. The verb is often used reflexively, meaning 'get one's bearings' or 'adjust oneself to new surroundings': □ *They found it difficult to orient/orientate themselves in the unfamiliar town.*

The past participle is increasingly used in the sense of 'inclined towards': □ *a commercially orientated service* □ *a science-oriented course.* Many people dislike this usage, which is generally avoidable and often quite superfluous: examples include the local government service designed *to meet locality-oriented needs* rather than 'to meet the needs of the locality' and job advertisements that call for experience in *product-orientated development* (product development) or *engineering-orientated environments* (engineering).

See also **DISORIENT OR DISORIENTATE**?

orthopaedic or **paediatric**? Both these adjectives are used in medical contexts and they are often confused. *Orthopaedic* refers to the treatment of bones, joints, muscles, etc.; *paediatric* refers to the treatment of children.

◆ The *-paed-* element in both words is derived from the Greek word for 'child': an *orthopaedic* specialist was originally concerned with the bones, joints, etc., of children but now treats people of all ages. Note that there is no connection with the *ped-* element of *pedestrian* and *pedal*, which is derived from the Latin word for 'foot'.

In American English the *-ae-* of *orthopaedic* and *paediatric* is reduced to *-e-* (see also **-AE- AND -OE-**).

ostensible or **ostentatious**? *Ostensible* means 'apparent'; *ostentatious* means 'showy': □ *the ostensible reason for her absence* □ *an ostentatious display of grief.*

◆ Both adjectives are ultimately derived from the Latin verb *ostendere*, meaning 'show', and neither is complimentary: *ostensible* has connotations of falseness or deception; *ostentatious* suggests pretentiousness or vulgarity.

other than The use of *other than* as an adverbial phrase is disliked by some users: □ *They were unable to escape other than by squeezing through the narrow window.*

◆ Its adjectival use, however, is acceptable to all: □ *There was no means of escape other than the narrow window.*

Other than is best avoided where *apart from* would be more appropriate: □ *There was a narrow window; apart from* [not *other than*] *that, there was no means of escape.*

The construction *other ... than* should not be replaced by *other ... but* or *other ... except*: □ *He had no other friend than* [not *but*] *me.* □ *Every other card than* [not *except*] *yours arrived on time.* If the word *other* is omitted, however, *but* or *except* may be substituted for *than.*

otherwise Some people object to the frequent use of *otherwise* as an adjective or pronoun: □ *All essays, finished or otherwise, must be handed in tomorrow morning.* □ *The entire workforce, union* *members and otherwise, went on strike. Otherwise* may be replaced by *not* in the first of these examples and by *others* in the second.

◆ The use of *otherwise* in combination with an adverb is acceptable to all: □ *The window was broken, accidentally or otherwise, by one of your children.*

In the sense of 'or else', *otherwise* should not be preceded by *or*: □ *Turn the volume down, otherwise you'll wake the baby.*

OTT see **OVER THE TOP.**

ought The auxiliary verb *ought*, expressing duty, obligation, advisability, expectation, etc., is always followed by an infinitive with *to*: □ *They ought to visit her more often.* □ *Ought we to have invited your sister?* □ *You oughtn't to leave your car unlocked.* □ *The meat ought to be cooked by now.*

◆ The negative and interrogative forms *didn't ought to, hadn't ought to, did we ought to, had I ought to,* etc., are regarded as wrong by careful users.

Ought to can occasionally be replaced by *should*: □ *The meat should be cooked by now.* In most contexts, however, *ought* expresses a stronger sense of duty, obligation, advisability, etc., than *should*. See also **SHOULD OR WOULD?**

our or **us?** see **-ING FORMS.**

out The verb *out*, meaning 'expose the homosexuality of', is a relatively recent coinage derived from the phrase *come out (of the closet)*, meaning 'reveal one's homosexuality': □ *The militant gay group which threatened to 'out' MPs and other leading figures for not disclosing their homosexuality ... said it was all a hoax (The Guardian).*

◆ The verb *out* and its associated noun *outing* are increasingly used in other contexts: □ *Indiscriminate 'outings'* [of people alleged to have collaborated with the former communist secret police] *prompted Mr Havel to announce that he himself had been listed as a 'candidate for collaboration' in 1965 (The Guardian).*

outdoor or **outdoors?** *Outdoor* is an adjective, *outdoors* is an adverb: □ *outdoor sports* □ *outdoor pursuits* □ *to play outdoors* □ *Outdoor clothes are worn outdoors.*

◆ The word *outdoors* is also used as a noun: □ *the great outdoors.*

outing see **OUT.**

outlet Some people object to the frequent use of the noun *outlet* in place of *shop*: □ *The product is available at a number of retail outlets in London.*

◆ In commercial contexts *outlet* also means 'market': □ *The company has yet to find outlets for its solar-powered torches.*

outplacement The noun *outplacement* refers to advice and assistance given to people who have been made redundant (or who are about to be made redundant): □ *outplacement counselling* □ *Outplacement consulting came to Britain from the US in the 1970s and has grown from a £2 million turnover in 1978 to about £55 million now (The Guardian).*

◆ The use of the noun *outplacement* as a euphemism for 'making redundant' is best avoided.

outrageous This word, meaning 'shocking or unconventional': □ *outrageous manners*, is sometimes misspelt. The *e* of *outrage* is retained before the suffix *-ous* to indicate the softness of the *g*.

outside of Many people dislike the prepositional phrase *outside of*, in which the word *of* is incorrect. The phrase is best avoided in formal contexts: □ *There was a taxi outside* [not *outside of*] *the house.*

◆ The addition of this superfluous *of* to the preposition *outside* may be influenced by the prepositional phrase *out of* or by the phrase *on the outside*, which is followed by *of* when it is used prepositionally: □ *a label on the outside of the box.*

outward or **outwards**? In British English *outward* is principally used as an adjective, *outwards* being the usual form of the adverb meaning 'towards the outside': □ *the outward journey* □ *to pull outwards.*

◆ The adverb *outward* is more frequently used in American English. See also -WARD OR -WARDS?

over see ABOVE OR OVER?

overall The word *overall* is best avoided where *total, whole, comprehensive, general, average, inclusive, altogether,* etc., would be adequate or more appropriate: □ *his general* [not *overall*] *appearance* □ *the total* [not *overall*] *cost of the project* □ *The journey will take five days altogether* [not *overall*].

◆ In some contexts *overall* is superfluous: □ *an overall increase in production.*

The use of the word *overall* in its original sense of 'from end to end' is acceptable to all users: □ *the overall length of the room.*

overkill The frequent use of the noun *overkill* in the sense of 'excess' is disliked by some users: □ *In the coverage of the election the media have been accused of overkill.*

◆ The noun is particularly undesirable in contexts that may be associated with the literal meaning of the verb *kill*: □ *We must avoid overkill in the presentation of our anti-abortion campaign.*

The term *overkill* originally denoted a greater capacity than necessary for destruction, with specific reference to nuclear weapons: □ *The de-escalation of the arms race has reduced the problem of overkill.*

overly Many people object to the use of the adverb *overly* in place of *too, excessively,* etc.: □ *She was not overly enthusiastic about my idea.* □ *He is overly sensitive to the slightest criticism.*

◆ In some contexts the need for *overly* can be obviated by attaching the prefix *over-*, with or without a hyphen, to the relevant adjective: □ *overenthusiastic* □ *oversensitive.*

over the top The cliché *over the top* and its slang abbreviation *OTT*, meaning 'excessive' or 'outrageous', should not be overused: □ *The restaurant sketch was a bit OTT.*

overtone or **undertone**? In the figurative sense of 'implicit shade of meaning or feeling', these two nouns are virtually synonymous, although *overtone* may convey an additional effect and *undertone* an underlying effect. Both are more frequently used in the plural: □ *overtones of malice* □ *undertones of discontent* □ *political overtones* □ *religious undertones.*

◆ The words are not interchangeable in their other meanings; *overtone* is a technical term in music and *undertone* denotes a hushed voice: □ *to speak in an undertone.*

overview The noun *overview* is best avoided where *survey, summary,* etc., would be adequate or more appropriate: □ *a general overview of the situation.*

owing to see DUE TO, OWING TO, OR BECAUSE OF?

pace The Latin word *pace*, usually printed in italics, means 'with due respect to' and is used when stating an opinion contrary to that of the specified person: □ *The teaching profession*, pace *George Bernard Shaw, is not a refuge for those who cannot do anything else.*

◆ *Pace* is a two-syllable word with at least two accepted pronunciations, [*pays*i] and [*pah*chay]. Since the word is largely restricted to formal written contexts, the problem of pronunciation does not frequently arise.

package The word *package* and the expression *package deal* are widely used to denote a set of proposals or offers that must be accepted or rejected as a whole: □ *a new package of measures dealing with pay and working conditions.*

◆ In other contexts *package* is often better omitted or replaced by a more appropriate noun: □ *Japan's recent announcement of a substantial package of extra spending* (Sunday Times). □ *Hammicks has spent over £100,000 on a retail design package* (The Bookseller).

Some people also object to the frequent use of the verb *package* in place of *present*: □ *the different ways in which the major political parties were packaged during the election campaign.*

paediatric see ORTHOPAEDIC OR PAEDIATRIC?

palate This word, meaning 'the top part of the inside of one's mouth' or 'sense of taste': □ *a cleft palate* □ *He has a sensitive palate*, is sometimes misspelt. It should not be confused with *palette*, the board on which an artist mixes colours, or *pallet*, a flat platform used in stacking and moving stored goods, and also a hard bed or straw mattress.

pallor The noun *pallor*, meaning 'paleness', is sometimes misspelt. Note the final *-or*, as in *stupor*, rather than *-our*.

palpable The use of the adjective *palpable* in the extended sense of 'easily perceived', in place of *obvious, manifest, plain*, etc., is disliked by some people: □ *a palpable lie.*

◆ Derived from the Latin verb *palpare*, meaning 'touch', *palpable* was originally restricted to what could be touched or felt: □ *palpable warmth.*

panacea The noun *panacea* denotes a universal remedy for all ills; it should not be used with reference to individual problems or troubles: □ *Efficient use of energy saves money but is not a panacea for solving carbon dioxide pollution* (Daily Telegraph).

◆ Often used disparagingly, the word is more frequently found in figurative contexts than in its literal sense of 'cure-all'.

Note the spelling of *panacea*, which is derived from the prefix *pan-*, meaning 'all', and the Greek word for 'cure'. It is pronounced [pan*à*see*à*].

panic The word *panic* adds a *k* before the suffix *-y* and suffixes beginning with an *e* or *i* such as *-ed*, *-er*, and *-ing*: □ *panicky* □ *They* *panicked.* □ *Stop panicking!* See also SPELLING 1.

paradigm The noun *paradigm* is best avoided where *example, model, pattern*, etc., would be adequate or more appropriate: □ *a paradigm of enterprise and initiative* □ *a paradigm of the problems faced by the unemployed.*

◆ *Paradigm* specifically denotes a clear or typical example; it should not be confused with the noun *paragon*, meaning 'model of excellence'.

The *g* of *paradigm*, pronounced [parrȧdīm], is silent. In the adjective *paradigmatic*, pronounced [parrȧdigmatik], the *g* is sounded.

paraffin This word is sometimes misspelt. Note the single *r* and *-ff-*, as in *raffle.*

paragon see PARADIGM.

paragraphs A *paragraph* is a subdivision of a written passage, which usually deals with one particular point or theme. It expresses an idea which, though it relates to the sense of the whole passage, can to some extent stand alone.

◆ There is no specified length for a paragraph. It can be one sentence or over a page long. However, very short successive paragraphs, as found in advertisements and popular journalism, can have a rather disjointed effect; while very long paragraphs can give the impression of heavy material that can be read through only in a slow, laborious manner. The most effective writing usually mixes longer and shorter paragraphs.

A paragraph starts on a new line and is usually indented. In a passage of dialogue each act of speech normally starts a new paragraph.

parallel This word is sometimes misspelt. Note the single *r, -ll-*, and then the single *l*.

◆ The spelling of some derived forms and compounds varies: □ *paralleling* or *parallelling* □ *paralleled* or *parallelled* □ *parallelism* □ *parallelogram* □ *unparalleled.*

paralyse This word is sometimes misspelt. The spelling in British English is *paralyse* [not *-yze*], in American English, *paralyze.*

◆ See also -IZE OR -ISE?

parameter Many people object to the frequent use of the noun *parameter*, a mathematical term, as a synonym for 'limit', 'boundary', 'framework', 'characteristic', or 'point to be considered': □ *A business must operate within the parameters of time, money, and efficiency.* □ *We keep on refining our mailing selection parameters* (*The Bookseller*). □ *What are the parameters of the problem?*

◆ Note the pronunciation of *parameter*, which is stressed on the second syllable [pȧramitèr].

paranoid The adjective *paranoid* principally relates to a mental disorder (*paranoia*) characterized by delusions of persecution or grandeur: □ *Often, he* [a schizophrenic] *feels himself to be persecuted – a paranoid delusion that occasionally leads to violence* (*Reader's Digest*).

◆ Some people object to the frequent use of *paranoid* and *paranoia* with reference to any intense suspicion, distrust, anxiety, fear, obsession, etc.: □ *It gives me an interest-free overdraft of £250 so I don't have to get paranoid at the end of the month* (Midland Bank advertisement, *Sunday Times*).

The word *paranoid* is also used as a noun. Its synonym *paranoiac*, pronounced [parrănoīk] or [parrănoīak], is less frequent.

Note the spelling of *paranoia*, particularly the last three vowels.

paraphernalia The noun *paraphernalia*, sometimes used with derogatory connotations, denotes all the miscellaneous items associated with a particular activity: □ *the paraphernalia of photography*. It is also used in more abstract contexts: □ *the paraphernalia of buying a new house. Paraphernalia* is a plural noun, but it is frequently used with a singular verb: □ *His camping paraphernalia is stored in the attic*. This usage is generally acceptable.

◆ Note the spelling of the word, particularly the unstressed syllable *-phern-*.

parenting The word *parenting*, which means 'being a parent' or 'parental care', is increasingly used to emphasize the joint responsibility of both parents in all aspects of a child's upbringing and to avoid the sexual stereotypes and traditional roles associated with the words *mother* and *father* and their derivatives: □ *the advantages of shared parenting* □ *a guide to parenting the gifted child*.

◆ This expression is disliked by those who object to the use of nouns as verbs.

parliament The noun *parliament*, meaning 'legislative authority, assembly, or body', is usually written with a capital *P* when it denotes a specific parliament, especially that of the United Kingdom: □ *The issue will be debated in Parliament this afternoon*.

◆ The usual pronunciation of *parliament* is [parlămĕnt]; the pronunciations [*par*limĕnt] and [*parl*yămĕnt] are accepted variants. Note the spelling of the word, particularly the central vowels.

parlour see LOUNGE.

partially or **partly**? Both adverbs mean 'not completely' or 'to some extent', but there are differences of sense, usage, and application between them: □ *facilities for the blind and partially sighted* □ *The course consists partly of oral work and partly of written work*.

◆ In some contexts the two adverbs are virtually interchangeable: □ *a partly/partially successful attempt*. It can be helpful to think of *partly* as meaning 'concerning one part; not wholly': □ *The woman's face was partly hidden* [i.e. only part of her face was hidden] *by her veil*. □ *The art treasures were partly on permanent loan to the museum and partly in the possession of the Adams family. Partially* may then be used to mean 'to a limited extent; not completely': □ *The woman's face was partially hidden* [i.e. her whole face may have been hidden but to a limited degree] *by her veil*. □ *His hopes were partially frustrated by the lack of full commitment by his fellow workers*.

However, in actual usage such guidelines tend to be ignored, and the words are used interchangeably, with *partly* being the more frequent. The H.M. Customs and Excise VAT notice on Partial Exemption (1984), for example, describes those registered for VAT as *partly exempt*, even though the notice is titled *Partial* Exemption.

participles All verbs have *present participles*, which are formed with *-ing*: □ *seeing* □ *walking*, and *past participles*, formed with *-d* or *-ed* for regular verbs and in other ways for irregular verbs: □ *loved* □ *finished* □ *given* □ *gone* □ *thought*.

◆ Participles are often used as adjectives: □ *broken promises* □ *a leaking tap*. They are also used, with an inversion of the usual sentence construction, to introduce a sentence such as: □ *Sitting in* the corner was an old man. □ *Attached to his wrist was a luggage label.* Care should be taken with such introductory participles, as they are sometimes used to link items that are quite unrelated: see DANGLING PARTICIPLES.

The pronunciation most frequently used is [par*t*isipl]; [*par*tisipl] is an older variant. See also STRESS.

See also -ED OR -T?; -ING FORMS.

particular Used for emphasis, the adjective *particular* is often superfluous: □ *Do you have any particular preference?* □ *This particular dress was worn by Vivien Leigh in 'Gone with the Wind'.*

◆ Many people dislike this usage, reserving the adjective for what is exceptional, special, specific, or worthy of note: □ *This discovery is of particular importance.*

partly see PARTIALLY OR PARTLY?

passed or **past**? These spellings are sometimes confused. *Passed* is the past tense and past participle of *pass*: □ *We passed the station.* □ *The years have passed by so quickly.*

◆ *Past* is used for all other forms: noun, adjective, preposition, and adverb: □ *Your past is catching up with you.* □ *the past weeks* □ *She ran past the sign.* □ *It's five past three.* □ *The plane flew past.*

passive A passive verb is one in which the SUBJECT receives the action of the verb (compare ACTIVE). The sentence □ *The play was written by Oscar Wilde* contains the passive verb *was written.*

◆ The subject of a passive verb is the direct object of the verb in a corresponding active sentence. The subject of the above example, *the play,* is the direct object of the active equivalent *Oscar Wilde wrote the play.*

A passive verb is usually formed from part of the verb *be* followed by a past participle: □ *The woman was struck on the head.* □ *The house had been demolished.*

Many users prefer to replace a passive clause or sentence with its simpler active equivalent, but this is not always possible. One cannot convert the two examples in the previous paragraph into the active unless one knows who or what struck the woman and demolished the house.

past see PASSED OR PAST?

patent This word may be pronounced [*pay*tĕnt] in all senses in British English: □ *to patent/apply for a patent for a new invention* □ *patent leather shoes,* and as the adverb *patently* [*pay*tĕntli]: □ *It is patently obvious she's lying.*

◆ In legal and official contexts, the noun and verb senses of the word, (obtaining) the official rights to a product, *patent* is pronounced [*pat*ĕnt].

In American English [*pat*ĕnt] is used for all senses.

pathetic The use of the adjective *pathetic* in the derogatory sense of 'contemptible' or 'worthless' is best restricted to informal contexts: □ *The comedian made a pathetic attempt to mimic the president.* □ *Don't be so pathetic!*

◆ The principal sense of *pathetic* is 'arousing pity or sorrow': □ *The sick child made several pathetic attempts to stand up.*

patriot This word, meaning 'one who loves his or her country', has two acceptable pronunciations [*pay*triŏt] or [*pat*riŏt].

patron see CLIENT OR CUSTOMER?

PC see POLITICAL CORRECTNESS.

peaceable or **peaceful**? The adjective *peaceable,* meaning 'disposed to peace', 'peace-loving', or 'not aggressive', is principally applied to people: □ *the peaceable inhabitants of the town* □ *a peaceable temperament. Peaceful*, the more frequent of the two adjectives, means 'characterized by peace', 'calm', or 'not violent': □ *a peaceful scene* □ *a peaceful demonstration* □ *peaceful coexistence*.

◆ Note the spelling of *peaceable*, particularly the second *e* (see also SPELLING 3).

pedal or **peddle**? The word *pedal* relates to a foot-operated lever: □ *the soft pedal on a piano* □ *a pedal bin* □ *to pedal a bicycle*. To *peddle* is to sell small articles or illegal goods, such as drugs, or to put forward ideas or information: □ *to peddle brushes/heroin/gossip*. The two verbs should not be confused.

◆ The verb *peddle* is a BACK FORMATION from the noun *pedlar*, denoting a person who goes from place to place selling goods. In other senses of the verb *peddle* the spelling *peddler* is often used in place of *pedlar*: □ *a drug peddler* □ *a peddler of ideas*. In American English *peddler* is preferred for all senses; in British English *pedlar* is usually retained in its original sense. Note the single *d* and the *-ar* ending of *pedlar*.

In British English the final *l* of the verb *pedal* is doubled before a suffix beginning with a vowel: □ *pedalled* □ *pedalling*. The American spellings are *pedaled*, *pedaling*, etc. See also SPELLING 1.

pedigree The noun *pedigree* denotes an ancestral line or line of descent, specifically that of a purebred animal; its use as a synonym for 'record' or 'background' is disliked by some users: □ *a pedigree of success spanning over 50 years in the radio and television rental and retail field* (*Executive Post*).

pedlar see PEDAL OR PEDDLE?

pejorative This word, meaning 'disparaging', can be pronounced in two ways. The pronunciation [pijorrătiv] is used more frequently than the more traditional [peejŏrătiv].

pence As *pence* is one of the plural forms of the noun *penny*, many people object to the use of the term *one-pence piece* to denote a penny coin: □ *Does the machine still take one-pence pieces?* The plural noun *pennies* is used with reference to a number of coins, whereas *pence* usually refers to a sum of money: □ *My purse is full of pennies.* □ *The envelopes cost four pence each.* □ *Can you give me ten pennies in exchange for a ten-pence piece?*

◆ After the decimalization of British currency in 1971 the abbreviation *p*, pronounced [pee], was often used in speech to distinguish between old and new pennies or pence: □ *The bus fare used to be ninepence; now we have to pay five p.* This usage has continued, but is best restricted to informal contexts.

The pronunciation of the word *pence* has also been affected by decimalization: the sum of *6d* was pronounced [sikspēns], with the stress on the first syllable, whereas *6p* is usually pronounced [siks pens], with equal stress on both syllables.

penchant The noun *penchant*, meaning 'inclination' or 'liking', is of French origin and is pronounced [pon(g)shon(g)], an anglicized form of the French pronunciation, in British English.

pendant or **pendent**? The noun *pendant*, denoting a type of necklace, has the rare variant spelling *pendent*. The word *pendent* is also used as an adjective, in the sense of 'hanging', with the (less frequent) variant spelling *pendant*.

peninsula or **peninsular**? These two spellings are sometimes confused. A *peninsula* is a long narrow section of land that is almost surrounded by water but which is joined to the mainland. The adjective is *peninsular*: □ *the Peninsular War of 1808 to 1814.*

pennies, penny see PENCE.

pensioner see SENIOR CITIZEN OR OLD AGE PENSIONER?

people *People* is usually a plural noun, but in the sense of 'nation', 'race', or 'tribe' it may be singular or plural: □ *a nomadic people of Africa* □ *all the peoples of the world* □ *The French people are renowned for their culinary expertise.* The use of the alternative plural form *persons* to denote a number of human beings is best restricted to formal contexts: □ *No more than eight persons may use the lift.* □ *There are four people* [not *persons*] *in the waiting room.*

◆ With reference to a group or body of human beings, the word *people* is preferred in all contexts: □ *a meeting place for young people* □ *representatives of the people.*

per The preposition *per*, meaning 'for each' or 'in each', is often better replaced by *a* or *an*: □ *four times a* [not *per*] *month* □ *60p a* [not *per*] *metre.* In some contexts, however, *per* must be retained: □ *Use two ounces of cheese per person.* □ *The left-luggage attendant charges one pound per item per day.*

◆ Many people consider the use of *per* in place of *by* to be excessively formal or affected: □ *The parcel will be sent per Datapost.*

See also AS PER; PER ANNUM; PER CAPITA; PER CENT; PER SE.

per-, pre-, or **pro-**? These three prefixes sometimes cause confusion in the spelling and usage of certain pairs of words.

◆ See PERSECUTE OR PROSECUTE?; PERSPECTIVE OR PROSPECTIVE?; PRECEDE OR PROCEED?; PREREQUISITE OR PERQUISITE?; PRESCRIBE OR PROSCRIBE?

per annum The Latin phrase *per annum*, meaning 'for each year', is best restricted to formal contexts: □ *You will be paid a salary of £12,000 per annum.*

◆ In other contexts the more informal phrase *a year* is preferred: □ *It costs several hundred pounds a year, excluding petrol, to keep this car on the road.* See also PER.

per capita The adverbial or adjectival phrase *per capita* is widely used in English in the sense of 'for each person': □ *the minimum cost per capita* □ *a per capita allowance of ten pounds.*

◆ Some people object to this usage as an inaccurate translation of the Latin phrase, which literally means 'by heads': □ *The estate will be divided per capita.*

per cent The phrase *per cent* is used adverbially, in combination with a number, in the sense of 'in or for each hundred': □ *an increase of 25 per cent* □ *75 per cent of the students.*

◆ The use of *per cent* as a noun, meaning 'one-hundredth' or 'a percentage', is disliked by some users: the phrase *half a per cent*, for example, is better replaced by *half of one per cent.* See also PERCENTAGE.

In American English *per cent* is usually written as one word. In British English the two-word form is preferred.

See also SINGULAR OR PLURAL?

percentage Many people object to the use of *a percentage* to mean 'a small part', 'a little', or 'a few': □ *Only a percentage of the workforce will be present.* A percentage may be as small as 1% or as large as 99%; in the sense of 'proportion' the noun often needs a qualifying adjective for clarity: □ *A small percentage of the money is used for administration costs.* □ *A large percentage of* *the stock was damaged in the fire.*

◆ *Percentage* is sometimes better replaced by *number, amount, part,* or *proportion*; *a high percentage* by *many* or *much*; *a lower percentage* by *fewer* or *less,* etc.

The use of the noun *percentage* as a synonym for 'advantage' or 'profit' is best restricted to informal contexts: □ *There's no real percentage in sending your children to a private school.*

perceptible, perceptive, or **percipient**? The adjective *perceptible* means 'perceivable', 'noticeable', or 'recognizable'; *perceptive* means 'observant', 'discerning', or 'sensitive': □ *a perceptible change* □ *a perceptive remark.*

◆ *Percipient,* which is virtually synonymous with, but less frequent than, *perceptive,* is largely restricted to formal contexts: □ *a percipient writer.*

The adverbs *perceptibly* and *perceptively* are often confused, being similar in spelling and pronunciation: □ *The children were perceptibly quieter when their teacher was present.* □ *She spoke perceptively of the composer's orchestral works.*

peremptory or **perfunctory**? *Peremptory* means 'commanding; dogmatic; positive; decisive': □ *a peremptory order* □ *a peremptory man* □ *in a peremptory tone of voice* □ *a peremptory knock at the door.* *Perfunctory* means 'quick; careless; cursory; superficial': □ *a perfunctory glance at the letter.* Both adjectives are largely restricted to formal contexts; they should not be confused.

◆ *Peremptory* is usually pronounced [pĕ*remp*tŏri], with the stress on the second syllable, but [*perr*ĕmptŏri], stressed on the first syllable, is an acceptable alternative.

perestroika *Perestroika,* a Russian word, is used to denote the restructuring or economic and social reform programme in the Soviet Union under Mikhail Gorbachev in the late 1980s. *Perestroika* was also the title of a book by Gorbachev published in 1987: □ *the main thrust of the book is to argue that without the full-blooded economic and political reforms of his* [Gorbachev's] *perestroika, the Soviet Union would face a desperate crisis* (*The Guardian*).

◆ Like **GLASNOST**, *perestroika* is increasingly used in the Western world: □ *The chief executive* [of Abbey National], *Mr Peter Birch, referred to the ballot result as a financial perestroika* (*The Guardian*).

perfect Many people avoid using such adverbs as *very, rather, more, most, less, least,* etc., to qualify the adjective *perfect,* meaning 'faultless', 'unblemished', 'complete', or 'utter': □ *This book is in less perfect condition than that one.* □ *It was the most perfect diamond that he had ever seen.* The expressions *nearly perfect* and *almost perfect,* however, are generally acceptable.

◆ The pronunciation of the adjective *perfect* is different from that of the verb. The adjective is stressed on the first syllable [*per*fikt]; the verb is stressed on the second syllable [pĕr*fekt*].

perfunctory see PEREMPTORY OR PERFUNCTORY?

perk see PREREQUISITE OR PERQUISITE?

permissible or **permissive**? These two adjectives are derived from the verb *permit,* meaning 'allow' or 'authorize'. *Permissible* means 'permitted'; *permissive* means 'tolerant': □ *the smallest permissible investment* □ *a permissive attitude.* *Permissive* sometimes implies disapproval of such tolerance (or of the thing tolerated), especially when it is used with reference to sexual indulgence: □ *the permissive society.*

◆ Note the spelling of *permissible,* particularly the *-ible* ending.

perpetrate or **perpetuate**? *Perpetrate* means 'commit' or 'perform';

perpetuate means 'cause to continue' or 'make perpetual': □ *to perpetrate a crime* □ *to perpetuate a tradition.* The two verbs should not be confused.

per pro. see **P.P.**

perquisite see **PREREQUISITE OR PERQUISITE?**

per se The Latin phrase *per se*, meaning 'by itself' or 'in itself', is best restricted to formal contexts: □ *The discovery is of little importance per se.*

◆ Note the spelling and pronunciation of the word *se* [say].

persecute or **prosecute?** *Persecute* means 'harass' or 'oppress'; *prosecute* means 'take legal action against': □ *They were persecuted for their beliefs.* □ *Trespassers will be prosecuted.* The two verbs should not be confused.

perseverance The noun *perseverance* is sometimes misspelt. A common error is the addition of an extra *-r-* before the *-v-*. Note also the *-ance* ending.

person Many people prefer to use the noun *person*, rather than *man*, to denote a human being whose sex is unspecified: □ *We need to take on another person to deal with the backlog.*

◆ The substitution of *person* for *man* in such words as *chairman, salesman, statesman, spokesman, layman, craftsman*, etc., is a more controversial issue: □ *Margaret Thatcher, world statesperson mingling with her peers at the summit in Venice (The Guardian).* □ *Mrs Liz Forsdick ... will act as 'linesperson' in the third qualifying round game (The Guardian).*

Some users apply the terms *chairman, salesman*, etc., to both men and women: □ *The chairman of the CBI's Smaller Firms Council, Mrs Jean Parker (The Guardian).* Others use the more or less acceptable feminine forms *chairwoman, saleswoman*, etc., for women: □ *The appointment was announced yesterday by ChildLine's chairwoman, Miss Esther Rantzen (The Guardian).* See also **CHAIR; MAN; SEXISM.**

As a general rule the substitution of *person* for *man*, in any context, is best avoided if a simpler or more idiomatic solution can be found: the use of *someone else* instead of *another person, nobody* instead of *no person, crew of four* instead of *four-person crew*, etc.

Person has two plurals, *persons* and *people*: see also **PEOPLE.**

personage or **personality?** Both nouns are applied to famous people, but they are not synonymous. *Personage* is used in formal contexts to refer to an important or distinguished person; a *personality* is a famous person from the world of show business, sport, etc.: □ *members of the royal family and other personages* □ *The shop will be opened by a TV personality.*

◆ The principal meaning of the noun *personality* is 'character': □ *She has a delightful personality.* □ *Personality is more important than looks.*

personal see **PERSONALLY; PERSONNEL.**

personality see **PERSONAGE OR PERSONALITY?**

personally The use of the adverb *personally* for emphasis is disliked by some users: □ *I personally prefer to spend my holidays at home.*

◆ Similar objections may be raised to the unnecessary use of the adjective *personal* in such expressions as: □ *a personal friend* □ *her personal opinion* □ *a personal visit*, etc.

In some contexts, however, *personally* and *personal* may serve the useful purpose of distinguishing between the unofficial and the official, the private and the professional, etc.: □ *I personally think you* should accept their offer, but as your solicitor I must advise you to make further enquiries. □ He is a business acquaintance but not a personal friend.

personate, personify see IMPERSONATE, PERSONATE, OR PERSONIFY?

personnel Many people object to the frequent use of the noun *personnel* in place of *staff, workforce, workers, employees, people,* etc.: □ *They do not have enough personnel to cope with the increased workload.* The word *personnel* is principally used to denote the employees of a large company or organization, considered collectively, or the department that is concerned with their recruitment and welfare: □ *hospital personnel* □ *the personnel officer.*

◆ *Personnel* may be a singular or plural noun, but it should not be used with a specific number: □ We are moving four people [not personnel] from the sales office to the production department.

Note the spelling of *personnel*, particularly the -*nn*- and the second *e*, and the pronunciation of the word, with the primary stress on the last syllable [persŏnel]. *Personnel* is sometimes confused with the adjective *personal*: □ There will be strong prospects of long-term personnel development for ... the truly commercial engineer (Sunday Times).

persons see PEOPLE.

perspective or **prospective**? *Perspective* is a noun, meaning 'view', 'aspect', or 'objectivity'; it should not be confused with the adjective *prospective*, meaning 'expected', 'likely', or 'future': □ *a different perspective* □ *a prospective employer.*

◆ In painting, drawing, etc., the noun *perspective* principally refers to the representation of three-dimensional objects and their relative sizes and positions on a flat surface. Its figurative use in the phrase *in perspective* is derived from this sense: □ You must try to put things in perspective: the loss of one customer is relatively unimportant when the future of the company is at stake.

perturb see DISTURB OR PERTURB?

perverse or **perverted**? *Perverse* means 'obstinate' or 'contrary'; *perverted* means 'corrupt' or 'characterized by abnormal sexual behaviour': □ *a perverse refusal* □ *a perverted attack.* The two adjectives should not be confused: to call a man *perverted* is a more serious and offensive accusation than to call him *perverse.*

◆ Both adjectives may be applied to the same noun in different contexts: □ He took a perverse delight in making her wait. □ He took a perverted delight in torturing his victims.

phase see FAZE OR PHASE?

phenomena see PHENOMENON OR PHENOMENA?

phenomenal The use of the adjective *phenomenal* as a synonym for 'extraordinary', 'remarkable', 'prodigious', or 'outstanding' is disliked by some: □ *a phenomenal achievement.*

phenomenon or **phenomena**? *Phenomena* is the plural form of the noun *phenomenon*: □ *This phenomenon is of great interest to astronomers.* □ *Such phenomena are not easy to explain.*

◆ The use of *phenomena* as a singular noun, a frequent error, is wrong: □ 'The development of the Muslim community in Britain is only a recent phenomena and needs proper research,' Mr Ayman Ahwal, London spokesman of the World Muslim League, said (The Times).

philosophy The noun *philosophy* is best avoided where *idea, view, policy,* etc., would be adequate or more appropriate: □ *My philosophy is that children should be seen and not heard.* □ *The company has a philosophy of sound management practices at* *the local level.*

phlegm This word causes problems with spelling and pronunciation. Note the initial *ph-* spelling, pronounced [f], and the silent *g*. The word is pronounced [flem].

phobia A *phobia* is an abnormal or irrational fear or aversion: □ *He has a phobia about flying.* □ *She has a phobia of spiders.*

◆ The noun should not be used as a synonym for 'dislike', 'dread', 'obsession', 'inhibition', etc.: □ *She has a phobia of losing her car keys.* □ *He has a phobia about undressing in front of other people.*

phone The use of the noun and verb *phone* in place of *telephone* is becoming increasingly frequent and acceptable: the telephone directory is now officially entitled 'The Phone Book', the term long used to describe it in informal contexts. The shortened form *phone* is best avoided, however, in formal contexts: □ *The phone's ringing.* □ *You'd better phone the doctor.* □ *The cost of your telephone call will be refunded.* □ *Please write or telephone for an application form.*

◆ See also ABBREVIATIONS; APOSTROPHE.

phoney or **phony**? The more frequent spelling of this word, meaning 'fake', is *phoney* in British English, and *phony* in American English.

photo The use of the noun *photo* in place of *photograph* is best restricted to informal contexts: □ *Did you take a photo of the baby?* □ *This pass is not valid without a photograph of the holder.* The plural of *photo* is *photos*.

◆ The word *photo* is not generally used as a shortened form of the verb *photograph*. See also ABBREVIATIONS; APOSTROPHE.

photo-opportunity *Photo-opportunity* (or *photocall*) is a vogue term used for an allegedly spontaneous but invariably prearranged event for press and television photographers: □ *Now the gloves are off, life is one endless round of photo-opportunities, media calls, ... and hectic journeys across the country* (The Times) □ *Whirling from photocall to photocall, now cutting a birthday cake, now smiling coyly by a What-the-Butler-Saw machine, ...* (The Guardian). The *opportunity* is ostensibly for the camera operators, but in fact is created by and for the politician or media star being photographed in order to obtain favourable visual publicity.

◆ Both *photo-opportunity* and *photocall* may be spelt as two-word compounds, without hyphens.

phrase A *phrase* is a group of words that function together as a noun, verb, adjective, adverb, preposition, etc.: □ *the red car* □ *give up* □ *highly polished* □ *at the back of the room* □ *with reference to.* See also CLAUSE; SENTENCES.

physician or **physicist**? A *physician* is a doctor of medicine; a *physicist* is a scientist who has specialized in physics: □ *the number of physicians in the National Health Service* □ *physicists involved in nuclear research.* The two nouns should not be confused.

◆ The term *physician* is chiefly used to distinguish qualified medical practitioners in nonsurgical fields from surgeons. In everyday usage the term *doctor* is preferred; *physician* sounds formal or old-fashioned in British English.

physiognomy Note the spelling of this word, which means 'the outward appearance of a person considered to show the person's character'. The most frequent error is to omit the silent *g*.

picnic This word adds a *k* before the suffixes *-er, -ed, -ing*: □ *picnickers* □ *They picnicked in the woods.* See also **SPELLING 1.**

pidgin or **pigeon**? These two words may sometimes be confused. *Pidgin* is a language that is a mixture of two other languages: □ *pidgin English.* A *pigeon* is a grey bird with short legs and compact feathers: □ *the pigeons of Trafalgar Square.*

◆ *Pigeon* also has the informal, rather old-fashioned sense of 'concern': □ *that's his pigeon.*

pièce de résistance The phrase *pièce de résistance*, meaning 'main dish of a meal; most outstanding or impressive item', is of French origin and is sometimes written or printed in italics in English texts: □ *The designer's pièce de résistance was the exquisite dress worn by the princess at her wedding.* Note the accents, which serve to distinguish *pièce*, pronounced [pyes], from the English word *piece* [pees], and *résistance* [rezi*stahns*] from the English word *resistance* [rizi*stäns*]; these accents should never be omitted.

◆ The plural is formed by adding *-s* to the first word, *pièces de résistance.*

pigmy see **PYGMY OR PIGMY?**

piteous, pitiable, or **pitiful**? All these adjectives mean 'arousing or deserving pity', in which sense they are virtually interchangeable in many contexts. There are, however, slight differences of usage and application between them: □ *a piteous cry* □ *a pitiable figure* □ *a pitiful sight.*

◆ Note the spelling of *piteous*, the least frequent of the three adjectives, in which the *t* is followed by *e* rather than *i* (as in *pitiable* and *pitiful*).

Pitiable and *pitiful* have the additional meaning of 'arousing or deserving contempt': □ *Their pitiful offer of a two per cent pay rise was immediately rejected by the union.*

pivotal The frequent use of the adjective *pivotal* in the sense of 'crucial or very important' is disliked by some users: □ *to come to a pivotal decision.*

◆ Note the pronunciation of *pivotal*, which is stressed on the first syllable [*piv*ötäl].

plain or **plane**? These words are sometimes confused. The main noun sense of *plain* is 'level, treeless expanse of land': □ *the vast plains of the prairies.* *Plane* as a noun is a shortened form of *aeroplane*, a carpenter's tool, or a surface in geometry. See also **PLANE.**

◆ *Plain* has several adjectival senses, including 'straightforward', 'simple', and 'clear'; the adjectival use of *plane* means 'flat': □ *a plane surface.*

The idiomatic expression *plain sailing* is used to describe easy progress: □ *Once I've mended this switch, the rest will be plain sailing.*

plaintiff or **plaintive**? These words are sometimes confused. A *plaintiff* is the person who commences legal action in a court; *plaintive* means 'mournful and melancholy': □ *a plaintive song.*

plane The use of the noun *plane* as a shortened form of *aeroplane* is acceptable in most contexts: □ *What time does your plane leave?* □ *More than 250 people were killed in the plane crash.*

◆ See also **ABBREVIATIONS; APOSTROPHE; PLAIN OR PLANE?**

plastic The first syllable of the word *plastic* may be pronounced with the short *a* of *plan*, or with the long *a* of *plant*. The first of these pronunciations, [*plas*tik], is more frequent than the second, [*plah*stik].

◆ Many people object to the informal use of the noun *plastic* to mean '(payment by) credit cards': □ *I very rarely pay by cash these days – I usually use plastic.*

platform The use of the noun *platform* to denote the declared policies and principles of a political party or candidate is disliked by some users as an Americanism but is acceptable to most: □ *Their unilateralist platform will win them few votes in the forthcoming election.*

playwright see DRAMATIST OR PLAYWRIGHT?

plc This abbreviation for *public limited company* is often written or printed in lower-case letters, without full stops.

◆ A *public limited company* is a company whose shares can be bought and sold on the stock exchange, as opposed to a private limited company, which has the abbreviation *Ltd* (spelt with a capital *L*- and usually without a full stop) after its name.

pleaded or **pled**? In British English *pleaded* is the usual form of the past tense and past participle of the verb *plead*: □ *'Save my child,' she pleaded.* □ *They had pleaded with him to stay.*

◆ *Pled* is an American, Scottish, or dialectal variant of *pleaded*.

pleasantness or **pleasantry**? *Pleasantness* is an uncountable noun, meaning 'the state of being pleasant': □ *the pleasantness of the weather. Pleasantry* is chiefly used in more formal English in the plural form *pleasantries,* meaning 'polite, casual, friendly, agreeable, or amusing remarks': □ *to exchange pleasantries.*

plenitude *Plenitude* means 'abundance': □ *religious adornments in great plenitude.* A formal word, it is best avoided where *plenty* would be adequate or more appropriate.

◆ The word *plenitude* is sometimes misspelt, the most frequent error being the insertion of a *t* after the *n*, as in *plenty.* It is pronounced [*pleni*tewd].

plenty The use of *plenty* as an adverb, in place of *quite* or *very*, is regarded by some as nonstandard: □ *The house is plenty big enough for us.* □ *She was plenty upset when she heard the news.*

◆ The second of these uses is generally considered to be an Americanism.

The adjectival use of *plenty* without *of* is also unacceptable to many users: □ *They have plenty toys to play with.*

plethora The phrase *a plethora of* implies excess or superfluity; it should not be used as a pretentious synonym for 'a large number of' or 'plenty of': □ *a plethora of houses for sale,* for example, describes a situation in which there are too many houses on the market, far more than the number of prospective buyers, with the result that many will remain unsold.

plurals The regular way of forming plurals for English words is to add an *-s,* except for words ending in *-s, -x, -ch, -sh,* and *-z,* where *-es* is added: □ *ships* □ *houses* □ *buses* □ *foxes* □ *churches* □ *sashes* □ *buzzes.* Of course, there are many irregularly formed plurals. Words ending in a consonant and then *-y* have *-ies* in the plural: □ *fairies* □ *ponies,* except for proper nouns, which have *-s* or *-ies:* □ *I've invited the Joneses and the Hartys.* □ *the Two Sicilies.* Some words ending in *-f* or *-fe* have *-ves* in the plural: □ *halves* □ *wives,* while others simply add *-s,* and others allow a choice: □ *beliefs* □ *hoofs – hooves.* Some words ending in *-o* add *-es,* others just an *-s.* It is impossible to formulate a general rule here, although note the frequently used *potatoes* and *tomatoes,* which both end *-es.* Note also that shortened forms ending in *-o* just add

-s: □ *photos* □ *pianos* □ *radios* □ *stereos* □ *videos*. Some nouns ending in *-s* are already plural and cannot be pluralized: □ *trousers* □ *spectacles* □ *scissors*. With various animal names the plural form is the same as the singular: □ *deer* □ *sheep* □ *bison*.

◆ Several English words have plurals not formed in any of the ways described above: □ *man* – *men* □ *child* – *children* □ *mouse* – *mice* □ *goose* – *geese* □ *foot* – *feet*. There is no rule about these words and one cannot generalize from them; the plural of *mongoose* is *mongooses* [not *mongeese*].

Foreign words sometimes take a regular English plural and sometimes the plural of the appropriate language. Often either is regarded as correct: □ *châteaus/châteaux*. Latin or Greek words often take the plural of their original language. The *-is* ending of such nouns as *analysis* and *thesis* changes to *-es* in the plural: □ *analyses* □ *theses*. The endings *-ix* and *-ex* may change to *-ices* (see **APPENDIXES OR APPENDICES?**; **INDEXES OR INDICES?**); the ending *-a* may add an *-e* (see **FORMULAE OR FORMULAS?**); the endings *-on* and *-um* may change to *-a* (see **MEDIA**; **PHENOMENON OR PHENOMENA?**); and the ending *-us* may change to *-i* (see **FUNGI**).

Difficulties often arise with the plurals of compound nouns. The general rule is that when the qualifying word is an adjective then the noun is made plural: □ *courts martial* □ *poets laureate*, though in less formal usage, the second word is made plural: □ *poet laureates*. If both words are nouns the second is made plural: □ *town clerks*, although *woman teacher* becomes *women teachers*. In compounds of a noun and a prepositional phrase or adverb, the noun is made plural: □ *mothers-in-law* □ *hangers-on* □ *men of war*. If no words in the compound are nouns, then *-s* is added at the end: □ *forget-me-nots* □ *go-betweens* □ *grown-ups*.

On using singular or plural verbs, see **SINGULAR OR PLURAL?**

plus The prepositional use of *plus* in the sense of 'with the addition of' is acceptable in all contexts: □ *My savings, plus the money my grandmother left me, are almost enough to buy a car.*

◆ Note that the verb agrees with *savings*; if the sentence is reordered to make *money* the principal subject a singular verb must be used: □ *The money my grandmother left me, plus my savings, is almost enough to buy a car.*

Some people avoid using the noun *plus* as a synonym for 'advantage' in formal contexts: □ *Being within walking distance of the station is one of the pluses of living on this estate.*

The expression *an added plus* is tautological and should be avoided.

The use of *plus* in the sense of 'and' or 'with' is best restricted to informal contexts: □ *He's afraid to go sailing because he can't swim, plus he suffers from seasickness.* □ *She was met at the airport by her son plus his new girlfriend.*

See also **MINUS**.

p.m. see **A.M. AND P.M.**

pneumatic and **pneumonia** Note the spelling of these words, particularly the silent initial *p-* and the *-eu-* of the first syllable.

◆ The prefix *pneum-* is derived from a Greek word meaning 'air', as in *pneumatic*, 'using compressed air', or 'breath', as in *pneumonia*, 'inflammation of the lungs'.

poetess see **-ESS**.

poignant This word, meaning 'distressing', is usually pronounced [*poyn*yănt] although [*poyn*ănt] is also acceptable. The *g* is silent.

politic or **political**? *Politic* means 'prudent', 'shrewd', or 'cunning'; *political* means 'of politics, government, policy-making, etc.': □ *a politic decision* □ *a political party.* The two adjectives should not be confused.

◆ *Politic* was originally synonymous with *political*. This sense of the word survives only in the expression *the body politic*, meaning 'the state'.

Note the different stress patterns of the two words: *politic* is stressed on the first syllable, *political* on the second.

political correctness *Political correctness,* or *PC,* is the avoidance of words, phrases, or actions that may be deemed offensive by a particular section of society, such as ethnic minorities, homosexuals, women, blind people, deaf people, or old people: □ *Traditional industrial terms such as 'blackleg', the 'black economy' and 'blacklisted' have been banned because they might offend TUC delegates from ethnic minorities. Speakers have been asked not to use descriptions deemed politically incorrect on grounds of race, disability and gender* (*Daily Telegraph*). □ *Lynx ... enjoyed phenomenal early success in its drive to transform fur from an elegant status symbol into a 'politically incorrect' badge of cruelty* (*Sunday Times*). The term is most frequently used in situations where this anxiety to avoid offence seems excessive: □ *It is a pretty nonsensical aspect of 'political correctness' to worry about the sex of a reviewer* (*The Bookseller*). □ *The legions of the politically correct continue to direct their accusations of racism, sexism, stoutism and inappropriate body language at every area of our public and private life, sniffing out imaginary insults and creating antagonism in their wake* (*Daily Telegraph*).

◆ Political correctness also strives to project a more positive image of negative or undesirable qualities such as dishonesty or failure, with the substitution of such euphemisms as *ethically disoriented* for *dishonest* and *deficiency achievement* for *failure*. Of American origin, political correctness is often regarded in Britain as unacceptable interference with English usage and the natural development of the English language. See also **ABLED; ABLEISM; AGEISM; CHALLENGED; SEXISM.**

politics see -**ICS.**

poltergeist The word *poltergeist,* denoting a mischievous spirit, is sometimes misspelt. Note the *er* in the middle and the *ei* in the final syllable. The word is pronounced [pŏltĕrgīst].

pomegranate Note the spelling of this word, particularly the single *m* and the *-ate* ending (not *-ite,* as in *granite*). Note also the first *e,* which is usually sounded in British English [*pom*igranit], but is often dropped in the American English pronunciation [*pom*granit].

pore or **pour**? These spellings are sometimes confused. *Pore* as a verb means 'look intently': □ *They pored over the map*; *pour* means 'cause to flow': □ *She poured the tea.* The noun *pore* refers to a minute opening in the skin.

portmanteau word see **BLENDS.**

Portuguese This word is sometimes misspelt; note the *-e-* following the second *u.*

position To *position* is to put carefully and deliberately in a specific place; the verb is best avoided where *place, put, post, situate, locate,* etc., would be adequate or more appropriate: □ *She positioned the mat on the carpet to hide the stain.* □ *He put* [not *positioned*] *his dirty plate on top of the others.* □ *The offices are situated* [not *positioned*] *in the town centre.*

◆ Some people also dislike the unnecessary use of the noun *position* in many contexts. It is usually possible to replace the verbal phrase *be in a position to*, for example, with *be able* or *can*: □ *I am not in a position to answer your questions.*

possessives The two ways of showing that a noun is one of possession are the apostrophe and the use of the word *of*: □ *Anne's car* □ *the company's profits* □ *the rabbits' burrow* □ *soldiers of the Queen.*

◆ The apostrophe is used more frequently than *of* and there is no firm rule as to where it is appropriate to use *of*. One can say either: □ *the table's leg* or *the leg of the table*, but where there is a recognized phrase containing *of*: □ *the Valley of the Rocks*, an apostrophe cannot be substituted. *Of* is usually used of inanimate things; when it is used of people an apostrophe is generally used as well: □ *a friend of Peter's*. It is also often used for geographical regions: □ *the wines of France* □ *the cities of Europe*.

In cases of joint possession the apostrophe belongs to the last owner mentioned: □ *Tom and Lucy's house* □ *Beaumont and Fletcher's plays*. With a compound noun the last word takes the apostrophe: □ *the lady-in-waiting's dress* □ *the county court's judge*.

Care should be taken with such phrases as: *one of the residents' dogs* which might mean 'the dog belonging to one of the residents' or 'one of the dogs belonging to one of the residents' or 'one of the dogs jointly owned by the residents'. It is better to rephrase such an expression to avoid ambiguity. See also **APOSTROPHE**; **'S OR S'**?

post- Some people object to the frequent use of the prefix *post-*, meaning 'after', to coin new adjectives, often of a futuristic nature: □ *post-nuclear Britain* □ *post-feminist literature* □ *Mr Steel said the aim would be to create an 'effective and electable alternative to government in the post-Thatcher period'* (*Daily Telegraph*).

posthumous This word causes problems with spelling and pronunciation. In speech the *h* is silent [*post*ewmŭs]; the first syllable is not as in *post*, but as in *possible*.

post-traumatic stress disorder The phrase *post-traumatic stress disorder* (or *syndrome*) denotes a combination of largely psychological symptoms, such as irrational fear, feelings of guilt, depression, nightmares, etc., resulting from the shock of being involved in a highly distressing situation, such as a rail or plane crash, a major fire, a terrorist bomb attack, or warfare: □ *The ... constable has been diagnosed as having post-traumatic stress syndrome resulting from her experiences while on the Stevens investigation into links between the security forces and loyalist groups* (*Daily Telegraph*).

◆ Originally applied to American veterans of the Vietnam War, the term is sometimes regarded as a modern or pretentious synonym for *shell shock* or *battle fatigue*.

pour see **PORE OR POUR?**

power The word *power* is sometimes used adjectivally to refer to an important business occasion. For example □ *a power breakfast* [or *lunch*] is a meeting of influential people from e.g. politics, business, or the media that is held over breakfast (or lunch). This vogue usage is best restricted to informal contexts.

p.p. The abbreviation *p.p.* (or *per pro.*), short for the Latin phrase *per procurationem*, is used when signing a letter on behalf of somebody else. The Latin phrase means 'by proxy' or 'through the agency of', and the abbreviation should precede the name of the person signing the letter.

◆ In modern usage the abbreviation is frequently interpreted as 'for and on behalf of' and placed before the name of the person on whose behalf the letter is signed. This 'incorrect' sequence is so well-established that the correct usage could lead to misunderstanding.

practical or **practicable**? The adjective *practical* has a wide range of senses; the principal meaning of *practicable* is 'capable of being done or put into practice'. A *practicable* suggestion is simply possible or feasible; a *practical* suggestion is also useful, sensible, realistic, economical, profitable, and likely to be effective or successful: □ *It may be practicable to create jobs for everyone but this would not be a practical solution to the problems of unemployment.*

◆ Careful users maintain the distinction between the two words, which is also applicable to their antonyms, *impractical* and *impracticable*: □ *It's impractical to use the washing machine when you only have a couple of shirts to wash.* □ *It's impracticable to use the washing machine when there is a power cut.* Unpractical, a less frequent antonym of *practical*, may refer to a person who lacks practical abilities.

Additional senses of *practical* include 'not theoretical', 'suitable for use', 'skilled at doing or making things', and 'virtual': □ *a practical course in first aid* □ *a more practical layout for the kitchen* □ *My brother is not a very practical man.* □ *She has practical control of the company.* See also PRACTICALLY.

practically The adverb *practically* is widely used as a synonym for 'almost', 'nearly', 'virtually', etc.: □ *I practically broke my ankle.*

◆ Some people dislike this usage, which can lead to confusion with one of the more literal senses of the word: □ *It is practically impossible,* for example, may mean 'it is impossible in practice' or 'it is almost impossible'.

See also PRACTICAL OR PRACTICABLE?

practice or **practise**? The noun is *practice*, the verb is *practise*: □ *the doctor's practice* □ *the doctor who practises in our town.*

◆ In American English both the noun and verb are spelt *practice.*

practitioner This word is sometimes misspelt, the most frequent error being the substitution of *c* or *s* for the final *t*.

pray or **prey**? These spellings are sometimes confused. The verb *pray* means 'speak to God': □ *pray for forgiveness.* The verb *prey*, which is usually followed by *on* or *upon*, means 'hunt' or 'obsess': □ *The lion preys on other animals.* □ *The problem is preying on my mind.* The noun *prey* means 'animals hunted for food': □ *birds of prey.*

◆ Spelling mistakes may be avoided if *pray* is associated with *prayer.*

pre- see HYPHEN 1; PER-, PRE-, OR PRO-?; PRE-WAR.

precautionary measure The phrase *precautionary measure* can usually be replaced by the noun *precaution*, which denotes a measure taken to avoid something harmful or undesirable: □ *The police closed the road as a precaution(ary measure) against flooding.*

precede or **proceed**? *Precede* means 'come before', 'go before', or 'be before'; *proceed* means 'continue', 'go on', or 'advance': □ *September precedes October.* □ *The text is preceded by an introduction.* □ *I am unable to proceed with this work.* □ *They proceeded to dismantle the car.*

◆ The two verbs should not be confused or misspelt: note the different spelling but identical pronunciation of the second syllables, -*cede* and -*ceed* [-*seed*].

precedence or **precedent**? The noun *precedence* means 'priority' or 'superiority'; the noun *precedent* denotes a previous example that may serve as a model (in a court of law or elsewhere): □ *Should this work take precedence over our other commitments?* □ *The guests were seated in order of precedence.* □ *The committee's decision has set a precedent for future claims.* □ *This result is without precedent.*

◆ Both nouns are derived from the verb *precede* (see **PRECEDE OR PROCEED**?); to interchange them is wrong.

The pronunciation of *precedence* is [*presi*dĕns]. The noun *precedent* is pronounced [*presi*dĕnt], but the rarer adjective is pronounced [pri*seed*ĕnt].

precipitate or **precipitous**? The adjective *precipitate* means 'rushing', 'hasty', 'rash', or 'sudden'; *precipitous* means 'like a precipice' or 'very steep': □ *a precipitate decision* □ *their precipitate departure* □ *a precipitous slope.*

◆ The substitution of *precipitous* for *precipitate* is disliked by some users but acknowledged by most dictionaries. *Precipitate*, however, should not be used used in the sense of 'precipitous'.

The word *precipitate* is also used as a verb and as a noun. In the pronunciation of the adjective and noun the final syllable is unstressed [pri*sip*ităt]. The verb has the same primary stress pattern but the final syllable is pronounced to rhyme with *gate* [pri*sip*itayt].

preclude see **EXCLUDE OR PRECLUDE**?

precondition see **CONDITION OR PRECONDITION**?

predecessor The noun *predecessor* denotes the previous holder of an office, post, etc.: □ *Her predecessor had left the accounts in a mess.* Although the words *predecessor* and *decease* (meaning 'death') are both derived from the Latin verb *dēcēdere*, a predecessor is not necessarily dead: the Latin verb means 'go away', not 'die'.

◆ Note the spelling of *predecessor*, particularly the -*c*- and -*ss*- and the -*or* ending.

predicative see **ADJECTIVES**.

predict or **predicate**? To *predict* is to foretell; the verb *predicate* means 'affirm', 'declare', or 'imply': □ *It is impossible to predict the result of tomorrow's match.* □ *They predicated that the accident had been caused by negligence.*

◆ In British English the verb *predicate* is rare and largely restricted to formal contexts. In American English, however, it is widely used as a synonym for 'base' or 'found': □ *Her decision was predicated on past experience.*

In grammar and logic the word *predicate* is also used as a noun. In grammar the *predicate* is the part of a clause or sentence that is not the subject; namely, the verb and its complement or object.

The verb *predicate* is pronounced [*predi*kayt]; the noun is pronounced [*predi*kăt].

preface see **FOREWORD OR PREFACE**?; **PREFIX OR PREFACE**?

prefer The elements that follow the verb *prefer* should be separated by *to*, not *than*: □ *I prefer cricket to football.* □ *She prefers watching television to reading a book.*

◆ If these elements are infinitives, the preposition *to* (and the second infinitive marker) may be replaced by *rather than* in informal contexts: □ *He prefers to walk rather than (to) drive.* In formal contexts the

sentence should be rephrased: □ *He would rather walk than drive.*
□ *He prefers walking to driving.*

Careful users avoid qualifying the verb *prefer* and its derived
adjective *preferable* with such adverbs as *more, most,* etc.: □ *Which
dress do you prefer* [not *prefer most*]*?* □ *Quiet background music is
acceptable but complete silence is preferable* [not *more preferable*].

The verb *prefer* is stressed on the second syllable; the final *r* is
doubled before *-ed, -ing,* and *-er.* In the adjective *preferable,* the
adverb *preferably,* and the noun *preference,* the stress shifts to the
first syllable and the second *r* is not doubled. The pronunciation of
preferable with the stress on the second syllable [priferàbl] is widely
disliked. See also SPELLING 1.

prefix or **preface**? The words *prefix* and *preface* are most frequently
used as nouns (see FOREWORD OR PREFACE?; PREFIXES AND SUF-
FIXES). As verbs, both can mean 'add at the beginning' or 'put
before', although *preface* is more common: □ *She prefaced/pre-
fixed her speech with a few words of welcome.*

◆ Some users dislike this use of the verb *prefix,* reserving it for the
literal sense 'add as a prefix': □ *The word 'organized' may be prefixed
by 'dis-' or 'un-'.*

prefixes and suffixes Prefixes and suffixes are elements attached to a
word in order to form a new word. Prefixes are attached to the
beginnings of words and include: □ *un-* □ *dis-* □ *anti-* □ *non-* □ *ex-.*
Suffixes are attached to the ends of words and include:
□ *-ism* □ *-ful* □ *-dom* □ *-ology* □ *-ship.*

◆ Prefixes are sometimes used with hyphens, sometimes not:
□ *disenchanted* □ *ex-husband*: see HYPHEN 1.

There are some cases where a word cannot stand alone without its
prefix: □ *uncouth* □ *disgruntled* □ *dishevelled* □ *unkempt,* although
gruntled, kempt, etc., are occasionally used jocularly.

Most affixes are in productive use: they can be attached to any
appropriate noun. However, new coinages involving affixes are often
disliked: see, for example, MACRO- AND MICRO-.

prelude The frequent use of the noun *prelude* in the sense of 'introduction' is disliked by some users: □ *The leaders had an informal
meeting this morning as a prelude to next week's summit in
Geneva.*

◆ The noun *prelude* is principally used to denote a piece of music:
□ *one of Chopin's preludes.*

premier The adjective *premier* is best avoided where *foremost, principal, first,* etc., would be adequate or more appropriate: □ *We consulted one of the country's premier authorities on the subject.*

◆ *Premier* is pronounced [premyèr] or [premièr], the first syllable
having the short *e* of *them,* not the long *e* of *theme.* It should not be
confused with PREMIERE, which is sometimes pronounced in the
same way.

premiere Some people dislike the use of the word *premiere* as a verb,
meaning 'give the first performance of': □ *The film will be premiered in New York.*

◆ The verb is also used intransitively: □ *The play premiered in the
West End.*

The noun *premiere,* meaning 'first performance', is acceptable to all
users: □ *the world premiere of Andrew Lloyd Webber's latest musical.*

Premiere may be pronounced [premiair] or [premièr]. It is
sometimes spelt with a grave accent on the second *e,* as in the French

word from which it is derived: *première*. See also **ACCENTS**.

premises The noun *premises*, denoting a building (or buildings) and any accompanying land or grounds, is always plural: □ *Their new premises are on the other side of the railway line.*

◆ The singular noun *premise*, which is not used in this context, means 'assumption' or 'proposition'; it has the variant spelling *premiss*.

premiss see **PREMISES**.

preoccupied see **OCCUPIED OR PREOCCUPIED?**

preparation The noun *preparation* is sometimes misspelt, a frequent error being the substitution of *-per-* for *-par-*, as in *desperation*.

prepositions *Prepositions* are such words as: □ *at* □ *with* □ *of* □ *up* □ *before* that show the relation of a noun or noun equivalent to the rest of the sentence.

◆ One often hears of the grammatical rule that sentences should never end with a preposition. It is true that prepositions, as their name implies, usually precede the noun or pronoun to which they are attached: □ *It was under the chair.* □ *They drove to Birmingham*, but it certainly does not have to be in this position. □ *Which village did you stay in?* and *In which village did you stay?* are both possible, although the latter sounds more formal. In some cases it is hardly possible to put the preposition anywhere but at the end of the sentence: □ *What is he up to?* □ *It isn't worth worrying about.* A reliable rule is that the preposition should be placed where it sounds most natural.

The 'rule' about not ending a sentence with a preposition originated in the fact that a Latin sentence cannot end with a preposition, but there is no reason for this to have any implication for English usage.

A preposition does not need to be repeated when it applies to two elements of a sentence: □ *They went to France and Italy.* □ *He behaved with tact and discretion*, although the preposition must be repeated if ambiguity might otherwise arise. □ *They were arguing about physical fitness and about drinking spirits* could have a different meaning if the second *about* were omitted.

PREPOSITIONS

The following table lists mainly verbs, adjectives, and nouns that have a choice of two interchangeable prepositions. Entries are in alphabetical order, showing the preposition that is recommended for the particular meaning of the word shown. If you want further details on the meaning, context, and use of the expressions listed, then you should consult a good dictionary.

Where there is a fuller discussion, cross-references, e.g., see **ADMIT**, are also included to main entries in the *Guide to Better English*.

abound to abound with *or* in: □ *The river abounds with* [or in] *salmon.*

absolve to absolve somebody of *or* from: □ *They absolved us of* [or from] *blame.*

acquit I to acquit somebody of *or* on (a charge): □ *She was acquitted of* [or on] *all charges.* **II** to acquit somebody of (a crime): □ *She was acquitted of manslaughter.*

adjunct an adjunct to *or* of: □ *as an adjunct to* [or of] *the normal service.*

admit (to; of) see **ADMIT**.

affiliated affiliated to *or* with: □ *organizations affiliated to* [or with] *the union.*

affinity (with; for) see AFFINITY.

afraid I afraid of (something frightening): □ *I'm afraid of the dark.* **II** afraid for (something at risk): □ *I'm afraid for his safety.*

allied I allied with *or* to (another country, etc.): □ *Britain was allied with* [*or to*] *France in both world wars.* **II** (= connected) allied to: □ *The rise in crime is allied to the increase in poverty.*

alternate I to alternate between (two things): □ *Control of the council has alternated between Labour and the Conservatives for the past 20 years.* **II** to alternate with (another thing): □ *Joy alternated with sorrow.*

analogous analogous to *or* with: □ *This phenomenon is analogous to* [*or with*] *the reproductive process in animals.*

angry I angry about *or* at (something): □ *She was angry about* [*or at*] *the way they had treated him.* **II** angry with (somebody): □ *Are you angry with me?*

antidote an antidote to *or* for: □ *Alcohol should not be used as an antidote to* [*or for*] *depression.*

antipathy (an) antipathy to *or* towards: □ *a general feeling of antipathy to* [*or towards*] *the new manager.*

appropriate appropriate to *or* for: □ *language that is appropriate to* [*or for*] *the situation in which it is used.*

approval approval of *or* for: □ *They expressed their approval of* [*or for*] *our plan.*

arise to arise from *or* out of: □ *issues arising from* [or *out of*] *the discussion.*

assist to assist in *or* with: □ *He assisted her in* [or *with*] *her research.*

attempt I an attempt at (something): □ *Her first attempt at setting up a business ended in failure.* **II** an attempt on (somebody's life, a record, etc.): □ *He had survived two earlier attempts on his life.*

attribute (to, *not* with) see ATTRIBUTE.

averse (to *or* from) see ADVERSE OR AVERSE?

beg to beg (something) from *or* of: □ *She begged food from* [or *of*] *her neighbours.*

begin I to begin with (something): □ *The word 'knee' begins with the letter 'k'.* **II** to begin by (-ing): □ *He began by thanking the visiting speaker.*

benefit to benefit from *or* by: □ *Most old age pensioners will benefit from* [or *by*] *these changes in taxation.*

blow a blow on *or* to: □ *a blow on* [or *to*] *her left shoulder.*

book a book about *or* on: □ *a book about* [or *on*] *motor sport.*

born I (from the parents' point of view) born to: □ *Three daughters were born to them, but no sons.* **II** (from the child's point of view) born of: □ *He was born of wealthy parents.*

borrow (from, *not* off) see BORROW.

bridge a bridge over *or* across: □ *a bridge over* [or *across*] *the railway line.*

burden a burden on *or* to: □ *The unemployed are a burden on* [or *to*] *the taxpayer.*

care I (= feel affection) to care for *or* about: □ *Most people care for* [or *about*] *their family.* **II** (= like) to care for: □ *I don't care for foreign food.* **III** (= look after) to care for: □ *He cared for the wounded fox.* **IV** (= be concerned) to care about: □ *She doesn't care about the cost.*

cater to cater for *or* to: □ *The leisure centre caters for* [or *to*] *the needs of the local people.*

centre (on, *not* around) see CENTRE ON OR CENTRE AROUND?

chat to chat to *or* with: □ *chatting to* [or *with*] *his friend on the phone.*

cheat to cheat somebody of *or* out of: □ *She had been cheated of* [or *out of*] *her inheritance.*

clever I clever at (something): □ *He's not very clever at maths.* **II** clever with (a tool, one's hands, etc.): □ *She's clever with a needle.*

coat to coat something in *or* with: □ *Coat the fish in* [or *with*] *breadcrumbs.*

collaborate to collaborate in *or* on: □ *They have collaborated in* [or *on*] *a number of musicals.*

commensurate commensurate with: □ *a position commensurate with his abilities.*

communicate I to communicate with: □ *They communicated with each other through an interpreter.* **II** to communicate something to: □ *She communicated the news to her staff.*

compare (to; with) see **COMPARE TO** OR **COMPARE WITH?**

compete to compete with *or* against: □ *We found ourselves competing with* [or *against*] *three other companies for the contract.*

competent competent at *or* in: □ *Applicants must be competent at* [or *in*] *word processing.*

concerned (about *or* for; with) see **CONCERNED.**

conducive conducive to: □ *an environment conducive to mental concentration.*

confide I to confide in: □ *He confided in his sister.* **II** to confide something to: □ *He confided his problems to his sister.*

conform to conform to *or* with: □ *The results did not conform to* [or *with*] *our expectations.*

connect I (= join) to connect something to *or* with: □ *A narrow lane connects the farm to* [or *with*] *the village.* **II** (= associate) to connect something with: □ *The broken window may not be connected with the robbery.*

consist (of; in) see **CONSIST OF** OR **CONSIST IN?**

contingent contingent on: □ *The success or failure of the strike is contingent on these negotiations.*

convenient convenient for *or* to: □ *Come whenever it is convenient for* [or *to*] *you.*

conversant conversant with: □ *She is not yet conversant with the procedure.*

correspond (with; to) see **CORRESPOND.**

cover to cover something in *or* with: □ *The floor was covered in* [or *with*] *sawdust.*

criterion a criterion of *or* for: □ *the only criterion of* [or *for*] *success.*

culminate to culminate in: □ *The rebellion culminated in civil war.*

date to date from *or* back to: □ *This custom dates from* [or *back to*] *the 16th century.*

deal I to deal in (something bought and sold): □ *They deal in antique furniture.* **II** to deal with (a situation, problem, subject, person, etc.): □ *The police were called in to deal with the riot.*

defer to defer to: □ *She deferred to our wishes.*

desert to desert from (the armed forces): □ *He deserted from his regiment.*

detrimental detrimental to: □ *Smoking is detrimental to health.*

devoid devoid of: □ *The landscape is devoid of interesting features.*

die I to die of *or* from: □ *Thousands died of* [or *from*] *starvation during the drought.* **II** to die from (an injury): □ *He died from his wounds.*

different (from *or* to *or* than) see **DIFFERENT FROM, DIFFERENT TO,** OR **DIFFERENT THAN?**

disappointed I disappointed with *or* at (something): □ *She was disappointed with* [or *at*] *her results.* **II** disappointed in *or* with (somebody): □ *I felt that my parents were disappointed in* [or *with*] *me.*

disparity I a disparity between (two or more people or things): □ *the disparity between the upper and lower classes.* **II** a disparity in (size, age, income, etc.): □ *The disparity in their ages did not affect their performance in the tests.*

dissimilar dissimilar to *or* from: □ *The flavour is not dissimilar to* [or *from*] *that of yoghurt.*

dream to dream of *or* about: □ *I often dream of* [or *about*] *the house where I used to live.* □ *She dreamt of* [or *about*] *becoming a brain surgeon.*

due I due to (a cause): □ *The change in the weather may be due to global warming.* **II** due for (something owed, deserved, etc.): □ *I'm due for a pay rise in September.*

end I to end in *or* with: □ *words ending in* [or *with*] *'-er'.* **II** (= have as result) to end in: □ *Their marriage ended in divorce.* **III** (= finish) to end (something) with: □ *He ended his speech with a vote of thanks.*

endemic endemic in *or* to: □ *The disease is endemic in* [or *to*] *Africa.*

engrossed engrossed in: □ *She was engrossed in her work and didn't hear the doorbell.*

engulfed engulfed in: □ *The car was engulfed in flames.*

entangled I entangled in (something): □ *His fishing line was entangled in the seaweed.* **II** entangled with (another thing): □ *His fishing line was entangled with mine.* **III** (= involved in difficulties) entangled in: □ *become entangled in criminal activities.* **IV** (= involved in a difficult relationship) entangled with: □ *get entangled with some idle young man.*

entrance the entrance to *or* of: □ *the entrance to* [or *of*] *the theatre.*

equal (to; with) see **EQUAL TO OR EQUAL WITH?**

essential essential to *or* for: □ *Money is not essential to* [or *for*] *happiness.*

excel to excel at *or* in: □ *She excels at* [or *in*] *creative writing.*

expert I an expert on *or* in (a subject): □ *We need the advice of an expert on* [or *in*] *commercial law.* **II** an expert at *or* in (an activity): □ *He's an expert at* [or *in*] *problem-solving.*

explanation I an explanation for *or* of (an occurrence, situation, behaviour, etc.): □ *There's no scientific explanation for* [or *of*] *the phenomenon.* **II** an explanation of (something complicated): □ *an explanation of the theory of relativity.*

familiar I familiar to (somebody): □ *Her name is familiar to me.* **II** familiar with (something): □ *I'm not familiar with her poetry.*

fed up fed up with: □ *I'm fed up with his rude remarks.*

fight to fight with *or* against (an opponent, enemy, etc.): □ *The Cavaliers fought with* [or *against*] *the Roundheads.*

fill (in; out) see **FILL IN OR FILL OUT?**

free free of *or* from: □ *The path is free of* [or *from*] *obstacles.*

fret to fret about *or* over: □ *Don't fret about* [or *over*] *it.*

friend I a friend of: □ *a friend of Mary's.* **II** a friend to (somebody who needs help): □ *a friend to the needy.*

fuss a fuss about *or* over: □ *There's no need to make such a fuss about* [or *over*] *such a trivial matter.*

gamble I to gamble with (what is at stake): □ *Don't gamble with your health.* **II** to gamble on (what is uncertain): □ *I'm gambling on her accepting my offer.*

grieve to grieve for *or* over: □ *She grieved for* [or *over*] *the death of her horse.*

grounded I grounded on (a foundation): □ *The story is grounded on*

fact. **II** grounded in (a subject): □ *The children are grounded in road safety.*

guilty I guilty of (a crime): □ *He was found guilty of manslaughter.* **II** to plead guilty to (a crime): □ *He pleaded guilty to all the charges.* **III** to feel guilty about (something): □ *She felt guilty about taking time off work.*

hanker to hanker after *or* for: □ *those who hanker after* [or for] *power.*

happy happy about *or* with: □ *Are you happy about* [or with] *the arrangements?*

hatred hatred for *or* of: □ *Her hatred for* [or of] *her father.*

hazardous hazardous to *or* for: □ *These sharp edges can be hazardous to* [or for] *young children.*

hear I (= receive news from) to hear from: □ *I've not heard from her for years.* **II** (= know about) to hear of: □ *I'd never heard of the disease before.* **III** (= find out about) to hear about *or* of: □ *I only heard about* [or of] *his promotion yesterday.*

identical (with *or* to) see **IDENTICAL WITH OR IDENTICAL TO**?

ignorant I ignorant of (a fact): □ *foreign tourists who are ignorant of the law.* **II** ignorant about (a subject): □ *I'm pretty ignorant about football.*

immune (to; from) see **IMMUNE FROM OR IMMUNE TO**?

impervious impervious to: □ *She is impervious to criticism.*

incentive (an) incentive to *or* for: □ *an incentive to* [or for] *their employees to work harder.*

indifferent (to, *not* about) see **INDIFFERENT**.

indignant I indignant at *or* about (something): □ *He was indignant at* [or about] *having to do the washing-up.* **II** indignant with (somebody): □ *She seemed indignant with me.*

inferior inferior to: □ *This novel is inferior to his last one.*

information information on *or* about: □ *Do you have any information on* [or about] *the company?*

infringement (an) infringement of *or* on: □ *an infringement of* [or on] *our privacy.*

insulate to insulate something from *or* against: □ *The cupboard next to the cooker is insulated from* [or against] *the heat of the oven.*

intended I intended as (something): □ *The message was intended as a warning.* **II** intended for (a person, a purpose): □ *The table is not intended for sitting on.*

interfere I (= meddle) to interfere with: □ *Don't interfere with my papers.* **II** (= intrude) to interfere in: □ *The police are reluctant to interfere in a domestic dispute.* **III** (= abuse sexually) to interfere with: □ *He denied interfering with the girl.*

involved I (= concerned; taking part) involved in *or* with: □ *a meeting of all the people involved in* [or with] *the project.* **II** (= having a close relationship) involved with: □ *She's involved with a married man.*

jealous jealous of: □ *He was jealous of her success.*

judging judging by *or* from: □ *Judging by* [or from] *the design, I'd say this chair was at least 50 years old.*

land I to land somebody in (a situation): □ *You'll land yourself in trouble.* **II** to land somebody with (something unwanted): □ *I was landed with the job of clearing up the mess.*

learn I (= receive information) to learn of *or* about: □ *When did you learn of* [or about] *the accident?* **II** (= gain knowledge) to learn about: □ *We learnt about the Vikings last week.*

liable I (= responsible) liable for: □ *She is liable for their debts.* **II** (= susceptible) liable to: □ *He is liable to epileptic attacks.*

linger I (= be slow) to linger over: □ *He lingered over his breakfast.* **II** (= dwell) to linger on: □ *Don't let your mind linger on the unpleasant details.*

live I to live on (money, food): □ *We can't live on my wages.* **II** to live off (a source of income): □ *She lived off her parents for many years.*

love I love for (somebody): □ *his love for his children.* **II** love of (something): □ *her love of tennis.*

lust to lust for *or* after: □ *He lusted for* [*or* after] *fame.*

make to make something from *or* out of: □ *She made a model of the Eiffel Tower from* [*or* out of] *matchsticks.*

mediate I to mediate in (a situation): □ *An independent adviser was called in to mediate in the dispute.* **II** to mediate between (people): □ *Who will mediate between the union and the management?*

memory I a memory of (a particular thing): □ *I have no memory of the incident.* **II** a memory for (a particular type of thing): □ *I have a very poor memory for names.*

merge I to merge with *or* into (something else): □ *On the horizon, the sea appeared to merge with* [*or* into] *the sky.* **II** to merge with (another business, company, etc.): □ *Cadbury merged with Schweppes.* **III** to merge into (the combined group): □ *The three companies merged into one.*

militate to militate against: □ *His left-wing opinions militated against his appointment as headmaster.*

mixed up I (= involved) mixed up in: □ *Several of the president's aides were mixed up in the conspiracy.* **II** (= confused) mixed up with: □ *You've got Jane's telephone number mixed up with Sarah's.*

name I (in British English) to name somebody or something after: □ *He was named after his grandfather.* **II** (in American English) to name somebody or something for: □ *The airport is named for John F. Kennedy.*

native I (noun) a native of: □ *She's a native of Sweden.* **II** (adjective) native to: □ *The bird is native to Australia.*

nominate I (= propose) to nominate somebody for (a position, office, etc.): □ *He was nominated for the post of treasurer.* **II** (= propose) to nominate somebody as (the holder of a position, office, etc.): He was nominated as treasurer. **III** (= appoint) to nominate somebody to: □ *She was nominated to the board of directors.*

oblivious (of, *not* to) see OBLIVIOUS.

opinion an opinion of *or* about: □ *What's your opinion of* [*or* about] *their proposal?*

opposite (of; to) see OPPOSITE.

parallel parallel to *or* with: □ *The shelf should be parallel to* [*or* with] *the bottom of the cupboard.*

partake I to partake of (food, drink, etc.): □ *She partook of a glass of wine.* **II** to partake in (an activity): □ *I did not partake in the ceremony.*

persevere to persevere in *or* with: □ *They persevered in* [*or* with] *their efforts to dam the stream.*

pivot to pivot on: □ *Everything pivots on his response.*

possessed I (= having) possessed of: □ *He is possessed of an ability to communicate with animals.* **II** (= dominated) possessed by: □ *She was possessed by a desire for revenge.*

precondition a precondition of *or* for: □ *Freedom of speech is a precondition of* [*or* for] *true democracy.*

predispose to predispose somebody to: □ *His background predisposed him to a life of crime.*

prefer (to, *not* than) see PREFER.

prerequisite a prerequisite of or for: □ *A good education is not a prerequisite of* [or *for*] *a successful career.*

preside to preside at or over: □ *The chairman presided at* [or *over*] *the meeting.*

proficient proficient in or at: □ *Applicants must be proficient in* [or *at*] *French and German.*

proportion I in proportion to: □ *The cost of the project will increase in proportion to the time spent on it.* **II** out of proportion to: □ *The animal's head looks out of proportion to its body.*

protect to protect somebody or something from or against: □ *This vaccination will protect you from* [or *against*] *a number of tropical diseases.*

quest I a quest for: □ *The never-ending quest for truth.* **II** in quest of: □ *She travelled the world in quest of her missing brother.*

quibble to quibble about or over: □ *Let's not quibble about* [or *over*] *the details.*

rail to rail at or against: □ *Protesters railed at* [or *against*] *the reform of the abortion law.*

rankle to rankle with: □ *Her attitude rankled with him.*

recoil to recoil from or at: □ *She recoiled from* [or *at*] *the prospect of meeting him again.*

reconcile I to reconcile something or somebody with: □ *I cannot reconcile this theory with scientific fact.* **II** to reconcile oneself to: □ *We must reconcile ourselves to a lower standard of living.*

reek I to reek of: □ *His breath reeked of alcohol.* **II** (in figurative use) to reek of or with: □ *The affair reeks of* [or *with*] *corruption.*

relation in relation to: □ *The price of these video games seems excessively high in relation to the cost of producing them.*

remind I (= cause to think of) to remind somebody of: □ *The smell of pine forests reminds me of my childhood in Scotland.* **II** (= cause to remember) to remind somebody about or of: □ *She reminded me about* [or *of*] *the promise I had made.*

renege to renege on: □ *They reneged on the deal.*

repentance repentance for: □ *repentance for her past misdemeanours.*

replace (with; by) see **REPLACE OR SUBSTITUTE?**

reproach to reproach somebody with or for: □ *She reproached me with* [or *for*] *my carelessness.*

resign I to resign or to resign from (a position, office, etc.): □ *She resigned (from) the presidency.* **II** to resign as (the holder of a position, office, etc.): □ *She resigned as president.*

respect I in respect of: □ *In respect of value for money, this package is the best buy.* **II** with respect to: □ *With respect to your letter of 24 July, ...*

responsible I responsible for (something): □ *The landlord is responsible for the maintenance of the building.* **II** responsible to (somebody): □ *The directors of the company are responsible to the shareholders.*

result I to result in (the effect): □ *Drug abuse resulted in her premature death.* **II** to result from (the cause): □ *Her premature death resulted from drug abuse.*

rob to rob somebody of: □ *The incident robbed him of his dignity.*

satire a satire on: □ *The novel is a satire on totalitarianism.*

saturate to saturate something with or in: □ *The rug was saturated with* [or *in*] *dirty water.*

scared I (adjective) scared of: □ *He's scared of spiders.* **II** (past participle) scared by: □ *We were scared by their threats.*

sceptical sceptical about or of: □ *I remain sceptical about* [or *of*] *her motives.*

sell to sell for or at (a price): □ *These houses normally sell for* [or *at*] *around £100,000.*

sensitive I (= affected by) sensitive to: □ *He is too sensitive to criticism.* **II** (= self-conscious about) sensitive about: □ *She is very sensitive about her large nose.*

separate separate from: □ *Keep raw meat separate from cooked meat.*

serve to serve as or for: □ *The sofa serves as* [or *for*] *a spare bed.*

share I to share in (something): □ *We shared in the household chores.* **II** to share something with somebody: □ *I shared the household chores with my flatmate.*

sick sick of (something boring or annoying): □ *I'm sick of hearing about your problems.*

similar similar to: □ *Their car is similar to ours.*

skill skill at or in: □ *The job requires considerable skill at* [or *in*] *dealing with difficult people.*

smothered smothered in or with: □ *The vegetables were smothered in* [or *with*] *cheese sauce.*

sorry sorry for or about: □ *I'm sorry for* [or *about*] *what I said yesterday.*

speak I (= address) to speak to: □ *He hasn't spoken to his daughter for years.* **II** (= have a conversation) to speak to or with: □ *I spoke to* [or *with*] *the manager on the phone.*

speculate to speculate on or about: □ *There's no point in speculating on* [or *about*] *what might happen.*

sponge to sponge off or on: □ *You can't sponge off* [or *on*] *your family for the rest of your life.*

strive to strive for or after: □ *Some minority groups are still striving for* [or *after*] *equality of opportunity.*

stumble to stumble across or on: □ *I stumbled across* [or *on*] *the solution to the problem.*

substitute (for) see REPLACE OR SUBSTITUTE?

suited suited to or for: □ *She's not suited to* [or *for*] *this type of work.*

superior superior to: □ *This wine is superior to the one we had in the restaurant.*

surprised (by; at) see SURPRISED.

susceptible (to; of) see SUSCEPTIBLE.

symbol I (= emblem) a symbol of: □ *An olive branch is a symbol of peace.* **II** (= sign) a symbol for: □ *A diagonal cross is the symbol for multiplication.*

tantamount tantamount to: □ *Her offer was tantamount to bribery.*

think I (= ponder) think about: □ *I've been thinking about your idea.* **II** (= formulate) think of: □ *Can you think of a better idea?* **III** (= have an opinion) think of: □ *What do you think of the idea?*

thirst to thirst for or after: □ *They thirsted for* [or *after*] *revenge.*

tired tired of: □ *I'm tired of waiting.*

tower to tower above or over: □ *The cliff towered above* [or *over*] *him.*

tremble I to tremble at (something frightening): □ *I trembled at the thought.* **II** to tremble with (fear, excitement, etc.): □ *The children were trembling with fear.*

turn I (= change) to turn to or into: □ *The snow had turned to* [or *into*] *slush.* **II** (= be transformed) to turn into: □ *The frog turned into a handsome prince.*

uncertain uncertain of or about: □ *She was uncertain of* [or *about*] *the* *terms of the contract.*

unfair unfair to or on: □ *The present system is unfair to* [or *on*] *the self-employed.*

upsurge an upsurge in or of: □ *an upsurge in* [or *of*] *enthusiasm for the project.*

use I to use something as (something): □ *I use this cloth as a duster.* **II** to use something for (-ing): □ *I use this cloth for dusting.*

variation I (= change) a variation in or of: □ *The machine responds to variations in* [or *of*] *temperature.* **II** (= different form) a variation on: □ *a variation on the usual theme.*

vital vital to or for: □ *Their cooperation is vital to* [or *for*] *the success of the mission.*

war I a war with or against: □ *wars with* [or *against*] *neighbouring countries.* **II** at war with: □ *France was at war with Spain.* **III** to declare war on: □ *Britain declared war on Germany.*

wary wary of or about: □ *She's wary of* [or *about*] *giving her address to strangers.*

wonder I (= marvel) to wonder at: □ *I wondered at his strength.* **II** (= speculate) to wonder about: □ *I wondered about the reason for his departure.*

wring to wring something from or out of: □ *They tried in vain to wring the truth from* [or *out of*] *her.*

---

prerequisite or **perquisite**? A *prerequisite* is a precondition; a *perquisite* is a benefit, privilege, or exclusive right: □ *A degree is not a prerequisite for a career in journalism.* □ *A company car is often regarded as a perquisite.*

◆ In the sense of 'incidental benefit' the noun *perquisite* is largely restricted to formal contexts, the abbreviation *perk* being the usual form elsewhere: □ *one of the perks of the job.*

See also **PREREQUISITE OR REQUISITE?**

prerequisite or **requisite**? Both these words may be used as nouns or adjectives. *Requisite* relates to anything that is required, necessary, essential, or indispensable; *prerequisite* relates to something that is required in advance: □ *Does the building have the requisite number of fire exits?* □ *The shop sells pens, paper, and other writing requisites.* □ *Physical fitness is prerequisite to/a prerequisite of success at sport.* See also **PREREQUISITE OR PERQUISITE?**

prescribe or **proscribe**? To *prescribe* is to lay down as a rule or to advise or order as a remedy; to *proscribe* is to condemn, prohibit, outlaw, or exile: □ *The union has prescribed a new procedure for dealing with complaints.* □ *Surrogate motherhood has been proscribed in Britain.* □ *Proscribing the doctor's habit of prescribing* (*Daily Telegraph* headline).

◆ The two verbs are similar in pronunciation but almost opposite in meaning: a *prescribed* book is recommended, a *proscribed* book should not be read; a *prescribed* drug should be taken, a *proscribed* drug is banned.

presently Some people object to the increasingly frequent use of the adverb *presently* in place of *currently, at present,* or *now*: □ *Mr John Smith, presently leader of the opposition.* □ *The company presently manufactures components for the electronics industry.*

◆ The word has long been used in this sense in Scotland and America.

The principal meaning of *presently* in British English is 'soon': □ *We walked on a little further and presently we reached the inn.* □ *I'll phone him presently.*

pressure or **pressurize**? The verb *pressure*, which literally means 'apply pressure to', is frequently used in the figurative sense of 'coerce': □ *They were pressured into accepting the pay rise.*

◆ The literal meaning of the verb *pressurize* is 'increase the pressure in', but it is also used figuratively in British English: □ *Aircraft cabins are pressurized to maintain normal atmospheric pressure at high altitudes.* □ *They were pressurized into accepting the pay rise.*

The figurative use of *pressurize* and *pressurized* is disliked and avoided by some users, especially in potentially ambiguous contexts: □ *The ability to work effectively in a pressurised stimulating environment is essential* (*Daily Telegraph*).

prestige The noun *prestige*, denoting the high status, esteem, or renown derived from wealth, success, or influence, is usually pronounced [pres*teezh*].

◆ *Prestige* is also used adjectivally: □ *a prestige company* □ *a prestige car*. See also **PRESTIGIOUS**.

prestigious The adjective *prestigious* is frequently used in the sense of 'having or conferring prestige': □ *new ways of raising money for the country's most prestigious opera house* □ *The company will shortly be relocating to prestigious new offices in the City.*

◆ The original meaning of *prestigious* was less complimentary: derived from the Latin word for 'conjuring tricks', it was used as a synonym for 'fraudulent' or 'deceitful'.

Unlike *prestige*, *prestigious* has the anglicized pronunciation [pres*tijǔs*].

presume see **ASSUME OR PRESUME?**

presumptuous or **presumptive**? *Presumptuous* means 'bold', 'forward', or 'impudent'; *presumptive* means 'based on presumption or probability' or 'giving reasonable grounds for belief': □ *It's rather presumptuous of him to make such a request.* □ *This is only presumptive evidence.*

◆ The adjective *presumptive* is also used in the term *heir presumptive*, which denotes a person whose right to succeed or inherit may be superseded by the birth of another.

Note the spelling of *presumptuous*, particularly the second *u*.

pretence, pretension, or **pretentiousness**? The noun *pretence* denotes the act of pretending; a *pretension* is a claim; *pretentiousness* means 'ostentation' or 'affectation': □ *She made a pretence of closing the door.* □ *He has no pretensions to fame.* □ *Their pretentiousness does not impress me.*

◆ In some contexts *pretence* may be used in place of *pretension*, especially to denote a false or unsupported claim; both nouns may be used in the sense of 'pretentiousness'.

Compare the spellings of *pretension* and *pretentiousness*, particularly the *s* of the former and the second *t* of the latter. In American English the *c* of *pretence* is replaced by *s*.

prevaricate or **procrastinate**? To *prevaricate* is to be evasive, misleading, or untruthful; to *procrastinate* is to delay, defer, or put off: □ *She prevaricated in order to avoid revealing her husband's whereabouts.* □ *He procrastinated in the hope of avoiding the work altogether.*

◆ The two verbs should not be confused: *prevaricate* is partially derived from the Latin word *varus*, meaning 'crooked'; *procrastinate* contains the Latin word *cras*, meaning 'tomorrow'.

prevent When the verb *prevent* is followed by an *-ing* form in formal contexts, the *-ing* form should be preceded either by *from* or by a possessive adjective or noun: □ *They prevented me from winning.* □ *They prevented Andrew from winning.* □ *They prevented my winning.* □ *They prevented Andrew's winning.*

◆ In informal contexts the last example may be considered unnatural or unidiomatic and the word *from* may be omitted from the first two examples: □ *They prevented me/Andrew winning.* See also **-ING FORMS**.

preventive or **preventative**? Either word may be used as an adjective or noun, but *preventive* is the more frequent: □ *preventive measures* □ *preventative surgery* □ *This drug is used as a preventive/preventative.*

◆ Some users consider *preventative* to be a needlessly long variant.

In medical and technical contexts the adjective is used with reference to procedures that forestall disease, damage, breakdown, etc., rather than curing or repairing it: □ *preventive medicine* □ *preventive maintenance.*

pre-war This word is usually hyphenated, although some dictionaries list it as a one-word compound. See also **HYPHEN 1**.

◆ *Pre-war* is generally used as an adjective: □ *pre-war conditions* □ *reverting to pre-war practices.* Its adverbial use is less frequent, the phrase *before the war* being preferred by some users: □ *These houses were built pre-war/before the war.*

In general usage *pre-war* usually refers to the period preceding World War II, but in some contexts the reference may be to World War I or, more rarely, to a different war. This can occasionally lead to ambiguity or confusion: □ *pre-war house prices in the Falkland Islands.*

prey see **PRAY OR PREY?**

price see **COST OR PRICE?**

prima facie This Latin phrase is used adverbially or adjectivally in the sense of 'at first sight', '(based) on first impressions', or 'apparently true': □ *Her argument seems reasonable prima facie.* □ *There is prima facie evidence to support his case.*

◆ Largely restricted to formal contexts, the phrase is pronounced [*prīmā fayshee*].

primarily Many users prefer to stress this word on the first syllable [*prīmărĕli*], but this is very difficult to say unless one is speaking slowly and carefully. The pronunciation with the stress on the second syllable [*prīmerrĕli*] is becoming increasingly common in British English, although it is disliked by many. It is the standard pronunciation in American English. See also **STRESS**.

prime Some people dislike the frequent use of the adjective *prime* in the sense of 'best', 'most important', 'principal', etc., especially when it is applied to something that is not of the highest quality, significance, or rank: □ *in prime condition* □ *the prime position* □ *a prime example.*

primeval This word, meaning 'of the first ages', is usually spelt *primeval* but in British English may also be spelt *primaeval*. See also **-AE- AND -OE-**.

principal or **principle**? These two spellings are often confused. The adjective *principal* means 'of the most importance': □ *the principal cause*; the noun *principal* refers to the head of an organization: □ *the principal of a college. Principle* is always a noun and refers to a fundamental truth or standard: □ *moral principles.* The adjectival form is *principled.*

◆ *In principle* means 'in theory', *on principle* means 'because of the principle'.

principal parts The *principal parts* of a verb are the main inflected forms from which all the other verb forms can be derived. In English they usually include the infinitive, the present participle, the past tense, and past participle. The principal parts of *give,* for example, would be: □ *give, giving, gave, given.* Often the past tense and past participle are the same, and do not both have to be listed: □ *walk, walking, walked.* The present participle is not always included when it is derived regularly, as in: □ *know, knew, known.*

principle see PRINCIPAL OR PRINCIPLE?

prioritize The verb *prioritize,* meaning 'put in order of priority' or 'give priority to', is disliked by some users as an example of the increasing tendency to coin new verbs by adding the suffix *-ize* to nouns and adjectives: □ *The methods of increasing industrial output have been prioritized.* □ *Where women are, in fact, seen to prioritise their career, they are considered in some way 'unnatural', 'unfeminine' or 'on the shelf'* (*The Bookseller*).

◆ An editorial comment in the *Oxford English Dictionary* notes that this is a word 'that at present sits uneasily in the language'. See also -IZE OR -ISE?

prior to Many people object to the unnecessary use of the phrase *prior to* in place of the simpler and more natural preposition *before*: □ *Players and singers rehearsed the works during the afternoon prior to performing them in the evening* (*Chichester Observer*).

◆ The use of *prior* as an adjective is acceptable to all: □ *I would like to come but unfortunately have a prior engagement.*

prise or **prize**? For the meaning 'to force open', either spelling can be used in British English, but *prise* is more common: □ *In the end we managed to prise the lid off.*

◆ *Prize* is the only possible spelling for the noun meaning 'a reward' and the verb 'value greatly': □ *Gloria won first prize in the competition.* □ *The thieves made off with most of their prized possessions.* In American English, the spelling *prize* is more common than *prise* for the sense 'force open'.

pristine The use of *pristine* to mean 'spotlessly clean', 'pure', or 'as good as new' is acceptable to most users: □ *a pristine tablecloth* □ *He made the packet look untouched and in pristine condition* (*Daily Telegraph*).

◆ A few people object to this usage, restricting the adjective to its earlier sense of 'original' or 'primitive': □ *The pristine severity of the Benedictine rule was moderated in the course of time.*

The second syllable of *pristine* may be pronounced to rhyme with *mean* or *mine.*

privacy This word has two pronunciations: [*prĭvăsi*] and [*prīvăsi*] in British English.

◆ The standard American English pronunciation is [*prīvăsi*].

privatization or **denationalization**? Both these nouns refer to the transfer or restoration by a government of nationalized industries to private ownership: □ *the privatization of British Telecom* □ *the denationalization of the iron and steel industry* □ *Electricity charges are likely to rise by 15 to 20 per cent after privatisation to ensure that de-nationalisation is successful*

(Daily Telegraph).

◆ John Silverlight (*Words*) suggests that *denationalization* covers outright disposal of government interest whereas *privatization* covers part disposal. The two words also have political connotations: *denationalization* emphasizes the reversal of Labour's work of nationalization and *privatization* emphasizes private ownership – a major tenet of Conservative policy.

privilege This word, meaning 'special right or advantage', is often misspelt. Note particularly the second *-i-* and the first *-e-*. Remember also that there is no *d* as in *ledge*.

prize see PRISE OR PRIZE?

pro- see PER-, PRE-, OR PRO-?

proactive *Proactive*, a technical term in psychology, is entering general usage as a vogue word, meaning 'taking the initiative; acting in anticipation rather than reacting after the event': □ *a proactive approach to business* □ *a proactive role in the marketplace.* This word is disliked by many people and should not be overused in this sense.

probe In the headline language of popular newspapers the noun *probe* is often used in place of the longer *enquiry* or *investigation*: □ *Crucial questions the BBC poll probe must answer (Sunday Times).* See also JOURNALESE.

◆ In medicine a *probe* is a slender instrument for examining a wound or cavity; *space probes* examine and investigate the expanse beyond the earth's atmosphere.

In nontechnical contexts *probe* is more frequently used as a verb: □ *After further gentle probing, Mark revealed some new details of the incident.*

procedure or **proceeding**? The noun *procedure* denotes a way of doing something; the noun *proceeding* (or, more frequently, *proceedings*) means 'something that is done': □ *to follow the established procedure* □ *to take part in the proceedings.* The two words should not be confused.

◆ Note the difference in spelling between the two words, particularly the *-ced-* of *procedure* and the *-ceed-* of *proceeding*.

proceed see PRECEDE OR PROCEED?

proceeding see PROCEDURE OR PROCEEDING?

process The noun *process* is always pronounced with the stress on the first syllable, [*prōses*]. (The pronunciation [*proses*], with a short *-o-*, is largely restricted to American English.) The verb *process* is also stressed on the first syllable in most contexts; however, in the rare sense 'move (as if) in a procession': □ *They processed down the avenue,* the second syllable is stressed, [*prōses*].

◆ This rare sense, a BACK FORMATION from *procession*, is etymologically distinct from the noun and other meanings of the verb.

pro-choice see PRO-LIFE.

procrastinate see PREVARICATE OR PROCRASTINATE?

prodigal *Prodigal* means 'recklessly wasteful', 'extravagant', or 'lavish': □ *Her brother has always been prodigal with his money.* □ *They were prodigal of praise.*

◆ The use of the adjective *prodigal* to mean 'returning home after a long absence' (based on a misunderstanding of the word in the New Testament parable of the prodigal son, Luke 15:11–32) is disliked and avoided by some careful users: □ *Prodigal performers from the Bosham Players are to return home 40 years on (Chichester*

Observer).

The use of the noun *prodigal*, however, in the extended sense of 'returned wanderer' or 'repentant sinner', rather than the traditional sense of 'spendthrift', is acceptable to most: □ *The prodigal has returned*.

prodigy or **protégé**? The noun *prodigy*, meaning 'marvel', is used to denote an exceptionally talented person, especially a child: □ *Tracy Austin, then 14, was starting to be acknowledged as one of the first child prodigies in professional tennis* (*Daily Telegraph*). A *protégé* is someone who receives help, guidance, protection, patronage, etc., from a more influential or experienced person: □ *one of Lord Olivier's protégés*. The two nouns should not be confused.

◆ Derived from the French word *protéger*, meaning 'protect', the noun *protégé* has the (optional) feminine form *protégée*.

produce or **product**? Both these nouns denote something that is produced. *Produce* refers to things that have been produced by growing or farming, whereas *product* usually refers to industrially produced goods: □ *farm produce* □ *the company's latest product*.

◆ The noun *product* is also used in more abstract senses: □ *He is a product of the public-school system.* □ *the product of a vivid imagination* □ *Such attitudes are the product of ignorance and suspicion.*

Both nouns are pronounced with the stress on the first syllable. The verb *produce*, however, is stressed on the second syllable, [prŏdews].

productivity The noun *productivity*, frequently used in industrial contexts, relates to efficiency or rate of production; it is not synonymous with *output*, which denotes the amount produced: □ *a productivity bonus* □ *The installation of new machinery will increase the company's productivity; employing more workers will only increase its output.*

professional The adjective *professional* is applied to people who are engaged in a profession or who take part in a sport or other activity for gain: □ *doctors, lawyers, and other professional people* □ *a professional golfer/actor/writer/musician*. The noun *professional* is used to denote such people.

◆ In general usage the word *professional*, in the sense of '(person) engaged in a profession', may refer to any career that requires advanced learning and/or special training, such as law, medicine, theology, accountancy, engineering, teaching, nursing, and the armed forces. Many users object to the wider application of the term to include other middle-class occupations: □ *a marketing professional* □ *sales professionals* □ *recruitment professionals*.

Note the spelling of the word *professional*, which has one *f* and *-ss-*.

professor This word is sometimes misspelt. Note the single *f*, *-ss-*, and the *-or* ending.

proffer see OFFER OR PROFFER?

profile The noun *profile* is widely used in the expression *keep a low profile*, meaning 'be inconspicuous or unobtrusive' or 'avoid attention or publicity': □ *The group has kept a low profile since the arrest of its leader*. This usage is disliked by some.

◆ Two adjectival compounds, *low-profile* and *high-profile*, have developed from this use: □ *a low-profile investigation* □ *In Glasgow on Monday, he* [Neil Kinnock] ... *continued his high-profile, ticket-*

only rallies with his wife, Glenys (Sunday Times). See also
VISIBLE.

The noun *profile* is also used alone in a further extension of this
sense: □ *She* [Joan Bakewell] *is credited with raising the profile of arts
coverage on television (Sunday Times)*. □ *You can't risk loss of profile,
market share, and media appeal (The Bookseller)*.

prognosis see DIAGNOSIS OR PROGNOSIS?

program or **programme**? Both these words may be used as nouns or
verbs. In British English the spelling *program* is restricted to the
computing sense of '(provide with) a series of coded instructions': □ *a computer program* □ *to program a computer. Program*
is also the American spelling of the word *programme*.

◆ The noun *programme* has a variety of senses and uses, such as
'broadcast', 'list', 'plan', and 'schedule': □ *a television programme* □ *a
theatre programme* □ *the programme for tonight's concert* □ *a
research programme* □ *a housing programme* □ *the programme of
events.*

The verb *programme* means 'plan', 'schedule', or 'cause to conform
to particular instructions', though some object to this usage: □ *The
new road is programmed for completion next spring.* □ *He has been
programmed to respond in this way.*

In British English the final *m* of *program* is doubled before *-ed, -ing,
-er,* and *-able.* In American English *programmed, programming,* etc.,
are sometimes spelt with a single *m.*

The spelling *programme* was adopted from the French in the 19th
century; *program,* which is now regarded as an Americanism, was the
original spelling of the word in British English.

prohibit see FORBID OR PROHIBIT?

project The word *project,* as a noun, meaning 'scheme or plan', is usually pronounced [projekt]. The alternative [prōjekt] is sometimes
heard but is avoided by careful users.

◆ The verb *project* meaning 'protrude' or 'estimate for the future' is
pronounced [prōjekt].

pro-life The adjective *pro-life* is used to describe an organization,
movement, etc., that supports the right to the maintenance of the
life of the unborn. Those with *pro-life* views are in favour of limi-
tations on the availability of legal abortions and a ban on exper-
iments on human embryos: □ *The controversial Human Fertili-
sation and Embryo Bill faces new dissent from pro-life MPs (The
Guardian).*

◆ *Pro-life* is considered by many people to be a euphemism for
anti-abortion. The term *pro-choice,* describing the opposite point of
view, may be considered a euphemism for *pro-abortion:* □ *The
pro-choice movement believes that women have a right to choose
whether to have an abortion or not.*

prolific The adjective *prolific* means 'very productive'; it is applied to
the person or thing that produces rather than to what is produced: □ *A prolific author, she writes two or three new novels
every year.*

◆ Many people object to the use of *prolific* as a synonym for
'abundant' or 'numerous': □ *Her prolific novels deal with a wide range
of subjects.*

prone see LIABLE OR LIKELY?; PROSTRATE, PRONE, OR SUPINE?

pronouns *Pronouns* are words that are used to replace nouns or noun
phrases to refer to something or someone: □ *I* □ *she* □ *him* □ *it*
□ *you* □ *they,* etc. The main difficulty that arises with pronouns

is in the use of the personal pronoun, where many people are confused between the subject and object forms. Such phrases as: □ *Everything comes to he who waits.* □ *It was up to Julia and I,* though incorrect, are frequently used. Remember that after verbs and prepositions, the object pronoun (*me, him, her, us, them*) should be used: □ *Everything comes to him who waits.* □ *It was up to Julia and me.* The confusion can be resolved by mentally changing the sentence slightly: □ *Things come to him* [not *he*]. □ *It was up to me* [not *I*]. Before verbs the subject pronouns (*I, he, she, we, they*) should be used: □ *I* [not *me*] *and my friend will come.* □ *She* [not *her*] *and her colleague are arguing.* See also **I OR ME?**

◆ Perhaps because of this uncertainty about the personal pronoun, another frequent mistake is the use of a reflexive pronoun instead of a personal pronoun: □ *It was written by another author and me* [not *myself*].

A further difficulty with pronouns is that of uncertainty of reference. This can occur in sentences containing *it*: □ *We took the bus although it was late.* It is unclear whether the bus was late or the time was late.

See also **I OR ME; IT; THEM.**

pronunciation The recommended pronunciation of English words found in dictionaries and grammar books is usually what is known as *RP* or *received pronunciation*, which more or less represents the speech of educated middle-class people from the South-East of England. Until comparatively recently, RP was regarded as 'correct' and other pronunciations were sometimes thought of as, if not actually incorrect, at least inferior. Most people now accept that there is no one standard form of English pronunciation which is correct. There is great regional variety within the United Kingdom and further variations in the speech of other English-speaking countries, and there is nothing incorrect about a pronunciation that is standard to a particular community or region.

◆ It is perfectly valid, then, to say [bath] instead of [bahth] if one comes from northern England, or for an American to say [misl] instead of [misīl]. There is, however, still the possibility of mispronunciations, where a certain pronunciation is not an accepted regional variation and would generally be regarded as a mistake, for example, pronouncing *gist* as [gist] instead of [jist]. It should also be noted, though, that pronunciation is not static; it changes over the years and new pronunciations which were originally resisted by careful speakers sometimes eventually become the standard form.

A frequent mistake is to misspell *pronunciation* as *pronounciation*. The recommended pronunciation is [prănunsiayshăn], not [prănownsiayshăn].

See also **LAW AND ORDER** and other individual entries.

propeller This word for a rotating device with blades is usually spelt with the ending *-er*, though *-or* is occasionally found.

proper nouns see **CAPITAL LETTERS; NOUNS.**

prophecy or **prophesy**? These spellings and pronunciations are sometimes confused. The noun meaning 'prediction' is spelt *prophecy* and pronounced [profisi]. The verb meaning 'utter predictions' is spelt *prophesy* and pronounced [profisī].

◆ *Advice* and *advise* are a similar noun-verb combination, spelt with a *c* for the noun and an *s* for the verb.

proportion The noun *proportion* denotes a ratio; it is best avoided where *part, number, some*, etc., would be adequate or more appropriate: □ *The proportion of female students to male students has increased.* □ *Some* [not *A proportion*] *of his friends are unemployed.*

◆ Such phrases as *a small(er) proportion* and *a large(r) proportion* may be replaced by *few, less, many, more*, etc.: □ *many* [not *a large proportion*] *of our employees* □ *less* [not *a smaller proportion*] *of their money.*

Some people also dislike the use of the plural noun *proportions* in place of *size* or *dimensions*: □ *Men of his proportions have difficulty finding clothes that fit.* □ *They set sail in a ship of enormous proportions.*

proportional or **proportionate**? The adjectives *proportional* and *proportionate* are virtually synonymous in the sense of 'in proportion': □ *a proportionate* [or *proportional*] *increase in spending* □ *the cooking time is proportional* [or *proportionate*] *to the size of the joint of meat.*

◆ In the phrase *proportional representation*, denoting a type of electoral system, the adjective *proportional* cannot be replaced by *proportionate*.

proposal or **proposition**? Both these nouns can mean 'something that is proposed, suggested, or put forward for consideration', but they are not always interchangeable: □ *the government's latest proposal/proposition* □ *That's an interesting proposition/proposal.* □ *an insurance proposal* □ *a business proposition.*

◆ The two words have other specific senses that should not be confused: a *proposal* is an offer of marriage; a *proposition* is an invitation to extramarital sex. The verb *proposition* usually relates to this meaning of the noun (and is much more common than the noun in this sense): □ *He propositioned his secretary*; it should not be used in place of *propose.*

Some people dislike the informal use of the noun *proposition* in the sense of 'person', 'thing', etc.: □ *The new manager is a formidable proposition.* □ *Recycling may not be an economic proposition.* In both these examples the adjective phrase could be replaced by the adjective alone.

proprietary Note the spelling of this word, which is used to refer to goods sold under a particular trade name, especially the second *r*, the *ie*, and the *-ary* ending. The *a* is not always sounded in speech.

proscribe see PRESCRIBE OR PROSCRIBE?

prosecute see PERSECUTE OR PROSECUTE?

prospective see PERSPECTIVE OR PROSPECTIVE?

prostate or **prostrate**? The word *prostate* refers to a gland around the neck of the bladder in men and other male mammals: □ *He's going into hospital to have his prostate (gland) removed.*

◆ It should not be confused with the adjective *prostrate*, which means 'lying face downwards', 'exhausted', or 'overcome': □ *He stepped over the prostrate body of the prisoner.* □ *They were prostrate with anguish.*

The word *prostrate* is also used as a verb. The adjective is stressed on the first syllable; the verb is stressed on the second syllable.

prostrate, prone, or **supine**? *Prostrate* and *prone* mean 'lying face downwards'; *supine* means 'lying face upwards'. In these senses the adjectives *prone* and *supine* are largely restricted to formal or literary usage, or to contexts where the distinction between 'face downwards' and 'face upwards' is particularly important or relevant. Elsewhere, the adjective *prostrate* (with its additional meanings of 'exhausted' or 'overcome': see **PROSTATE OR PROSTRATE?**) is more frequent than *prone* and may also be used in place of *supine* or in the general sense of 'lying flat': □ *She lay prostrate with exhaustion.*

protagonist Some people object to the frequent use of the noun *protagonist* to denote a supporter, especially a leading or notable supporter, of a cause, movement, idea, political party, etc.: □ *British Rail has been the chief protagonist of the pro-Tunnel view over recent years* (*The Guardian*). □ *I would find myself a protagonist of a movement to introduce sanctions on those who do not use these established trade tools* (*The Bookseller*). In such contexts *protagonist* may be better replaced by an appropriate synonym, such as *champion*, *advocate*, or *proponent*.

◆ The traditional meaning of *protagonist* is 'the leading or principal character in a play, story, etc.': □ *Wheeler and Webb then added a third series, starting with 'Murder Gone to Earth' (1937), ... in which the protagonist was a country doctor* (*Daily Telegraph*). In this sense it should not be necessary to qualify the noun with such adjectives as *chief, main, leading, principal,* etc.

protégé see **PRODIGY OR PROTÉGÉ?**

protein Note the spelling of this word, especially the *-ein* ending. It is an exception to the '*i* before *e*' rule (see **SPELLING 5**).

pro tem The expression *pro tem* is a shortened form of the Latin phrase *pro tempore*, meaning 'for the time being' or 'temporarily': □ *Mr Jones will take charge of the sales department pro tem.*

proved or **proven**? *Proved* is the past tense of the verb *prove* and the usual form of its past participle in British English: □ *They (have) proved their innocence.*

◆ As a variant form of the past participle, *proven* is largely restricted to the Scottish legal phrase *not proven*. In British English it is more frequently used as an adjective: □ *a proven remedy* □ *proven skills* □ *a proven liar.*

The accepted pronunciation of the word *proven* is [proovĕn], although the pronunciation [prōvĕn] is also heard from time to time, particularly in the Scottish legal phrase *not proven.*

proverbial The cliché *the proverbial ...* is often used when (part of) a proverb or other idiomatic expression is quoted: □ *It's like taking the proverbial horse to water.* □ *We found ourselves up the proverbial creek.*

◆ The use of the adjective *proverbial* as a synonym for 'famous' or 'notorious' is disliked by some: □ *the proverbial British weather.*

provided or **providing**? The expressions *provided (that)* and *providing (that)* mean 'on the condition (that)': □ *You may have a dog provided/providing that you look after it yourself.*

◆ Some consider *provided (that)* more acceptable than *providing (that).* The inclusion or omission of *that* is optional in most contexts.

The use of *provided* or *providing* in place of *if* is usually unnecessary and sometimes wrong: □ *I'll clean the windows this afternoon if/provided/providing it doesn't rain.* □ *We'll miss our train if* [not *provided/providing*] *we don't leave soon.*

provident or **providential**? These two adjectives, both used in formal contexts, should not be confused. *Provident* means 'showing or exercising foresight' or 'thrifty'; *providential* means 'fortunate' or 'relating to divine providence': □ *They should have been more provident with their resources.* □ *A providential shower of rain brought the game to an end.*

providing see PROVIDED OR PROVIDING?

psychedelic The adjective *psychedelic,* describing hallucinogenic drugs or their effects, is sometimes spelt *psychodelic.* This spelling is acknowledged by some dictionaries but is unacceptable to many users, on the grounds that the adjective is derived from the word *psyche* rather than the prefix *psycho-.*

◆ The use of the adjective *psychedelic* in the sense of 'vividly coloured or patterned' should be restricted to informal contexts.

psychiatry The branch of medicine dealing with problems of the mind is known as *psychiatry.* Note the spelling of the first syllable: *psych-,* which is from the Greek *psychē* 'soul'.

◆ Other words which have the same stem include: □ *psychic* □ *psychiatrist* □ *psychoanalysis* □ *psychological.*

psychological moment The phrase *psychological moment,* of German origin, is generally used with reference to the most appropriate time to produce the desired effect: □ *He waited until she had digested the news of his promotion and then, at the psychological moment, he proposed to her.*

◆ This usage derives from a misinterpretation of the German original, which would have been more accurately translated as *psychological momentum.*

The expression should not be used in place of *turning point, nick of time,* etc., or in contexts where the noun *moment* would be better qualified by a different adjective, such as *crucial, critical, exact,* or *precise:* □ *She lost her concentration at the critical* [not *psychological*] *moment.*

publicly This word is frequently misspelt; there is no *-k-* before the suffix *-ly.*

◆ This word does not conform to the normal rule that adjectives ending in *-ic* have an adverb ending in *-ically,* as in *tragic–tragically.*

pudding see DESSERT, SWEET, PUDDING, OR AFTERS?

punctilious or **punctual**? These two adjectives should not be confused. *Punctilious* is the more formal of the two and means 'scrupulously correct' or 'attentive to detail'; *punctual* means 'prompt; exactly on time': □ *He is very punctilious about etiquette.* □ *If you're called for an interview, be punctual.*

punctuation The primary purpose of punctuation is to clarify the writer's meaning. In speech the meaning is conveyed by the use of emphasis and pauses; punctuation has to serve the same purpose with written language. Lack of punctuation or incorrect punctuation can lead to misunderstanding and ambiguity.

◆ The importance of punctuation in conveying meaning can be illustrated by the various levels of punctuation in the following sentences: □ *My son who is a psychiatrist said Geoff is insane.* The sense here is that one of my sons was commenting on Geoff's mental state. □ *My son, who is a psychiatrist, said Geoff is insane.* The suggestion here is that I have only one son and he was commenting on Geoff's mental state. □ *'My son, who is a psychiatrist,' said Geoff, 'is insane.'* Here Geoff is commenting on his son's mental state.

Punctuation is sometimes a matter of rules and sometimes a matter of style or personal preference. A heavily punctuated passage of writing is unpleasant to read and, in general, it is preferable to use the minimum amount of punctuation consistent with conveying the meaning clearly.

See also **APOSTROPHE; BRACKETS; CAPITAL LETTERS; COLON; COMMA; DASH; ELLIPSIS; EXCLAMATION MARK; FULL STOP; HYPHEN; ITALICS; PARAGRAPHS; QUESTION MARK; QUOTATION MARKS; SEMICOLONS; SOLIDUS.**

pupil or **student**? In British English the noun *pupil* denotes a child at school or a person receiving instruction from an expert; a *student* is a person who studies at an institute of further or higher education, such as a college or university: □ *a pupil at the local infant school* □ *a painting by one of Michelangelo's pupils* □ *while she was a student at Oxford.*

◆ Influenced by American usage, the application of the noun *student* to schoolchildren, especially the older pupils at a secondary school, is becoming increasingly frequent in British English.

purposely or **purposefully**? *Purposely* means 'on purpose; intentionally' and usually refers to the reason for doing something; *purposefully* means 'in a determined way; with a definite purpose in mind' and usually indicates the manner in which something is done: □ *He purposely left his umbrella behind.* □ *She strode purposefully into the room.* The two adverbs are sometimes confused.

pusillanimous The adjective *pusillanimous,* used in formal contexts to mean 'timid' or 'cowardly', is sometimes misspelt. Note the *-ll-*, the single *-n-*, and the *-ous* ending.

putrefy This word, used in formal English to mean 'decompose' or 'rot', is sometimes misspelt. Note the ending *-efy* (like *stupefy*), in spite of the spelling of the related word *putrid.*

pygmy or **pigmy**? Both of these spellings are acceptable, although the *y* spelling is preferred by some users as it shows the word's Greek origins, *pygmaios* 'dwarfish'.

◆ *Pygmy* should be written with an initial capital letter when it is used to refer to a member of one of the tribes of equatorial Africa.

quality The word *quality* is often used adjectivally as a synonym for 'excellent' or 'of superior quality': □*quality goods* □*quality fiction* □*a quality newspaper*. Some people object to this usage on the grounds that the noun *quality* does not always denote excellence: the quality of a product, service, etc., may be good, mediocre, or bad.

quality time The phrase *quality time* is a vogue expression applied to time spent in personal relationships, e.g., by working parents with their children; a comparatively small amount of time exclusively devoted to the needs and interests of the children: □*an hour's quality time with the twins before they go to bed.*

quantum leap Many people object to the frequent use of the term *quantum leap* (or *quantum jump*) to denote a great change or advance: □*Sir Geoffrey has failed to convince the South African Government that it must make the 'quantum leap' to negotiations with Mr Nelson Mandela and the African National Congress* (*The Guardian*).
   ◆ The term is borrowed from the field of physics, where it refers to a sudden transition that is discernible but far from great.

quasi The Latin word *quasi*, meaning 'as if', may be combined with adjectives, in the sense of 'seemingly', 'partly', or 'almost', or with nouns, in the sense of 'resembling', 'so-called', or 'apparent': □*quasi-religious* □*quasi-official* □*quasi-republics.*
   ◆ The hyphen is sometimes omitted but the words are never written as a one-word compound.
   Quasi may be pronounced [*kwayzī*], [*kwaysī*], or [*kwahzi*].

quay This word for 'landing place' is sometimes misspelt. Although pronounced like *key*, note its totally different spelling.

queer The use of *queer* as an informal, often derogatory, synonym for 'homosexual', dates back to the early 20th century. In recent years it has been replaced by the word GAY, which is not derogatory.
   ◆ Although the term *queer* sounds dated in modern usage when used by a heterosexual, it is increasingly used in a non-derogatory manner by homosexuals amongst themselves.

query The verb *query* is best avoided where *ask* or *question* would be more appropriate: □*'Where do you live?' she asked* [not *queried*].
   ◆ The word *query* has connotations of doubt: a *query* is a question prompted by doubt; to *query* is to cast doubt on: □*They accepted his statement without query.* □*We queried the bill.*

question see BEG THE QUESTION; LEADING QUESTION; QUESTION MARK; QUESTIONS; RHETORICAL QUESTION.

question mark The primary use of the question mark is as a substitute for a full stop at the end of a sentence that is a direct question: □*Where are you going?*, and at the end of a quoted question, within the quotation marks: □*'Where are you going?' he asked.*

It is not used for an indirect question: □ *He asked me where I was going.*

◆ A question mark may appear after a question that is not a complete sentence: □ *Beer? Wine? Red or white?* It may also appear after a sentence which is not actually in question form but where the rising intonation of speech would indicate a question: □ *You can't mean that?* □ *She's really going to do it?*

A question mark usually follows a request: □ *Could I possibly have a cup of tea?* If the request is more of an instruction, especially if it is lengthy, it normally ends with a full stop, not a question mark: □ *Would all ladies who wish to travel to the gardens by coach kindly remain here for a short time.*

If a verb of thinking follows a direct question it takes a question mark unless the question is in the past, where it has the force of reported speech: □ *Where are they now, I wonder?* □ *Where were they now, I wondered.* One would not write: □ *Where are they now? I wonder*, although it is occasionally possible for a question mark to appear in the middle of a sentence: □ *The question Why me? is one that cannnot be answered.* This is disliked by some people who insist that, as a question mark has the force of a full stop, it cannot appear except at the end of a sentence, or in quotation marks or parentheses.

A question mark can be used to show that a fact is dubiously true: □ *Ambrose Bierce (1842–?1914).* It is sometimes also used, humorously or ironically, to express doubt: □ *my devoted (?) little brother*, but only in very informal contexts. Similarly, doubled question marks and the combination of question marks and exclamation marks should be avoided in formal writing.

questionnaire This word is sometimes misspelt. Note the *-nn-*, unlike the single *n* in *millionaire*.

◆ The traditional pronunciation of the first syllable was [kest-] but in contemporary usage the first syllable is generally pronounced as in *question*: [kweschōnair].

questions A *question* is a word, phrase, or sentence that asks for information and requires an answer (see also RHETORICAL QUESTION). Questions often begin with *how, what, when, where, which, who,* or *why*: □*How did you find out?* □ *Where is it?* □ *Which one?* □ *Why?*, or with an inverted verb: □*Is he old enough?* □*Are you hungry?* □*Must she?* □ *Will the car be ready tomorrow?* Direct questions are always followed by a QUESTION MARK.

◆ Indirect questions, which occur in REPORTED SPEECH, do not have a question mark at the end: □ *She asked me what I was doing.*

Other words, phrases, and sentences may become questions by the addition of a question mark in written or printed texts or by INTONATION in speech: □ *You've sold it?* □ *Coffee?*

A *tag question* is an inverted form of the verb *be, have, do, can, must,* etc., that is added to a statement. Usually a positive statement is followed by a negative tag question, and vice versa: □ *He's tall, isn't he?* □ *You work in a bank, don't you?* □ *She can't swim, can she?* □ *The clock hasn't stopped, has it?* Tag questions usually require a 'yes' or 'no' answer but they are sometimes rhetorical. A positive statement followed by a positive tag question may be more of an exclamation than a question: □ *They want higher wages, do they!* Negative tag questions usually contain the contraction *-n't*; the full form *not* is heard only in very formal contexts or in dialectal English: □ *You left the car unlocked, did you not?*

quick The use of the word *quick* as an adverb should generally be avoided in formal contexts: □ *Please reply quickly* [not *quick*] *to avoid disappointment.* □ *Come quick!*

◆ The comparative and superlative forms *quicker* and *quickest* are more informal than *more quickly* and *most quickly*: □ *Some plants grow more quickly/quicker than others.* □ *The East German athlete ran the quickest/most quickly. Quicker* may be preferred to *more quickly* when the adverb is preceded by *any*: □ *Can you drive any quicker?*

The use of the adverb *quick* in fixed combinations, such as *quick-drying paint, quick-frozen food,* etc., is acceptable in all contexts.

quiet or **quieten**? Both these verbs may be used to mean 'soothe, calm, or allay' or 'make or become quiet'; in the second of these senses the verb is often followed by *down*.

◆ In British English the verb *quiet* is largely restricted to the first sense and formal usage and *quieten* to the second: □ *We must try to quiet his doubts.* □ *The children quietened down when their mother appeared.* In American English the verb *quiet* is preferred in both senses.

quit or **quitted**? Either word may be used as the past tense and past participle of the verb *quit.*

◆ In British English *quitted* is preferred by some users in formal contexts, but the American variant *quit* is becoming increasingly frequent, particularly in informal contexts: □ *They quitted/quit the building without delay.* □ *He has quit/quitted his job.*

quite In the sense of 'completely', 'totally', or 'entirely', the adverb *quite* is generally used with adjectives that cannot be qualified by *very*: □ *a quite excellent result* □ *a quite unnecessary remark* □ *It is quite impossible!* □ *The ring is quite worthless.* Used with other adjectives, *quite* usually has the meaning 'somewhat', 'fairly', or 'rather': □ *They are quite useful.* □ *The film is quite frightening.*

◆ In some contexts, however, the adverb may be ambiguous: □ *The room is quite clean.* □ *The bucket is quite full.*

In the sense of 'fairly', the adverb *quite* usually precedes the indefinite article: □ *quite an easy question* □ *quite a long time.* The adjectival use of the expression *quite a/an,* meaning 'remarkable' or 'exceptional', is best restricted to informal contexts: □ *She has quite a collection.* □ *That was quite a meal.*

quitted see QUIT OR QUITTED?

quiz Some people dislike the use of the verb *quiz* in the sense of 'interrogate': □ *The police quizzed him about his involvement in the affair.* This usage is widely regarded as JOURNALESE.

◆ A further objection to the verb is raised by those who feel that the lighthearted connotations of the noun *quiz* (in the sense of 'general knowledge game or competition') are inappropriate to the seriousness of a police interrogation.

quotation marks Quotation marks are used at the beginning and end of direct quotations: □ *He said, 'I'm going out now.'* □ *'All right,' she replied, 'but don't be late.'* Only the words actually spoken are placed within the quotation marks; they are not used in reported speech: □ *'I am tired,' she said.* □ *She said that she was tired.* However, in reported speech, one might use quotation marks in order to draw attention to the fact that the speaker has used certain words, particularly if one wished to dissociate oneself from the expression used: □ *He said he was in an 'ongoing situation'.*

◆ The convention in British English has been for punctuation to come inside the quotation marks only when it is part of the actual quotation. However, the comma usually also comes within the quotation marks when it is followed by *he said*, *Martha replied*, etc.: □ *'I wish,' she said, 'you would go away.'* In sentences where the quoted matter is not followed by *he said* or similar, then the comma takes its logical position: □ *He loves Kipling's 'If', and is constantly quoting it.* In American English the comma would appear within the quotation marks in the last example. Full stops also always appear within the quotation marks in American English: □ *See Fowler's section on 'hackneyed phrases.'* whereas in British English when the quoted material is not a complete sentence or utterance the full stop falls outside the quotation marks: □ *He said I should work at 'improving my image'.*

Either single or double quotation marks can be used but when there is a quotation within a quotation, double marks must be used inside single ones, or vice versa: □ *She commented, 'I wish he wouldn't call me "sweetie".'*

Quotation marks are used instead of italics for various short literary and musical works (see TITLES). They are also sometimes used by writers to indicate slang or as an apology for using a particular word or expression: □ *I gather my writing is thought to lack 'pizzazz'.* They are also used in various specialized writings to indicate meanings or interpretations: □ The word *hence* means 'from this time'.

quote The noun *quote* (short for *quotation*) and the plural form *quotes* (short for *quotation marks*) are best restricted to informal contexts: □ *It's a quote from Shakespeare.* □ *We'd better get a quote for having the fence repaired.* □ *Should the last sentence be in quotes?*

◆ The word *quote* is also used in speech to introduce a direct quotation: □ *The chairman said, quote, there will be no further redundancies this year, unquote.* (The addition of *unquote* at the end is optional.)

racism or **racialism**? Both these nouns are used in the sense of 'racial prejudice or discrimination', *racism* being more frequent than *racialism* in modern usage: □ *The company was accused of racism in its recruitment policy.*

◆ *Racism* and *racialism* also refer to the theory that some races (or one particular race) are superior to others. See also **BLACK**.

rack or **wrack**? These two words are sometimes confused. *Rack* is used for a framework for storing or displaying things: □ *a luggage rack* □ *a shoe rack*. *Rack* is also used for the torturing frame: □ *on the rack*. As a verb *rack* means 'cause to suffer pain': □ *racked with uncertainty;* one also *racks one's brains.* The expression *rack and ruin*, 'a state of collapse', may also be spelt *wrack and ruin*; *nerve-racking*, 'causing great anxiety and tension', has the variant spelling *nerve-wracking. Wrack* is seaweed.

racket or **racquet**? Either spelling is acceptable for describing the implement used in sport for striking the ball: □ *tennis racket/racquet* □ *the game of rackets/racquets.*

◆ The spelling *racket* has the additional noun senses 'loud noise': □ *That music is a terrible racket,* and 'illegal business': □ *involved in a drugs racket.*

rad The adjective *rad* and its full form *radical* are slang terms of approval used especially by young people: □ *a rad new video game.*

rainbow coalition The phrase *rainbow coalition* is a vogue expression of American origin, denoting a political alliance of minority groups (such as ethnic minorities, pressure groups, or minor political parties): □ *a rainbow coalition of New Agers, peace campaigners, and animal rights activists.*

raise or **raze**? The verb *raise* means 'move to a higher position': □ *He raised the trophy high; raze* means 'destroy completely': □ *The city was razed to the ground.* The two spellings should not be confused.

◆ The verb *raze* has the variant spelling *rase. Raze* is more frequent than *rase* in modern usage.

raise or **rise**? Both these verbs mean 'move to a higher or upright position' or 'increase'. *Raise* is transitive, *rise* is intransitive: □ *She raised her arm.* □ *They may raise the price.* □ *I watched the smoke rise.* □ *The temperature was rising.*

◆ The verb *raise* is also used in the sense of 'bring up', 'rear', or 'breed': □ *He was raised in Cornwall.* □ *We raise Highland cattle.* (Some people regard this usage as an Americanism.) *Rise,* an irregular verb, has a number of specialized uses: □ *She rose at dawn.* □ *The dough has risen.*

The noun *rise* means 'increase': □ *a pay rise* □ *a rise in unemployment.* In American English *raise* is used in place of *rise* to denote an increase in salary, wages, etc.: □ *He asked for a raise;* this usage is now gradually coming into British English, but is disliked by many.

See also ARISE OR RISE?; RAISE OR RAZE?

raison d'être The phrase *raison d'être*, of French origin, is used in English to denote a reason or justification for existence; it is best avoided where *reason, explanation,* etc., would be adequate or more appropriate: □ *Helping the bereaved is the organization's raison d'être.* □ *The Prime Minister explained the reason* [not *raison d'être*] *for the government's change of policy.*

◆ Note the spelling of the phrase, particularly the circumflex accent on the first *e*. The anglicized pronunciation is [*rayzon detrè*].

rang see RINGED, RANG, OR RUNG?

rapt or **wrapped**? These spellings are sometimes confused. The adjective *rapt* means 'engrossed or absorbed': □ *rapt with wonder* □ *They listened with rapt attention. Wrapped* is the past tense of the verb *wrap*, meaning 'enfold': □ *She wrapped the shawl round the baby.*

◆ Note that *wrapped* can also be used figuratively: □ *He is completely wrapped up in his work.*

rara avis The phrase *rara avis*, denoting a rare or unusual person or thing, is often better replaced by the noun *rarity*: □ *The dedicated employee who is prepared to work long hours without reward is a rara avis.*

◆ Of Latin origin, the phrase literally means 'rare bird'.

The usual pronunciation of *rara avis* is [*rairă ayvis*] or [*rară ayvis*].

rarefy This word, meaning 'make rare or less dense', is sometimes misspelt. Note the *-efy* ending, unlike *purify, intensify,* etc. The variant spelling *rarify* is acknowledged by some dictionaries but is best avoided.

◆ The past participle *rarefied*, used as an adjective meaning 'exalted', 'exclusive', or 'thin', is the most frequent form: □ *rarefied atmosphere.*

rateable or **ratable**? Both spellings of this word are acceptable, but *rateable* is preferred by some users: □ *rateable value.* See SPELLING 3.

rather The adverb *rather* may be used with *would* or *had*, but *would* is more frequent in modern usage, *had* being rather formal: □ *They would/had rather watch television than listen to the radio.* □ *She would/had rather you stayed at home.*

◆ The contraction *'d*, which may represent either *would* or *had*, is often used in informal contexts: □ *I'd rather write than telephone.* See also SHOULD OR WOULD?

The substitution of *rather than* for *than* after a comparative is wrong: □ *He is more interested in the customs and traditions of Elizabethan times than* [not *rather than*] *in the political events of the period.*

Some people object to the use of *rather* before *a* or *an* when the following noun is qualified by an adjective, preferring *it's a rather expensive car* to *it's rather an expensive car.* If the noun is not qualified by an adjective, *rather* must precede the indefinite article: □ *He's rather a coward.*

ravage or **ravish**? These two verbs should not be confused. *Ravage* means 'cause great damage to' and 'devastate'; to *ravish* is 'to delight or enrapture': □ *The country was ravaged by war.* □ *They were ravished by the beauty of the sunset.*

◆ *Ravish* has the additional meaning of 'rape' or 'carry off by force': □ *She was ravished by her captors.*

Both verbs are largely restricted to formal contexts. The word *ravage* is also used as a noun, in such phrases as *the ravages of time*, and the word *ravish* in the adjectival form *ravishing*: □ *You look ravishing in that dress.*

raze see RAISE OR RAZE?

re The use of the preposition *re*, meaning 'with reference to' or 'in the matter of', should be restricted to the heading or opening of a business letter: □*Re: Interest rates for personal loans.* □Re your advertisement in *Country Life.*

◆ In other contexts *re* can usually be replaced by *about, concerning,* etc.: □ *I am producing a documentary about* [not *re*] *the problems faced by single parents.* □ *We have received many complaints concerning* [not *re*] *the proposed route for the new bypass.*

Re is usually pronounced to rhyme with *bee*. The pronunciation [ray] is also heard from time to time, but is incorrect.

See also COMMERCIALESE.

re- The prefix *re-*, meaning 'again', should be followed by a hyphen in compounds that might be confused with existing or more familiar words. Such verbs as *re-sound*, *re-lease*, and *re-sign* (meaning 'sound again', 'lease again', and 'sign again'), for example, are thus distinguished from the verbs *resound*, *release*, and *resign*.

◆ See also REBOUND OR RE-BOUND?; RECOUNT OR RE-COUNT?; RECOVER OR RE-COVER?; RECREATION OR RE-CREATION?; REFORM OR RE-FORM?; RELAY OR RE-LAY?; REPRESENT OR RE-PRESENT?; RESORT OR RE-SORT?

The use of a hyphen in the words *re-educate, re-election, re-entry, re-examine*, etc., is optional (see also HYPHEN 1). Some people prefer to retain the hyphen in such words as *re-invent, re-arrest*, etc., to avoid confusion with *rein, rear*, etc.

Careful users avoid the tautological addition of the adverbs *back* and *again* to verbs that begin with the prefix *re-*: □ *She returned* [not *returned back*] *to England in 1945.* □ *I refer you to the opening paragraph* [not *I refer you back*]. □ *We are redecorating the lounge* [not *redecorating again*]. □ *He made me rewrite the article* [not *rewrite again*]. The use of *again* in the last example would imply that the article had been written more than twice: □ *He was not satisfied with my second draft and made me rewrite the article again.*

reaction The noun *reaction*, which denotes a spontaneous or automatic response, is best avoided where *reply, response, answer, opinion*, etc., would be more appropriate: □ *On hearing the alarm his reaction was one of panic.* □ *We had hoped for a more favourable response* [not *reaction*] *from the committee.* □*Please study these proposals and give me your opinion* [not *reaction*].

◆ A *reaction* can only occur in response to something else; the word should not be used in place of *effect, influence*, etc.: □ *What was the effect* [not *reaction*] *of the news on her family?*, but: □ *What was the reaction of her family to the news?*

readable see LEGIBLE OR READABLE?

real Many people object to the frequent use of the adjective *real* in place of *important, serious*, etc., or simply for emphasis: □*a real achievement* □*a real problem* □*the real facts* □*in real life.*

◆ The adverbial use of *real* in the sense of 'really' or 'very' is an American or dialectal usage: □ *He's real clever.*

realism or **reality**? *Reality* is the state of being real, or the state of things as they really are: □*Daydreams are an escape from reality.* □ *We* *must face reality. Realism* is the acceptance of reality, a practical rather than idealistic attitude of mind: □ *Problems like this must be approached with realism and common sense.*

◆ In art, literature, etc., the term *realism* denotes a style in which things are depicted as they really are, as opposed to abstract art, romantic literature, etc.

realistic The frequent use of the adjective *realistic* as a synonym for 'sensible', 'practical', 'reasonable', etc., is disliked by many users: □ *a realistic proposal* □ *a realistic alternative* □ *a realistic offer.*

reality see REALISM OR REALITY?

really The excessive use of the adverb *really* is best avoided, even in informal contexts. *Really* can often be replaced by a different intensifier, such as *very, extremely, thoroughly, truly,* etc., or omitted altogether: □ *It was really late when they arrived and we were really worried.* □ *Wait until the paint is really dry.* □ *I really enjoyed that holiday.* □ *She really hates her job.*

reason Careful users regard the tautological construction *the reason is/was because* as wrong, preferring *the reason is/was that* or a simpler paraphrase using *because* alone: □ *The reason for the delay is that* [not *because*] *there are road works in the town centre.* □ *The reason I opened the window was that* [not *because*] *there was a wasp in the room.* □ *I opened the window because there was a wasp in the room.*

◆ Similar objections are raised to the use of such constructions as *the reason is due to, the reason was on account of,* etc.

The phrase *the reason why* is acceptable to some users but disliked by others: □ *the reason why he resigned.* In such contexts *why* may be replaced by *that* or omitted altogether; if a noun can be substituted for the verb, the phrase *the reason for* may be used instead: □ *the reason (that) he resigned* □ *the reason for his resignation.*

rebound or **re-bound**? These two spellings are sometimes confused. The verb *rebound* means 'spring back': □ *The ball rebounded. Re-bound,* spelt with a hyphen, is the past tense and past participle of the verb *re-bind* (or *rebind*), meaning 'bind again': □ *The book has been re-bound.*

receipt This word, meaning 'written confirmation that something has been paid or received', is sometimes misspelt. Note the *-ei-* spelling, and the silent *p*. See also SPELLING 5.

receive This word is often misspelt. Note the *-ei-* spelling, which conforms to the rule '*i* before *e* except after *c*'. See also SPELLING 5.

recess The noun *recess* may be pronounced [ri*sess*] or [*rees*es]. The first pronunciation, with the stress on the second syllable, is preferred by some users of British English, but the second pronunciation, stressed on the first syllable, is becoming increasingly frequent.

reciprocal see MUTUAL, COMMON, OR RECIPROCAL?

reckon The use of the verb *reckon* in place of *think*, expressing a personal opinion, is best restricted to informal contexts: □ *He reckons the other team will win.*

◆ In the sense of 'consider' or 'regard', however, *reckon* is acceptable in all contexts: □ *She is reckoned to be one of the most talented musicians of her generation.*

recommend This word, meaning 'praise or suggest as suitable', is often misspelt. Note the single *c* and *-mm-*.

reconnaissance This word, meaning 'exploration or survey of an area for military intelligence purposes', is often misspelt. Note the

recount 292

-nn- and -ss-.

◆ Note also the spelling of the verb *reconnoitre* meaning 'make a reconnaissance'.

recount or **re-count**? These two spellings are sometimes confused. The verb *recount* means 'narrate': □*He recounted his experiences during the war.* The verb *re-count*, with a hyphen, means 'count again', and the noun *re-count*, which is used more frequently than the verb, means 'second count': □ *to demand a re-count of the votes.*

recourse, resort, or **resource**? Similarities in the sense, usage, form, and pronunciation of these words may lead to confusion. All three can refer to a source of help or an expedient: □ *Violence was our only recourse/resort/resource.*

◆ In the expressions *have recourse/resort to* and *without recourse/resort to, recourse* and *resort* are virtually interchangeable but cannot be replaced by *resource. Recourse* is the more frequent noun in such contexts, *resort* being used as a verb in similar constructions: □ *I hope he will not have recourse to violence. – I hope he will not resort to violence.* □ *They settled the dispute without recourse to violence. – They settled the dispute without resorting to violence.*

In the expression *as a last resort/resource* the nouns *resort* and *resource* are interchangeable but cannot be replaced by *recourse. Resort* is generally considered to be the more idiomatic choice in such contexts: □ *She turned to violence as a last resort.*

recover or **re-cover**? These two spellings are sometimes confused. *Recover* means 'regain': □ *She recovered her health. Re-cover*, with a hyphen, means 'give a new cover to': □ *The firm re-covered the chair.*

recreation or **re-creation**? The spellings of these words are sometimes confused. *Recreation* means 'relaxation; leisure (pursuit)': □ *a recreation ground. Re-creation*, with a hyphen, is a word less frequently used and means 'a new creation': □ *the re-creation of the Wild West for the film set.*

recuperate The verb *recuperate*, meaning 'recover', is sometimes misspelt, a common error being the substitution of -coup- for -cup-, as in the verb *recoup.*

redouble or **reduplicate**? The verb *redouble* means 'increase' or 'intensify': □ *We redoubled our efforts.* The rarer and more formal verb *reduplicate* means 'repeat' or 'double'; it also has the specialized sense of 'repeat (a syllable)', as in the words *bye-bye, papa*, etc.

◆ Note that in general usage *redouble* does not refer to the act of doubling something.

redundant Some people object to the frequent use of the adjective *redundant* in place of *unnecessary, superfluous, irrelevant, unimportant*, etc.: □ *Our second car will become redundant when my husband starts commuting by train.* □ *The cancellation of the dinner dance made the baby-sitting problem redundant.*

reduplicate see REDOUBLE OR REDUPLICATE?

refer The verb *refer* is stressed on the second syllable; the final *r* is doubled before -ed, -ing, and -er. In the noun *reference* the stress shifts to the first syllable, and the second *r* is not doubled.

◆ See also SPELLING 1.

For the use of the adverb *back* with the verb *refer* see RE-.

referee or **umpire**? Both nouns denote a person who ensures that a game is played according to the rules and settles any disputes that arise during the course of the game. A *referee* supervises such sports as football, boxing, etc.; an *umpire* supervises such sports as tennis, cricket, baseball, hockey, etc.

◆ A *referee* is also a person who supplies a professional or character reference for a job applicant, prospective tenant, etc. The noun *umpire* is not used in this sense.

referendum The noun *referendum* has two plural forms, *referendums* and *referenda*. *Referendums* is the more frequent in general usage: □ *Their proposed referendums on nuclear disarmament and the return of capital punishment will be welcomed by many.*

reflective or **reflexive**? These two adjectives should not be confused. *Reflective* is used in the literal sense of 'reflecting light' or the figurative sense of 'thoughtful; contemplative': □ *a reflective stripe across the back of the jacket* □ *in a reflective mood*. *Reflexive* is a grammatical term (see REFLEXIVE): □ *reflexive verb* □ *reflexive pronoun*.

reflexive A *reflexive verb* is a transitive verb in which the subject and object are the same: □ *I washed myself.* □ *She hid herself behind a tree.* □ *He perjured himself.* □ *The directors awarded themselves large pay increases.* The pronouns *myself, yourself, himself, herself, itself, oneself, ourselves, yourselves*, and *themselves* are called *reflexive pronouns*.

◆ See also SELF; VERBS.

reform or **re-form**? These spellings are sometimes confused. The verb *reform* means 'change by improvement': □ *plans to reform the tax system*. *Re-form*, with a hyphen, means 'form again': □ *After a lapse of ten years, the club decided to re-form.*

refrigerator Note the spelling of this word, particularly the *-er-* in the middle and the *-or* at the end. There is no *d* in *refrigerator*, unlike the informal short form *fridge*.

refute or **deny**? The verb *refute* means 'prove to be false'; *deny* means 'declare to be false': □ *He refuted their accusations by producing a receipt for the camera.* □ *He denied their accusations but was unable to prove his innocence.* The use of *refute* in place of *deny* is avoided by many careful users but nevertheless occurs with some frequency.

regard In the sense of 'consider' the verb *regard* should be used with the preposition *as*: □ *She regards her mother as her friend.* □ *This novel is regarded as the author's masterpiece.* Compare CONSIDER:

◆ The verb *regard* has a number of other senses and is also used in the prepositional phrase *as regards*, meaning 'with respect to', 'about', or 'concerning': □ *As regards your suggestion, the committee will discuss it at tomorrow's meeting*. *As regards* should not be confused with the phrases *with regard to* and the less frequent *in regard to*, used in similar contexts, in which the word *regard* is a noun and does not end in *s*. In mid-sentence these compound prepositions are often better replaced by *about, concerning*, or *regarding*.

The noun *regard* is used in a variety of other expressions. *Have regard for* means 'show consideration for': □ *They have no regard for her safety*. The plural noun *regards*, meaning 'greetings', occurs in such expressions as *with kind regards* (used to close a letter) and *give one's regards to*: □ *Please give my regards to your daughter when you next see her.*

regardless see IRRESPECTIVE.

registry office or **register office**? Both these terms are used to denote the place where civil marriages are conducted and where births, marriages, and deaths are recorded. *Registry office* is the more frequent term in general usage, *register office* being largely restricted to formal contexts.

regrettably or **regretfully**? These two adverbs are sometimes confused. *Regrettably* relates to something that causes regret; *regretfully* relates to somebody who feels regret: □ *This year's profits are regrettably low.* □ *She regretfully turned down their offer.*

◆ *Regrettably*, not *regretfully*, may be used to mean 'it is regrettable that': □ *Regrettably, the house does not have a garage.* The increasing use of *regretfully* in place of *regrettably* in this sense may be due to confusion with **HOPEFULLY, THANKFULLY,** etc.

rein or **reign**? These spellings are sometimes confused. *Reins* are the leather straps that control a horse; a *reign* is the period of a monarch's rule: □ *pull at the reins* □ *the reign of King Henry VIII.*

◆ The noun *rein* is also used in such expressions as *give free rein to* 'allow freedom to' and *keep a tight rein on* 'control strictly'. The verb *reign* means 'exercise royal authority': □ *King Henry VIII reigned from 1509 to 1547. Reign* is also used to describe a powerful prevalent power or influence: □ *the reign of terror in Uganda under Idi Amin.* □ *Peace has reigned in Europe since 1945.*

reiterate The verb *reiterate* means 'repeat' or 'say or do repeatedly'; it should not be used with the adverb *again* (see also **RE-**): □ *The Prime Minister was simply reiterating the promises made in the party manifesto.*

relation or **relationship**? Both these nouns may be used in the sense of 'connection' but they are not interchangeable in all contexts: □ *Is there any relation/relationship between unemployment and crime?* □ *This evidence bears no relation* [not *relationship*] *to the case.* □ *What is his relationship* [not *relation*] *to the deceased?*

◆ The noun *relationship* is preferred for human connections, *relation* for more abstract connections.

A similar distinction may be applied to the use of *relationship* and the plural noun *relations* in the sense of 'mutual feelings or dealings': □ *business relations* □ *an intimate relationship* □ *the government's relations with the unions* □ *his relationship with his wife.* See also **RELATION OR RELATIVE?**

relation or **relative**? Either noun may be used to denote a person connected to another by blood, marriage, or adoption: □ *Most of her relations/relatives are going to the wedding.* □ *I have a distant relation/relative in Canada.*

◆ See also **RELATION OR RELATIONSHIP?**

relative clause see **CLAUSE; COMMA; THAT OR WHICH?**

relatively The adverb *relatively* implies comparison; many people object to its use as a synonym for 'fairly', 'somewhat', 'rather', etc., where there is no comparison: □ *After the heat of the kitchen the lounge felt relatively cool.* □ *Our records are fairly* [not *relatively*] *up to date.*

relay or **re-lay**? These two spellings are sometimes confused. The verb *relay* means 'pass on': □ *to relay a message.* The verb *re-lay*, spelt with a hyphen, means 'lay again': □ *to re-lay a carpet.*

◆ The past tense and past participle of *relay* is *relayed*; the past tense and past participle of *re-lay* is *re-laid*.

The word *relay* is also used as a noun: □ *The switch is operated by a relay.* □ *They worked in relays.* In this usage, and in such phrases as *relay race, relay* is stressed on the first syllable. The verbs *relay* and *re-lay* may be stressed on either syllable; *re-lay* is sometimes stressed on both.

relevant This word is sometimes misspelt. Note particularly the second *e*.

reliable or **reliant**? The adjective *reliable* means 'dependable' or 'able to be trusted': □ *a reliable car* □ *Some of the author's sources are not very reliable.* The adjective *reliant*, meaning 'dependent', is chiefly used in the phrase *be reliant on*: □ *We were reliant on their assistance.*

relocate The verb *relocate*, frequently used in business and industrial contexts, is widely regarded as a pretentious synonym for 'move': □ *the latest major firm to relocate to Basingstoke* □ *Unemployment in the North is forcing many families to relocate.*

remedial or **remediable**? *Remedial* means 'intended as a remedy'; *remediable* means 'able to be remedied': □ *remedial treatment* □ *a remediable problem.* The two adjectives should not be confused.

◆ *Remedial* is specifically applied to the teaching of slow learners: □ *remedial education* □ *a remedial course.*
  Remediable is less frequent than its antonym *irremediable*: □ *The damage is irremediable.*
  Both adjectives are stressed on the second syllable, unlike the word *remedy* from which they are derived. *Remedial* is pronounced [rimeediăl], *remediable* is pronounced [rimeediăbl].

remembrance The noun *remembrance*, meaning 'the act of remembering', 'memory', or 'memento', is often misspelt, the most frequent error being the substitution of -*ber*- for -*br*-, as in the verb *remember.* Note also the -*ance* ending.

reminiscent This word is sometimes misspelt. Note particularly the -*sc*-, as in *scent.*

remission or **remittance**? Both these nouns are derived from the verb *remit. Remittance* is largely restricted to official contexts, in the sense of 'payment': □ *Please enclose this counterfoil with your remittance. Remission* has a wider range of uses and meanings, such as 'reduction in the length of a prison sentence', 'abatement of the symptoms of a disease', 'discharge; release': □ *the remission of sins.*

◆ Careful users maintain the distinction between the two words.

remit The noun *remit* is best avoided where *task, responsibility, brief,* etc., would be adequate or more appropriate: □ *The quality control function will also be part of your remit (Executive Post).*

◆ As a synonym for the wordy expression *terms of reference*, however, denoting the scope of an investigation, *remit* is welcomed by many users: □ *Financial matters are not part of the inquiry's remit.*
  The verb *remit* is pronounced [rimit]. The noun may also be stressed on the second syllable, but its usual pronunciation is [reemit]. See also **STRESS.**

remittance see **REMISSION OR REMITTANCE?**

renege The traditional pronunciation of this word, which means 'not keep (a promise, agreement, etc.)' is [rineeg], but [rinayg] is also frequently used and is acceptable.

◆ Note the spelling of *renege*, particularly the -*ege* ending. The spelling *renegue* is a less frequent variant.

rent see **HIRE OR RENT?**

repair see **FIX OR REPAIR?**

repairable or **reparable**? Both these adjectives mean 'able to be repaired'; careful users apply *repairable* to material objects and *reparable* to abstract nouns: □ *The car is badly damaged but repairable.* □ *His loss is scarcely reparable.*

◆ The two adjectives relate to different senses of the verb *repair*: 'mend' or 'restore' (*repairable*) and 'remedy' or 'make good' (*reparable*).

Reparable, which is stressed on the first syllable [repărăbl], is less frequent than its opposite *irreparable*: □ *These allegations have done irreparable harm to his political career.*

Repairable is stressed on the second syllable [ripairăbl]; its opposite is *unrepairable*: □ *These shoes are unrepairable.*

repel see REPELLENT OR REPULSIVE?

repellent or **repulsive**? *Repellent* and *repulsive* mean 'causing disgust or aversion'. *Repulsive* is the stronger of the two adjectives, both of which are ultimately derived from the Latin verb *repellere*, meaning 'repel': □ *His deformed body was a repellent sight.* □ *The partially decomposed corpse was a repulsive sight.* □ *The principles of Communism are repellent to some; the doctrines of Nazism were repulsive to many.*

◆ The adjective *repellent* is also used in combination to mean 'driving away' or 'resistant': □ *insect-repellent cream* □ *water-repellent fabric.* *Repellant* is a less frequent spelling of the noun and adjective *repellent*.

The verb *repel* is a weaker synonym of *repulse*. The use of the verb *repulse* in the sense of 'disgust' or 'cause aversion' is disliked by some users, who restrict it to the sense of 'drive back' or 'rebuff': □ *The inhabitants repulsed the invading army.* □ *He repulsed her offer of friendship. Repel* may be used in any of these senses.

repercussions The word *repercussions* is best avoided where *result, consequence, effect,* etc., would be adequate or more appropriate: □ *the repercussions of a ban on smoking in restaurants.*

◆ The noun *repercussion* literally means 'reverberation' or 'rebound'; in figurative contexts it should be restricted to indirect or far-reaching effects: □ *the repercussions of a serious accident at one of Britain's nuclear power stations.*

repertoire or **repertory**? The noun *repertoire* principally denotes the musical or dramatic works, poems, jokes, etc., that a person or group is able or prepared to perform: □ *That song is not in her repertoire.*

◆ The word *repertory* is also used in this sense but is more frequently applied to a company of actors that presents a *repertoire* of plays at the same theatre: □ *a repertory company* □ *a repertory theatre* □ *to act/be performed in repertory.*

repetitious or **repetitive**? The adjective *repetitive* means 'characterized by repetition'; *repetitious* means 'characterized by unnecessary or tedious repetition': □ *a repetitive rhythm* □ *repetitious arguments.*

◆ *Repetitive*, the more frequent of the two adjectives, is also sometimes used in the derogatory sense of *repetitious*, but careful users avoid this usage: □ *a lengthy repetitious* [not *repetitive*] *description of the ceremony.*

Note the spellings of *repetitious, repetitive,* and the related noun *repetition*, particularly the second *-e-* which is sometimes wrongly replaced by *-i-*.

replace or **substitute**? The verb *replace* means 'take the place of'; the verb *substitute* means 'put in the place of': □ *I substituted his*

painting for her photograph. □*Her photograph was replaced
with his painting.* □*His painting was substituted for her photograph.* □*His painting replaced her photograph.*

◆ *Substitute* is always used with the preposition *for*; *replace* may be
used with the preposition *with* or *by* (especially in passive sentences):
□*Her photograph was replaced by his painting.*

All the examples above refer to the act of removing *her photograph*
and putting *his painting* in its place. The two verbs are often confused
in such contexts, *substitute* being used instead of *replace*, but careful
users maintain the distinction between them.

replica Some people object to the frequent use of *replica* in place of
copy, duplicate, reproduction, model, etc.: □*He bought a plastic
replica of the Eiffel Tower.* □*This article is a replica of yesterday's editorial.*

◆ The noun *replica* principally denotes an exact copy of a work of art,
especially one made by the original artist. The phrase *exact replica* is
therefore tautologous.

reported speech Reported speech, also called indirect speech, differs
from direct speech in a number of ways. In direct speech the
actual words of the speaker are given, enclosed in QUOTATION
MARKS in written or printed texts: □*Mary said, 'I've lost my ring.'*
In reported speech quotation marks are not used for this purpose:
□*Mary said that she had lost her ring.*

◆ Note the differences between the two examples above. The subject
pronoun *I* usually changes to *he* or *she* in reported speech; *we* often
changes to *they*. The subject pronoun *you* may change to *I* in reported
speech if it refers to the person who is reporting the speech: □*Peter
said, 'You need a new battery.'* □*Peter said that I needed a new
battery.*

The use of the word *that* to introduce reported speech is optional. In
formal contexts *that* is usually included.

Note also the change of TENSE in reported speech: *I've lost*
becomes *she had lost*; *you need* becomes *I needed*. Thus the present
tense usually changes to the simple past; *has* and *have* change to
had; *will* changes to *would*: □*He said, 'Anne will be late.'* □*He said
that Anne would be late; am* and *is* change to *was*; *are* changes to
were; etc.

represent or **re-present**? These spellings are sometimes confused.
Represent means 'act in place of': □*The team will represent the
whole school. Re-present,* with a hyphen, means 'present again':
□*He re-presented the series of lectures the following autumn.*

repress see OPPRESS, REPRESS, OR SUPPRESS?

repulse, repulsive see REPELLENT OR REPULSIVE?

reputable The adjective *reputable* should be stressed on the first syllable, [*repyuutäbl*]. The pronunciation [ri*pewt*äbl], with the
stress on the second syllable, is incorrect.

requisite see PREREQUISITE OR REQUISITE?

resin or **rosin**? *Resin* is a natural substance exuded by plants, insects,
etc., or a synthetic substance that resembles natural resin. *Rosin*
is a type of natural resin used on the bow of a stringed instrument
to increase friction, on the hands of a gymnast to increase grip,
etc.

◆ *Resin* is pronounced [*rezin*]; *rosin* is pronounced [*rozin*].

resort or **re-sort**? The noun *resort* means 'place of rest or recreation':
□*seaside resorts.* The verb *resort* means 'turn to': □*I hope he will
not resort to violence.* The verb *re-sort,* with a hyphen, means

'sort again': □ *re-sort all the index cards.*

◆ *Resort*, both as a noun and as a verb, is pronounced with a z [ri*zort*]; *re-sort* is pronounced with an s [ree*sort*].

resort, resource see RECOURSE, RESORT, OR RESOURCE?

respectable, respectful, or **respective**? These three adjectives should not be confused. *Respectable* means 'worthy of respect'; *respectful* means 'showing respect'; *respective* means 'separate; several' (see RESPECTIVE OR RESPECTIVELY?): □ *In those days acting was not considered a respectable profession.* □ *a respectful silence* □ *Jane and Michael collected their respective children and went home.*

respective and **respectively** The words *respective* and *respectively* should be used only where there would be a risk of ambiguity or confusion in their absence: □ *The workers explained their respective problems to the shop steward.* □ *Toys and furniture are sold on the second and third floors respectively.* Without *respective*, the first example could imply that all the workers had the same problems; without *respectively*, the second example might suggest that toys and furniture are sold on both floors.

◆ In other contexts the words are often unnecessary or inappropriate: □ *Paul and Sarah got into their (respective) cars and drove away.* □ *Each book must be returned to its (respective) shelf.* □ *She worked (respectively) in Paris, Vienna, and Rome.*

respite This word, meaning 'relief, delay': □ *no respite from the toil,* is often mispronounced. The stress falls on the first syllable, unlike *despite,* which has the stress on the second syllable.

◆ The second syllable may be pronounced [*resp*it] or [*resp*īt] although some users prefer the former pronunciation.

restaurateur Note the spelling of this formal word for a person who runs a restaurant. There is no *n* as in *restaurant.*

◆ *Restaurateur* is pronounced [restårå*ter*].

restive or **restless**? The adjective *restive* means 'resisting control'; *restless* means 'fidgety' or 'agitated': □ *The teacher tried to discipline his restive pupils.* □ *Some of the congregation became restless during the long sermon.* The use of *restive* in place of *restless* is disliked by careful users.

◆ The two adjectives are etymologically unrelated: *restive,* which originally meant 'refusing to move', is derived from the same Latin source as the noun *rest* (meaning 'remainder'); *restless,* the opposite of *restful,* is derived from the noun *rest* (meaning 'repose'), which is of Germanic origin.

restrain see CONSTRAIN OR RESTRAIN?

resuscitate This word, meaning 'revive': □ *All attempts to resuscitate him with the kiss of life failed,* is often misspelt. Note particularly the *-sc-* in the middle of the word.

retread The noun *retread* denotes an old tyre with a new outer surface; it is synonymous with *remould.* Many people object to the metaphorical application of the word *retread* to people, such as politicians returning to parliament after a spell out of office or retired people returning to paid employment: □ *There will be a number of retreads in the new government.*

retro The prefix *retro-,* meaning 'backwards', is increasingly used as an adjective in its own right, describing fashions, styles, ideas, etc., that have been revived from the past: □ *the retro look/sound* □ *His latest film is unashamedly retro.*

return see RE-.

returner A *returner* is a person who returns to work after an extended period of absence from paid employment, such as a woman who resumes her career after spending a number of years bringing up her children: □*Few employers are actually offering women returners a new deal ... but a wealth of information on the subject is available* (*The Guardian*). □*Current trends are centring on more widely appealing 'returner schemes' which offer career breaks of between two and five years* (*The Guardian*).

reveille This word may be pronounced [rivali] or [riveli], the former being the more frequent pronunciation.

◆ Note also the spelling; the word is derived from the French *réveiller* 'awaken'.

revenge or **avenge**? Both these verbs refer to the act of repaying a wrong. The person who *revenges* is usually the offended or injured party; a person who *avenges* is usually a third party acting on behalf of another: □*I will revenge myself on those who cruelly humiliated me.* □*He planned to avenge his brother's death by drowning the murderer's daughter.* □*He avenged his murdered brother.*

◆ This distinction is not observed by all users in all contexts, however, and *revenge* is often interchangeable with *avenge*. See also **REVENGE OR VENGEANCE?**

revenge or **vengeance**? Both these nouns may be used in the sense of 'retaliation' or 'retribution': □*The destruction of her parents' home was an act of revenge/vengeance.*

◆ Some users associate *revenge* with the subjective or personal act of revenging and *vengeance* with the objective or impersonal act of avenging (see **REVENGE OR AVENGE?**): □ *They humiliated me, but I will take my revenge.* □ *He sought vengeance for the murder of his brother.*

reversal or **reversion**? *Reversal* is the act of reversing; *reversion* is the act of reverting: □*the reversal of this trend* □*reversion to his former way of life.* The two nouns should not be confused.

reverse see CONVERSE, INVERSE, OBVERSE, OR REVERSE?

reversion see REVERSAL OR REVERSION?

review or **revue**? These two spellings are sometimes confused. *Review*, as a noun, is a 'critical appraisal': □*a review of her latest novel* or a 'reassessment': □*The minister ordered an urgent review of prison security.* A *revue* is a light theatrical show consisting of sketches, songs, etc.: □*the annual Christmas revue.*

◆ *Revue* may also be spelt *review*, but this is best avoided in order to maintain the distinction between the two words.

rhetorical question A *rhetorical question* is one which is asked for effect, and to which no answer is expected: □ *What is the world coming to?* □*How can people behave like that?* The question is sometimes asked so that it can be answered immediately by the speaker: □ *Why are we on strike? I will tell you why ....*

◆ A rhetorical question is sometimes just a rephrased statement, put in question form for greater emphasis: □ *Was there ever a more unfortunate person?*

rheumatism This word for an illness that causes pain in the muscles or joints is sometimes misspelt. Note particularly the first syllable *rheum-*.

rhinoceros The name of this animal is often misspelt. Note particularly the *rh-*, and the *c* in the middle of the word.

rhythm This word is frequently misspelt. Note particularly the first *h* and the *y*.

ribald This adjective, meaning 'coarse or crude': □ *ribald language*, is often mispronounced. The pronunciation is [ríbăld].
◆ The alternative [rībawld] is regarded as unacceptable by careful users.

ricochet This word, used to describe bullets, etc., that rebound, is usually pronounced [rikŏshay] although [rikŏshet] is also acceptable. There are alternative present and past participles: *ricocheting* [rikŏshaying] or *ricochetting* [rikŏsheting] and *ricocheted* [rikŏshayd] or *ricochetted* [rikŏshetid].

right or **rightly**? Both these adverbs may be used in the sense of 'correctly' or 'properly'. *Right* is generally placed after the verb, *rightly* before the verb: □ *Have I spelt your name right?* □ *He rightly stopped at the zebra crossing.* □ *You're not holding your fork right.* □ *She rightly held her fork in her left hand.*
◆ The phrase *if I remember right/rightly* is a notable exception to this rule.
Right has a number of other adverbial uses: □ *Turn right at the next junction.* □ *They went right home.* □ *We live right at the top of the hill.* *Rightly* also means 'justly' or 'suitably': □ *She was rightly annoyed by their behaviour.* □ *Am I rightly dressed for the trip?* The two adverbs are not interchangeable in any of these senses.
In informal contexts *right* is sometimes used to mean 'very' and *rightly* to mean 'with certainty': □ *We're right pleased to see you.* □ *He doesn't rightly know.*

rigor see RIGOUR OR RIGOR?

rigorous This word is sometimes misspelt. The *u* of *rigour* is dropped in front of the suffix *-ous*.

rigour or **rigor**? *Rigour*, meaning 'harsh conditions; severity': □ *the rigours of winter*, should not be confused in British English with the medical *rigor*: □ *rigor mortis*.
◆ Note, however, that in American English *rigour* is spelt *rigor*.

ring or **wring**? These two verbs are sometimes confused, being identical in pronunciation. *Ring* means 'make a resonant sound' or 'surround or mark with a ring'; *wring* means 'twist' or 'squeeze': □ *to ring a bell* □ *I asked her to ring any errors in red ink.* □ *to wring one's hands* □ *Shall I wring out the wet clothes?*
◆ The past tense and past participle of *wring* is *wrung*, which should not be confused with *rung* (see RINGED, RANG, OR RUNG?)

ringed, rang, or **rung**? *Ringed* is the past tense and past participle of the verb *ring* in the sense of 'surround or mark with a ring': □ *He ringed all the words that had been misspelt.* □ *The birds have been ringed for identification.* *Rang* is the past tense and *rung* the past participle of the verb *ring* in the sense of 'sound (a bell)': □ *She rang the bell.* □ *The telephone has not rung.*
◆ The substitution of *rung* for *rang* is now restricted to dialectal usage; it is considered incorrect in formal British English.

rip-off Derived from the slang verb *rip off*, meaning 'steal' or 'cheat', the noun *rip-off* is principally applied to overpriced goods or the practice of charging exorbitant prices: □ *This handbag is an absolute rip-off – it's not even made of real leather.* □ *I had to pay £10 to get in – it's a rip-off!*
◆ Extending this sense of 'exploitation', *rip-off* is also used to denote an inferior film, book, etc., that seeks to exploit the success of another by imitation.
The noun *rip-off* should not be used in formal contexts.

rise see ARISE OR RISE?; RAISE OR RISE?

road or **street**? Generally the noun *road* is used to denote a thoroughfare between towns or cities or in the suburbs of a town or city; a *street* is a thoroughfare in the town or city centre: □ *a country road* □ *a one-way street* □ *the road to Brighton* □ *the streets of London* □ *a new housing estate on Park Road* □ *their Oxford Street store*. There are, however, numerous exceptions to this rule, especially in the naming of roads and streets.

◆ Through its association with inner-city areas the word *street* has acquired certain negative connotations, and it is rarely used in the names of thoroughfares on new estates. It is used in a number of words and expressions related to prostitution: □ *on the streets* □ *streetwalker*, and also in neutral idioms such as *streets ahead*, meaning 'much better': □ *She's streets ahead of her sister at maths*, and *(right) up one's street*, meaning 'suited to one's interests or experience': □ *This project is right up my street*. See also **STREET-**.

rob, robbery see **BURGLE, ROB, OR STEAL?**

role Some people object to the frequent use of the noun *role* as a synonym for 'place', 'function', 'position', 'part', etc.: □ *the role of religion in modern society* □ *a proven track record in a technical sales role* □ *A new manager is now sought to play a key role in determining the company's future strategy*. The noun *role* is principally used to denote the part played by an actor. In psychology and sociology it refers to the part played by an individual in a social situation: □ *role reversal* □ *role-playing*.

◆ The word is sometimes spelt with a circumflex accent over the *o*, as in the French word from which it is derived: □ *rôle*. It should not be confused with the English noun *roll*, to which it is etymologically related.

roofs or **rooves**? The plural of the word *roof*, 'covering of a building', is usually *roofs*, pronounced [roofs] or [roovz].

◆ The spelling of the plural *rooves* is less frequent.

root see **ROUT OR ROUTE?**

rosin see **RESIN OR ROSIN?**

roughage This word, meaning 'coarse food; dietary fibre', is sometimes misspelt. Note the *-gh-* in the middle of the word.

round see **AROUND OR ROUND?**

rouse see **AROUSE OR ROUSE?**

rout or **route**? The noun *rout* means 'overwhelming defeat' or 'disorderly retreat'; the noun *route* means 'road' or 'course': □ *They put the enemy to rout*. □ *The procession took a different route this summer*.

◆ The risk of confusion is greater when the words are used as verbs, especially in the past tense: □ *They routed the enemy*. □ *The procession was routed along a different road*. The *e* of *route* is sometimes retained in the spelling of the present participle.

The phrasal verb *rout out*, meaning 'find by searching' or 'force out', is a variant of the verb *root*, meaning 'rummage', and is etymologically unrelated to the verb *rout* discussed above.

Rout is pronounced [rowt], rhyming with *out*, in all its senses and uses. The pronunciation of *route* is identical with that of *root* in British English; in American English *route* may be pronounced [root] or [rowt].

rowlock This word, for the device in a boat that holds an oar in place, is usually pronounced [rolŏk].

◆ In nontechnical contexts, *rowlock* is sometimes pronounced [rōlok].

RSI The abbreviation *RSI* is short for *repetitive strain injury*; injury to

muscles or tendons caused by repetitive action, such as using a
computer keyboard: □ *Repetitive Strain Injury (RSI) is an
umbrella term for a series of musculo-skeletal complaints now
affecting the newspaper industry – among others* (*The Guardian*).

rubbish The use of the word *rubbish* as a verb, meaning 'criticize
severely' or 'condemn as worthless', is disliked by many users
and should be avoided in formal contexts: □ *The report rub-
bishes the new GCSE examinations.*

rung see RINGED, RANG, OR RUNG?

run-up Some people dislike the frequent use of the noun *run-up*,
adopted from the field of athletics, to denote the period preceding an important event: □ *the last few days in the run-up to the
general election* □ *The run-up to the anniversary of soldiers
being deployed on the streets of Northern Ireland* (*BBC TV*).

rural or **rustic**? Both these adjectives relate to the countryside, country
life, country people, farming, etc. *Rural* is used as a neutral opposite of *urban*; *rustic* has the connotations of simplicity, crude-
ness, quaintness, or lack of sophistication: □ *rural schools* □ *a
rural setting* □ *rural areas* □ *rustic food* □ *a rustic cottage* □ *rustic
manners.* Careful users maintain the distinction between the two
words.

Russian or **Soviet**? The word *Russian* relates to the country of Russia,
which formed the major part of the Soviet Union from 1922 to
1991, and its people: □ *the Russian composer Rimsky-Korsakov*
□ *a Russian manufacturing company.* The word *Soviet* is used
with reference to people and events of the years when the Soviet
Union was in existence: □ *Soviet space missions* □ *a Soviet
politician.*

◆ The noun and adjective *Russian*, formerly loosely applied to all the
constituent republics of the Soviet Union and their people, should not
be used with reference to (the people of) Ukraine, Lithuania, etc.,
since their independence in 1991.

's or s'? Possessive nouns are usually formed by adding *'s* to singular nouns, an apostrophe to plural nouns that end in *s*, and *'s* to irregular plural nouns that do not end in *s*: □ *Jane's pen* □ *the boy's father* □ *the directors' cars* □ *women's clothes*.

◆ In the possessive form of a name or singular noun that ends in *s*, *x*, or *z*, the apostrophe may or may not be followed by *s*. The final *s* is most frequently omitted in names, especially names of three or more syllables that end in the sound [z]: □ *Euripides' tragedies* □ *Berlioz' operas*. For words of one syllable *'s* is generally used: □ *St James's Palace* □ *the fox's tail* □ *Liz's house* □ *the boss's secretary*. The presence or absence of the final *s* in other possessives of this group depends on usage, convention, pronunciation, etc.: □ *the princess's tiara* □ *Jesus' apostles* □ *the rhinoceros'(s) horn* □ *Nostradamus'(s) prophecies*.

See also **APOSTROPHE**; **CONTRACTIONS**; **-ING FORMS**; **POSSESSIVES**; **SAKE**.

sac or sack? These two spellings are sometimes confused. The noun *sac* is largely restricted to scientific contexts, where it denotes a baglike part of an animal or plant: □ *a fluid-filled sac*. A *sack* is a large bag used to hold coal, potatoes, etc.

◆ In informal contexts *sack* is also a noun or verb referring to dismissal from employment: □ *They got the sack.* □ *We sacked them.* The word *sac*, of French origin, occurs in the compound *cul-de-sac*, meaning 'dead end'.

saccharin or saccharine? The sweet powder that is used as a sugar substitute is spelt *saccharin*, without a final *-e*; *saccharine* is an adjective meaning 'excessively sweet': □ *The drink is sweetened with saccharin.* □ *a saccharine smile.*

◆ The noun *saccharin* is frequently misspelt as *saccharine*. Note also the *-cc-* and *-ar-* of both words.

sack see **SAC OR SACK?**

sacrilegious This word, which means 'showing disrespect towards something holy', sometimes causes problems with spelling. Note the position of the first *i* and *e*, which are in the opposite order in the word *religious*.

sake The noun *sake* is usually preceded by a possessive adjective or noun: □ *for their sake* □ *for Edward's sake* □ *for pity's sake* □ *for old times' sake*.

◆ If the preceding noun ends in the sound [s] the possessive form is not used, although an apostrophe may be added: □ *for goodness sake* □ *for conscience' sake.*

Such expressions as *for all our sakes* and *for both their sakes*, using the plural form of *sake*, are disliked by some users but acceptable to most. They may be replaced by *for the sake of us all, for the sake of both of them*, etc.

salable see **SALEABLE OR SALABLE?**

salary or **wage**? Both these nouns denote the money paid to employees at regular intervals in return for their services. A *salary* is usually paid monthly to professional people or nonmanual workers; a *wage* is usually paid weekly to manual workers or servants: □ *My salary barely covers our mortgage repayments and living expenses.* □ *the minimum wage for factory workers.*

◆ The noun *wage* is often used in the plural form *wages*: □ *a bricklayer's wage(s)* □ *He seems to spend most of his wages on cigarettes and alcohol.* The noun *wages* is not used with a singular verb, except in the well-known biblical quotation *the wages of sin is death* (Romans 6:23).

saleable or **salable**? Both spellings of this word are acceptable, but *saleable* is the more frequent in British English. See SPELLING 3.

salivary This word has two possible pronunciations. The more traditional pronunciation has the stress on the first syllable [*sali*vări]. The pronunciation [să*lī*vări], with the stress on the second syllable, is perfectly acceptable and is more frequently used.

salmonella This word is sometimes mispronounced. The correct pronunciation is [salmŏ*nel*ă].

◆ Unlike the *-l-* in *salmon*, the first *-l-* in *salmonella* is clearly sounded. The word *salmonella* has in fact nothing to do with *salmon*; it is named after the American veterinary surgeon Daniel Elmer Salmon (1850–1914), who first identified this genus of bacteria.

salon or **saloon**? *Saloon* is the anglicized form of the French word *salon*. Both words entered the English language in the 18th century and have developed a number of individual meanings. *Salon* is most frequently found in the names of certain places of business, such as: □ *beauty salon* □ *hairdressing salon.* A *saloon* is a large room in a public house or on a ship: □ *We went into the saloon (bar)*; it also denotes a type of car: □ *the most popular saloon (car).*

◆ A *salon* is also a room for receiving visitors in a large house or an assembly of important political or artistic guests: □ *the literary salons of 17th-century Paris.*

salubrious or **salutary**? *Salubrious* means 'wholesome' or 'conducive to health'; *salutary* means 'beneficial', 'causing improvement', or 'remedial': □ *a salubrious climate* □ *a salutary warning* □ *We decided to look for a more salubrious hotel.* □ *Spending a few days in prison can be a salutary experience for young offenders.*

◆ The adjective *salutary* was formerly synonymous with *salubrious* but is rarely used in this sense today. Both adjectives are ultimately derived from the Latin word *salus*, meaning 'health'.

Note the spelling of *salutary*, which ends in *-ary*, not *-ory*.

same The use of *same* as a pronoun is best restricted to business or official contexts: □ *I enclose my passport, as requested; please return same by registered post.* This usage is widely regarded as COMMERCIALESE. Another pronoun, such as *it* or *them*, can usually be substituted for *same*: □ *He found an old blanket and used it* [not *same*] *to line the dog's basket.*

◆ Nouns qualified by the adjective *same* are usually followed by *as*: □ *He works for the same company as his brother-in-law.* □ *She sent me the same book as you gave her last Christmas.* In the second example and similar sentences *as* is often omitted or replaced by *that*: □ *the same suit that he wore for his wedding.* This usage is disliked and avoided by a few users.

sanatorium A *sanatorium* is a medical establishment for the treatment

305 **scam**

and care of people, especially those suffering from long-term illnesses. Note the spelling of this word in British English, particularly the second *a* and the *o*. The spelling *sanitarium* is an American English variant.

◆ The plural forms of both spellings may end in *-riums* or *-ria*.

sanction The noun *sanction* has two senses that appear to contradict each other. It may mean 'official authorization or permission': □ *The project has been given the sanction of the board of directors*. This use is largely restricted to formal contexts, and the noun is perhaps more frequently found in the plural form *sanctions*, referring to coercive measures taken against a state or institution: □ *economic sanctions against Iraq* □ *to impose political sanctions*.

◆ The verb *sanction* means 'permit' or 'authorize': □ *The law does not sanction the use of violence in such cases*. It should not be used in the sense of 'impose sanctions'.

sank, sunk, or **sunken?** The past tense of the verb *sink* is *sank* or *sunk*, *sank* being the more frequent. The usual form of its past participle is *sunk*, *sunken* being largely restricted to adjectival use: □ *The dog sank its teeth into the man's leg.* □ *One of the boats has sunk.* □ *We are diving for sunken treasure.*

sarcasm, sarcastic see IRONY.

sat see SITTING OR SAT?

sate, satiate, or **satisfy?** The verb *satisfy* means 'supply' or 'fulfil': □ *Her needs had been satisfied.* □ *This should satisfy their demands*. The verbs *sate* and *satiate* may mean 'satisfy fully', but are more frequently used in the sense of 'supply or fulfil to excess': □ *to satiate a person's appetite* □ *Television viewers are sated with imported comedy shows*. A person who is *satisfied* has had enough; a person who is *sated* or *satiated* has usually had too much. *Sate* and *satiate* are used in formal contexts and are largely synonymous, but *sate* is very rarely used as an active verb.

◆ The nouns *satiety* and *satiation* are derived from *satiate*. *Satiation* means 'the act of satiating' or 'the state of being satiated'; *satiety* is used only in the second of these senses. Both nouns are used only in formal contexts.

Note the change in pronunciation of the first *-t-* in *satiate* [sayshiayt] and *satiety* [sătīĕti].

satire or **satyr?** *Satire* is the use of irony or parody to mock folly and evil in human behaviour, politics, religion, etc.; a *satyr* is a mythological creature in the form of a goatlike man, associated with lechery. The two nouns should not be confused in usage or pronunciation: *satyr* rhymes with matter, whereas the second syllable of *satire* rhymes with *fire*.

satisfy see SATE, SATIATE, OR SATISFY?

satyr see SATIRE OR SATYR?

says This word is sometimes mispronounced. The form of the verb *say* used in the present tense with *he, she,* or *it* is *says*, pronounced [sez].

scallop The standard pronunciation of this word, which means 'a shellfish with two flat fan-shaped shells', is [skolŏp]. An alternative which rhymes with *gallop* is often heard, but avoided by careful users.

scam The noun *scam* means 'swindle', 'trick', 'racket', or 'hoax': □ *This* [the Enterprise Allowance Scheme] *was a government* *scam to get the unemployed off the register and pretend they were all setting up small businesses in the thriving enterprise culture instead (The Guardian).*

◆ A vogue word of American origin, *scam* is disliked by some people and should not be overused.

scant or **scanty**? Both these adjectives mean 'limited', 'barely enough', or 'meagre'. *Scant* is more formal and less frequent than *scanty*, being chiefly used in front of certain abstract nouns: □ *He paid scant attention to my words.* □ *She has scant regard for the law. Scanty* is used before or after a wider range of nouns: □ *Their knowledge is rather scanty.* □ *a scanty bikini* □ *a scanty collection of books.*

◆ *Scant* is also used with units of measurement to mean 'barely' or 'slightly less than': □ *a scant two ounces.*

scarcely see HARDLY.

scarfs or **scarves**? Either *scarfs* or *scarves* is acceptable as the plural of the noun *scarf,* denoting a piece of cloth worn around the neck or on the head.

scarify The verb *scarify* should not be used in place of *scare,* to which it is unrelated in meaning and origin. *Scarify* tends to be used in formal contexts and means 'scratch or break up the surface of': □ *to scarify the skin before administering a vaccine* □ *to scarify the topsoil of a field.* In figurative contexts it is used in the sense of 'wound with harsh criticism': □ *a scarifying review.*

◆ The traditional pronunciation of *scarify* is [skarrifī], the pronunciation [skairifī] being an accepted and frequent variant.

scarves see SCARFS OR SCARVES?

scenario The noun *scenario* is frequently used to denote a projected or imagined future state of affairs or sequence of events: □ *a scenario in which the superpowers would have recourse to nuclear weapons.* Many people object to the frequency of this usage, especially in contexts where *plan, programme, scene, situation,* etc., would be adequate or more appropriate. The clichés *nightmare scenario* and *worst-case scenario,* both of which mean 'the worst thing that could happen', are also best avoided wherever possible.

◆ The principal meaning of *scenario* is 'outline or synopsis of a play, film, opera, etc.'. The word is usually pronounced [sinariō]; the variant pronunciation [sinairiō] is disliked by some users.

sceptic or **septic**? The pronunciation of these two words is sometimes confused. A *sceptic* (American English, *skeptic*) is a person who has doubts about accepted beliefs or principles, and is pronounced [skeptik].

◆ *Septic* is an adjective meaning 'infected with harmful bacteria': □ *a septic wound,* and is pronounced [septik].

sceptical see CYNICAL OR SCEPTICAL?

schedule This word, meaning 'plan or timetable': □ *The train was behind schedule again,* is usually pronounced [shedyool] in British English. The word may also be pronounced [skedyool], particularly in American English.

◆ The verb *schedule,* 'to plan', should not be overused.

schism The traditional pronunciation of this word, meaning 'separation into opposed groups', is [sizm], with a silent *ch*. The alternative pronunciation [skizm] is perfectly acceptable.

schizophrenic The adjective *schizophrenic* relates to the mental disorder *schizophrenia,* which is characterized by hallucinations, delusions, social withdrawal, emotional instability, loss of contact with reality, etc.: □ *Another sufferer believes during a schizophrenic attack that he is in command of a spaceship, 2,000 years in the future* (*Reader's Digest*).

◆ The use of the adjective *schizophrenic* in the extended sense of 'inconsistent', 'contradictory', 'unpredictable', 'capricious', etc., is disliked and avoided by most users.

Note the spelling of *schizophrenic* and *schizophrenia* and the difference in pronunciation between the two words: *schizophrenic* is pronounced [skitsŏfrenik], with a short *e*; *schizophrenia* [skitsŏfreeniă] has a long *e*.

scone The pronunciation of this word is a favourite topic for debate; both [skon] and [skōn] are equally acceptable.

◆ The parish of *Scone* in East Scotland, the original site of the stone on which Scottish kings were crowned, is pronounced [skoon].

Scotch, Scots, or **Scottish**? All these adjectives mean 'of Scotland', but there are differences of usage and application between them.

◆ *Scottish*, the most frequent, is used in a wide range of contexts: □ *Scottish history* □ *a Scottish town* □ *Scottish Gaelic* □ *a Scottish name* □ *Scottish dancing* □ *a Scottish poet*.

The adjective *Scotch* was formerly used for such purposes but is now restricted to a number of fixed phrases, in the sense of 'produced in Scotland' or 'associated with Scotland': □ *Scotch whisky* □ *Scotch broth* □ *Scotch mist*.

Scots is usually applied to people: □ *the Scots Guards* □ *a Scotsman* □ *a Scotswoman*. The last two examples may be replaced by the noun *Scot*, which means 'a native or inhabitant of Scotland': □ *She married a Scot*. The collective name for the people of Scotland is *the Scots* or *the Scottish*. The noun *Scots* also denotes a variety of English spoken in Scotland.

In some contexts two of the adjectives are interchangeable: □ *a Scots/Scotch pine* □ *a Scottish/Scotch terrier* □ *a Scottish/Scots accent*.

sculpt or **sculpture**? The verbs *sculpt* and *sculpture* are synonymous and virtually interchangeable in all contexts: □ *He sculpted/ sculptured a copy of the Venus de Milo in marble*. □ *She paints and sculpts/sculptures in her attic studio*.

seasonal or **seasonable**? *Seasonal* means 'of or occurring in a particular season'; *seasonable* means 'suitable for the season' or 'opportune': □ *seasonal vegetables* □ *seasonal work* □ *seasonable weather* □ *seasonable advice*. The two adjectives should not be confused.

secateurs This word, meaning 'pruning shears', is sometimes misspelt. Note the single -*c*- and the -*eurs* ending.

second or **secondly**? see FIRST OR FIRSTLY?

second-guess The verb *second-guess*, of American origin, means 'predict', 'anticipate', or 'evaluate with hindsight': □ *On a scale of difficulty of one to 10, second-guessing the travel market this year is 12* (*The Guardian*).

◆ Some people object to the use of this Americanism in British English.

secretary The word *secretary* is sometimes misspelt. Note the -*ary* ending, which is attached to the letters of the word *secret*.

◆ The *a* of *secretary* is rarely sounded in the British English pronunciation [sekrĕtri]. Careful users always sound the first *r*, however, and object to the pronunciation [sekĕtri]. The usual

American English pronunciation is [*sekrèterri*].

seem When the verb *seem* is used in the negative, the word *not* (or other negative element) may be placed before or after the verb: □ *She didn't seem to understand.* □ *She seemed not to understand.* □ *The weather doesn't seem likely to improve.* □ *The weather seems unlikely to improve.* The use of *didn't seem, doesn't seem,* etc., is best avoided in formal contexts.

◆ Similarly, the phrases *cannot seem, can't seem, couldn't seem,* etc., should be restricted to informal speech: □ *He couldn't seem to hear us.* □ *I cannot seem to find the key.* In formal writing such phrases may be replaced by *seem unable* or simply *cannot*: □ *He seemed unable to hear us.* □ *I cannot find the key.*

seize This word, meaning 'take eagerly or by force': □ *He seized the money and ran,* is sometimes misspelt. Note the order of the vowels *-ei-* which does not correspond to the usual '*i* before *e*' rule. See also **SPELLING 5**.

self The use of the word *self* as a pronoun is disliked and avoided by many users, even in informal contexts: □ *tickets for husband and self.*

◆ The noun *self* and its plural form *selves* are acceptable to all users: □ *his usual self* □ *their true selves.*

The suffixes *-self* and *-selves* are used to form the reflexive pronouns *myself, yourself, ourselves, themselves,* etc.: □ *She killed herself and her three children.* Some people object to the use of these pronouns for emphasis: □ *The house itself will be demolished next week.* □ *He has not driven the car himself.* See also **MYSELF**.

The prefix *self-* is always attached with a hyphen: □ *self-catering* □ *self-confident* □ *self-propelled* □ *self-sufficient.* See also **HYPHEN 1**. Some people object to the increasing use of the prefix *self-* to coin new verbs: □ *self-pick strawberries* □ *We teach them to be aware, to self-market, to look at the future, perhaps in a slightly different way* (*The Guardian*). □ *Farmers may one day be able to graze 'self-dipping' sheep which do not need to be dunked in chemicals to deter attacks by pests and parasites* (*Daily Telegraph*). Such verbs can often be replaced by a more acceptable phrase using a reflexive pronoun, such as *market oneself* in place of *self-market.*

self-starter The frequent use of the noun *self-starter,* especially in job advertisements, to denote a person with initiative who can work without supervision, is disliked by many users: □ *We need an ambitious self-starter with experience in production control and man-management.*

sell-by date This phrase literally means 'the date by which perishable goods should be sold', but it is increasingly used in figurative contexts, meaning 'no longer useful or effective; out-of-date': □ *The government is past its sell-by date.* □ *ideas that have passed their sell-by date.* The phrase should not be overused in this sense.

◆ Other phrases adopted from commercial usage include *best-before date* and *shelf-life*: □ *the best-before date for new entrants to the profession* □ *Despite passionate loyalty to Mrs Thatcher and the broad drift of her policies, he had in the last couple of years become convinced that her shelf-life was exhausted* (*The Guardian*).

semantics, semiotics, or **semiology**? *Semiotics* (or *semiology*) is the study of the properties of sign systems, especially as used in human communication. *Semantics,* one part of semiotics, is the study of the meaning of linguistic signs. For example, discussion of the meaning of the words *book*, *the moon*, or *yellow* belongs to semantics, whereas the wider cultural aspects of raising one's eyebrows when people greet each other at a distance belongs to semiotics.

semi- see DEMI-, HEMI-, OR SEMI-?

semicolons The semicolon is a useful punctuation mark but, unlike many of the other punctuation marks, there is no occasion when its use is compulsory. It is mainly used between clauses that are linked by sense but are not joined by a conjunction, and that could each stand as a separate sentence: □ *I am very tired; I am also hungry.* □ *The night was dark; the rain fell in torrents.*

◆ It is frequently used before such phrases as *however, none the less, nevertheless:* □ *This precaution is recommended; however, it is not compulsory.*

The semicolon can sometimes be replaced by a comma, but in sentences where clauses already contain commas, the semicolon is often used to separate the clauses: □ *Eliot, though born in America, was a British subject; he lived, worked, and died in England.* The semicolon can also be used in order to establish subsets in a long list or series separated by commas: □ *Applicants must have a good honours degree, preferably in English; a lively writing style, a knowledge of magazine publishing, and proven editorial experience; an ability to work under pressure, to cooperate with colleagues, and to work flexible hours.*

semiotics, semiology see SEMANTICS, SEMIOTICS, OR SEMIOLOGY?

senior citizen or **old age pensioner**? Both these expressions are used with reference to people who are over the age of retirement. The expression *senior citizen* is considered a euphemism by most: □ *There are courses for senior citizens at the university.* □ *Senior citizens are entitled to reduced bus and train fares.* The term *old age pensioner* specifically denotes a person who receives a state retirement pension.

◆ *Old age pensioner*, often shortened to *pensioner* or abbreviated to *OAP*, may have connotations of dependence: □ *helping old age pensioners in the community* □ *pensioners who are unable to pay their fuel bills.*

sensible or **sensitive**? The most frequent meaning of *sensible* is 'having or showing common sense; not foolish; practical': □ *a sensible child* □ *sensible advice* □ *the sensible thing to do* □ *sensible shoes.* *Sensitive* means 'easily hurt or irritated', 'having awareness', 'delicate', or 'reacting to very small differences': □ *sensitive skin* □ *He's very sensitive about his large nose.* □ *We are sensitive to your problems.* □ *a sensitive issue* □ *a sensitive instrument.*

sensual or **sensuous**? Both these adjectives relate to the gratification of the senses. Something that is *sensual* appeals to the body, arousing or satisfying physical appetites or sexual desire; something that is *sensuous* appeals to the senses, sometimes especially the mind, being aesthetically pleasing or spiritually uplifting: □ *to indulge in the sensual pleasures of eating and drinking* □ *the sensual movements of the striptease artist* □ *the sensuous movements of the ballerina* □ *to appreciate the sensuous music of Elgar's cello concerto.*

◆ The use of the adjective *sensual* sometimes implies disapproval, whereas *sensuous* is generally used in a favourable manner.

sentences A *sentence* can be defined as 'a grammatically complete unit consisting of one or more words, which starts with a capital letter and ends with a full stop, question mark, or exclamation mark'.

◆ The old rule that 'all sentences must contain a verb' holds good for most kinds of writing but it is a rule that is often legitimately broken, for example: □ *Whatever for?* □ *For heaven's sake!* □ *Yes, of course.* Verbless sentences are often used for stylistic effect, particularly in order to emphasize or qualify a previous statement: □ *It was an illusion, he told himself. A trick of the light.* □ *He's as rich as Croesus. Possibly richer.*

Sentence structure and word order in English are partly a matter of rules and partly a matter of style. The normal word order is subject-verb-object; for example: □ *The dog bit the postman* cannot be changed to *The postman bit the dog* without changing the sense of the sentence. However, one can choose one's word order in sentences like: □ *After lunch we could go for a walk. – We could go for a walk after lunch.* □ *Even more delicious is her chocolate mousse. – Her chocolate mousse is even more delicious.* See also **INVERSION**.

sentiment or **sentimentality**? A *sentiment* is a feeling, emotion, attitude, or opinion: □ *anti-communist sentiment* □ *These are my sentiments on the matter. Sentimentality* is the state of being sentimental, with particular reference to excessive indulgence of the emotions: □ *the sentimentality of the film* □ *She kept his handkerchief under her pillow for reasons of sentimentality.*

◆ *Sentiment* may also refer to indulgence of the emotions, but it is more neutral than *sentimentality*: □ *He seems to be totally lacking in sentiment.*

separate This word is often misspelt. Note the vowels; the most frequent error is to replace the first *-a-* with *-e-*. It may help to associate the central syllable *-par-* with the central letters of the word *apart*.

septic see **SCEPTIC OR SEPTIC?**

sergeant The spelling of *sergeant* is often a source of error. A *sergeant* is a middle-ranking noncommissioned officer in an army, etc., or an officer in a police force. A *sergeant-major* is a noncommissioned officer of the highest rank. A *serjeant-at-arms* is an officer in a parliament; a *serjeant-at-law* a former rank of barrister.

serial see **CEREAL OR SERIAL?**

seriously The adverb *seriously* is best avoided where *very* or *extremely* would be adequate or more appropriate: □ *They seemed to be having a very* [not *seriously*] *good time.* □ *Her parents are extremely* [not *seriously*] *rich.*

◆ The adjective *serious* is also overused in the sense of 'great', especially in the phrase *serious money*, meaning 'a large amount of money'.

service The verb *service* is best avoided where *serve* would be adequate or more appropriate: □ *Labour MPs have accused Thames Water officials of spending too much time on privatisation issues rather than servicing customers* (*Daily Telegraph*). □ *A national organization has been formed to service the local groups.*

◆ The principal meanings of the verb *service* are 'overhaul': □ *The mechanic serviced the car*, and 'pay interest on a debt'.

serviceable This word, meaning 'ready to be used; durable': □ *The television had been repaired and was now serviceable*, is sometimes misspelt. The *e* is retained before the suffix *-able* in order to retain the soft *c* sound.

◆ See also **SPELLING 3**.

session see **CESSION OR SESSION?**

sewed or **sewn?** Either word may be used as the past participle of the verb *sew*: □ *I have sewn/sewed a patch over the hole. Sewn* is often preferred to *sewed*, especially when the participle is used as an adjective: □ *a neatly sewn hem.*

◆ The past tense of *sew* is always *sewed*: □ *She sewed the lace along the edge.*

The verb *sew* and its derivatives should not be confused with *sow* (see **SOWED OR SOWN?**).

sexism The use of sexist language can often be avoided by the substitution of neutral synonyms or simple paraphrases, without recourse to clumsy or controversial neologisms. Those opponents of sexism who coin such expressions as *the artist's mistress-piece* and *to person the telephones* do little to further their cause. See also **POLITICAL CORRECTNESS**.

◆ The most frequent examples of sexism include the use of the noun *man* in place of *person*; *lady* or *girl* in place of *woman*; *he*, *him*, and *his* as pronouns of common gender; and the titles *Mrs* and *Miss*. See **HE OR SHE; MAN; MS, MRS, OR MISS?; WOMAN**.

The problems of sexism arising from occupational titles fall into three categories. The words *engineer* and *nurse*, for example, are of neutral gender but are traditionally associated with men and women respectively. For this reason the terms *female engineer*, *male nurse*, etc., are sometimes used to avoid confusion. This is often quite unnecessary: □ *Dr Tony Butterworth, 40, a former male nurse, has been appointed Britain's first Professor of Community Nursing at Manchester University* (*Daily Telegraph*).

The ban on sexual discrimination in job advertisements has encouraged the substitution of neutral synonyms for occupational titles that specify sex: *foreman* and *charwoman*, for example, may be replaced by *supervisor* and *cleaner*; *fireman* and *cameraman* by *fire fighter* and *camera operator*; *policeman* and *policewoman* by *police officer*; *salesman* and *saleswoman* by *sales representative* or *shop assistant*. See also **PERSON**.

The use of feminine suffixes is also disliked by some users: □ *The fête was opened by the comedienne Victoria Wood.* □ *Her sister is an usherette at the local cinema.* □ *He married a successful authoress.* See also **-ESS**.

sexy *Sexy*, an informal adjective meaning 'arousing sexual interest' or 'sexually aroused', is increasingly used as a synonym for 'attractive', 'enjoyable', 'exciting', or 'fashionable' in contexts that are completely devoid of sexual connotations: □ *'Crime,' according to an independent television producer recently, 'is very sexy this year.'* (*The Guardian*). □ *Boots wanted a presence in some of the sexier parts of the retailing business* (*The Guardian*).

◆ This vogue usage is disliked and avoided by most people.

Shakespearean or **Shakespearian?** This word, meaning 'of or having the characteristics of Shakespeare': □ *a Shakespearean sonnet*, may end with *-ean* or with *-ian*.

shall or **will?** The traditional distinction between *shall* and *will* is that *shall* is used in the first person and *will* in the second and third persons as the future tense of the verb *to be* and that *will* is used to express determination, compulsion, intention, willingness, commands, promises, etc.: □ *I shall wash the dishes later.* □ *He will come back tomorrow.* □ *We will not obey you.* □ *They shall apologize immediately.*

◆ In informal contexts the problem rarely arises, the contraction *'ll* being used to represent both *shall* and *will* in all persons.

Outside England, especially in American, Scottish, and Irish English, the distinction between *shall* and *will* is more simply defined, *shall* being used in all persons to express determination, compulsion, etc., and *will* as the future tense of the verb *to be*, with an increasing tendency to use *will* in all senses. Modern usage in England is following this trend, although *shall* is retained in official contexts: □ *Passengers shall remain seated until the vehicle is stationary.*

The use of *shall* and *will* in questions is a more complex issue. □ *Shall I stay?* means 'Do you want me to stay?' □ *Shall we go?* is a suggestion or proposition. □ *Will I/we win?* means 'Am I/Are we going to win?' □ *Shall you pay the bill?* means 'Are you going to pay the bill?' □ *Will you pay the bill?* is a request.

shaved or **shaven**? *Shaved* is the past tense of the verb *shave* and the usual form of the past participle: □ *He (has) shaved off his beard. Shaven*, a variant form of the past participle, is largely restricted to adjectival use: □ *the shaven heads of the monks* □ *a clean-shaven young man.*

she see HE OR SHE.

sheared or **shorn**? *Sheared* is the past tense of the verb *shear; shorn* is the usual form of its past participle: □ *They sheared the sheep.* □ *They have shorn the sheep.* □ *You will be shorn of your power.*

◆ The past participle *sheared* is used in the technical sense of 'deformed', 'distorted', 'fractured', or 'broken': □ *The head of the screw has sheared off.*

Shorn is also used as an adjective: □ *a shorn lamb* □ *his shorn hair.*

sheikh The preferred pronunciation of this word, which means 'an Arab chief or ruler', is [shayk]. The alternative pronunciation [sheek] is not generally accepted.

◆ Note the spelling of this word; the spelling *sheik* is an accepted variant.

shelf-life see SELL-BY DATE.

shibboleth The noun *shibboleth* is frequently used to denote a catch-word, slogan, maxim, cliché, etc., especially one that is old-fashioned or obsolescent: □ *We were unimpressed by his speech, in which he did little more than repeat the old shibboleths of the party.*

◆ *Shibboleth* traditionally refers to a custom or practice that serves to distinguish the members of one party, sect, race, etc., from those of another. In the Old Testament (Judges 12:6) the word is used as a test to distinguish the Ephraimites, who could not pronounce the sound [sh], from the Gileadites.

shined or **shone**? *Shone* is the past tense and past participle for most senses of the verb *shine; shined* is restricted to the meaning 'polished': □ *The sun (has) shone all day.* □ *He shone his torch on the statue.* □ *They (have) shined our shoes.*

ship see BOAT OR SHIP?

shone see SHINED OR SHONE?

shorn see SHEARED OR SHORN?

should or **would**? In reported speech, conditional sentences, and other indirect constructions, the use of *should* and *would* follows the pattern of *shall* and *will* (as the future tense of the verb *to be*); *would* is always used in the second and third persons and often replaces *should* in the first person: □ *We said we should/would stay until Saturday.* □ *She thought you would fail.* □*If you were in trouble I should/would help you.* □*He would open the door if he had the key.* See also SHALL OR WILL?

◆ A similar convention applies to the use of *should* and *would* in polite or formal constructions: □ *We should/would be delighted to see you.* □ *I should/would like to buy a pair of sandals.* □ *She would be pleased to oblige.* □ *They would prefer to play outside.*

In informal contexts, the distinction between *should* and *would* does not arise, the contraction *'d* being used to represent both *should* and *would* in all persons.

In the sense of 'ought to' *should* is used in all persons: □ *We should visit her more often.* □ *You should be able to see it from here.* There is sometimes a risk of ambiguity in the first person: □ *I thought I should accept their offer* may be a paraphrase of 'I thought I ought to ...' or the past tense of 'I think I shall ...'.

In the sense of 'used to' *would* is used in all persons: □ *When we were on holiday we would sometimes spend all day on the beach.* □ *Before his retirement he would always get up at seven o'clock.* See also RATHER; SUBJUNCTIVE.

shrank, shrunk, or **shrunken**? *Shrank* is the past tense of the verb *shrink* and *shrunk* the usual form of its past participle, the variant *shrunken* being more frequently used as an adjective: □*He shrank from telling her the truth.* □*My pullover has shrunk.* □*A shrunken old woman stood in the doorway.*

◆ The use of *shrunk* in place of *shrank* is also acknowledged by some authorities.

sibling The noun *sibling*, which denotes a brother or sister, is a useful word that is unfortunately disliked by many users and largely restricted to formal contexts and sociological jargon: □ *the twins' relationship with their siblings* □*sibling rivalry.*

◆ The use of *sibling* and *siblings* to simplify such sentences as: □ *He would like to have a sibling* [rather than *a brother or sister*] *to play with* and: □ *All her siblings* [rather than *brothers and sisters*] *have left home* has yet to gain general acceptance.

sic The Latin word *sic*, meaning 'so' or 'thus', is used in printed or written text (often in a quotation) to indicate that an unlikely, unexpected, questionable, or misspelt word or phrase has in fact been accurately transcribed: □*He spoke of a need for 'more thorough analysation [sic]' of the results.*

◆ *Sic* is enclosed in square brackets and inserted immediately after the word or phrase it refers to. The use of italics is optional.

sick or **ill**? In British English to feel *sick* is to feel nauseated or queasy, to feel *ill* is to feel unwell: □*She was sick yesterday* usually means 'she vomited yesterday'; □*She was ill yesterday* means 'she was not well yesterday'.

◆ The adjective *ill* is not usually used in this sense before a noun, *sick* being preferred: □ *a sick* [not *ill*] *man.* (*Ill* may, however, precede a noun in the sense of 'bad': □*ill fortune* □*ill treatment* □*ill health.*) *Sick* is also used with reference to absence from work because of illness: □*to go sick* □*off sick* □*sick pay* □*sick leave.*

In American English *sick* and *ill* are interchangeable in most contexts, *ill* being the more formal of the two adjectives.

sideline Some people dislike the increasing use of the verb *sideline*, meaning 'prevent from taking part' or 'put out of action': □ *In his warmest speech yet on European integration, Mr Major set out his determination not to allow Britain to be sidelined in Europe* (*The Guardian*). □ *A 100-day counter revolution to undo the Conservatives' local government reforms, including sidelining Thatcherite civil servants, is being prepared by Labour for immediate implementation if returned in April* (*The Guardian*).

◆ Of sporting origin, the verb *sideline* has been used in American English since the 1940s, usually with reference to illness or injury that puts a player out of action.

siege This word, meaning 'the surrounding of a fortified place to force a surrender', is sometimes misspelt. Note the order of the vowels *-ie-*, which conforms to the normal '*i* before *e*' rule. See also SPELLING 5.

significant The adjective *significant* means 'having meaning': □ *a significant detail* □ *a significant gesture*.

◆ Its frequent use as a synonym for 'important', 'large', 'serious', etc., is disliked by some users: □ *a significant writer* □ *a significant increase* □ *a significant problem*.

silhouette This word, meaning 'outline; shadow', is sometimes misspelt, the most frequent error being the omission of the silent *-h-*. Note also the *-ette* ending.

◆ The word derives from the name of the French politician Étienne de *Silhouette* (1709–67), perhaps because of his small-minded economies.

silicon or **silicone**? *Silicon* is an element that occurs in sand and is used in alloys, glass manufacture, and the electronics industry: □ *silicon chip*. *Silicone* is a compound that contains silicon and is used in lubricants, polishes, and cosmetic surgery: □ *silicone rubber*.

◆ The two words should not be confused. The final syllable of *silicon* is unstressed; the final syllable of *silicone* rhymes with *bone*.

similar Note the spelling of this adjective, particularly the single *-m-* and *-l-* and the *-ar* ending.

similes A *simile* is a figure of speech which, like a metaphor, suggests a comparison or analogy, but a simile expresses the comparison explicitly and is usually introduced by *like* or *as*: □ *teeth like pearls* □ *wide as the ocean*.

◆ Similes are used in many well-known idioms: □ *good as gold* □ *dry as dust* □ *bold as brass*, and many similes are so overworked as to have become clichés: □ *to run like the wind* □ *a voice like thunder* □ *eyes like stars*.

Similes can, however, be used to good effect, particularly in humorous or ironical prose: □ *Jeeves coughed one soft, low, gentle cough like a sheep with a blade of grass stuck in its throat* (P.G. Wodehouse, *The Inimitable Jeeves*). □ *A laugh swept through the conference hall as a drip of water might sweep through the Kalahari* (*The Times*). They are more often used seriously in poetry:

Life, like a dome of many-coloured glass,
　　Stains the white radiance of Eternity.
(Shelley, *Adonais*)

simplistic The adjective *simplistic* means 'oversimplified' or 'naive'; it should not be used in place of *simple*: □ *a simplistic explanation of the theory of relativity* □ *a simple* [not *simplistic*] *explanation for her behaviour*.

◆ *Simplistic* is generally used in a derogatory manner: □ *His simplistic solution to the problem was rejected without further discussion.*

simulate or **stimulate**? These two verbs are sometimes confused. *Simulate* means 'feign', 'imitate', or 'reproduce for the purpose of study, training, experiment, etc.': □ *to simulate indifference* □ *simulated leather* □ *The process is simulated in the laboratory.* *Stimulate* means 'arouse' or 'excite': □ *He stimulated his pupils' interest.* □ *a stimulating experience.* See also DISSEMBLE, DISSIMU-LATE, OR SIMULATE?

simultaneity The traditional pronunciation of this noun, derived from SIMULTANEOUS, is [simŭltăneeiti], although [simŭltănayiti] is also heard. The American English pronunciation is [sīm-].

simultaneous This word, meaning 'happening at the same time', may cause problems with pronunciation. The usual pronunciation is [simŭltayniĕs]. The American English pronunciation is [sīm-].

since see AGO OR SINCE?; BECAUSE, AS, FOR, OR SINCE?

sincerely The adverb *sincerely* is sometimes misspelt. Note the *-cere-* in the middle, and the *-ly* (not *-ley*) ending.

sinecure The noun *sinecure*, meaning 'a job or position in which pay-ment is received for little or no work', is often mispronounced. The correct pronunciation of this three syllable word is [sīnikewr]: the *-i-* is long, as in *wine*, and the first *-e-* is not silent.

sine qua non The expression *sine qua non*, which is largely restricted to formal contexts, denotes an essential or indispensable condi-tion or requirement: □ *Mutual trust is a sine qua non of a success-ful marriage.*

◆ Of Latin origin, the phrase literally means 'without which not'. The word *sine* may be pronounced [sīni], [sini], or [sinay]; *qua* may be pronounced [kway] or [kwah]; *non* may rhyme with *gone* or *bone*.

singeing or **singing**? *Singeing* is the present participle of the verb *singe*, meaning 'burn slightly': □ *It is difficult to iron this blouse without singeing the lace.* The *-e* of *singe* is retained in *singeing* to keep the *-g-* soft and to distinguish it from *singing*, the present participle of the verb *sing*: □ *The birds were singing in the trees.*

◆ *Singeing* is pronounced [sinjing]; *singing* is pronounced [singing]. Careful speakers do not insert the hard *g* sound, as in *single,* into *singing, singer,* etc.

singular or **plural**? As a general rule a singular verb is used with a sin-gular subject and a plural verb is used with a plural subject. Problems arise when the subject is a noun or phrase that can be singular or plural and when a singular subject is separated from the verb by a number of plural nouns (or vice versa): □ *A list of the names and addresses of new members is* [not *are*] *available on request.*

◆ Such nouns as *audience, government, jury, committee, family, crowd, herd,* etc., and other collective nouns followed by *of (a bunch of flowers, a flock of geese, a gang of thieves,* etc.), are used with a singular verb if the people or items in question are considered as a group and with a plural verb if they are considered as individuals. See also COLLECTIVE NOUNS; COMMITTEE; GOVERNMENT; -ICS; KIND OF; MAJORITY AND MINORITY; NUMBER. Any corresponding pronouns or possessive adjectives should agree with the chosen verb: □ *The audience were asked to remain in their* [not *its*] *seats.* □ *The jury has to consider all the evidence before it* [not *they*] *can reach a verdict.* American English treats groups as singular more than British English does: □ *Harvard plays Yale,* but: *Oxford play Cambridge.*

Measurements, sums of money, percentages, etc., are used with a singular verb if they are considered as a single entity: □ *Four metres is all we need.* □ *Ten pounds is not enough.* □ *Fifteen per cent is a generous increase.*

Two or more nouns joined with *and* are used with a plural verb unless they represent a single concept: □ *His sister and her friend were killed in the accident.* □ *Gin and tonic is a popular drink.* However, nouns and phrases joined to the principal subject with *as well as, together with, plus,* etc., are regarded as parenthetical; the verb agrees with the principal subject alone: □ *A valuable painting, as well as her engravings, was destroyed in the fire.* □ *Her engravings, together with a valuable painting, were destroyed in the fire.*

See also **ANY; EITHER; FOOT OR FEET?; MORE; NEITHER; NONE; ONE; OR; PLUS; THERE IS OR THERE ARE?; TOGETHER WITH.**

siphon or **syphon**? This word, meaning '(draw off liquid by means of a) tube using atmospheric pressure', can be spelt with an *i* or a *y*.
◆ Some users prefer the *i*-spelling, since this reflects the original Greek *siphōn*.

Sir *Sir* is a polite term of address for a man: □ *Thank you very much, sir.* The word is usually written with a lower-case *s*- in such contexts, but as an impersonal salutation in **LETTER WRITING** it is always written with a capital *S*-: □ *Dear Sir.*
◆ *Sir*, with a capital *S*-, is also the title of knights and baronets: □ *Sir Lancelot* □ *Sir Humphrey Appleby.* Note that it is correct to use *Sir* with a person's first name alone but not with his surname alone: □ *Sir Humphrey* [not *Sir Appleby*].

sitting or **sat**? The substitution of *sat*, the past participle of the verb *sit*, for the present participle *sitting* is found in some dialects of English: □ *They were sitting* [in some dialects *sat*] *in the garden.*
◆ *Sat* is correctly used in the passive form of the transitive verb *sit*: □ *We were sat at this table by the head waiter.*

sitting room see **LOUNGE.**

situation In the sense of 'state of affairs' the noun *situation* often serves a useful purpose, but it should not be used to excess: □ *We discussed our financial situation with the bank manager.* □ *They are trying to improve the unemployment situation.*
◆ In some contexts *situation* is quite superfluous: □ *a crisis situation* is a crisis; □ *an interview situation* is an interview. See also **ONGOING.**

sixth This word may be pronounced [siksth] or [sikth], although some people dislike the omission of the second [s] sound.

sizeable or **sizable**? Both spellings of this word are acceptable. See **SPELLING 3.**

skilful The adjective *skilful*, meaning 'possessing skill', is sometimes misspelt. The final *l* of *skill* is dropped in British English before the suffix *-ful*. In American English, the *-ll-* is retained: *skillful.*

slander see **LIBEL OR SLANDER?**

slang *Slang* is unauthorized language, often but not necessarily coarse, which stands in the linguistic hierarchy between general informal speech and the specific vocabularies of professional and occupational jargon. Innovative and dramatic, slang is the most ephemeral of language, continually coining new terms and discarding old ones, which are either abandoned to obscurity or transferred into the respectability of the standard language.
◆ Slang includes shortening of words: □ *biz* (business) □ *vibes* (vibrations); onomatopoeic words: □ *zap*; rhyming slang or abbreviations of it: □ *skin and blister* (sister) □ *plates* (feet, from *plates of meat*); terms from the criminal and drug subcultures: □ *grass* (a

police informer, or alternatively marijuana) □ *porridge* (time spent in prison) □ *speed* (an amphetamine drug).

A sparing use of slang can be effective, except when the context is too formal for it to be appropriate. However, slang often becomes obsolete or old-fashioned very quickly and the use of out-of-date or overworked slang can make speech or writing seem dated and tedious.

sled, sledge, or **sleigh?** All these nouns denote vehicles that are used on snow for transport or recreation.

◆ *Sledge*, the most frequent in British English, is replaced by *sled* in American English. *Sleigh* usually refers to a large sledge that is pulled by animals; the smaller sledge that is used for sliding downhill is also known as a *toboggan*: □ *a picture of Father Christmas on his sleigh* □ *children playing on their sledges/sleds.*

sleight The word *sleight*, most frequently used in the phrase *sleight of hand* ('dexterity in using the hands to perform conjuring tricks, etc.') is sometimes misspelt and mispronounced. Note the *-ei-* spelling and the pronunciation [slīt] not [slayt].

slough *Slough* is pronounced [slow], rhyming with *how*, in the sense 'swamp; state of hopeless dejection': □ *in the slough of despond*, and [sluf] when referring to the cast-off skin of a snake or the verb 'shed or abandon'.

slow The use of the word *slow* as an adverb should generally be avoided in formal contexts: □ *Time passes slowly* [not *slow*] *in prison.* □ *You'd better drive slow in this fog.*

◆ The comparative and superlative forms *slower* and *slowest* are more informal than *more slowly* and *most slowly*: □ *She eats more slowly/slower than you.* □ *Michael works the slowest/most slowly.* *Slower* may be preferred to *more slowly* when the adverb is preceded by *any*: □ *I can't walk any slower.*

The use of the adverb *slow* in fixed combinations, such as *slow-moving traffic, a go-slow*, etc., is acceptable in all contexts.

smart In modern usage the adjective *smart*, meaning 'intelligent', is often applied to devices that use sophisticated electronic technology: □ *smart card* (a plastic bank card with an integral microprocessor) □ *smart house* (a house with computer-controlled heating, lighting, etc.) □ *smart weapon* (a bomb or other missile that can be automatically guided to its target).

smear The increasing use of the noun *smear* to denote a defamatory attack, often involving slander or libel, is disliked by many users: □ *Their allegations of professional misconduct are the latest in a series of smears.* □ *the victim of a smear campaign.*

◆ The noun is particularly frequent in the headline language of popular newspapers.

smelled or **smelt?** Either word may be used as the past tense and past participle of the verb *smell*: □ *The cake smelled/smelt delicious.*

◆ See also **-ED OR -T?**

Smelled may be pronounced [smelt] or [smeld]; *smelt* is always pronounced [smelt].

so The phrase *so that*, expressing purpose, is sometimes reduced to *so* in informal contexts. In formal speech and writing the word *that* should be retained: □ *The gate had been left open so (that) we could drive in.*

◆ To introduce a result or consequence *so* may be used alone in all contexts: □ *The gate had been left open, so we drove in.*

The phrase *so as*, which also expresses purpose, is followed by an infinitive with *to* and should not be confused with *so that*: □ *She wore gloves so as not to leave fingerprints.* □ *She wore gloves so that* [not as] *she would not leave fingerprints. So as to* is best avoided where *to* would be adequate: □ *He closed the window (so as) to keep out the rain.*

See also **AS**; **IN ORDER THAT** AND **IN ORDER TO**; **SO-CALLED**.

so-called The adjective *so-called* is generally used in an ironic sense, implying that the following word is inaccurate or inappropriate: □ *a so-called friend* □ *their so-called supporters* □ *This year's so-called disastrous summer was actually quite good, the London Weather Centre said yesterday* (*Daily Telegraph*).

◆ The increasing use of the adjective in neutral contexts is disliked by some users: □ *The so-called black economy regularly comes under fire.*

Used without a hyphen after the noun it qualifies, *so called* may be interpreted more literally: □ *the peewit, so called because of its characteristic cry.*

sociable or **social**? *Sociable* means 'friendly', 'companionable', or 'convivial'; *social* means 'of society' or 'promoting companionship': □ *a sociable guest* □ *a sociable dinner party* □ *a social worker* □ *a social club.*

◆ The two adjectives are not interchangeable in these senses, although both may be applied to the same noun: □ *a sociable evening with friends at the pub* □ *a social evening for new members.*

Both words also mean 'gregarious', *sociable* being used in the sense of 'liking the company of others' and *social* in the sense of 'living with others': □ *She is more sociable than her sister, who hardly ever goes out.* □ *Ants are social insects.*

See also **ANTISOCIAL, ASOCIAL, UNSOCIAL, OR UNSOCIABLE**?

solidus The solidus is also known as the *stroke, slant, slash mark, oblique,* or *virgule.* Its main use is in separating alternatives: □ *A doctor must use his/her diagnostic skill in such cases.* □ *You need butter and/or margarine to make pastry.*

◆ It is also used, as in this book, to indicate that both of two alternatives are correct or appropriate: □ *a terrible/terrific amount of work.*

The solidus is used in the percentage sign %, and is sometimes used for writing fractions: □ *2/3.* It is used instead of the word *per* in expressions like: □ *35 km/hr.* It is used in certain abbreviations: □ *a/c* □ *c/o.* It is also used to separate successive time units: □ *the financial year 1994/95* □ *July/August* and in dates: □ *1/4/95.*

A further use of the solidus is to indicate the breaks in lines of verse, when a poem is not set out in its separate lines: □ *We are the hollow men/We are the stuffed men/Leaning together* (T.S. Eliot).

soluble or **solvable**? Either adjective may be used to describe something that can be solved: □ *a soluble/solvable problem. Soluble* is more frequently used to describe something that can be dissolved, especially something that dissolves easily in water: □ *soluble aspirin.*

somebody or **someone**? The pronoun *somebody* and its synonym *someone* are interchangeable in all contexts.

◆ Both are used with a singular verb but are sometimes followed by a plural personal pronoun or possessive adjective (see **THEY**): □ *Somebody/Someone has parked their car in our drive.*

somersault Note the spelling and pronunciation of this word, which means 'acrobatic roll'. The first two syllables are pronounced like *summer*, but are spelt *somer*-; the last syllable is pronounced like *salt*, but spelt *-sault*.

-something Many people dislike the frequent use of the words *twen-tysomething, thirtysomething, fortysomething*, etc., with refer-ence to people in their twenties/thirties/forties/etc. These words may be used as adjectives or nouns: □ *The studio panel was formed ... of five well-heeled thirtysomething artsy liberals (Sun-day Times)*. □ *If you admit to being thirtysomething ... the chances are that you'll have vivid memories of the Pathe News (Insight)*. □ *Are the thirtysomethings leaving childbearing too late for safety? (The Guardian)*.

◆ The expression derives originally from the popular 1980s American television series *Thirtysomething* that described the lives and lifestyles of a group of people born in the late 1940s or early 1950s and who had therefore reached their thirties during the 1980s.

sometime or **some time**? These spellings are occasionally confused. *Sometime* is used as an adverb to mean 'at some point in time': □ *I'll come and see you sometime*, and as an adjective to mean 'former': □ *Sir Percy Cooper, the sometime President of the Yachting Association*. *Some time* means 'a period of time': □ *I need some time to think.* □ *I've been worried about her for some time now.*

sooner see HARDLY.

sophisticated The adjective *sophisticated* is frequently applied to machines or devices, in the sense of 'complex' or 'advanced': □ *Our client ... develops and manufactures sophisticated electri-cal and electronic products and systems (Sunday Times)*.

◆ This usage may be extended to the methods or techniques involved in producing such equipment: □ *sophisticated technology*. When it is extended to people, however, there is a risk of confusion with the principal sense of the adjective, 'refined' or 'cultured': □ *the best-documented UFO case in history – one which has managed to perplex and astonish some of the most sophisticated scientists in the world (The Bookseller)*.

sort of see KIND OF.

sound bite A *sound bite* is a segment of a speech, especially one made by a politician, specifically designed to be extracted for news reports and media coverage. An example of a sound bite is the statement made by the then US President George Bush: □ *Read my lips: no new taxes*. Of American origin, the term is a vogue expression that is becoming increasingly common in Britain: □ *John Major has yet to come to terms with the vital technique of the prime ministerial sound bite (The Guardian)*.

source The use of the word *source* as a verb, meaning 'find a source', is disliked by many users: □ *He had difficulty sourcing the material for his thesis.*

◆ In commercial contexts the term *sourcing* is used with reference to the discovery of suppliers: □ *Responsible for a team of buyers and accountable for the effective sourcing and procurement of all the company's supplies (Executive Post)*.

south, South, or **southern**? As an adjective, *south* is always written with a capital *S* when it forms part of a proper name: □ *South Africa* □ *the South Pole*. The noun *south* is usually written with a capital *S* when it denotes a specific region, such as the southern states of the USA: □ *The secession of the South precipitated the American Civil War.*

◆ In other contexts, and as an adverb, *south* is usually written with a lower-case *s*: □ *Many birds fly south for the winter.* □ *Only the south wall of the city remains intact.* □ *The island of Tasmania lies to the south of Australia.*

The adjective *southern* is more frequent and usually less specific than the adjective *south*: □ *the southern slopes* □ *in southern Italy.*

Like *south*, *southern* is written with a capital *S* when it forms part of a proper name, such as *the Southern Cross.* With or without a capital *S*, it also means 'of the South': □ *speaking with a southern/Southern drawl.*

Soviet see RUSSIAN OR SOVIET?

sowed or **sown**? Either word may be used as the past participle of the verb *sow*, but *sown* is the more frequent: □ *I have sown/sowed some more parsley in the herb garden.*

◆ The past tense of the verb *sow* is always *sowed*: □ *They sowed the field with wheat.*

The verb *sow* and its derivatives should not be confused with *sew* (see SEWED OR SEWN?).

span see SPUN OR SPAN?

spatula The noun *spatula*, meaning 'flat-bladed utensil', is sometimes misspelt. Note that the word ends in -*a*, not -*ar* or -*er*.

-speak Some people object to the overuse of the suffix -*speak*, meaning 'jargon' or 'characteristic language', which is attached to nouns, proper names, or prefixes and is derived from the term *newspeak* coined by George Orwell in his novel *Nineteen Eighty-Four*: □ *computerspeak* □ *Thatcherspeak* □ *techspeak* □ *econospeak* □ *Joy-rides bill themselves as 'the travel sickness tablet for children', which is, to say the least, a cheeky bit of marketing-speak* (*Sunday Times*). See also -BABBLE.

◆ In view of its etymology, it is appropriate that the suffix should have established itself in the English language during the 1980s.

spearhead The verb *spearhead* is best avoided where *lead* would be adequate: □ *an opportunity exists for a profit-oriented manager who can spearhead the Company's continued expansion.*

speciality or **specialty**? *Speciality* is used in British English and *specialty* in American English to denote a special skill or interest or a product, service, etc., that is specialized in: □ *Wildlife photography is his speciality.* □ *Steak tartare is a speciality of the house.*

◆ In British English the noun *specialty* is sometimes used in place of *speciality.*

specially see ESPECIALLY OR SPECIALLY?

specialty see SPECIALITY OR SPECIALTY?

species This word is normally pronounced [*speesheez*]. The alternative pronunciation [*speeseez*] is avoided by careful users.

spectrum The noun *spectrum* is best avoided where *range* would be adequate or more appropriate: □ *a wide spectrum of experience* □ *across the whole spectrum* □ *at the other end of the political spectrum.*

◆ The noun *spectrum* principally denotes the series of colours produced when white light is dispersed. It has two plural forms, *spectra* and *spectrums.*

speeded or **sped**? *Sped* is the past tense and past participle of the verb *speed* in the sense of 'move or go quickly'; *speeded* relates to the sense of 'drive at excessive speed' and to the phrasal verb *speed up*, meaning 'accelerate': □ *We sped through the water.* □ *The days have sped by.* □ *He has never speeded on a motorway.* □ *The* *workers speeded up when the supervisor arrived.*

spelled or **spelt**? Either word may be used as the past tense and past participle of the verb *spell*: □ *Have I spelt/spelled your name right?*

◆ See also -ED OR -T? *Spelled* may be pronounced [spelt] or [speld]; *spelt* is always pronounced [spelt].

spelling English spelling is notoriously difficult to learn, for native English speakers as well as foreign students. However, it is to some extent governed by rules, some of which are described below.

◆ **1 Doubling of consonants** Final consonants are sometimes doubled when a suffix starting with a vowel is added. With single-syllable words this applies when the final consonant is preceded by a single vowel: □ *hit – hitting* □ *drop – dropped.* If the word has more than one syllable, the consonant is doubled if the last syllable is stressed and the final consonant is preceded by a single vowel: □ *refer – referred* □ *commit – committed.* Exceptions are words with a final -*l*, which is doubled even if the syllable is unstressed: □ *traveller* (but *traveler* in American English); and □ *worshipped* □ *handicapped* □ *kidnapped* (not always doubled in American English) □ *leapfrogged* □ *jetlagged* □ *outfitter.* A final -*c* is not doubled, but is changed to *ck* before a suffix beginning with a vowel: □ *panic – panicked.*

2 y and i When a suffix is added to a word that ends in -*y*, the *y* becomes an *i* only if the preceding letter is a consonant: □ *silly – sillier* □ *hurry – hurried.* Exceptions are: □ *said* □ *laid* □ *paid* and in words where a suffix beginning with an *i* is added, such as -*ing*: □ *try – trying.*

3 Final -e When a suffix beginning with a vowel is added to a word with a silent final -*e*, the *e* is dropped: □ *rate – rating.* A growing trend is to drop the -*e*- before the suffixes -*able* and -*age*: □ *likeable – likable* □ *sizeable – sizable* □ *mileage – milage.* If the word ends in -*ge* or -*ce* the *e* is not dropped before *a* and *o*: □ *outrageous* □ *peaceable.* The *e* is not dropped if the suffix begins with a consonant: □ *excitement*, except -*ly* (see **4** below).

4 -ly suffix When -*ly* is added to a word it remains unchanged except for the endings -*ll* and -*le* which change to -*lly* and -*ly*: □ *nice – nicely* □ *full – fully* □ *noble – nobly.* Exceptions are: □ *truly* □ *duly* □ *wholly.*

5 ie and ei The rule '*i* before *e* except after *c*' applies to most words where the sound those letters represent is [ee]: □ *believe* □ *grief* □ *deceive* □ *ceiling. Caffeine, protein, seize, species, weir,* and *weird* are exceptions. When the sound represented is [ay] then *ei* is used: □ *beige* □ *reign.*

See also -ABLE OR -IBLE?; -AE- AND -OE-; AMERICANISMS; -ANT OR -ENT?; -IZE OR -ISE?; PLURALS; and individual entries.

spelt see SPELLED OR SPELT?

spend The use of the word *spend* as a noun, meaning 'amount spent' or 'amount to be spent': □ *an advertising spend of £20,000*, is disliked by many people and is best replaced by an appropriate synonym or paraphrase.

spilled or **spilt**? Either word may be used as the past tense and past participle of the verb *spill*: □ *He has spilt/spilled his coffee.* □ *The children spilled/spilt out of the school.*

◆ See also -ED OR -T?

Spilt is the usual form of the adjective in British English: □ *It's no use crying over spilt milk.*

Spilled may be pronounced [spild] or [spilt]; *spilt* is always pronounced [spilt].

spin doctor A *spin doctor* is a person employed by a political party, government department, etc., to present or interpret facts or events in a favourable light: □ *Almost everyone who took part in the travelling circus of the election became so bewitched by the spin doctors, photo opportunities and in-jokes of each campaign that we lost sight of one fundamental reality (The Observer).* □ *He received help from Scotland Yard's own spin doctors (The Independent).* The term is a vogue expression of American origin, which is becoming increasingly common in Britain.

◆ The expression derives from the spin given to a ball in certain sports in order to control its direction through the air or the way in which it bounces.

split infinitive A *split infinitive* occurs when an adverb is inserted between *to* and the infinitive form of a verb: □ *to boldly go.* The practice is widely disliked but very widely used: □ *Captains on the bridge would be able to visually check what was happening on the car decks (The Guardian).*

◆ Split infinitives have a long history and the objection to them is comparatively recent. As with the opposition to ending sentences with prepositions, grammarians based their objections on the rules of Latin grammar.

Since so many people dislike split infinitives it is probably best to try to avoid them, at least in formal speech and writing. They can sound awkward or unpleasant, particularly when more than one word comes between *to* and the verb: □ *He tries to on the one hand explain* .... However, there are some sentences where it is preferable to split an infinitive in order to avoid ambiguity: □ *He failed to entirely comprehend me.* The revised ordering *He entirely failed to* ... or *He failed to comprehend me entirely* would suggest complete, not partial, failure. □ *We expect to further modernize our services.* The revised ordering *We expect further to modernize* ... suggests *moreover*. □ *They were plotting secretly to destroy the files.* Was the plotting or the intended destruction secret? □ *I would not expect anyone who has not read Joyce fully to understand the play.* Read Joyce fully or understand fully?

Another argument for disregarding the rule is that sometimes the rhythm of spoken English makes the split infinitive sound natural and its avoidance awkward. Compare: □ *I hope to really enjoy myself* with *I hope really to enjoy myself.*

spoiled or **spoilt**? Either word may be used as the past tense and past participle of the verb *spoil*: □ *The bad weather spoiled/spoilt our holiday.*

◆ See also **-ED OR -T**?

Spoilt is the usual form of the adjective in British English: □ *a spoilt child.*

Spoiled may be pronounced [spoild] or [spoilt]; *spoilt* is always pronounced [spoilt].

spontaneity The traditional pronunciation of this noun, meaning 'the quality of behaving in a natural, impulsive way', is [spon-tă*nee*iti] but the pronunciation [spontă*nay*iti] is probably more frequently heard.

spoonful Most users prefer to form the plural *-fuls*: □ *spoonfuls.* See **-FUL**.

spouse The use of the noun *spouse* in place of *husband* or *wife* is best avoided where the sex of the person is known: □ *The broadcaster Sue Baker and her husband* [not *spouse*] *were the guests of honour.*

◆ The words *spouse* and *spouses* may, however, serve as useful replacements for the phrases 'husband or wife', 'husbands and wives', etc., especially in formal contexts: □ *Please give details of any other properties owned by you or your spouse.* □ *Use of the car park is restricted to members and their spouses.*

The noun *spouse* is usually pronounced [spows], the pronunciation [spowz] being an accepted variant.

spun or **span**? *Spun* is the past tense and part participle of the verb *spin* in modern usage; *span* is an archaic form of the past tense: □ *He spun the wheel.* □ *This yarn has been spun by hand.*

squalor This word, meaning 'dirtiness; wretchedness': □ *the squalor of the slums*, is sometimes misspelt. In both British and American English the ending is *-or* as in *tremor*, not *-o(u)r* as in *colour*.

squeaky clean The adjective *squeaky clean*, which originated in advertising, is often used in the figurative sense of 'beyond reproach' or 'above suspicion': □ *the squeaky clean image of this generation of pop-stars* □ *The president must be squeaky clean.* Users of this expression should be aware of its possible derogatory connotations: there may be an implication that the person or thing so described is too good to be true.

stadiums or **stadia**? *Stadiums* is the more usual plural of the noun *stadium*, but either word may be used: □ *Safer soccer stadiums should be built throughout Britain in the wake of the Hillsborough disaster .... The task of providing appropriate stadia for the 1990s is almost beyond the ability of anyone (The Guardian).*

stalactite or **stalagmite**? *Stalactites* and *stalagmites* are tapering masses of calcium carbonate that form in limestone caves. A *stalactite* hangs from the roof; a *stalagmite* rises from the floor.

◆ The classic method of distinguishing between the two words is to associate the *c* of *stalactite* with that of *ceiling* and the *g* of *stalagmite* with that of *ground*.

stanch or **staunch**? Either word may be used as a verb, meaning 'stop (the flow of)', *staunch* being more frequent than *stanch* in modern usage: □ *I staunched/stanched the flow of blood with a handkerchief.* □ *She staunched/stanched the wound.* □ *This offer is no remedy to recruitment and retention problems within our universities:* □ *It won't staunch the brain drain (The Guardian).*

◆ *Stanch* is also a rare variant of the adjective *staunch*, meaning 'loyal' or 'firm': □ *a staunch supporter.*

The word *stanch* is pronounced [stahnch]. *Staunch* is occasionally pronounced in the same way, but its usual pronunciation is [stawnch], rhyming with *launch*.

standing or **stood**? The substitution of *stood*, the past participle of the verb *stand*, for the present participle *standing* is found in some dialects of English: □ *She was standing* [in some dialects *stood*] *in front of the mirror.*

◆ *Stood* is correctly used in the passive form of the transitive verb *stand*: □ *The bottle should be stood in a cool place for two hours.*

stank or **stunk**? Either word may be used as the past tense of the verb *stink*, but *stunk* is the only form of its past participle: □ *The room stank/stunk of cigarette smoke.* □ *These boots have stunk* [not *stank*] *of manure since my visit to the farm last week.*

state-of-the-art The adjective *state-of-the-art*, which relates to the current level of technical achievement, development, knowledge, etc., is disliked by some users: □ *Heart of the system is a state-of-the-art desktop copier with a host of time-saving features* (*Sunday Times*). □ *state-of-the-art computer technology.*

◆ It is best avoided where *modern* or *up-to-date* would be adequate or more appropriate: □ *They* [Venture Scouts] *use state-of-the-art camp stoves for cooking* (*Daily Telegraph*).

stationary or **stationery**? These two words are often confused. *Stationary* means 'not moving': □ *a stationary car*; *stationery* means 'writing materials': □ *office stationery.*

◆ To avoid confusion remember that *stationery* is sold by a *stationer*, a trader whose name, like *baker* and *grocer*, ends in *-er*.

statistics see -ICS.

status In British English the word *status* should be pronounced [*stay*tŭs], with the first syllable like *state*. The pronunciation [*stat*ŭs], with the first syllable as in *static*, is an American English variant.

staunch see STANCH OR STAUNCH?

stay or **stop**? The substitution of the verb *stop* for *stay* in the sense of 'reside temporarily' or 'remain' is found in some dialects of English: □ *We stayed* [in some dialects *stopped*] *with my sister for a few days.*

◆ The use of the verb *stop* with reference to a break in a journey is generally acceptable: □ *We stopped at my sister's house for a cup of tea on the way home.*

steal see BURGLE, ROB, OR STEAL?

step- see HALF- OR STEP-?

stereo- This word has the alternative pronunciations [*ster*riō] and [*steer*iō], both of which are acceptable, although the former is more frequent in contemporary usage.

stiletto Note the spelling of this word, which refers to a woman's shoe with a high narrow heel, particularly the *-l-* and the *-tt-*.

◆ The plural is either *stilettos* or *stilettoes*, the former being accepted by more authorities.

stimulant or **stimulus**? Both these nouns are used to denote something that stimulates activity. *Stimulant* is specifically applied to drugs, alcohol, etc., whereas *stimulus* is a more general synonym for 'incentive': □ *Caffeine is a stimulant.* □ *They responded to the stimulus of competition.* A *stimulant* increases activity; a *stimulus* initiates activity.

◆ The plural of *stimulus* is *stimuli*, which may be pronounced [*stimewlī*] or [*stimewlee*].

stimulate see SIMULATE OR STIMULATE?

stimulus see STIMULANT OR STIMULUS?

stoical The adjective *stoical*, meaning 'resigned to or unaffected by suffering': □ *a stoical attitude to death*, is pronounced [*stō*ikl]. The *-o-* and *-i-* are pronounced separately, not as the *oi* sound of *soil*.

◆ The word *stoic* may be used as a variant of *stoical* or as a noun: □ *She's a real stoic.*

Spelt with a capital *S-*, the noun and adjective *Stoic* refer to a school of ancient Greek philosophy.

stood see STANDING OR STOOD?

stop see STAY OR STOP?

storey or **story**? These two spellings are sometimes confused. The word *storey*, meaning 'level of a building': □ *He lives on the* *second storey.* □*a multi-storey car park*, is spelt with an *e*; the plural is *storeys*. A *story* means 'a tale': □*Tell me a story*; its plural is *stories*.

◆ In American English the sense 'level of a building' may also be spelt *story*, with the plural *stories*.

straight or **strait**? The word *straight* is most frequently used as an adjective or adverb: □*a straight line* □*I went straight there*. It is sometimes used as a noun, meaning 'straight line or part': □*the home straight* (of a racecourse). The word *strait* is an archaic adjective meaning 'narrow; restricted'; in modern usage it is most frequently found in the form of the plural noun *straits*, meaning 'difficult circumstances': □*in dire straits*. In the sense of 'narrow channel', the noun *strait* (or *straits*) also occurs in proper names: □*the Straits of Dover*.

◆ The two words have different origins: *straight* comes from the Old English *streccan* 'to stretch', whereas *strait* is ultimately derived from the Latin *stringere* 'to bind tightly'.

The two spellings are interchangeable only in certain compound words (see STRAITJACKET AND STRAITLACED). See also STRAIGHTENED OR STRAITENED?

straightaway or **straight away**? This expression, meaning 'without delay': □*I'll be going to the shops straightaway*, may be written as one word or two.

straightened or **straitened**? These words are sometimes confused. *Straightened* means 'made straight': □*The road has been straightened. Straitened*, which is derived from the archaic adjective *strait* (see STRAIGHT OR STRAIT?), means 'restricted': □*in straitened circumstances*.

strait see STRAIGHT OR STRAIT?

straitened see STRAIGHTENED OR STRAITENED?

straitjacket and **straitlaced** A *straitjacket*, a constricting jacket used to restrain a violent person, and also in extended senses, 'something that restricts', may also be spelt *straightjacket*: □*Eurotunnel will overnight make cross-Channel communications fast, efficient and dependable. A change from the straightjacket we're in now* (*Sunday Times*). In the same way, *straitlaced*, meaning 'puritanical', may also be spelt *straightlaced*: □*a very straitlaced maiden aunt*. See also STRAIGHT OR STRAIT?

strata see STRATUM OR STRATA?

stratagem or **strategy**? A *stratagem* is a scheme, trick, or ruse; *strategy* is the art of planning a campaign: □*to devise a new stratagem* □*the strategy involved in a game of chess*.

◆ The use of *strategy* in the extended sense of 'plan' or 'method' overlaps with that of *stratagem*.

Both nouns are ultimately derived from the Greek word for 'a general' and are principally applied to warfare, a *stratagem* being an artifice for deceiving the enemy and *strategy* being the science or art of conducting a war.

stratum or **strata**? *Strata* is the plural form of the noun *stratum*: □*from a different social stratum* □*in one of the upper strata of the rock*.

◆ The use of *strata* as a singular noun is wrong, but nevertheless is occurring with increasing frequency, especially in figurative contexts: □*that strata of society*.

street see ROAD OR STREET?

street- In such words and phrases as *streetwise* and *street credibility*, *street-* refers to the culture of young people, especially young

working-class inhabitants of the inner cities: □*a streetwise kid.*
□*This year's batch of school-leavers are optimisic and streetwise, according to a study commissioned by the TSB bank* (*The
Guardian*). The meaning has recently widened to include the
culture of those familiar with the latest trends, fashions, topical
issues, etc.: □*To be successful in the public relations industry,
you need more than just street credibility.* □*Ladas and Skodas
snubbed as car thieves opt for 'street cred'* (headline, *The Guardian*). See also -**CRED.**

◆ *Street* is occasionally used as an adjective in slang usage in its own
right, meaning 'accepted by young people or those familiar with the
latest trends, etc.': □*He isn't street enough.*

strength This word is sometimes mispronounced [strenth]. The correct pronunciation is [strength], but the variant pronunciation
[strenkth] is acceptable to most users.

stress Some languages have a fairly regular stress pattern but English
stress patterns are varied and subject to change over time. As
foreign words become absorbed into the English language they
often change their stress to a more English-sounding one:
□*bureau* □*chauffeur.*

◆ Two-syllable words are more likely to be stressed on the first
syllable, but when a word serves as both a noun (or adjective) and a
verb it is normally stressed on the first syllable as a noun (or adjective),
but the second as a verb: □*permit* □*rebel* □*present* □*conflict* □*insult*
□*absent.*

Most three-syllable words have their stress on the first syllable, and
several of those words which have their stress on the second are
widely coming to be pronounced with the stress on the first:
□*contribute* □*subsidence.* Words with four or more syllables usually
have their stress on the second or third syllable. Some people find
difficulty in pronouncing those multisyllabic words that traditionally
have been stressed on the first syllable and such words are coming
to be pronounced with the stress on a later syllable: □*applicable*
□*demonstrable* □*formidable.*

Individual words may be stressed in speech for emphasis. In written
and printed texts such words are indicated by italics: □I *like* walking
in the rain. See also **INTONATION.**

stringed or **strung**? *Stringed* is an adjective derived from the noun
string; *strung* is the past tense and past participle of the verb
string: □*a stringed instrument* □*a twelve-stringed guitar* □*His
squash racket was strung by an expert.* □*The children (have)
strung decorations around the room.*

◆ *Strung* is also used adjectivally before a noun, often in combination
with an adverb: □*a newly strung violin.*

student see **PUPIL OR STUDENT?**

stunk see **STANK OR STUNK?**

stupefy This word, meaning 'bewilder or amaze', is sometimes misspelt. Note the ending -*efy* (like *putrefy*), in spite of the spelling
of the related word *stupid.*

stupor This word, meaning 'a drowsy dazed state': □*in a drunken
stupor*, is sometimes misspelt. Note the final -*or*, as in *torpor*,
rather than -*our.*

subconscious or **unconscious**? Both these adjectives mean 'without
(full) awareness', but *subconscious* implies a greater degree of
consciousness than *unconscious*: □*a subconscious desire* □*unconscious resentment.*

◆ In psychology both words relate to parts of the mind that can influence behaviour.

Unconscious has the additional senses of 'not conscious', 'unaware', and 'unintentional': □ *He lay unconscious for two hours.* □ *They were unconscious of the danger.* □ *It was an unconscious insult.*

subject The *subject* of a clause or sentence is the noun, pronoun, or phrase that controls the verb (see also ACTIVE; PASSIVE). The subject usually precedes the verb, unless the clause or sentence is a question. In the sentence: □ *The dog buried the bone, the dog* is the subject. In the sentence: □ *Does he like them?*, the pronoun *he* is the subject.

◆ In more complex sentences, the subject may be a clause, such as *Why she resigned* in the sentence: □ *Why she resigned remains a mystery.*

The subject determines the form of the verb: a singular subject is used with a singular verb and a plural subject is used with a plural verb: □ *She often goes to the cinema* [singular subject *she*, singular verb *goes*]. □ *The children go to school by bus* [plural subject *children*, plural verb *go*]. □ *The legs of the table are loose.* In the last example, note that the verb agrees with *the legs*, not with *the table.*

Compare OBJECT. See also SINGULAR OR PLURAL?

subjective see OBJECTIVE OR SUBJECTIVE?

subjunctive The *subjunctive* is the grammatical set ('mood') of forms of a verb used to express possibilities or wishes rather than facts. With most verbs the subjunctive form is its basic form minus the *-s* ending of the third person singular, but *to be* has the past tense subjunctive *were*. The subjunctive is largely falling into disuse but survives in such idioms as: □ *be that as it may* □ *as it were* □ *far be it from me* □ *come what may.*

◆ The main use of subjunctives is in clauses introduced by *that* and expressing a proposal, desire, or necessity: □ *It is vital that she leave immediately.* □ *I suggested to Mark that he drop in for a coffee sometime.* □ *They demanded that he answer their questions.* This usage is more popular in American English than in British English, where *should* is often inserted before the verb: □ *It is vital that she should leave immediately.*

The other use of subjunctives is in clauses introduced by *if, though,* or *supposing*: □ *If you were to go, you might regret it.* □ *It's not as though he were a bachelor.* It is now very unusual to use such a construction with any subjunctive form other than *were.*

See also IF; WERE OR WAS?

subordinate clause see CLAUSE.

subpoena This word, as a noun referring to a writ requiring a person to appear in court, is sometimes misspelt. Note particularly the *-oe-*. The pronunciations [sŭb*pee*nă] or [sŭ*pee*nă] are both acceptable.

◆ The word comes from the Latin *sub poena*, meaning 'under penalty'.

The present participle of the verb *subpoena* 'issue with a subpoena' is *subpoenaing*; the past tense and past participle are *subpoenaed*, pronounced [*-pee*nĕd].

subsequent see CONSEQUENT OR SUBSEQUENT?

subsidence The traditional pronunciation of this word, which means 'falling or sinking': □ *cracks due to subsidence*, is [sŭb*sī*dĕns].

◆ The alternative pronunciation [*subsi*dĕns] is also widely used and is generally acceptable.

subsidiarity The noun *subsidiarity* is often used in the context of the

European Community, where it refers to the principle that political decisions should be made at the lowest level. Thus some issues may be dealt with by countries that belong to the EC rather than by the EC itself.

subsidiary The noun and adjective *subsidiary*, which means 'auxiliary; subordinate', is sometimes misspelt. Note that the word ends in *-iary*, not *-uary* or *-ary*.

substantial or **substantive**? Both these adjectives refer to the basic substance or essence of something, but neither is in frequent use in this sense. *Substantial* usually means 'of considerable size, importance, etc.': □ *a substantial improvement* □ *a substantial meal*. *Substantive*, a rarer word, is used to mean 'real; firm': □ *substantive measures to curb inflation*.

◆ In grammar, the word *substantive* is a noun or adjective relating to words that have the function of a noun.

Note that *substantial* is stressed on the second syllable [sŭb*stan*shăl] and *substantive* on the first syllable [*sub*stăntiv].

Some people object to the use of *substantial* as a pretentious synonym for 'large', 'big', etc.: □ *a substantial pay rise*.

substitute see REPLACE OR SUBSTITUTE?

subsume The verb *subsume* means 'incorporate within a larger category or group' or 'classify under a general rule or heading'; it should not be used as a pretentious synonym for 'include' or 'contain': □ *The concept of a classless society is subsumed within the doctrine of Marxism*.

succeed see ACCEDE OR EXCEED?

successfully or **successively**? These two adverbs are sometimes confused. *Successfully* means 'with success'; *successively* means 'in succession': □ *The surgeons operated successfully*. □ *The sales figures fell for several months successively*.

such The use of the construction *such ... that* (or *such ... who*) in place of *such ... as* is avoided by careful users: □ *such tools as* [not *that*] *are needed for the job* □ *such people as* [not *who*] *are eligible for supplementary benefit*.

◆ The construction *such ... that* may, however, be used to indicate a result: □ *He earns such a pittance that he can't afford to buy food for his family*.

The use of *such* or *such a/an* before an adjective preceding a noun, in the sense of 'so' or 'very', is disliked by a few users but acceptable to most: □ *Such careless driving should not go unpunished*. □ *I have never seen such a small house*. □ *You have such beautiful clothes*. □ *It was such a difficult question*.

See also SUCH AS OR LIKE?

such as or **like**? *Such as* introduces an example; *like* introduces a comparison: □ *Dairy products, such as milk and cheese, should be kept in a cool place*. □ *Dairy products, like fresh meat, should be kept in a cool place*. □ He directed several horror films, such as *Dracula*. □ He directed several horror films like *Dracula*.

◆ The potentially ambiguous use of *like* in place of *such as* is disliked by some people but frequently occurs in general usage: □ *He gave Danielle gifts like a £1,500 ruby and diamond necklace, a matching ring and earrings* (*Daily Telegraph*). The use of *such as* in place of *like* is largely restricted to formal contexts: □ *Shoes such as these are ideal for indoor sports*.

Careful users avoid substituting *such as* for *as*: □ *When the Post Office is closed, as* [not *such as*] *on Sundays, stamps may be obtained from the machine outside.* □ *The pizza can be cooked in a number of ways, as by* [not *such as by*] *baking it in a hot oven for twenty minutes.* In the second example *as by* may be replaced by *such as.*

suffer from or **suffer with**? *Suffer from* means 'have (an illness or disability)'; *suffer with* means 'experience pain or discomfort because of (an illness or disability)': □ *I suffer from hay fever.* □ *I have been suffering with my hay fever today.*

◆ *Suffer with* is often followed by a possessive. It should not be used in place of *suffer from.*

suffixes see PREFIXES AND SUFFIXES.

suit or **suite**? These two nouns should not be confused. A *suit* is a set of clothes, one of the four sets of playing cards, or an action in a court of law: □ *a trouser suit* □ *to follow suit* □ *a lawsuit.* A *suite* is a set of furniture, a set of rooms, or a musical composition with several movements: □ *to reupholster a suite* □ *the honeymoon suite* □ *a ballet suite.*

◆ *Suit* and *suite* are most frequently confused in the expressions *three-piece suit* (a pair of trousers, a jacket, and a waistcoat) and *three-piece suite* (a sofa and two armchairs).

Note the difference in pronunciation between the two words: *suite* is pronounced [sweet]; *suit* is pronounced [soot] or [syoot], although the last of these pronunciations is becoming less frequent and may be considered old-fashioned.

summon or **summons**? To *summon* is to send for, call upon, or muster; to *summons* is to serve with a legal summons (an order to appear in court): □ *I was summoned to the managing director's office.* □ *He was summonsed for speeding.*

◆ The verb *summon* may be used in place of the verb *summons*: □ *He was summoned for speeding.*

Of the two words only *summons* is used as a noun: □ *I received a summons from the managing director.* □ *He received a summons for speeding.*

sunk, sunken see SANK, SUNK, OR SUNKEN?

super- Some people object to the frequent use of the prefix *super-*, in the sense of 'surpassing all others' or 'to an excessive degree', to coin new nouns and adjectives: □ *a superbug that is resistant to most antibiotics* □ *those superfit people who put the rest of us to shame.*

◆ See also MACRO- AND MICRO-; MEGA-.

supercilious This word, meaning 'haughty in a condescending disdainful manner', is sometimes misspelt. Note the single *c* and single *l.*

superlative see COMPARATIVE AND SUPERLATIVE.

supersede This word, meaning 'replace', is sometimes misspelt. The most frequent mistake is to confuse the *-sede* ending with the -*cede* ending of *precede.*

◆ *Supersede* comes from the Latin *supersedēre,* 'to sit above'.

supervise *Supervise*, meaning 'oversee': □ *She supervised the plans for the party,* is sometimes misspelt; the *-ise* ending cannot be spelt *-ize*: see -IZE OR -ISE?

◆ Note also the *-or* ending of *supervisor*, not *-er.*

supine see PROSTRATE, PRONE, OR SUPINE?

supper see DINNER, LUNCH, TEA, OR SUPPER?

supplement see COMPLEMENT OR SUPPLEMENT?

suppose or **supposing**? Either word may be used to introduce a suggestion or hypothesis, *suppose* being preferred by some users in formal contexts: □ *Suppose/Supposing we sell the car?* □ *Suppose/Supposing the train is late.*

◆ Only *supposing* can be used in the sense of 'if' or 'assuming': □ *I'll buy her some chocolates on the way home, supposing the corner shop is still open.*

suppress see OPPRESS, REPRESS, OR SUPPRESS?

surprised *Surprised* is followed by the preposition *by* in the sense of 'taken unawares' and by *at* in the sense of 'amazed': □ *The thief was surprised by the owner of the car.* □ *I was surprised at her ignorance.*

◆ In the second sense *surprised* may also be followed by an infinitive with *to* or a clause introduced by *that*: □ *He was surprised to see you.* □ *They were surprised that we won.*

The idiomatic use of a **DOUBLE NEGATIVE** in such sentences as *I shouldn't be surprised if it doesn't rain* is acceptable to most users in informal contexts, provided that the meaning is clear. The construction is best avoided if there is a risk of ambiguity.

surveillance This word, meaning 'careful observation', is usually pronounced [servaylĕns]. The pronunciation [servayĕns], imitating the French original, sounds rather affected.

susceptible The adjective *susceptible* is followed by the preposition *to* in the sense of 'easily influenced or affected' and by *of* in the formal sense of 'capable' or 'admitting': □ *susceptible to flattery* □ *susceptible to hay fever* □ *susceptible of a different interpretation.*

◆ Note that *susceptible* ends in *-ible*, not *-able*. The *-sc-* combination can also cause spelling mistakes.

suspect or **suspicious**? The word *suspect* may be used as a verb, noun, or adjective. *Suspicious* functions only as an adjective. In its adjectival sense of 'causing suspicion' or 'open to suspicion', *suspect* is sometimes virtually synonymous with *suspicious*: □ *a suspect/suspicious package* □ *The scheme sounds rather suspect/suspicious.* However, only *suspicious* can be used in the sense of 'feeling or showing suspicion': □ *The police were suspicious* [not *suspect*] *of her behaviour.* Similarly, only *suspect* can be used in the sense of 'possibly false or unreliable': □ *a suspect banknote* □ *The braking system is suspect.*

◆ Note the difference in pronunciation between the verb *suspect*, which is stressed on the second syllable [sŭs*pekt*], and the noun and adjective, stressed on the first syllable [*sus*pekt].

suspense or **suspension**? Both these nouns are derived from the verb *suspend*, meaning 'hang'. *Suspense* is largely restricted to the figurative sense of 'a state of uncertainty, anxiety, insecurity, or excitement': □ *Don't keep me in suspense any longer! Suspension* means 'the act of suspending' or 'the state of being suspended'; it is also used in the figurative senses of 'interruption; deferment; postponement' and 'temporary debarment or expulsion': □ *the suspension of an insurance policy* □ *The offending players face suspension from the team.* The two nouns are not interchangeable in any context.

suspicious see SUSPECT OR SUSPICIOUS?

sustainable In modern usage the adjective *sustainable* has developed a specialized application to natural resources that can be renewed: □ *sustainable forests,* and to activities that do not damage the environment: □ *sustainable development.*

swam or **swum**? *Swam* is the past tense of the verb *swim*; *swum* is the past participle: □ *The dog swam to the shore.* □ *the lake where they had swum.*

swap or **swop**? Both spellings are acceptable for this informal word meaning 'exchange': □ *to swap stamps* □ *swop homes for a holiday. Swap* is the more traditional spelling, but *swop* is a frequently used variation.
◆ The Middle English *swappen* from which the word originates meant 'to strike' from the custom of striking or shaking hands on a bargain.

swat or **swot**? These spellings are sometimes confused. *Swat* means 'strike with a blow': □ *to swat flies.* This word may also be spelt *swot*, although this spelling is disliked by many careful users. *Swot* is an informal word meaning 'study hard': □ *swotting for exams.*

sweet see DESSERT, SWEET, PUDDING, OR AFTERS?

swelled or **swollen**? Either word may be used as the past participle of the verb *swell. Swelled* is the more neutral form; *swollen* often indicates an undesirable or harmful increase or expansion: □ *The population has swelled in recent years.* □ *The disaster fund was swelled by a generous contribution from the mayor.* □ *His wrist has swollen to twice its normal size.* □ *The stream was swollen by the melted snow.*
◆ The past tense of *swell* is always *swelled*: □ *The population swelled.* □ *His wrist swelled.*
Swollen is the usual form of the adjective: □ *She crammed a few more sweets into her swollen pockets.* □ *My ankle is badly swollen.* The adjective *swelled* is largely restricted to the informal American English phrase *swelled head*, denoting conceit, which is usually replaced by *swollen head* in British English.

swingeing Note the pronunciation and spelling of this word, which means 'severe': □ *swingeing cuts in public expenditure* □ *swingeing tax increases.* The word is pronounced [*swin*jing]; the *-e-* distinguishes it from *swinging* and indicates the softness of the *g*. See also SPELLING 3.
◆ The word derives from Old English *swengan* 'to beat or flog'.

swollen see SWELLED OR SWOLLEN?

swop see SWAP OR SWOP?

swot see SWAT OR SWOT?

syllable A *syllable* is a unit of a word that contains a vowel sound or something that resembles a vowel sound. The words *by, tune,* and *through* have one syllable; the words *doctor, table,* and *open* have two syllables; the word *secretary* has three syllables if the *a* is not sounded and four syllables if the *a* is sounded.

syllabus The plural of this word, which means 'the subjects studied in a particular course', is usually *syllabuses. Syllabi*, pronounced [-bī], is the less frequent plural form.

symbol see CYMBAL OR SYMBOL?

syndrome Some people object to the frequent use of the noun *syndrome* in nonmedical contexts to denote any set of characteristics, actions, emotions, etc.: □ *She is suffering from the only-child syndrome.*
◆ In medicine the noun *syndrome* denotes a group of signs and symptoms that indicate a physical or mental disorder: □ *Down's syndrome.*

synergy In technical contexts the noun *synergy*, pronounced with a soft *g* sound [*sin*ĕji], denotes the combined action and increased effect of two or more drugs, muscles, etc., working together. The introduction of the noun *synergy* into general usage is disliked by some: □ *Synergy, as business people know, is bringing several elements together to make a product greater than the parts* (Islwyn Borough Council advertisement). □ [of the Cadbury-Schweppes merger] *The growth of vending machines has provided the magic synergy which such mergers are always supposed to produce* (*The Guardian*).

◆ The concept of synergy is sometimes explained in mathematical terms as $2 + 2 = 5$.

synonymous Note the spelling of this word, particularly the vowel sequence *-y-o-y-o-*.

◆ The phrase *synonymous with* literally means 'being a synonym of', but in general contexts it is frequently used in the sense of 'closely associated with': □ *The verb 'jump' is synonymous with 'leap'.* □ *Our name is synonymous with excellence.* □ *The Porsche car is synonymous with the yuppie lifestyle.*

syphon see SIPHON OR SYPHON?

systematic or **systemic**? The adjective *systematic* means 'methodical; well-ordered; well-planned': □ *a systematic approach to the problem* □ *You must try to be more systematic.* A rare synonym of *systematic*, the adjective *systemic* is most frequently found in biological contexts in the sense of 'affecting or spreading through the whole system, body, plant, etc': □ *a systemic disease* □ *a systemic fungicide.*

-t see -ED OR -T?

tactics see -ICS.

tag question see QUESTIONS.

take on board The informal phrase *take on board* means 'accept (a situation, new idea, etc.)': □ *We can't ignore the fact that there has been an over-production of titles, and this is a lesson everyone is having to take on board* (*The Bookseller*). This vogue expression is disliked by some people and should not be overused.

tall see HIGH OR TALL?

target The noun *target* is now most frequently used in its metaphorical meaning of 'an aim or goal'. The verb form is more recent, and is often followed by *on* or *at*: □ *The advertising campaign is to be carefully targeted at the 18–25 age group.* □ *a benefit which is easy to understand, popular, fair, ... and actually targets those who genuinely need it* (*The Guardian*).

◆ Although many people object to the use of *target* as a verb, it has a long history: the *Oxford English Dictionary* cites an example from 1837.

Note that the final *t* is not doubled in front of suffixes: □ *targeted* □ *targeting*.

Target is often used in expressions such as *target date*, meaning 'the date set for the completion of work, etc.': □ *target markets* □ *consumer-targeted material*.

tariff This word is sometimes misspelt. Note the single *r* and the *-ff* ending.

task force A *task force* is a group of people formed in order to undertake a particular objective, usually of a military nature: □ *The captain led a task force to blow up the bridge.*

◆ The most frequent use refers to subsections of the armed forces dispatched to deal with particular crises. However, it is sometimes used in a civilian context: □ *A Home Office task force is to investigate the rise in crime*.

tasteful or **tasty**? These two adjectives relate to different senses of the word *taste*. *Tasteful* is applied to things that indicate good taste, in the sense of 'aesthetic discrimination'; *tasty* is applied to things that have a good taste, in the sense of 'flavour': □ *tasteful furnishings* □ *a tasty meal*. Careful users maintain the distinction between the two words.

◆ *Tasty* also has the slang meaning of 'sexually attractive', used by men when talking of women: □ *His sister's rather tasty*, and is sometimes used to mean 'excellent; notable': □ *a tasty song* □ *a tasty little villain*. Some people object to these extended usages.

tautology *Tautology* is the avoidable repetition of an idea already expressed in different words: □ *a new innovation* □ *a brief moment*. Many well-established English phrases contain

333

tautologies: □ *circle round* □ *free gift* □ *join together* □ *all-time record*, etc.

◆ It is not difficult to avoid the cruder tautologies: □ *a dead corpse* □ *an empty bottle with nothing in it*, but many tautologies arise unintentionally from carelessness about the meanings of words. To speak of *unlawful murder* is tautologous because *murder* means 'unlawful killing'. In □ *She repeated it again*, *again* is redundant as *repeat* means 'to say again'. People also speak of □ *SALT talks* □ *OPEC countries* □ *a YTS scheme*, presumably not realizing that the word following the abbreviation is a repetition of the final word of the abbreviation.

Tautologies are in general to be avoided but can sometimes be used deliberately for emphasis: □ *a tiny wee mite*.

tea see DINNER, LUNCH, TEA, OR SUPPER?

teach see LEARN OR TEACH?

team or **teem**? These two words are sometimes confused, being identical in pronunciation. *Team* is most frequently used as a noun, meaning 'group of people (or animals) who work or play together': □ *a valuable member of the sales team* □ *the captain of the hockey team* □ *a team of oxen*. *Teem* is a verb, meaning 'pour' or 'abound': □ *It was teeming with rain.* □ *The village was teeming with tourists.*

◆ The word *team* is also used as a verb, often followed by *up*, meaning 'join to make a team': □ *Michael teamed up with Peter*.

technical or **technological**? *Technical* means 'having or concerned with special practical knowledge of a scientific or mechanical subject'; *technological* means 'using science for practical purposes' and is used particularly of modern advances in technical processes: □ *technical skills* □ *a technical college* □ *a technological breakthrough*.

◆ A second meaning of the word *technical* is 'marked by a strict interpretation of law or a set of rules': □ *a technical offence* □ *a technical advantage*.

techno- The prefix *techno-* relates to art, craft, technology, or technical matters. Some people object to its frequent use in the coining of new words in the sense of 'relating to high technology, especially computers'. *Techno-* may be used with or without a hyphen: □ *technophobia* □ *technofreak* □ *techno-politics*. See also HI-TECH.

technological see TECHNICAL OR TECHNOLOGICAL?

teem see TEAM OR TEEM?

tele- The prefix *tele-*, from a Greek word meaning 'far', is found in such words as *television, telephone, telescope*, etc. It is increasingly used in the senses of 'relating to television' or 'by telephone': □ *telebook* □ *telecast* □ *televangelism* □ *teleshopping* □ *telemarketing* □ *teleworking* □ *Telecommuting is the name given to working from home by linking up to your office computer over the telephone line* (*The Guardian*). These neologisms are disliked by some people, despite the fact that most of them retain the original sense of 'far', since a thing transmitted by television or telephone must originate at a distance.

telephone see PHONE.

televise This word is often spelt incorrectly with a *z* instead of an *s*.

◆ To avoid mistakes remember that the *s* in *television* remains unchanged. *Televise* is one of the verbs ending in *-ise* that cannot be spelt *-ize*: see -IZE OR -ISE?

temerity or **timidity**? The word *temerity* is sometimes mistakenly used where *timidity* is intended, though their meanings are completely different. *Temerity* means 'audacity or recklessness'; *timidity* means 'lacking courage or self-confidence; easily frightened or alarmed'.

◆ The two words are not exact opposites. The opposite of *timidity* is *courage* or *confidence*, which have positive connotations, whereas *temerity* has negative ones. It suggests a rash contempt of danger or disapproval, with a lack of reserve that may be interpreted as ill-mannered: □ *He had the temerity to interrupt the meeting.*

temperature *Temperature* can mean 'the degree of heat or cold as measured on, for example, a thermometer'; 'the degree of heat natural to the body'; 'abnormally high body heat'. To *take someone's temperature* means 'to use a thermometer to find the person's body heat'.

◆ The word is often used as a synonym for *fever*: □ *running a temperature* □ *She's got a temperature*, but this is best avoided in writing and formal contexts. A metaphorical use of *temperature* describes the emotional state of a group of people: the *temperature* is raised or low according to whether they are agitated or calm.

temporary The adjective *temporary* may be pronounced as a three- or four-syllable word, with the stress on the first syllable: [*tem*prări] or [*tem*pŏrări]. The four-syllable pronunciation is preferred by some careful users.

◆ The pronunciation [*tem*pări], omitting the [-(ŏ)r-] sound, is widely regarded as careless or incorrect.

The adverb *temporarily* should be stressed on the first syllable in British English; the pronunciation [tempŏ*rai*rili] is restricted to American English.

temporize see EXTEMPORIZE OR TEMPORIZE?

tense The *tense* of a verb is a set of forms expressing distinctions of time. Some modern grammarians tend to say that fundamentally there are only two real tenses in English, the *present*: □ *It is hot today*, and the *past*: □ *It was cloudy yesterday*. The *future* is simply formed by the addition of *will* or *shall*, etc.: □ *It will be fine tomorrow*, and all other changes of tense are marked by using *be*, *have*, or both combined, with the past or present participle of the verb: □ *She is dancing.* □ *He was talking.* □ *I'll be thinking of you.* □ *They had ridden for three days.* □ *I shall have finished it by then.* □ *They had slept until noon.* □ *He had been praying.* □ *She has been working.* □ *They will have been travelling all day.*

◆ The tense system becomes more complicated when there is more than one verb in a sentence. In such sentences there is a main clause, containing the most important verb, and a subordinate clause or clauses containing the other verb(s): □ *I thought that I knew him*. Here the main clause *I thought* is in the past tense, and the subordinate clause *that I knew him* follows the lead of the main clause and is in the same tense. This is by no means always the case, for it is quite possible for the clauses to refer to different times: □ *I believe I met him last week*. When the main clause is in the future, the verb of the subordinate clause is usually in the present: □ *I will look him up when I go to London*. When the main clause is in the past but the subordinate clause expresses some permanent fact, then that clause can be in the present: □ *She had learnt that Paris is a capital city*. In sentences referring to the future as viewed from the past, the subordinate verb

usually changes to the past tense: □ *I hope they will succeed*
becomes *I hoped they would succeed.*

The present tense is not used solely in expressions of events in the
present. It is frequently used to express the future: □ *I leave on
Thursday.* □ *The President speaks to the nation tonight.* The present
is also habitually used in newspaper headlines to describe past
events: □ *Van makes U-turn into path of coach* (*The Times*).

The tense that is generally used for expressing recent events or
actions is the *present perfect*, which is formed by adding *have* to the
past participle of a verb: □ *You've already told me.* □ *He's just seen his
mother.* □ *Has she turned up yet?* In informal American English the
simple past tense is used in such sentences: □ *You already told me.*
□ *He just saw his mother.* □ *Did she turn up yet?* and this form is also
beginning to be used in British English. See also **PARTICIPLES**;
SUBJUNCTIVE; **VERBS**.

terminal or **terminus**? Used as a noun meaning 'end or finishing point'
these words are often synonymous. Both can mean the finishing
point of a transport line, but in Britain *terminal* is used for air-
lines, *terminus* for railways, while either can be used for bus
routes. *Terminal* as an adjective can mean 'of, at, the end' or
'leading to death': □ *a terminal illness.*
◆ Other meanings of *terminal* as a noun include: 'a device on a wire
or battery for an electrical connection', and 'an instrument through
which a user can communicate with a computer'.

terminate *Terminate*, meaning 'bring to an end, form the ending
of, close', is increasingly used in the context of ending employment. From speaking of *terminating someone's contract*, etc.,
some people have gone on to use *terminated* as a synonym for
dismissed: □ *The workers were terminated when profits fell.*
◆ *Terminate* is also used of buses and trains to mean 'stop at a
particular place and go no further': □ *This train terminates here.*
Another popular use relates to ending pregnancies. A *termination* is
synonymous with an *abortion*.
Terminated, with the addition of *with* or *in*, is a fashionable
alternative to *resulted in* in sports commentaries: □ *The match
terminated in a draw.*

terminus see **TERMINAL** OR **TERMINUS**?

terrible or **terrific**? *Terrible* can be used as a general term of disapproval or can mean 'very bad' or 'causing distress': □ *a terrible
singer* □ *a terrible accident* □ *a terrible sight.* *Terrific*, on the other
hand, expresses approval: □ *Chartres has a terrific cathedral.*
Both can mean 'unusually great': □ *There's a terrible/terrific
amount of paperwork here.*
◆ The adverbs *terribly* and *terrifically* may be used as intensifiers to
express either approval or disapproval: □ *a terribly/terrifically dull
lecture* □ *a terribly/terrifically good book.*
While both words derive from *terror*, they are now far removed from
any suggestion of fear. Both should be restricted to informal contexts.

tête-à-tête This compound, meaning 'intimate conversation between
two people', is of French origin. Note the accents, which should
not be omitted when the term is used in English texts.
◆ The anglicized pronunciation is [taytah*tayt*].

than *Than* is used to link two halves of comparisons or contrasts:
□ *Jack is taller than Jill.* □ *I am wiser now than I was at that time.*
◆ Care must be taken with pronouns following *than*. The general rule
is to remember the missing verb: □ *You are older than I (am).* If there

is no obvious implied verb the object form follows: □ *Rather you than me!* However, the form that is considered correct by careful users sometimes sounds stilted: □ *She runs faster than he* is correct, but *She runs faster than him* is more frequently used. □ *She runs faster than he does* is both correct and natural-sounding.

thankfully As an adverb from *thank*, *thankfully* means 'in a thankful, relieved, or grateful way': □ *They received the good news thankfully*. It is also used to mean 'it is a matter of relief that': □ *Thankfully, he has survived the operation.*

◆ Many people dislike the second use of *thankfully*, although it is not as widely objected to as the similar use of **HOPEFULLY**. It can also occasionally lead to such ambiguous statements as: □ *Thankfully, she went to church on Sunday.*

thank you *Thank you, thanks, many thanks*, etc., are expressions of gratitude: □ *Thank you for a lovely evening.* They are also used in acceptance: □ *'Have a sweet.' 'Thanks, I will.'*, as a polite refusal in conjunction with *no*: □ *'Have a sweet.' 'No, thanks.'*, in a firm and less polite refusal: □ *I can manage without your advice, thank you very much*, and to show pleasure: □ *Now David's got a new job, we're doing very nicely, thank you very much.*

◆ *Thanks* can indicate responsibility or blame: □ *Thanks to your coaching, I passed my exam.* □ *Thanks to their incompetence, we lost the contract.* Thank heavens, thank goodness, and thank God are general expressions of relief: □ *Thank heavens you're all right.* □ *'Peace has been declared.' 'Thank goodness!'*

Thank you is sometimes spelt as one word or hyphenated, when it is used as a noun or attributively: □ *We said our thankyous and left.* □ *a thank-you letter.*

that *That* is used as a conjunction or relative pronoun to introduce various types of clause, and in some cases can be omitted, both in written and spoken English. As a conjunction it can usually be omitted: □ *I'm sure (that) you're lying.* It cannot be left out when used with a noun: □ *the fact that grass is green*, or with certain verbs, usually of a formal nature, for example *assert, contend*. It must not be left out when its omission could lead to ambiguity: □ *I said last week you were wrong* might mean either 'I said that last week you were wrong' or 'I said last week that you were wrong'.

◆ Used as a relative pronoun *that* can be omitted when it is the object: □ *the man (that) I love*, but not when it is the subject: □ *the thing that upsets me.*

The use of *that* as an adverb: □ *He's not that fat* is best avoided in formal contexts.

that or **this**? The difference between the pronouns *that* and *this*, referring to objects or people, is one of distance. *That* is further away from the speaker than *this*: □ *Give me that.* □ *Take this.*

◆ When the pronouns represent abstract concepts, *that* traditionally refers to something in the past (or something previously mentioned), whereas *this* refers to something in the future (or something about to be mentioned): □ *This is what I want you to do.* □ *That is what I expected you to do.* The use of *this* in place of *that* in such contexts may be ambiguous and is best avoided.

that or **which**? Whether to use *that* or *which* depends on whether it appears in a defining or non-defining clause. *That* and *which* are both used in defining clauses: □ *the school that/which they go to.* Note that a defining clause is not preceded by a comma. In non-defining clauses, those conveying parenthetical or incidental information, only *which* can be used: □ *The programme, which was broadcast by the BBC, caused much controversy.* Non-defining clauses are always preceded by a comma and, unless at the end of a sentence, followed by one. On the use of *that* or *who/whom*, see **WHO**.

◆ Some people dislike the use of *which* in defining clauses, maintaining that only *that* can be used. However, the usage described above is widespread and generally accepted. *Which* is also useful to relieve a sentence that already has several *that*'s: □ *His Ford Capri. He remembered that that was the car which* [not *that*] *had run out of petrol on the M1.*

the *The* is the most frequently used word in the English language. Its pronunciation is usually a straightforward matter. Before consonants it is pronounced [dhĕ]; before vowels or an unaspirated *h* it is pronounced [dhee]. The use of [dhee] before consonants has become frequent in recent years, particularly by broadcasters, but it is disliked by many people.

◆ One use of *the* is to single out one of a class as the best or most significant of a class: □ *Is that* the *Harold Wilson?* □ *It's the place to go for curry.* In these cases *the* is emphasized and pronounced [dhee].

theft see **BURGLE, ROB, OR STEAL?**

their, **there**, or **they're**? These three words are sometimes confused. *Their* means 'of them or belonging to them': □ *their house.* *There* means 'in or to that place': □ *over there. They're* is a contraction of *they are*: □ *They're/They are always late.*

◆ Another frequent mistake is the wrong spelling of *theirs* as *their's.* The correct usage is as in: □ *The car was theirs.*
See also **THEY**.

them or **their**? see **-ING FORMS**.

theme park A *theme park* is an amusement park in which the displays and entertainments are organized round one particular idea or group of ideas, e.g. space travel or the Wild West.

◆ The expression is of American origin, and, according to the *Oxford English Dictionary*, the earliest quotation of its usage is 1960.

themself The reflexive pronoun *themself* is unacceptable to careful users, being associated with the controversial singular usage of *they, them, their*, etc. (see **THEY**): □ *Somebody has been helping themself to my whisky.* □ *Walking through Pilsen, the casual observer might easily think themself back in 1945* (*The Times*, cited in *English Today*).

◆ The plural reflexive pronoun *themselves* is no more correct in such contexts, and *themself* should be replaced by *himself* or *herself* or the sentence rephrased.

thence *Thence* is a formal and almost archaic word with three meanings: 'from there, from that place': □ *We drove to York and thence to Scotland*; 'from that premise, or for that reason': □ *She proved that x was an even number and thence that it must be 42*; and 'from that time': □ *His wife died ten years ago and thence he has become a recluse.*

◆ As *from* is contained in the meaning of *thence* it is incorrect to say *from thence* (see **HENCE; WHENCE**).
Thence is sometimes mistakenly used to mean 'to there', instead of the even more archaic *thither*.

there see **THEIR, THERE, OR THEY'RE?**
there are see **THERE IS OR THERE ARE?**

therefore *Therefore* means 'for that reason, consequently, as this proves': □ *I dislike worms; therefore I avoid digging the garden.* □ *Scotland is part of Great Britain; therefore the Scots are British.*

◆ *Therefore* normally appears at the beginning of a clause and is not followed by a comma. If it appears parenthetically within a clause it has a comma before and after: □ *It appears, therefore, that he must be guilty.*

there is or **there are**? Normally, *there is* should precede a singular noun, and *there are* a plural: □ *There is a pine.* □ *There are cedars.* However, *there is* is widely used in various expressions where *there are* is formally correct.

◆ These include situations where the plural noun is regarded as a single unit: □ *There is three tons of coal here*; where the first of a list of nouns is singular: □ *There is a rabbit, two gerbils, and some white mice*; where two nouns are regarded as a single entity: □ *There is fish and chips for supper*; and where one is considering a situation in its entirety: □ *There is my job and career prospects at stake.*

The use of the contraction *there's* followed by a plural is almost universal in informal speech: □ *There's two good films showing*, although unacceptable in formal speech and writing.

they *They, them, their*, etc., are increasingly being used to refer to singular entities: □ *Anyone can apply if they have the qualifications.*

◆ Such use, in conjunction with *anyone, someone, no one, everyone*, is well-established and in formations such as: □ *No one's seen John, have they?* is becoming generally acceptable. However, many careful users object to such phrases as *a person on their own*. The use of *he* and *his* has a male bias unacceptable to many, while *he or she* or *his or her* often sounds stilted. Probably the best solution is to make the noun plural to agree with *they* or *their*: □ *people on their own*. See also HE OR SHE; THEMSELF.

they're see THEIR, THERE, OR THEY'RE?

third or **thirdly**? see FIRST OR FIRSTLY?

this see NEXT OR THIS?; THAT OR THIS?

thoroughfare The noun *thoroughfare*, meaning 'way through', is sometimes misspelt and/or mispronounced, the most frequent error being the substitution of *through-* for *thorough-*.

though see ALTHOUGH OR THOUGH?

thrash or **thresh**? The verb *thrash* means 'flog or beat with repeated blows' or 'defeat': □ *He was thrashed by the headmaster.* □ *We thrashed the opposition. Thresh* means 'separate seeds of cereal from husks by beating'.

◆ *Thrash*, usually with *about*, can also mean 'move violently': □ *He thrashed his arms about like a windmill*, and is used in the idiomatic phrasal verb *thrash out* meaning 'discuss in detail until a solution is found': □ *Let's thrash out this problem together.*

The two words are occasionally confused, partly because *thresh*, with the meaning given above, is sometimes spelt *thrash*.

threshold Note that there is only one *h* in the middle of this word, unlike in the word *withhold*.

◆ *Threshold* may be pronounced either [threshhōld] or [threshōld].

thus The slightly formal adverb *thus* means 'in such a manner, in the way indicated, consequently': □ *His father died in a hunting accident and he thus became a baron.*

◆ *Thus far* means 'to this extent, up to now': □ *Thus far we have succeeded.* □ *Go thus far but no further.*

till 340

The word *thusly*, sometimes used in American English, is unacceptable in written or spoken British English.

till or **until**? Both words mean 'up to the time that, up to as far as': □ *I will work until I drop.* □ *Carry on till you reach the traffic lights.*

◆ They are interchangeable although *until* is slightly more formal and *till* is more likely to be used in speech. *Until* is usually more appropriate as the first word of a sentence: □ *Until they go we shall have no peace.* *Till* is not an abbreviation of *until* so *'til* and *'till* are incorrect.

timidity see TEMERITY OR TIMIDITY?

titillate or **titivate**? Literally, *titillate* means the same as *tickle* but it is almost always used figuratively in the sense of 'stimulate or arouse pleasantly': □ *Her interest titillated his vanity.* *Titivate* is occasionally confused with *titillate*, but its meaning is 'tidy or smarten up': □ *I must titivate myself for the party.*

◆ *Titillate* is sometimes used to mean 'excite mild sexual pleasure' and modern usage often has negative connotations of superficiality or self-indulgence: □ *Readers of sensationalist tabloids are titillated by reports of sexual offences.*

Note the spelling of *titillate*, especially the *-t-* and *-ll-* (unlike the single *-v-* of *titivate*).

titles Generally the titles of literary works, musical works, works of art, films, etc., are set in italics or, in handwriting and typescript, underlined: □ *I saw King Lear last night.* □ *She sang the title role in Carmen.* □ *Constable's Flatford Mill.*

◆ The Bible and the names of its individual books are not set in italics, and neither are the Talmud, the Torah, or the Koran.

Newspapers and periodicals are set in italics. Normally the definite article before a paper's name is not italicized: □ the *Daily Mail*. *The Times* and *The Economist* are exceptions.

The titles of long poems are usually set in italics, but short ones in inverted commas: □ Keats's *Endymion* □ Keats's 'To Autumn'.

See also MS, MRS, OR MISS?

to or **too**? These two spellings are sometimes confused. *To* is used with the infinitive and as a preposition; *too* is an adverb, meaning 'also' or 'excessively': □ *to go home* □ *Give it to me.* □ *too much noise* □ *Mary came too.*

tobacconist This word, for a person or shop that sells tobacco, cigarettes, cigars, etc., is sometimes misspelt. Like *tobacco*, there is a single *-b-* and *-cc-*; note also the single *-n-*.

together with *Together with* means 'in addition to': □ *The chairman of the company, together with three of the directors, has resigned.* Note that the verb *has* agrees with the singular noun *chairman*: the phrase introduced by *together with* does not form part of the subject of the sentence.

◆ If *together with* is replaced by *and*, the verb becomes plural: □ *The chairman of the company and three of the directors have resigned.*

toilet, lavatory, loo, or **bathroom**? *Toilet, lavatory,* and *loo* are virtually interchangeable in British English: □ *I need the toilet.* □ *We're out of lavatory paper.* □ *Where's the loo? Bathroom* is used in American English as a synonym for *toilet*, but in Britain its main meaning is a room containing a bath but not necessarily a toilet.

◆ *Toilet* is probably the most widely used term in British English, although *loo* is very commonly used in all but the most formal situations.

Toilets is usually used on signs in public places.

The use of *toilet* or *lavatory* is often considered a class marker in

Britain. Upper- and middle-class people tend to use *lavatory*, while lower-middle and working-class people use *toilet* and regard *lavatory* as affected or impolite. *Loo* is classless.

tolerance or **toleration**? Both these words are nouns from *tolerate*, but *tolerance* is 'the capacity to tolerate', while *toleration* is 'the act of tolerating': □ *His tolerance is unlimited.* □ *Her toleration of his habits demonstrates her good nature.*

◆ *Tolerance* is generally used with reference to respect for the beliefs of others, although in the context of official government policy, *toleration* is used: □ *religious toleration.*

Tolerance has several technical meanings in mathematics, statistics, physics, and medicine: an accepted deviation from a standard measurement; the ability of substances to endure heat, stress, etc., without being damaged; the capacity of a person's body to withstand harmful substances, etc.

too see TO OR TOO?

torpor This word, meaning 'inactive condition', is sometimes misspelt. Note the final *-or*, as in *stupor*, rather than *-our*.

tortuous or **torturous**? *Tortuous* means 'twisting; winding' and, figuratively, 'complex, devious, or overelaborate': □ *a tortuous road* □ *a tortuous policy. Torturous* comes from *torture* and means 'inflicting torture; agonizing or painful': □ *a torturous illness.*

◆ *Torturous* is sometimes used to mean 'complicated' or 'twisted', but careful users restrict it to the use suggesting physical or mental pain. The context often leads to confusion: □ *a tortuous decision* might mean a complex one or might be a mistake for *a torturous decision* – one that is painful to make.

total *Total* is used as a noun: □ *The total was 115*, a verb: □ *Profits this year total one million pounds*, and an intensifying adjective suggesting completeness: □ *a total failure* □ *a total stranger.*

◆ Some people dislike the use of *total* as an intensifying adjective synonymous with *utter* or *complete*, maintaining that the word should be used only when there is a sense of parts being added to produce a whole as in: □ *the total cost.*

Another disputed use is where the noun already suggests totality; some people think *total* is redundant in phrases like *total annihilation* or *the sum total.*

tourniquet This word, meaning 'a bandage tied tightly round an arm or leg to stop bleeding', may be pronounced [toornikay] or [tornikay] in British English.

◆ In American English the final *t* is often pronounced.

toward or **towards**? In British English *toward* is a rare adjective meaning 'afoot', 'imminent', or 'favourable' or a variant of *towards*, the usual form of the preposition meaning 'in the direction of' or 'with regard to': □ *They walked towards the hotel.* □ *What are his feelings towards her?*

◆ The preposition *toward* is more frequently used in American English. See also -WARD OR -WARDS?

The adjective *toward* is pronounced [tōărd]; the preposition *toward(s)* is pronounced [tōword(z)].

town see CITY OR TOWN?

town house A *town house* suggests an urban terraced house, usually with three or more storeys. However, when one speaks of someone's *town house* one can also mean a house in town belonging to a rich person whose main residence is in the country: □ *They* *used their town house for Veronica's ball.*

track record The phrase *track record*, meaning 'record of past performance', is frequently used as an unnecessary extension of the word *record* or synonym for 'experience', especially in job advertisements: □ *a sound track record in R&D* □ *a successful track record in sales and marketing.* Care should be taken to avoid overusing this expression.

trade names Trade names are names given to articles by their manufacturers. Some have become generic names for articles of their kind, even when the article does not actually bear the trade name in question: □ *Thermos flask* □ *Hoover* □ *Biro.*
◆ All nouns that are actually trade names should be spelt with an initial capital letter, although this is frequently overlooked, as in: □ *Please use a black fountain pen or biro.* □ *She wore a crimplene dress.* When the noun has given rise to a verb it is spelt with a lower-case initial letter: □ *He hoovered the carpet.*

trade union or **trades union**? The generally accepted singular noun is *trade union*, with the plural *trade unions.*
◆ There is no good grammatical reason for the use of *trades union* or *trades unions*, although both are frequently used. However, the official title of the TUC, the central association of British trade unions, is the *Trades Union Congress*, and this title should be used when referring to that organization.

trafficker This word is sometimes misspelt. The word *traffic* adds a *k* before the suffixes *-er*, *-ed*, and *-ing*: □ *drug traffickers* □ *illegal arms trafficking.* See also SPELLING 1.

trait This word may be pronounced [tray] or [trayt], although careful users prefer the first pronunciation.
◆ In American English [trayt] is standard.

tranche The noun *tranche* is best avoided where *section, group, portion*, or *instalment* would be adequate or more appropriate: □ *a tranche of the population* □ *payable in three tranches.*
◆ Of French origin, the word *tranche* entered the English language via the terminology of the Stock Market, where it means 'a block of bonds or government stock'.

tranquillity This word, meaning 'peaceful state': □ *the perfect tranquillity of the lake*, is often misspelt. Note the *-ll-* and the final single *t*.

transient or **transitory**? Both words mean 'short-lived, lasting only a brief time': □ *It is just a transient/transitory phase.*
◆ The words are virtually interchangeable but have a slightly different feel about them. *Transient* often suggests passing by quickly, perhaps because of rapid movement from place to place: □ *transient summer visitors. Transitory* often carries a suggestion of regret about the way desirable things change or disappear: □ *the transitory nature of human love.*
Transient is sometimes used as a noun to denote a person who stays for only a short time in any one place.

transitive see VERBS.

translate or **transliterate**? To *translate* is to express in a different language; to *transliterate* is to write or print using a different alphabet. The Greek word　　, for example, may be *transliterated* as *petra* and *translated* into English as 'rock'. The two verbs should not be confused.

transparent This word has various pronunciations, all of which are acceptable. The most frequent in contemporary usage is [trans-

*parr*ĕnt] but the pronunciations [trahns*parr*ĕnt] and [trans*pair*-ĕnt] are also heard. The -*s*- is sometimes pronounced with a *z* sound.

transpire *Transpire* means 'become known; come to light': □ *It later transpired that the President had known of the plan all along.* It is also widely used to mean 'happen or occur': □ *I will let you know what transpires.* This second use is disliked by many careful users, although it has a well-established history.

◆ *Transpire* is also sometimes used to mean 'turn out or prove to be': □ *He transpired to be her cousin*, and even 'arrive or turn up': □ *Subsequently dozens of letters transpired*. Both such uses are incorrect.

transport or **transportation**? *Transport* is used in British English both for the system and means of conveying: □ *public transport* □ *I have my own transport.* In American English *transportation* is often used: □ *the fastest form of transportation* □ *The goods were packed ready for transportation*, and this usage is now occasionally found in British English.

◆ *Transportation* is used in both British and American English to mean 'the banishment of convicts': □ *The sentence was transportation to Australia.*

Transport is also used in formal English to mean 'the state of being carried away by emotion': □ *a transport of joy.*

transverse or **traverse**? *Transverse* is an adjective meaning 'lying or set across; at right angles': □ *a transverse section. Traverse* is a verb meaning 'cross; go across' or a noun meaning 'way or path across': □ *The river traverses two counties.* □ *The traverse of this mountain is dangerous to inexperienced climbers.*

traumatic *Traumatic* is the adjective from *trauma*, which means 'a wound or injury' and it is still used in this sense in medical contexts: □ *traumatic fever.* However its main use is with the figurative meaning of 'causing great and deeply disturbing emotional shock': □ *a traumatic bereavement* □ *the traumatic effects of divorce* □ *the traumatic experience of a concentration camp.*

◆ Both *traumatic* and *trauma* have become very much overworked and are often used for cases of mild distress or annoyance: □ *I spent a traumatic evening filling in my tax return.* □ *the trauma of moving house.*

The usual pronunciation of *trauma* is [*traw*mä]; the pronunciation [*trow*mä] is used less frequently.

travel This word is sometimes misspelt. In British English the final *l* is doubled before the suffixes -*ed*, -*ing*, and -*er*: □ *well-travelled* □ *travelling fast along the motorway* □ *commercial travellers.*

◆ American English retains the single *l*: □ *traveled* □ *traveler* □ *traveling*. See also **SPELLING 1**.

traverse see **TRANSVERSE OR TRAVERSE**?

treble or **triple**? Both words can be used as a noun, verb, and adjective and are virtually interchangeable in meaning. However, *treble* is preferred by many careful users when the meaning is 'three times as great': □ *treble the sum*, and *triple* when the meaning is 'consisting of three parts': □ *a triple jump.*

◆ The words have distinctly different meanings in the context of music. *Treble* refers to a high-pitched voice or instrument, or a singer who performs at this pitch, whereas *triple* is used of rhythm: □ *a treble recorder* □ *triple time.*

tremor This word, meaning 'shaking or quivering action': □ *earth tremors*, is sometimes misspelt. Note the ending -*or*, not -*our*.

triple see TREBLE OR TRIPLE?

triumphal or **triumphant**? These adjectives are often confused. *Triumphal* is connected with the celebration of a victory, usually of a military nature: □ *triumphal arch* □ *A triumphal march was played as the victorious army paraded through the streets.* *Triumphant* means 'victorious, exulting or rejoicing in success': □ *The team were triumphant.* □ *Having succeeded in her task, she returned with a triumphant smile.*

◆ *Triumphant* is the more frequently used word, *triumphal* being restricted to narrower, more formal contexts.

trivia *Trivia* means 'matters of very minor importance': □ *the trivia of village gossip* □ *Why waste hours fussing over the trivia of every-day life?*

◆ The word is actually a plural, so careful users would not say for example: □ *Such trivia is beneath my notice.* However, *Such trivia are beneath my notice* has a stilted and unnatural sound, so most users would substitute such phrases as: □ *trivial matters* □ *trivial issues* □ *trivial things* for *trivia* in the preceding example.

troop or **troupe**? These words are sometimes confused. A *troop* is a military unit or group of people or things: □ *troops of soldiers* □ *a Scout troop.* *Troop* is also used as a verb in informal English to mean 'move as a large group': □ *Then they all trooped off home.* A *troupe* is a group of actors or performers: □ *a troupe of travel-ling acrobats.*

◆ The words *trooper* and *trouper* are also sometimes confused. A *trooper* is a cavalry soldier, especially a private, and in American and Australian English a mounted policeman: □ *swear like a trooper* means 'swear a lot'. A *trouper* is a member of a *troupe* of dancers, singers, etc.

trooping the colour To *troop the colour* is to parade the flag of a regi-ment ceremonially along the ranks of soldiers of that regiment: □ *trooping the colour* □ *the trooping of the colour.* Written with capital initials, the phrase *Trooping the Colour* refers to the annual parade in London, usually attended by the Queen, the Prime Minister, and other dignitaries: □ *We went to watch the ceremony of Trooping the Colour.*

◆ Since the ceremony is officially called *Trooping the Colour,* some people object to the phrase *the Trooping of the Colour*: □ *We went to watch the Trooping of the Colour.* However, this example reads awkwardly without the *of* (or the first *the*): □ *We went to watch (the) Trooping the Colour.* A possible solution is to use *Trooping the Colour* adjectivally: □ *We went to watch the Trooping the Colour ceremony.*

troupe see TROOP OR TROUPE?

truculent This adjective, which means 'sullenly or defiantly aggress-ive', is sometimes misspelt. Note the *-ucu-* and the *-ent* ending. The correct pronunciation is [trukyuulĕnt].

truism The narrower meaning of *truism* is 'a statement of self-evident truth, one containing superfluous repetition of an idea': □ *It is a truism to speak of single bachelors.* The word is more widely used to mean 'a statement of a fact that is too obvious to be thought worth stating': □ *the truism that stars are only visible at night.*

◆ *Truism* is sometimes used as though it were a synonym for *fact* or *truth* in such phrases as: □ *the truism that heterosexuals can contract AIDS,* but such use is widely regarded as unacceptable.

truly The adverb *truly* is sometimes misspelt. Note that the final *-e* of *true* is dropped when the adverbial suffix *-ly* is added.

try and or **try to**? The two expressions are virtually interchangeable: □ *Try and catch me!* □ *Try to tell the truth.* *Try and* is colloquial and is very frequently used; it is unacceptable only in formal written English.

◆ Note that *try to* sounds better in a negative context: □ *She didn't even try to be polite* and only *try to* can be used in the past tense: □ *They tried to break into the house.*

tsar or **czar**? This word, the title of any of the former Russian emperors, is spelt *tsar*, *czar*, or, rarely, *tzar*. It is pronounced [zah].

◆ Many users prefer the spelling *tsar*, because it more accurately reflects the Russian word as written in the Cyrillic script. The spelling *czar* shows the origin of the word from the Gothic *kaisar*, and ultimately the Latin *Caesar*.

turbid, turbulent, or **turgid**? The adjective *turbid*, used in formal contexts, is sometimes confused with *turbulent* or *turgid*. *Turbid* means 'opaque; cloudy; muddy; dense': □ *a turbid pool.* The adjective *turbulent* means 'in a state of agitated movement or confusion': □ *turbulent seas* □ *a politically turbulent period of history.* The adjective *turgid* means 'swollen' or 'distended': □ *The turgid river had overflowed its banks.*

◆ Both *turbid* and *turgid* may be applied in formal and figurative contexts to linguistic or literary style, *turbid* meaning 'confused' and *turgid* 'bombastic': □ *turbid/turgid prose.*

turbo- The prefix *turbo-* is applied to a machine that is driven by a turbine: □ *turbofan* □ *turbojet.* Its association with turbocharged cars, in which performance is improved by the use of a turbine, sometimes leads to a mistaken interpretation and application of the prefix in the sense of 'fast' or 'powerful': □ *a turbo model of a computer.* This extension of usage is best avoided.

turbulent, turgid see TURBID, TURBULENT, OR TURGID?

turquoise The name of this greenish-blue mineral has various pronunciations. The most frequent in contemporary usage is [*terk*woiz], but [*terk*wahz], [*terk*wois], and [*terk*oiz] are also heard.

twelfth Careful users avoid dropping the *f* in the pronunciation of this word [twelfth]. The word is, however, frequently pronounced without the *f*.

type of see KIND OF.

ultimate *Ultimate* is used mainly as an adjective meaning 'last, final, eventual': □*the ultimate goal*, or 'fundamental': □*ultimate truths*. As a noun it has traditionally simply meant 'something ultimate' or 'the extreme': □ *the ultimate in wickedness*. This last use is increasingly being extended, particularly in advertising and journalism, to mean 'the best possible; the most modern or advanced thing': □*the ultimate in swimming pools* □*the ultimate in high technology*.
◆ This vogue use, disliked by some, has some similarity with the phrase *the last word*.

ultra *Ultra* is an adjective meaning 'going beyond' or 'extreme' and is also used as a prefix with other words, either with or without a hyphen. In the sense of 'extremely' it is used in such words as: □*ultra-modern* □*ultra-radical*.
◆ In the sense of 'beyond the range of' it is used in: □*ultrasonic* □*ultramicroscopic*. *UHT* stands for *ultraheat-treated* and *UHF* for *ultrahigh frequency*.

umbilical This word may be stressed on the second syllable [um*bil*ikl] or on the third [umbi*lik*l].

umpire see **REFEREE OR UMPIRE?**

un- see **NON-**.

unanimous *Unanimous* means 'of one mind; in complete agreement': □ *The committee reached a unanimous decision*. It can only be used when several people all agree about something, and cannot be used as a synonym for *wholehearted* or *enthusiastic* as in: □*Many of the group were prepared to give the project their unanimous backing*.
◆ When a vote is taken someone can only be said to have been *elected unanimously*, or a motion *passed unanimously*, if every person present voted in favour. If there are any abstentions the motion is said to be passed *nem con*, which is an abbreviation of the Latin *nemine contradicente*, 'no one contradicting'.

unaware or **unawares**? *Unaware* is an adjective meaning 'not aware; not knowing about; not having noticed': □*I was unaware that you were coming*. □*He seemed unaware of the reaction he was causing*. It is occasionally used as an adverb, but the usual adverb is *unawares*, meaning 'unexpectedly, without warning', often in *caught unawares* or *taken unawares*: □ *The landslide caught the villagers unawares*.
◆ *Unaware* is often followed by *of* or *that* but *unawares* cannot precede another word in that way.

unconscious see **SUBCONSCIOUS OR UNCONSCIOUS?**

under see **BELOW, BENEATH, UNDER, OR UNDERNEATH?**

under foot or **underfoot**? This term should be spelt as one word, not as two separate words: □*It was rather wet underfoot*.

underhand or **underhanded**? Both *underhand* and *underhanded* are used as adjectives to mean 'sly; marked by dishonesty, trickery, and deception': □ *They used the most underhand/underhanded methods in their campaign.*

◆ Both words can be used in the context of some sports, meaning 'with the hand below the shoulder or elbow': □ *underhand shooting* □ *aiming underhanded. Underhanded* is also occasionally used to mean 'short of the required number of workers'.

underneath see BELOW, BENEATH, UNDER, OR UNDERNEATH?

underprivileged *Underprivileged* has become a fashionable adjective to use in connection with those lacking the standard of income and opportunities enjoyed by other members of the society in which they live: □ *She started a clinic for underprivileged children.* □ *Many young criminals come from underprivileged backgrounds.* It is used as a noun as well as an adjective: □ *His concern for the underprivileged drew him towards social work as a career.*

◆ Its real meaning is not 'lacking in privileges' but rather, 'lacking in rights; disadvantaged' or at least lacking in those social and economic rights considered to be fundamental in Western developed society.

undertone see OVERTONE OR UNDERTONE?

underway or **under way**? Careful users prefer to write this expression, meaning 'moving; in progress', as two words: □ *Preparations for the new project are now well under way.* The expression is, however, increasingly being spelt as one word.

◆ The spelling *under weigh* is wrong. This spelling probably arises from confusion with the nautical expression *weigh anchor*, meaning 'raise anchor'.

undiscriminating see INDISCRIMINATE OR UNDISCRIMINATING?

undoubtedly *Undoubtedly, no doubt, doubtless, without (a) doubt* are all adverbs expressing that something is not disputed. However, *undoubtedly* and *without a doubt* express that idea much more positively and strongly than the other expressions: □ *She is undoubtedly the best student in her year. No doubt* and *doubtless* are much weaker expressions, often suggesting that the user is in fact not completely certain, or is even harbouring doubts: □ *No doubt he is very clever but I still can't understand what he is saying.*

◆ As *doubtless* is an adverb, *doubtlessly* is incorrect.

Some people mistakenly spell *undoubtedly* as *undoubtably*, perhaps confused with *indubitably*, which is a more formal and even stronger expression, suggesting that something cannot possibly be doubted: □ *It was indubitably evident that he had acted in a manner which was utterly unacceptable.*

uneatable see EATABLE OR EDIBLE?

unequivocally Note that the adverb *unequivocally* has the ending *-ally*, not *-ably*. It is derived from the adjective *unequivocal*, meaning 'clear; plain'.

unexceptionable or **unexceptional**? *Unexceptionable* means 'inoffensive; not liable to be criticized or objected to': □ *His behaviour had been unexceptionable, so he could not understand how he could have offended his hosts. Unexceptional* means 'usual, normal, or ordinary': □ *The weather was unexceptional for the time of year.* It is, however, more frequently used to suggest that something is dull or disappointingly commonplace: □ *I had heard enthusiastic reports of his playing, but I found this an unexceptional performance.*

◆ The words are often confused, partly because it is quite possible for something to be both inoffensive and rather dull.

-unfriendly see FRIENDLY.

uninterested see DISINTERESTED OR UNINTERESTED?

unique *Unique* means 'being the only one of its kind': □ *Every snow-flake has a unique pattern.* A thing is either unique or it is not, so careful users dislike such expressions as *so unique, rather unique, very unique,* etc., and something cannot be *more unique* or *less unique* than something else. *Almost* and *nearly* are the only modifiers generally acceptable with *unique.*

◆ The word is widely used with a weaker meaning of 'unrivalled; outstanding', but many people object to such use. Intensifiers are often used with *unique*: □ *It was absolutely unique*, but such expressions should be restricted to informal use.

United Kingdom see BRITAIN.

United States, United States of America see AMERICA.

unmistakable or **unmistakeable**? Both spellings of this word are acceptable, but *unmistakable* is the more frequent in British English. See SPELLING 3.

unnecessary The adjective *unnecessary* is sometimes misspelt. Note the *-nn-* (from the addition of the prefix *un-* to the adjective *necessary*), the single *-c-*, and the *-ss-*.

unorganized see DISORGANIZED OR UNORGANIZED?

unpractical see PRACTICAL OR PRACTICABLE?

unprecedented A *precedent* is 'an earlier example or occurrence of a similar thing', so *unprecedented* means 'never having happened before; completely new or original': □ *His score was unprecedented in the history of cricket.*

◆ It has recently become a popular word, particularly in the media where its meaning has weakened to 'extremely great': □ *The film is enjoying an unprecedented success.*

unreadable see ILLEGIBLE OR UNREADABLE?

unrepairable see REPAIRABLE OR REPARABLE?

unsociable, unsocial see ANTISOCIAL, ASOCIAL, UNSOCIAL, OR UNSOCI-ABLE?

until see TILL OR UNTIL?

unused Like USED, the word *unused* may be pronounced with the [s] sound of the noun *use* or the [z] sound of the verb *use.* In the phrase *unused to,* meaning 'unaccustomed to', *unused* is pronounced [un*yoost*]: □ *I am unused to driving on the righthand side of the road.* The adjective *unused,* meaning 'not being used' or 'never having been used', is pronounced [un*yoozd*]: □ *Many of the rooms are unused.* □ *Unused pills and tablets should be returned to the pharmacy for safe disposal.*

unwaged The adjective and noun *unwaged* refers to anybody who does not receive a wage or salary. Such people include the unemployed, full-time mothers or housewives, students, and old age pensioners: □ *The membership fee is £5 (or £3 for the unwaged).* The euphemistic use of the term *unwaged* in place of *unemployed,* with reference to those who are out of work and seeking employment, could be misleading and is best avoided.

unwanted or **unwonted**? *Unwanted* means simply 'not wanted': □ *She gave her unwanted clothes to the Oxfam shop. Unwonted* means 'out of the ordinary; unusual': □ *The drug gave him an unwonted feeling of euphoria.*

◆ The two words are confused because people sometimes mistakenly spell *unwanted* as *unwonted*, and frequently pronounce *unwonted* as *unwanted*. *Unwanted* should be pronounced [unwŏntid] and *unwonted* [unwŏntid], with the stressed syllable pronounced the same as the word *won't*.

up-front Some people dislike the increasing use of the term *up-front*, meaning 'paid in advance, at the beginning, or as a deposit': □ *an up-front payment* □ *They want £500 up-front and the remainder in monthly instalments.* The term should not be overused, and is best restricted to informal contexts.

upon or **on**? These two words are synonyms and virtually indistinguishable in use: □ *She threw herself upon the sofa.* □ *He walked on the beach. Upon* has a more formal sound and, particularly in spoken English, *on* is more frequently used.

◆ In some cases usage is dictated by the fact that one or the other word is normal in a particular idiom: □ *once upon a time* □ *on the contrary.*

Upon is used between two repeated nouns to suggest large numbers: □ *We walked mile upon mile.*

upward or **upwards**? In British English *upward* is principally used as an adjective, *upwards* being the usual form of the adverb meaning 'to a higher level': □ *an upward trend* □ *to float upwards.*

◆ The adverb *upward* is more frequently used in American English. See also **-WARD OR -WARDS**?

The phrase *upwards of*, meaning 'more than', is disliked by some users: □ *The newly privatised company is in contention with America's Pratt & Whitney to supply the engines for upwards of 100 Boeing 757s that Texas Air is planning to order (Sunday Times).*

upwardly mobile This is a very fashionable modern expression, used of ambitious, usually young, people who are moving into a higher class, income bracket, etc.: □ *These days the City is thought to be full of upwardly mobile men and women trying to enhance their status in society.*

urban or **urbane**? *Urban* means 'of a town or city': □ *Unemployment is higher in urban areas. Urbane* is used of someone who is sophisticated and polite, with a smooth and easy manner in any social situation: □ *He turned out to be an elegant and urbane man who charmed them all.*

◆ *Urbane* actually derives from *urban* for it describes a manner which was thought to be characteristic of a person who came from a city.

urinal This word may be stressed on either the second syllable [yuurīnl] or the first syllable [yoorinl] in British English.

◆ The American English pronunciation is stressed on the first syllable.

us see **WE**.

us or **our**? see **-ING FORMS**.

US, USA see **AMERICA**.

usable or **useable**? Both spellings of this word are acceptable, but *usable* is the more frequent in British English. See **SPELLING 3**.

usage or **use**? *Usage* is the way in which something, especially language, is used; the noun *use* denotes the act of using: □ *This book deals with problems of usage.* □ *in contemporary usage* □ *the use of wood as an insulator* □ *The photocopier is in use.* Careful users maintain this distinction between the two words, avoiding such phrases as: □ *a ban on the usage of hosepipes.*

◆ Either *usage* or *use* may be used in the sense of 'amount or degree to which something is used': □ *increased usage/use of electricity,* although some people dislike the use of *usage* in this context.

Usage also means 'treatment': □ *rough/gentle usage.* The noun *use* has a variety of other meanings, such as 'usefulness': □ *What's the use of trying?*, 'wear': □ *to deteriorate through use*, 'need': □ *Do you have a use for this box?*, and 'the right to use': □ *to have the use of a company car.*

Note the difference in pronunciation between the noun *use* [yoos] and the verb *use* [yooz]. *Usage* may be pronounced [*yoo*sij] or [*yoo*zij].

useable see USABLE OR USEABLE?

used In the phrase USED TO, *used* is pronounced [yoost]. *Used* as an adjective, for example in: □ *used cars*, and as the past tense and past participle of the verb *use* is pronounced [yoozd].

used to *Used to* either means 'accustomed to': □ *I have got used to the noise by now*, or refers to a habitual action or situation in the past: □ *She used to play squash regularly.*

◆ Difficulties arise over negative and question forms of the phrase in its second meaning. In negative forms the more formal *used not to* or the more informal *did not/didn't use to* are both acceptable: □ *He used not to be so aggressive.* □ *She did not use to like fish.* Both *usen't to* and *didn't used to* are heard, but are avoided by careful users.

In the question form the formal and rather old-fashioned *used X to?* and the less formal *did X use to?* are both correct: □ *Used there to be a lake in that wood?* □ *Did Henry use to visit you? Did X used to?* or *didn't X used to?* are frequently heard, though disliked by many careful users. As no form sounds completely natural and correct many people would reconstruct the sentence and say, for example: □ *Was there once a lake in that wood?*

See also USED.

user-friendly *User-friendly* is a term used in computing to describe software that is simple to use, being designed to assist the user and forestall any potential problems: □ *a user-friendly program.*

◆ The term is increasingly found in other fields, meaning 'easy to operate or understand', and describing electrical appliances, cars, books, etc.: □ *A drive to make the National Health Service 'user-friendly' was launched yesterday* (*Daily Telegraph*). This implied association with advanced technology may impress some people but will alienate others; it is therefore advisable to reserve the term for its original purpose. See also -FRIENDLY.

User-hostile, the opposite of *user-friendly*, is also found in certain contexts: □ *complex, user-hostile systems which require complicated languages to programme and are hard to understand* (*The Guardian*).

utilize *Utilize* means 'use in a practical and effective, profitable or productive way': □ *They utilized every machine that was available.* It can also mean 'make good use of something not intended for the purpose': □ *She utilized her tights when the fan belt broke*; or 'make use of something that might be thought useless': □ *She utilized all the scraps for stuffing cushions.*

◆ *Utilize* is often used, particularly in business jargon, as though it were merely a synonym for *use*: □ *Successful applicants will be able to utilize their experience and skills in this field.* However, careful users restrict the word to the narrower senses described above.

vacant or vacuous? Both these adjectives mean 'empty', but they are not generally interchangeable in usage. The adjective *vacant* is most frequently applied to a flat, room, seat, post, etc., that is not occupied by a person or people: □ *a hotel with vacant rooms* □ *The post remained vacant for several months after her resignation.* The adjective *vacuous* is used in formal contexts often in the derogatory sense of 'apparently devoid of intelligence; inane; mindless': □ *a vacuous remark* □ *Modern pop music is vacuous, repetitive, and uninspiring.*

◆ Both *vacant* and *vacuous* may also be applied to a person's expression, or to a gaze or stare: □ *a vacant expression* suggests a temporary lack of concentration, attention, or awareness; □ *a vacuous expression* suggests a lack of intelligence.

vacation In British English the primary meaning of the noun *vacation* is 'the period when universities and law courts are not officially working': □ *She went home for the Christmas vacation.*

◆ Students often shorten the word informally to *vac.*

In American English the main meaning of *vacation* is 'a holiday': □ *They took a vacation in Miami.* It is also used as a verb: □ *We vacationed in Europe last year.*

A further meaning of the word is 'vacating; making vacant or empty': □ *The landlord insisted on immediate vacation of the house.*

vaccinate see INOCULATE OR VACCINATE?

vacuous see VACANT OR VACUOUS?

vagary The noun *vagary*, meaning 'whim', 'caprice', or 'unpredictable change': □ *the vagaries of the weather,* causes problems of pronunciation. In British English the noun is usually pronounced [*vay*gări]; the pronunciation [vă*gai*ri] is less frequent and may be regarded as an Americanism.

vain, vane, or vein? These three words are sometimes confused, being identical in pronunciation. *Vain* is an adjective, meaning 'conceited; excessively proud' or 'worthless; futile': □ *the vain parents of talented children* □ *a vain attempt to increase productivity.* *Vane* and *vein* are nouns. A *vane* is a flat blade moved by wind or water: □ *a weather vane*; a *vein* is a blood vessel, a thin layer of ore in rock, etc.

◆ *Vain* is also used in the phrase *in vain,* meaning 'to no avail': □ *She tried in vain to dissuade him.* *Vein* is also used in figurative contexts, referring to a style, mood, quality, or trait: □ *another remark in the same vein* □ *a vein of irony in the novel.*

vantage see ADVANTAGE OR VANTAGE?

vaporize Note the spelling of the verb *vaporize,* meaning 'change into vapour'. The *-u-* of *vapour* is dropped before the suffix *-ize.*

◆ The variant spelling *vaporise* is equally correct (see -IZE OR -ISE?).

variegated This word, meaning 'having different colours; diverse': □ *variegated leaves,* is sometimes misspelt. Note the *e* between 've

352

the *i* and the *g*.

've see OF.

vein see VAIN, VANE, OR VEIN?

venal or **venial**? *Venal* means literally 'for sale' and it is used either of individuals who are capable of being 'bought' or corrupted, or of systems which operate by bribery and corruption: □ *Their legal system is so venal that criminals openly offer bribes in court.* *Venial* means 'pardonable; excusable' and is applied to minor faults and offences: □ *He was inclined to be thoughtless but that was a venial fault in one so young.*

◆ In Roman Catholic theology a *venial sin* is one that does not deprive the soul of divine grace, as opposed to a *mortal sin.*

vengeance see REVENGE OR VENGEANCE?

venial see VENAL OR VENIAL?

venison This word, meaning 'the meat of a deer', is usually pronounced [*ven*isŏn] or [*ven*izŏn], although the traditional pronunciation is [*ven*zŏn].

venue The usual meaning of *venue* is 'the place where a meeting, event, or gathering happens': □ *We have not yet decided on the venue for the annual conference.*

◆ There is a sense of people coming together to a particular place for a purpose. However, recent usage, to the dislike of some, makes *venue* virtually synonymous with *place, scene,* or *setting,* as the site of any activity: □ *A valley in South Wales is the venue for this experiment in self-sufficient communal living.*

verbal or **oral**? *Verbal* means 'expressed in words' while *oral* means 'relating to the mouth' or 'expressed in speech'. Something *verbal* can be expressed in either speech or writing. However, a *verbal agreement* is generally understood to mean one that is spoken and not written.

◆ Some careful users feel that, despite the established use of *verbal* in this way, it is always better to use an *oral agreement,* as there is no risk of misunderstanding or ambiguity with the word *oral.*

verbal nouns see INFINITIVE; -ING FORMS.

verbs Verbs refer to actions, occurrences, or existence. They vary in form according to the tense or mood used, usually in a predictable way but, with irregular verbs, in various different ways which need to be learned.

◆ Verbs differ in their functions. One distinction is between *transitive* and *intransitive* verbs. A transitive verb is one that needs a direct object, for example, *like.* One cannot just like; one has to like someone or something. Either it must take a direct object: □ *He likes chocolate,* or it can be used in the passive: □ *She is liked by everyone.* Intransitive verbs do not take a direct object. *Fall,* for example, is an intransitive verb. Some verbs can be used both transitively and intransitively in different constructions: □ *Can the boat sail? – She sailed the boat.*

Some transitive verbs are *reflexive verbs,* where the subject and object are the same: □ *perjure oneself.* In this example the verb is always reflexive; one cannot perjure anyone or anything other than oneself. But some verbs are not always used reflexively: □ *I introduced myself to our hostess. – I introduced Chris to our hostess.*

Auxiliary verbs are those used with other verbs, enabling them to express variations in tense, mood, voice, etc. The most frequently used auxiliaries are *be, have,* and *do:* □ *He is tired.* □ *I have finished.* □ *We did not agree. Be* is used to form the passive: □ *It was discussed.* Other auxiliaries include: *shall, should, can, could, will, would, may,*

might, and must: □ *I shall accept the offer.* □ *You must stop
immediately.* This second group of auxiliary verbs, which cannot be
used as full verbs (unlike *be, have,* and *do*) are also called *modal
verbs.* See also **DARE; NEED.**

Phrasal verbs are verbs which include an adverb, preposition, or
both: □*give in* □*throw away* □*take to.* Many such verbs have
meanings which go beyond the sum of their parts, for example *came
by* as in: □*I came by* [i.e. obtained or received] *that engraving in
Venice.* Some mean no more than the words suggest: □*keep down*
□*stay away.* The modern trend to extend ordinary verbs so that they
become phrasal verbs, while adding nothing to their meaning:
□*I consulted (with) my accountant* is disliked by many.

New verbs are formed in various ways. One way is by converting
nouns: □*He serviced her car* (see NOUNS). A variation of this is the
formation of compound verbs: □ *to rubber-stamp* □*blue-pencil*
□*inflation-proof* □*top-score* □*fundraise* □*downgrade.* These verbs
are often disliked when first introduced but they have the advantage
of economy, if not of elegance. □ *I shall word-process the letters* is
briefer than *I shall produce the letters on a word processor.* See also
COMPOUND. For other ways of forming new verbs see **BACK
FORMATION; -IZE OR -ISE?**

See also **ACTIVE; FINITE VERB; INFINITIVE; -ING FORMS;
PARTICIPLES; PASSIVE; PRINCIPAL PARTS; SUBJUNCTIVE; TENSE.**

vermilion The noun and adjective *vermilion,* meaning 'bright red', is
sometimes misspelt. Note that *vermilion* has a single *-l-,* unlike
the word *million.*

vertex or **vortex?** A *vertex* is the highest point or a point where two or
more lines intersect; a *vortex* is the spiralling motion of a
whirlpool or whirlwind or, metaphorically, an activity that one
is drawn into like a whirlpool or whirlwind: □*the vertex of a
triangle* □*the vortex of rebellion.*

◆ The plural of *vertex* is *vertexes* or *vertices;* the plural of *vortex* is
vortexes or *vortices.*

very *Very* can be used as an intensifier before most adjectives and
adverbs: □*very unpleasant* □*very efficiently.* However, before
past participles *much* is used instead of *very:* □*It was much
improved.* The exception is when the past participle is used
adjectivally: □*She was very excited.*

◆ Some words come into a grey area where either *very* or *much* can be
used: □ *She was very/much distressed. Much* usually has a more formal
sound. There are other participles which cannot take either *very* or *much*
as an intensifier, although they can take *very* if an adverb is interposed:
one cannot be *very wounded* but can be *very badly wounded;* one
cannot say *very mended* but can say *very neatly mended.*

veterinary This word causes problems with spelling and pronunciation. Note the *-erin-* and the *-ary* ending. The word is frequently
pronounced [vetĕnri], [vetĕnĕri], or [vetrinri], although careful
users insist on the pronunciation with five syllables [vetĕrinĕri].

◆ The expression *veterinary surgeon* is usually shortened to *vet.*

via *Via* means 'by way of' and is used when talking of the route for a
journey: □ *They went to Australia via Hong Kong.* □ *Your best
route would be via the M6.*

◆ It is also used to mean 'by means of': □*I'll return it via Fred,* or to
speak of a means of transport: □ *We crossed the Channel via
hovercraft,* but many people dislike these usages, particularly the
latter one.

The pronunciation normally regarded as correct is [vīā] although [veeā] is sometimes heard.

viable *Viable* means 'capable of living or surviving independently': □ *a viable foetus.* It can be used figuratively in this sense of new communities: □ *When the colony shows itself to be viable, it will be granted independence.*

◆ The meaning has been extended to 'capable of carrying on without extra (financial) support': □ *The business is expected to be commercially viable within two years.*

In vogue use the meaning is even further extended to become synonymous with *workable, practicable, feasible:* □ *a viable partnership* □ *a viable plan.* This loose use of *viable* is objected to by many careful users.

vice versa This expression, meaning 'with the order reversed', is usually pronounced [vīsĕ versĕ]. Alternative pronunciations for the first word are: [vīsi] and [vis].

vicious or **viscous**? *Vicious* means 'wicked' or 'ferocious'; *viscous* describes a liquid that is thick and sticky: □ *a vicious dog* □ *viscous paint.*

◆ The two adjectives are sometimes confused, being similar in form and pronunciation. The *c* of *vicious* is soft [vishūs]; the *c* of *viscous* is hard [viskūs].

The word *vicious* also occurs in the expression *vicious circle,* denoting a problematic situation that creates new problems leading back to the original situation: □ *the vicious circle of debt.* The word *viscous* is largely restricted to formal or technical contexts.

victuals This word, meaning 'supplies of food', is pronounced [vitlz].

◆ A *victualler,* 'a licensed purveyor of spirits', is pronounced [vitlĕr].

vigorous This word, meaning 'healthy and strong', is often misspelt. Note that the *u* of *vigour* is dropped before the suffix *-ous.*

vilify Note the spelling of this verb, used in formal contexts to mean 'malign; defame', particularly the single *-l-.*

virtual reality *Virtual reality* is an interactive hypothetical environment created by sophisticated computer graphics and related technology: □ *ITV could be the first network to screen a game show using virtual reality, the emerging technology in which users become immersed in, and interact with, a world generated by computers* (*The Guardian*).

◆ *Virtual reality* is chiefly used in computer games, where the player's movements may be mirrored by a character in the computer-generated world.

virus A *virus* is the causative agent of a disease, but the word is frequently used of the disease itself: □ *He's recovering from a very nasty virus.*

◆ The word is also often used in a metaphorical sense for an influence or ideology that is thought to be corrupting people's minds: □ *the virus of anti-Semitism that spread throughout Germany in the 1930s.* A *computer virus* is a code or program that can spread through a computer system, corrupting or destroying data.

vis-à-vis *Vis-à-vis* literally means 'face to face' and is most frequently used as a preposition to mean 'in relation to': □ *We shall have to change our policy vis-à-vis the law.* It also means 'opposite' or 'face to face with' and is sometimes used as a noun to mean 'someone or something opposite another; a counterpart'. It is also occasionally used as a synonym for *tête-à-tête,* meaning 'a private conversation between two people'.

◆ It is pronounced [veezah*vee*].

viscous see VICIOUS OR VISCOUS?

visible There is a recent fashionable use of *visible* to mean 'in the public eye; well known': □*He's one of the more visible cabinet ministers.* It can also be more or less synonymous with *having a high profile*, with the meaning of 'being in a position where one's actions are liable to become subject to public comment or notice': □ *The role of Director of Social Services is an increasingly visible one.* As some object to these uses of *visible*, care should be taken to avoid overworking this word.

visit or **visitation**? In its most frequent use *visit* is a verb meaning 'pay a call on, stay with as a guest, stay somewhere temporarily' and a noun meaning 'an act of visiting': □*I will visit Venice when I am in Italy.* □*He was on a visit to his daughter.* A *visitation* is an official or formal act of visiting: □ *The vicar's work includes the visitation of parishioners in hospital*, and is often found in humorous use, referring to an unwelcome visit: □ *I'm awaiting a visitation from the VAT man.*

◆ *Visitation* can also refer to the visit of a supernatural being: □ *a visitation of angels*, and is also used in referring to an act of affliction, either natural or divine: □ *the visitation of the Black Death* □ *the visitation of God's wrath.*

vitamin The traditional British pronunciation of this word is [*vit*-ămin].

◆ The American English pronunciation [*vīt*ămin], the first syllable of which rhymes with *bite*, is now acceptable in British English although disliked by some people.

voluntarily Careful users of British English stress this word on the first syllable [*vol*ĕntĕrili].

◆ Such users object to the alternative pronunciation, with stress on the third syllable [volĕn*terr*ili], though this is acceptable in American English.

vortex see VERTEX OR VORTEX?

vowel A *vowel* is the sound represented by any of the letters *a, e, i, o,* and *u* in the English language. Compare CONSONANT.

◆ The presence of a vowel at the beginning of a word may affect the form or pronunciation of the preceding word (see A OR AN?; THE).

Note that in such words as □ *unit* and □ *uranium*, the letter *u*- produces the combined consonant and vowel sound [yoo-].

wage, wages see SALARY OR WAGE?

wait see AWAIT OR WAIT?

waive or **wave**? These two words are sometimes confused. The verb *waive* means 'relinquish': □ *The judge waived the penalty; wave* means 'move to and fro': □ *wave goodbye* □ *The corn waved in the wind.* The noun *wave* means 'ridge of water'.

◆ The noun *waiver* comes from the verb *waive*: □ *a waiver clause in a contract.* It must not be confused with the verb *waver* which means 'fluctuate or hesitate; become unsteady': □ *Throughout his suffering his faith never wavered.* □ *a wavering voice.*

wake, waken see AWAKE, AWAKEN, WAKE, OR WAKEN?

wander or **wonder**? These spellings are sometimes confused. *Wander* means 'roam aimlessly': □ *He wandered through the streets*; *wonder* means 'be astonished at' or 'think about': □ *I wonder where she is.*

◆ The pronunciation of *wander* is [wondĕr]; the pronunciation of *wonder* [wundĕr] rhymes with *thunder*.

wannabee A *wannabee* is a person who strives to emulate another, especially a young fan who mimics a famous person in appearance, behaviour, etc.: □ *a horde of Madonna wannabees.*

◆ The word *wannabee*, from the phrase *(I) want to be (like ...)*, is sometimes spelt *wannabe*. It is best restricted to informal contexts.

want As a verb the main meanings of *want* are 'to desire': □ *I want a bigger car*, 'to need': □ *That door wants mending*, and 'to lack': □ *The door wants a handle.* As a noun it means 'something desired; a desire for something; a lack' or is used as a synonym for *poverty*: □ *the want experienced by the unemployed. Want to* is often used in informal contexts to mean 'ought to': □ *You want to be more careful.*

◆ There is controversy over whether *want* can be used with a present participle as in: □ *I want my hair cutting.* This usage is a standard regional variation in British English, although more people would say *I want my hair cut.* This latter form can lead to ambiguity. □ *I want the picture fixing on the wall* is clearer than *I want the picture fixed on the wall*, which could indicate a desire for a particular picture. □ *I want the picture to be fixed on the wall* is unambiguous and avoids the use of the present participle, which is generally considered unsuitable for any but informal use.

-ward or **-wards**? The adverbial suffixes *-ward* and *-wards* are used to indicate direction. Both forms are equally correct, although *-wards* is usually preferred in British English and *-ward* in American English.

◆ Most of these adverbs have a related adjective ending in *-ward*. The adjectival suffix cannot be replaced by *-wards*.

For further discussion and additional information see AFTERWARD OR AFTERWARDS?, BACKWARD OR BACKWARDS?, and other

356

individual entries.

-ware or **-wear**? The ending *-ware* denotes goods of the specified type or material; the ending *-wear* denotes clothing: □ *glassware* □ *computer software* □ *knitwear* □ *leather footwear*. The two endings are sometimes confused: □ *Dawn French, who is planning to open a knitwear shop* (*The Bookseller*).

◆ In computing, the ending *-ware* has been used to coin a number of nouns on the model of *hardware* and *software*. These include: □ *groupware* (a set of related software) □ *courseware* (educational software) □ *vapourware* (software that has yet to be produced) □ *liveware* (human beings).

was see WERE OR WAS?

wastage or **waste**? *Waste* is used as a verb, noun, and adjective. As a noun its main meanings are 'squandering, using carelessly or ungainfully': □ *It was a complete waste of time and money*; or 'rubbish; unwanted material': □ *Get rid of all this waste*. *Wastage* is a noun meaning 'loss due to leakage, decay, erosion, evaporation, etc.' □ *the wastage of water from a reservoir* □ *Petrol stored in garages is subject to wastage*. Another meaning, usually occurring in the phrase *natural wastage*, refers to the loss of employees through resignation, retirement, or death.

◆ *Wastage* is sometimes used as a synonym for *waste* but it should be confined to the meanings outlined above.

wave, waver see WAIVE OR WAVE?

-ways see -WISE OR -WAYS?

we *We* is used to mean 'I and one or more other people': □ *We should get a divorce*. □ *Shall we all go for a walk?*

◆ It was formerly used to mean 'I' by monarchs: □ *We grant by royal decree* ..., and is sometimes used by writers to give an impression of impersonality: □ *We shall discuss this in a later chapter*. *We* is sometimes used to mean 'you', usually in addressing children or invalids in a somewhat patronizing manner: □ *We are in a nasty temper today, aren't we?* □ *Are we feeling better this morning?*

Mistakes are sometimes made in the use of *we* and *us*. *We* is correct with a plural noun as the subject: □ *We children used to play there*. *Us* is correct when the noun is the object: □ *It won't help us workers*.

weal, wheal, or **wheel**? The noun *wheel*, denoting a circular object, is by far the most common of these three words: □ *the wheels of a bicycle* □ *a steering wheel* □ *a spinning wheel*. The nouns *weal* and *wheal* are interchangeable in the sense of 'raised mark on the skin (usually caused by a blow from a whip, cane, etc.)', *weal* being the more frequent: □ *The weals* [or *wheals*] *on his back suggested that he had been beaten*.

◆ *Weal* is also an archaic or literary word meaning 'welfare' or 'prosperity': □ *the public weal* □ *the common weal*.

-wear see WARE OR WEAR?

weather, wether, or **whether**? These three spellings are sometimes confused. The noun *weather* (see WEATHER CONDITIONS) and the conjunction *whether* (see WHETHER) are far more common than the noun *wether*, which denotes a (castrated) male sheep.

weather conditions *Weather* means 'the condition of the atmosphere, especially in respect of sunshine, rainfall, wind, etc.' As the word contains *condition* in its meaning, careful users maintain that it is tautological to talk of *weather conditions*, as in: □ *The bad weather conditions stopped play*. □ *The freezing weather conditions in the North will not improve*.

weaved, wove, or **woven**? The usual past tense of *weave* is *wove*: □ *She wove the cloth herself.* □ *The spider wove its web. Woven* is the usual past participle of *weave*: □ *It was woven by hand.* □ *They were wearing woven garments.*

◆ In some senses of *weave*, *weaved* is used for the past tense or past participle, as when *weave* means 'contrive or produce a complicated story': □ *She weaved a sinister plot*; 'lurch or stagger': □ *He weaved drunkenly down the street*; and 'move around vehicles to avoid hitting them': □ *The car weaved in and out of all the traffic.*

wed or **wedded**? The use of the verb *wed* in the sense of 'marry' is rather old-fashioned, formal, or literary; in modern usage it is chiefly found in newspaper headlines: □ *Doctor weds former patient.* Either word may be used as the past tense or past participle of the verb *wed*, meaning 'marry': □ *They wed* [or *wedded*] the following spring. □ *They were wed* [or *wedded*] by her uncle.

◆ When the past participle is used adjectivally (often in combination with an adverb), *wed* is preferred to *wedded*: □ *the newlywed couple* □ *her twice-wed father.* In the formal and figurative sense of 'committed' or 'closely connected', the past participle *wedded* is preferred to *wed*: □ *He seems wedded to the idea.* □ *Malnutrition is wedded to poverty.*

Wednesday The name of this day of the week is usually pronounced [wenzdi], although careful users prefer to sound the *d* [wednzdi] or [wednzday].

weigh or **weight**? To *weigh* is to measure the weight of something; to *weight* is to add weight to something: □ *The box weighs 3 kg.* □ *We weighted the tarpaulin with stones so that it would not blow away.*

◆ Both words may be used in the figurative sense of 'oppress': □ *They were weighed/weighted down with problems.*

Weigh is the more frequent of the two verbs, being used in a variety of other senses: □ *to weigh* ['raise'] *anchor* □ *to weigh up* ['assess'] *the pros and cons* □ *to weigh* ['consider carefully'] *one's words.* The verb *weight* is also used in the sense of 'bias': □ *The legislation must not be weighted towards the rich.* A London *weighting* allowance is an extra sum of money paid to some people who work in London, where the cost of living is high.

Note the *-eigh-* spelling of the two words. *Weight* is sometimes misspelt with the ending *-th*, on the model of *length, width*, etc.

weird This word, meaning 'uncanny or extraordinary', is sometimes misspelt. Note the *-ei-* spelling.

were or **was**? Difficulty is sometimes experienced in the use of the subjunctive form *were* in phrases expressing supposition. The basic rule is that *were* is used when the suggestion is of something hypothetical, unlikely, or not actually the case: □ *If I were you, I'd leave him.* □ *She talks to me as if I were three years old.* If the supposition is factual or realistic then *was* is used: □ *I'm sorry if I was rude.*

◆ When a supposition might be possible or factual then either *was* or *were* may be used: □ *They behaved as if it was/were their own house.* The more doubt there is, the more appropriate it is to use *were*.

west, West, or **western**? As an adjective, *west* is always written with a capital *W* when it forms part of a proper name: □ *West Germany* □ *the West Country.* The noun *west* is usually written with a capital *W* when it denotes a specific region, such as the noncommunist countries of Europe and America: □ *She defected to the*

West in 1986.

◆ In other contexts, and as an adverb, *west* is usually written with a lower-case *w*: □ *Drive west until you reach the border.* □ *We camped on the west bank of the river.* □ *The sun sets in the west.*

The adjective *western* is more frequent and usually less specific than the adjective *west*: □ *the western side of the island* □ *in western Scotland.*

Like *west*, *western* is written with a capital *W* when it forms part of a proper name, such as *Western Australia.* With or without a capital *W*, it also means 'of the West': □ *western/Western technology.* A *western* is a film, novel, etc., about life in the western USA in the 19th century.

wet or **wetted**? The verb *to wet* means 'make wet': □ *Don't keep wetting your lips,* and 'urinate in or on something': □ *Children often wet their beds when they are anxious.* The usual past tense or participle is *wet*: □ *The baby has wet its nappy again.* However, in the passive, *wetted* is used. *The sheets have been wetted* is less ambiguous than *the sheets have been wet.*

wet or **whet**? These two spellings are sometimes confused. *Wet* means 'cover with moisture': □ *to wet one's lips*; *whet* means 'stimulate or sharpen': □ *whet someone's appetite.*

◆ A *whetstone* is a stone used for sharpening knives, etc.; a *wet stone* is simply a stone that is damp.

wether see WEATHER, WETHER, OR WHETHER?

wetted see WET OR WETTED?

wharfs or **wharves**? Either *wharfs* or *wharves* is acceptable as the plural of the noun *wharf,* denoting a place where ships dock for loading and unloading. *Wharves* is the more frequent form.

what A difficulty in the use of the pronoun *what* is whether it should be followed by a singular or plural verb. In general the rule is that when *what* means 'that which' it takes a singular verb, even if the complement is plural, and when it means 'those which' it takes a plural verb: □ *What we need is a ladder.* □ *What he likes best is expensive restaurants.* □ *I mentioned what I thought were the most important points.*

◆ *What* cannot follow a noun or pronoun. Constructions such as: □ *the man what I was talking to* are wrong.

what or **which**? In a question, the use of *what* or *which* affects the interpretation of the meaning. *Which* chooses from a limited range of alternatives; *what* is used in more general enquiries.

◆ Thus □ *Which film are you going to see?* suggests that the speaker has several possible films in mind; whereas □ *What film are you going to see?* shows that the speaker is probably unaware of the choice of the various films.

whatever or **what ever**? If *ever* is used to intensify *what* the expression is written as two words in formal writing: □ *What ever* ['What on earth'] *did he say next?* In less formal writing, one word is sometimes used, but careful writers object to this usage. If *whatever* means 'no matter what', it is written as one word: □ *I'll write whatever I like.* □ *Whatever the weather he always wears a vest.* □ *There is no chance whatever of him winning.*

◆ A similar rule applies to the use of *how ever* and *however, when ever* and *whenever, where ever* and *wherever, which ever* and *whichever,* and *who ever* and *whoever*: □ *How ever did you find out? – However carefully I wash my hair, it always looks untidy.* □ *Where ever did you buy such a hat? – Wherever you travel, you'll find businesses that accept our credit card.* □ *Who ever told you that? – Whoever wrote this had a strange sense of humour.*

wheal, wheel see WEAL, WHEAL, OR WHEEL?

whence *Whence* is a formal, rarely used word meaning 'from where; from what place': □ *The monster returned to the swamp whence it had appeared.*

◆ *From whence* is more frequently used, as in: □ *The country from whence they came,* although the *from* is redundant, being contained in the meaning of *whence,* and many people consider *from whence* to be incorrect. However, as *whence* is now a word whose use tends to sound either old-fashioned, affected, or jocular it is probably better to avoid both *whence* and *from whence* altogether. See also HENCE; THENCE.

whenever or **when ever**? see WHATEVER OR WHAT EVER?

whereabouts The noun *whereabouts,* meaning 'place where somebody or something is', may be used with a singular or plural verb: □ *The whereabouts of the original manuscript remains* [or *remain*] *a secret.* □ *Her whereabouts are* [or *is*] *unknown.*

wherever or **where ever**? see WHATEVER OR WHAT EVER?

whet see WET OR WHET?

whether *Whether* can be used to introduce an indirect question: □ *He asked whether we were going.* Here it is synonymous with *if* but sounds rather more formal. *Whether* is also used to introduce alternatives or consider possibilities: □ *I wonder whether she'll come.* □ *I don't know whether it is correct.*

◆ In these cases there is some confusion concerning the use of *whether or not,* as in: □ *He has not decided whether (or not) to stay.* Here, where the sense is 'if he is staying' the *or not* can be considered redundant. It is only necessary when the sense is 'regardless of whether or not' as in: □ *He has decided to stay, whether or not he can afford it.*

See also WEATHER, WETHER, OR WHETHER?

which see THAT OR WHICH?; WHAT OR WHICH?

whichever or **which ever**? see WHATEVER OR WHAT EVER?

while or **whilst**? As a conjunction *while* means 'during the time that; as long as' and it is also used to mean 'although; whereas': □ *I shall be doing his work while he's away on holiday.* □ *Elizabeth votes Labour while her husband votes Conservative. Whilst* has the same meanings but is rarely used; it tends to sound formal and old-fashioned.

◆ Many people dislike the use of *while* or *whilst* in the sense of 'although; whereas' as it can give rise to ambiguity. □ *While she was studying literature she disliked poetry* could mean 'during the time she was studying literature' or 'although she was studying literature'.

whisky or **whiskey**? The alcoholic drink distilled in Scotland is spelt *whisky,* which is the more frequent spelling in British English. The alcoholic drink distilled in the USA or Ireland is spelt *whiskey,* the usual spelling in American English.

who The pronoun *who* is normally used in reference to human beings (*which* being used for nonhumans): □ *the man who runs the shop.* However, it is acceptable to use *who* in referring to animals, to countries in certain contexts, and to a group of people, especially when taking a plural verb: □ *cats who refuse to eat leftovers* □ *Iraq, who started the war* □ *the band who plays the loudest.*

◆ *That* can be used to refer to human beings and things in *defining clauses* (see THAT OR WHICH?): □ *the man that* [or *who*] *runs the shop*

□ *the band that* [or *who* or *which*] *plays the loudest* □ *the woman that* [or *who*, or the formally correct *whom*] *you just saw*.

Care must be taken with the punctuation of phrases containing *who*. □ *The boys, who attend public schools, regularly drink in pubs* changes its meaning if the commas are omitted. Without the commas, *who* introduces a defining clause, suggesting specific boys: those that attend public school. With commas, the additional clause merely adds extra information about the boys.

who or **whom**? *Who* is used when it is the subject of a verb and *whom* when it is the object of a verb or preposition: □ *the boy who delivers the papers* □ *the woman whom you just saw* □ *the people to whom I was talking. Whom* is falling into disuse, especially in questions. □ *Whom did you give it to?* is formally correct but most people would now use *who*. As a relative pronoun, *whom* should still be used, when correct, in all but informal speech.

◆ While many careful users feel that it is important to use *whom* when it is correct to do so, most would consider that the use of *who* for *whom* is far less of a mistake than the use of *whom* when *who* is correct, as in: □ *The children, whom she thought were dead, had been saved.* The temptation is to use *whom* because it is felt that this is the object of *she thought*, but it is not. *She thought* is a more or less independent part of the sentence; it could even be moved to another part of the sentence. It is not an object of *she thought* that is needed, but a subject (*who*) of the phrase *were dead*.

whodunit This word, used in informal contexts to describe a detective story, may be spelt *whodunit* or, less frequently, *whodunnit*.

◆ It is, of course, an abbreviation of the ungrammatical *who done it?*

whoever or **who ever**? see WHATEVER OR WHAT EVER?

wholly see HOLY, HOLEY, OR WHOLLY?; SPELLING 4.

whom see WHO OR WHOM?

whoop This word, meaning 'express delight', as in: □ *Sally whooped excitedly*, is sometimes mispronounced. The correct pronunciation is [woop].

◆ Note, however, that *whooping* as in *whooping cough* is pronounced [*hoop*ing].

whose or **who's**? These spellings are sometimes confused. *Whose* means 'of whom' or 'of which': □ *the children, whose father had left them* □ *political parties whose ideas are old-fashioned* □ *Whose book is that? Who's* is a contraction of *who is* or *who has*: □ *Who's coming to dinner tonight?*

◆ Some people object to the use of *whose* in the sense of 'of which', referring to things rather than people: □ *an old teapot, the handle of which* [not *whose handle*] *had been broken for many years*. Others, however, find the construction *the ... of which* an unnecessarily wordy substitute for *whose ....*

wicked Like BAD, the adjective *wicked* is used as slang term of approval, especially by young people: □ *His new bike is well wicked*.

◆ Jonathon Green in *Neologisms: new words since 1960* comments on its origin: 'The term has arrived via two borrowings: the first from standard English via black Americans, and subsequently by the white young from their black counterparts.'

wilful Note the spelling of this word, which has a single *l* in the middle and at the end in British English. In American English the *-ll* ending of *will* is retained in the spelling *willful*.

will see SHALL OR WILL?

window *Window* has various well-established metaphorical uses. It can mean 'something that allows people to see something they might otherwise not see': □ *The programme is a window on the closed world of the monastery*; or 'an opportunity to display something': □ *The exhibition is the annual window of domestic design.*

◆ A more recent use is 'a gap; an interval of time': □ *a window of opportunity,* though care should be taken to avoid overworking this expression: □ *Is there a window in my diary next week for that meeting with Dempster?* (Vodafone advertisement, *Daily Telegraph*). □ *Mr Ridley said that there would be a 'clear window' between Lord Justice Taylor's interim report and the bill's final stages in the Commons (The Guardian).*

-wise or **-ways**? The suffix *-ways* combines with certain abstract nouns to form an adverb meaning 'in (such) a way, direction, or manner': □ *sideways* □ *lengthways.* It has a more limited use than *-wise,* which can combine with various nouns to mean either 'in the position or direction of': □ *clockwise* □ *lengthwise* or 'in the manner of': □ *to walk crabwise.* The use of *-wise* to mean 'in respect of' in such expressions as: □ *moneywise* □ *weatherwise* □ *careerwise* □ *taxwise* □ *performancewise* is becoming increasingly popular, but is disliked by many people.

with When a singular subject is linked to something else by *with* it should take a singular verb: □ *The Prime Minister with senior members of the Cabinet has been considering the problem.*

◆ The usual pronunciation in British English is [widh]; [with] is a regional variation.

withhold This word, meaning 'keep back', is sometimes misspelt. Note the *-hh-* in the middle of this word, unlike the word *threshold.*

◆ The correct pronunciation [widh*hōld*] should ensure that the word is spelt correctly.

woman As a general term for an adult female human being, *woman* is more acceptable than *female, girl,* or *lady*: □ *The prize was won by a woman from Brighton.*

◆ The noun *female* is best reserved for animals and plants. It may be applied to human beings when the question of age makes *woman* or *women* inappropriate: □ *He shares the house with five females: his wife and their four young daughters.* In most other cases it is considered inelegant, contemptuous, or offensive. As an adjective, however, *female* is more acceptable than *woman* or *lady*: □ *There are two female doctors and one male doctor at the local surgery.* □ *Female drivers do not have more road accidents than male drivers.*

A *girl* is a female child or adolescent. The term is often used as a synonym for 'woman' but is considered patronizing or disrespectful by some people in some contexts, especially when used by men.

The word *lady* has connotations of nobility, dignity, and good manners: □ *the Lady of the manor.* □ *She may be wealthy but she's no lady!* It is used in polite address, as in formal or official contexts: □ *This lady would like to speak to the manager.* □ *Ladies and gentlemen ....* However, it is sometimes regarded as a term of condescension, especially in such phrases as *the cleaning lady,* which may be replaced by *the cleaning woman* or, more simply, *the cleaner.*

As a general rule, *female, girl,* and *lady* are best restricted to contexts where *male, boy,* or *gentleman* would be used of the opposite sex. See also **MAN; SEXISM.**

wonder see WANDER OR WONDER?

wont This old-fashioned word is used to mean 'inclined or accustomed': □ *They were wont to have tea at 4 o'clock every day* and in the expression *as is one's wont*. Its pronunciation is the same as that of the word *won't* [wōnt].

woolly Note the spelling of this word: *-oo-* and *-ll-* in British English; *-oo-* and single *-l-* in American English. Similarly, the adjective *woollen* has *-ll-* in British English and a single *-l-* in American English.

worship The single final *p* doubles in front of most suffixes beginning with a vowel in British English: □ *worshipped* □ *worshipper* □ *worshipping*. American English retains the single *p*.

◆ *Worshipful* retains the single *p*. See also SPELLING 1.

worthwhile or **worth while**? The traditional rule is that this expression is written as two words after a verb and as one word in front of a noun: □ *It is worth while spending a little more money.* □ *a project that is worth while – a worthwhile project.*

◆ Increasingly, however, the tendency is to write this expression as one word in all contexts.

would see SHOULD OR WOULD?

wove, woven see WEAVED, WOVE, OR WOVEN?

wrack see RACK OR WRACK?

wrapped see RAPT OR WRAPPED?

wring see RING OR WRING?

wrought *Wrought* is an archaic form of the past tense and past participle of the verb *work*. It is still used adjectivally in such expressions as *wrought iron*.

◆ *Wrought* is sometimes wrongly used as the past tense of *wreak*, meaning 'inflict; cause': □ *The hurricane wreaked* [not *wrought*] *havoc throughout the countryside.* □ *She wreaked* [not *wrought*] *vengeance on the bullies.*

wysiwyg The term *wysiwyg*, used in computing and pronounced [*wiz*iwig], is an acronym for *what you see is what you get*: the display on the computer screen is an exact representation of what will appear on the printout. The term is sometimes spelt *WYSIWYG* or *Wysiwyg*: □ *Offering full Wysiwyg (what you see is what you get), including the enhancements such as bold, italic, inverse, tone and outlines* (*Daily Telegraph*).

Xerox This word should be spelt *Xerox* if it is referring to the trademarked noun for a type of photographic copier or process. The verb, meaning 'copy on a Xerox machine', is spelt with a lower-case *x*.

◆ *Xerox* is pronounced [*zeer*oks].

Xmas *Xmas*, an abbreviation for *Christmas*, is used particularly in commercial contexts and newspaper headlines. The *X* derives from the Greek *chi*, the initial letter of *Christos*, the Greek for *Christ*.

◆ Some people, particularly Christians, find the word offensive and it is generally considered suitable only for informal writing. When reading the word aloud it is preferable to pronounce it as *Christmas*, and only actually to say [*eksmăs*] when this spelling is emphasized.

X-ray or **x-ray**? The noun is nearly always written with a capital *X*; the verb is written with a capital or lower-case letter: □ *He had an X-ray/He was X-rayed* [or *x-rayed*] *after the accident.*

364

yes and **no** In discussing affirmative or negative expressions one has the option of writing, for example, either: □ *She said yes to the offer* or: *She said, 'Yes' to the offer.* The latter carries more of an implication that the person actually used the word *yes* or *no*.

◆ In phrases where there is no suggestion of someone actually using the word, it is better not to have *yes* or *no* in inverted commas: □ *He says yes to life.* □ *She won't take no for an answer.*

Phrases such as: □ *He said (that) yes, he agreed* are acceptable. The *yes* is dispensable but adds emphasis.

yet *Yet* has various meanings: 'up till now; so far': □ *It has not yet been decided*, 'even': □ *a yet greater problem*, 'in addition': □ *yet more presents*, 'at some future time': □ *We'll do it yet*, and 'nevertheless': □ *slow, yet sure.*

◆ In several of its meanings *yet* is more or less interchangeable with *still*, but in the sense of 'as before': □ *It is yet raining, yet* is now archaic, and *still* is required.

When the meaning is 'so far' *yet* cannot be used with the simple past tense, except in informal American English: □ *Did she go yet?*

yoghurt The most frequent spelling of this word is *yoghurt*. Acceptable alternatives are *yogurt* and *yoghourt*. The usual pronunciation is [yogĕrt] in British English and [yōgĕrt] in American English.

yoke or **yolk**? These words are sometimes confused. *Yoke* means 'connecting bar or bond': □ *yoked oxen* □ *under the yoke of slavery.* A *yolk* is the yellow part of an egg: □ *Would you like your yolk hard?*

yoof *Yoof* is a phonetic respelling of the word *youth* (as pronounced by a Londoner), used with particular reference to contemporary youth culture: □ *Panels are a good idea, but they shouldn't all be authors who don't appeal to the 'yoof' culture (The Bookseller).*

◆ The vogue for such respellings as *yoof, lerv* (for love), and *meeja* (for media) is disliked by many people.

you *You* is often used to mean 'people in general' in place of the slightly more formal *one*: □ *You certainly get a good meal at that restaurant.* □ *You hold a hammer like this.* □ *They* [i.e. 'The authorities'] *fine you on the spot if you've not got a ticket.* □ *It's really embarrassing when you forget someone's name.* □ *Dentists say you should clean your teeth at least twice a day.* Although *one* is less frequently used than *you* it is sometimes better to use *one* to avoid possible confusion as to whether the speaker is talking personally or generally. It is also important to be consistent in the use of either *you* or *one* throughout a single piece of writing.

◆ The personal pronoun *you* is either singular or plural. All attempts to indicate that more than one person is being addressed: *you all, you lot, you guys*, etc., are informal.

See also -ING FORMS.

you know The expression *you know* is used by speakers who are not sure about what they have just said or who are not sure what to say next: □*I just wondered ... you know ... if you might like to come with me to the theatre.* The expression is frequently used with this function but is very widely disliked.

your or **you're**? These two words may be confused. *Your* means 'belonging to you': □*your house* □*your rights. You're* is a contraction of *you are:* □*Hurry up, you're going to be late!*

◆ Note also the spelling of *yours:* □ *That's mine not yours*; the spelling with an apostrophe, *your's*, is wrong.

yuppie *Yuppie*, often spelt *yuppy*, is a North American coinage which came into frequent use in Britain in the mid-1980s. It stands for 'young urban (or upwardly mobile) professional' and is used to designate well-educated young adults, living in cities, working in well-paid occupations, and enjoying a fashionable way of life.

◆ Unlike other vogue acronyms (see **DINKY**), *yuppie* has established itself in the English language with such derivatives as *yuppification* and *yuppiedom*. Other, more ephemeral, coinages include *buppie* (black yuppie), *guppie* (**GREEN** yuppie), and *Juppy* (Japanese yuppie).

The term *yuppie* is largely associated with those who enjoyed rapid career progress and financial success in the boom of the mid-1980s, at the peak of Margaret Thatcher's premiership. In the recession of the early 1990s it began to fall into disuse and to have mildly derogatory overtones.

zero The digit 0 has a variety of names. *Nought* (see also NAUGHT OR NOUGHT?) and (less frequently) *zero* are the general terms for this digit: □ *The number 1000 has three noughts* [or *zeros*]. □ *You've missed a nought off the end – it should be two hundred thousand, not twenty thousand.* In scientific contexts, and for expressing temperatures, etc., *zero* is preferred: □ *Water freezes at zero degrees Celsius.* Zero is also used in countdowns: □ *five, four, three, two, one, zero.*

♦ When 'spelling out' a number, such as a telephone number or account number, the name of the letter *O* (pronounced like the word *oh*) is used in British English: □ *The dialling code for Liverpool is oh-five-one.*

In sport, the terms *love* and *nil* are used for a score of 0: □ *four love in the final set.* □ *At half-time the score was two nil.*

The plural of *zero* is *zeros* or *zeroes*. Either form is acceptable, but *zeros* is the more frequent, being preferred by many users.

zoology This word, referring to the biological study of animals, has two pronunciations. The more frequent pronunciation is [zooo*l*ŏji], though careful users prefer [zōo*l*ŏji].